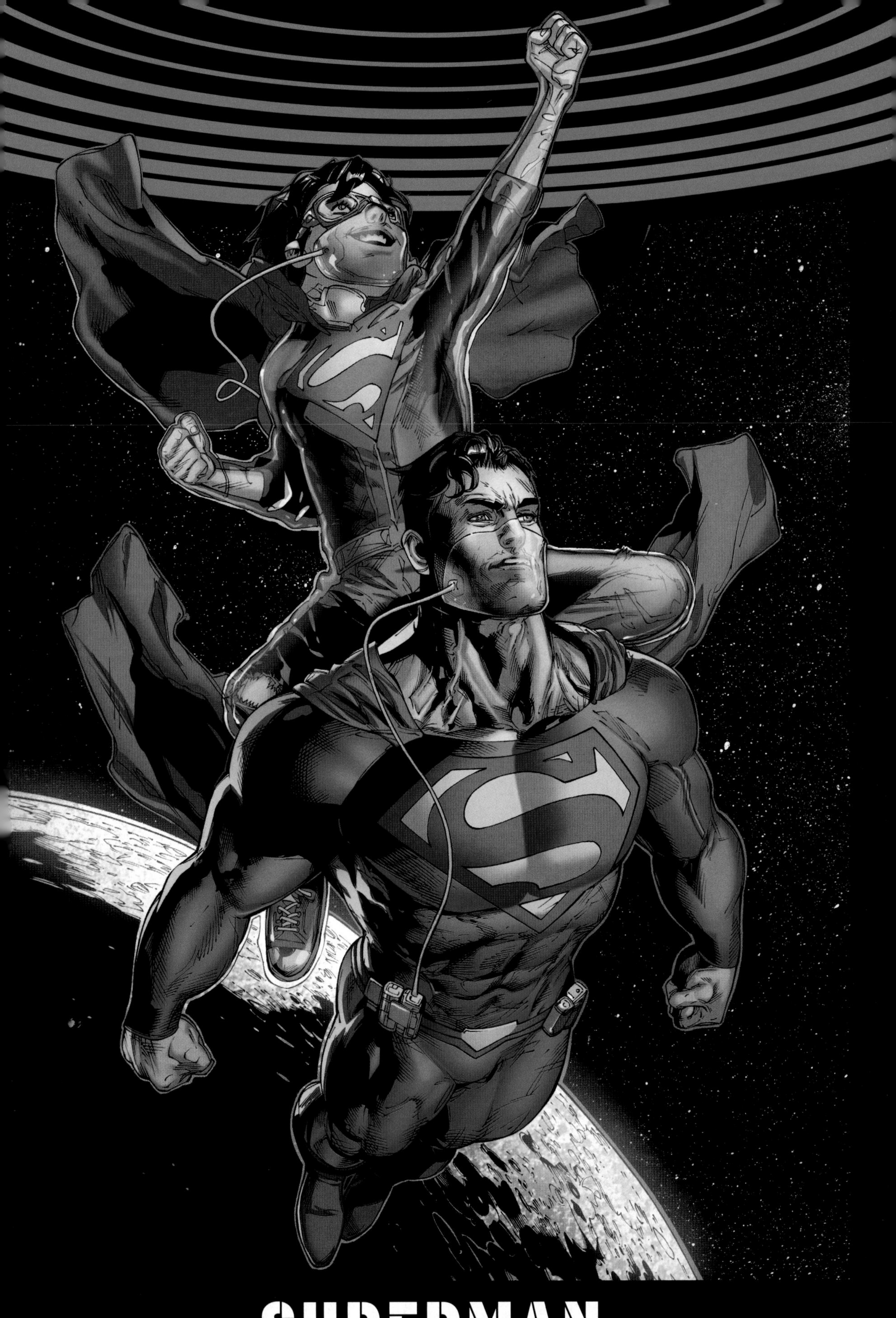

SUPERMAN

REBIRTH DELUXE EDITION

BOOK 4

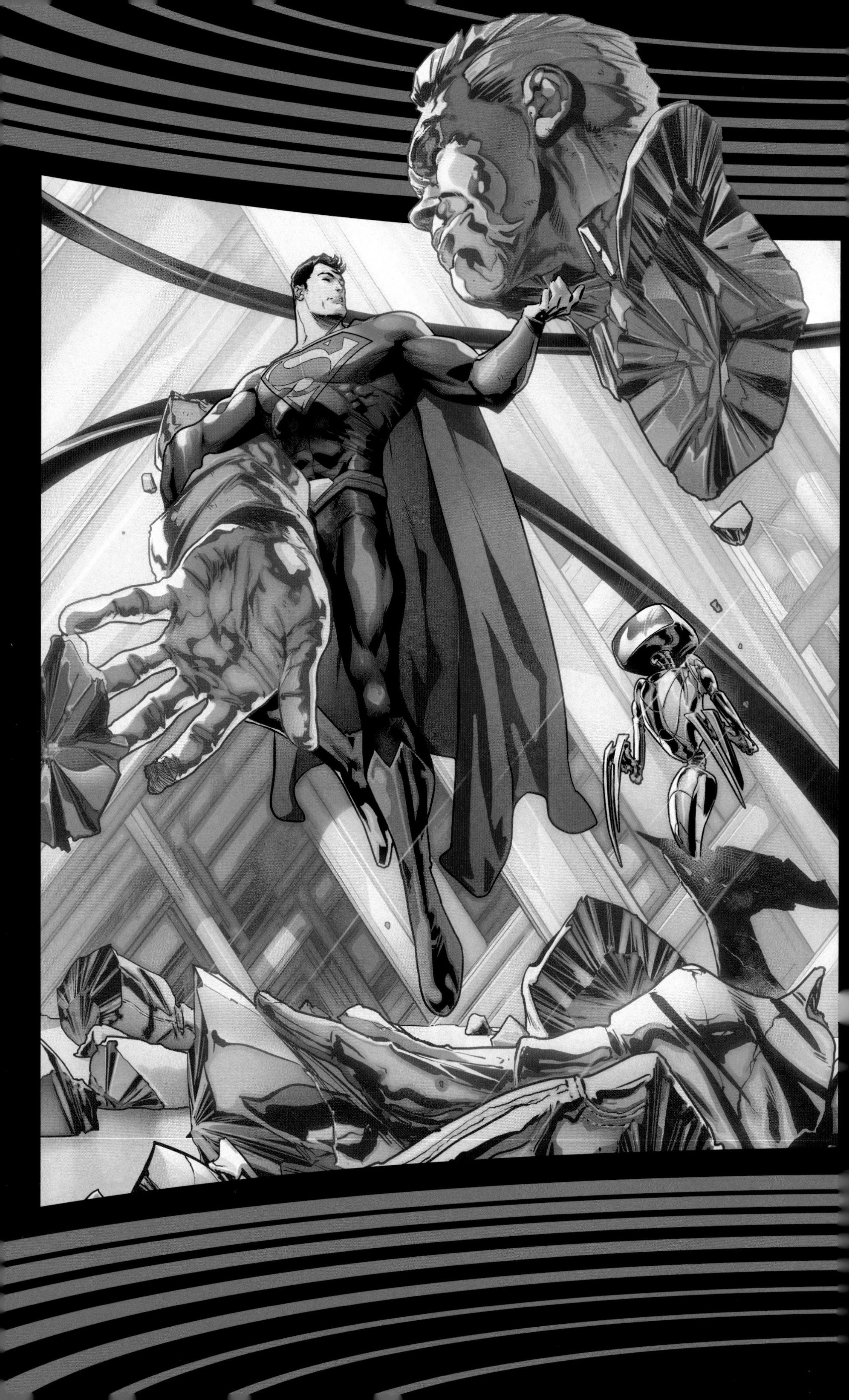

SUPERMAN
REBIRTH DELUXE EDITION
BOOK 4

PETER J. TOMASI ∗ **PATRICK GLEASON** ∗ **JAMES ROBINSON**

MARK RUSSELL ∗ **IAN FLYNN**

writers

PATRICK GLEASON ∗ **DOUG MAHNKE** ∗ **SCOTT GODLEWSKI** ∗ **JORGE JIMENEZ**
ED BENES ∗ **SERGIO DAVILA** ∗ **BARRY KITSON** ∗ **VICENTE CIFUENTES**
JAIME MENDOZA ∗ **SCOTT HANNA** ∗ **JOE PRADO**
BRYAN HITCH ∗ **KAARE ANDREWS**

artists

ALEJANDRO SANCHEZ ∗ **GABE ELTAEB** ∗ **WIL QUINTANA**
DINEI RIBEIRO ∗ **STEPHEN DOWNER**
ALEX SINCLAIR ∗ **KAARE ANDREWS**

colorists

ROB LEIGH ∗ **TOM NAPOLITANO**

letterers

PATRICK GLEASON and **ALEJANDRO SANCHEZ**

collection cover artists

SUPERMAN created by **JERRY SIEGEL** and **JOE SHUSTER**
SUPERBOY created by **JERRY SIEGEL**
By special arrangement with the Jerry Siegel family

ALEX ANTONE, PAUL KAMINSKI Editors - Original Series
BRITTANY HOLZHERR, JESSICA CHEN Associate Editors - Original Series * **ANDREW MARINO** Assistant Editor - Original Series
JEB WOODARD Group Editor - Collected Editions * **ERIKA ROTHBERG** Editor - Collected Edition
STEVE COOK Design Director - Books * **MEGEN BELLERSEN** Publication Design

BOB HARRAS Senior VP - Editor-in-Chief, DC Comics
PAT McCALLUM Executive Editor, DC Comics

DAN DiDIO Publisher * **JIM LEE** Publisher & Chief Creative Officer
AMIT DESAI Executive VP - Business & Marketing Strategy, Direct to Consumer & Global Franchise Management
BOBBIE CHASE VP & Executive Editor, Young Reader & Talent Development * **MARK CHIARELLO** Senior VP - Art, Design & Collected Editions
JOHN CUNNINGHAM Senior VP - Sales & Trade Marketing * **BRIAR DARDEN** VP - Business Affairs * **ANNE DePIES** Senior VP - Business Strategy, Finance & Administration
DON FALLETTI VP - Manufacturing Operations * **LAWRENCE GANEM** VP - Editorial Administration & Talent Relations * **ALISON GILL** Senior VP - Manufacturing & Operations
JASON GREENBERG VP - Business Strategy & Finance * **HANK KANALZ** Senior VP - Editorial Strategy & Administration * **JAY KOGAN** Senior VP - Legal Affairs
NICK J. NAPOLITANO VP - Manufacturing Administration * **LISETTE OSTERLOH** VP - Digital Marketing & Events * **EDDIE SCANNELL** VP - Consumer Marketing
COURTNEY SIMMONS Senior VP - Publicity & Communications * **JIM (SKI) SOKOLOWSKI** VP - Comic Book Specialty Sales & Trade Marketing
NANCY SPEARS VP - Mass, Book, Digital Sales & Trade Marketing * **MICHELE R. WELLS** VP - Content Strategy

SUPERMAN: REBIRTH DELUXE EDITION BOOK 4

DC Comics, 2900 West Alameda Ave., Burbank, CA 91505
Printed by Transcontinental Interglobe, Beauceville, QC, Canada. 4/12/19. First Printing.
ISBN: 978-1-4012-8935-5

Library of Congress Cataloging-in-Publication Data is available.

PEFC Certified
Printed on paper from sustainably managed forests and controlled sources
PEFC/01-31-106 www.pefc.org

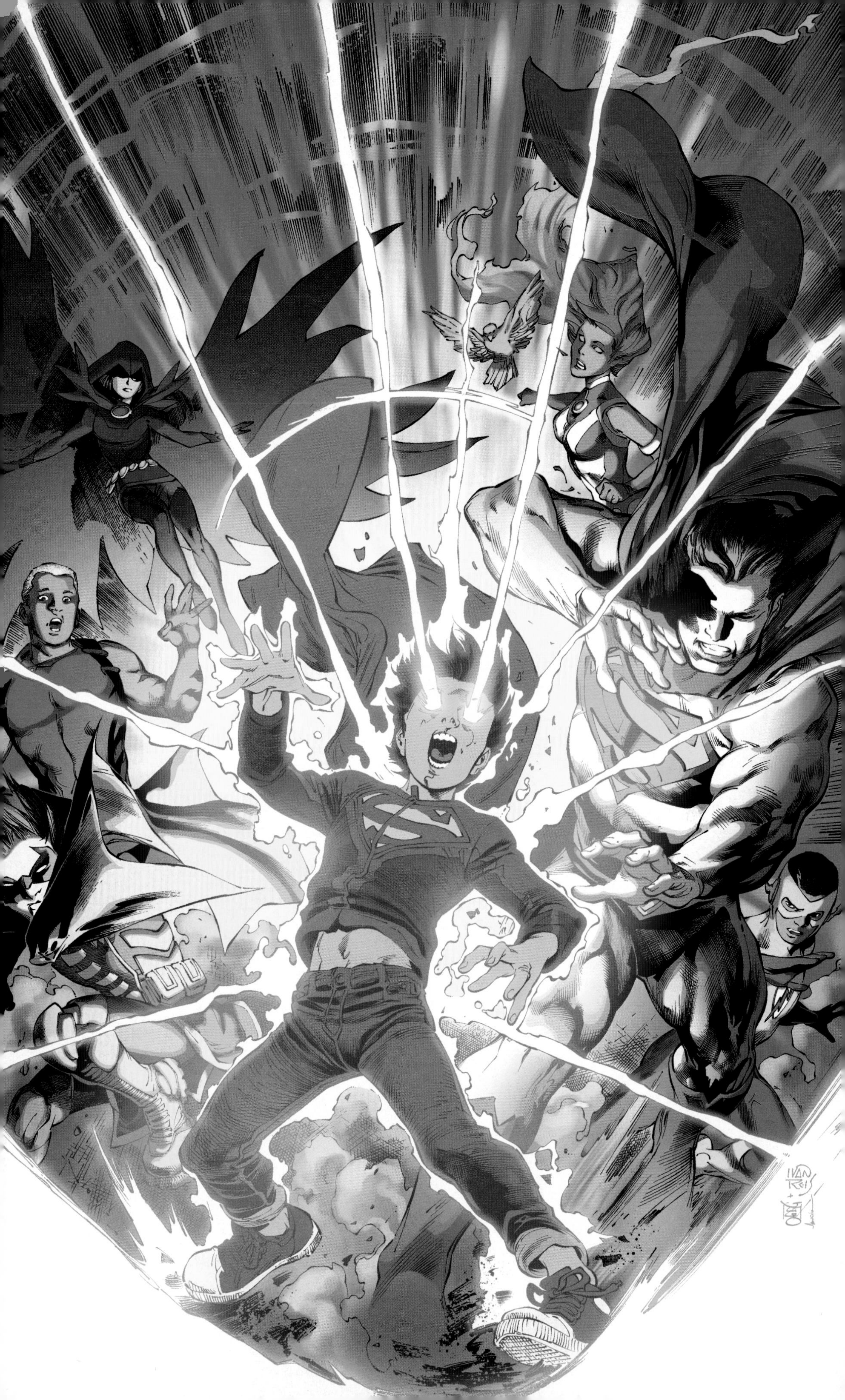
IVAN REIS

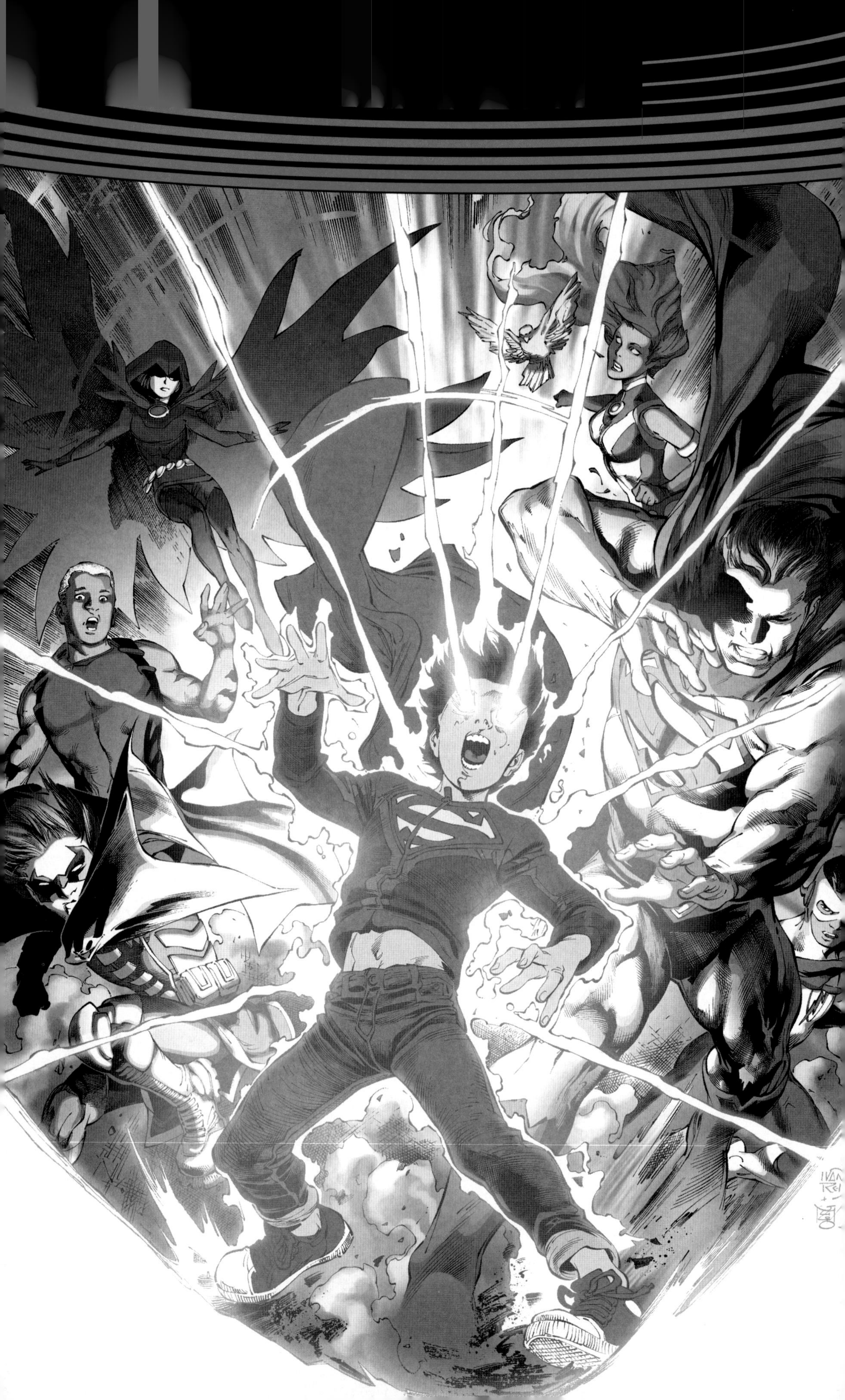

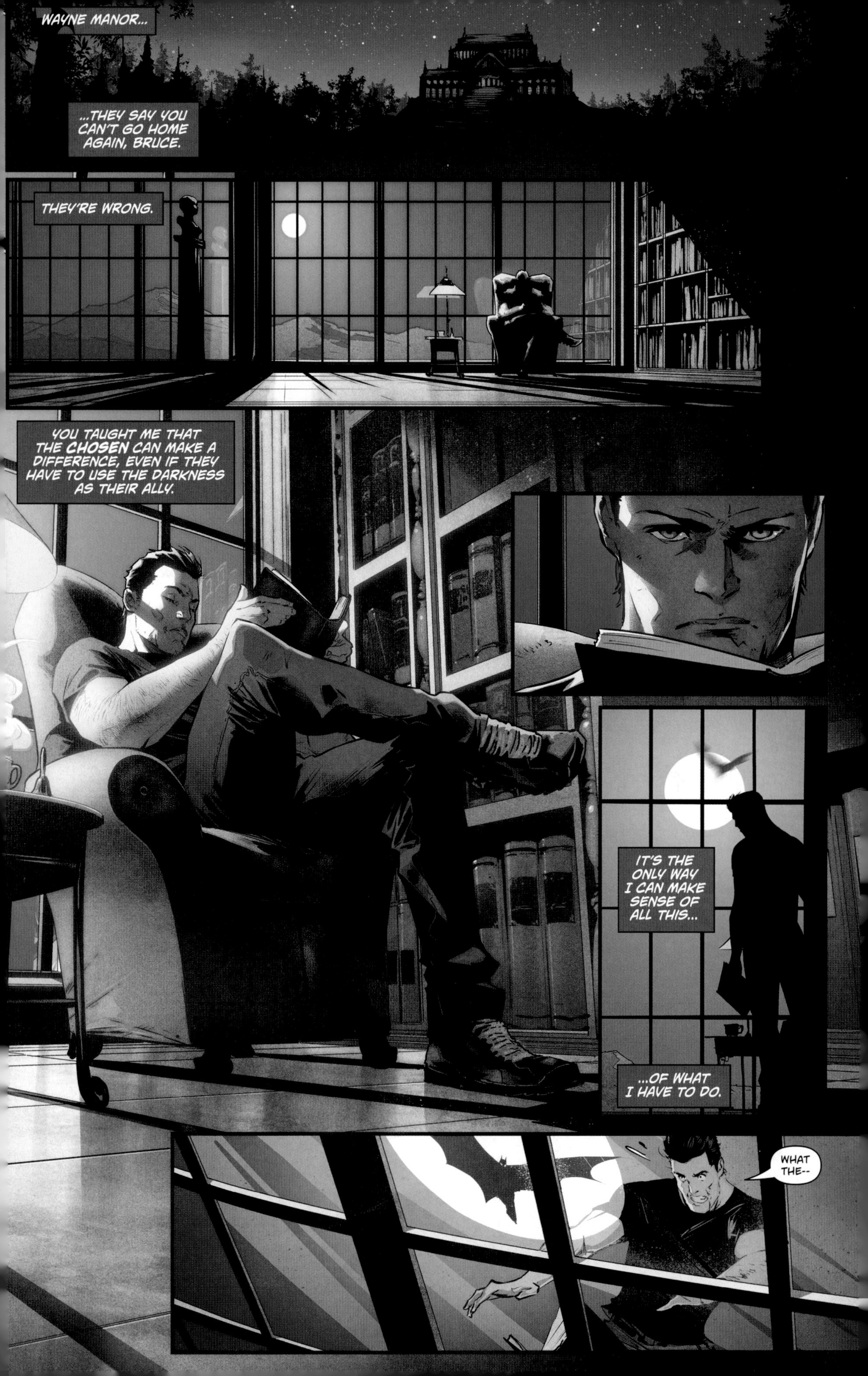
WAYNE MANOR...
...THEY SAY YOU CAN'T GO HOME AGAIN, BRUCE.
THEY'RE WRONG.
YOU TAUGHT ME THAT THE CHOSEN CAN MAKE A DIFFERENCE, EVEN IF THEY HAVE TO USE THE DARKNESS AS THEIR ALLY.
IT'S THE ONLY WAY I CAN MAKE SENSE OF ALL THIS...
...OF WHAT I HAVE TO DO.
WHAT THE--

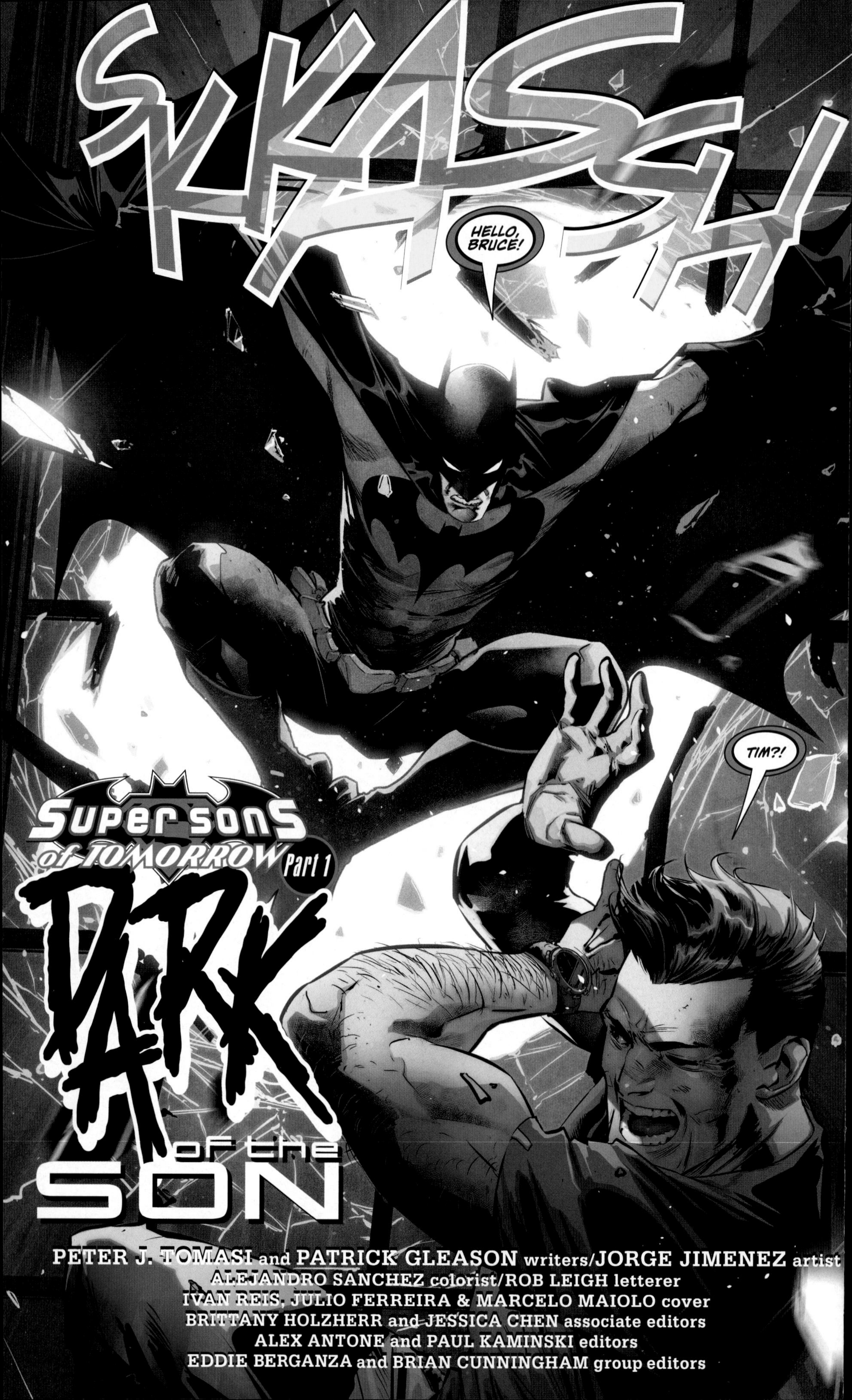
HELLO, BRUCE!
TIM?!
Super Sons of TOMORROW Part 1
DARK of the SON

PETER J. TOMASI and PATRICK GLEASON writers/JORGE JIMENEZ artist
ALEJANDRO SANCHEZ colorist/ROB LEIGH letterer
IVAN REIS, JULIO FERREIRA & MARCELO MAIOLO cover
BRITTANY HOLZHERR and JESSICA CHEN associate editors
ALEX ANTONE and PAUL KAMINSKI editors
EDDIE BERGANZA and BRIAN CUNNINGHAM group editors

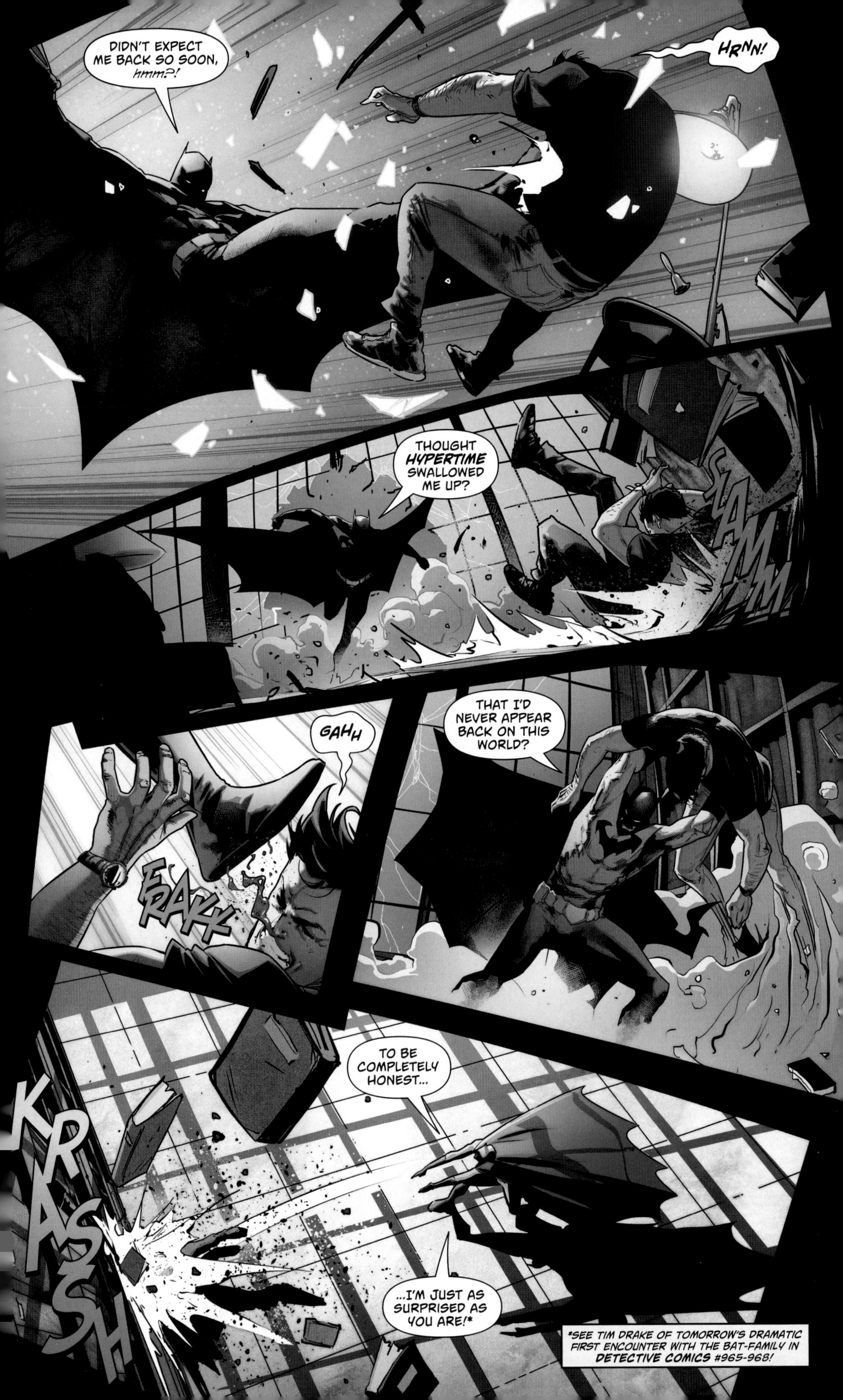
DIDN'T EXPECT ME BACK SO SOON, *hmm?!*
HRNN!
THOUGHT **HYPERTIME** SWALLOWED ME UP?
SLAMM
GAHH
FRAKK
THAT I'D NEVER APPEAR BACK ON THIS WORLD?
TO BE COMPLETELY HONEST...
KRASH
...I'M JUST AS SURPRISED AS YOU ARE!*
*SEE TIM DRAKE OF TOMORROW'S DRAMATIC FIRST ENCOUNTER WITH THE BAT-FAMILY IN **DETECTIVE COMICS** #965-968!

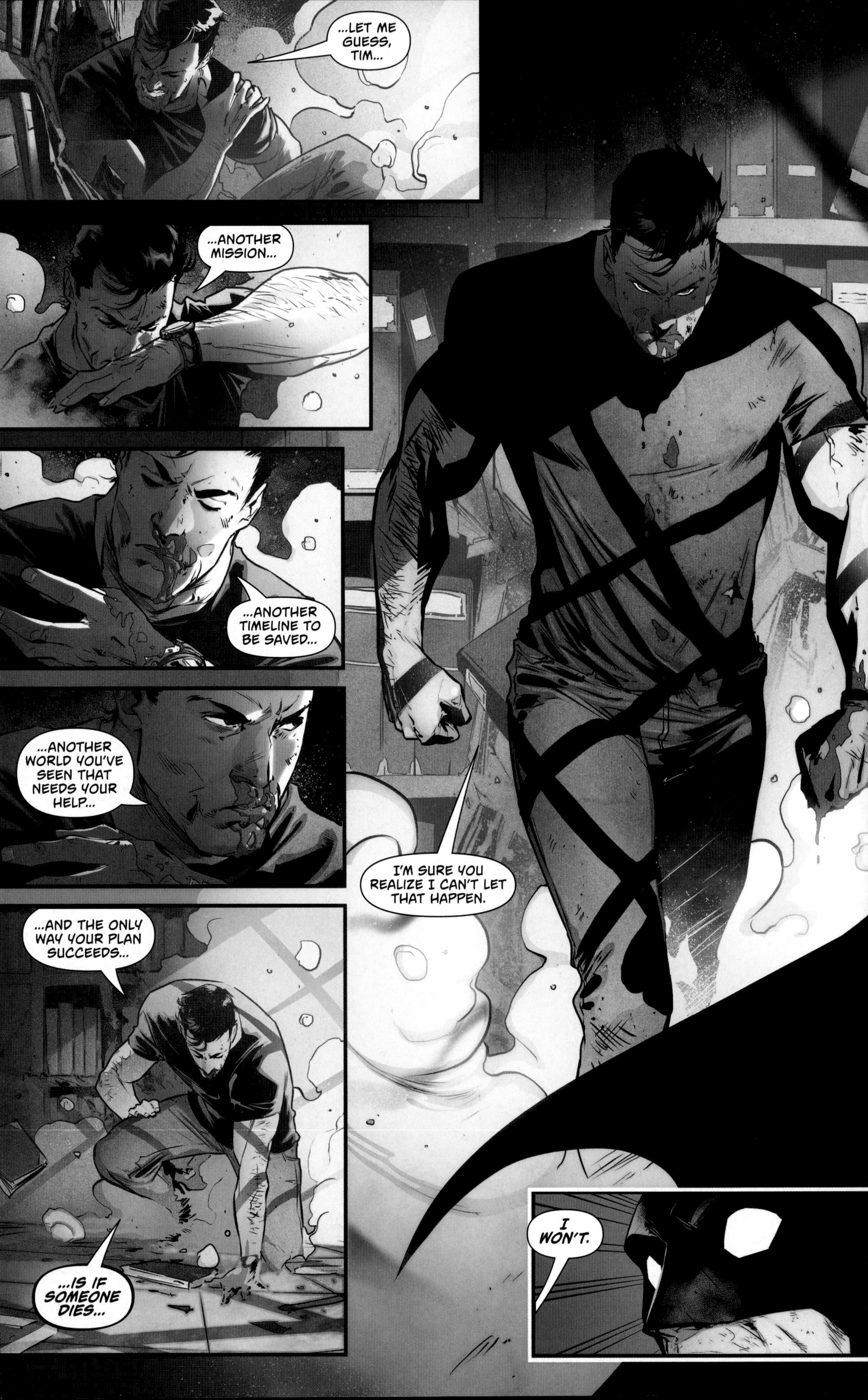
...LET ME GUESS, TIM...
...ANOTHER MISSION...
...ANOTHER TIMELINE TO BE SAVED...
...ANOTHER WORLD YOU'VE SEEN THAT NEEDS YOUR HELP...
...AND THE ONLY WAY YOUR PLAN SUCCEEDS...
...IS IF SOMEONE DIES...
I'M SURE YOU REALIZE I CAN'T LET THAT HAPPEN.
I WON'T.

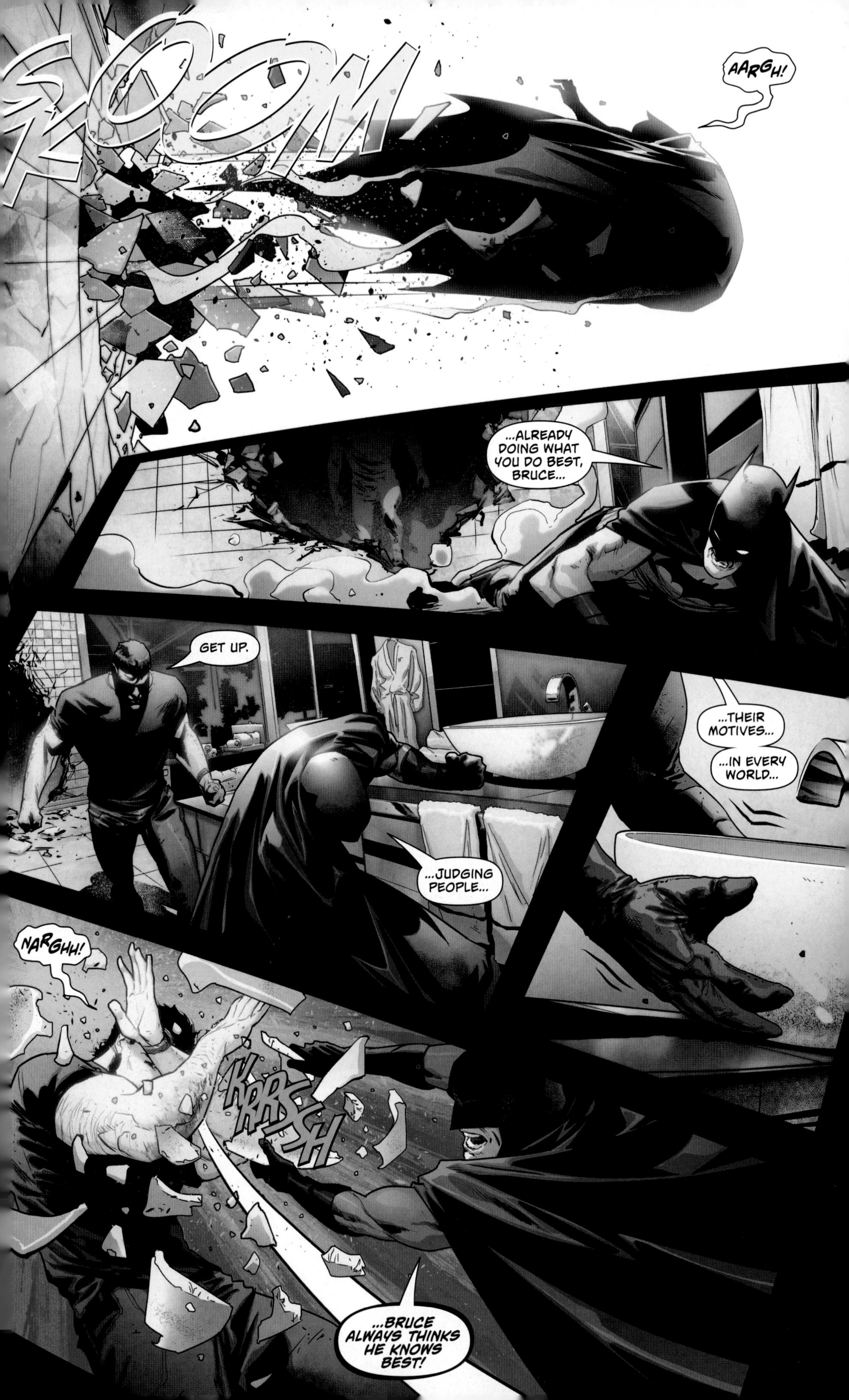
SKOOM
AARGH!
...ALREADY DOING WHAT YOU DO BEST, BRUCE...
GET UP.
...JUDGING PEOPLE...
...THEIR MOTIVES...
...IN EVERY WORLD...
NARGHH!
KRRSSH
...BRUCE ALWAYS THINKS HE KNOWS BEST!

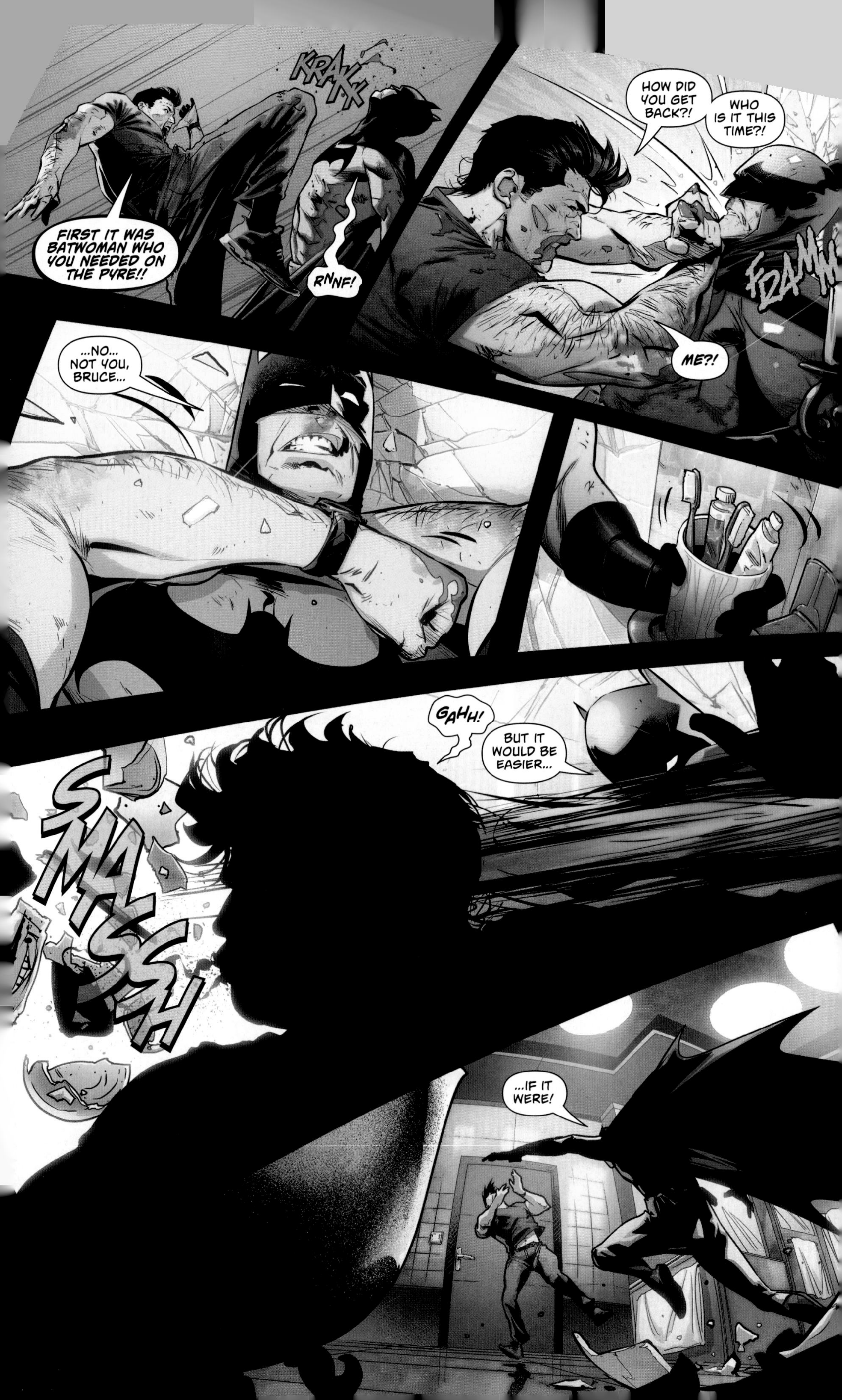
KRAKK
FIRST IT WAS BATWOMAN WHO YOU NEEDED ON THE PYRE!!
RNNF!
HOW DID YOU GET BACK?!
WHO IS IT THIS TIME?!
FDAMM
ME?!
...NO... NOT YOU, BRUCE...
GAHH!
BUT IT WOULD BE EASIER...
SMASSH
...IF IT WERE!

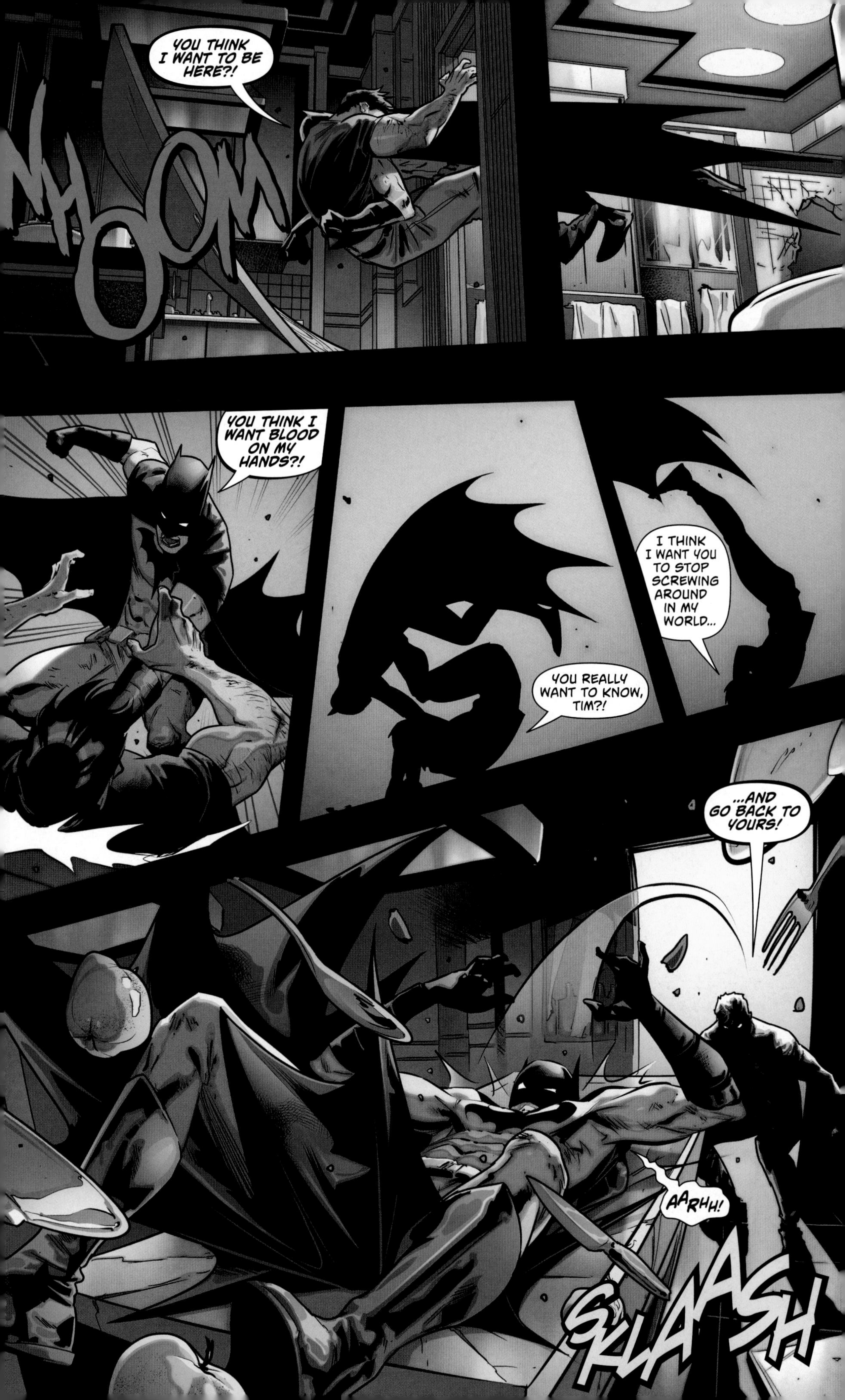

YOU THINK I WANT TO BE HERE?!
WHOOM
YOU THINK I WANT BLOOD ON MY HANDS?!
YOU REALLY WANT TO KNOW, TIM?!
I THINK I WANT YOU TO STOP SCREWING AROUND IN MY WORLD...
...AND GO BACK TO YOURS!
AARHH!
SKLAASH

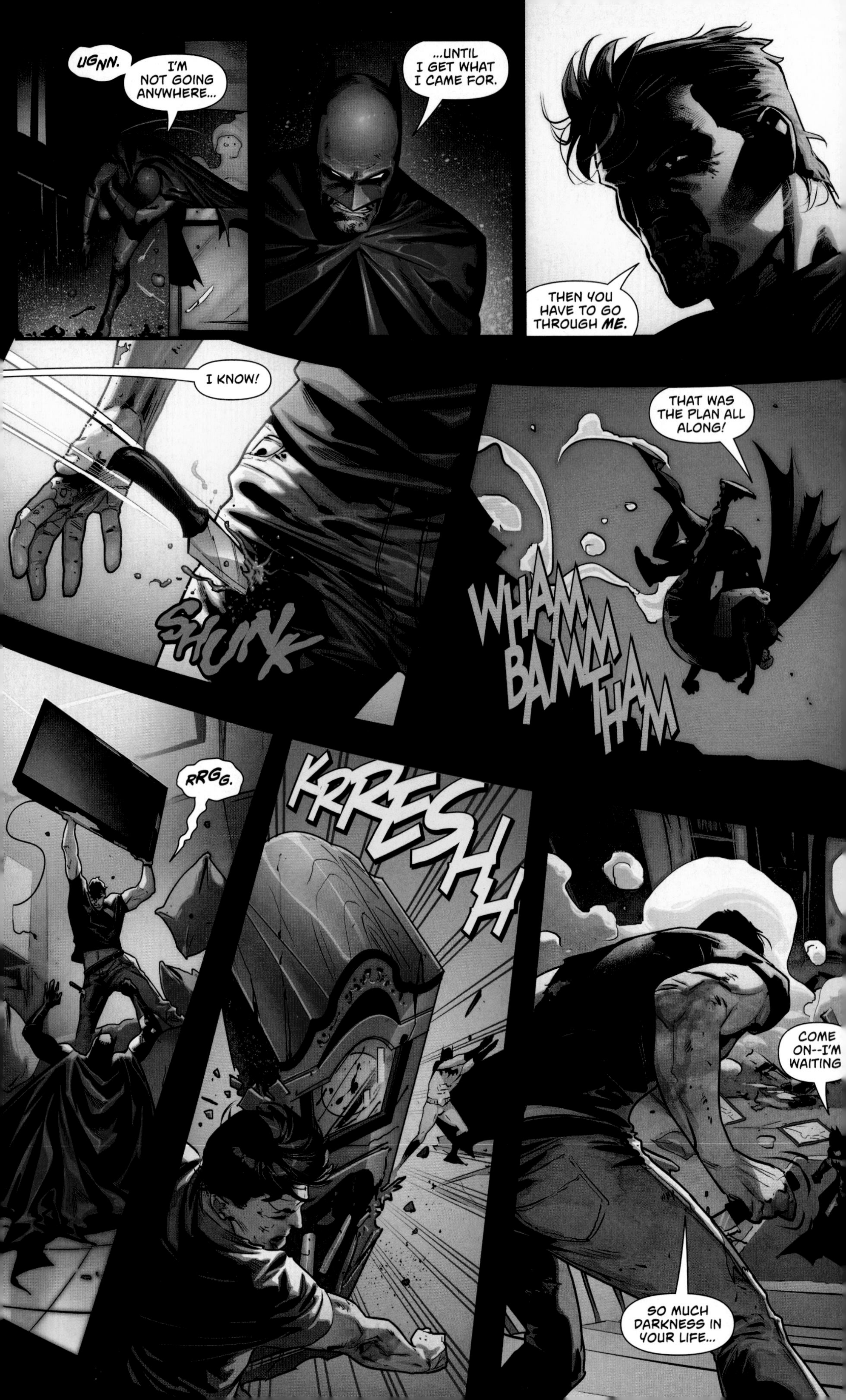
UGNN.
I'M NOT GOING ANYWHERE...
...UNTIL I GET WHAT I CAME FOR.
THEN YOU HAVE TO GO THROUGH ME.
I KNOW!
SHUNK
THAT WAS THE PLAN ALL ALONG!
WHAMM BAMM THAM
RRGG.
KRRESHH
COME ON--I'M WAITING
SO MUCH DARKNESS IN YOUR LIFE...

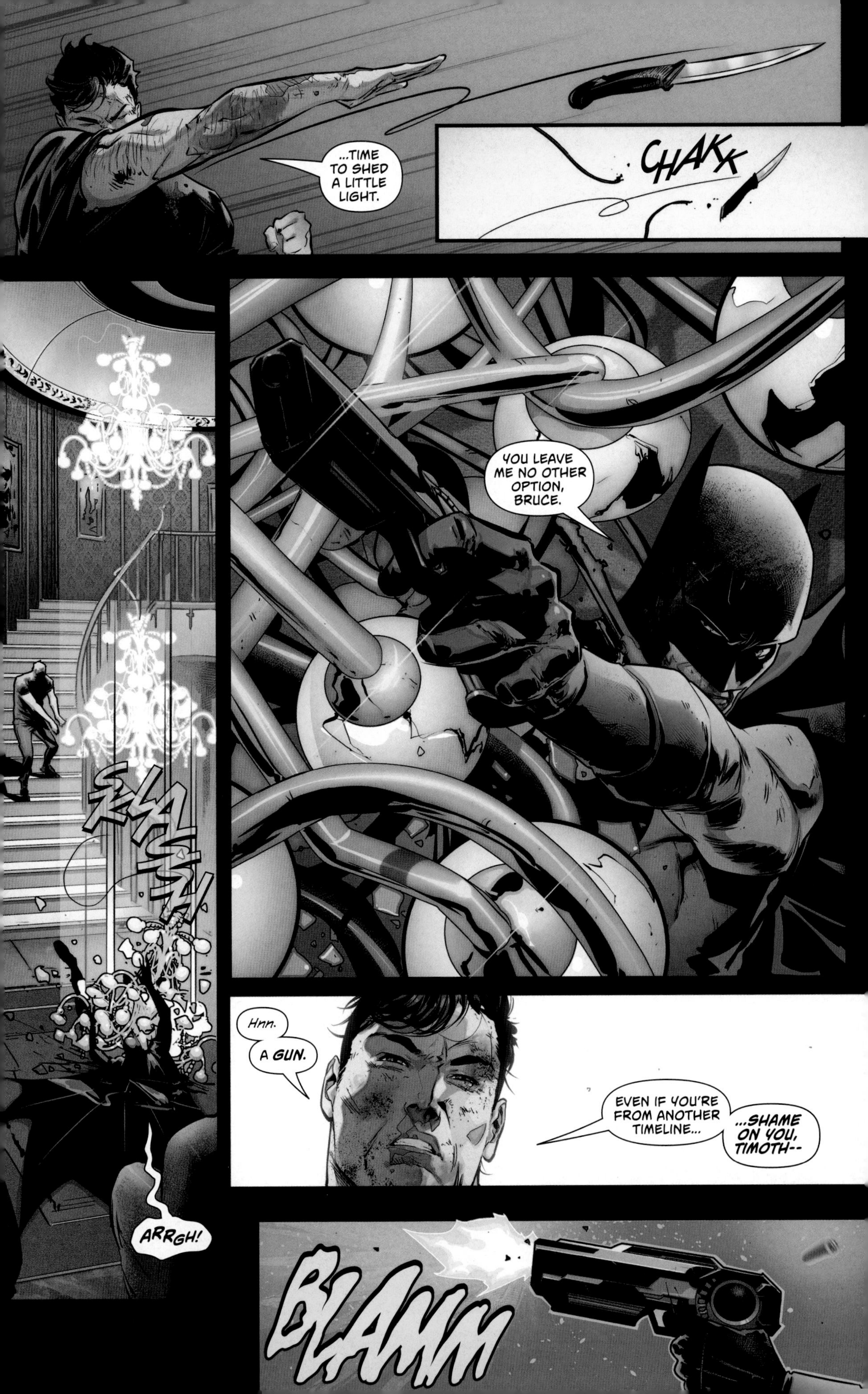
...TIME TO SHED A LITTLE LIGHT.
CHAKK
YOU LEAVE ME NO OTHER OPTION, BRUCE.
SHASHUNK
ARRGH!
Hnn.
A GUN.
EVEN IF YOU'RE FROM ANOTHER TIMELINE...
...SHAME ON YOU, TIMOTH--
BLAMM

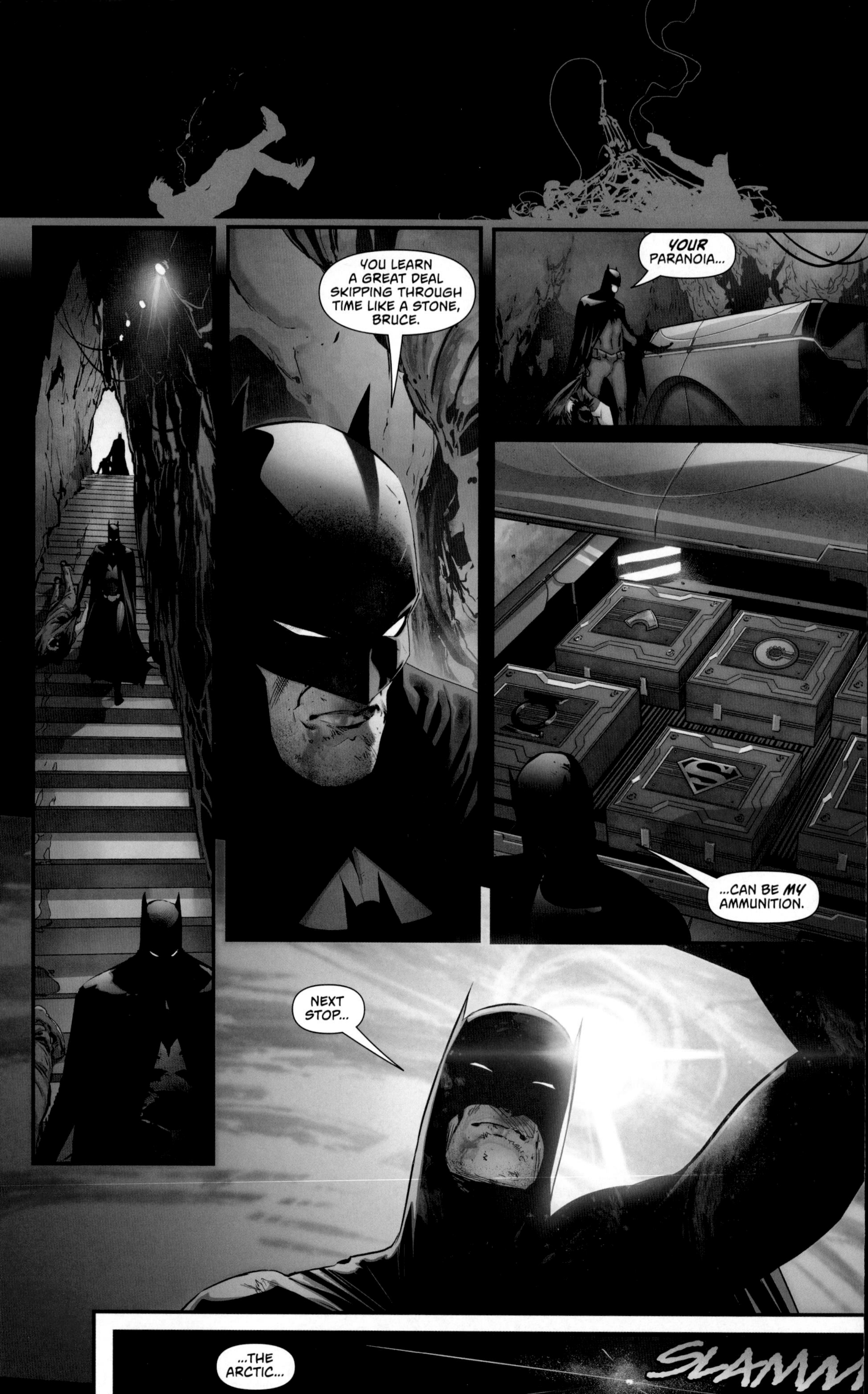
YOU LEARN A GREAT DEAL SKIPPING THROUGH TIME LIKE A STONE, BRUCE.
YOUR PARANOIA...
...CAN BE MY AMMUNITION.
NEXT STOP...
...THE ARCTIC...
SLAMM

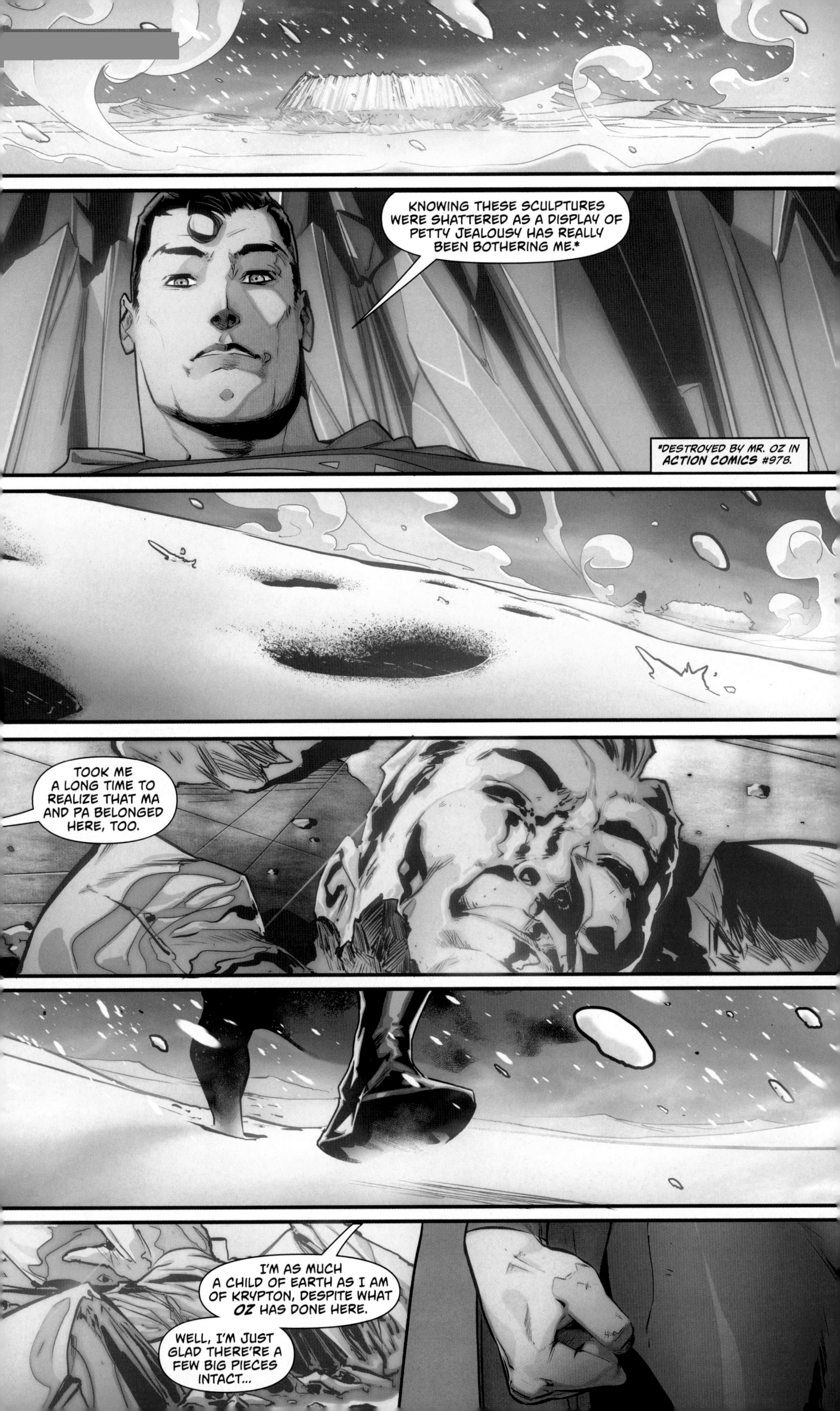
KNOWING THESE SCULPTURES WERE SHATTERED AS A DISPLAY OF PETTY JEALOUSY HAS REALLY BEEN BOTHERING ME.*
*DESTROYED BY MR. OZ IN ACTION COMICS #978.
TOOK ME A LONG TIME TO REALIZE THAT MA AND PA BELONGED HERE, TOO.
I'M AS MUCH A CHILD OF EARTH AS I AM OF KRYPTON, DESPITE WHAT OZ HAS DONE HERE.
WELL, I'M JUST GLAD THERE'RE A FEW BIG PIECES INTACT...

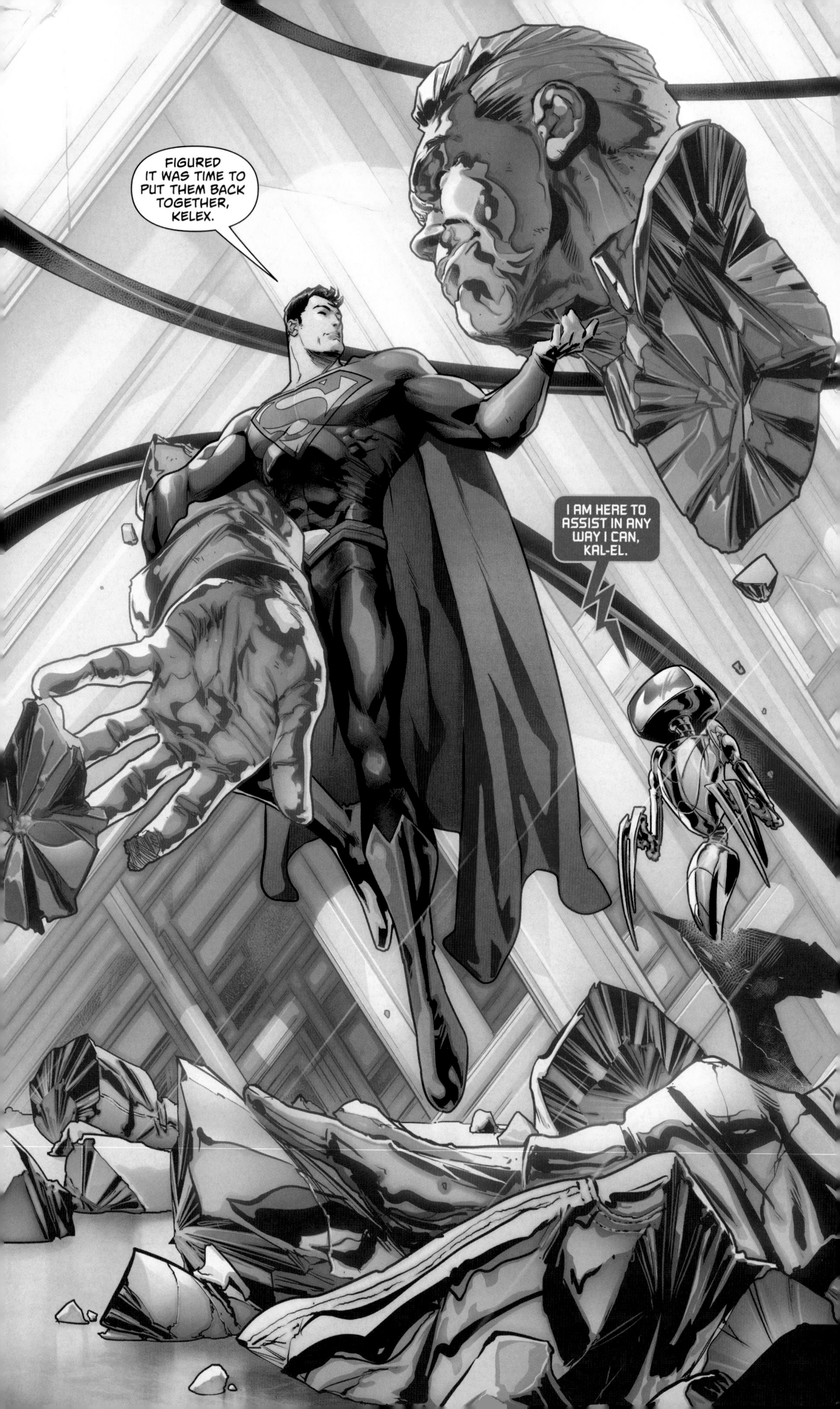
FIGURED IT WAS TIME TO PUT THEM BACK TOGETHER, KELEX.
I AM HERE TO ASSIST IN ANY WAY I CAN, KAL-EL.

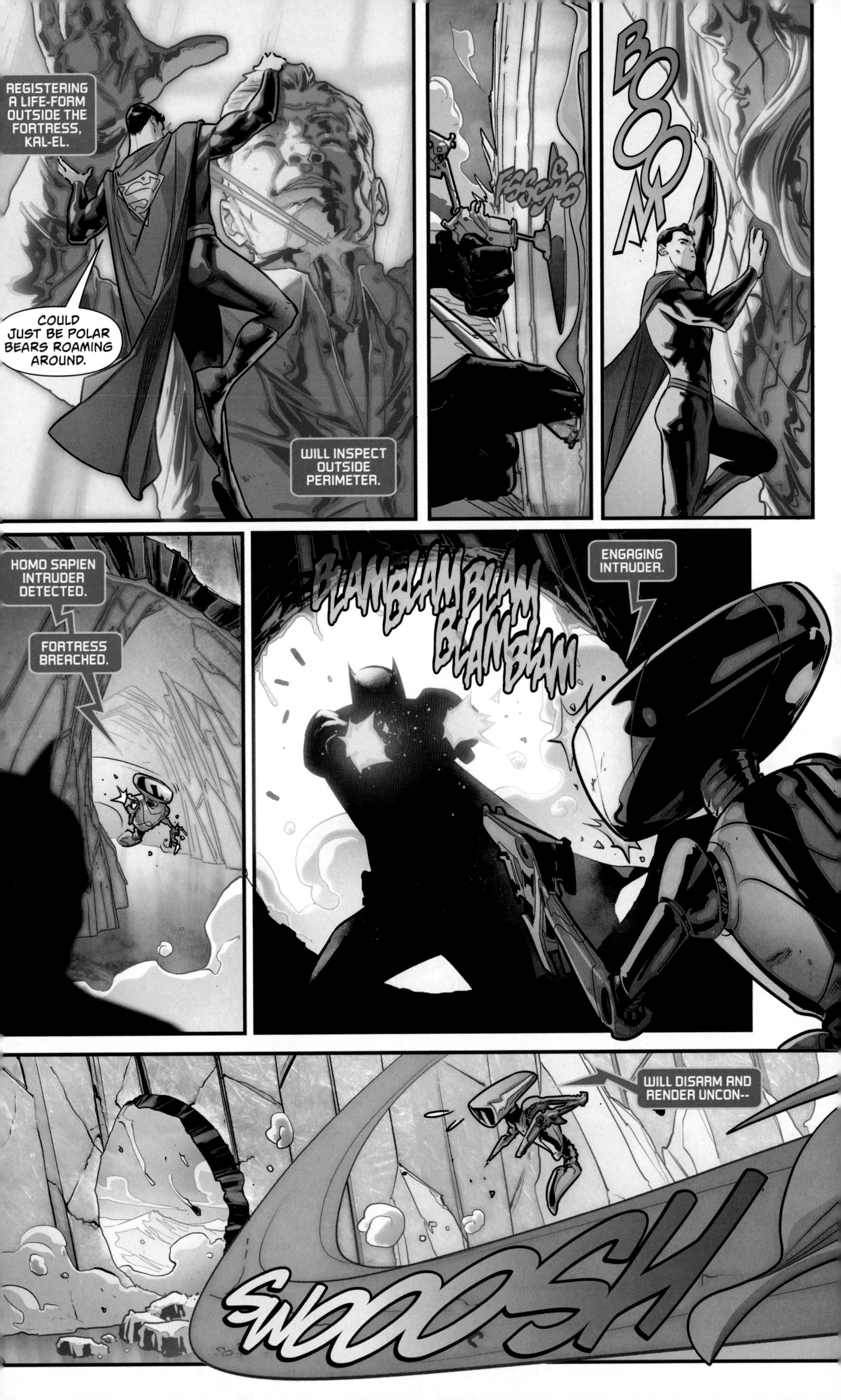
REGISTERING A LIFE-FORM OUTSIDE THE FORTRESS, KAL-EL.
COULD JUST BE POLAR BEARS ROAMING AROUND.
WILL INSPECT OUTSIDE PERIMETER.
BOOOM
HOMO SAPIEN INTRUDER DETECTED.
FORTRESS BREACHED.
BLAMBLAMBLAM
BLAMBLAM
ENGAGING INTRUDER.
WILL DISARM AND RENDER UNCON--
SWOOSH

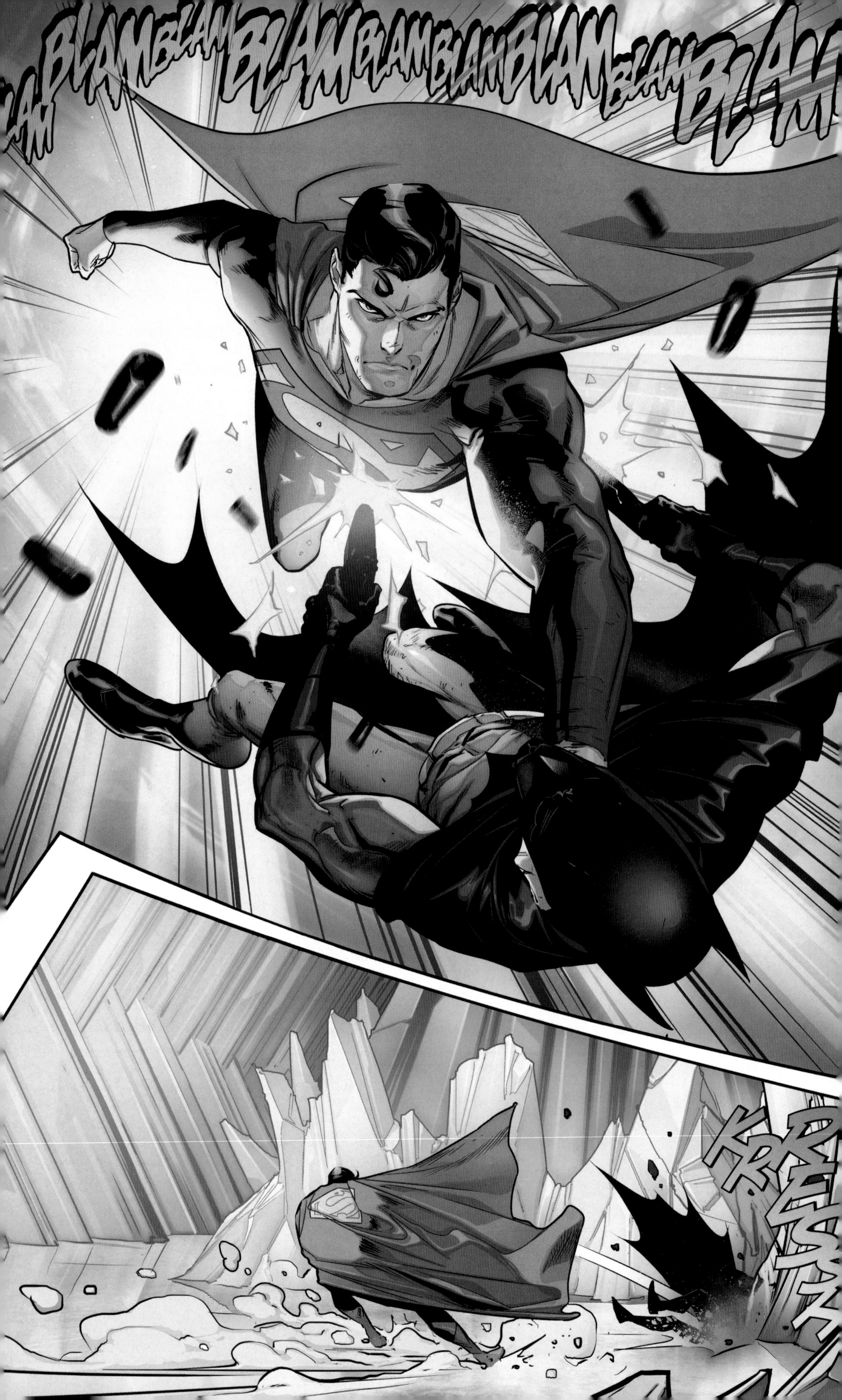

BLAMBLAMBLAMBLAMBLAMBLAMBLAMBLAM
KRRESSH

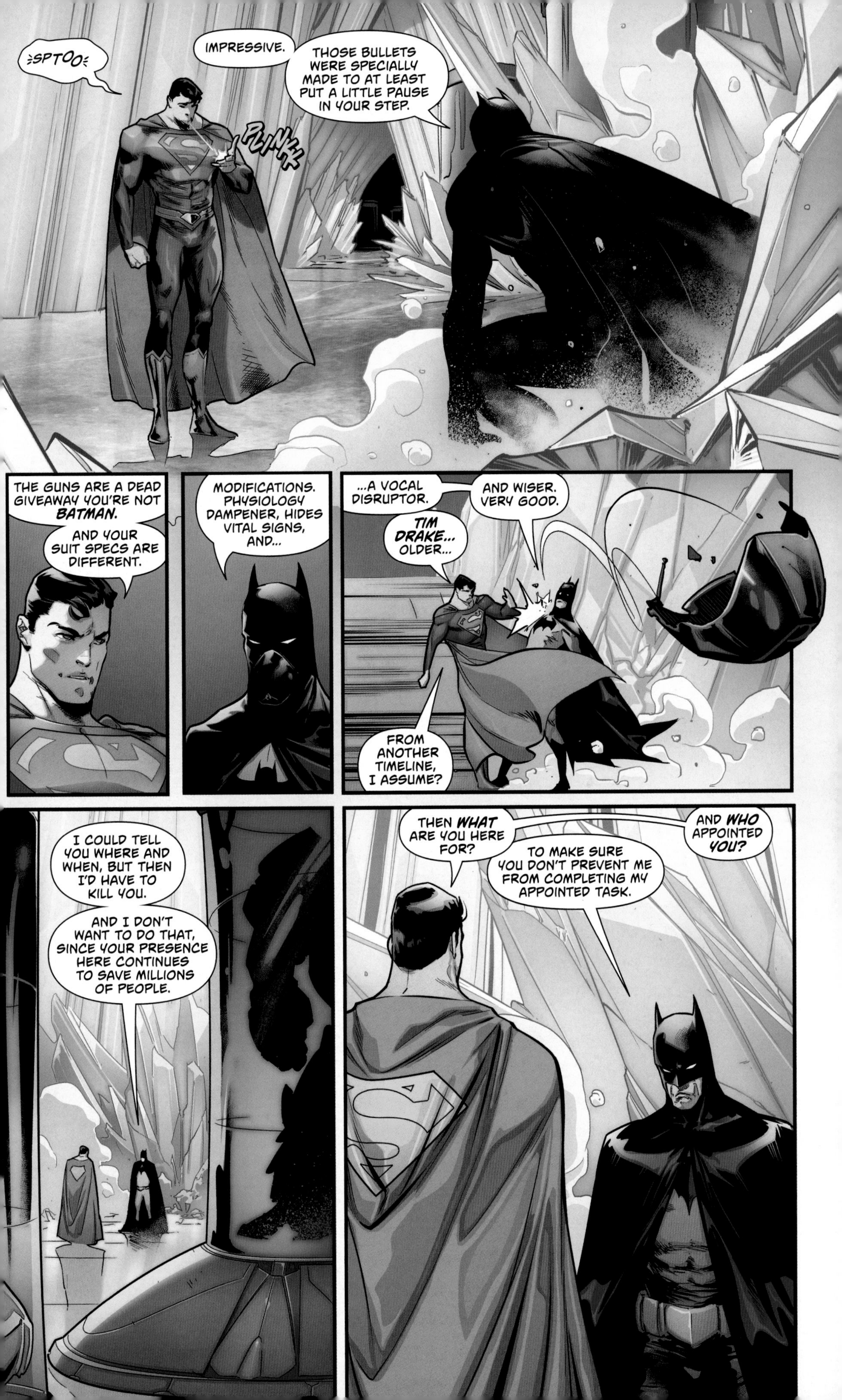

SPTOO
IMPRESSIVE.
THOSE BULLETS WERE SPECIALLY MADE TO AT LEAST PUT A LITTLE PAUSE IN YOUR STEP.
PLINKK
THE GUNS ARE A DEAD GIVEAWAY YOU'RE NOT BATMAN.
AND YOUR SUIT SPECS ARE DIFFERENT.
MODIFICATIONS. PHYSIOLOGY DAMPENER, HIDES VITAL SIGNS, AND...
...A VOCAL DISRUPTOR.
AND WISER. VERY GOOD.
TIM DRAKE... OLDER...
FROM ANOTHER TIMELINE, I ASSUME?
I COULD TELL YOU WHERE AND WHEN, BUT THEN I'D HAVE TO KILL YOU.
AND I DON'T WANT TO DO THAT, SINCE YOUR PRESENCE HERE CONTINUES TO SAVE MILLIONS OF PEOPLE.
THEN WHAT ARE YOU HERE FOR?
TO MAKE SURE YOU DON'T PREVENT ME FROM COMPLETING MY APPOINTED TASK.
AND WHO APPOINTED YOU?

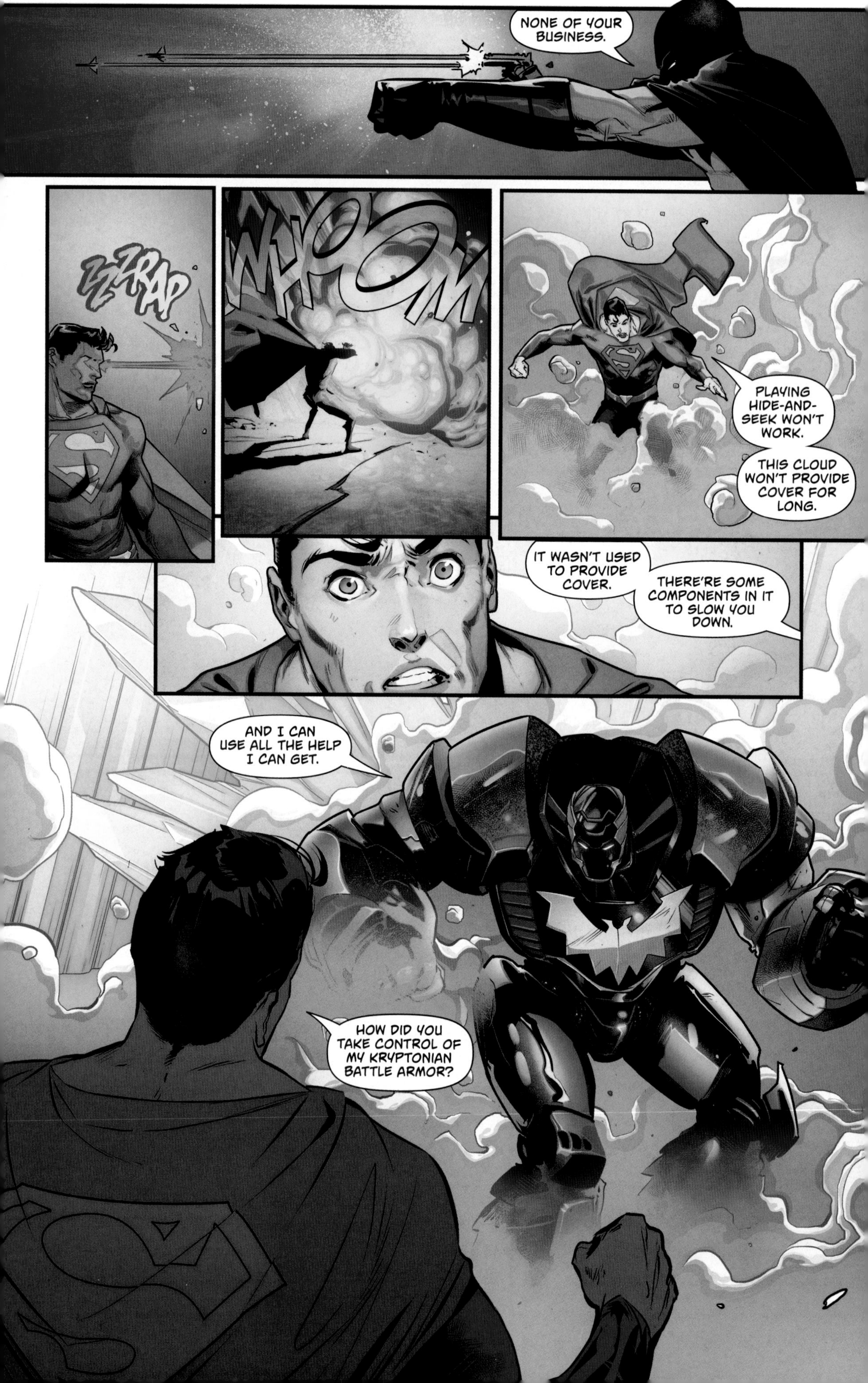
NONE OF YOUR BUSINESS.
ZZZRAP
WHOOM
PLAYING HIDE-AND-SEEK WON'T WORK.
THIS CLOUD WON'T PROVIDE COVER FOR LONG.
IT WASN'T USED TO PROVIDE COVER.
THERE'RE SOME COMPONENTS IN IT TO SLOW YOU DOWN.
AND I CAN USE ALL THE HELP I CAN GET.
HOW DID YOU TAKE CONTROL OF MY KRYPTONIAN BATTLE ARMOR?

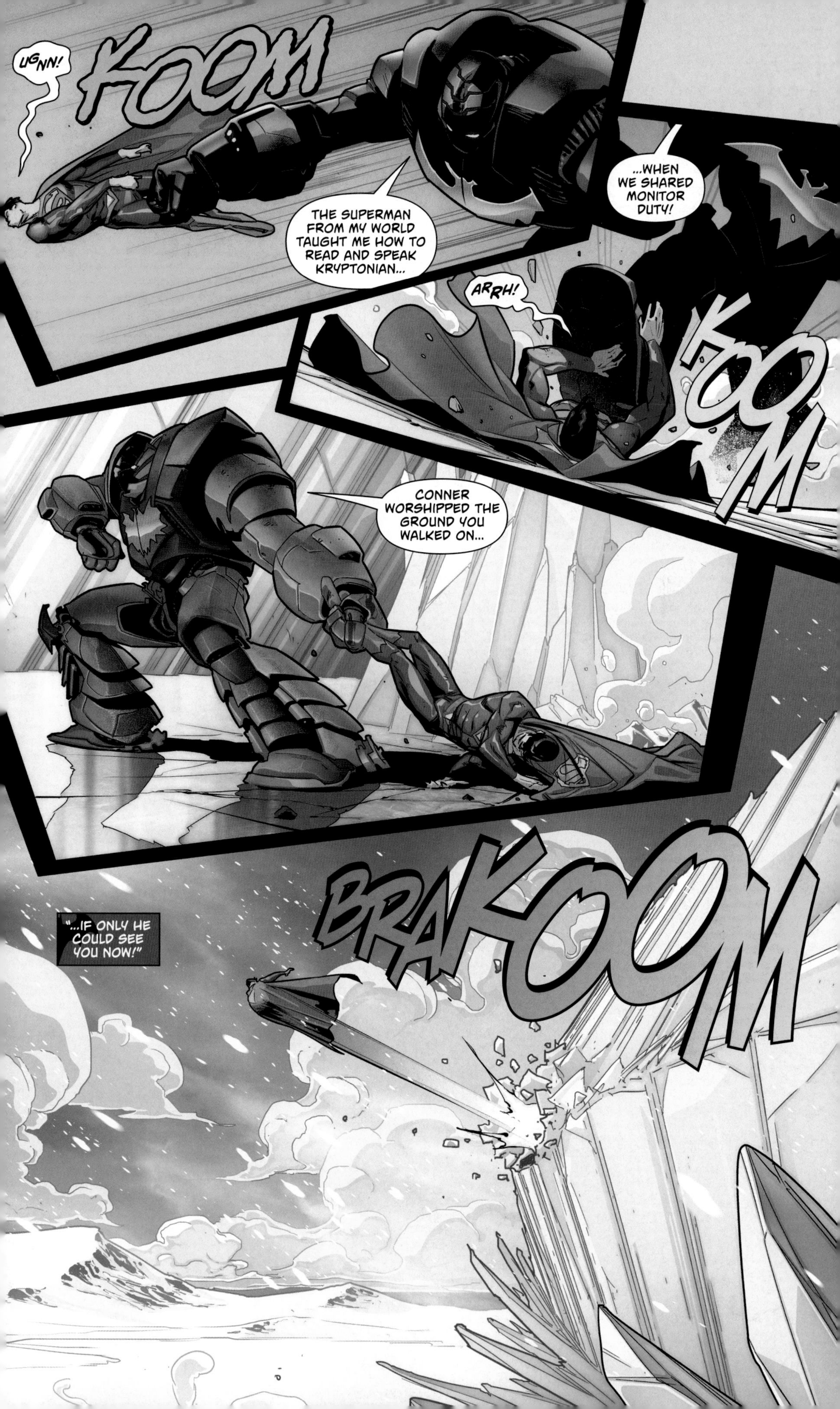
UGNN!
KOOM
THE SUPERMAN FROM MY WORLD TAUGHT ME HOW TO READ AND SPEAK KRYPTONIAN...
...WHEN WE SHARED MONITOR DUTY!
ARRH!
KOOOM
CONNER WORSHIPPED THE GROUND YOU WALKED ON...
BRAKOOOM
"...IF ONLY HE COULD SEE YOU NOW!"

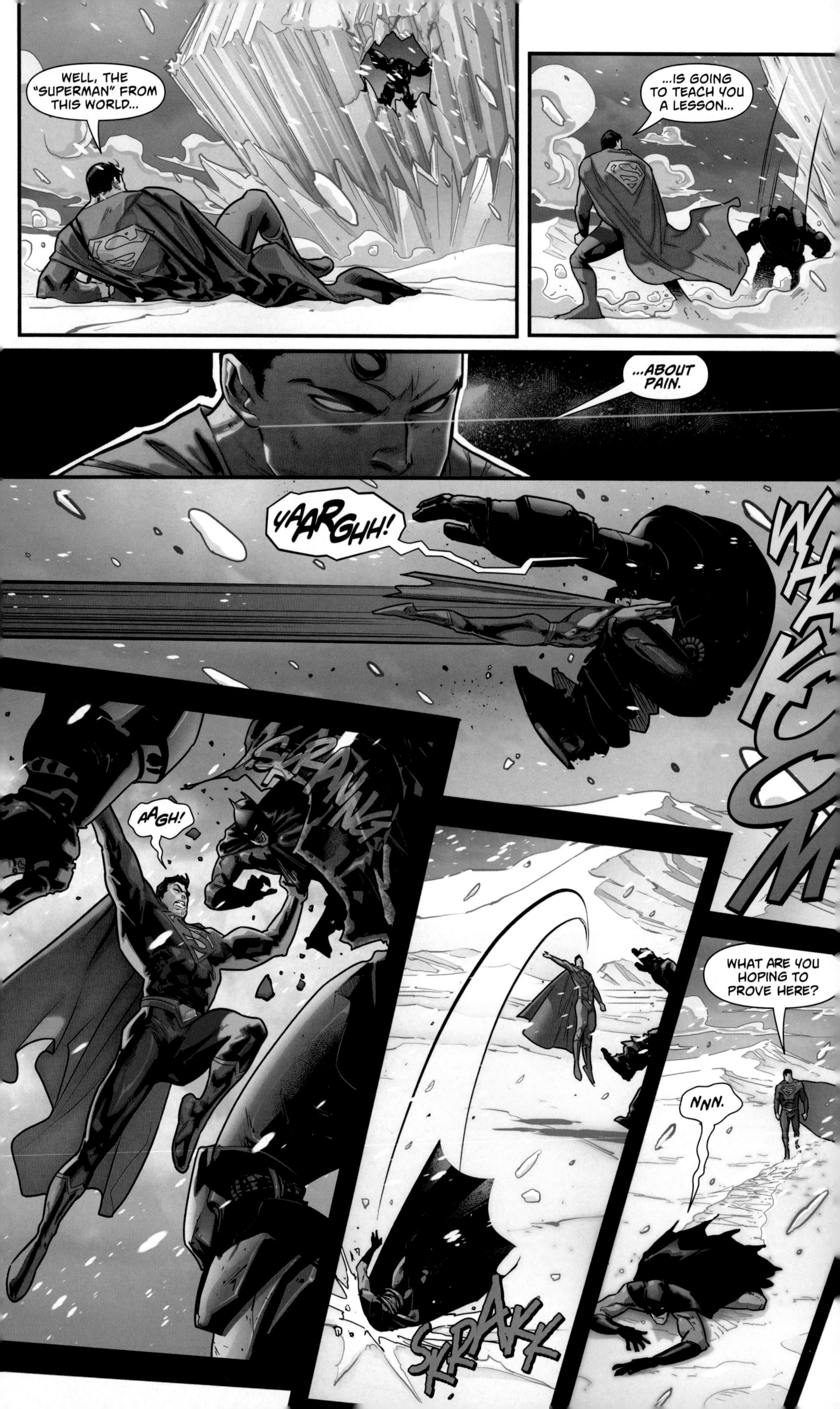
WELL, THE "SUPERMAN" FROM THIS WORLD...
...IS GOING TO TEACH YOU A LESSON...
...ABOUT PAIN.
YAARGHH!
WHAKOOM
SKRANNG
AAGH!
SKRAKK
WHAT ARE YOU HOPING TO PROVE HERE?
NNN.

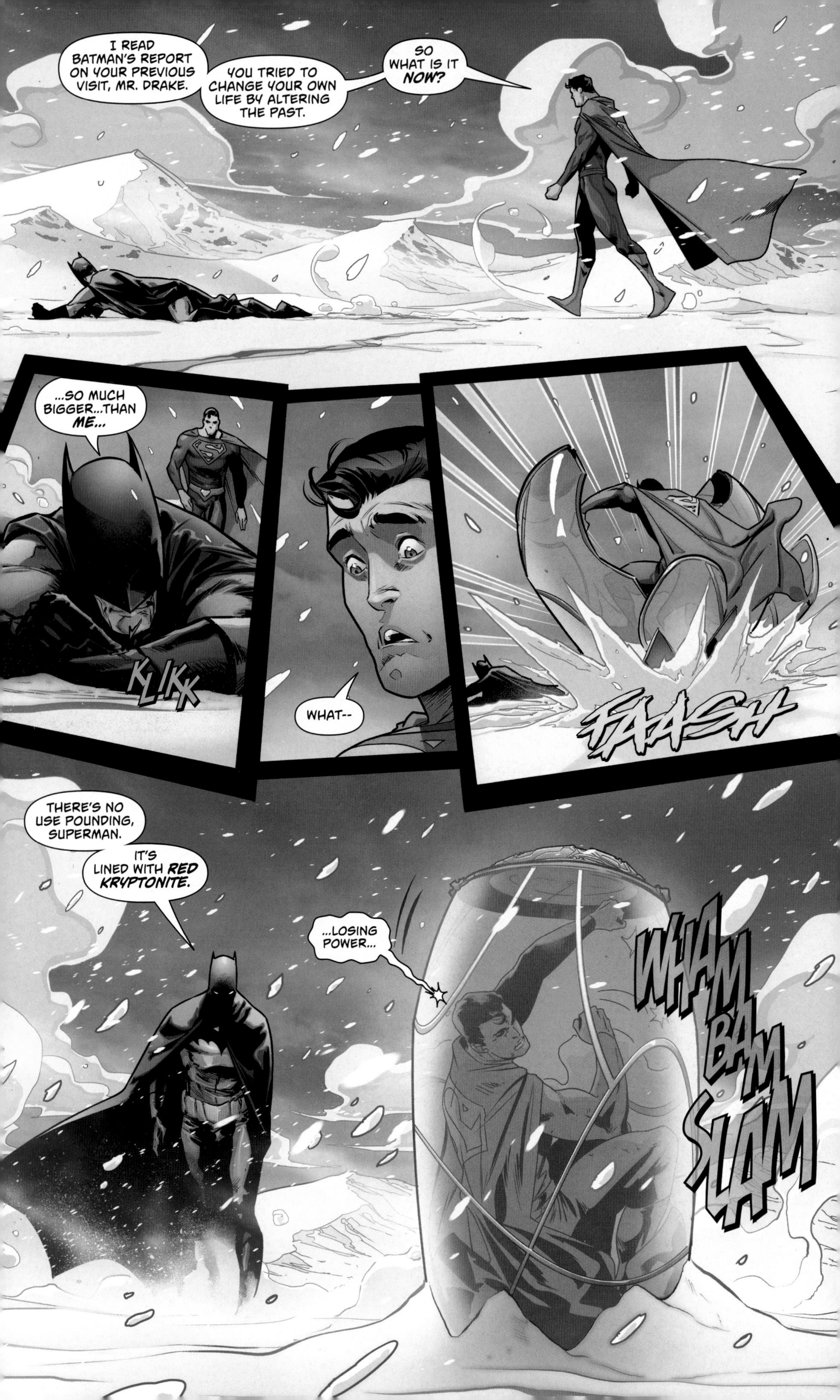
I READ BATMAN'S REPORT ON YOUR PREVIOUS VISIT, MR. DRAKE.
YOU TRIED TO CHANGE YOUR OWN LIFE BY ALTERING THE PAST.
SO WHAT IS IT NOW?
...SO MUCH BIGGER...THAN ME...
KLIKK
WHAT--
FAASH
THERE'S NO USE POUNDING, SUPERMAN.
IT'S LINED WITH RED KRYPTONITE.
...LOSING POWER...
WHAM
BAM
SLAM

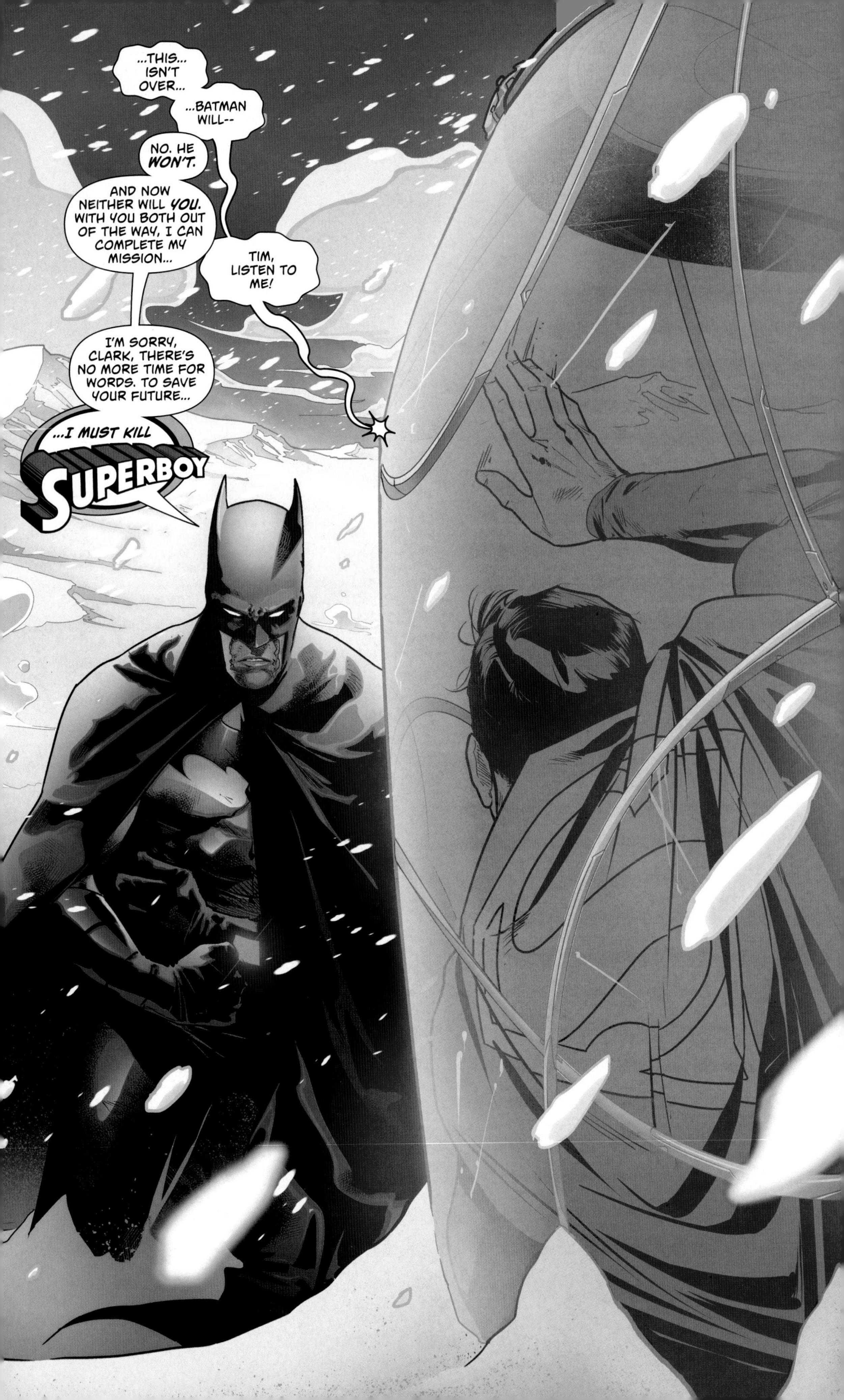
...THIS... ISN'T OVER...
...BATMAN WILL--
NO. HE WON'T.
AND NOW NEITHER WILL YOU. WITH YOU BOTH OUT OF THE WAY, I CAN COMPLETE MY MISSION...
TIM, LISTEN TO ME!
I'M SORRY, CLARK, THERE'S NO MORE TIME FOR WORDS. TO SAVE YOUR FUTURE...
...I MUST KILL
SUPERBOY

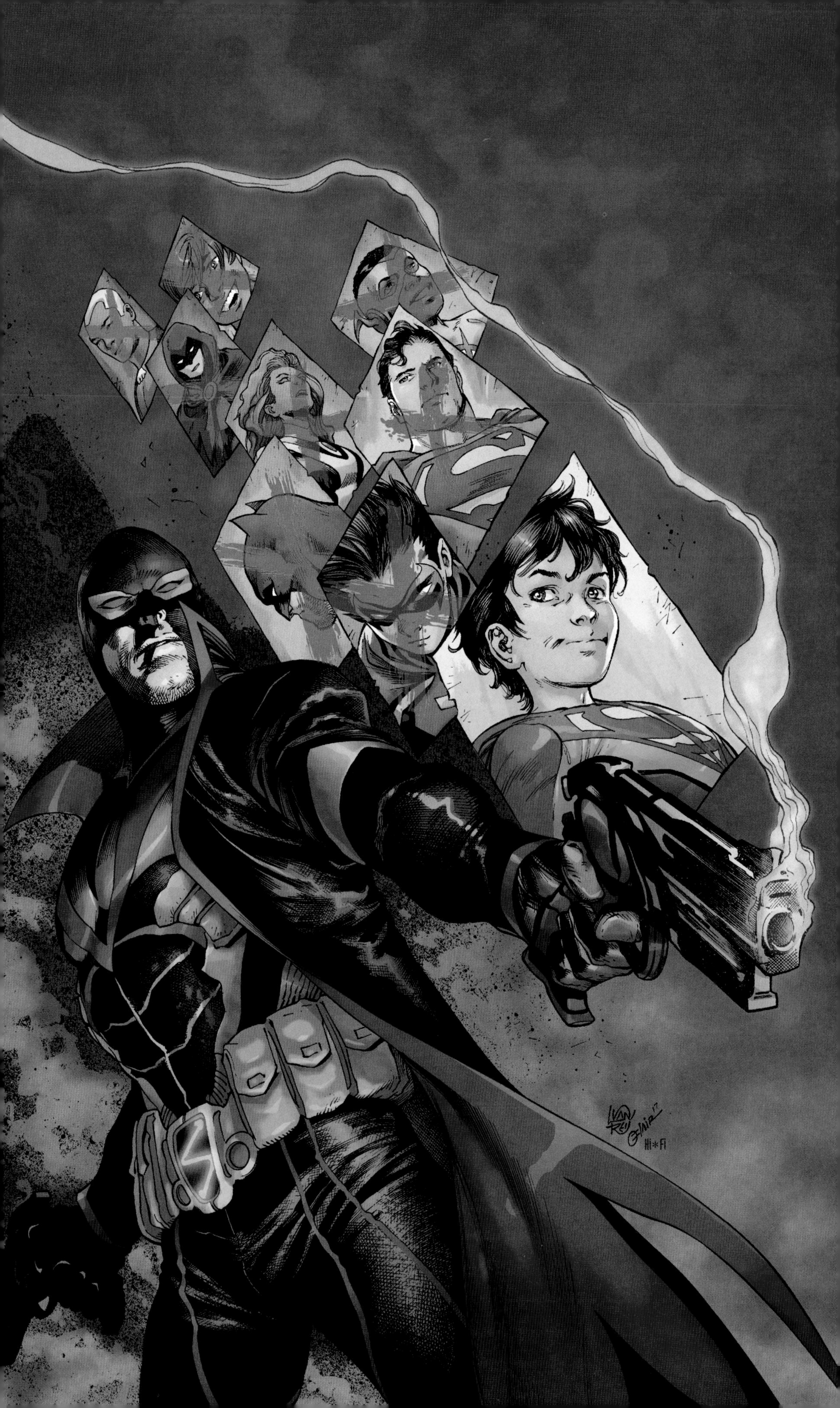

IN "SUPER SONS OF TOMORROW," PARTS TWO AND THREE:

Tim Drake, the Batman of Tomorrow, has one mission: to kill Superboy, in order to prevent a catastrophe Jon causes in the future that leaves millions dead. Tim's attack on Teen Titans Tower caused Superboy to accidentally release a huge energy wave that knocked the team unconscious. Robin whisked Superboy away from the chaos, and Tim begged Raven to track the duo in order to prevent another accident from hurting countless innocent people...

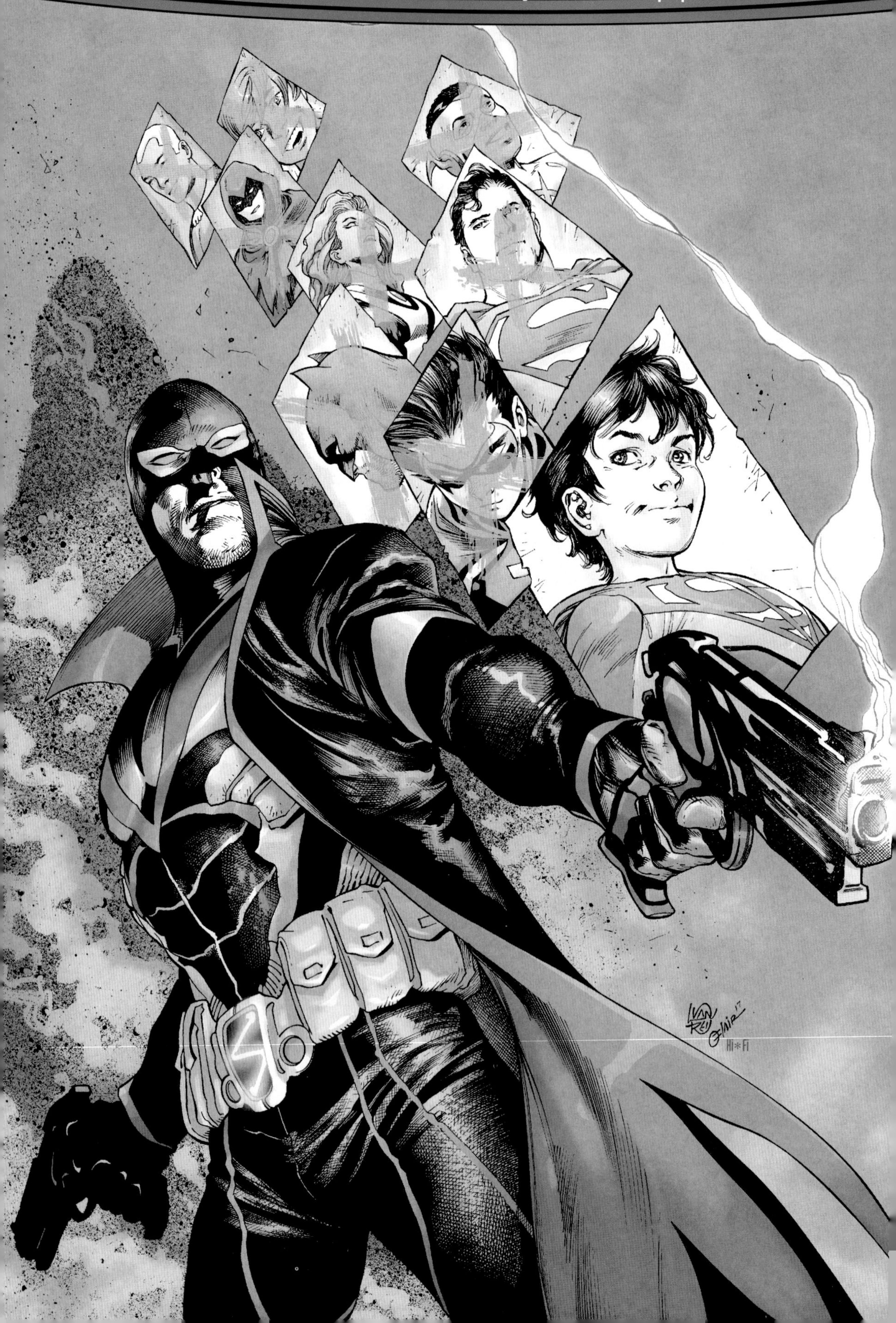

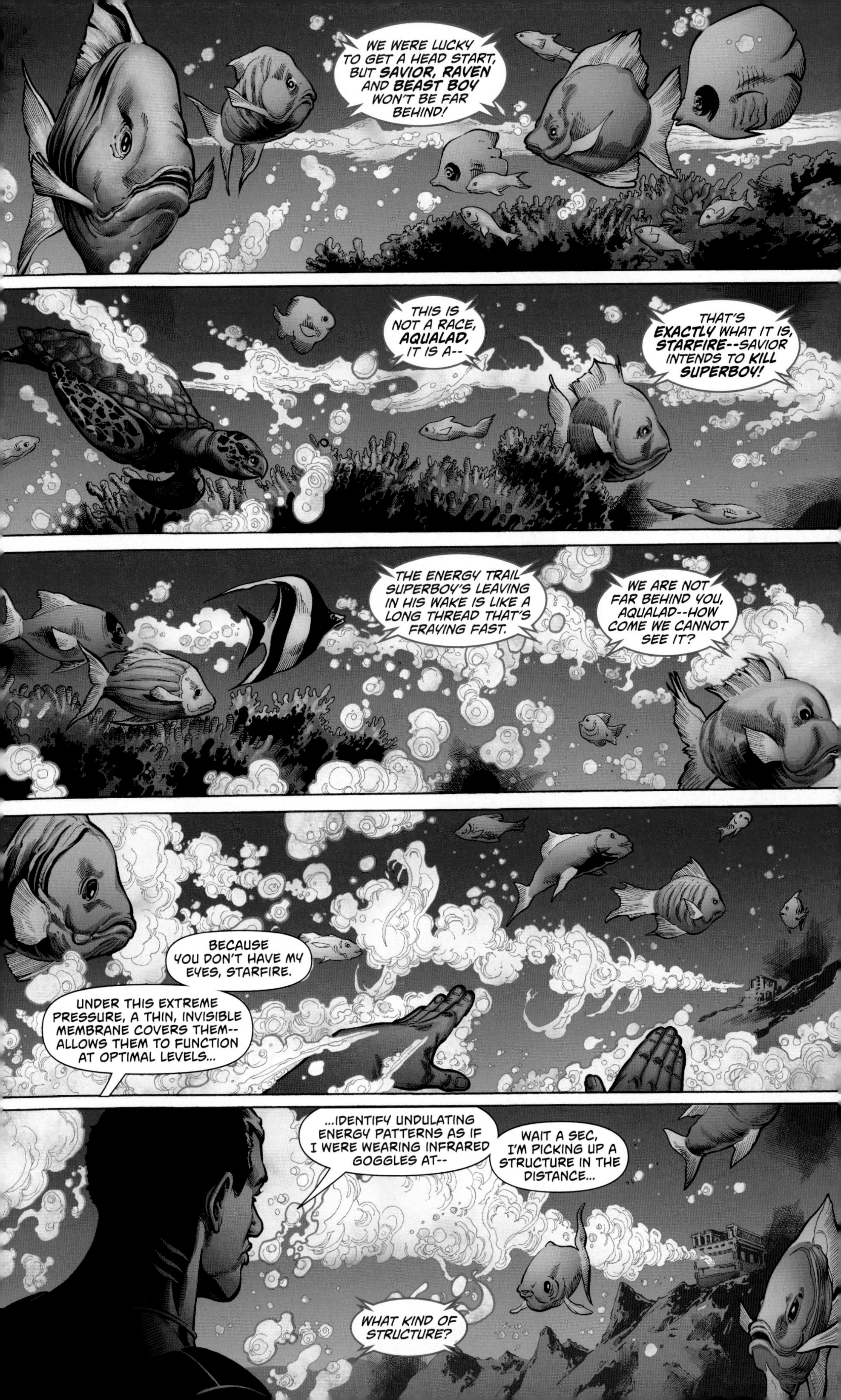
WE WERE LUCKY TO GET A HEAD START, BUT SAVIOR, RAVEN AND BEAST BOY WON'T BE FAR BEHIND!
THIS IS NOT A RACE, AQUALAD, IT IS A--
THAT'S EXACTLY WHAT IT IS, STARFIRE--SAVIOR INTENDS TO KILL SUPERBOY!
THE ENERGY TRAIL SUPERBOY'S LEAVING IN HIS WAKE IS LIKE A LONG THREAD THAT'S FRAYING FAST.
WE ARE NOT FAR BEHIND YOU, AQUALAD--HOW COME WE CANNOT SEE IT?
BECAUSE YOU DON'T HAVE MY EYES, STARFIRE.
UNDER THIS EXTREME PRESSURE, A THIN, INVISIBLE MEMBRANE COVERS THEM--ALLOWS THEM TO FUNCTION AT OPTIMAL LEVELS...
...IDENTIFY UNDULATING ENERGY PATTERNS AS IF I WERE WEARING INFRARED GOGGLES AT--
WAIT A SEC, I'M PICKING UP A STRUCTURE IN THE DISTANCE...
WHAT KIND OF STRUCTURE?

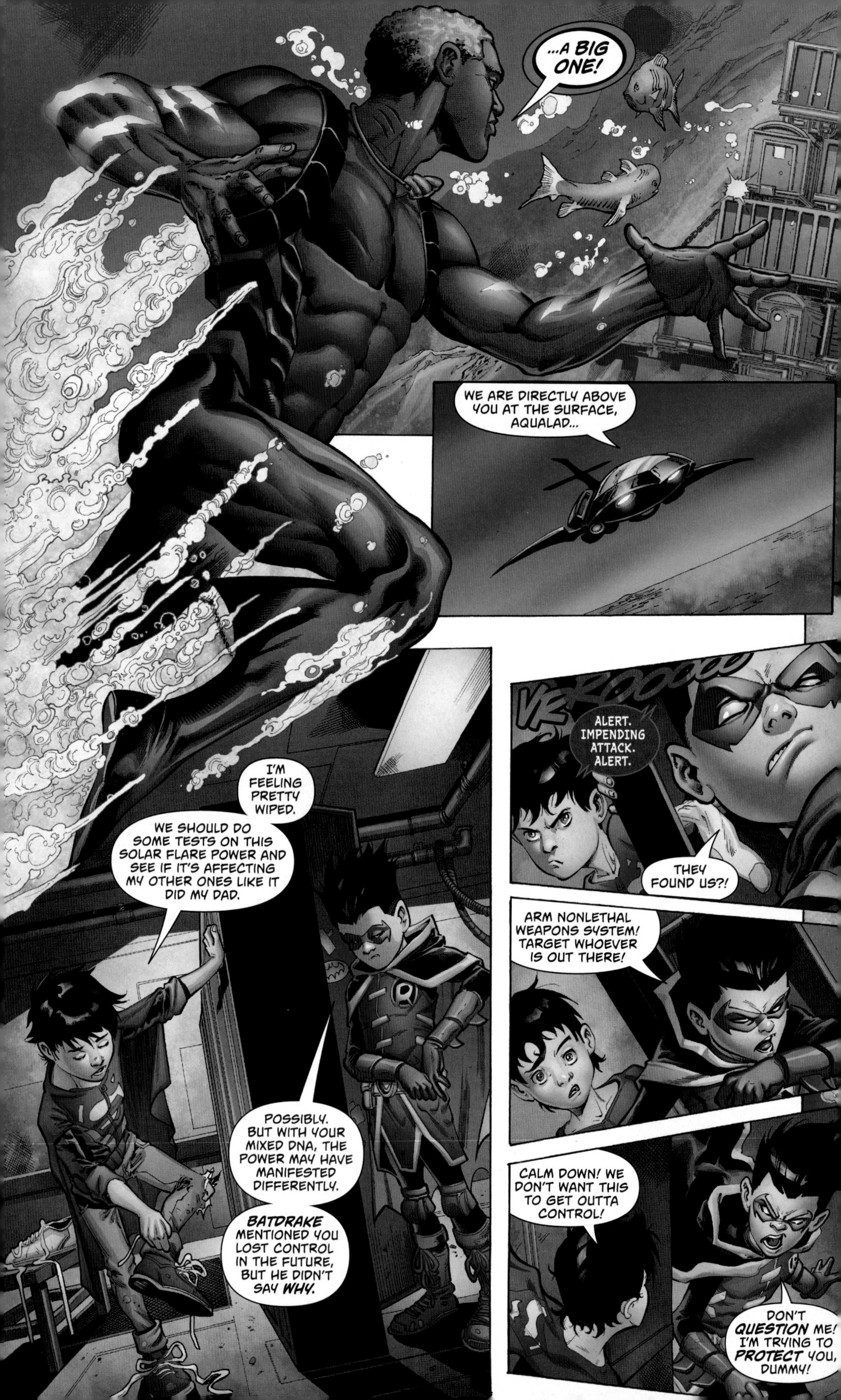

...A BIG ONE!
WE ARE DIRECTLY ABOVE YOU AT THE SURFACE, AQUALAD...
I'M FEELING PRETTY WIPED.
WE SHOULD DO SOME TESTS ON THIS SOLAR FLARE POWER AND SEE IF IT'S AFFECTING MY OTHER ONES LIKE IT DID MY DAD.
POSSIBLY. BUT WITH YOUR MIXED DNA, THE POWER MAY HAVE MANIFESTED DIFFERENTLY.
BATDRAKE MENTIONED YOU LOST CONTROL IN THE FUTURE, BUT HE DIDN'T SAY WHY.
VROOOOO
ALERT. IMPENDING ATTACK. ALERT.
THEY FOUND US?!
ARM NONLETHAL WEAPONS SYSTEM! TARGET WHOEVER IS OUT THERE!
CALM DOWN! WE DON'T WANT THIS TO GET OUTTA CONTROL!
DON'T QUESTION ME! I'M TRYING TO PROTECT YOU, DUMMY!

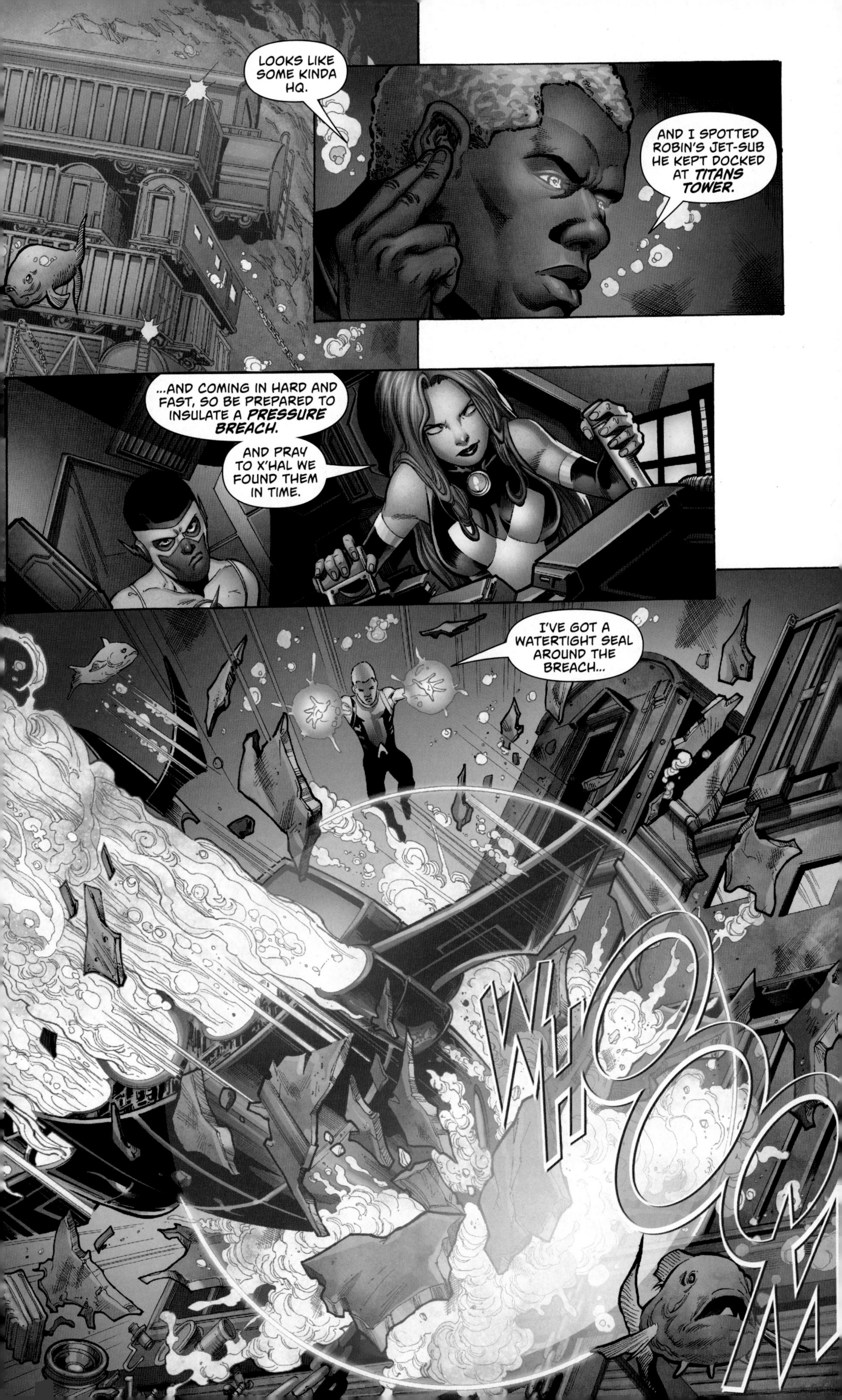

LOOKS LIKE SOME KINDA HQ.
AND I SPOTTED ROBIN'S JET-SUB HE KEPT DOCKED AT TITANS TOWER.
...AND COMING IN HARD AND FAST, SO BE PREPARED TO INSULATE A PRESSURE BREACH.
AND PRAY TO X'HAL WE FOUND THEM IN TIME.
I'VE GOT A WATERTIGHT SEAL AROUND THE BREACH...
WHOOOM

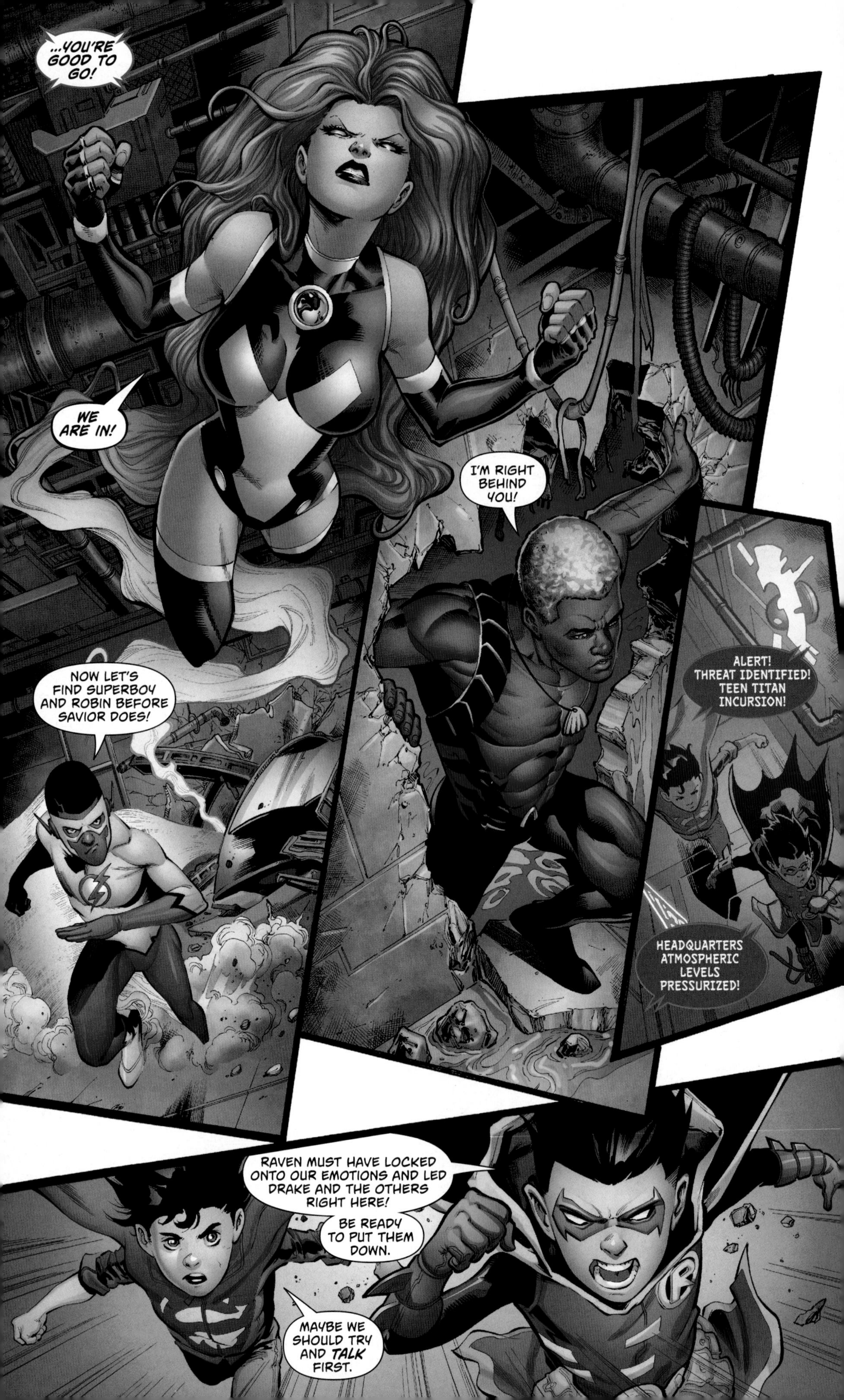
...YOU'RE GOOD TO GO!
WE ARE IN!
I'M RIGHT BEHIND YOU!
NOW LET'S FIND SUPERBOY AND ROBIN BEFORE SAVIOR DOES!
ALERT! THREAT IDENTIFIED! TEEN TITAN INCURSION!
HEADQUARTERS ATMOSPHERIC LEVELS PRESSURIZED!
RAVEN MUST HAVE LOCKED ONTO OUR EMOTIONS AND LED DRAKE AND THE OTHERS RIGHT HERE!
BE READY TO PUT THEM DOWN.
MAYBE WE SHOULD TRY AND TALK FIRST.

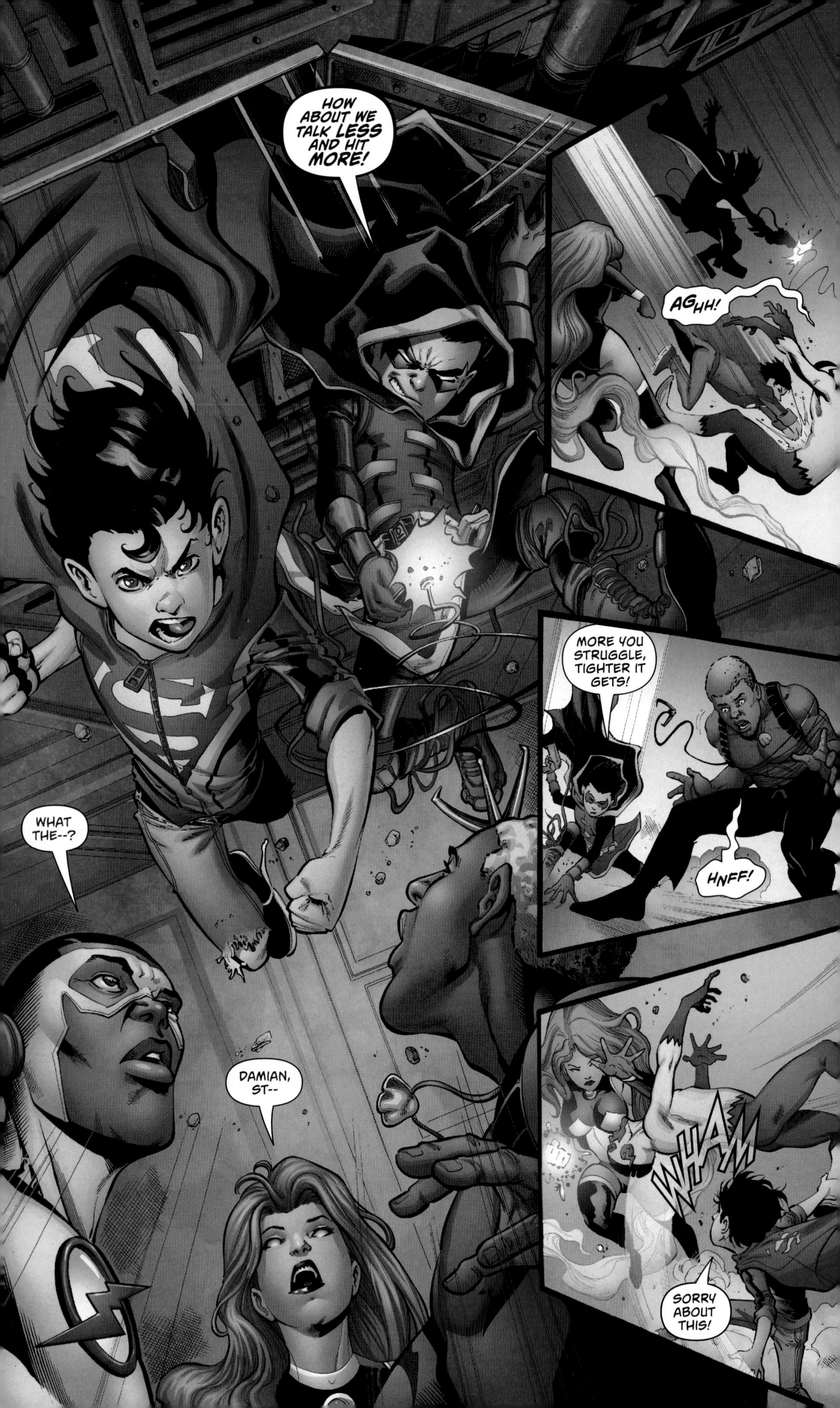
HOW ABOUT WE TALK LESS AND HIT MORE!
AGHH!
MORE YOU STRUGGLE, TIGHTER IT GETS!
HNFF!
WHAT THE--?
DAMIAN, ST--
WHAM
SORRY ABOUT THIS!

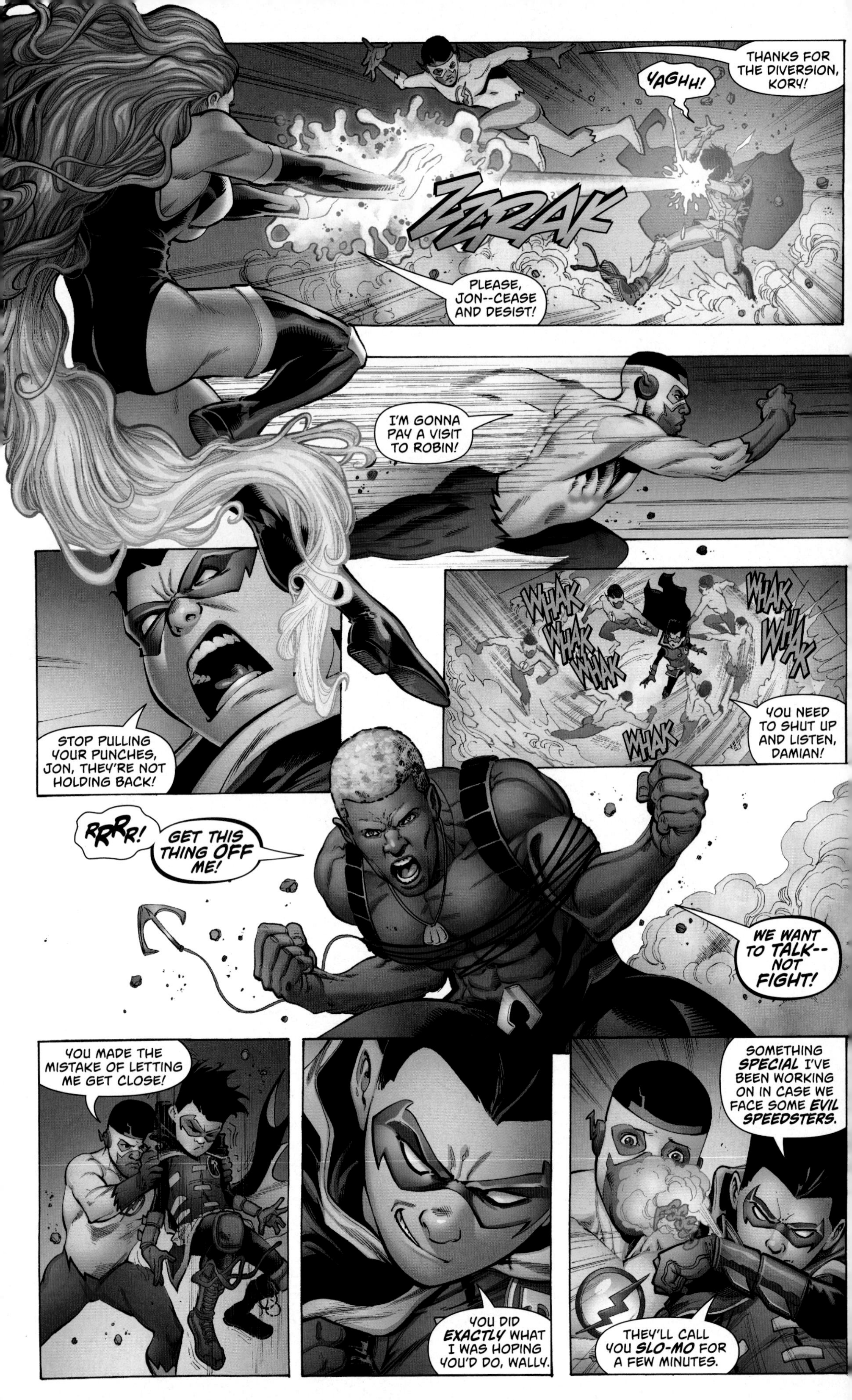
THANKS FOR THE DIVERSION, KORY!
YAGHH!
ZZRAK
PLEASE, JON--CEASE AND DESIST!
I'M GONNA PAY A VISIT TO ROBIN!
STOP PULLING YOUR PUNCHES, JON, THEY'RE NOT HOLDING BACK!
WHAK WHAK WHAK WHAK WHAK WHAK WHAK
YOU NEED TO SHUT UP AND LISTEN, DAMIAN!
RRRR!
GET THIS THING OFF ME!
WE WANT TO TALK--NOT FIGHT!
YOU MADE THE MISTAKE OF LETTING ME GET CLOSE!
YOU DID EXACTLY WHAT I WAS HOPING YOU'D DO, WALLY.
SOMETHING SPECIAL I'VE BEEN WORKING ON IN CASE WE FACE SOME EVIL SPEEDSTERS.
THEY'LL CALL YOU SLO-MO FOR A FEW MINUTES.

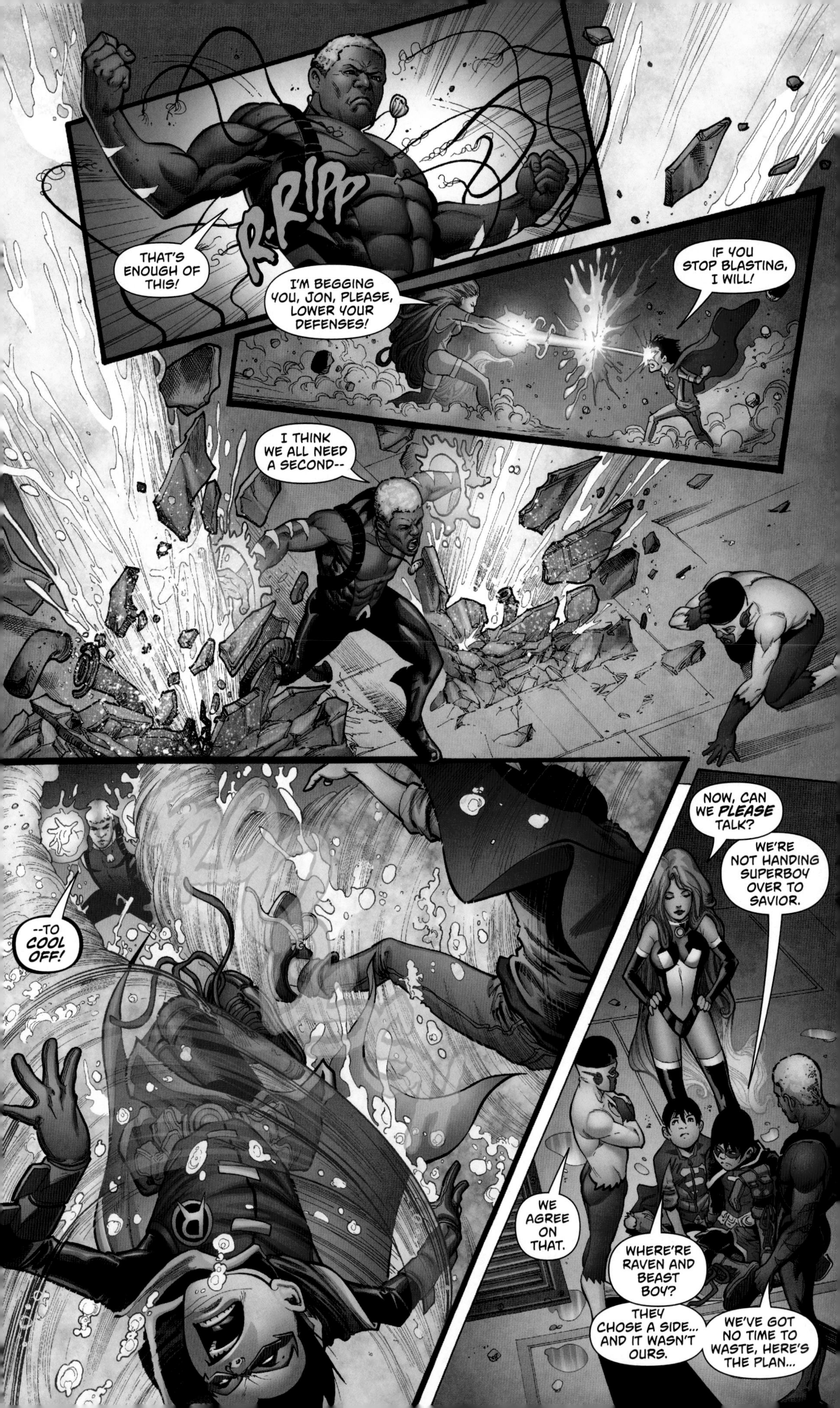
R-RIPP
THAT'S ENOUGH OF THIS!
I'M BEGGING YOU, JON, PLEASE, LOWER YOUR DEFENSES!
IF YOU STOP BLASTING, I WILL!
I THINK WE ALL NEED A SECOND--
--TO COOL OFF!
NOW, CAN WE PLEASE TALK?
WE'RE NOT HANDING SUPERBOY OVER TO SAVIOR.
WE AGREE ON THAT.
WHERE'RE RAVEN AND BEAST BOY?
THEY CHOSE A SIDE... AND IT WASN'T OURS.
WE'VE GOT NO TIME TO WASTE, HERE'S THE PLAN...

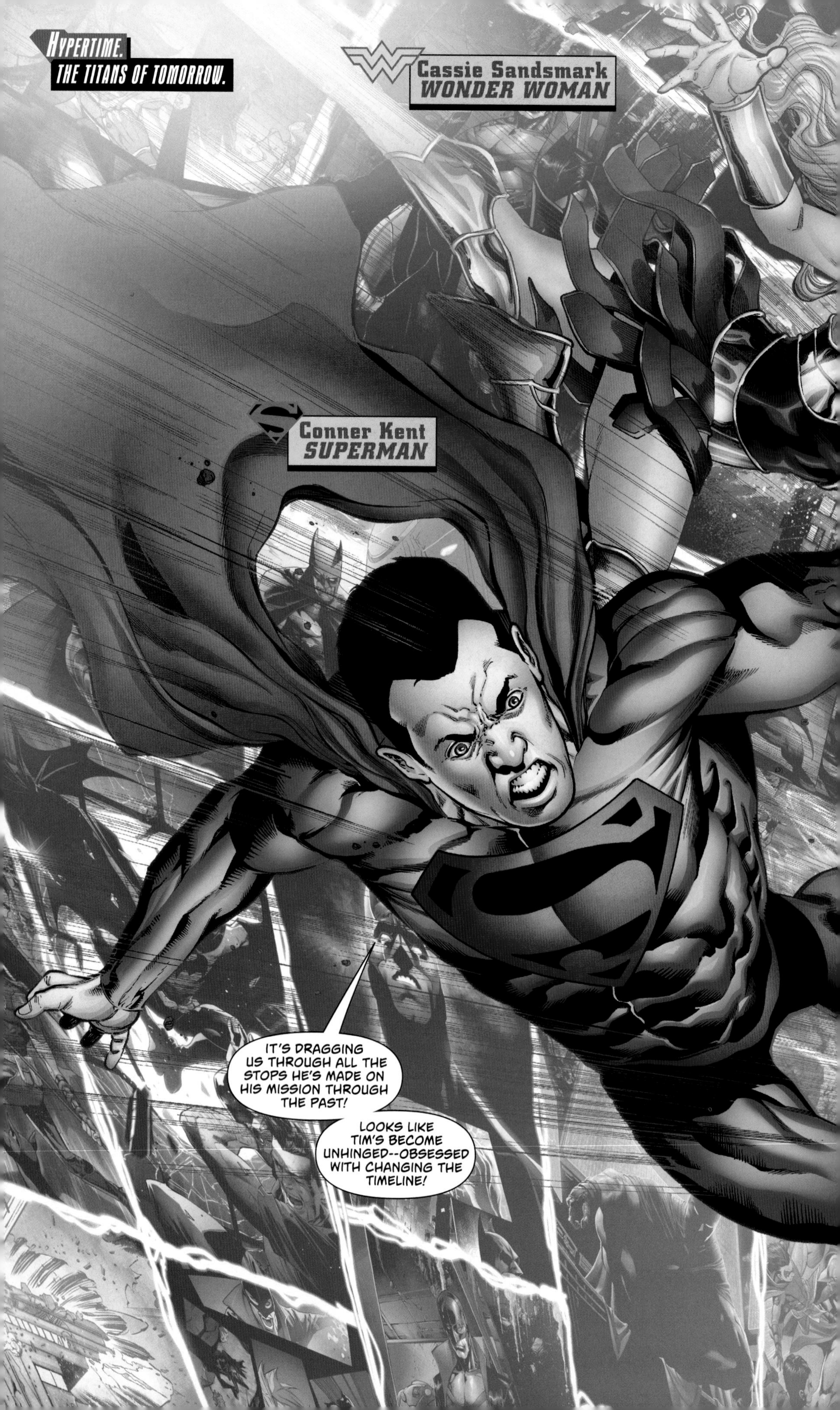
HYPERTIME.
THE TITANS OF TOMORROW.
Cassie Sandsmark
WONDER WOMAN
Conner Kent
SUPERMAN
IT'S DRAGGING US THROUGH ALL THE STOPS HE'S MADE ON HIS MISSION THROUGH THE PAST!
LOOKS LIKE TIM'S BECOME UNHINGED--OBSESSED WITH CHANGING THE TIMELINE!

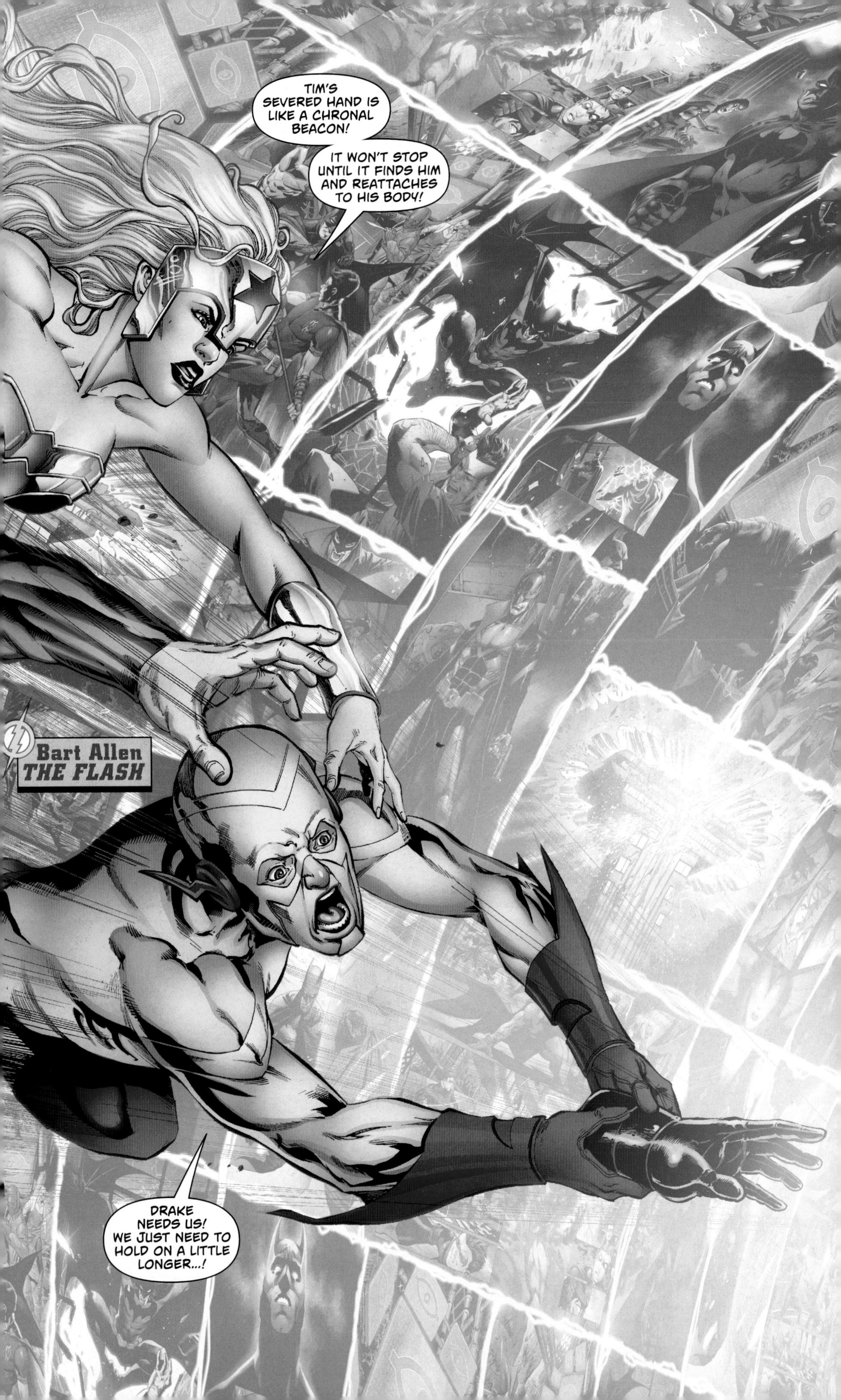
TIM'S SEVERED HAND IS LIKE A CHRONAL BEACON!
IT WON'T STOP UNTIL IT FINDS HIM AND REATTACHES TO HIS BODY!
Bart Allen THE FLASH
DRAKE NEEDS US! WE JUST NEED TO HOLD ON A LITTLE LONGER...!

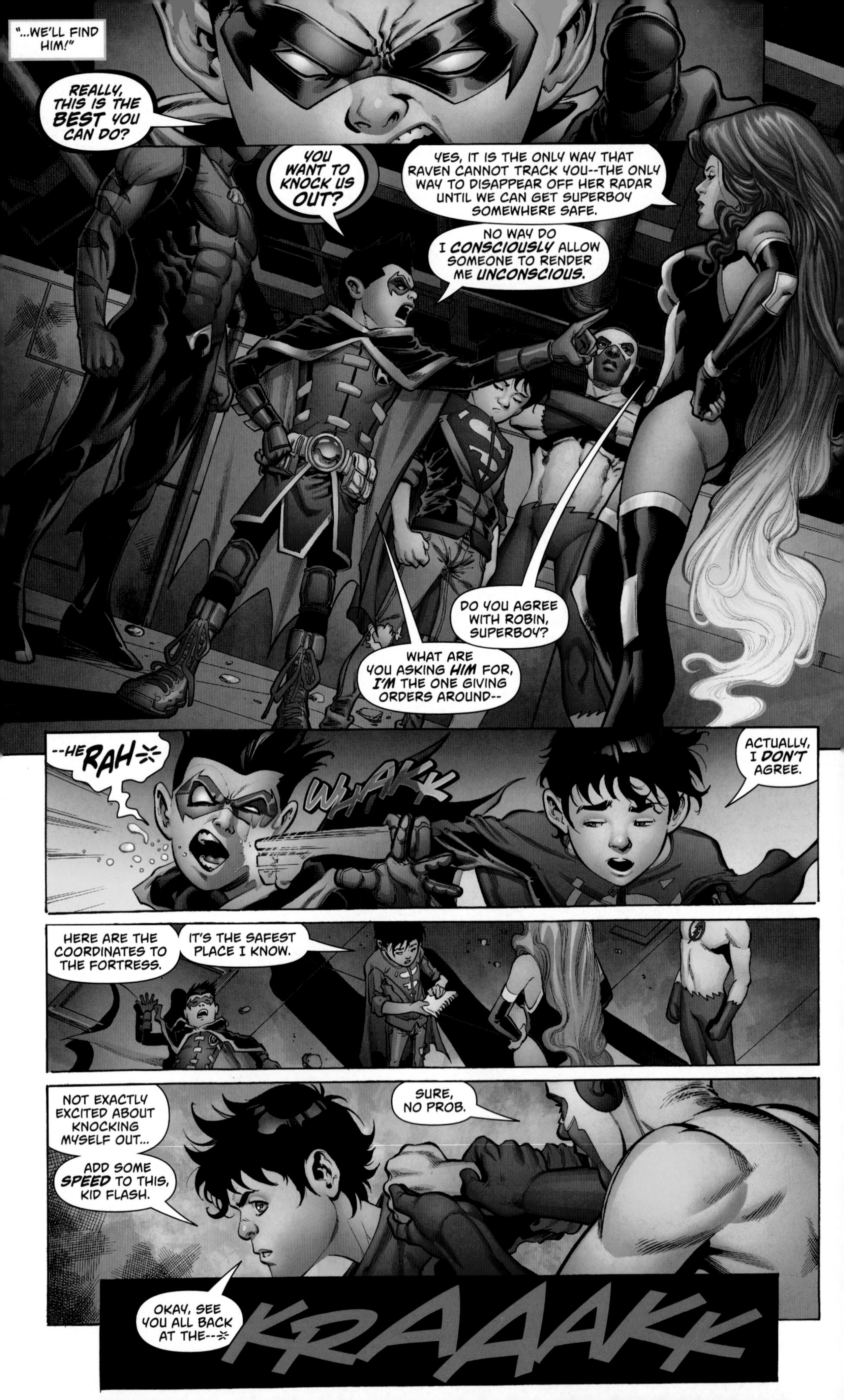
"...WE'LL FIND HIM!"
REALLY, THIS IS THE BEST YOU CAN DO?
YOU WANT TO KNOCK US OUT?
YES, IT IS THE ONLY WAY THAT RAVEN CANNOT TRACK YOU--THE ONLY WAY TO DISAPPEAR OFF HER RADAR UNTIL WE CAN GET SUPERBOY SOMEWHERE SAFE.
NO WAY DO I CONSCIOUSLY ALLOW SOMEONE TO RENDER ME UNCONSCIOUS.
DO YOU AGREE WITH ROBIN, SUPERBOY?
WHAT ARE YOU ASKING HIM FOR, I'M THE ONE GIVING ORDERS AROUND--
--HERAH
WHAKK
ACTUALLY, I DON'T AGREE.
HERE ARE THE COORDINATES TO THE FORTRESS.
IT'S THE SAFEST PLACE I KNOW.
NOT EXACTLY EXCITED ABOUT KNOCKING MYSELF OUT...
SURE, NO PROB.
ADD SOME SPEED TO THIS, KID FLASH.
OKAY, SEE YOU ALL BACK AT THE--
KRAAAKK

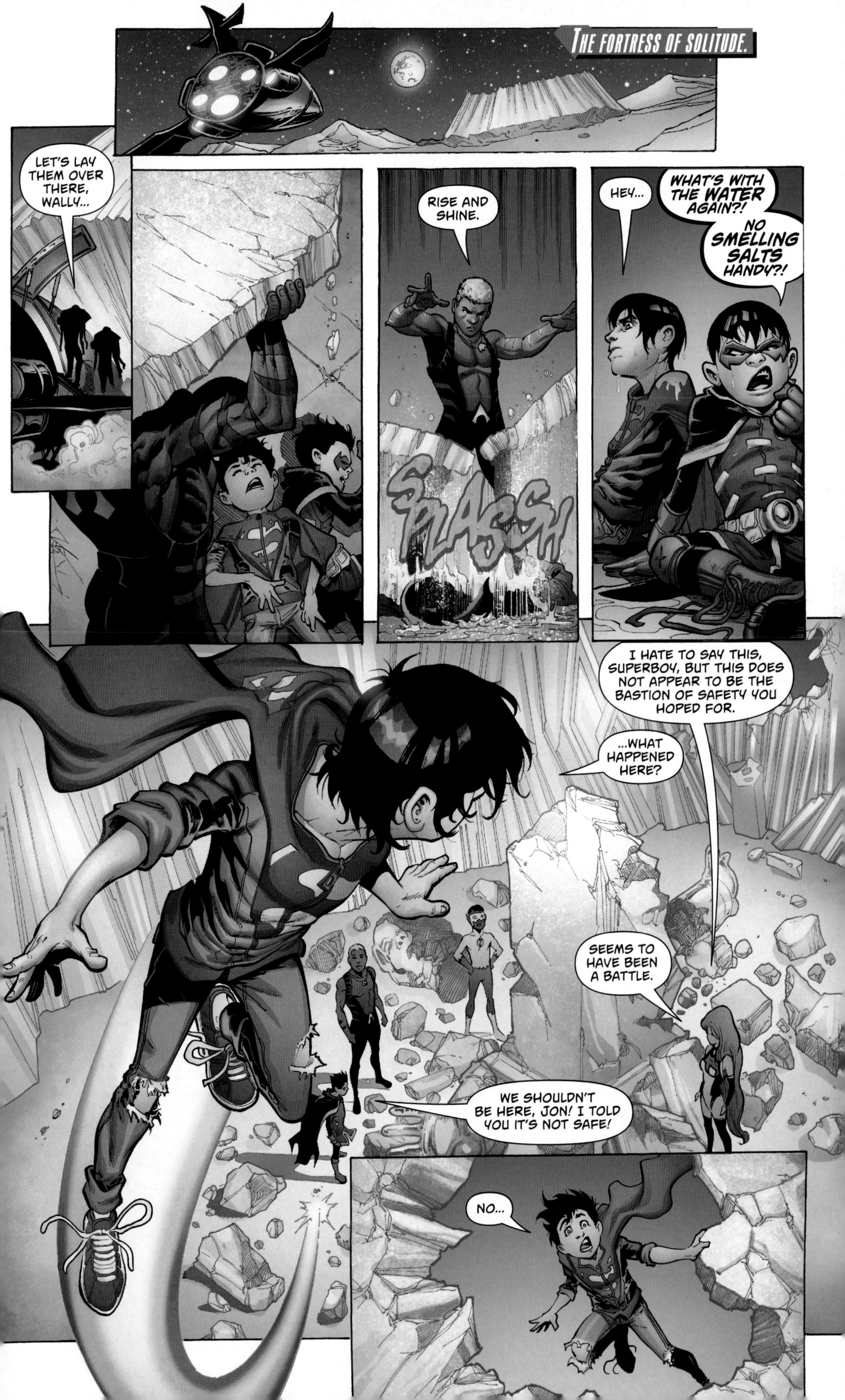

THE FORTRESS OF SOLITUDE.
LET'S LAY THEM OVER THERE, WALLY...
RISE AND SHINE.
SPLASSH
HEY...
WHAT'S WITH THE WATER AGAIN?!
NO SMELLING SALTS HANDY?!
I HATE TO SAY THIS, SUPERBOY, BUT THIS DOES NOT APPEAR TO BE THE BASTION OF SAFETY YOU HOPED FOR.
...WHAT HAPPENED HERE?
SEEMS TO HAVE BEEN A BATTLE.
WE SHOULDN'T BE HERE, JON! I TOLD YOU IT'S NOT SAFE!
NO...

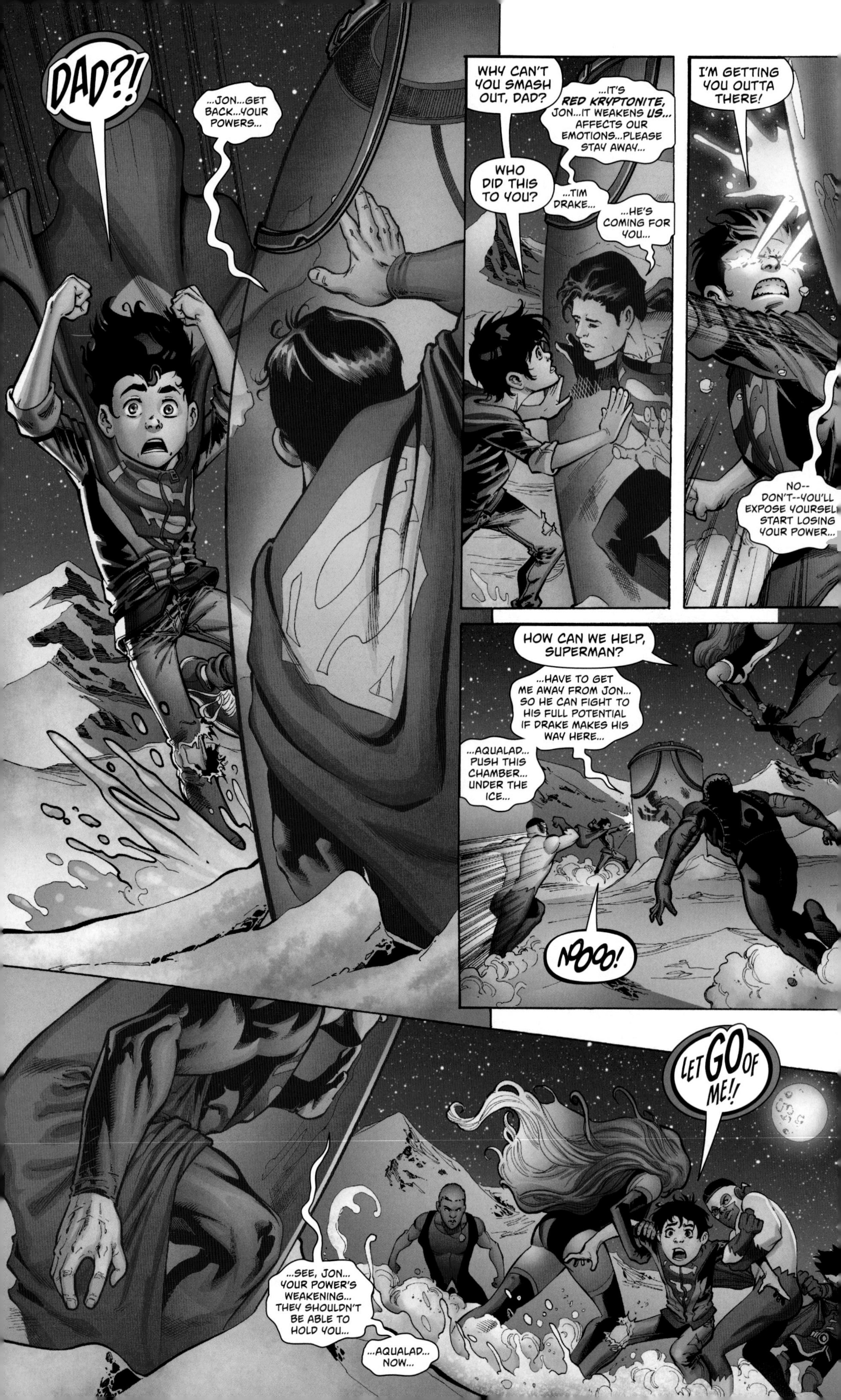
DAD?!
...JON...GET BACK...YOUR POWERS...
WHY CAN'T YOU SMASH OUT, DAD?
...IT'S RED KRYPTONITE, JON...IT WEAKENS US... AFFECTS OUR EMOTIONS...PLEASE STAY AWAY...
WHO DID THIS TO YOU?
...TIM DRAKE...
...HE'S COMING FOR YOU...
I'M GETTING YOU OUTTA THERE!
NO-- DON'T--YOU'LL EXPOSE YOURSEL START LOSING YOUR POWER...
HOW CAN WE HELP, SUPERMAN?
...HAVE TO GET ME AWAY FROM JON... SO HE CAN FIGHT TO HIS FULL POTENTIAL IF DRAKE MAKES HIS WAY HERE...
...AQUALAD... PUSH THIS CHAMBER... UNDER THE ICE...
NOOOO!
LET GO OF ME!!
...SEE, JON... YOUR POWER'S WEAKENING... THEY SHOULDN'T BE ABLE TO HOLD YOU...
...AQUALAD... NOW...

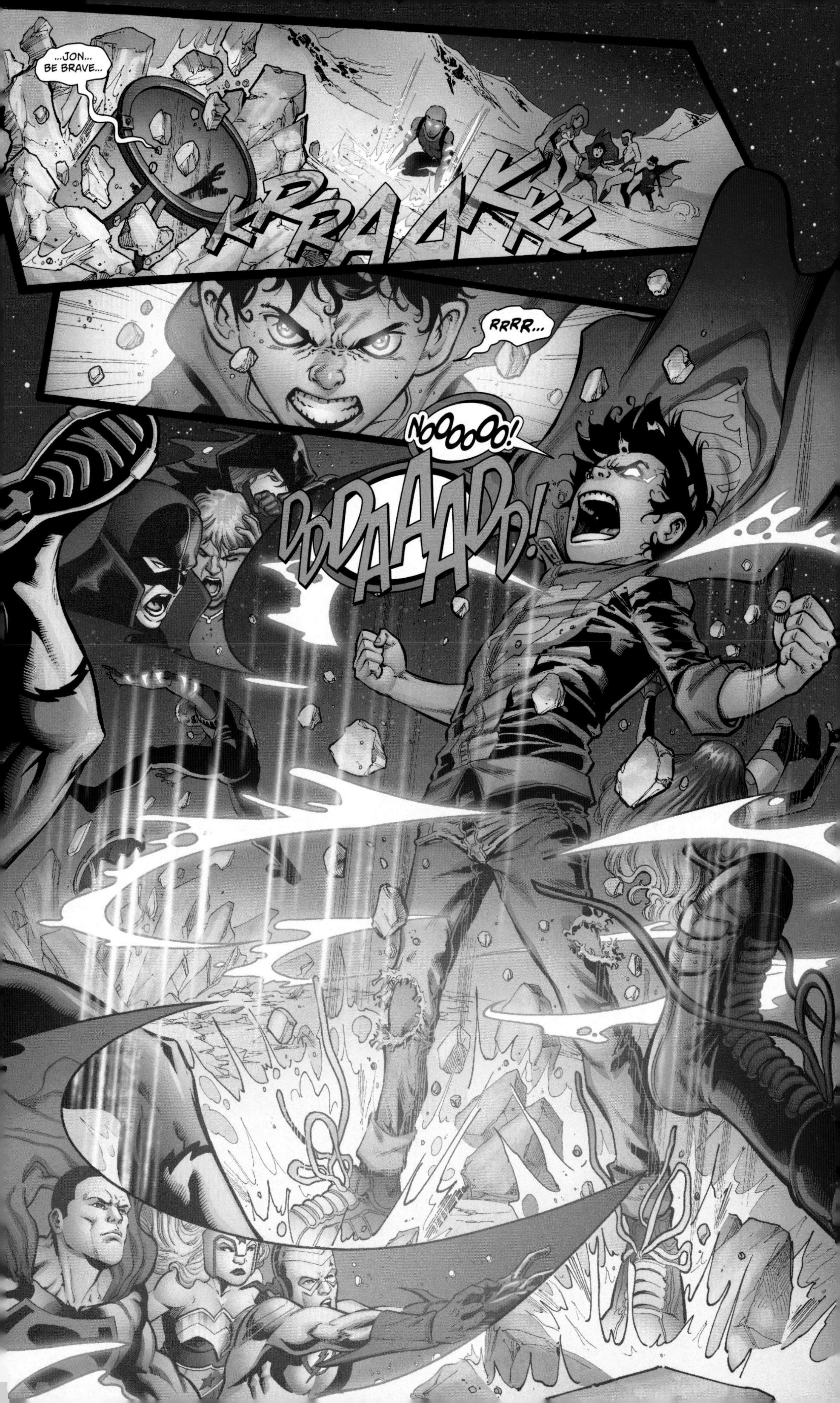
...JON... BE BRAVE...
KRRAAKKK
RRRR...
NOOOOOO!
DDDAAAADD!

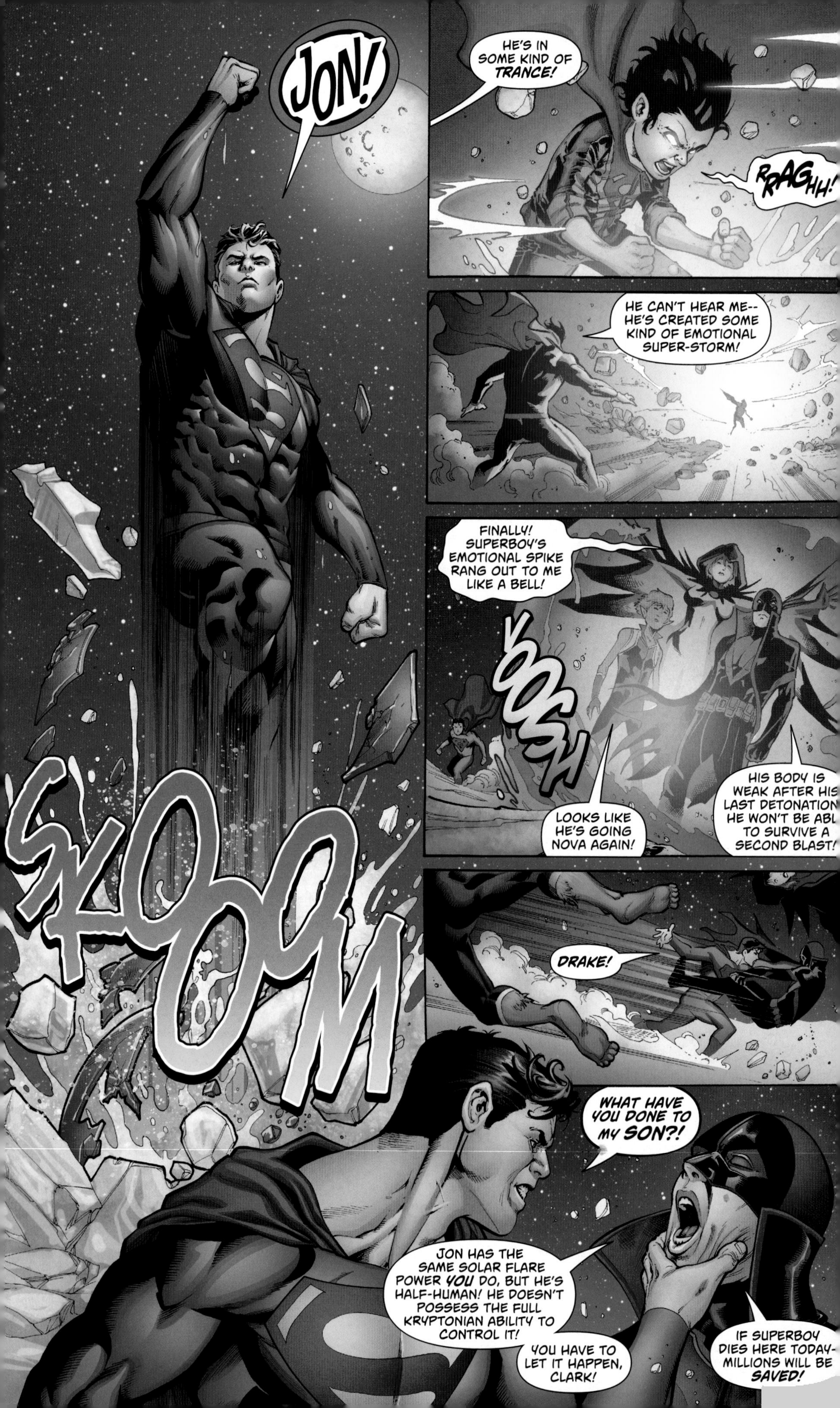
JON!
HE'S IN SOME KIND OF TRANCE!
RRAGHH!
HE CAN'T HEAR ME-- HE'S CREATED SOME KIND OF EMOTIONAL SUPER-STORM!
FINALLY! SUPERBOY'S EMOTIONAL SPIKE RANG OUT TO ME LIKE A BELL!
VOOSH
LOOKS LIKE HE'S GOING NOVA AGAIN!
HIS BODY IS WEAK AFTER HIS LAST DETONATION HE WON'T BE ABL TO SURVIVE A SECOND BLAST!
DRAKE!
SKOOM
WHAT HAVE YOU DONE TO MY SON?!
JON HAS THE SAME SOLAR FLARE POWER YOU DO, BUT HE'S HALF-HUMAN! HE DOESN'T POSSESS THE FULL KRYPTONIAN ABILITY TO CONTROL IT!
YOU HAVE TO LET IT HAPPEN, CLARK!
IF SUPERBOY DIES HERE TODAY-MILLIONS WILL BE SAVED!

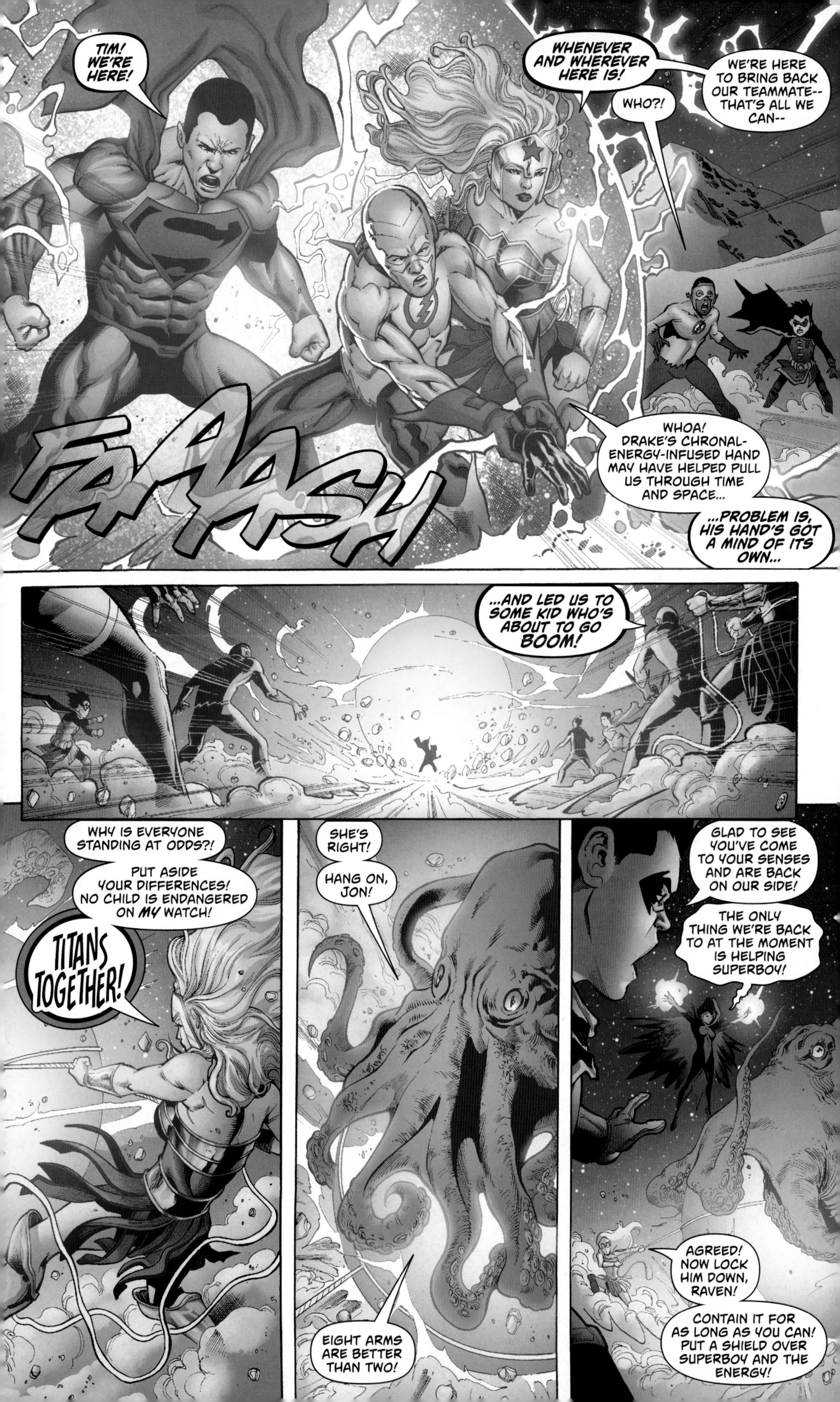
TIM! WE'RE HERE!
WHENEVER AND WHEREVER HERE IS!
WE'RE HERE TO BRING BACK OUR TEAMMATE-- THAT'S ALL WE CAN--
WHO?!
FAAASH
WHOA! DRAKE'S CHRONAL-ENERGY-INFUSED HAND MAY HAVE HELPED PULL US THROUGH TIME AND SPACE...
...PROBLEM IS, HIS HAND'S GOT A MIND OF ITS OWN...
...AND LED US TO SOME KID WHO'S ABOUT TO GO BOOM!
WHY IS EVERYONE STANDING AT ODDS?!
PUT ASIDE YOUR DIFFERENCES! NO CHILD IS ENDANGERED ON MY WATCH!
TITANS TOGETHER!
SHE'S RIGHT!
HANG ON, JON!
EIGHT ARMS ARE BETTER THAN TWO!
GLAD TO SEE YOU'VE COME TO YOUR SENSES AND ARE BACK ON OUR SIDE!
THE ONLY THING WE'RE BACK TO AT THE MOMENT IS HELPING SUPERBOY!
AGREED! NOW LOCK HIM DOWN, RAVEN!
CONTAIN IT FOR AS LONG AS YOU CAN! PUT A SHIELD OVER SUPERBOY AND THE ENERGY!

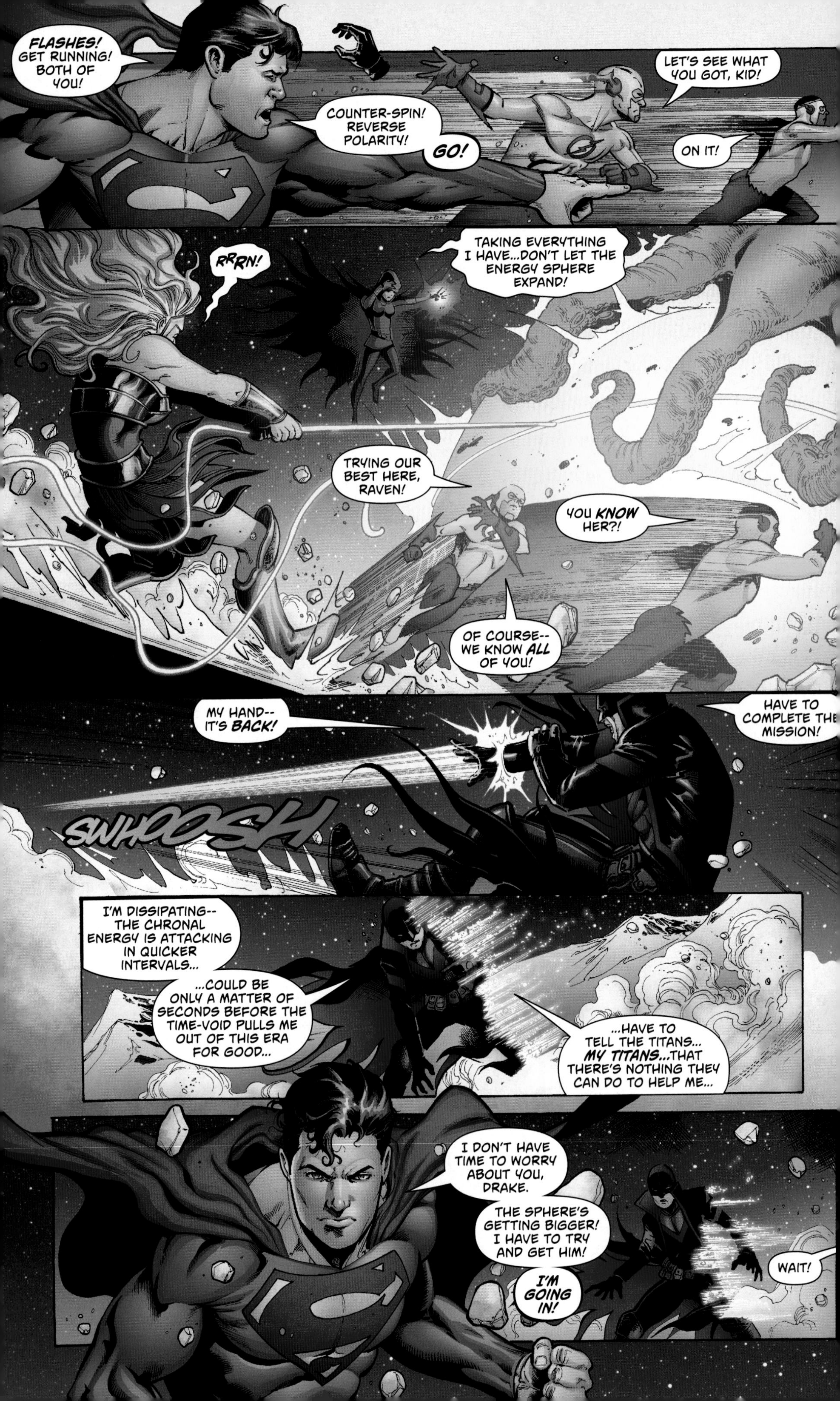
FLASHES! GET RUNNING! BOTH OF YOU!
COUNTER-SPIN! REVERSE POLARITY!
GO!
LET'S SEE WHAT YOU GOT, KID!
ON IT!
RRRN!
TAKING EVERYTHING I HAVE...DON'T LET THE ENERGY SPHERE EXPAND!
TRYING OUR BEST HERE, RAVEN!
YOU KNOW HER?!
OF COURSE-- WE KNOW ALL OF YOU!
MY HAND-- IT'S BACK!
HAVE TO COMPLETE THE MISSION!
SWHOOSH
I'M DISSIPATING-- THE CHRONAL ENERGY IS ATTACKING IN QUICKER INTERVALS...
...COULD BE ONLY A MATTER OF SECONDS BEFORE THE TIME-VOID PULLS ME OUT OF THIS ERA FOR GOOD...
...HAVE TO TELL THE TITANS... MY TITANS...THAT THERE'S NOTHING THEY CAN DO TO HELP ME...
I DON'T HAVE TIME TO WORRY ABOUT YOU, DRAKE.
THE SPHERE'S GETTING BIGGER! I HAVE TO TRY AND GET HIM!
I'M GOING IN!
WAIT!

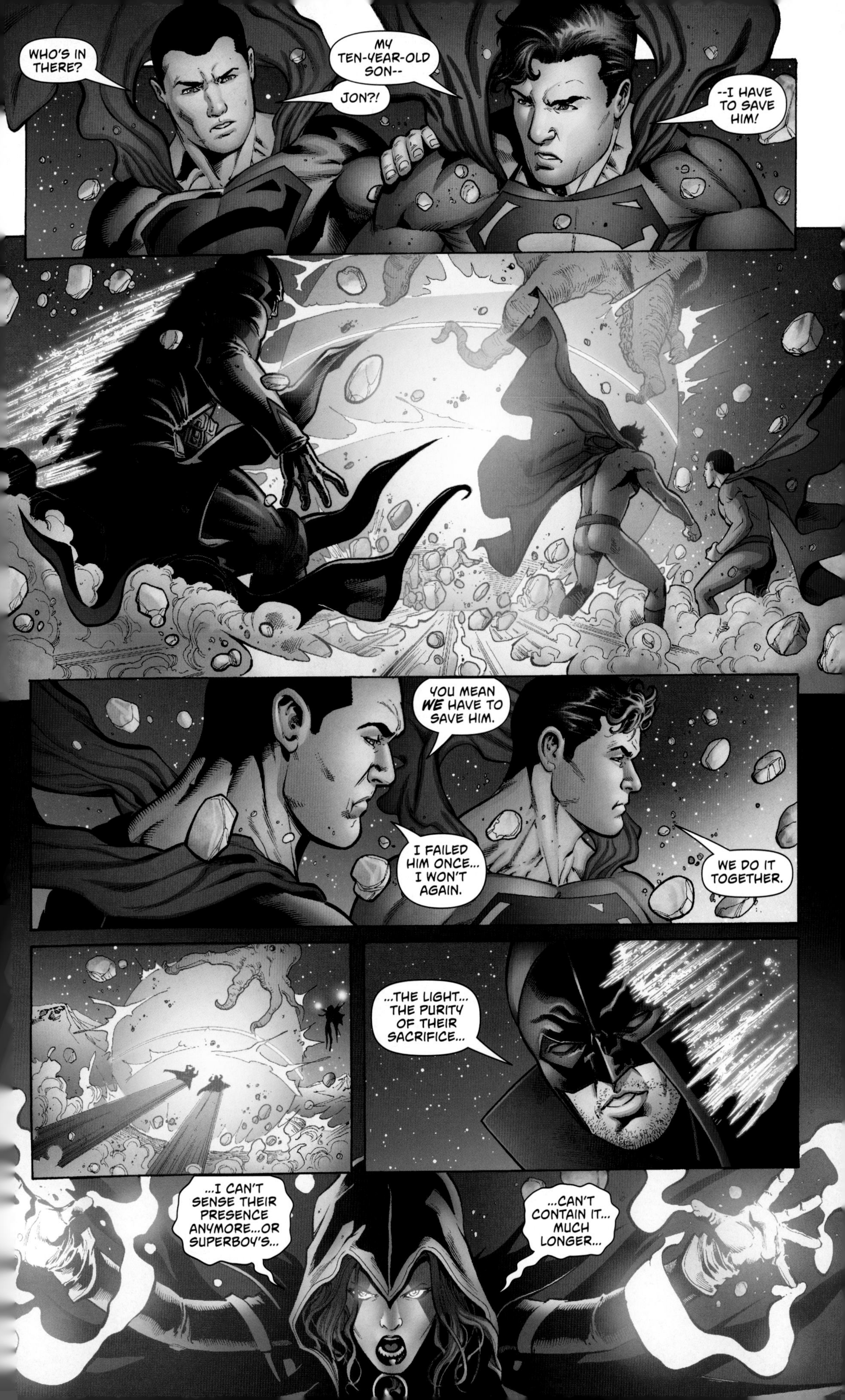
WHO'S IN THERE?
MY TEN-YEAR-OLD SON--
JON?!
--I HAVE TO SAVE HIM!
YOU MEAN WE HAVE TO SAVE HIM.
I FAILED HIM ONCE... I WON'T AGAIN.
WE DO IT TOGETHER.
...THE LIGHT... THE PURITY OF THEIR SACRIFICE...
...I CAN'T SENSE THEIR PRESENCE ANYMORE...OR SUPERBOY'S...
...CAN'T CONTAIN IT... MUCH LONGER...

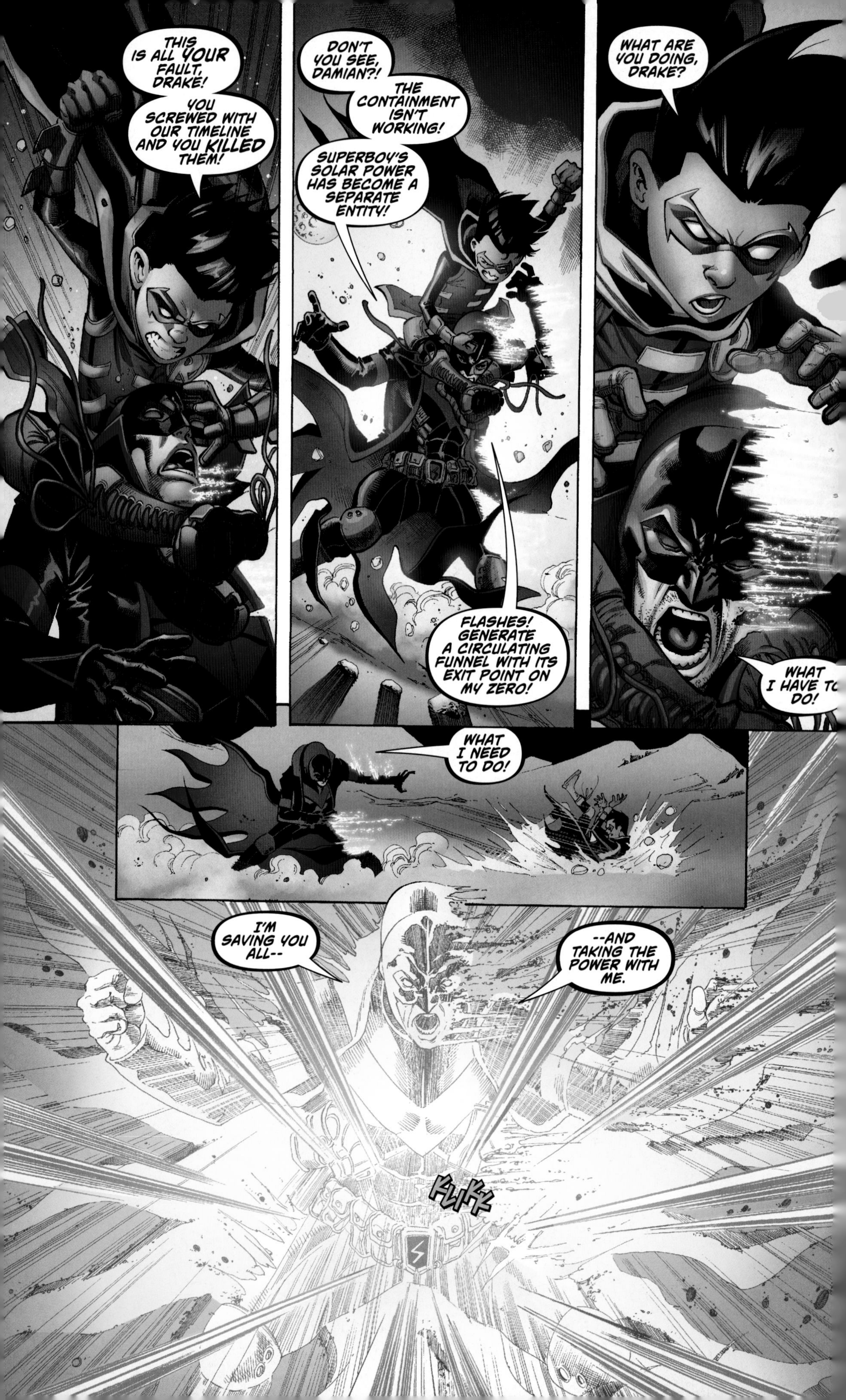
THIS IS ALL YOUR FAULT, DRAKE!
YOU SCREWED WITH OUR TIMELINE AND YOU KILLED THEM!
DON'T YOU SEE, DAMIAN?!
THE CONTAINMENT ISN'T WORKING!
SUPERBOY'S SOLAR POWER HAS BECOME A SEPARATE ENTITY!
FLASHES! GENERATE A CIRCULATING FUNNEL WITH ITS EXIT POINT ON MY ZERO!
WHAT ARE YOU DOING, DRAKE?
WHAT I HAVE TO DO!
WHAT I NEED TO DO!
I'M SAVING YOU ALL--
--AND TAKING THE POWER WITH ME.
KLIKK

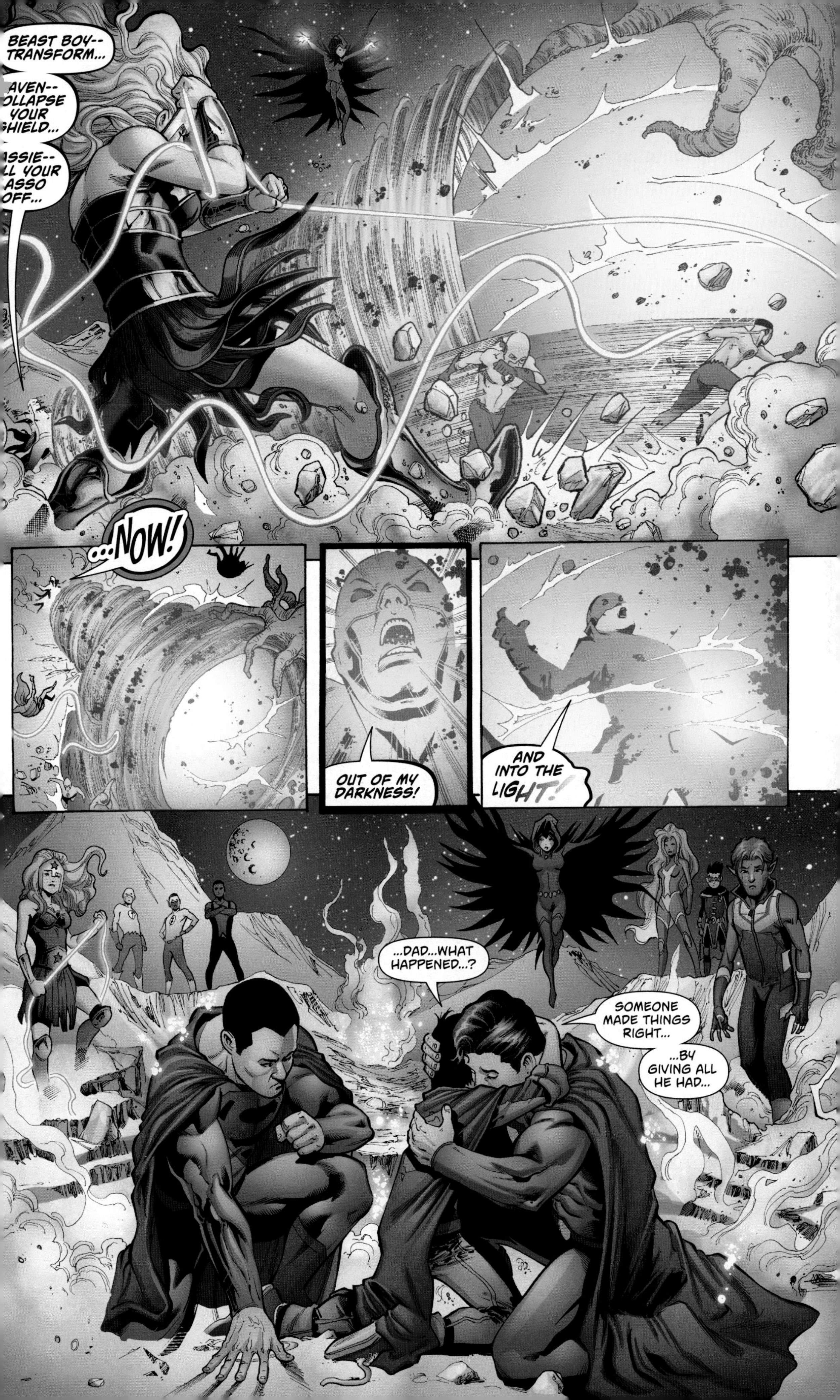

BEAST BOY-- TRANSFORM...
AVEN-- OLLAPSE YOUR SHIELD...
ASSIE-- LL YOUR ASSO OFF...
...NOW!
OUT OF MY DARKNESS!
AND INTO THE LIGHT!
...DAD...WHAT HAPPENED...?
SOMEONE MADE THINGS RIGHT...
...BY GIVING ALL HE HAD...

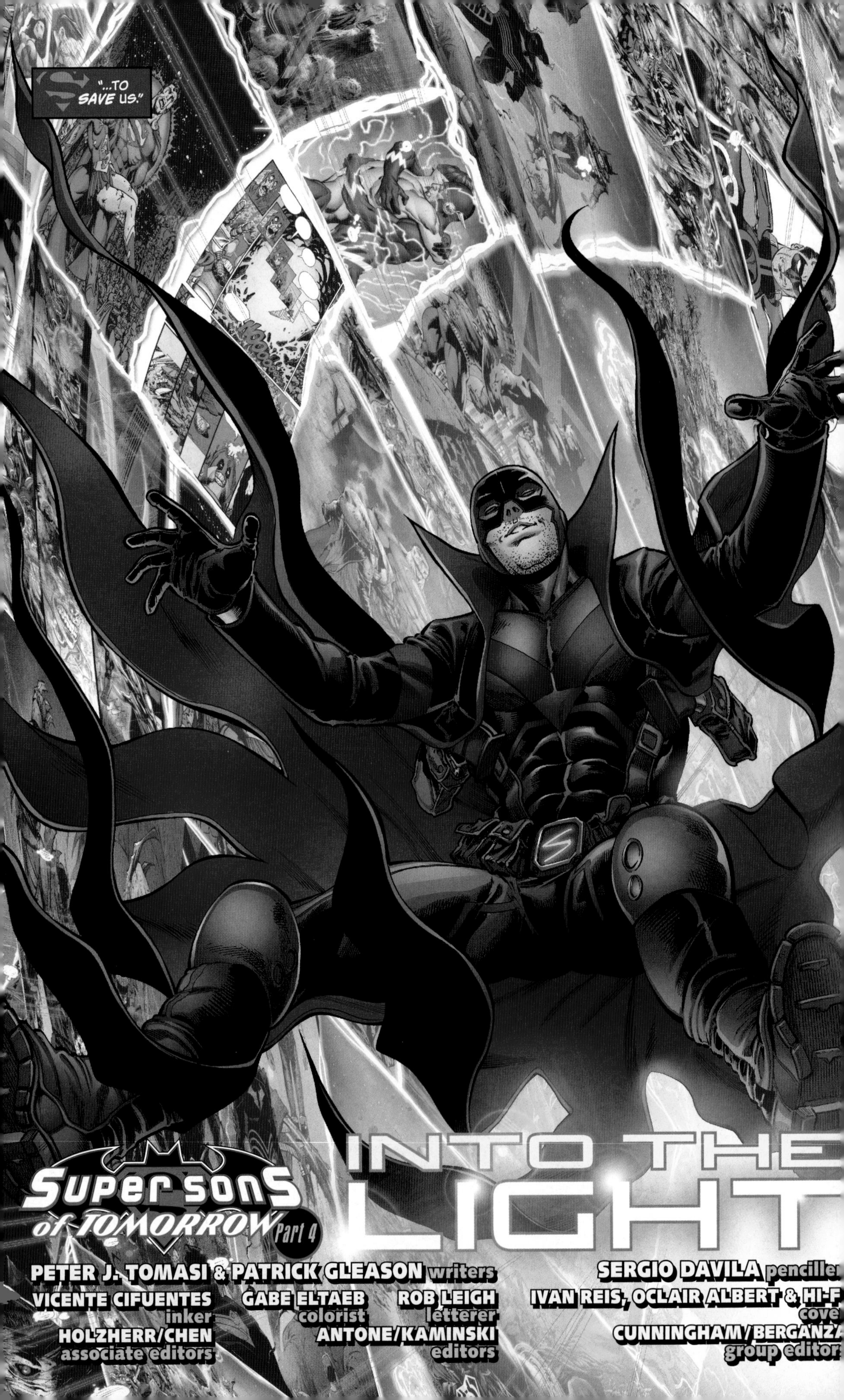
"...TO SAVE US."
Super sons of TOMORROW Part 4
INTO THE LIGHT
PETER J. TOMASI & PATRICK GLEASON writers
SERGIO DAVILA pencille
VICENTE CIFUENTES inker
GABE ELTAEB colorist
ROB LEIGH letterer
IVAN REIS, OCLAIR ALBERT & HI-F
cove
HOLZHERR/CHEN associate editors
ANTONE/KAMINSKI editors
CUNNINGHAM/BERGANZA group editor

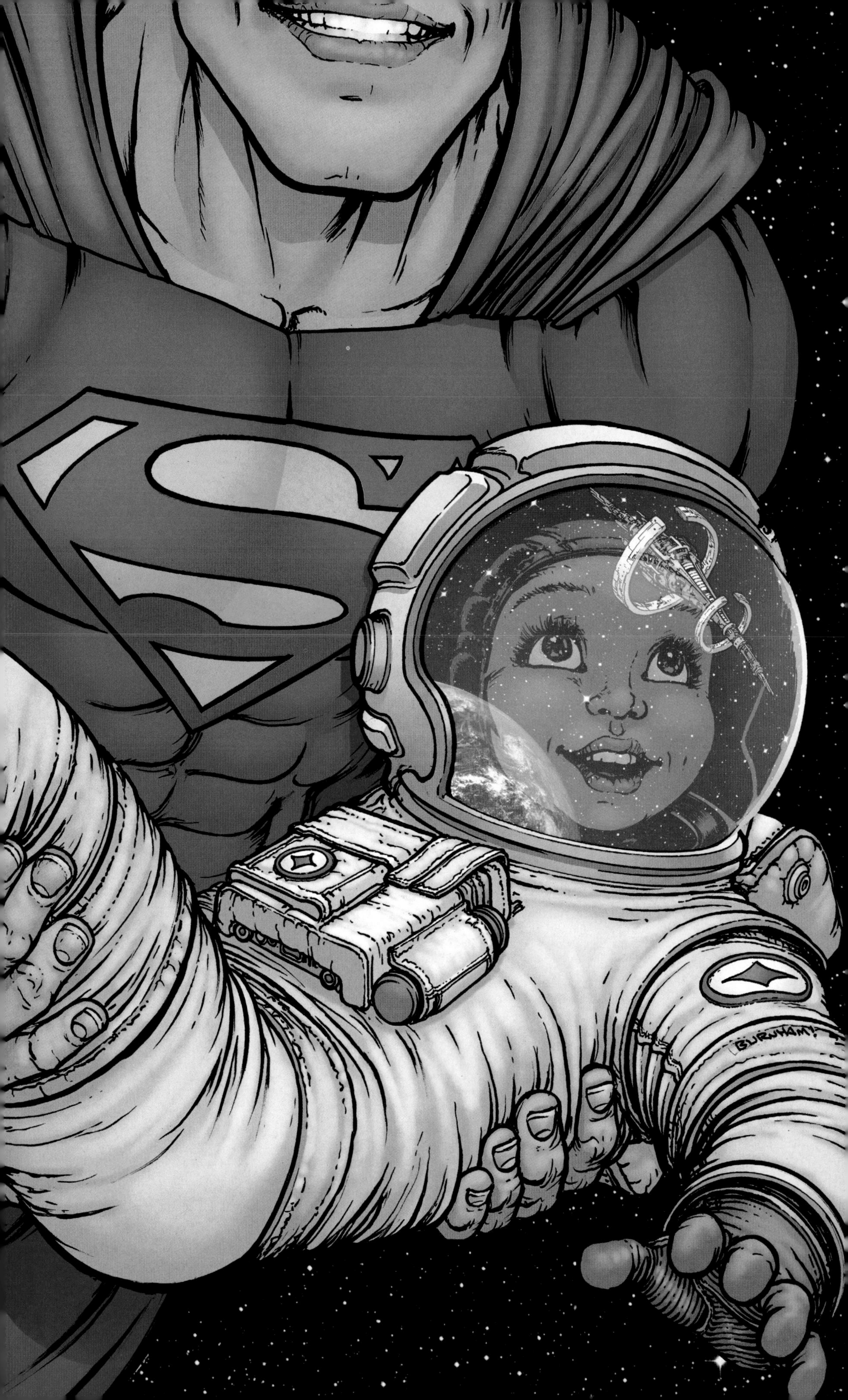
BURNHAM!

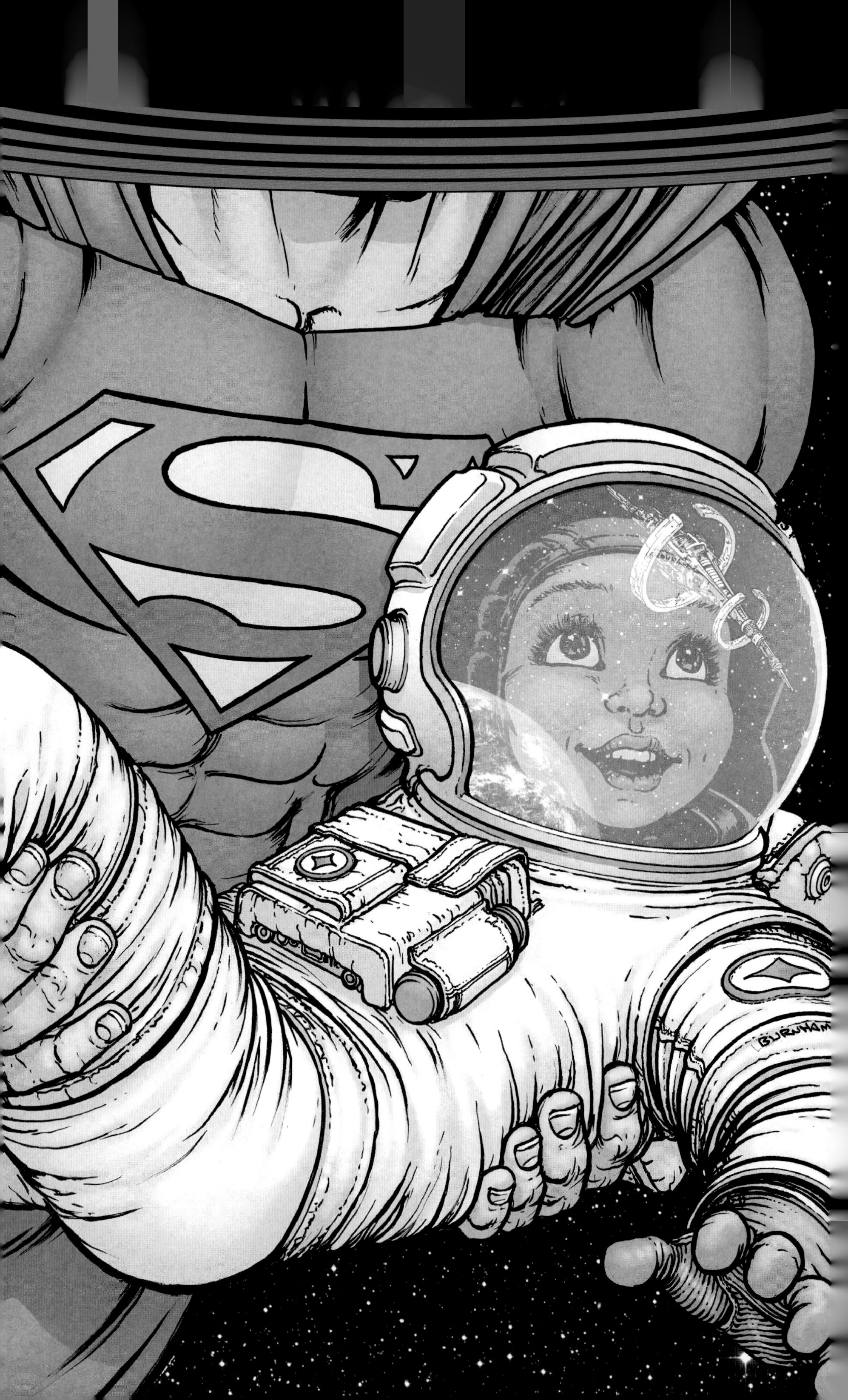
BURNHAM

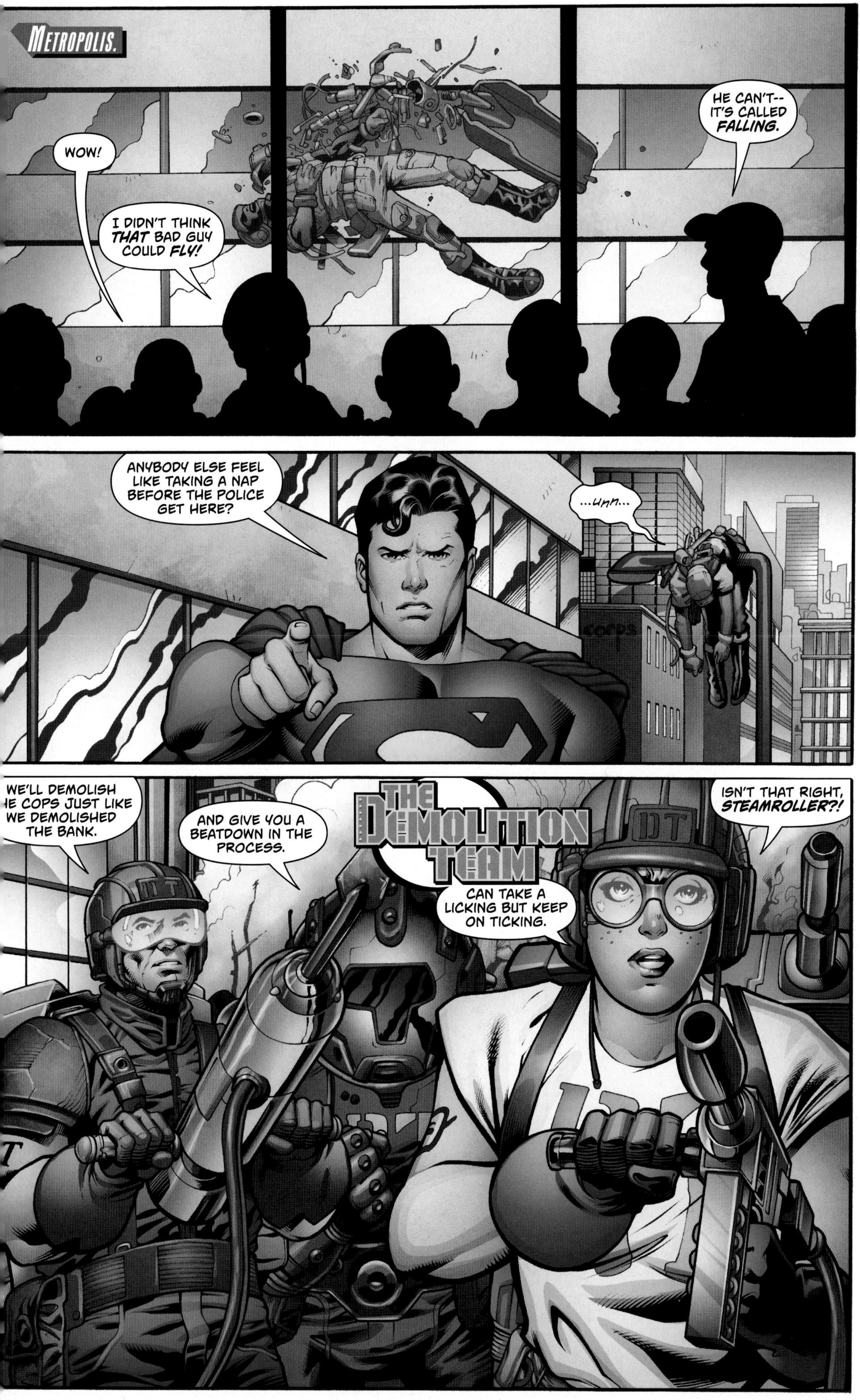
METROPOLIS.
WOW!
I DIDN'T THINK THAT BAD GUY COULD FLY!
HE CAN'T-- IT'S CALLED FALLING.
ANYBODY ELSE FEEL LIKE TAKING A NAP BEFORE THE POLICE GET HERE?
...unn...
WE'LL DEMOLISH HE COPS JUST LIKE WE DEMOLISHED THE BANK.
AND GIVE YOU A BEATDOWN IN THE PROCESS.
THE DEMOLITION TEAM
CAN TAKE A LICKING BUT KEEP ON TICKING.
ISN'T THAT RIGHT, STEAMROLLER?!

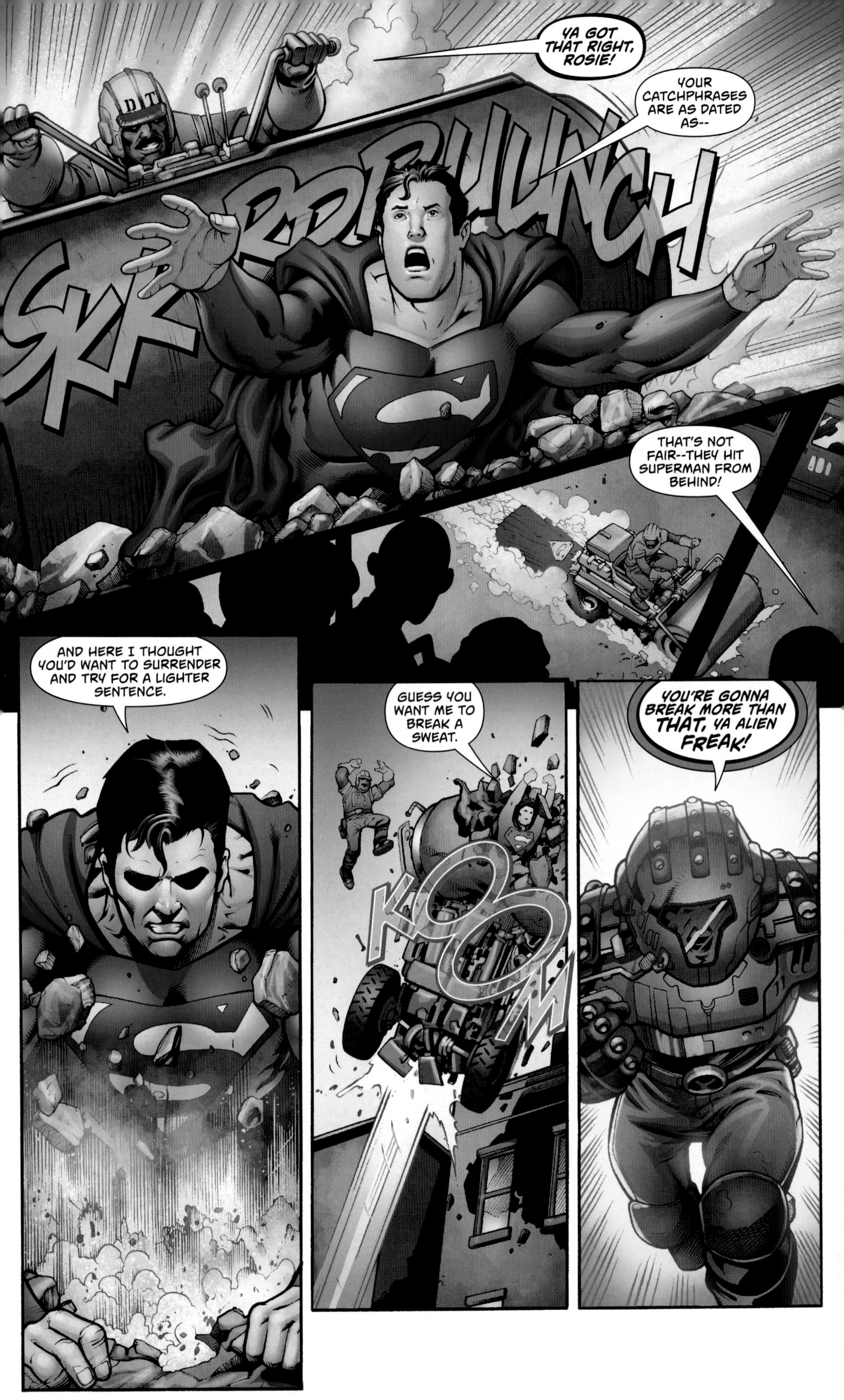
YA GOT THAT RIGHT, ROSIE!
YOUR CATCHPHRASES ARE AS DATED AS--
SKKRRRUNCH
THAT'S NOT FAIR--THEY HIT SUPERMAN FROM BEHIND!
AND HERE I THOUGHT YOU'D WANT TO SURRENDER AND TRY FOR A LIGHTER SENTENCE.
GUESS YOU WANT ME TO BREAK A SWEAT.
KOOM
YOU'RE GONNA BREAK MORE THAN THAT, YA ALIEN FREAK!

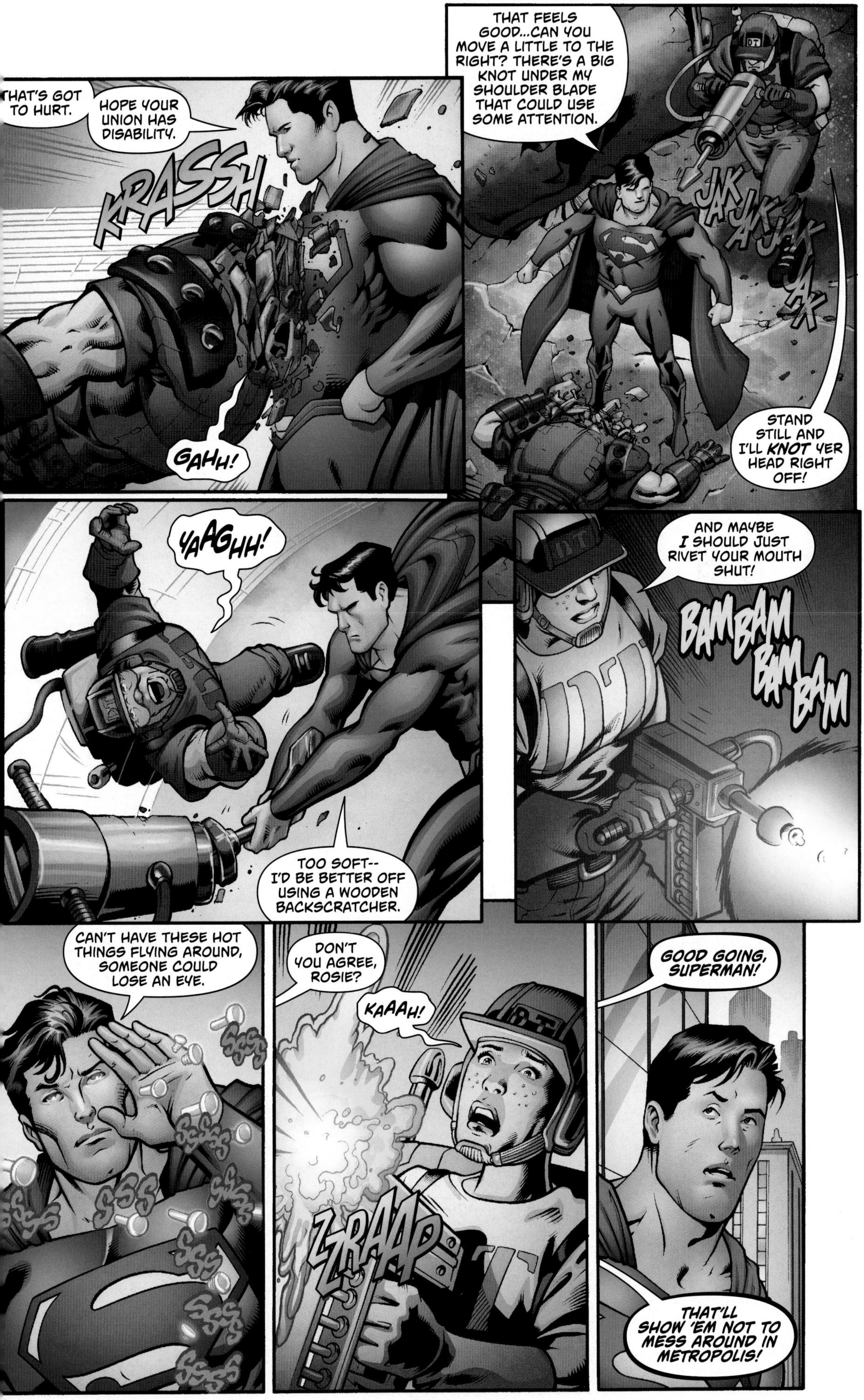
THAT'S GOT TO HURT.
HOPE YOUR UNION HAS DISABILITY.
KRASSH
GAHH!
THAT FEELS GOOD...CAN YOU MOVE A LITTLE TO THE RIGHT? THERE'S A BIG KNOT UNDER MY SHOULDER BLADE THAT COULD USE SOME ATTENTION.
JAKJAKJAKJAKJAK
STAND STILL AND I'LL KNOT YER HEAD RIGHT OFF!
YAAGHH!
TOO SOFT-- I'D BE BETTER OFF USING A WOODEN BACKSCRATCHER.
AND MAYBE I SHOULD JUST RIVET YOUR MOUTH SHUT!
BAM BAM BAM BAM
CAN'T HAVE THESE HOT THINGS FLYING AROUND, SOMEONE COULD LOSE AN EYE.
DON'T YOU AGREE, ROSIE?
KAAAH!
ZZRAAP
GOOD GOING, SUPERMAN!
THAT'LL SHOW 'EM NOT TO MESS AROUND IN METROPOLIS!

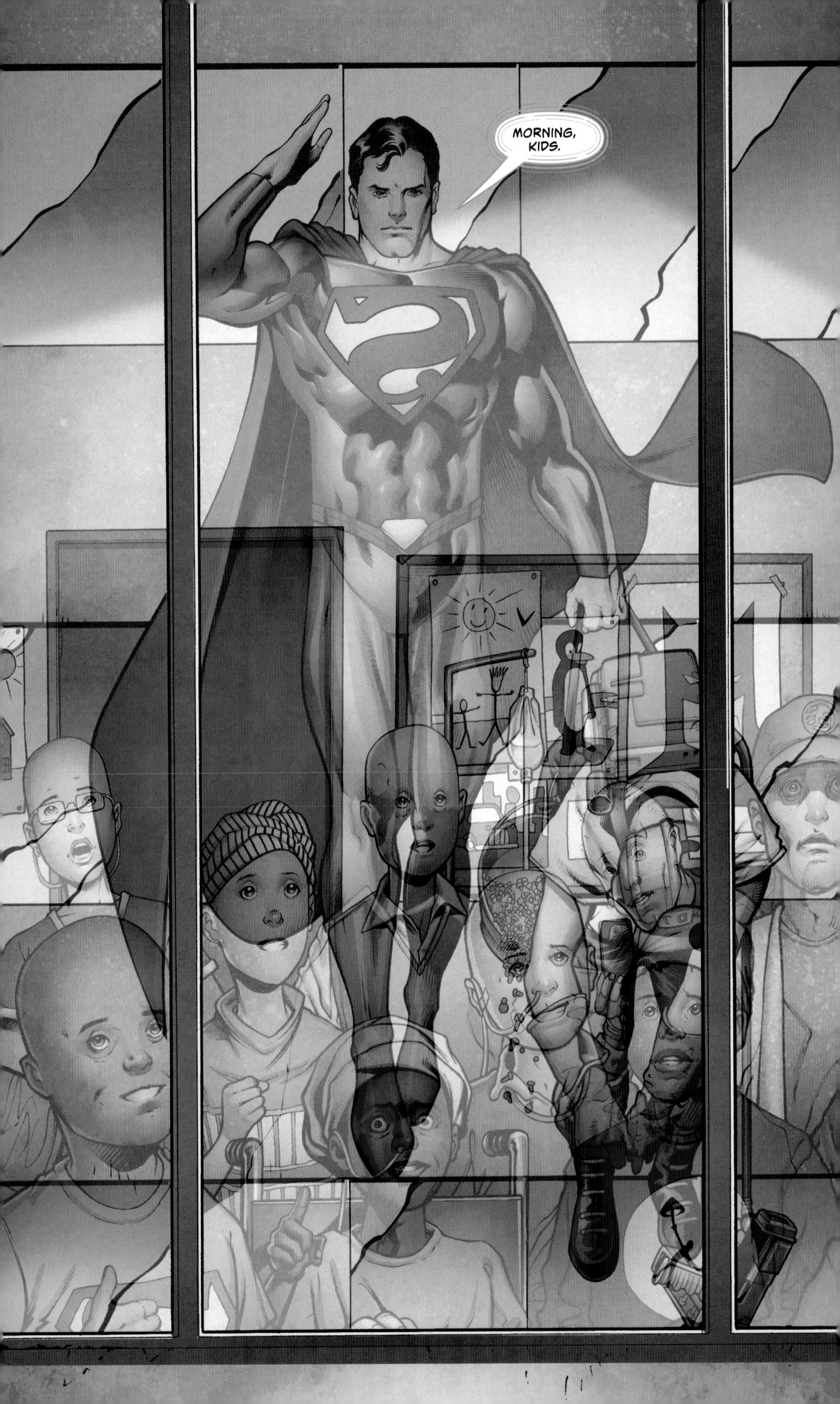
MORNING, KIDS.

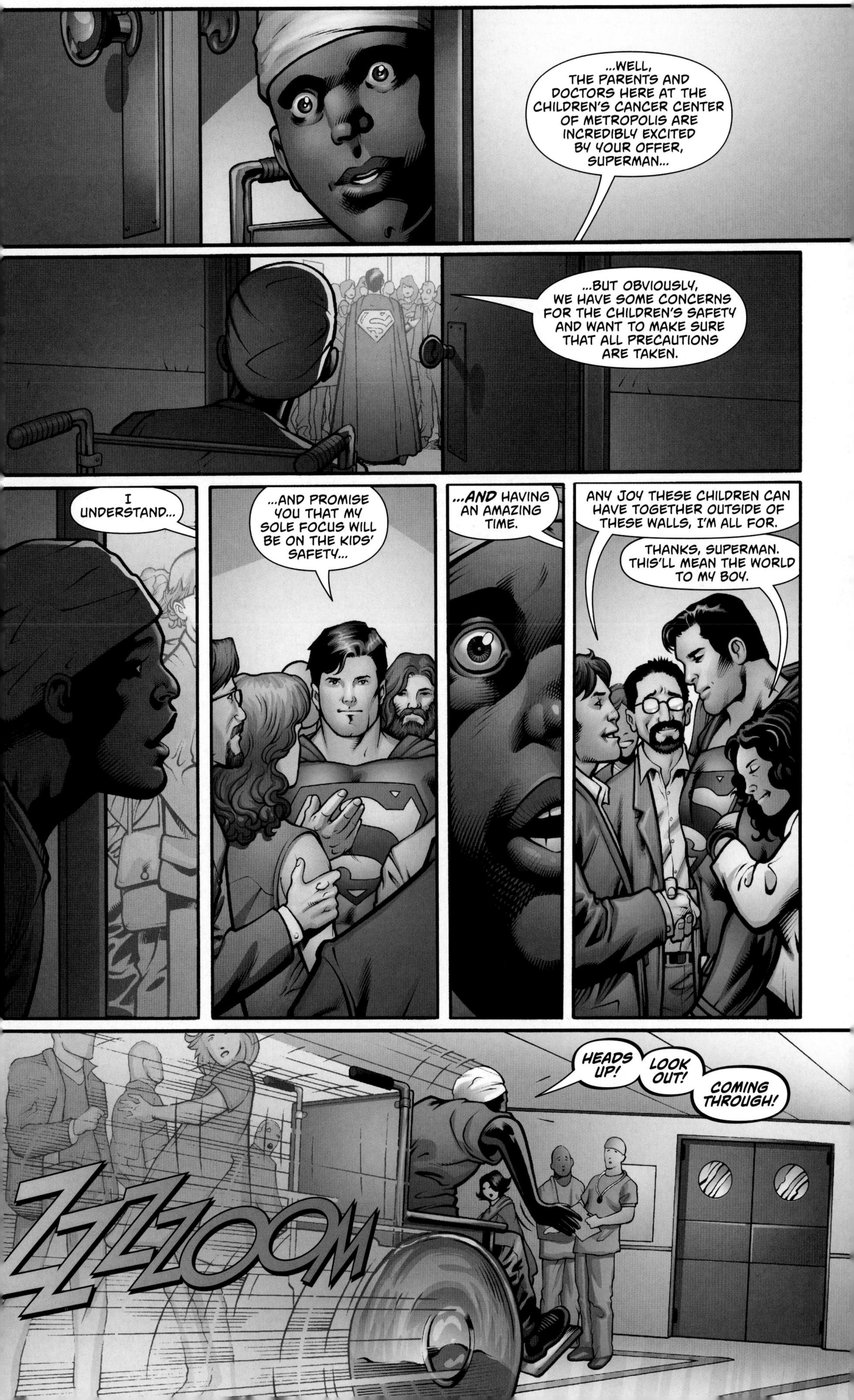
...WELL, THE PARENTS AND DOCTORS HERE AT THE CHILDREN'S CANCER CENTER OF METROPOLIS ARE INCREDIBLY EXCITED BY YOUR OFFER, SUPERMAN...
...BUT OBVIOUSLY, WE HAVE SOME CONCERNS FOR THE CHILDREN'S SAFETY AND WANT TO MAKE SURE THAT ALL PRECAUTIONS ARE TAKEN.
I UNDERSTAND...
...AND PROMISE YOU THAT MY SOLE FOCUS WILL BE ON THE KIDS' SAFETY...
...AND HAVING AN AMAZING TIME.
ANY JOY THESE CHILDREN CAN HAVE TOGETHER OUTSIDE OF THESE WALLS, I'M ALL FOR.
THANKS, SUPERMAN. THIS'LL MEAN THE WORLD TO MY BOY.
HEADS UP!
LOOK OUT!
COMING THROUGH!
ZZZOOM

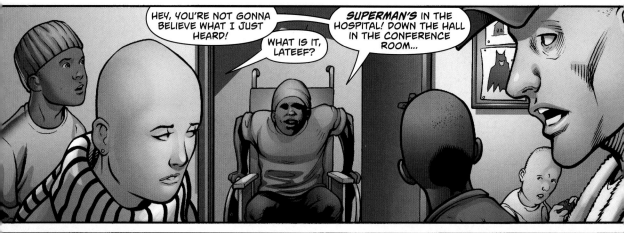

HEY, YOU'RE NOT GONNA BELIEVE WHAT I JUST HEARD!

WHAT IS IT, LATEEF?

SUPERMAN'S IN THE HOSPITAL! DOWN THE HALL IN THE CONFERENCE ROOM...

...TALKING WITH OUR PARENTS AND THE DOCS!

NO WAY!

WAY!

WE SAW SUPES FLY OFF AFTER HE BEAT DOWN THOSE DEMOLITION GUYS.

AND WHY WOULD HE HANG AROUND HERE WHEN HE CAN HANG WITH THE JUSTICE LEAGUE?

I'M TELLING YOU... YOU GOTTA BELIEVE ME...SUPERMAN'S HERE, AND...

AND I'VE BROUGHT SOME FRIENDS.

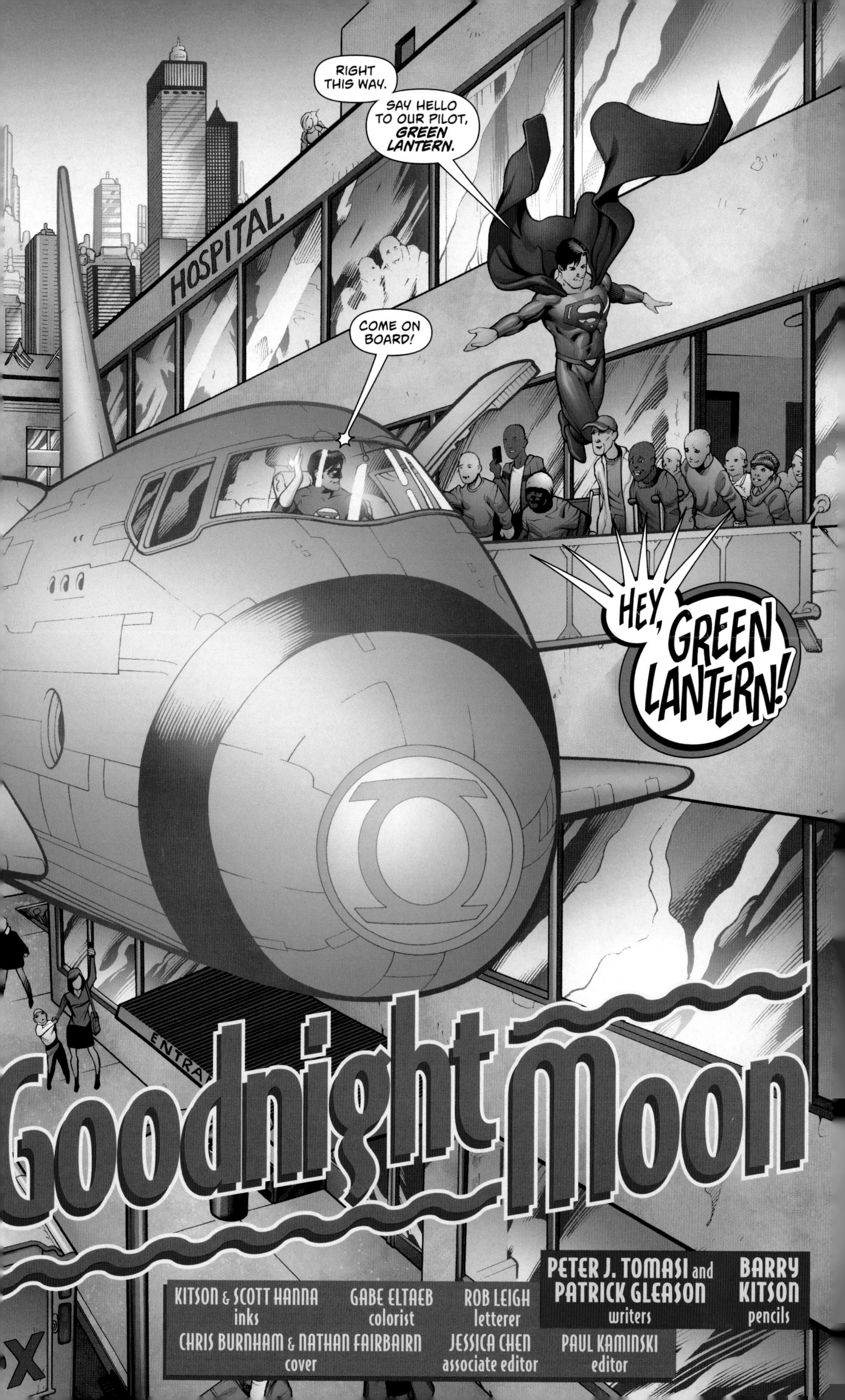

RIGHT THIS WAY.
SAY HELLO TO OUR PILOT, GREEN LANTERN.
HOSPITAL
COME ON BOARD!
HEY, GREEN LANTERN!
ENTRA
Goodnight Moon
PETER J. TOMASI and PATRICK GLEASON writers
BARRY KITSON pencils
KITSON & SCOTT HANNA inks
GABE ELTAEB colorist
ROB LEIGH letterer
CHRIS BURNHAM & NATHAN FAIRBAIRN cover
JESSICA CHEN associate editor
PAUL KAMINSKI editor

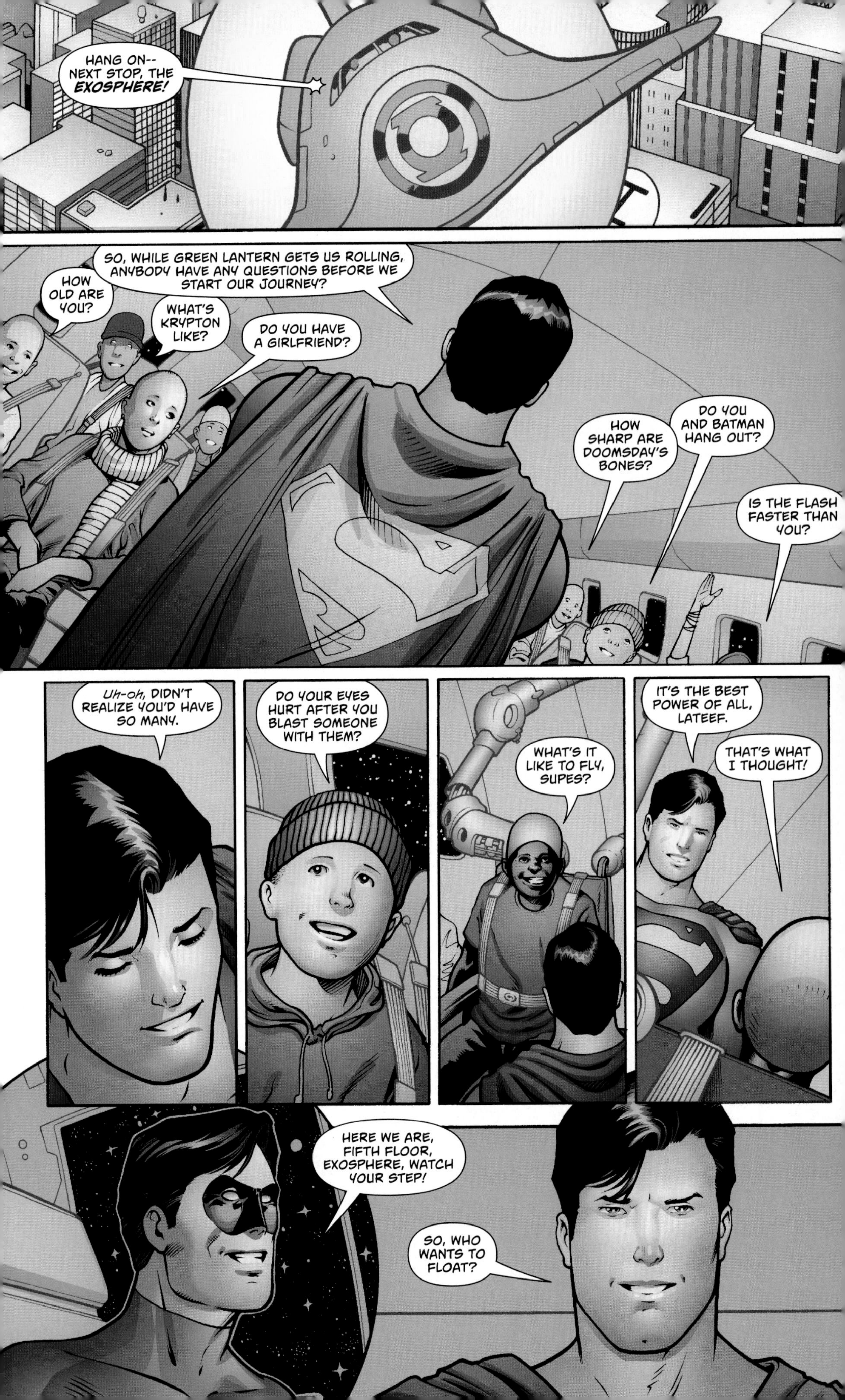
HANG ON-- NEXT STOP, THE *EXOSPHERE!*
SO, WHILE GREEN LANTERN GETS US ROLLING, ANYBODY HAVE ANY QUESTIONS BEFORE WE START OUR JOURNEY?
HOW OLD ARE YOU?
WHAT'S KRYPTON LIKE?
DO YOU HAVE A GIRLFRIEND?
HOW SHARP ARE DOOMSDAY'S BONES?
DO YOU AND BATMAN HANG OUT?
IS THE FLASH FASTER THAN YOU?
Uh-oh, DIDN'T REALIZE YOU'D HAVE SO MANY.
DO YOUR EYES HURT AFTER YOU BLAST SOMEONE WITH THEM?
WHAT'S IT LIKE TO FLY, SUPES?
IT'S THE BEST POWER OF ALL, LATEEF.
THAT'S WHAT I THOUGHT!
HERE WE ARE, FIFTH FLOOR, EXOSPHERE, WATCH YOUR STEP!
SO, WHO WANTS TO FLOAT?

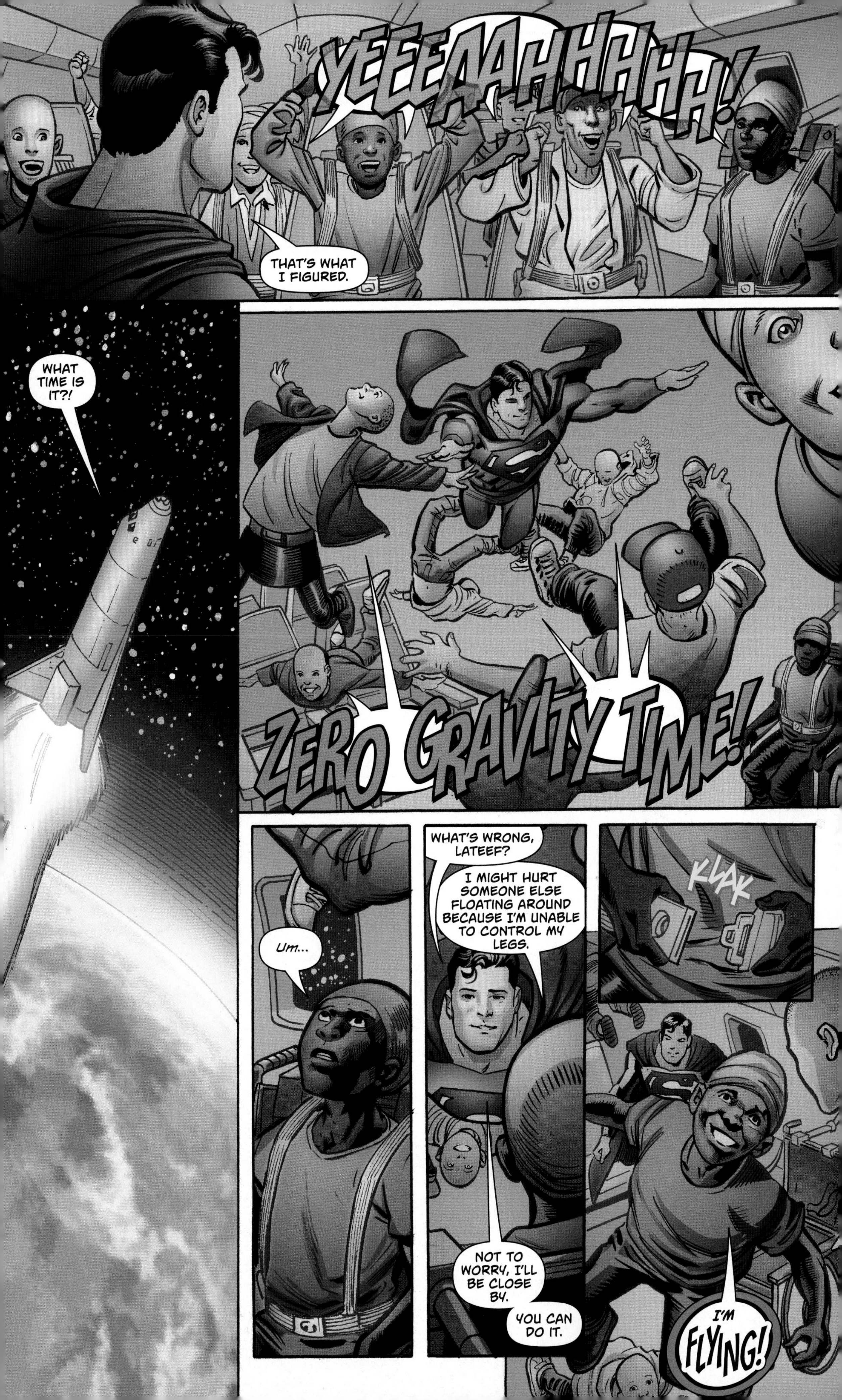
YEEEAAHHHHHH!
THAT'S WHAT I FIGURED.
WHAT TIME IS IT?!
ZERO GRAVITY TIME!
Um...
WHAT'S WRONG, LATEEF?
I MIGHT HURT SOMEONE ELSE FLOATING AROUND BECAUSE I'M UNABLE TO CONTROL MY LEGS.
NOT TO WORRY, I'LL BE CLOSE BY.
YOU CAN DO IT.
KLAK
I'M FLYING!

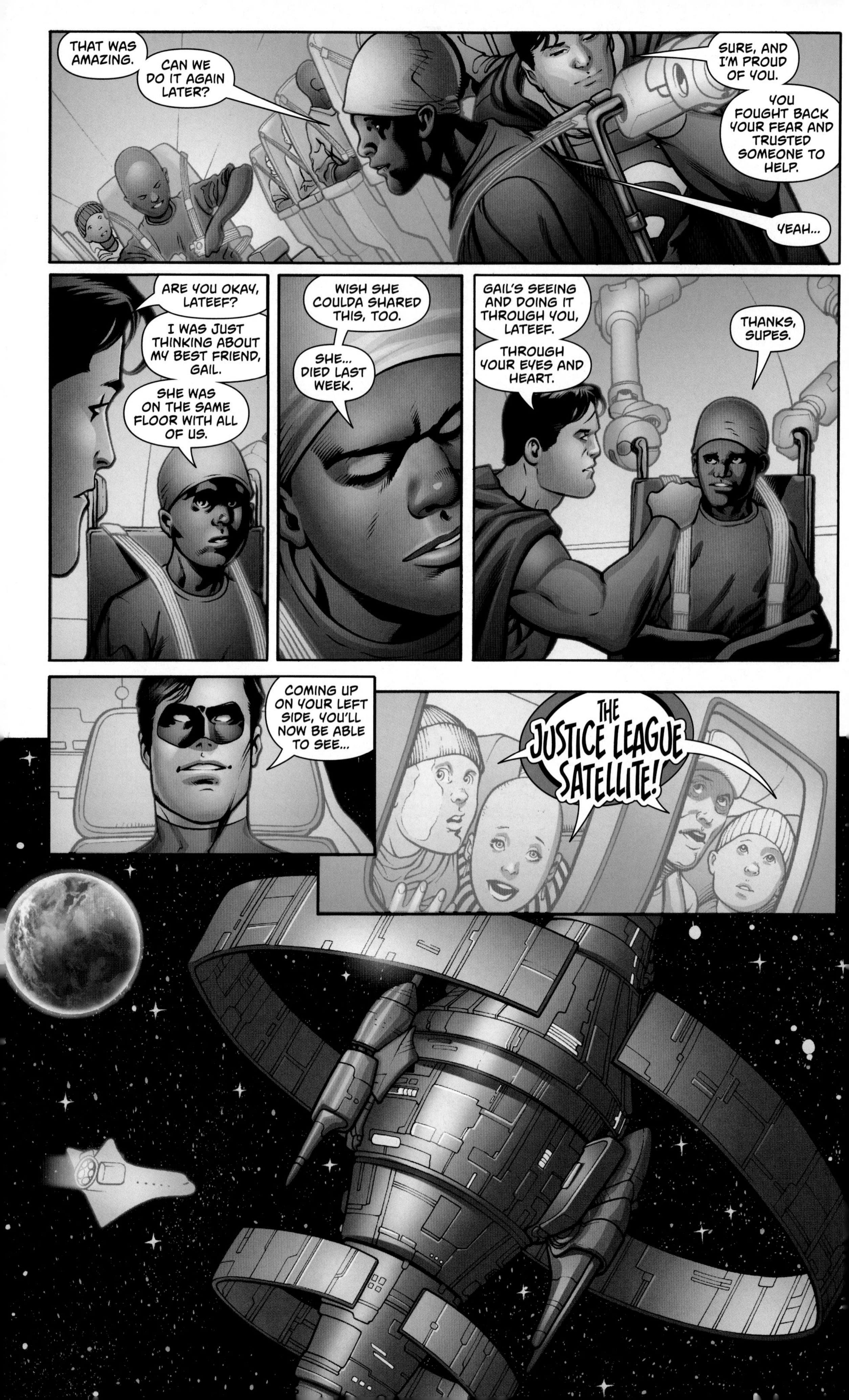
THAT WAS AMAZING.
CAN WE DO IT AGAIN LATER?
SURE, AND I'M PROUD OF YOU.
YOU FOUGHT BACK YOUR FEAR AND TRUSTED SOMEONE TO HELP.
YEAH...
ARE YOU OKAY, LATEEF?
I WAS JUST THINKING ABOUT MY BEST FRIEND, GAIL.
SHE WAS ON THE SAME FLOOR WITH ALL OF US.
WISH SHE COULDA SHARED THIS, TOO.
SHE... DIED LAST WEEK.
GAIL'S SEEING AND DOING IT THROUGH YOU, LATEEF.
THROUGH YOUR EYES AND HEART.
THANKS, SUPES.
COMING UP ON YOUR LEFT SIDE, YOU'LL NOW BE ABLE TO SEE...
THE JUSTICE LEAGUE SATELLITE!

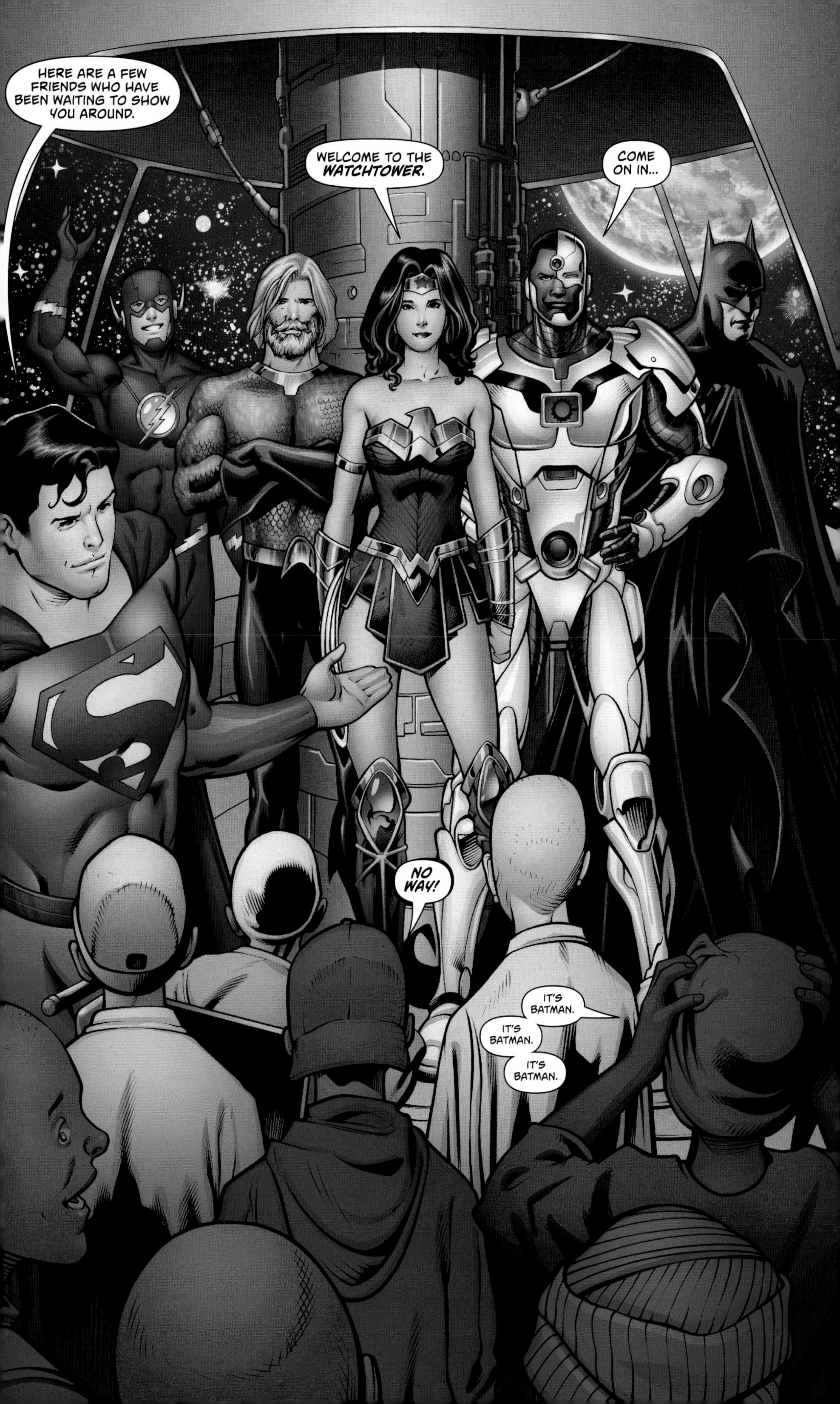
HERE ARE A FEW FRIENDS WHO HAVE BEEN WAITING TO SHOW YOU AROUND.
WELCOME TO THE *WATCHTOWER.*
COME ON IN...
NO WAY!
IT'S BATMAN.
IT'S BATMAN.
IT'S BATMAN.

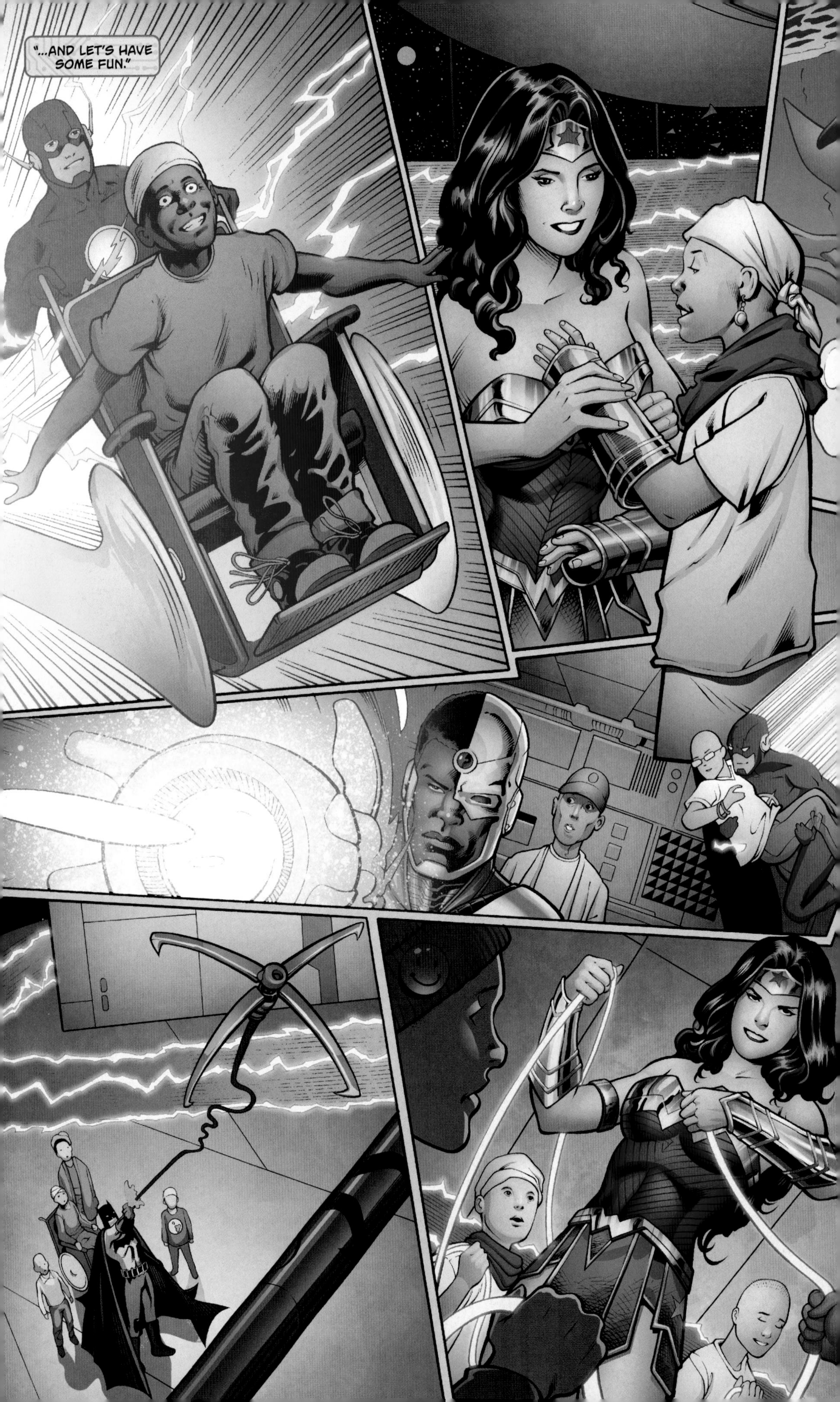
"...AND LET'S HAVE SOME FUN."

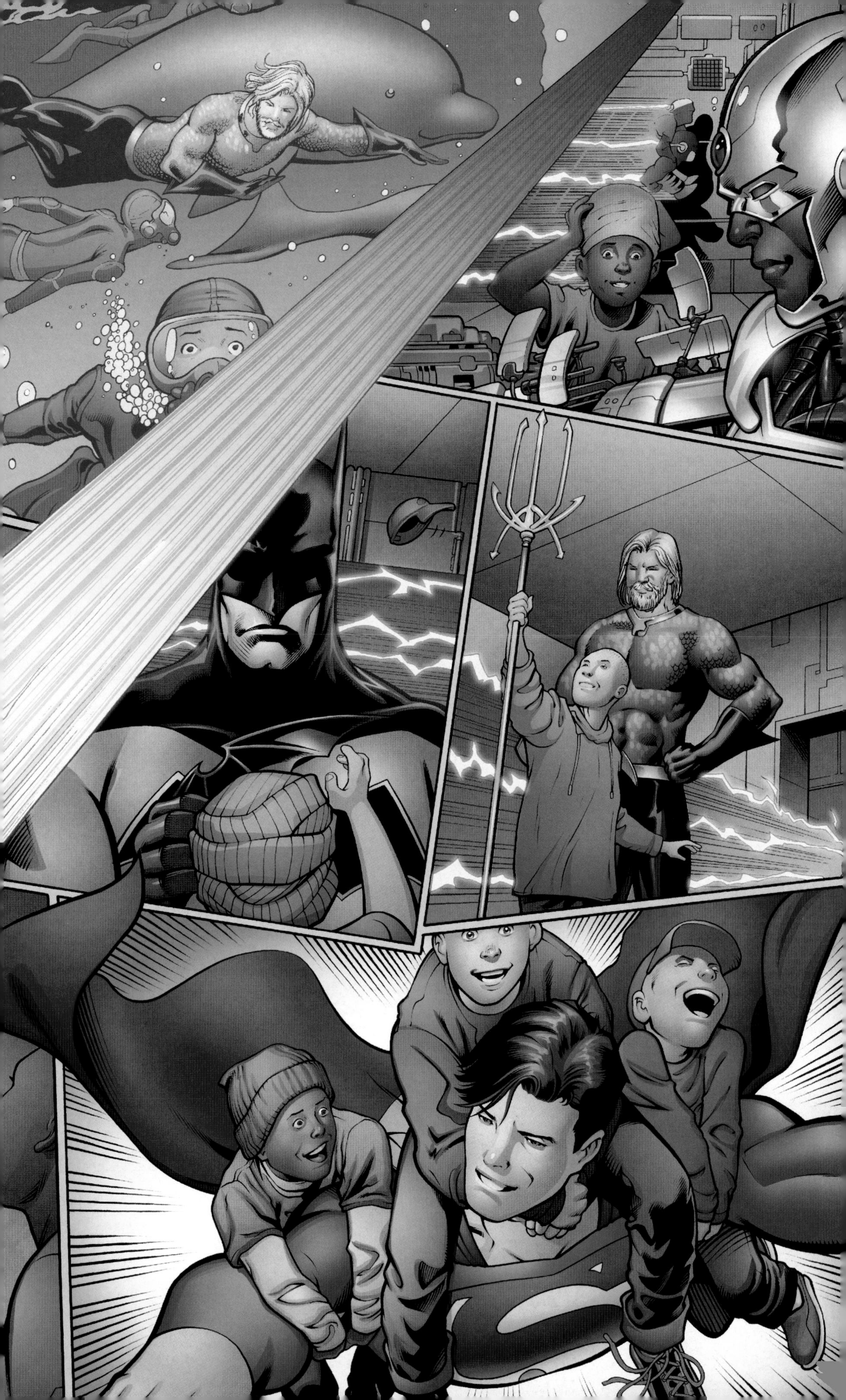

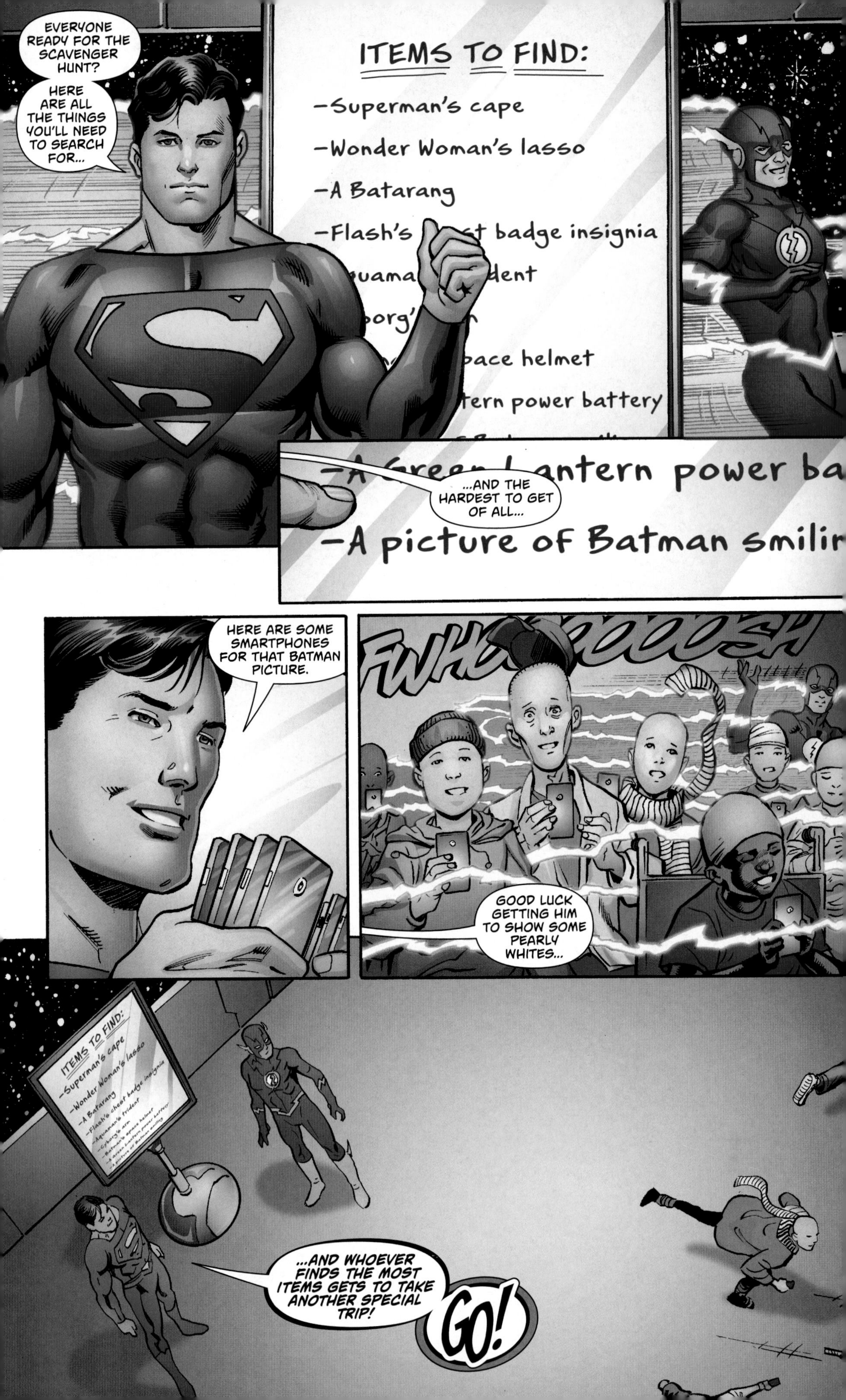
EVERYONE READY FOR THE SCAVENGER HUNT?
HERE ARE ALL THE THINGS YOU'LL NEED TO SEARCH FOR...
ITEMS TO FIND:
-Superman's cape
-Wonder Woman's lasso
-A Batarang
...AND THE HARDEST TO GET OF ALL...
HERE ARE SOME SMARTPHONES FOR THAT BATMAN PICTURE.
GOOD LUCK GETTING HIM TO SHOW SOME PEARLY WHITES...
...AND WHOEVER FINDS THE MOST ITEMS GETS TO TAKE ANOTHER SPECIAL TRIP!
GO!

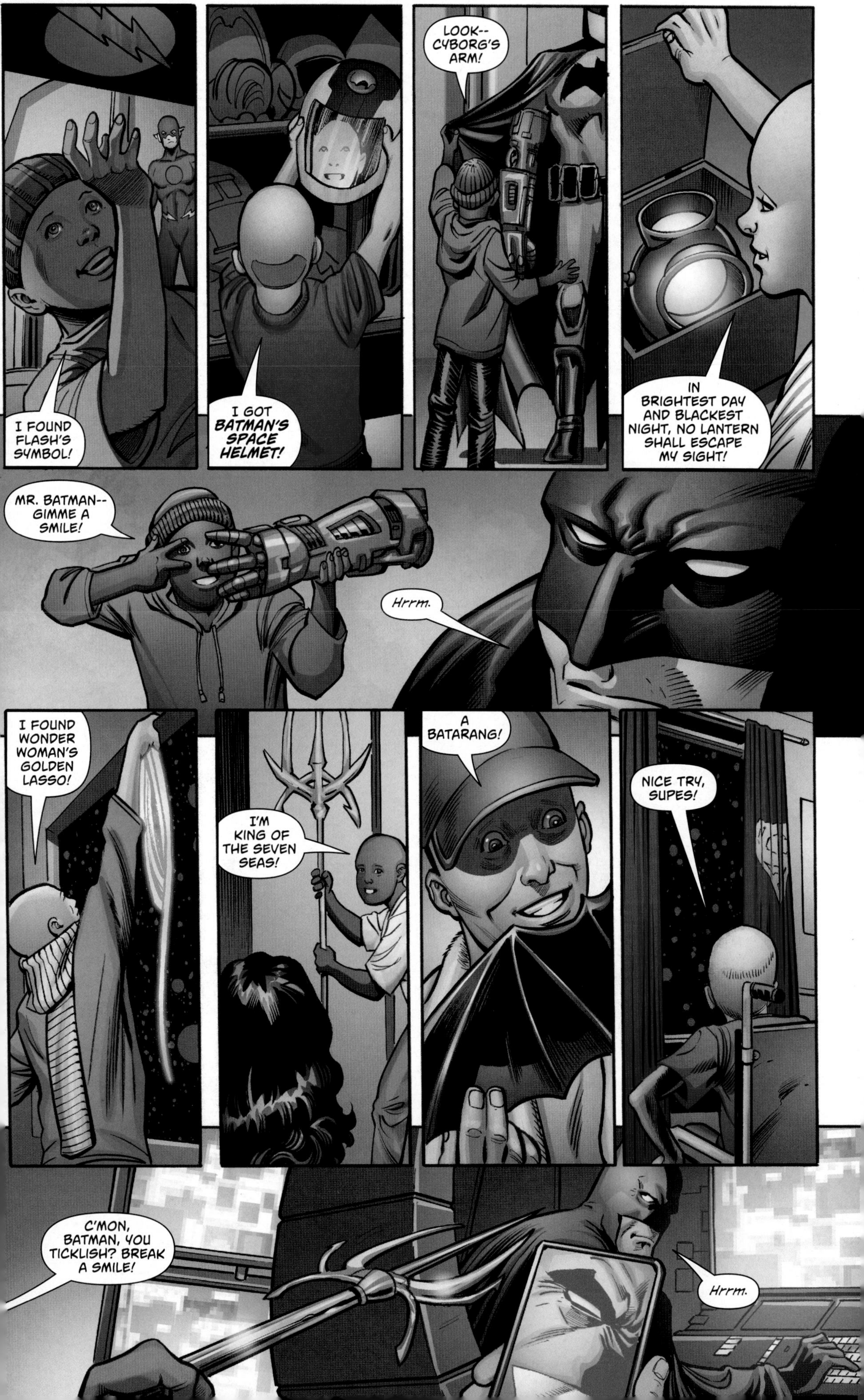
I FOUND FLASH'S SYMBOL!
I GOT BATMAN'S SPACE HELMET!
LOOK--CYBORG'S ARM!
IN BRIGHTEST DAY AND BLACKEST NIGHT, NO LANTERN SHALL ESCAPE MY SIGHT!
MR. BATMAN--GIMME A SMILE!
Hrrm.
I FOUND WONDER WOMAN'S GOLDEN LASSO!
I'M KING OF THE SEVEN SEAS!
A BATARANG!
NICE TRY, SUPES!
C'MON, BATMAN, YOU TICKLISH? BREAK A SMILE!
Hrrm.

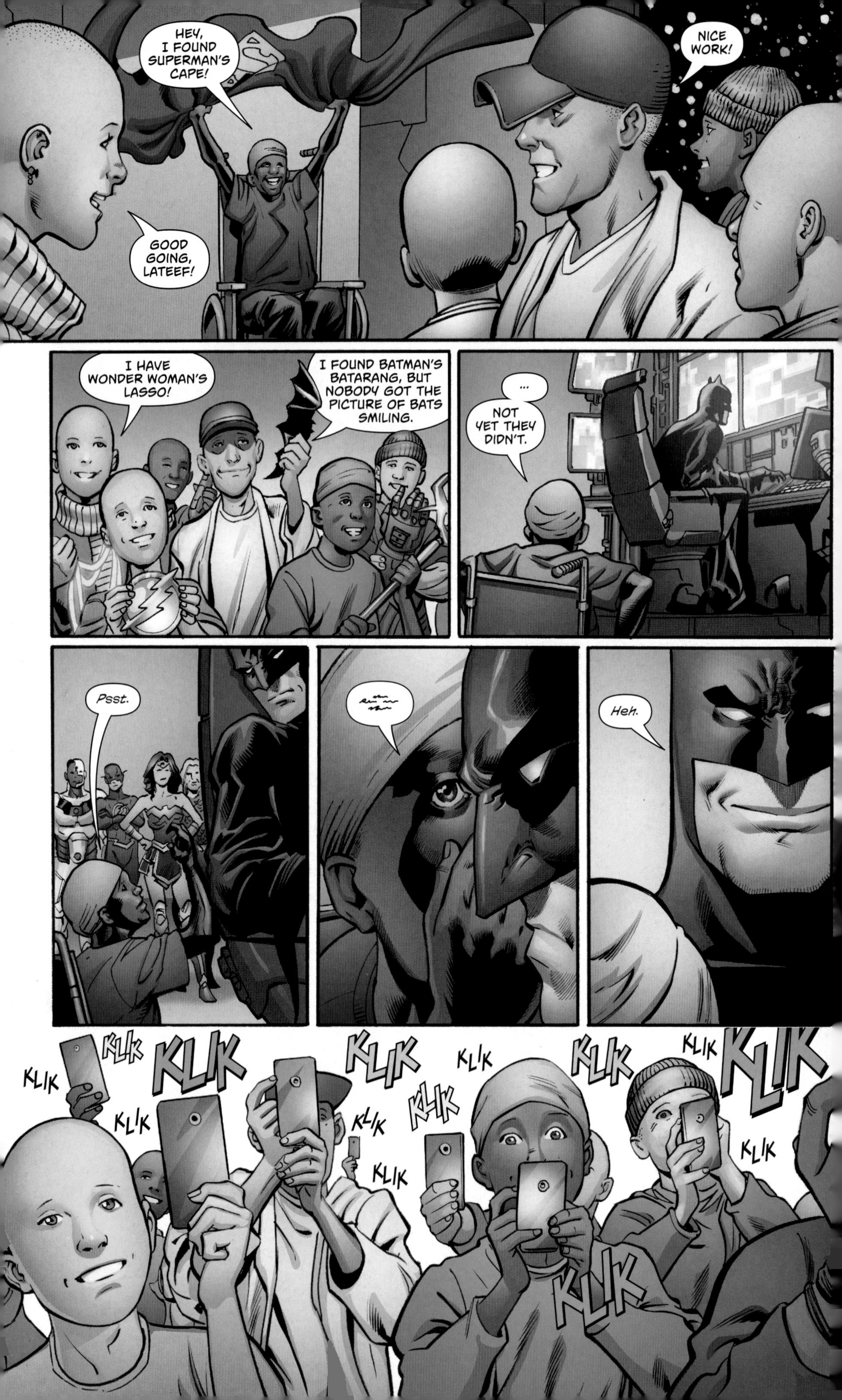
HEY, I FOUND SUPERMAN'S CAPE!
GOOD GOING, LATEEF!
NICE WORK!
I HAVE WONDER WOMAN'S LASSO!
I FOUND BATMAN'S BATARANG, BUT NOBODY GOT THE PICTURE OF BATS SMILING.
...
NOT YET THEY DIDN'T.
Psst.
Heh.
KLIK
KLIK
KLIK
KLIK
KLIK
KLIK
KLIK
KLIK
KLIK
KLIK
KLIK
KLIK
KLIK
KLIK

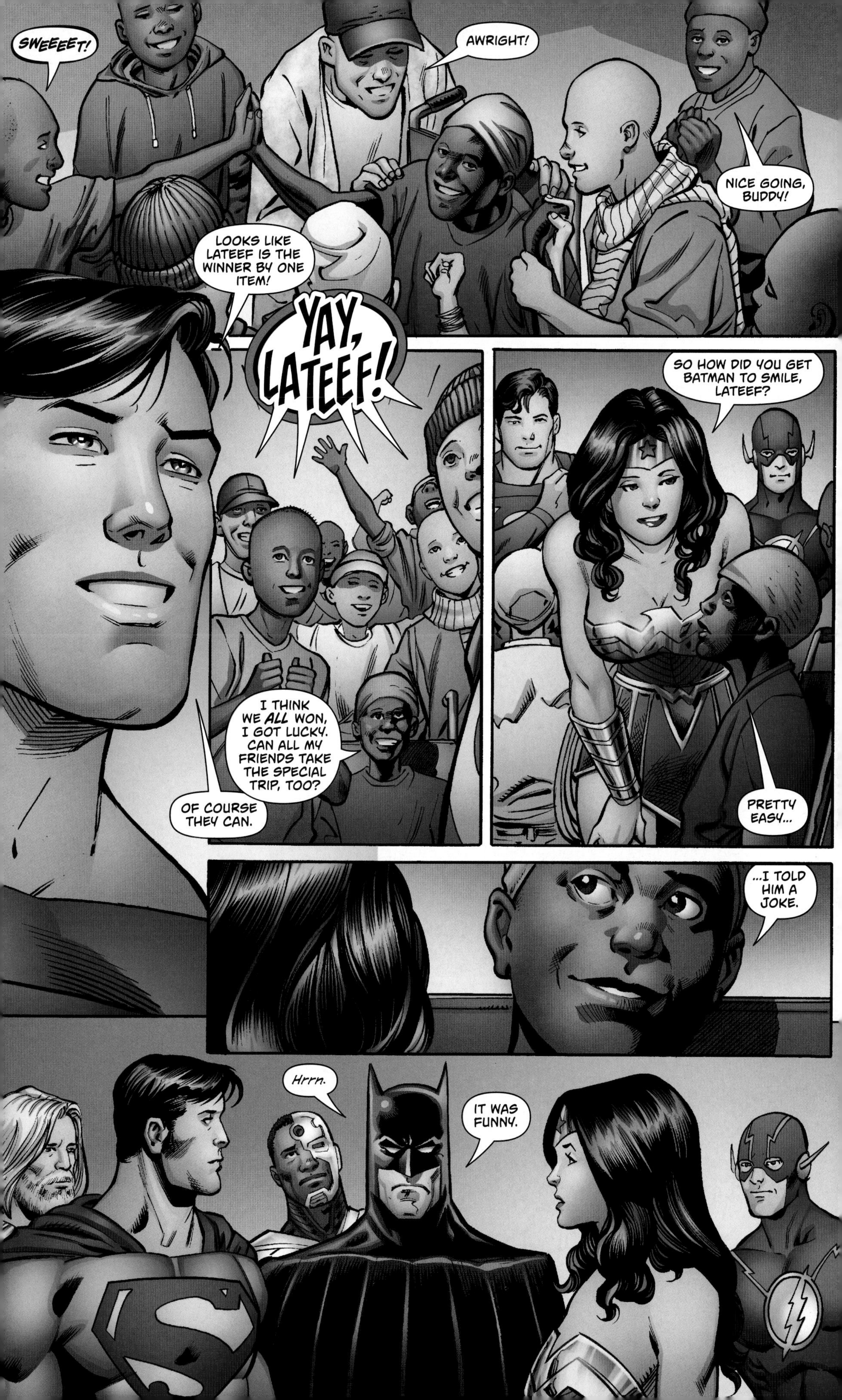
SWEEEEET!
AWRIGHT!
NICE GOING, BUDDY!
LOOKS LIKE LATEEF IS THE WINNER BY ONE ITEM!
YAY, LATEEF!
I THINK WE ALL WON, I GOT LUCKY. CAN ALL MY FRIENDS TAKE THE SPECIAL TRIP, TOO?
OF COURSE THEY CAN.
SO HOW DID YOU GET BATMAN TO SMILE, LATEEF?
PRETTY EASY...
...I TOLD HIM A JOKE.
Hrrn.
IT WAS FUNNY.

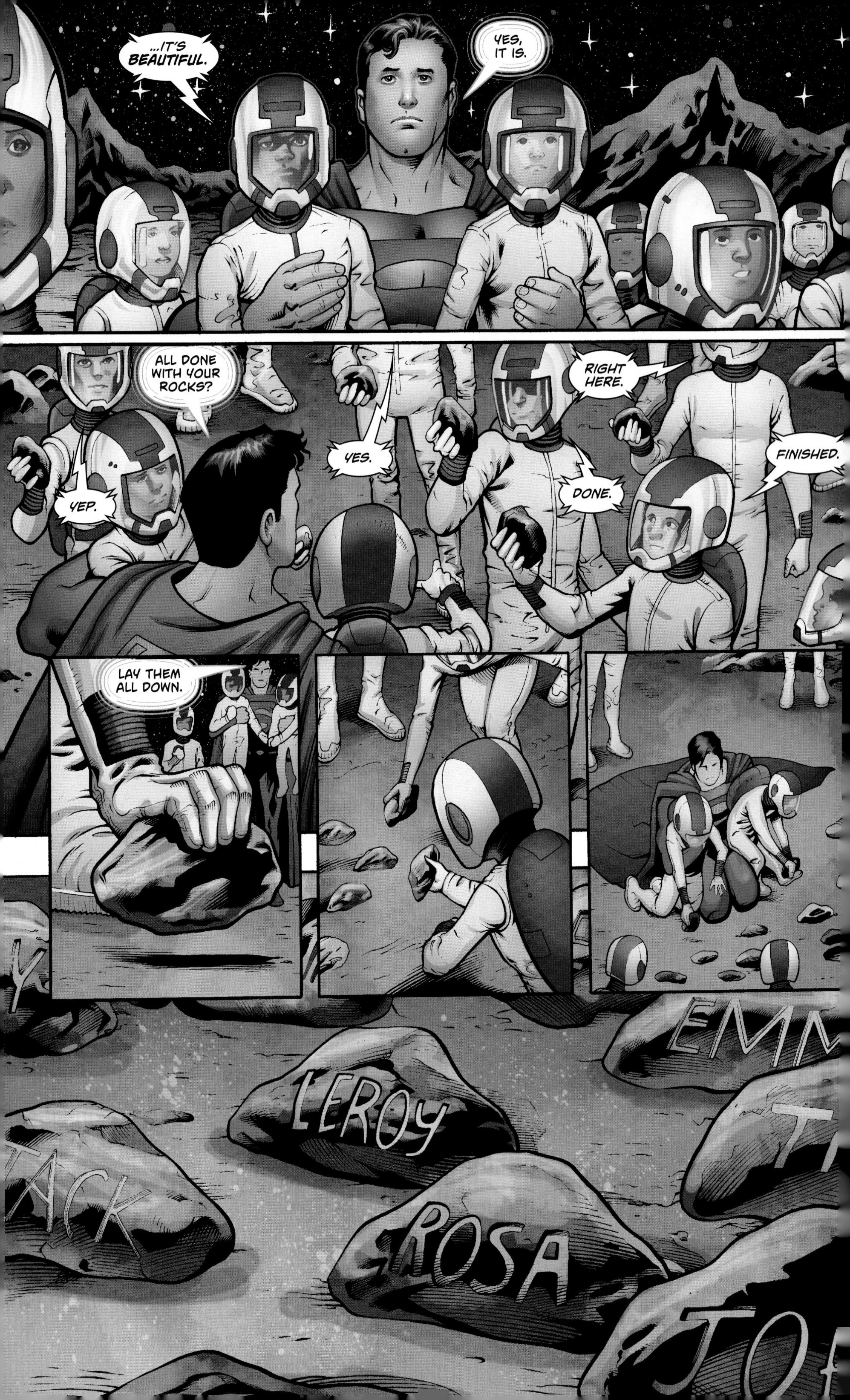

...IT'S BEAUTIFUL.
YES, IT IS.
ALL DONE WITH YOUR ROCKS?
YEP.
YES.
RIGHT HERE.
DONE.
FINISHED.
LAY THEM ALL DOWN.
LEROY
ROSA

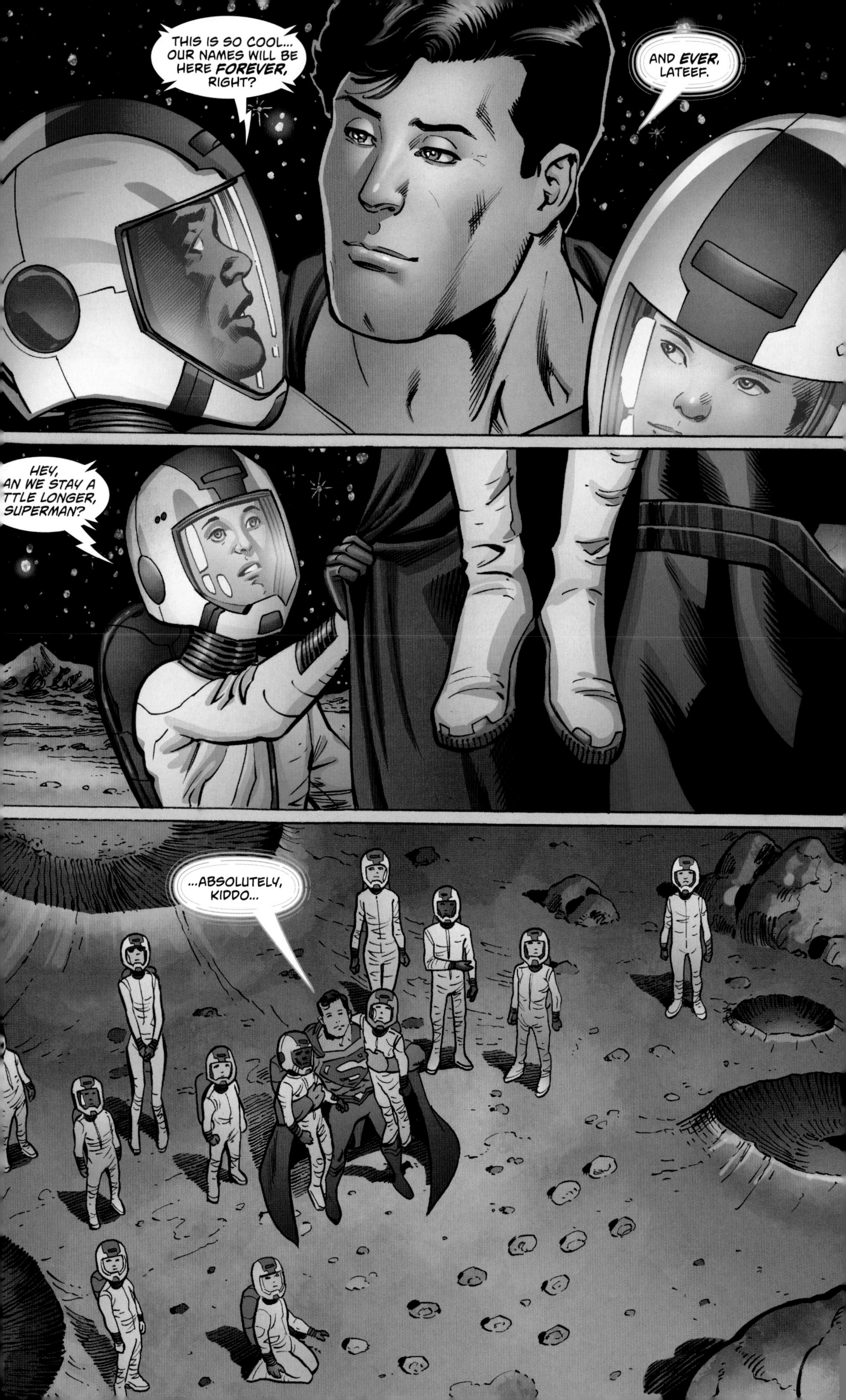
THIS IS SO COOL... OUR NAMES WILL BE HERE FOREVER, RIGHT?
AND EVER, LATEEF.
HEY, AN WE STAY A TTLE LONGER, SUPERMAN?
...ABSOLUTELY, KIDDO...

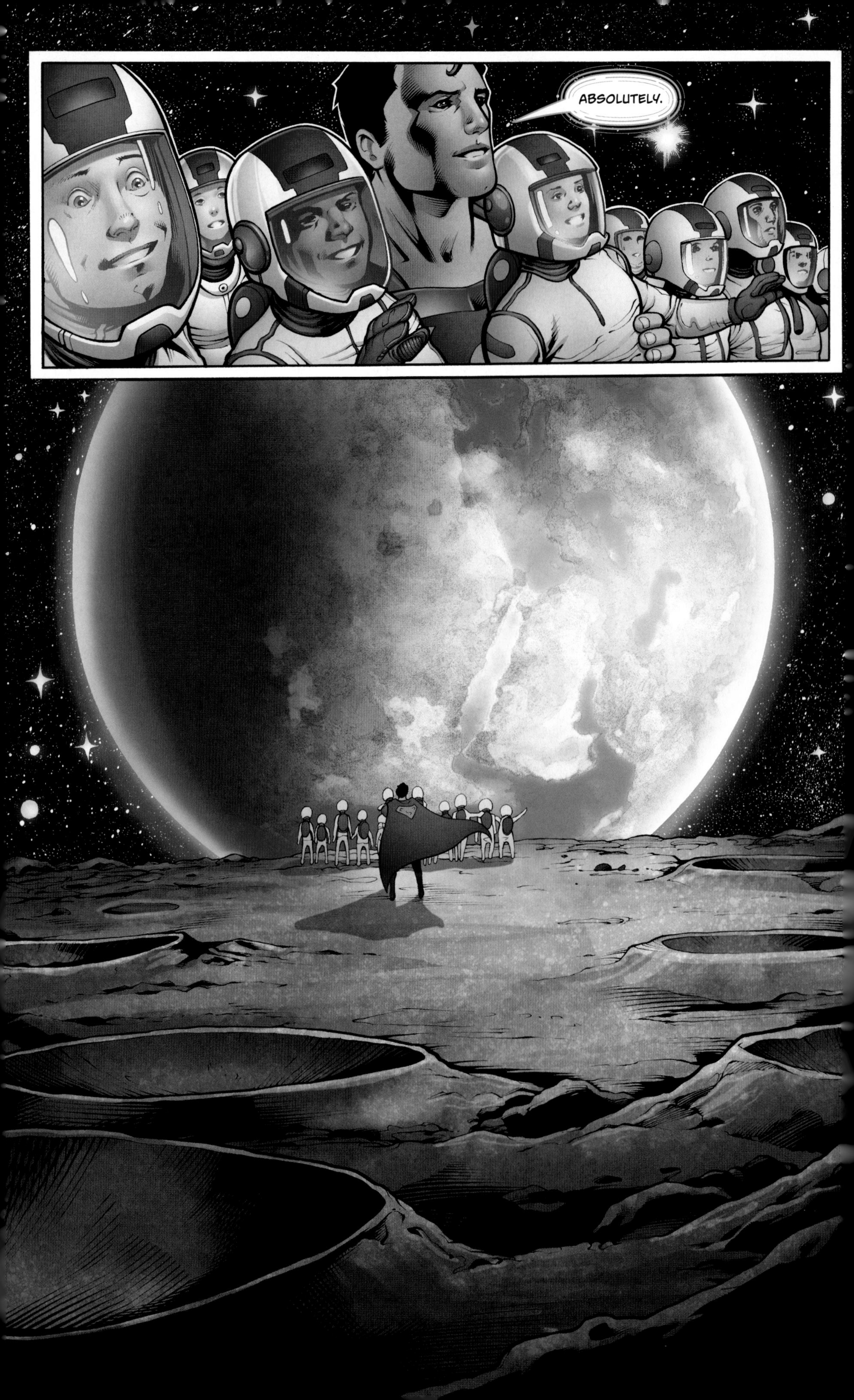
ABSOLUTELY.

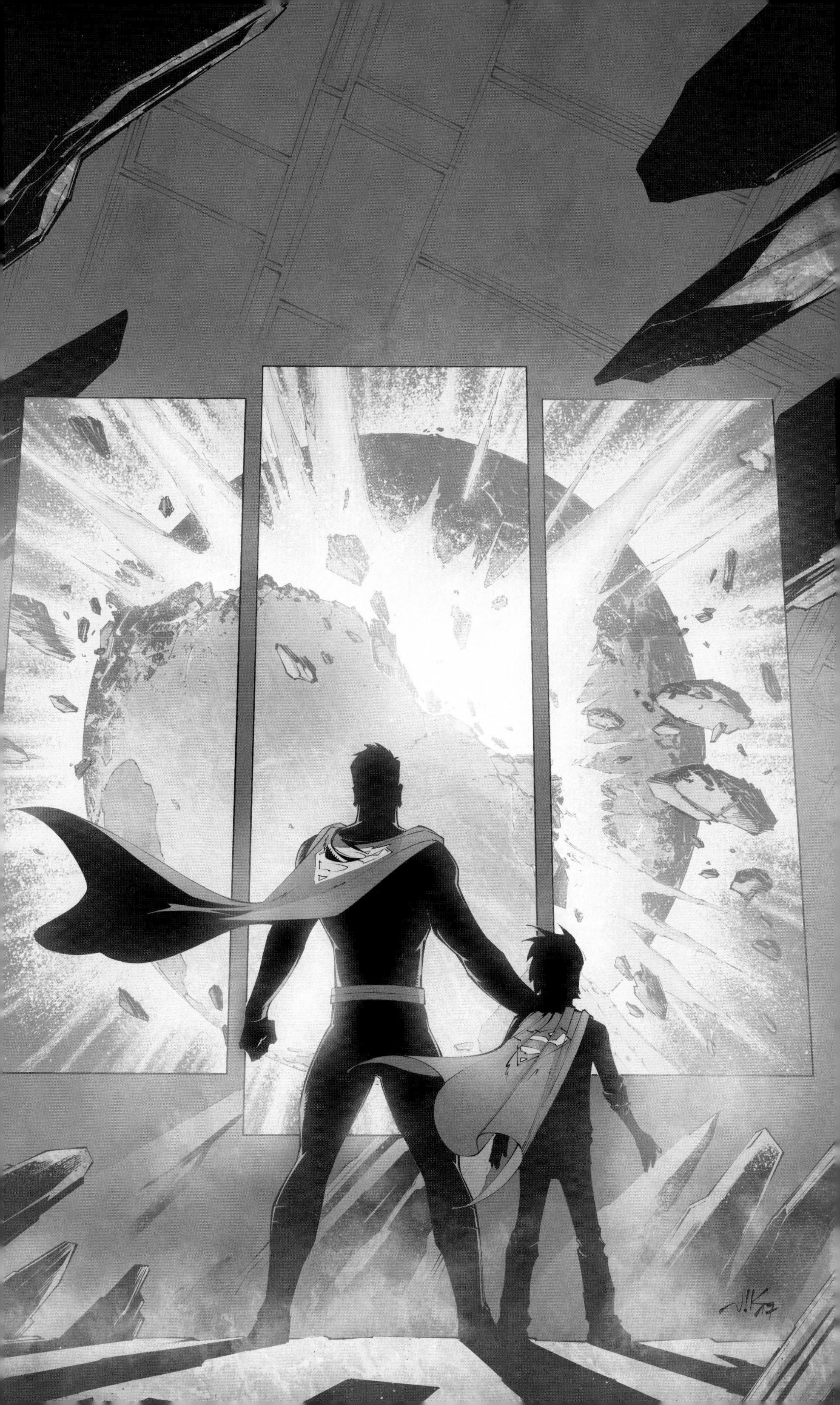

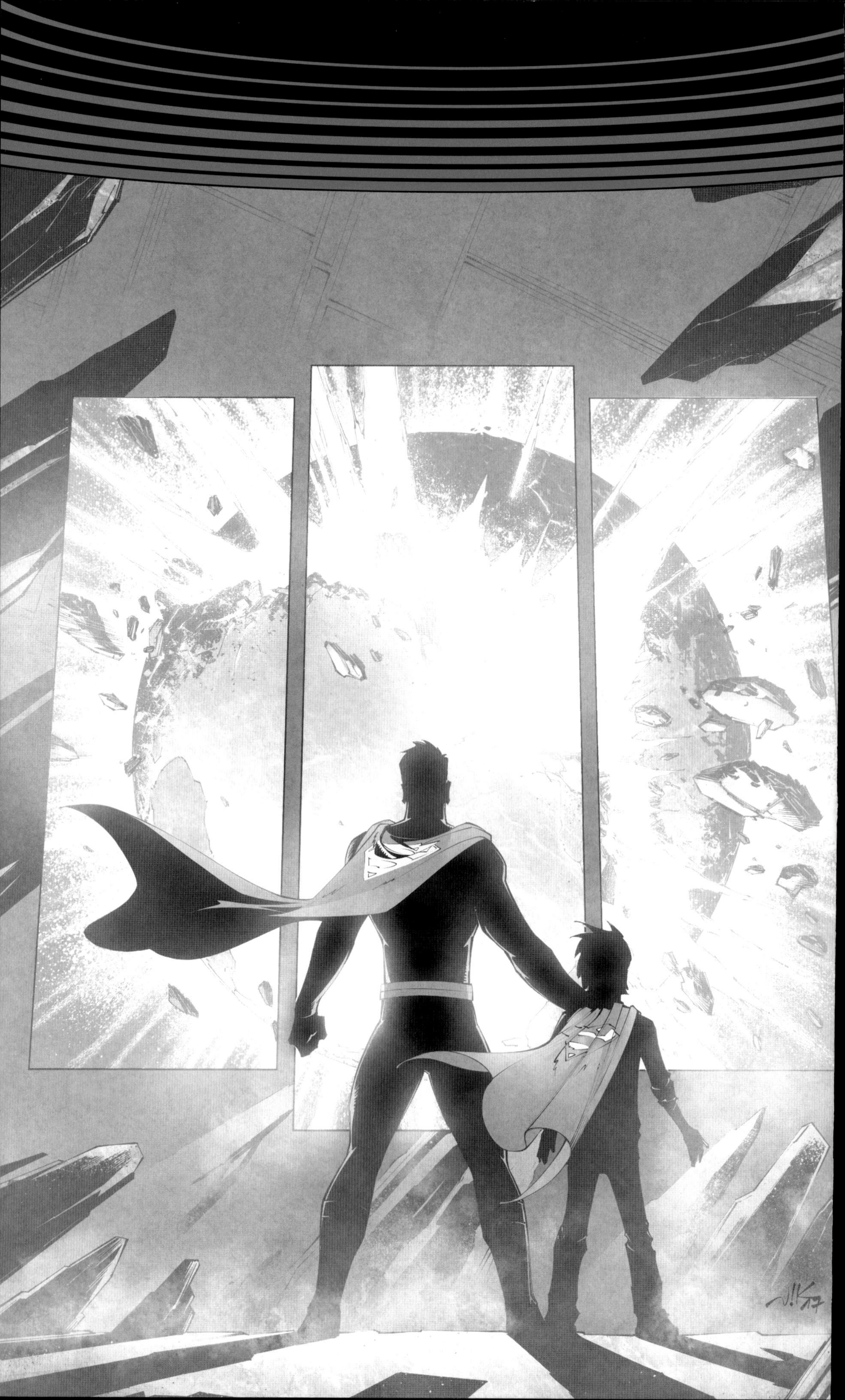

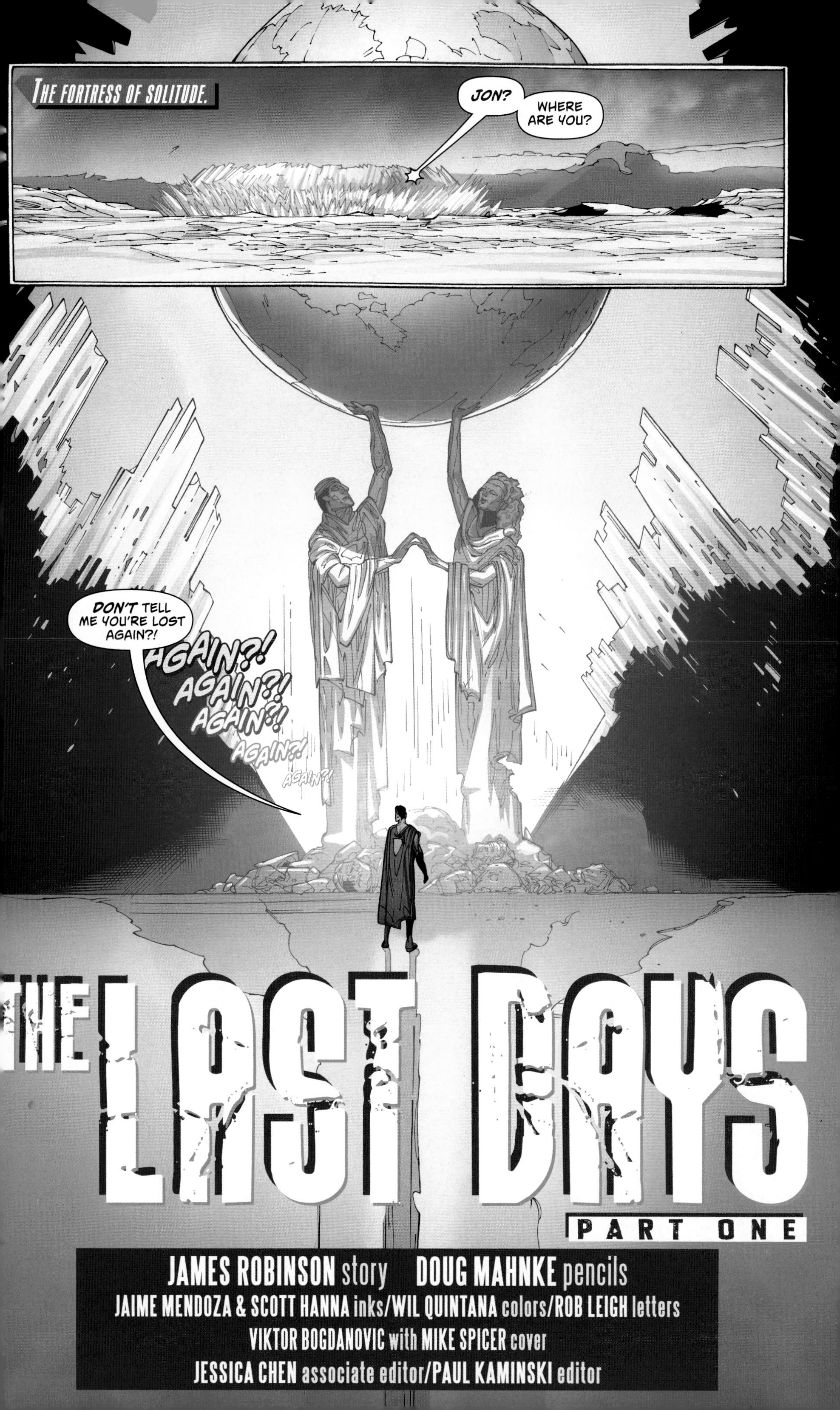

THE FORTRESS OF SOLITUDE.
JON?
WHERE ARE YOU?
DON'T TELL ME YOU'RE LOST AGAIN?!
AGAIN?! AGAIN?! AGAIN?! AGAIN?! AGAIN?!
THE LAST DAYS
PART ONE
JAMES ROBINSON story DOUG MAHNKE pencils
JAIME MENDOZA & SCOTT HANNA inks/WIL QUINTANA colors/ROB LEIGH letters
VIKTOR BOGDANOVIC with MIKE SPICER cover
JESSICA CHEN associate editor/PAUL KAMINSKI editor

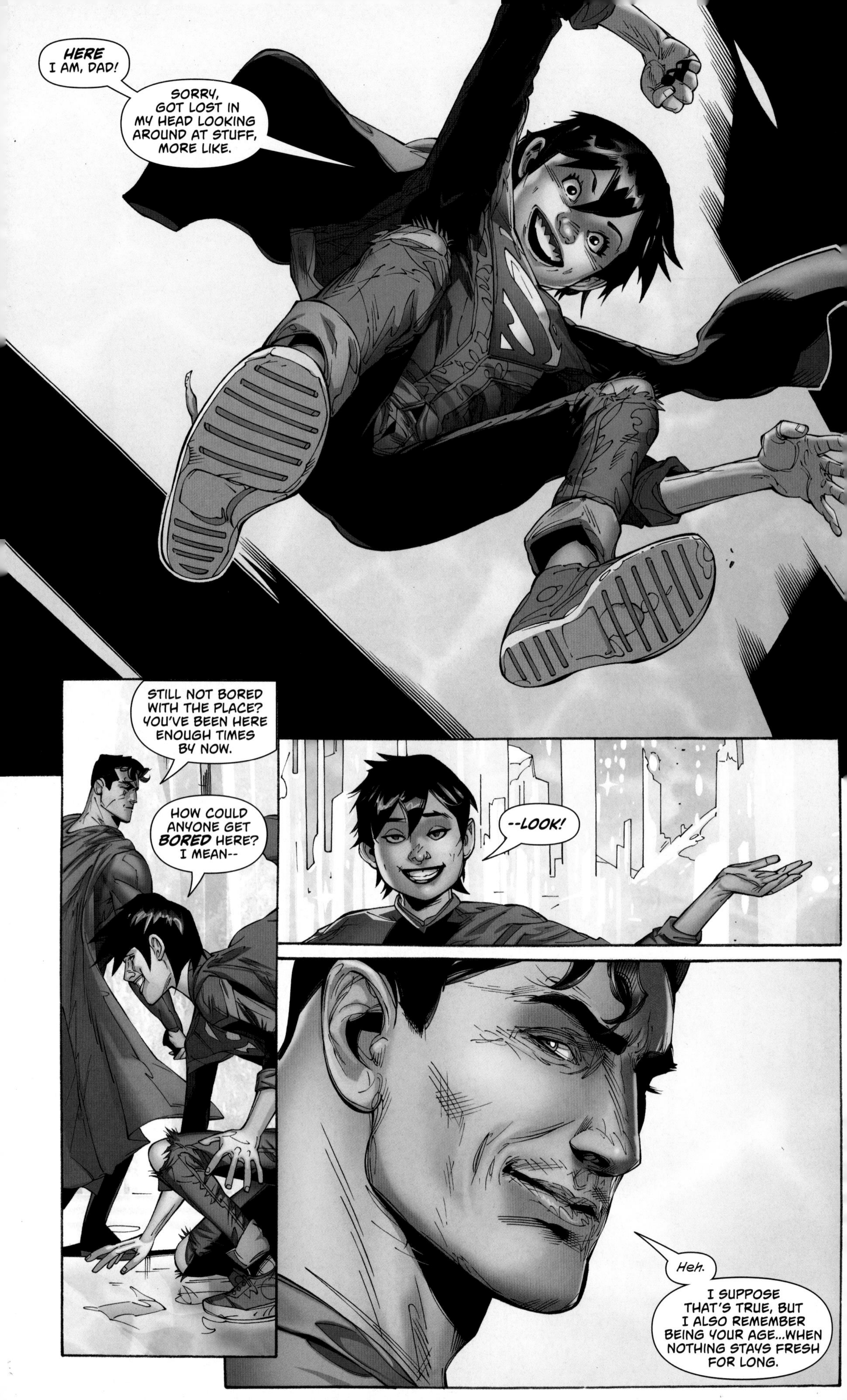
HERE I AM, DAD!
SORRY, GOT LOST IN MY HEAD LOOKING AROUND AT STUFF, MORE LIKE.
STILL NOT BORED WITH THE PLACE? YOU'VE BEEN HERE ENOUGH TIMES BY NOW.
HOW COULD ANYONE GET BORED HERE? I MEAN--
--LOOK!
Heh.
I SUPPOSE THAT'S TRUE, BUT I ALSO REMEMBER BEING YOUR AGE...WHEN NOTHING STAYS FRESH FOR LONG.

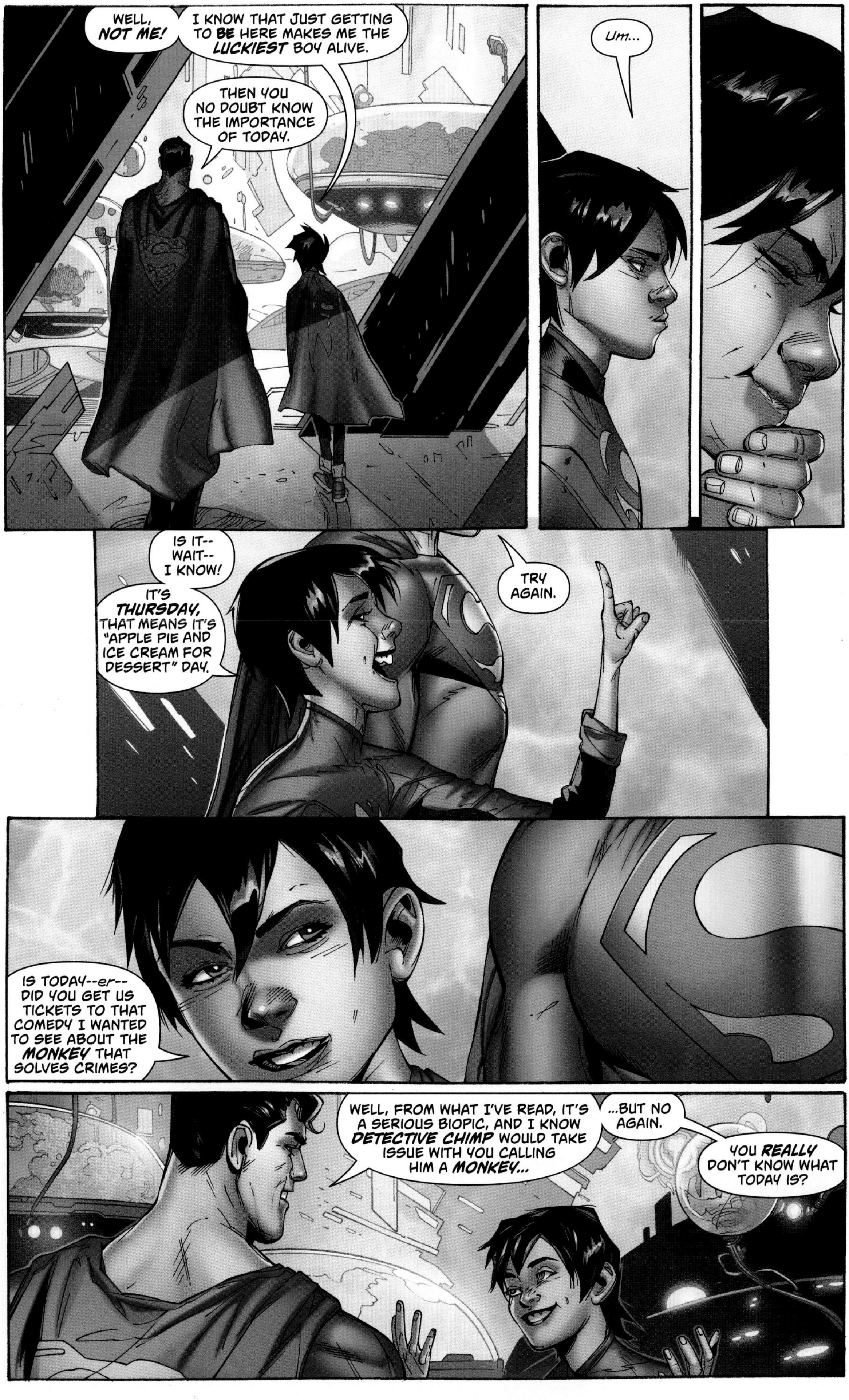

WELL, NOT ME!
I KNOW THAT JUST GETTING TO BE HERE MAKES ME THE LUCKIEST BOY ALIVE.
THEN YOU NO DOUBT KNOW THE IMPORTANCE OF TODAY.
Um...
IS IT-- WAIT-- I KNOW!
IT'S THURSDAY, THAT MEANS IT'S "APPLE PIE AND ICE CREAM FOR DESSERT" DAY.
TRY AGAIN.
IS TODAY--er-- DID YOU GET US TICKETS TO THAT COMEDY I WANTED TO SEE ABOUT THE MONKEY THAT SOLVES CRIMES?
WELL, FROM WHAT I'VE READ, IT'S A SERIOUS BIOPIC, AND I KNOW DETECTIVE CHIMP WOULD TAKE ISSUE WITH YOU CALLING HIM A MONKEY...
...BUT NO AGAIN.
YOU REALLY DON'T KNOW WHAT TODAY IS?

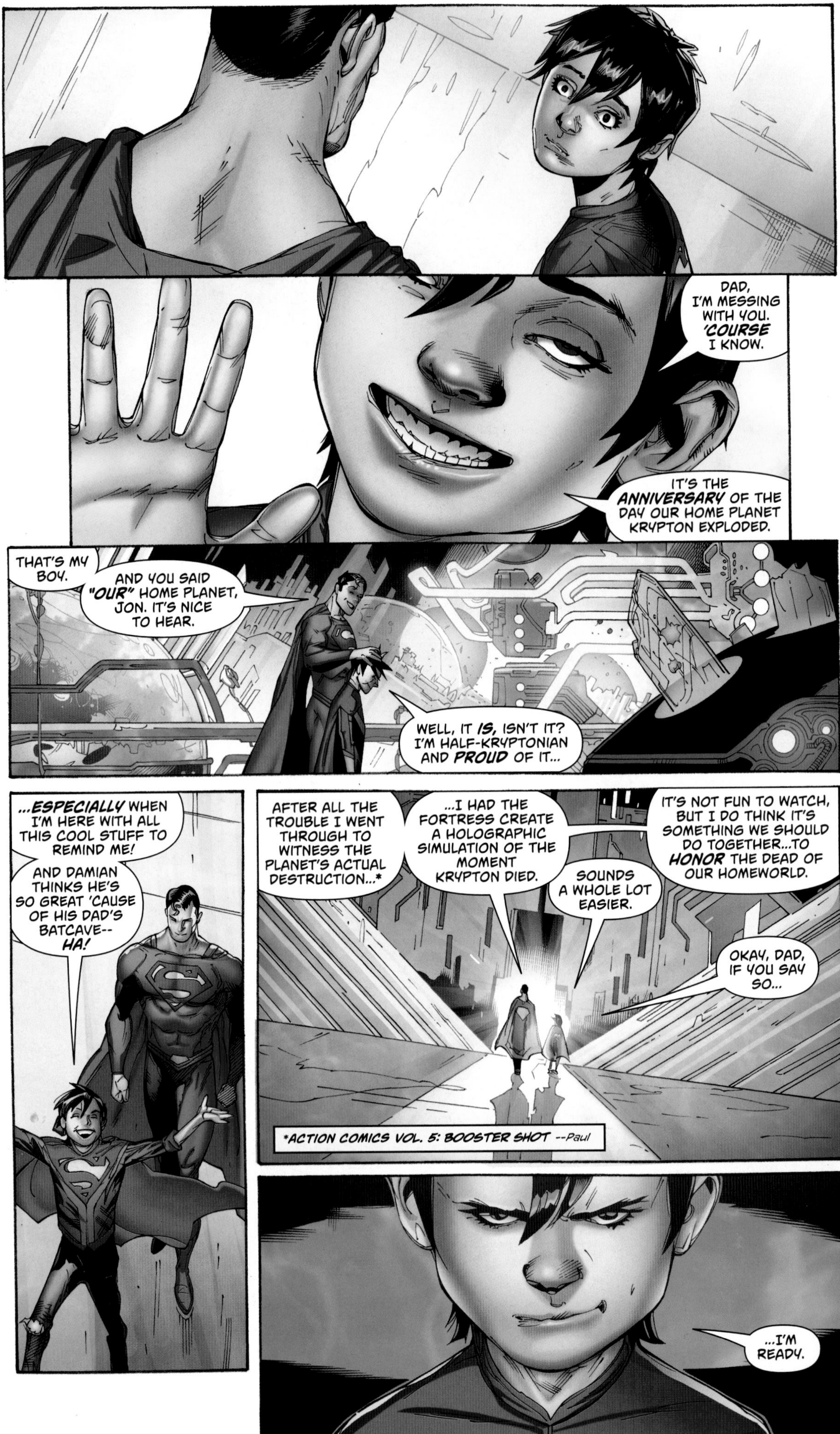
DAD, I'M MESSING WITH YOU. 'COURSE I KNOW.
IT'S THE ANNIVERSARY OF THE DAY OUR HOME PLANET KRYPTON EXPLODED.
THAT'S MY BOY.
AND YOU SAID "OUR" HOME PLANET, JON. IT'S NICE TO HEAR.
WELL, IT IS, ISN'T IT? I'M HALF-KRYPTONIAN AND PROUD OF IT...
...ESPECIALLY WHEN I'M HERE WITH ALL THIS COOL STUFF TO REMIND ME!
AND DAMIAN THINKS HE'S SO GREAT 'CAUSE OF HIS DAD'S BATCAVE--HA!
AFTER ALL THE TROUBLE I WENT THROUGH TO WITNESS THE PLANET'S ACTUAL DESTRUCTION...*
...I HAD THE FORTRESS CREATE A HOLOGRAPHIC SIMULATION OF THE MOMENT KRYPTON DIED.
SOUNDS A WHOLE LOT EASIER.
IT'S NOT FUN TO WATCH, BUT I DO THINK IT'S SOMETHING WE SHOULD DO TOGETHER...TO HONOR THE DEAD OF OUR HOMEWORLD.
OKAY, DAD, IF YOU SAY SO...
*ACTION COMICS VOL. 5: BOOSTER SHOT --Paul
...I'M READY.

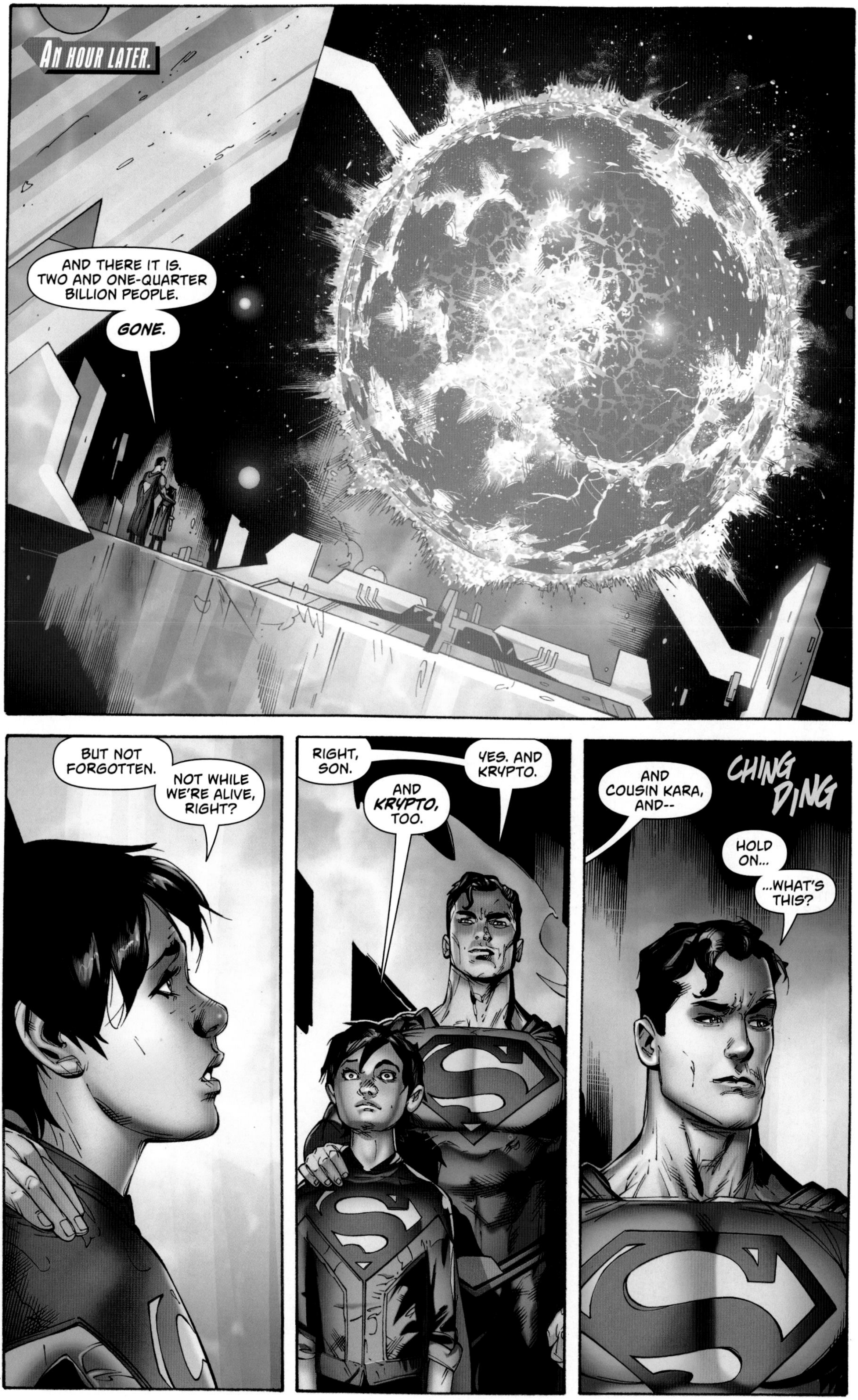
AN HOUR LATER.
AND THERE IT IS. TWO AND ONE-QUARTER BILLION PEOPLE.
GONE.
BUT NOT FORGOTTEN.
NOT WHILE WE'RE ALIVE, RIGHT?
RIGHT, SON.
YES. AND KRYPTO.
AND KRYPTO, TOO.
AND COUSIN KARA, AND--
CHING DING
HOLD ON...
...WHAT'S THIS?

CHING DING

I PROGRAMMED THE FORTRESS YEARS AGO TO SCAN THE STARS AND ALERT ME IF ANY OTHER PLANET FACED THE SAME END AS KRYPTON.

Hm.

OF COURSE, WHAT ARE THE CHANCES THAT *TODAY* OF ALL DAYS THE SENSORS WOULD DELIVER SUCH A REPORT?

WHERE IS IT, DAD?

THERE'S A POPULATED PLANET OUT THERE-- *GALYMAYNE*-- THAT'S ABOUT TO EXPLODE IN MUCH THE SAME WAY KRYPTON DID.

IS IT FAR AWAY?

FAR RELATIVE TO WHAT, JON? IT'S IN A DIFFERENT SOLAR SYSTEM, SO IT'S NOT EXACTLY A FIVE-MINUTE TRIP TO THE CORNER STORE. BUT...

...I COULD GET THERE EASILY ENOUGH--

--HOPEFULLY WORK OUT A WAY TO *SAVE* THE PLANET, OR AT THE VERY LEAST, ITS *POPULATION*.

THEN *WHAT* ARE WE WAITING FOR?!

"WE"? NO, YOU'RE GOING HOME. THIS IS A JOB FOR SUPERMAN--

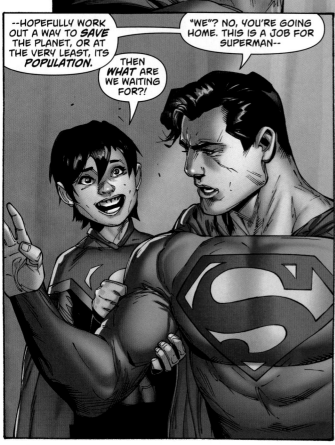

AND SON!

PLEASE, DAD. *PLEEEASE!*

I *PROMISE* I'LL BE GOOD. NO WANDERING OFF OR GOOFING AROUND.

AND LIKE *YOU* SAID, IT'S THE ANNIVERSARY OF KRYPTON'S PASSING. YOU WANTED ME TO EXPERIENCE THAT WITH YOU, SO LET ME DO THIS WITH YOU, TOO.

THIS IS A *SIGN*.

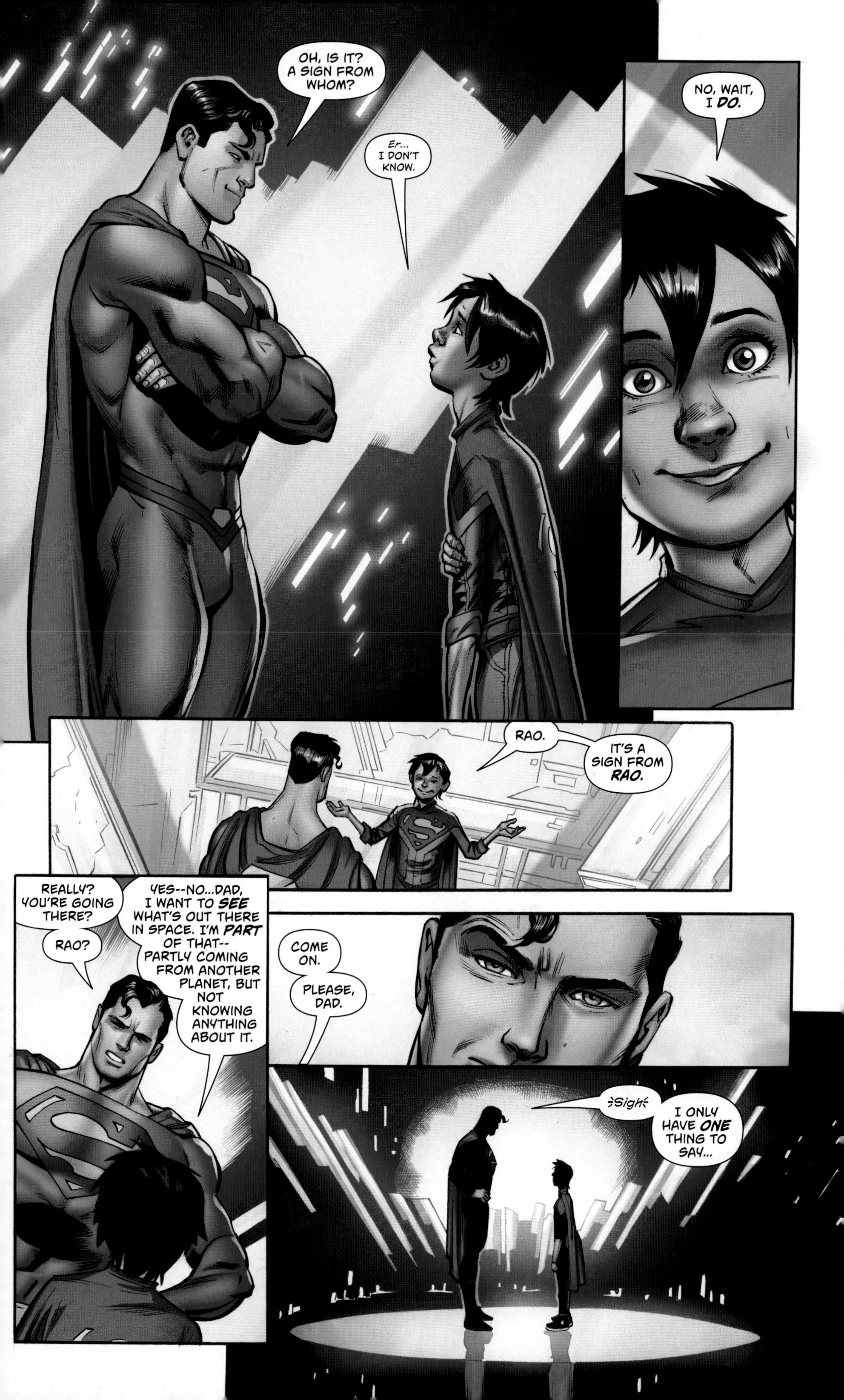
OH, IS IT? A SIGN FROM WHOM?
Er... I DON'T KNOW.
NO, WAIT, I DO.
RAO.
IT'S A SIGN FROM RAO.
REALLY? YOU'RE GOING THERE?
RAO?
YES--NO...DAD, I WANT TO SEE WHAT'S OUT THERE IN SPACE. I'M PART OF THAT-- PARTLY COMING FROM ANOTHER PLANET, BUT NOT KNOWING ANYTHING ABOUT IT.
COME ON.
PLEASE, DAD.
Sigh
I ONLY HAVE ONE THING TO SAY...

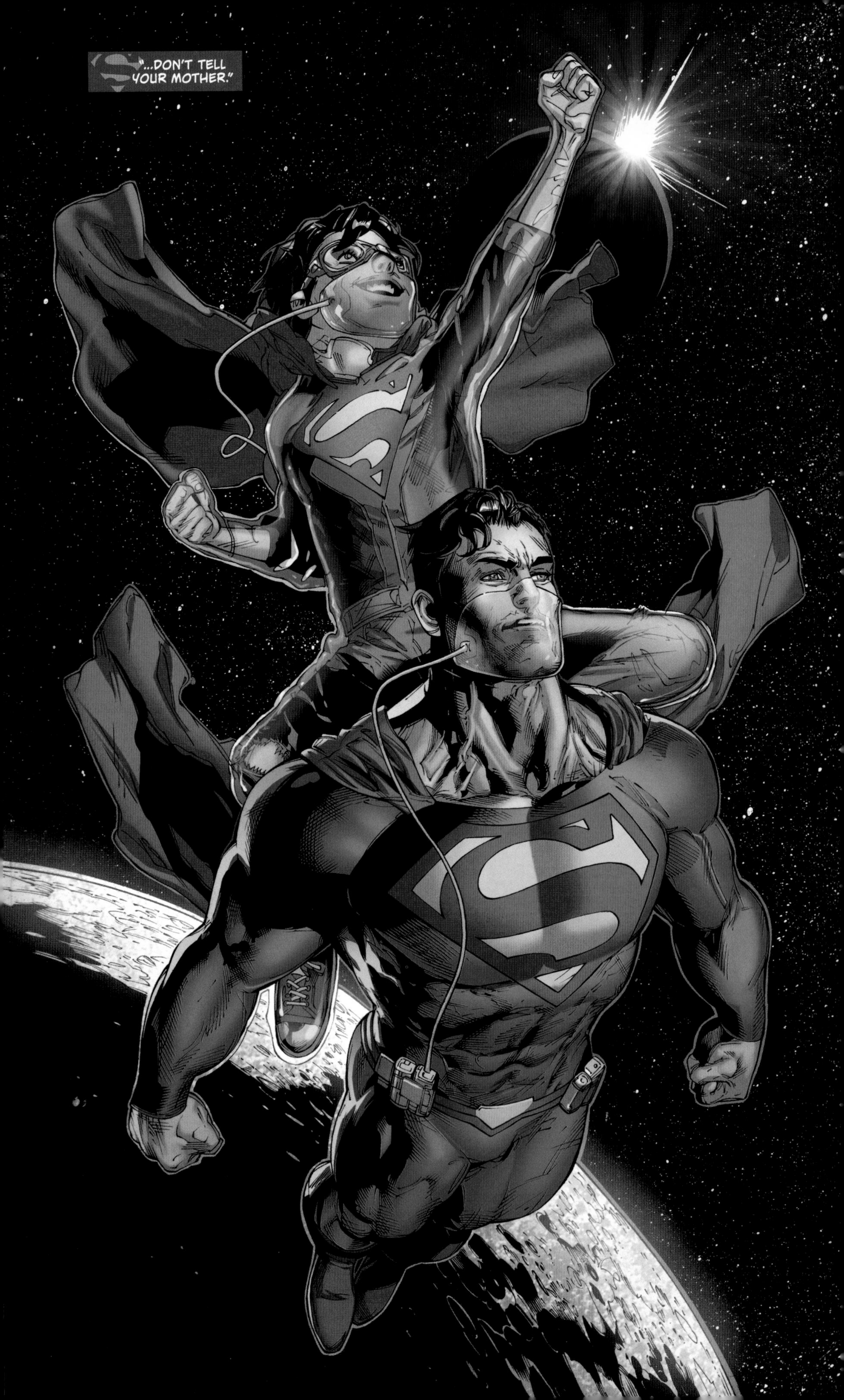
"...DON'T TELL YOUR MOTHER."

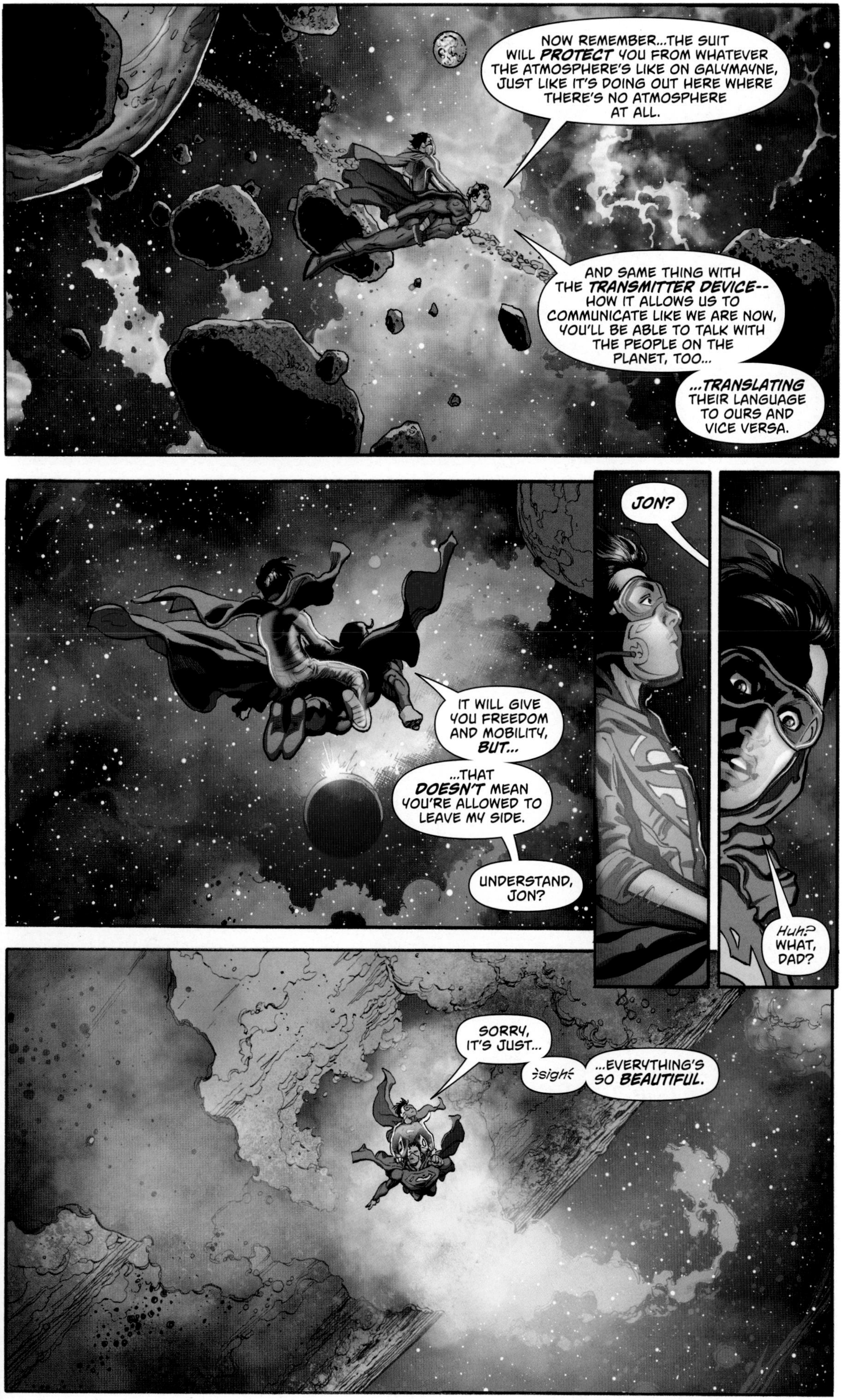
NOW REMEMBER...THE SUIT WILL PROTECT YOU FROM WHATEVER THE ATMOSPHERE'S LIKE ON GALYMAYNE, JUST LIKE IT'S DOING OUT HERE WHERE THERE'S NO ATMOSPHERE AT ALL.
AND SAME THING WITH THE TRANSMITTER DEVICE-- HOW IT ALLOWS US TO COMMUNICATE LIKE WE ARE NOW, YOU'LL BE ABLE TO TALK WITH THE PEOPLE ON THE PLANET, TOO...
...TRANSLATING THEIR LANGUAGE TO OURS AND VICE VERSA.
IT WILL GIVE YOU FREEDOM AND MOBILITY, BUT...
...THAT DOESN'T MEAN YOU'RE ALLOWED TO LEAVE MY SIDE.
UNDERSTAND, JON?
JON?
Huh? WHAT, DAD?
SORRY, IT'S JUST...
sigh
...EVERYTHING'S SO BEAUTIFUL.

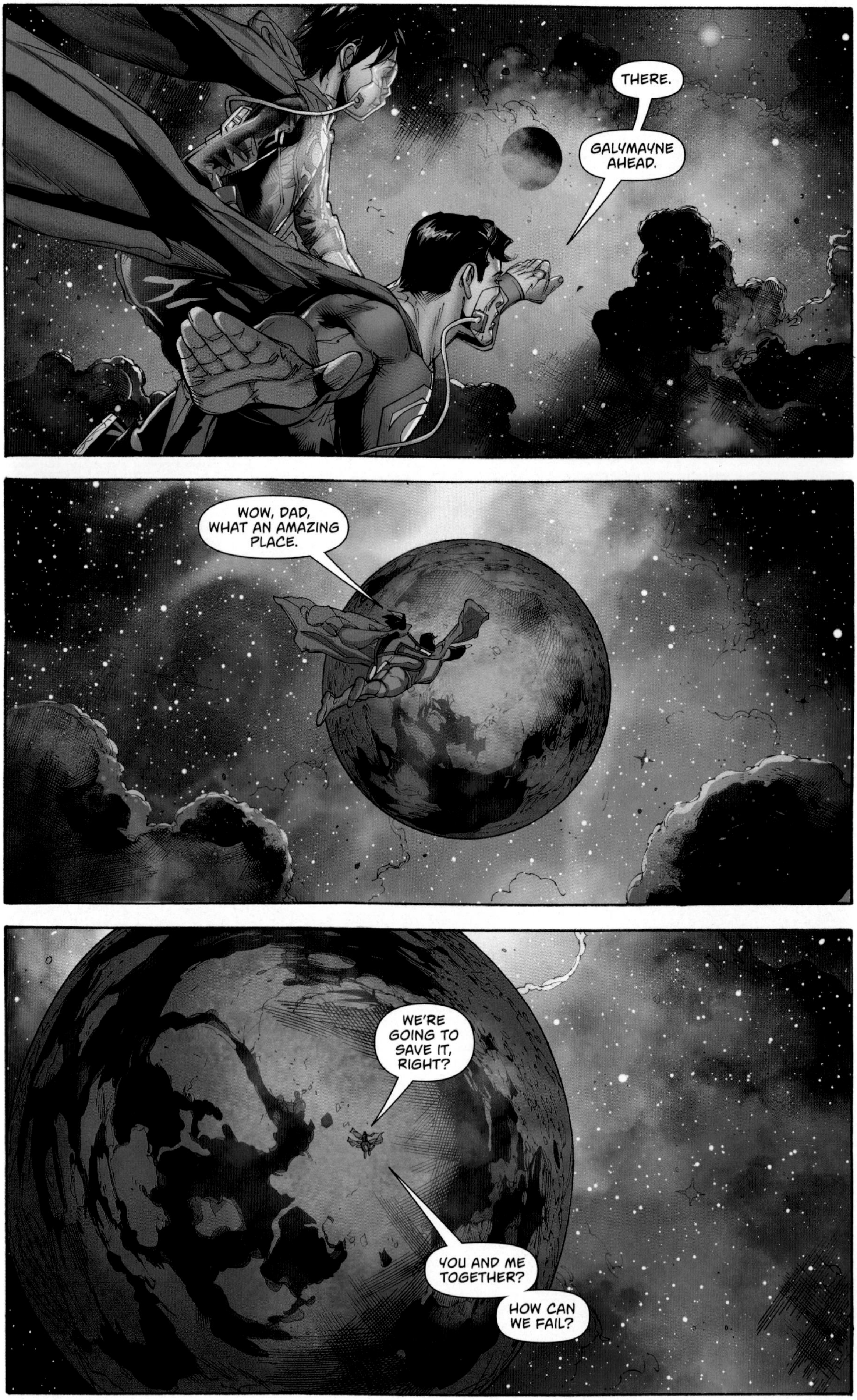
THERE.
GALYMAYNE AHEAD.
WOW, DAD, WHAT AN AMAZING PLACE.
WE'RE GOING TO SAVE IT, RIGHT?
YOU AND ME TOGETHER?
HOW CAN WE FAIL?

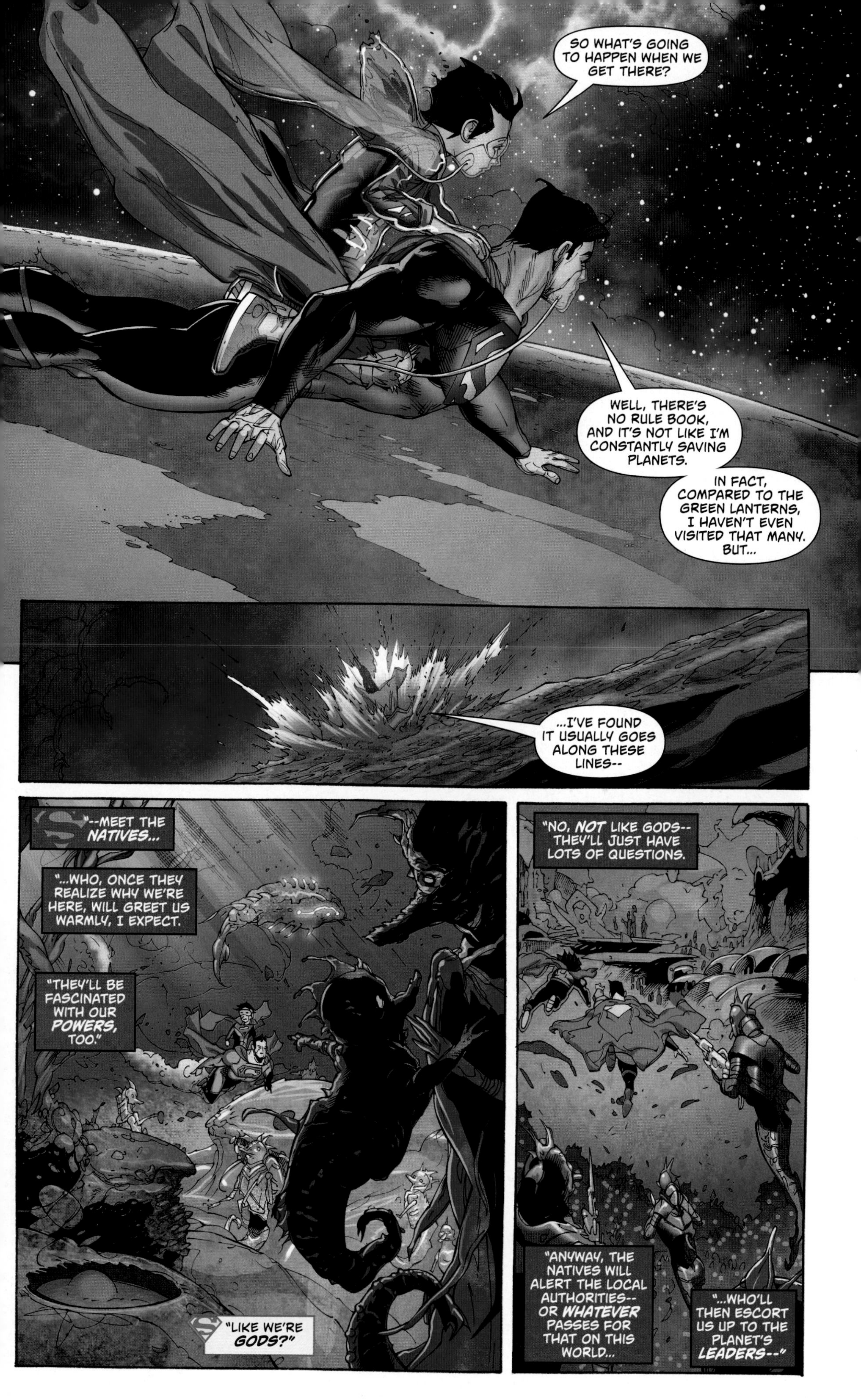
SO WHAT'S GOING TO HAPPEN WHEN WE GET THERE?
WELL, THERE'S NO RULE BOOK, AND IT'S NOT LIKE I'M CONSTANTLY SAVING PLANETS.
IN FACT, COMPARED TO THE GREEN LANTERNS, I HAVEN'T EVEN VISITED THAT MANY. BUT...
...I'VE FOUND IT USUALLY GOES ALONG THESE LINES--
"--MEET THE NATIVES...
"...WHO, ONCE THEY REALIZE WHY WE'RE HERE, WILL GREET US WARMLY, I EXPECT.
"THEY'LL BE FASCINATED WITH OUR POWERS, TOO."
"LIKE WE'RE GODS?"
"NO, NOT LIKE GODS-- THEY'LL JUST HAVE LOTS OF QUESTIONS.
"ANYWAY, THE NATIVES WILL ALERT THE LOCAL AUTHORITIES-- OR WHATEVER PASSES FOR THAT ON THIS WORLD...
"...WHO'LL THEN ESCORT US UP TO THE PLANET'S LEADERS--"

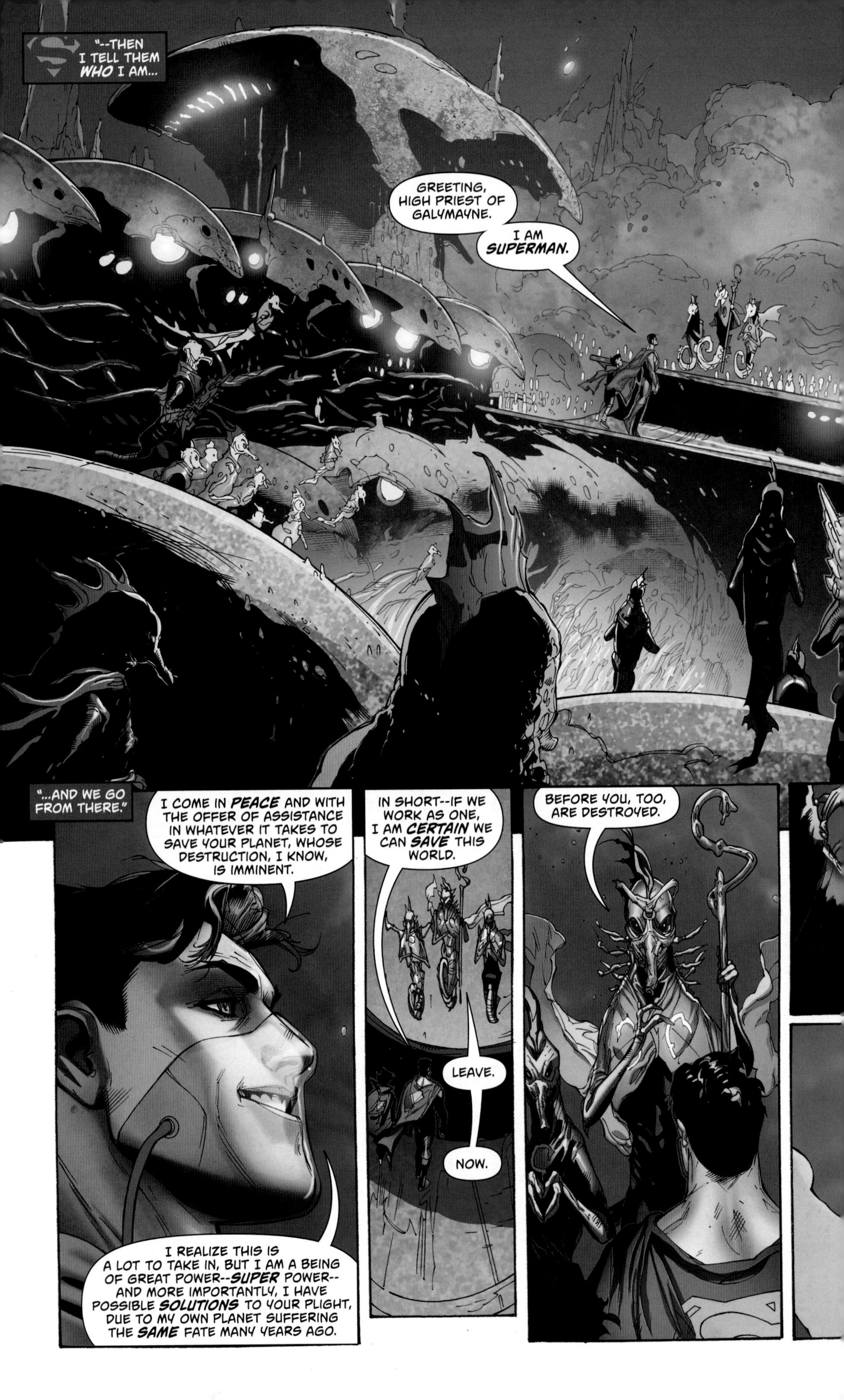
"--THEN I TELL THEM WHO I AM...
GREETING, HIGH PRIEST OF GALYMAYNE.
I AM SUPERMAN.
"...AND WE GO FROM THERE."
I COME IN PEACE AND WITH THE OFFER OF ASSISTANCE IN WHATEVER IT TAKES TO SAVE YOUR PLANET, WHOSE DESTRUCTION, I KNOW, IS IMMINENT.
I REALIZE THIS IS A LOT TO TAKE IN, BUT I AM A BEING OF GREAT POWER--SUPER POWER--AND MORE IMPORTANTLY, I HAVE POSSIBLE SOLUTIONS TO YOUR PLIGHT, DUE TO MY OWN PLANET SUFFERING THE SAME FATE MANY YEARS AGO.
IN SHORT--IF WE WORK AS ONE, I AM CERTAIN WE CAN SAVE THIS WORLD.
LEAVE.
NOW.
BEFORE YOU, TOO, ARE DESTROYED.

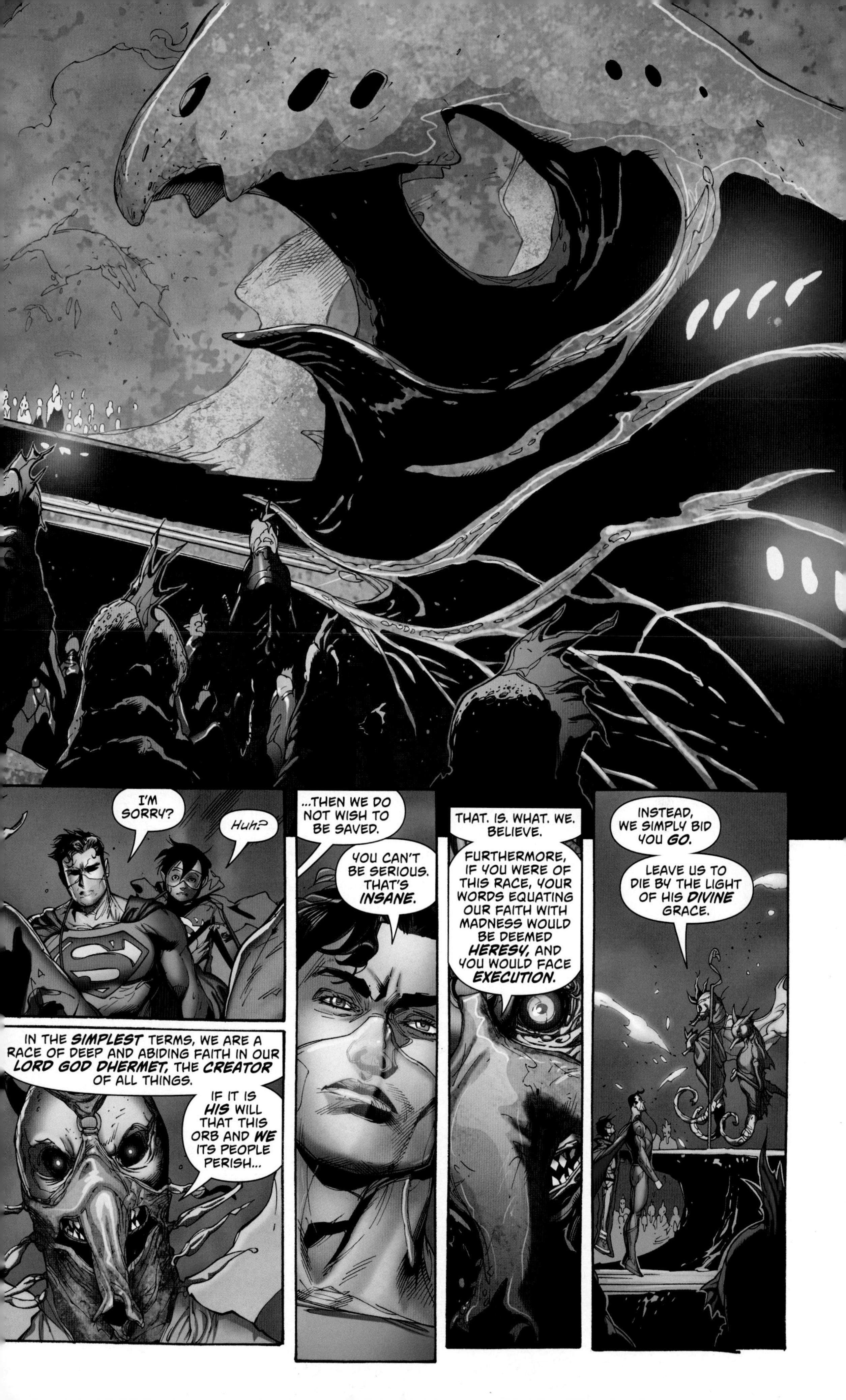
I'M SORRY?
Huh?
IN THE SIMPLEST TERMS, WE ARE A RACE OF DEEP AND ABIDING FAITH IN OUR LORD GOD DHERMET, THE CREATOR OF ALL THINGS.
IF IT IS HIS WILL THAT THIS ORB AND WE ITS PEOPLE PERISH...
...THEN WE DO NOT WISH TO BE SAVED.
YOU CAN'T BE SERIOUS. THAT'S INSANE.
THAT. IS. WHAT. WE. BELIEVE.
FURTHERMORE, IF YOU WERE OF THIS RACE, YOUR WORDS EQUATING OUR FAITH WITH MADNESS WOULD BE DEEMED HERESY, AND YOU WOULD FACE EXECUTION.
INSTEAD, WE SIMPLY BID YOU GO.
LEAVE US TO DIE BY THE LIGHT OF HIS DIVINE GRACE.

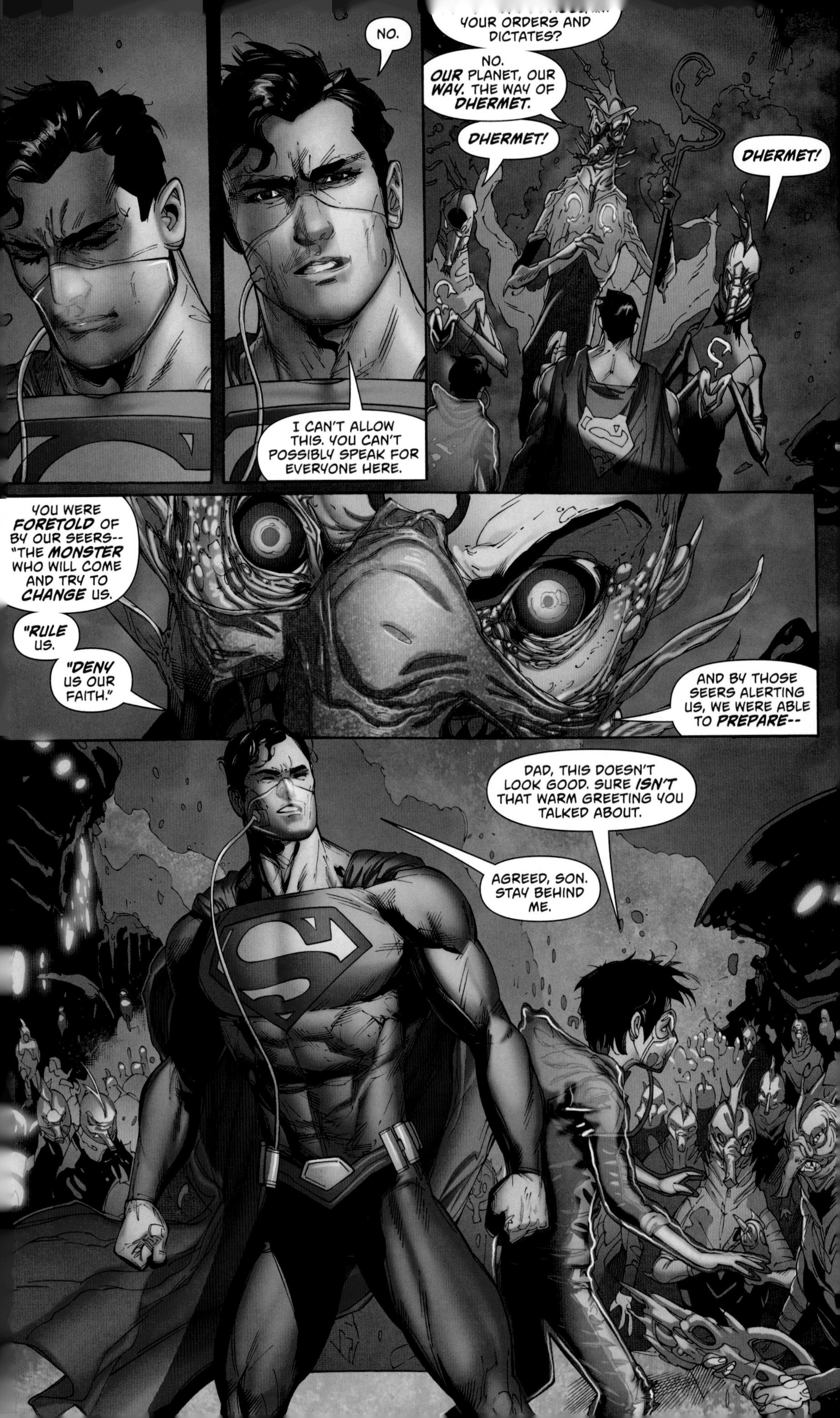

NO.
YOUR ORDERS AND DICTATES?
NO. OUR PLANET, OUR WAY. THE WAY OF DHERMET.
DHERMET!
DHERMET!
I CAN'T ALLOW THIS. YOU CAN'T POSSIBLY SPEAK FOR EVERYONE HERE.
YOU WERE FORETOLD OF BY OUR SEERS-- "THE MONSTER WHO WILL COME AND TRY TO CHANGE US.
"RULE US.
"DENY US OUR FAITH."
AND BY THOSE SEERS ALERTING US, WE WERE ABLE TO PREPARE--
DAD, THIS DOESN'T LOOK GOOD. SURE ISN'T THAT WARM GREETING YOU TALKED ABOUT.
AGREED, SON. STAY BEHIND ME.

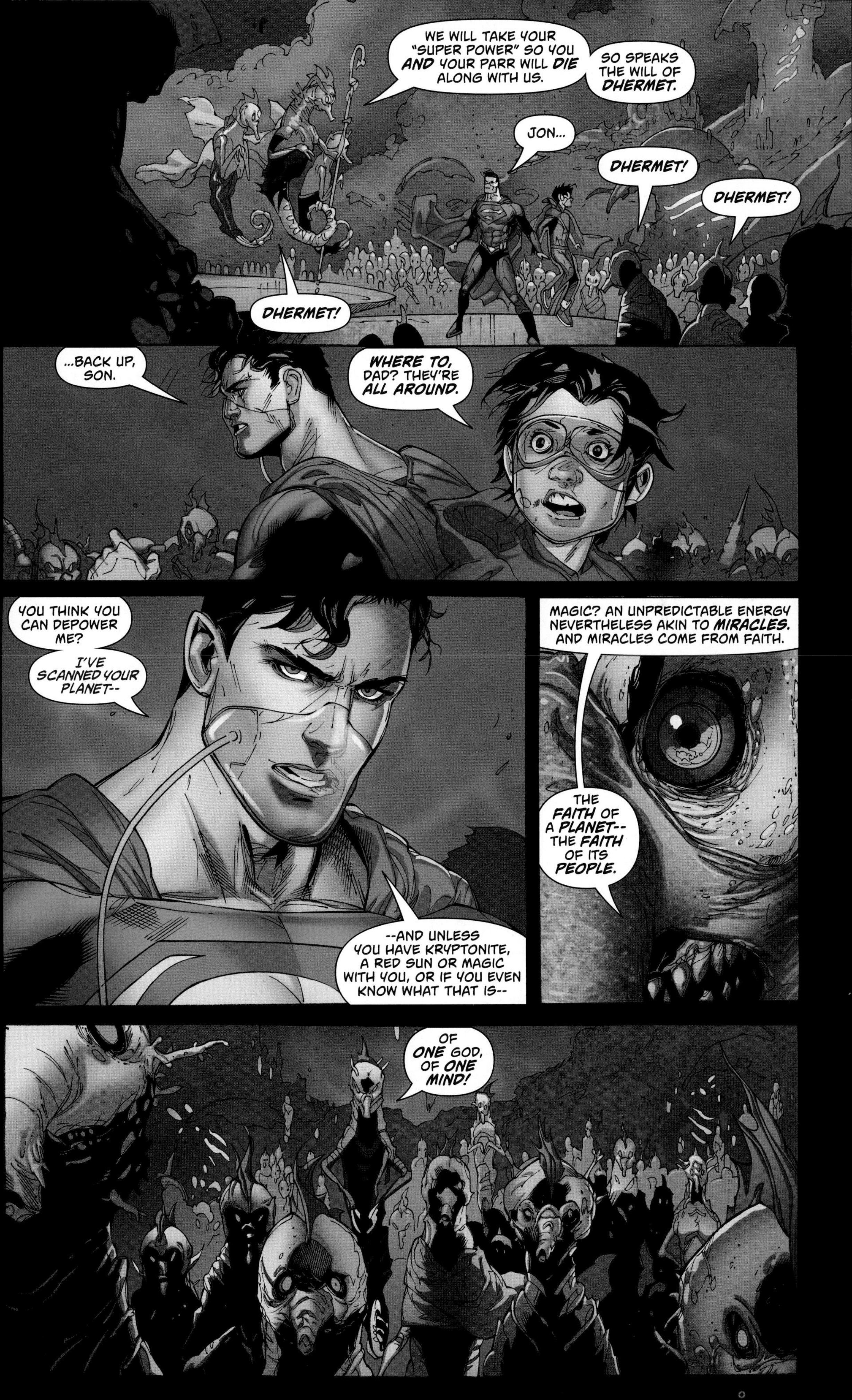

WE WILL TAKE YOUR "SUPER POWER" SO YOU AND YOUR PARR WILL DIE ALONG WITH US.
SO SPEAKS THE WILL OF DHERMET.
JON...
DHERMET!
DHERMET!
DHERMET!
...BACK UP, SON.
WHERE TO, DAD? THEY'RE ALL AROUND.
YOU THINK YOU CAN DEPOWER ME?
I'VE SCANNED YOUR PLANET--
--AND UNLESS YOU HAVE KRYPTONITE, A RED SUN OR MAGIC WITH YOU, OR IF YOU EVEN KNOW WHAT THAT IS--
MAGIC? AN UNPREDICTABLE ENERGY NEVERTHELESS AKIN TO MIRACLES. AND MIRACLES COME FROM FAITH.
THE FAITH OF A PLANET-- THE FAITH OF ITS PEOPLE.
OF ONE GOD, OF ONE MIND!

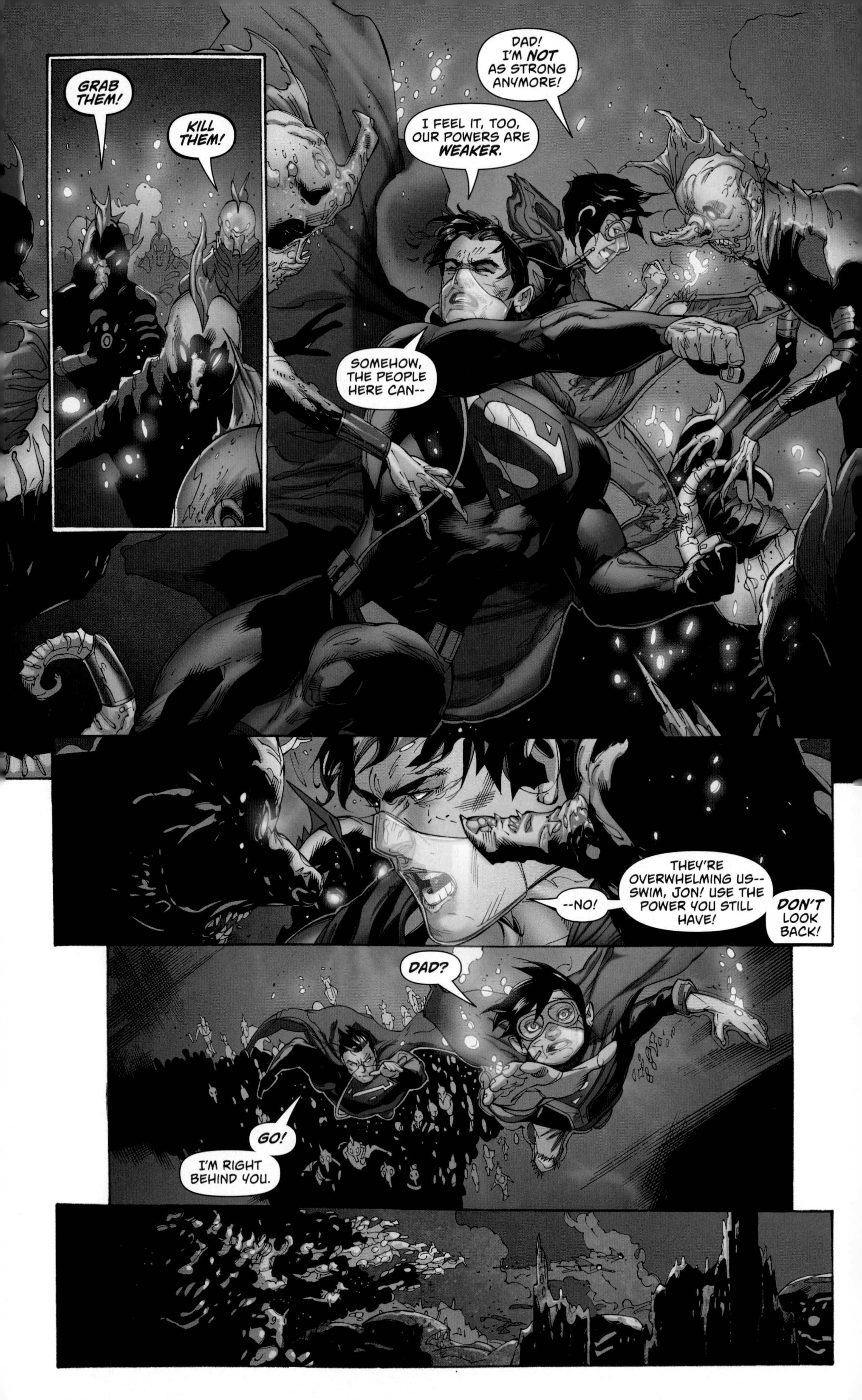
GRAB THEM!
KILL THEM!
DAD! I'M NOT AS STRONG ANYMORE!
I FEEL IT, TOO, OUR POWERS ARE WEAKER.
SOMEHOW, THE PEOPLE HERE CAN--
--NO!
THEY'RE OVERWHELMING US-- SWIM, JON! USE THE POWER YOU STILL HAVE!
DON'T LOOK BACK!
DAD?
GO!
I'M RIGHT BEHIND YOU.

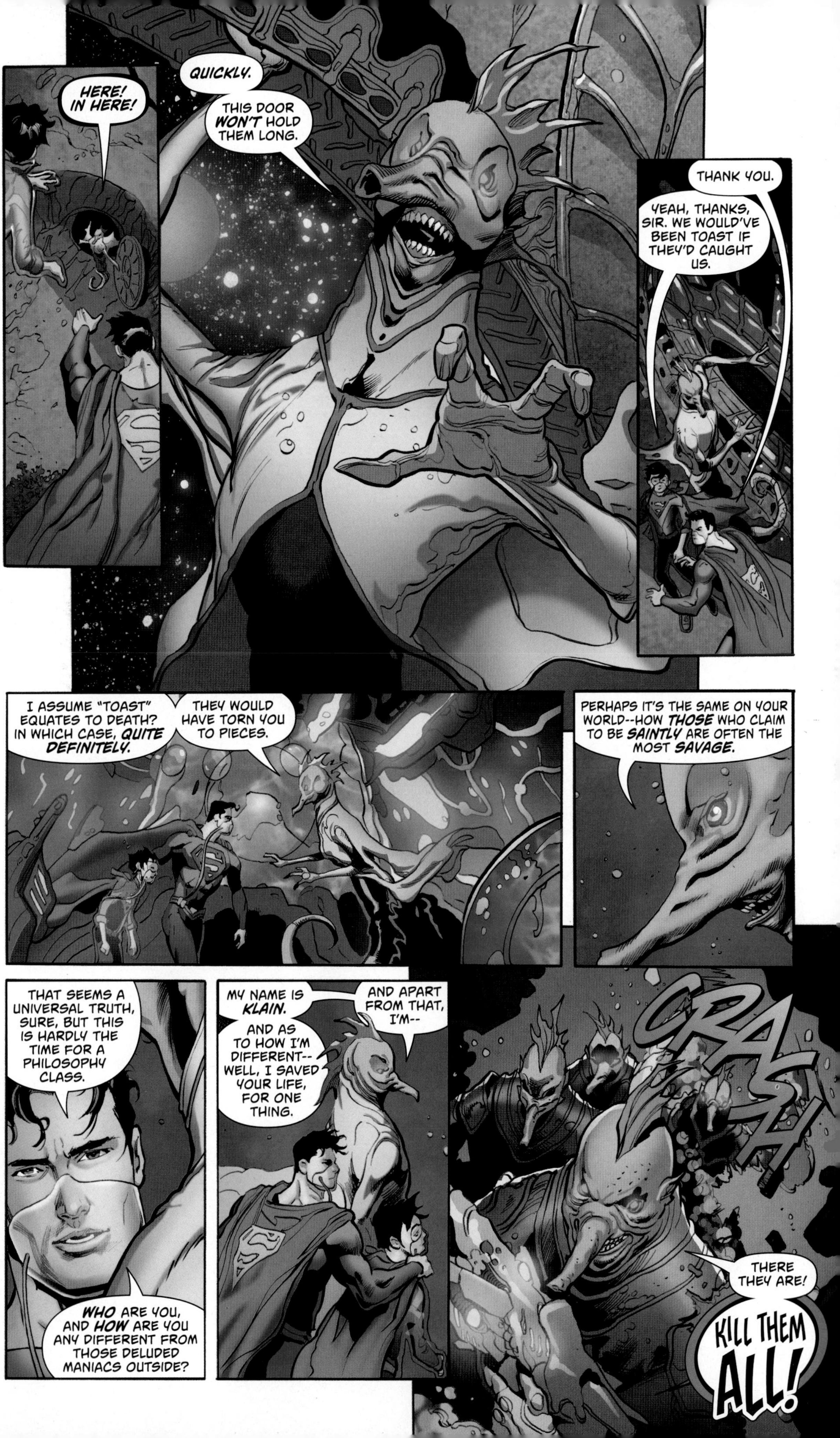

HERE! IN HERE!
QUICKLY.
THIS DOOR WON'T HOLD THEM LONG.
THANK YOU.
YEAH, THANKS, SIR. WE WOULD'VE BEEN TOAST IF THEY'D CAUGHT US.
I ASSUME "TOAST" EQUATES TO DEATH? IN WHICH CASE, QUITE DEFINITELY.
THEY WOULD HAVE TORN YOU TO PIECES.
PERHAPS IT'S THE SAME ON YOUR WORLD--HOW THOSE WHO CLAIM TO BE SAINTLY ARE OFTEN THE MOST SAVAGE.
THAT SEEMS A UNIVERSAL TRUTH, SURE, BUT THIS IS HARDLY THE TIME FOR A PHILOSOPHY CLASS.
WHO ARE YOU, AND HOW ARE YOU ANY DIFFERENT FROM THOSE DELUDED MANIACS OUTSIDE?
MY NAME IS KLAIN.
AND AS TO HOW I'M DIFFERENT-- WELL, I SAVED YOUR LIFE, FOR ONE THING.
AND APART FROM THAT, I'M--
CRASH
THERE THEY ARE!
KILL THEM ALL!

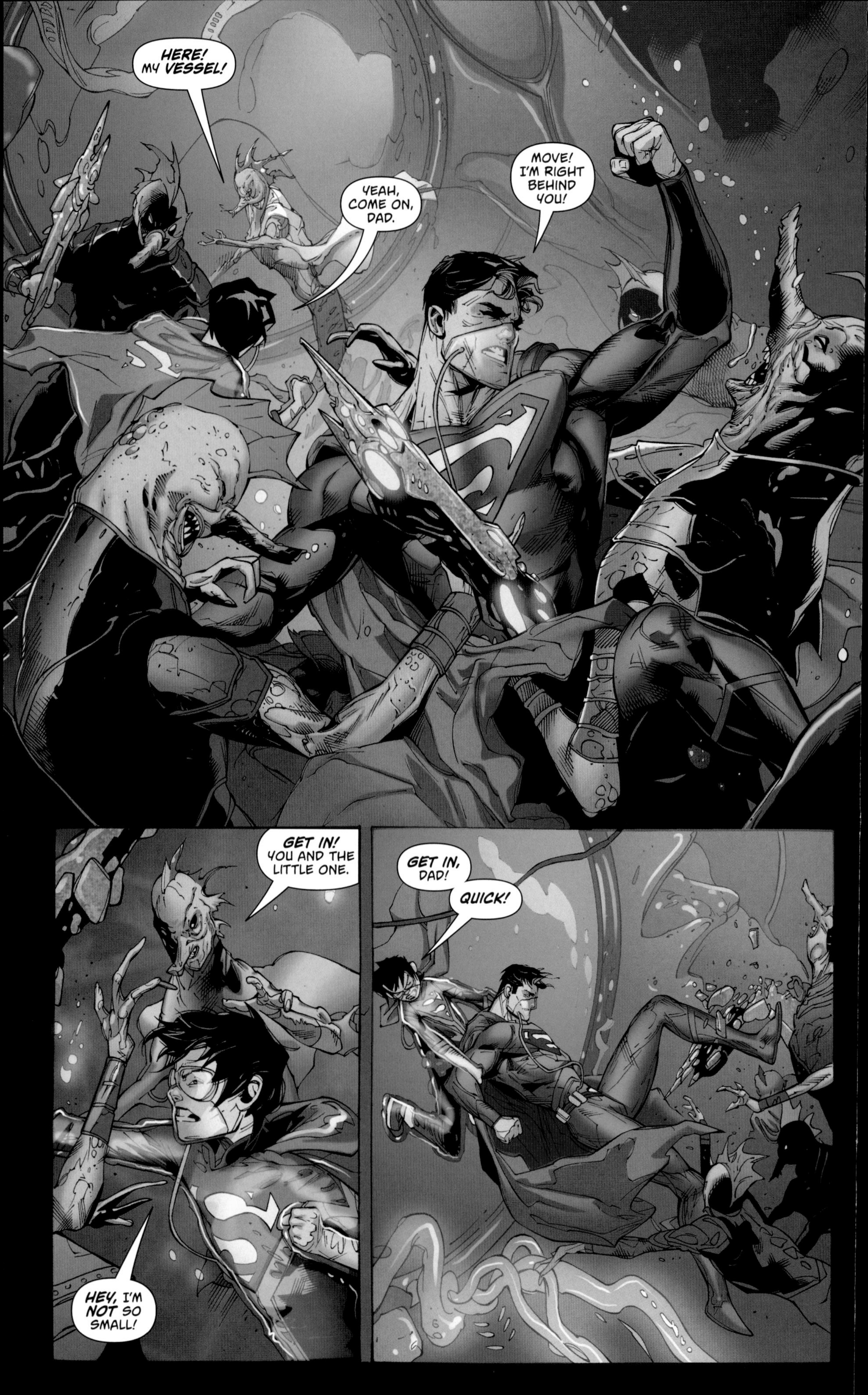
HERE! MY VESSEL!
YEAH, COME ON, DAD.
MOVE! I'M RIGHT BEHIND YOU!
GET IN! YOU AND THE LITTLE ONE.
HEY, I'M NOT SO SMALL!
GET IN, DAD!
QUICK!

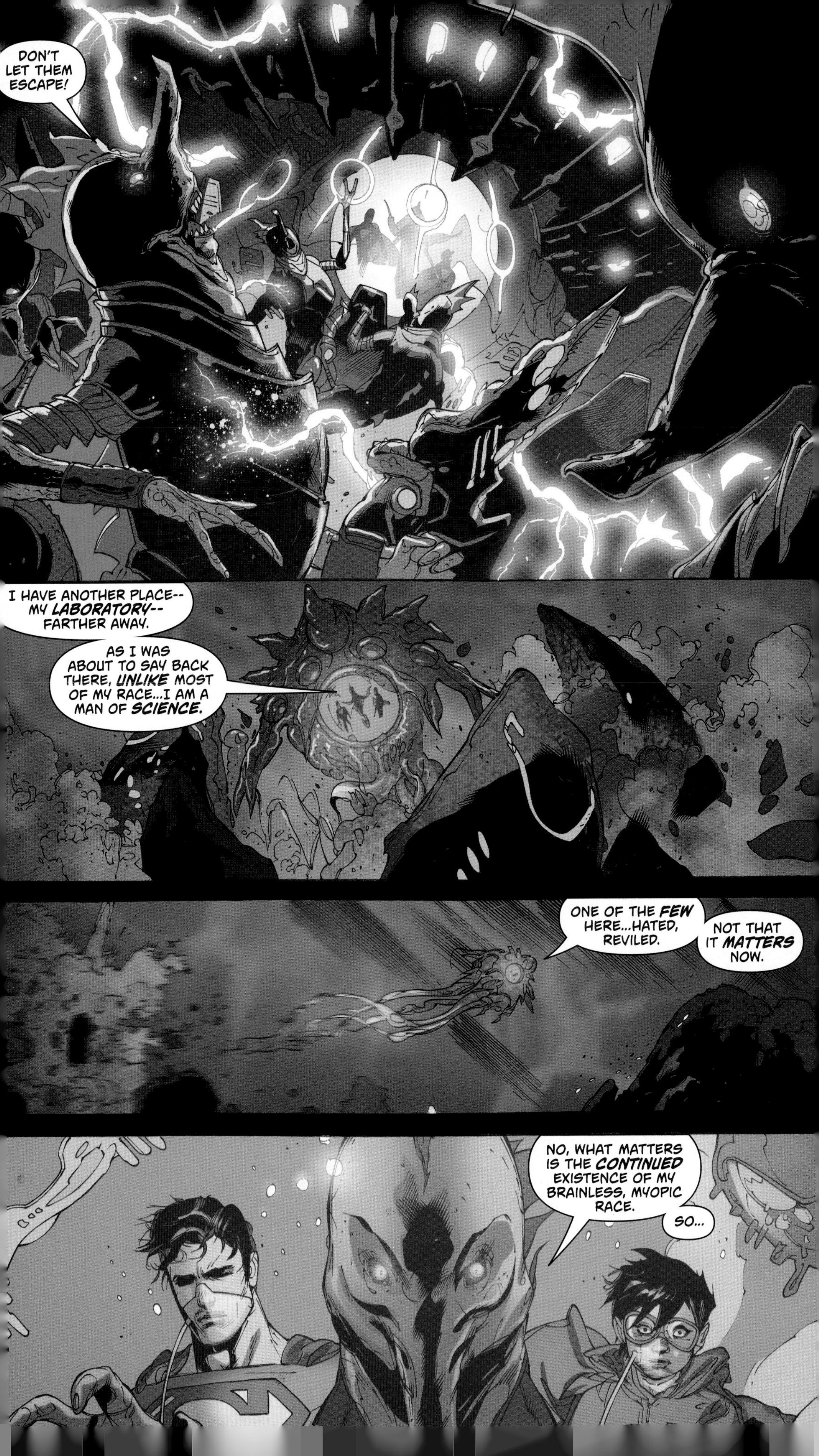
DON'T LET THEM ESCAPE!
I HAVE ANOTHER PLACE-- MY LABORATORY-- FARTHER AWAY.
AS I WAS ABOUT TO SAY BACK THERE, UNLIKE MOST OF MY RACE...I AM A MAN OF SCIENCE.
ONE OF THE FEW HERE...HATED, REVILED.
NOT THAT IT MATTERS NOW.
NO, WHAT MATTERS IS THE CONTINUED EXISTENCE OF MY BRAINLESS, MYOPIC RACE.
SO...

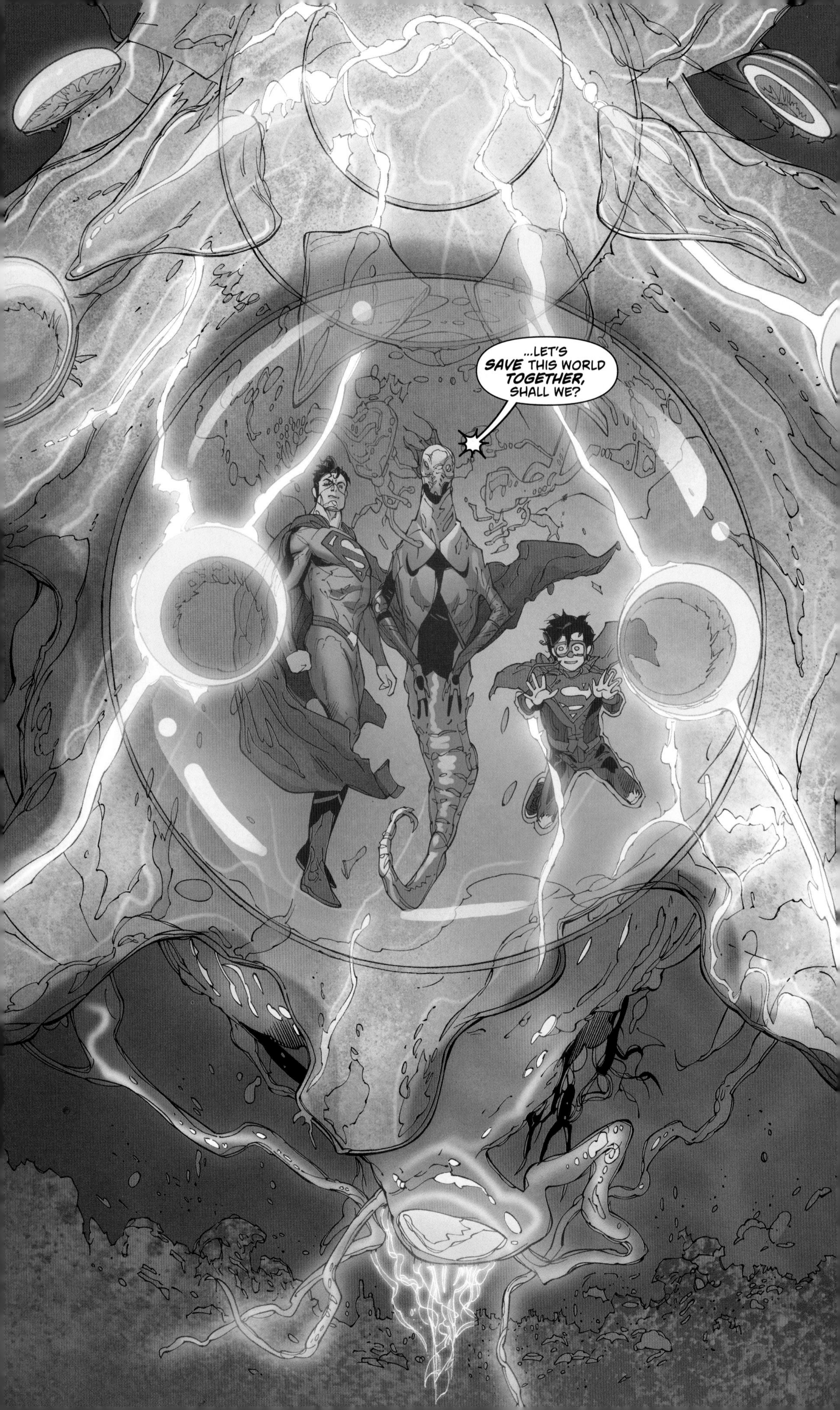
...LET'S SAVE THIS WORLD TOGETHER, SHALL WE?

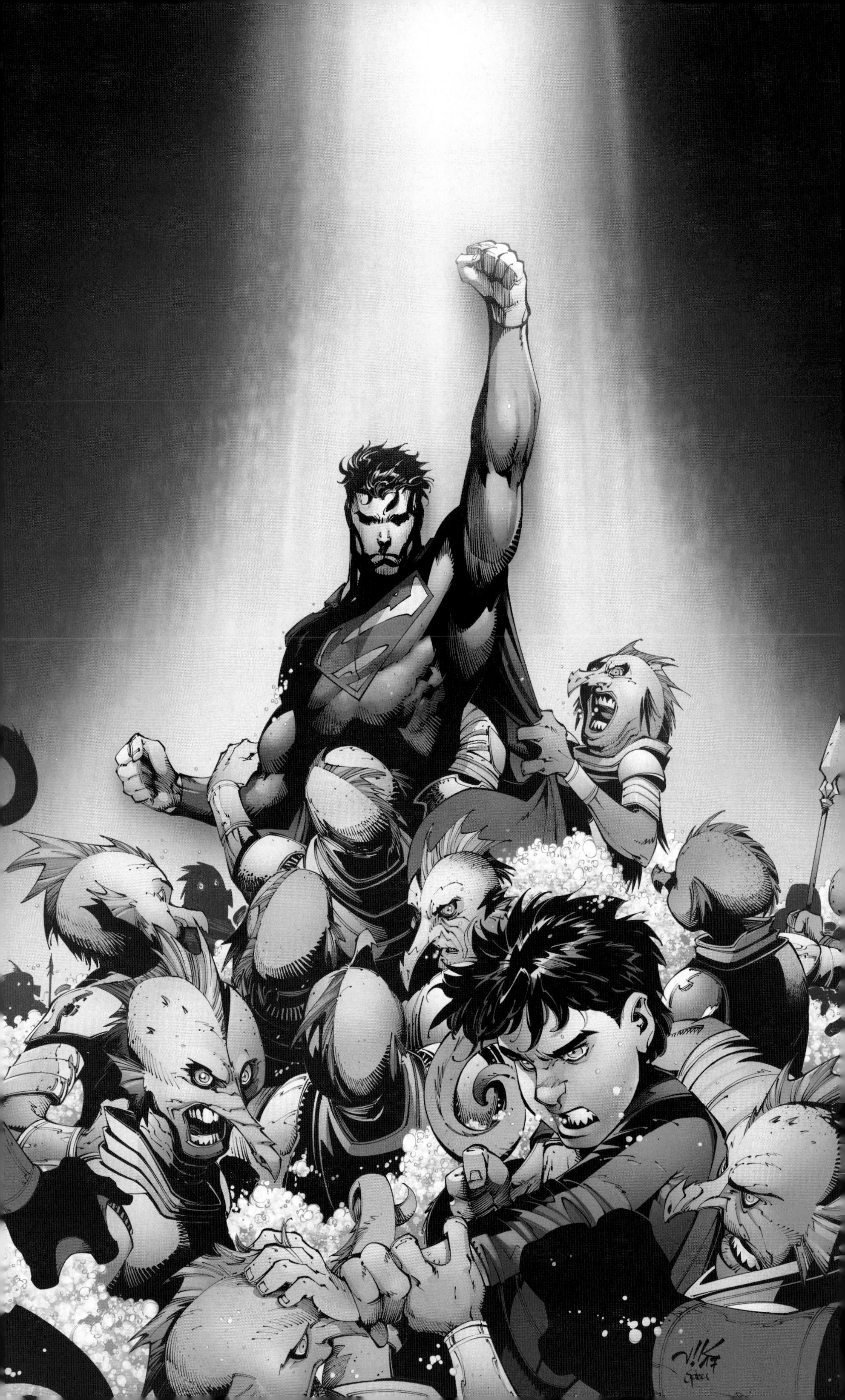

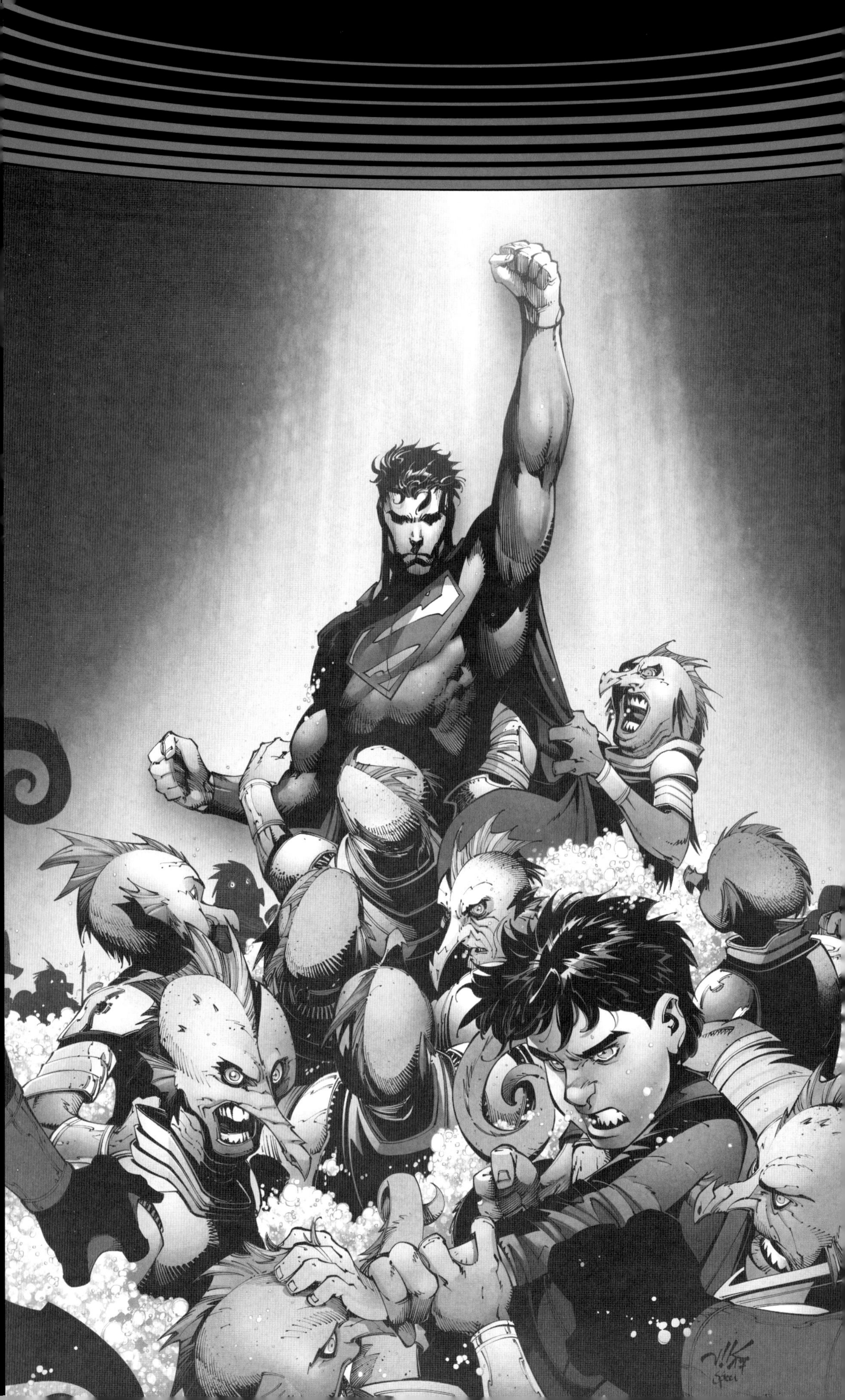

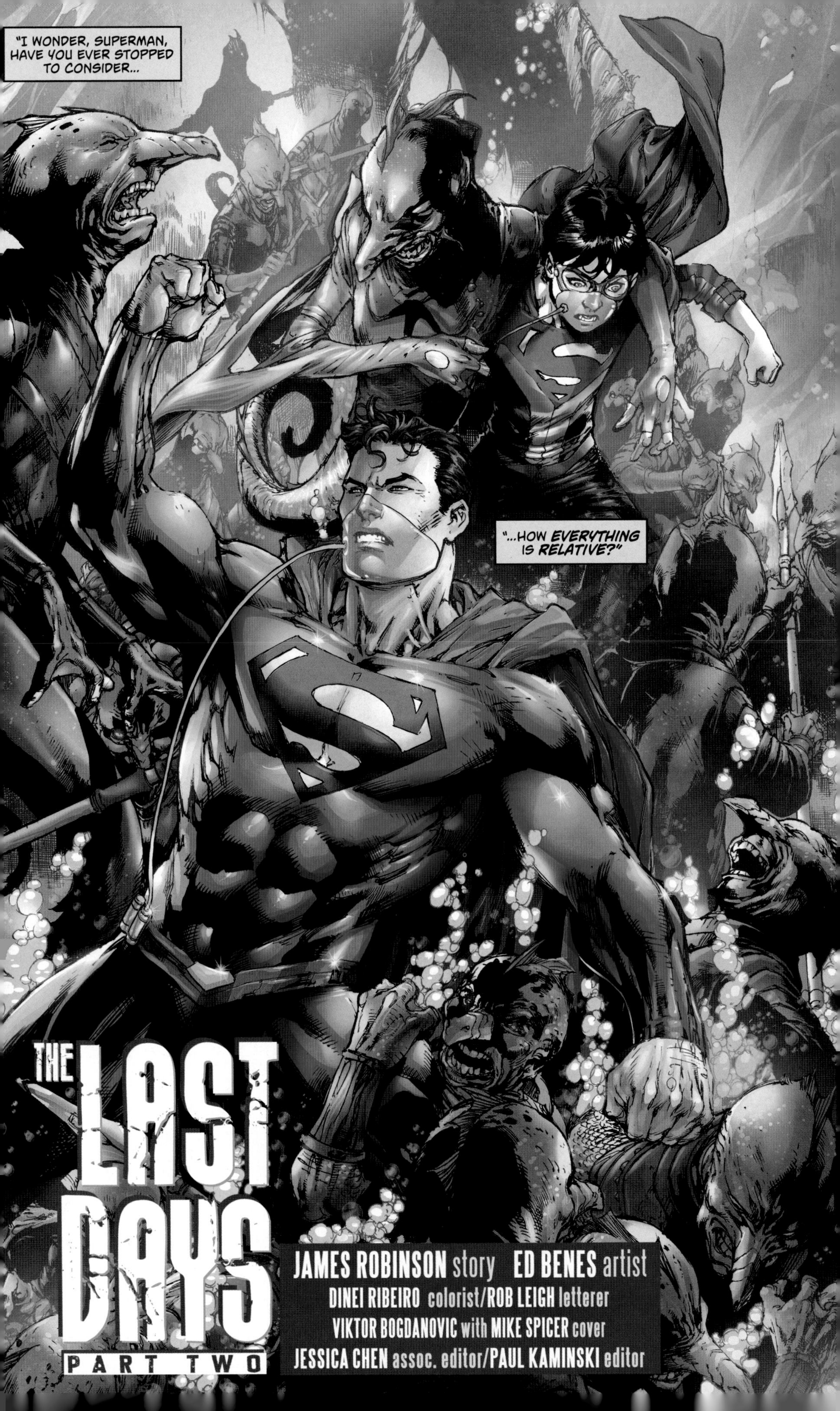
"I WONDER, SUPERMAN, HAVE YOU EVER STOPPED TO CONSIDER...
"...HOW EVERYTHING IS RELATIVE?"
THE LAST DAYS
PART TWO
JAMES ROBINSON story ED BENES artist
DINEI RIBEIRO colorist/ROB LEIGH letterer
VIKTOR BOGDANOVIC with MIKE SPICER cover
JESSICA CHEN assoc. editor/PAUL KAMINSKI editor

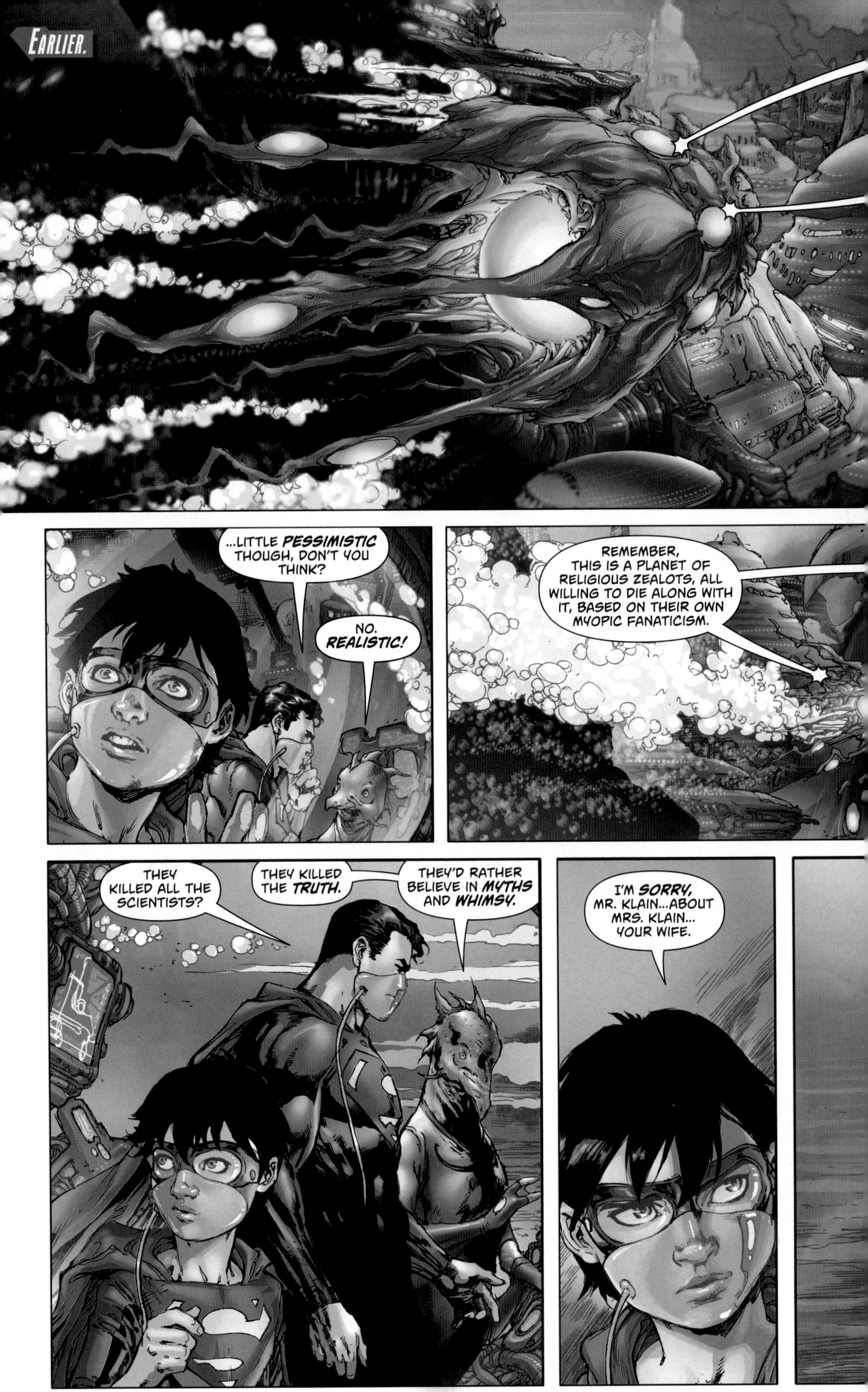
EARLIER.
...LITTLE PESSIMISTIC THOUGH, DON'T YOU THINK?
NO. REALISTIC!
REMEMBER, THIS IS A PLANET OF RELIGIOUS ZEALOTS, ALL WILLING TO DIE ALONG WITH IT, BASED ON THEIR OWN MYOPIC FANATICISM.
THEY KILLED ALL THE SCIENTISTS?
THEY KILLED THE TRUTH.
THEY'D RATHER BELIEVE IN MYTHS AND WHIMSY.
I'M SORRY, MR. KLAIN...ABOUT MRS. KLAIN... YOUR WIFE.

ACTUALLY, YES, KLAIN--IT'S CROSSED MY MIND ONCE OR TWICE.

THEN YOU'LL APPRECIATE THAT I WAS JUST ABOUT TO SAY, "WE'LL BE *SAFE* AT MY HIDDEN LABORATORY UP AHEAD"--

--BUT EVEN AS THE WORDS CAME TO MIND, I REALIZED THE MILITIA OF MY HOMEWORLD, GALYMAYNE, IS NO DOUBT ALREADY *SCOURING* EVERY TRENCH AND REEF ON THE PLANET TO FIND US.

AND THE PLANET'S ABOUT TO *EXPLODE*.

I GET IT-- SAFETY'S RELATIVE. FLEETING...

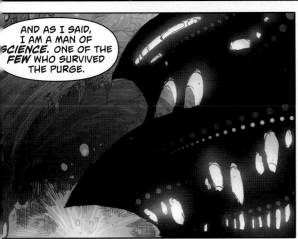

AND AS I SAID, I AM A MAN OF *SCIENCE*. ONE OF THE *FEW* WHO SURVIVED THE PURGE.

MY WIFE... WASN'T SO LUCKY.

THANK YOU, YOUNG MAN. I CAN TELL YOUR FATHER IS A CHAMPION OF GOOD HEART.

YOU HAVE THAT SAME LIGHT IN YOU.

HERE WE ARE.

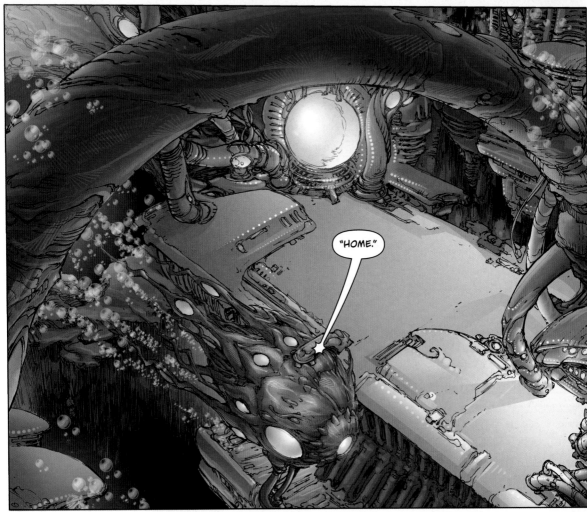

"HOME."

MY WIFE WAS MY LOVE. EVEN IN DEATH, SHE GIVES ME PURPOSE.

I MUST SAY, AFTER YOUR WIFE'S MURDER, THE FACT THAT YOU *STILL* WANT TO SAVE YOUR PEOPLE IS VERY ADMIRABLE.

DO YOU HATE A CHILD WHEN THEY BREAK SOMETHING, OR IS IT BETTER TO HOPE THAT THE CHILD WILL LEARN FROM ITS MISTAKE?

YOU'RE A GOOD MAN, KLAIN.

GOOD? TO *YOU*, PERHAPS.

TO MY PEOPLE, I AM THE EMBODIMENT OF *EVIL*. THEY THINK ME NOT JUST AN UNBELIEVER, BUT ONE WHO WOULD RIP APART THEIR CREDO.

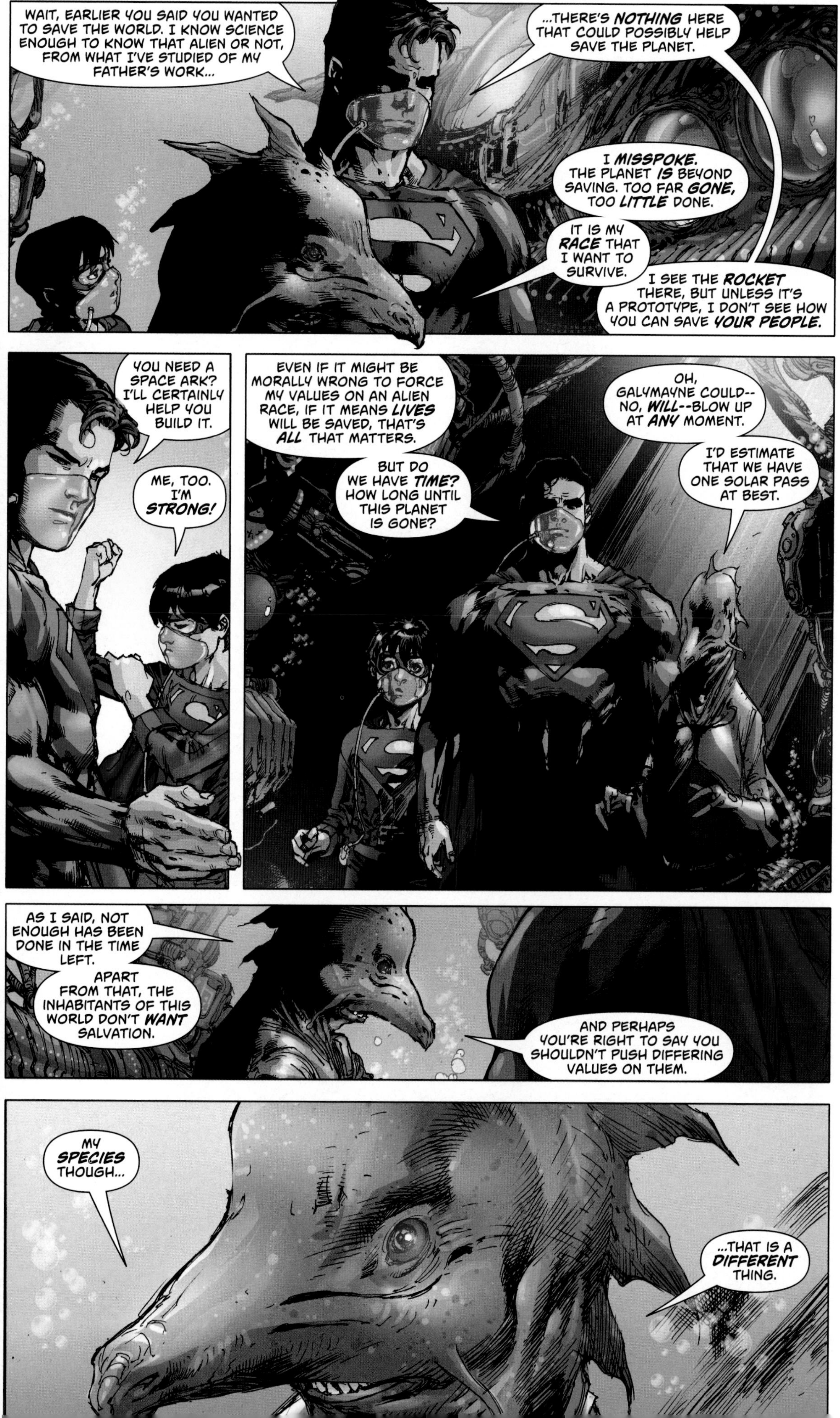
WAIT, EARLIER YOU SAID YOU WANTED TO SAVE THE WORLD. I KNOW SCIENCE ENOUGH TO KNOW THAT ALIEN OR NOT, FROM WHAT I'VE STUDIED OF MY FATHER'S WORK...
...THERE'S NOTHING HERE THAT COULD POSSIBLY HELP SAVE THE PLANET.
I MISSPOKE. THE PLANET IS BEYOND SAVING. TOO FAR GONE, TOO LITTLE DONE.
IT IS MY RACE THAT I WANT TO SURVIVE.
I SEE THE ROCKET THERE, BUT UNLESS IT'S A PROTOTYPE, I DON'T SEE HOW YOU CAN SAVE YOUR PEOPLE.
YOU NEED A SPACE ARK? I'LL CERTAINLY HELP YOU BUILD IT.
ME, TOO. I'M STRONG!
EVEN IF IT MIGHT BE MORALLY WRONG TO FORCE MY VALUES ON AN ALIEN RACE, IF IT MEANS LIVES WILL BE SAVED, THAT'S ALL THAT MATTERS.
BUT DO WE HAVE TIME? HOW LONG UNTIL THIS PLANET IS GONE?
OH, GALYMAYNE COULD-- NO, WILL--BLOW UP AT ANY MOMENT.
I'D ESTIMATE THAT WE HAVE ONE SOLAR PASS AT BEST.
AS I SAID, NOT ENOUGH HAS BEEN DONE IN THE TIME LEFT.
APART FROM THAT, THE INHABITANTS OF THIS WORLD DON'T WANT SALVATION.
AND PERHAPS YOU'RE RIGHT TO SAY YOU SHOULDN'T PUSH DIFFERING VALUES ON THEM.
MY SPECIES THOUGH...
...THAT IS A DIFFERENT THING.

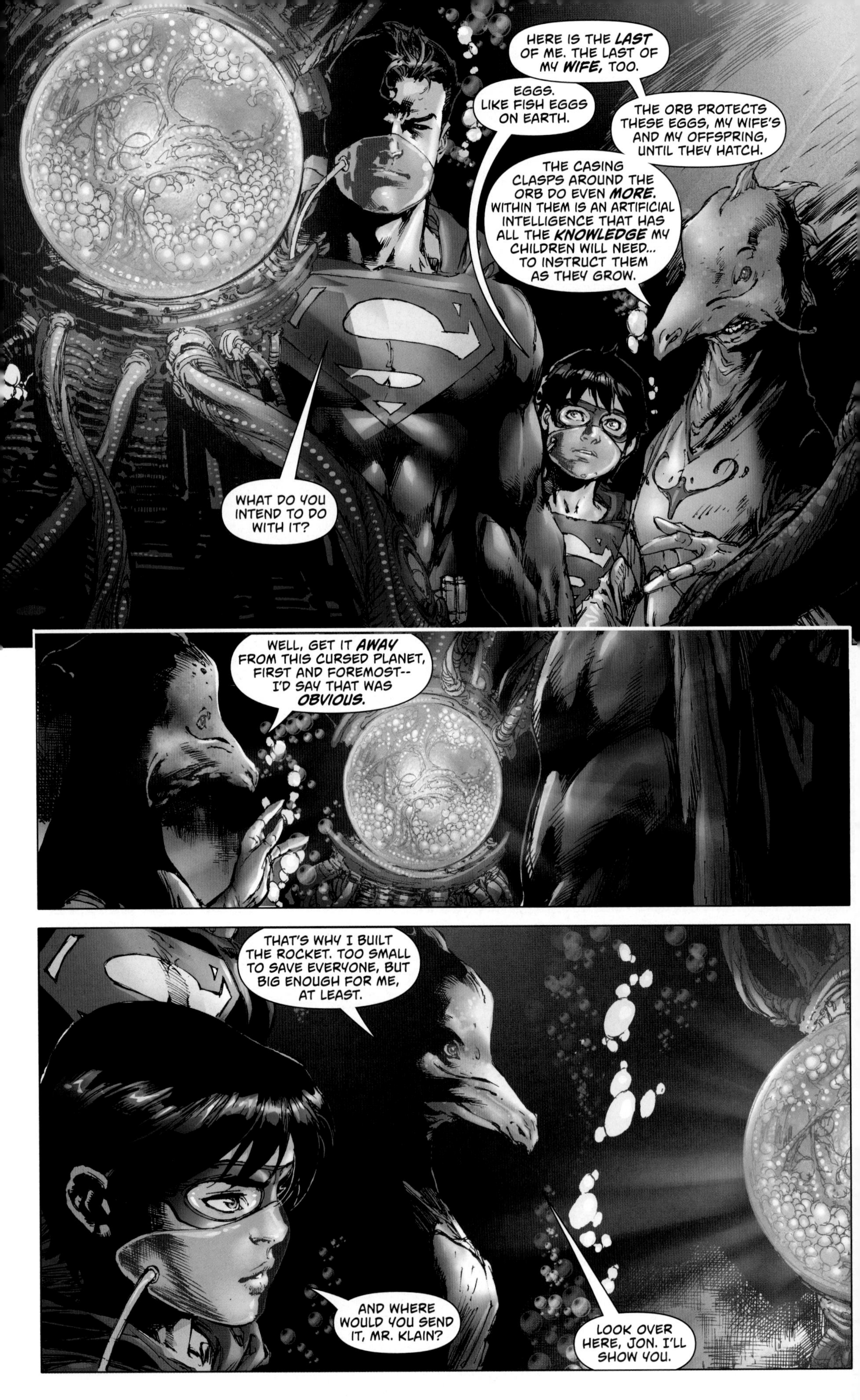
HERE IS THE LAST OF ME. THE LAST OF MY WIFE, TOO.
EGGS. LIKE FISH EGGS ON EARTH.
THE ORB PROTECTS THESE EGGS, MY WIFE'S AND MY OFFSPRING, UNTIL THEY HATCH.
THE CASING CLASPS AROUND THE ORB DO EVEN MORE. WITHIN THEM IS AN ARTIFICIAL INTELLIGENCE THAT HAS ALL THE KNOWLEDGE MY CHILDREN WILL NEED... TO INSTRUCT THEM AS THEY GROW.
WHAT DO YOU INTEND TO DO WITH IT?
WELL, GET IT AWAY FROM THIS CURSED PLANET, FIRST AND FOREMOST-- I'D SAY THAT WAS OBVIOUS.
THAT'S WHY I BUILT THE ROCKET. TOO SMALL TO SAVE EVERYONE, BUT BIG ENOUGH FOR ME, AT LEAST.
AND WHERE WOULD YOU SEND IT, MR. KLAIN?
LOOK OVER HERE, JON. I'LL SHOW YOU.

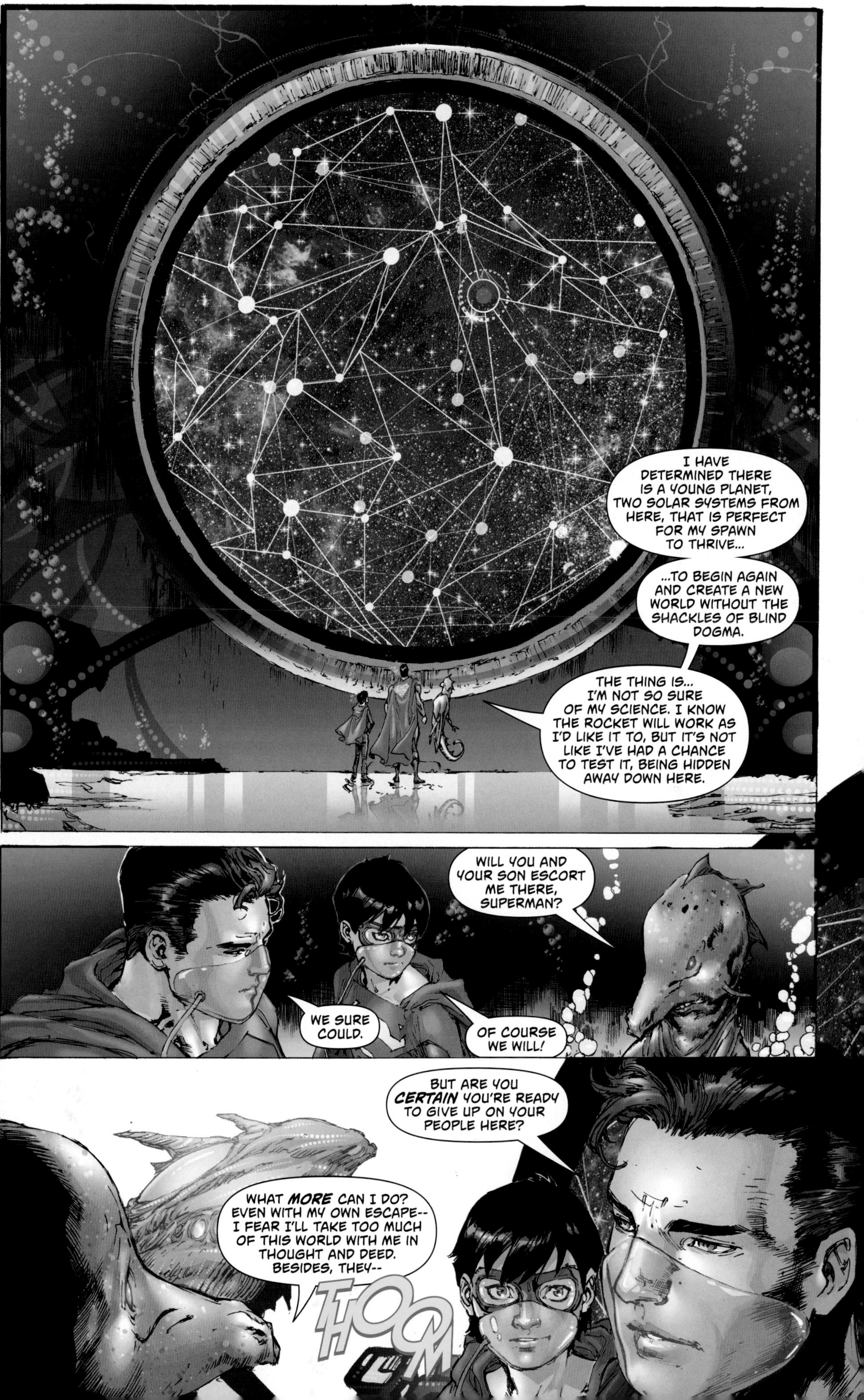

I HAVE DETERMINED THERE IS A YOUNG PLANET, TWO SOLAR SYSTEMS FROM HERE, THAT IS PERFECT FOR MY SPAWN TO THRIVE...
...TO BEGIN AGAIN AND CREATE A NEW WORLD WITHOUT THE SHACKLES OF BLIND DOGMA.
THE THING IS... I'M NOT SO SURE OF MY SCIENCE. I KNOW THE ROCKET WILL WORK AS I'D LIKE IT TO, BUT IT'S NOT LIKE I'VE HAD A CHANCE TO TEST IT, BEING HIDDEN AWAY DOWN HERE.
WILL YOU AND YOUR SON ESCORT ME THERE, SUPERMAN?
WE SURE COULD.
OF COURSE WE WILL!
BUT ARE YOU *CERTAIN* YOU'RE READY TO GIVE UP ON YOUR PEOPLE HERE?
WHAT *MORE* CAN I DO? EVEN WITH MY OWN ESCAPE-- I FEAR I'LL TAKE TOO MUCH OF THIS WORLD WITH ME IN THOUGHT AND DEED. BESIDES, THEY--
THOOM

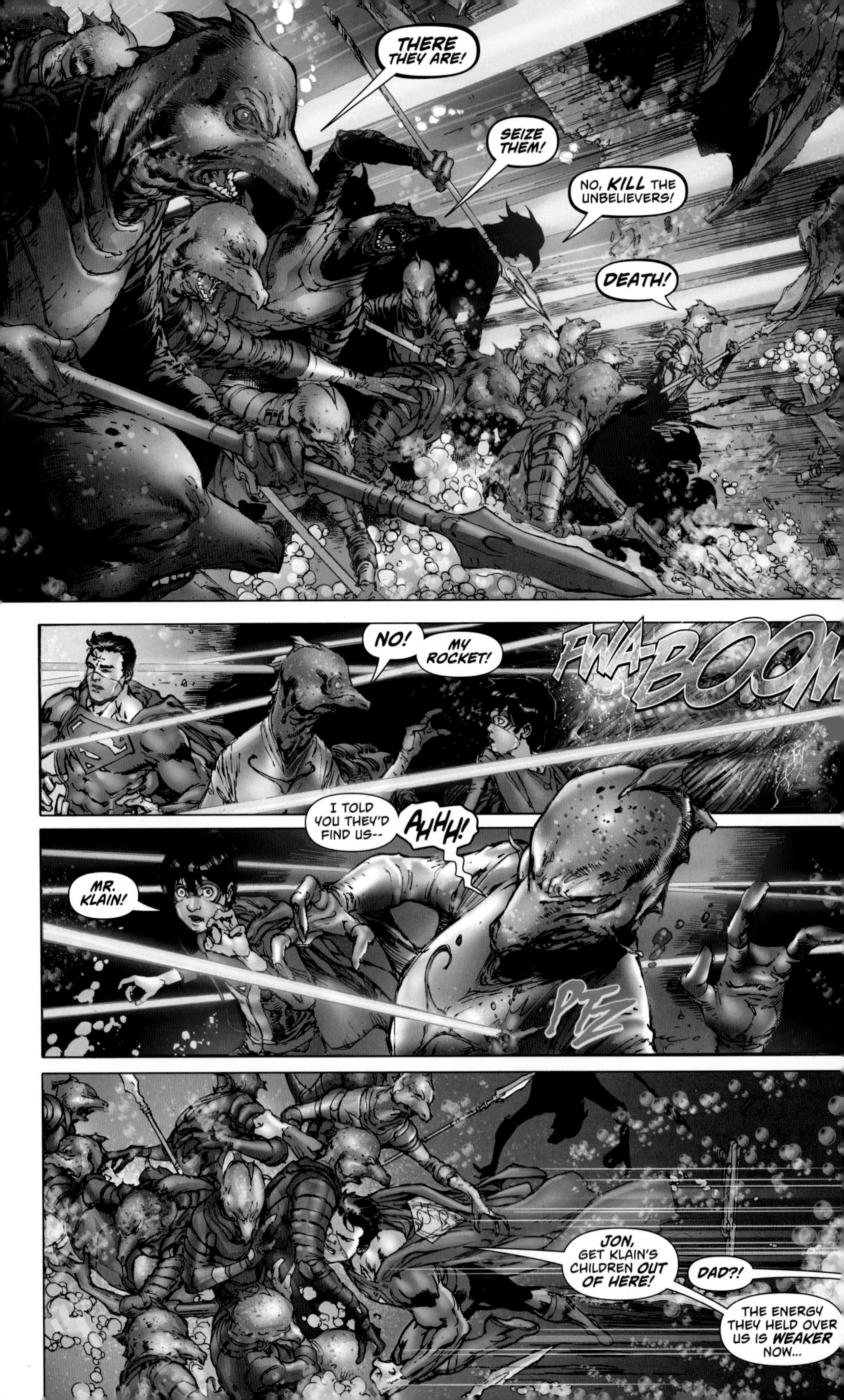
THERE THEY ARE!
SEIZE THEM!
NO, KILL THE UNBELIEVERS!
DEATH!
NO!
MY ROCKET!
FWA-BOOM
I TOLD YOU THEY'D FIND US--
AHHH!
MR. KLAIN!
PFZ
JON, GET KLAIN'S CHILDREN OUT OF HERE!
DAD?!
THE ENERGY THEY HELD OVER US IS WEAKER NOW...

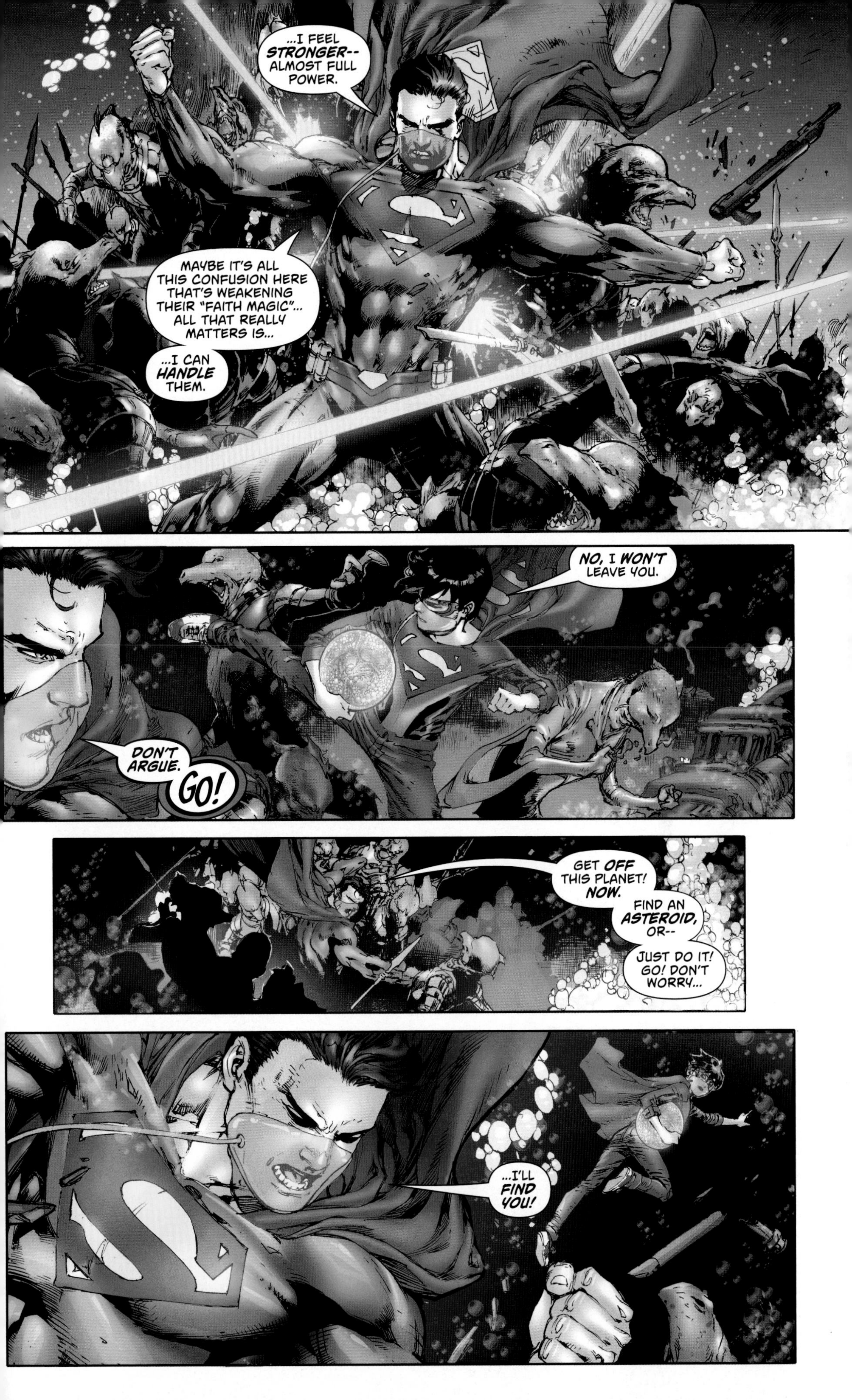
...I FEEL STRONGER-- ALMOST FULL POWER.
MAYBE IT'S ALL THIS CONFUSION HERE THAT'S WEAKENING THEIR "FAITH MAGIC"... ALL THAT REALLY MATTERS IS...
...I CAN HANDLE THEM.
NO, I WON'T LEAVE YOU.
DON'T ARGUE.
GO!
GET OFF THIS PLANET! NOW.
FIND AN ASTEROID, OR--
JUST DO IT! GO! DON'T WORRY...
...I'LL FIND YOU!

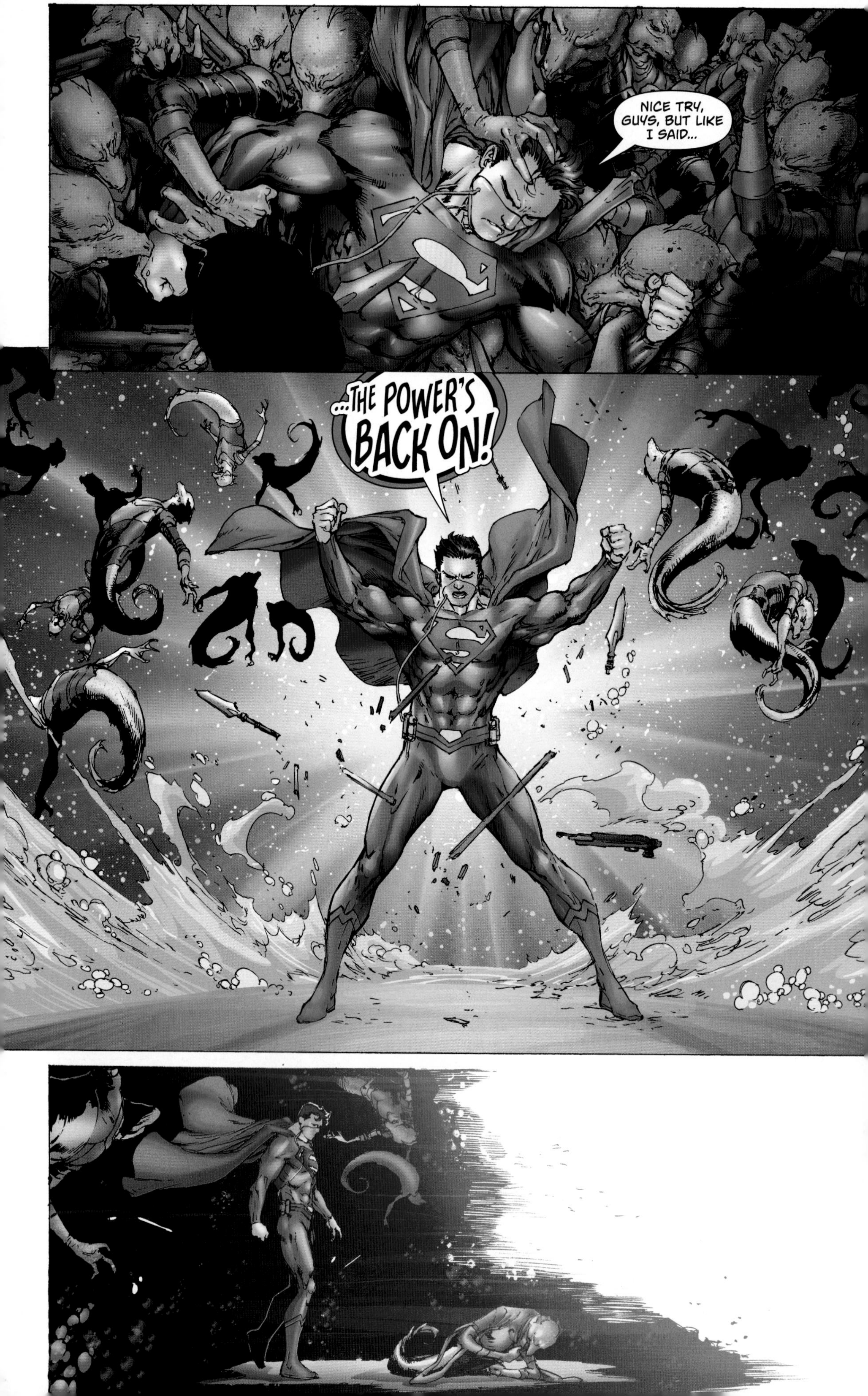
NICE TRY, GUYS, BUT LIKE I SAID...
...THE POWER'S BACK ON!

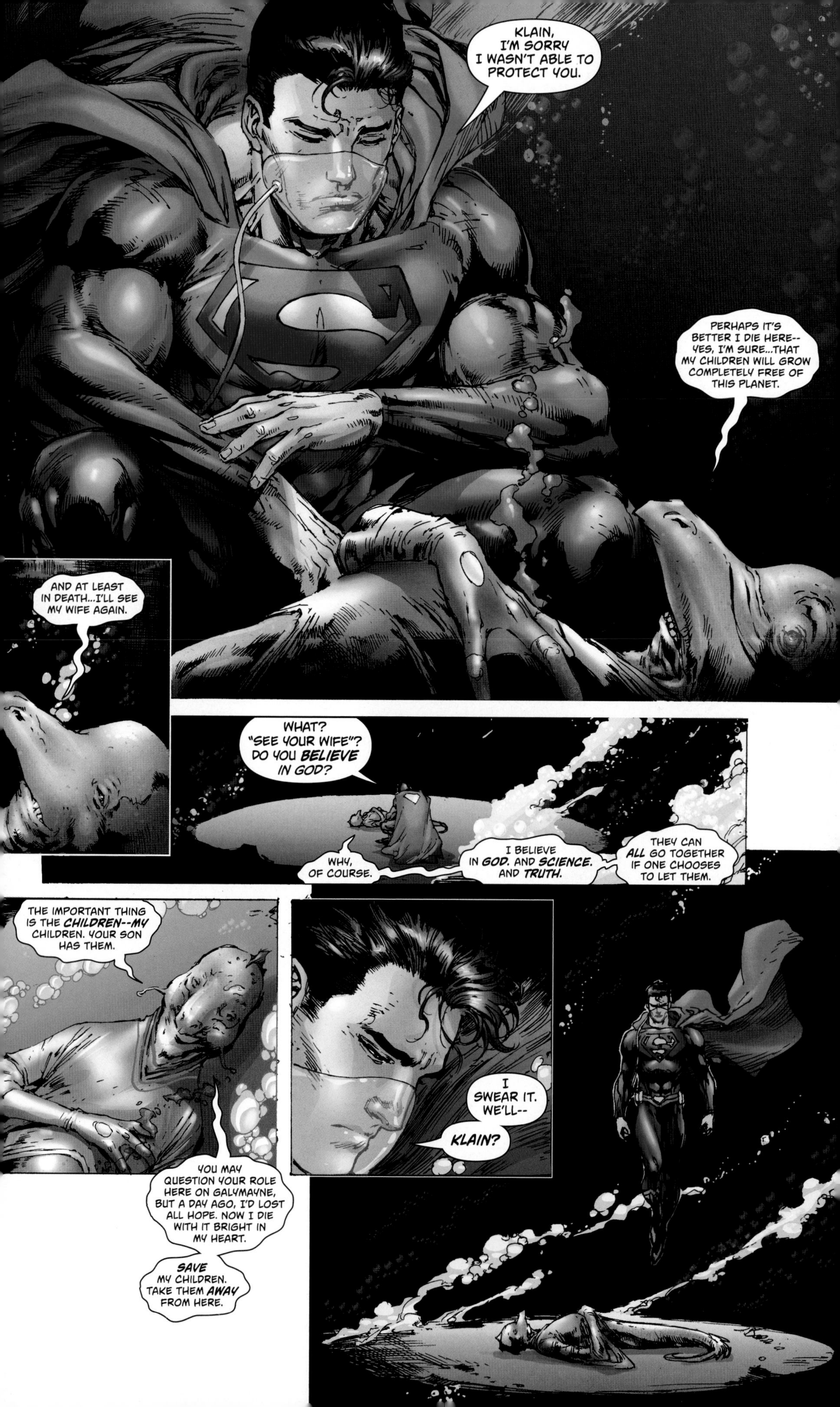
KLAIN, I'M SORRY I WASN'T ABLE TO PROTECT YOU.
PERHAPS IT'S BETTER I DIE HERE-- YES, I'M SURE...THAT MY CHILDREN WILL GROW COMPLETELY FREE OF THIS PLANET.
AND AT LEAST IN DEATH...I'LL SEE MY WIFE AGAIN.
WHAT? "SEE YOUR WIFE"? DO YOU BELIEVE IN GOD?
WHY, OF COURSE.
I BELIEVE IN GOD. AND SCIENCE. AND TRUTH.
THEY CAN ALL GO TOGETHER IF ONE CHOOSES TO LET THEM.
THE IMPORTANT THING IS THE CHILDREN--MY CHILDREN. YOUR SON HAS THEM.
YOU MAY QUESTION YOUR ROLE HERE ON GALYMAYNE, BUT A DAY AGO, I'D LOST ALL HOPE. NOW I DIE WITH IT BRIGHT IN MY HEART.
SAVE MY CHILDREN. TAKE THEM AWAY FROM HERE.
I SWEAR IT. WE'LL--
KLAIN?

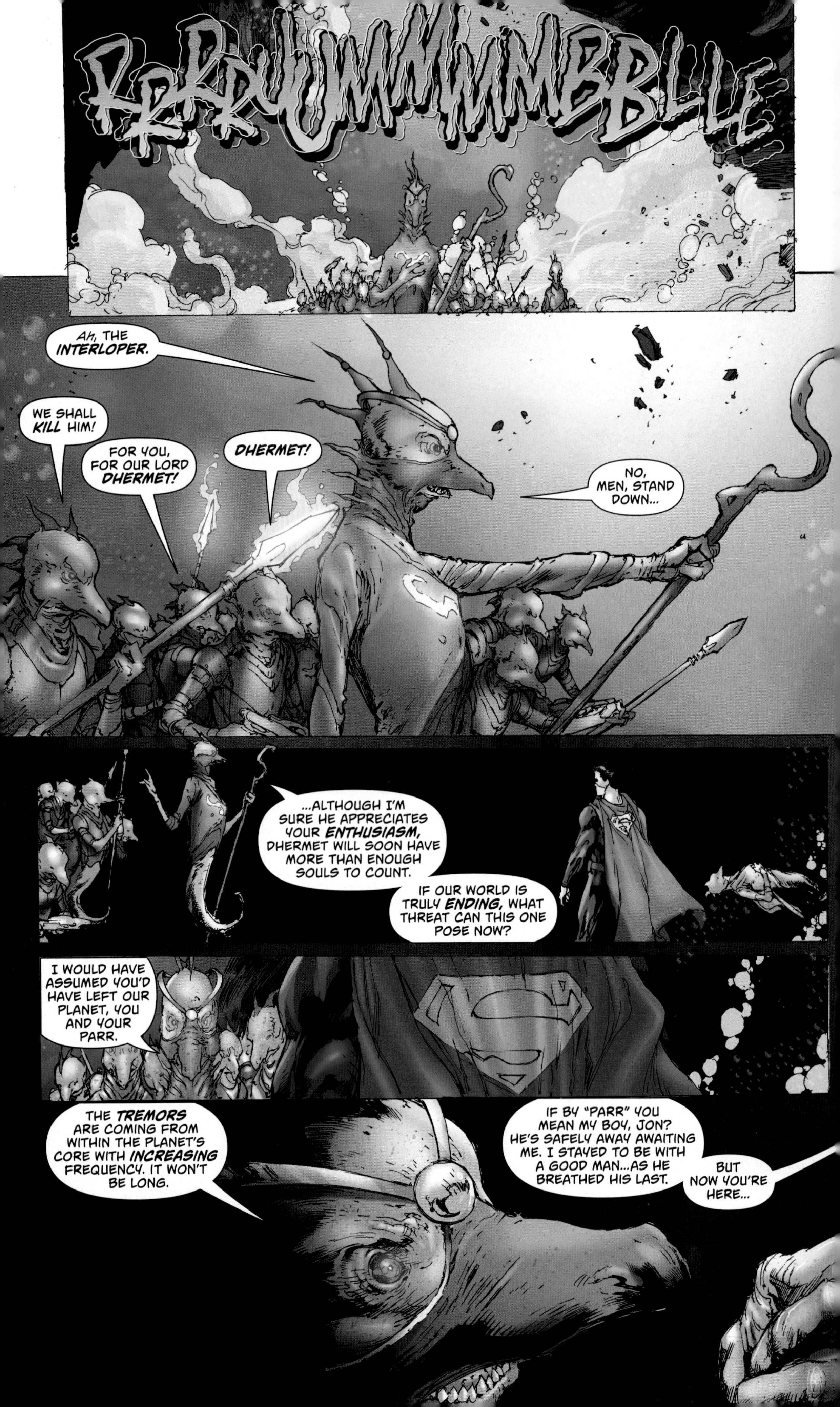
RRRRUUMMMMMBBLLE
AH, THE INTERLOPER.
WE SHALL KILL HIM!
FOR YOU, FOR OUR LORD DHERMET!
DHERMET!
NO, MEN, STAND DOWN...
...ALTHOUGH I'M SURE HE APPRECIATES YOUR ENTHUSIASM, DHERMET WILL SOON HAVE MORE THAN ENOUGH SOULS TO COUNT.
IF OUR WORLD IS TRULY ENDING, WHAT THREAT CAN THIS ONE POSE NOW?
I WOULD HAVE ASSUMED YOU'D HAVE LEFT OUR PLANET, YOU AND YOUR PARR.
THE TREMORS ARE COMING FROM WITHIN THE PLANET'S CORE WITH INCREASING FREQUENCY. IT WON'T BE LONG.
IF BY "PARR" YOU MEAN MY BOY, JON? HE'S SAFELY AWAY AWAITING ME. I STAYED TO BE WITH A GOOD MAN...AS HE BREATHED HIS LAST.
BUT NOW YOU'RE HERE...

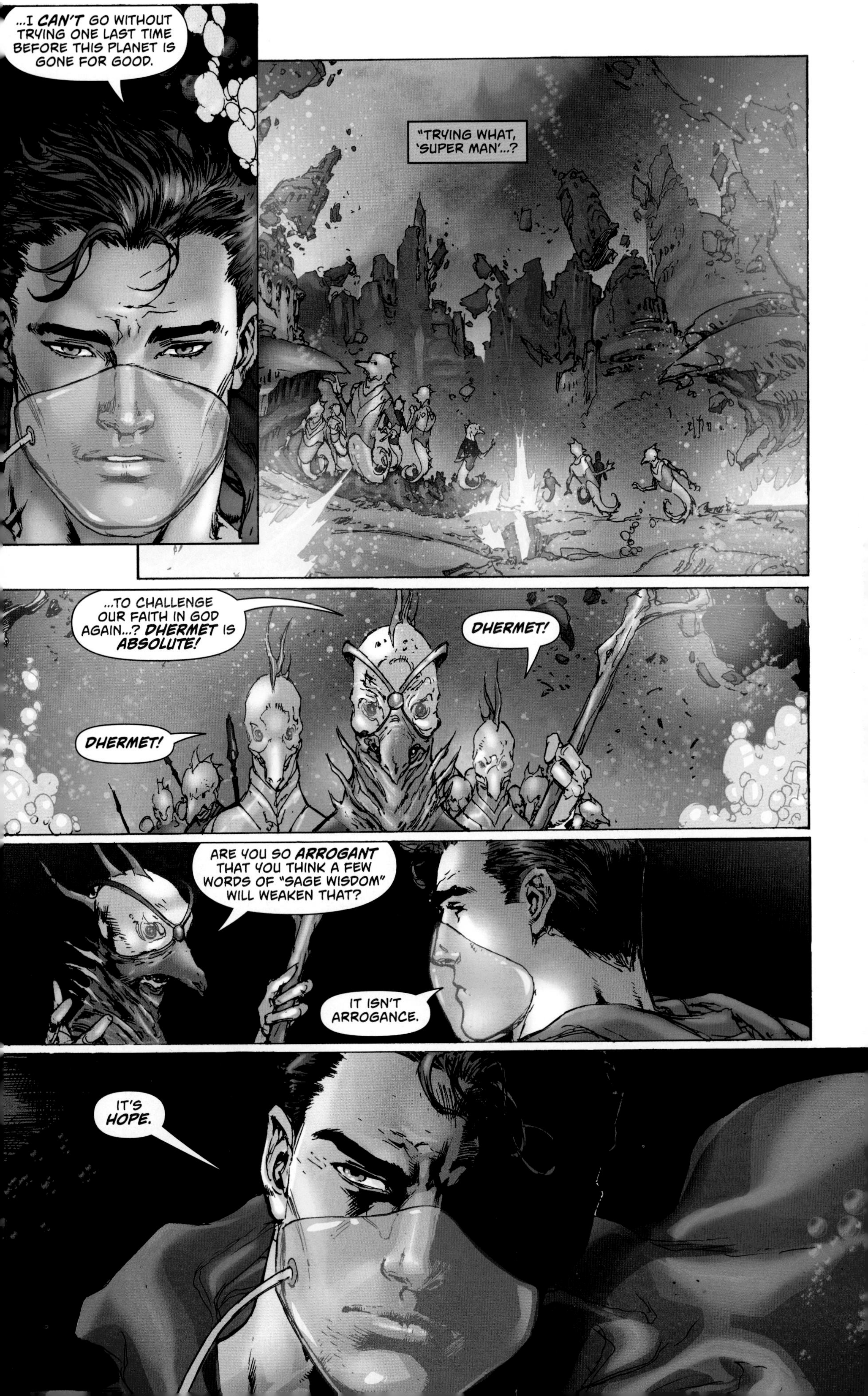
...I CAN'T GO WITHOUT TRYING ONE LAST TIME BEFORE THIS PLANET IS GONE FOR GOOD.
"TRYING WHAT, 'SUPER MAN'...?
...TO CHALLENGE OUR FAITH IN GOD AGAIN...? DHERMET IS ABSOLUTE!
DHERMET!
DHERMET!
ARE YOU SO ARROGANT THAT YOU THINK A FEW WORDS OF "SAGE WISDOM" WILL WEAKEN THAT?
IT ISN'T ARROGANCE.
IT'S HOPE.

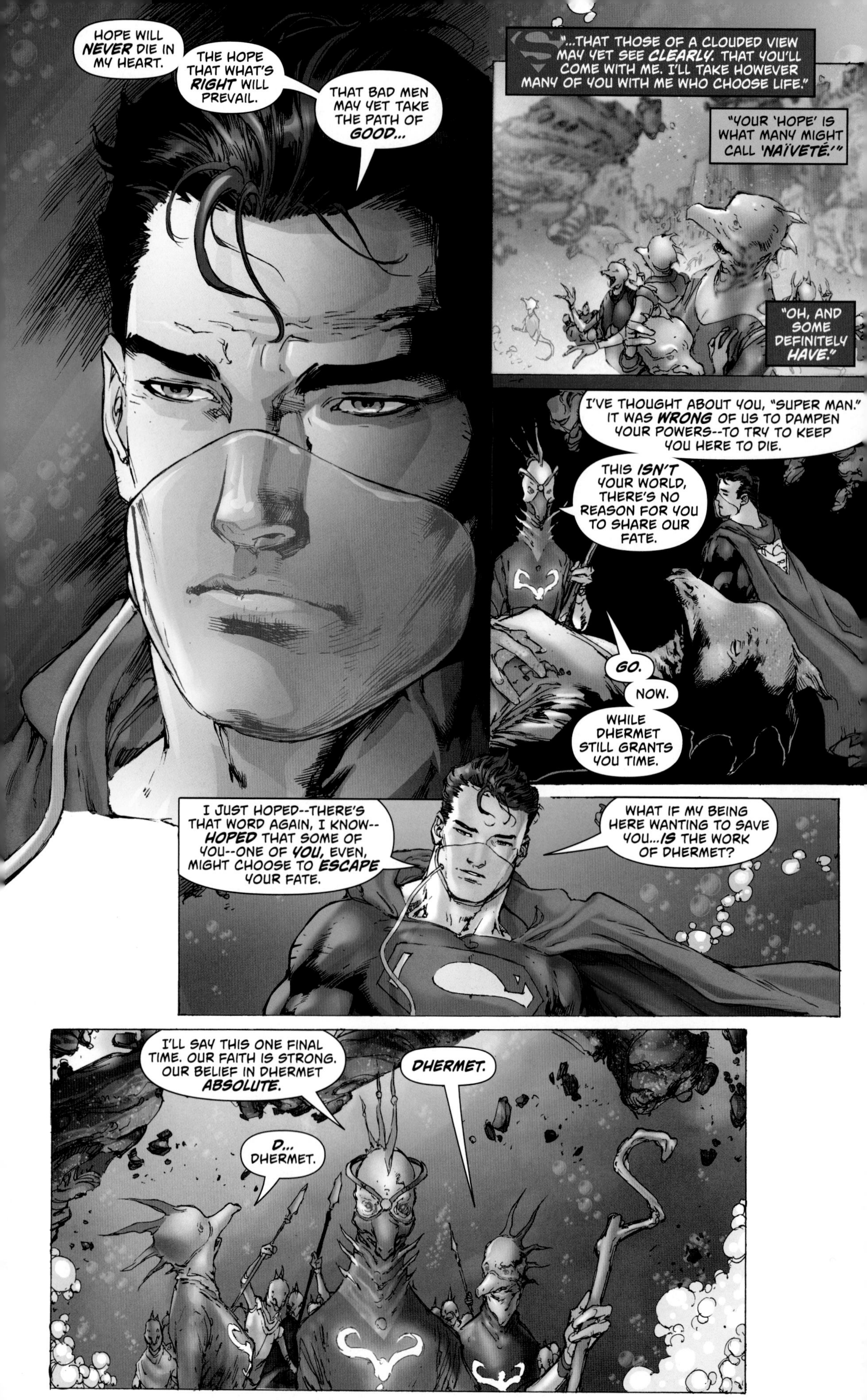
HOPE WILL NEVER DIE IN MY HEART.
THE HOPE THAT WHAT'S RIGHT WILL PREVAIL.
THAT BAD MEN MAY YET TAKE THE PATH OF GOOD...
"...THAT THOSE OF A CLOUDED VIEW MAY YET SEE CLEARLY. THAT YOU'LL COME WITH ME. I'LL TAKE HOWEVER MANY OF YOU WITH ME WHO CHOOSE LIFE."
"YOUR 'HOPE' IS WHAT MANY MIGHT CALL 'NAÏVETÉ.'"
"OH, AND SOME DEFINITELY HAVE."
I'VE THOUGHT ABOUT YOU, "SUPER MAN." IT WAS WRONG OF US TO DAMPEN YOUR POWERS--TO TRY TO KEEP YOU HERE TO DIE.
THIS ISN'T YOUR WORLD, THERE'S NO REASON FOR YOU TO SHARE OUR FATE.
GO.
NOW.
WHILE DHERMET STILL GRANTS YOU TIME.
I JUST HOPED--THERE'S THAT WORD AGAIN, I KNOW--HOPED THAT SOME OF YOU--ONE OF YOU, EVEN, MIGHT CHOOSE TO ESCAPE YOUR FATE.
WHAT IF MY BEING HERE WANTING TO SAVE YOU...IS THE WORK OF DHERMET?
I'LL SAY THIS ONE FINAL TIME. OUR FAITH IS STRONG. OUR BELIEF IN DHERMET ABSOLUTE.
DHERMET.
D... DHERMET.

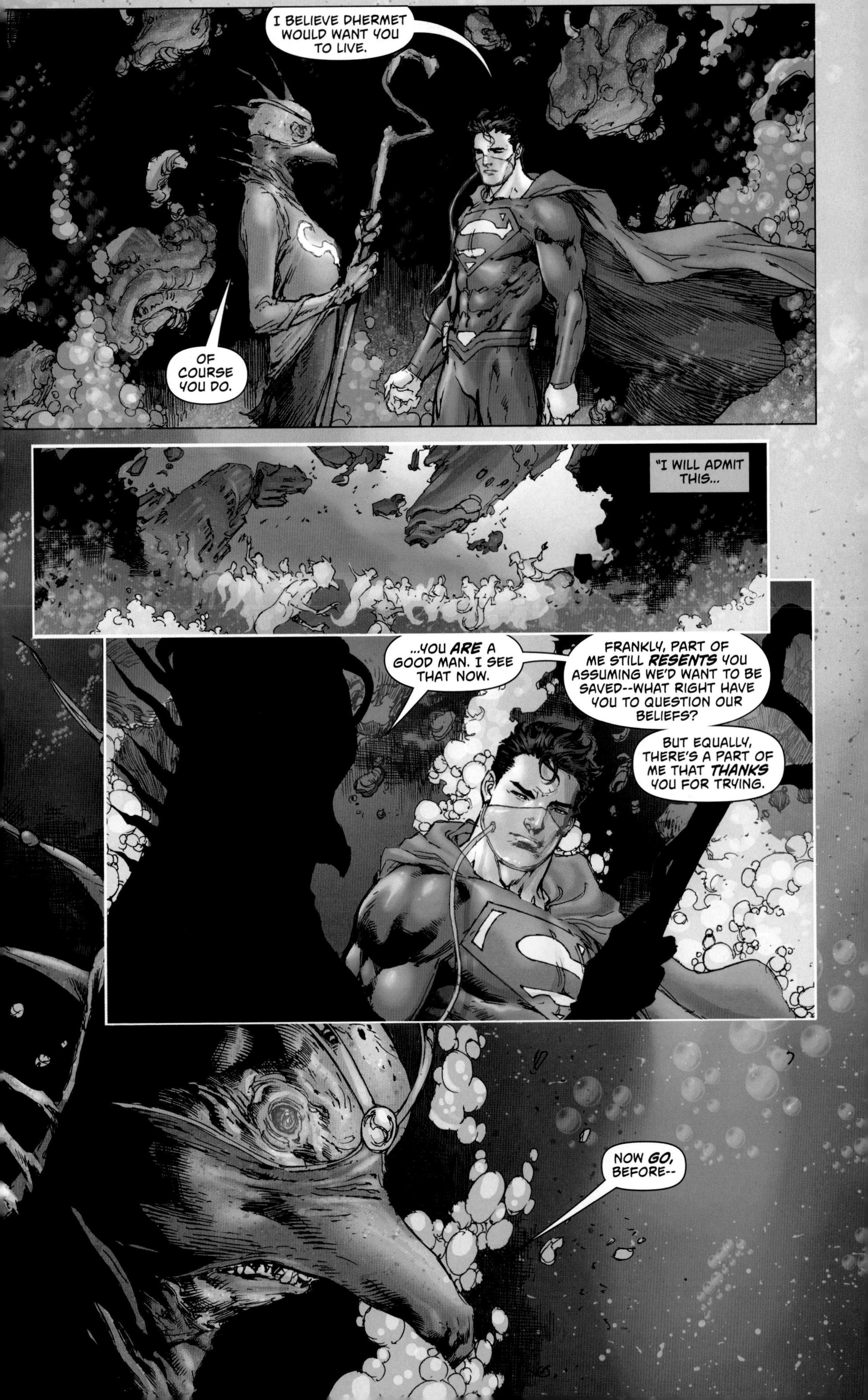
I BELIEVE DHERMET WOULD WANT YOU TO LIVE.
OF COURSE YOU DO.
"I WILL ADMIT THIS...
...YOU ARE A GOOD MAN. I SEE THAT NOW.
FRANKLY, PART OF ME STILL RESENTS YOU ASSUMING WE'D WANT TO BE SAVED--WHAT RIGHT HAVE YOU TO QUESTION OUR BELIEFS?
BUT EQUALLY, THERE'S A PART OF ME THAT THANKS YOU FOR TRYING.
NOW GO, BEFORE--

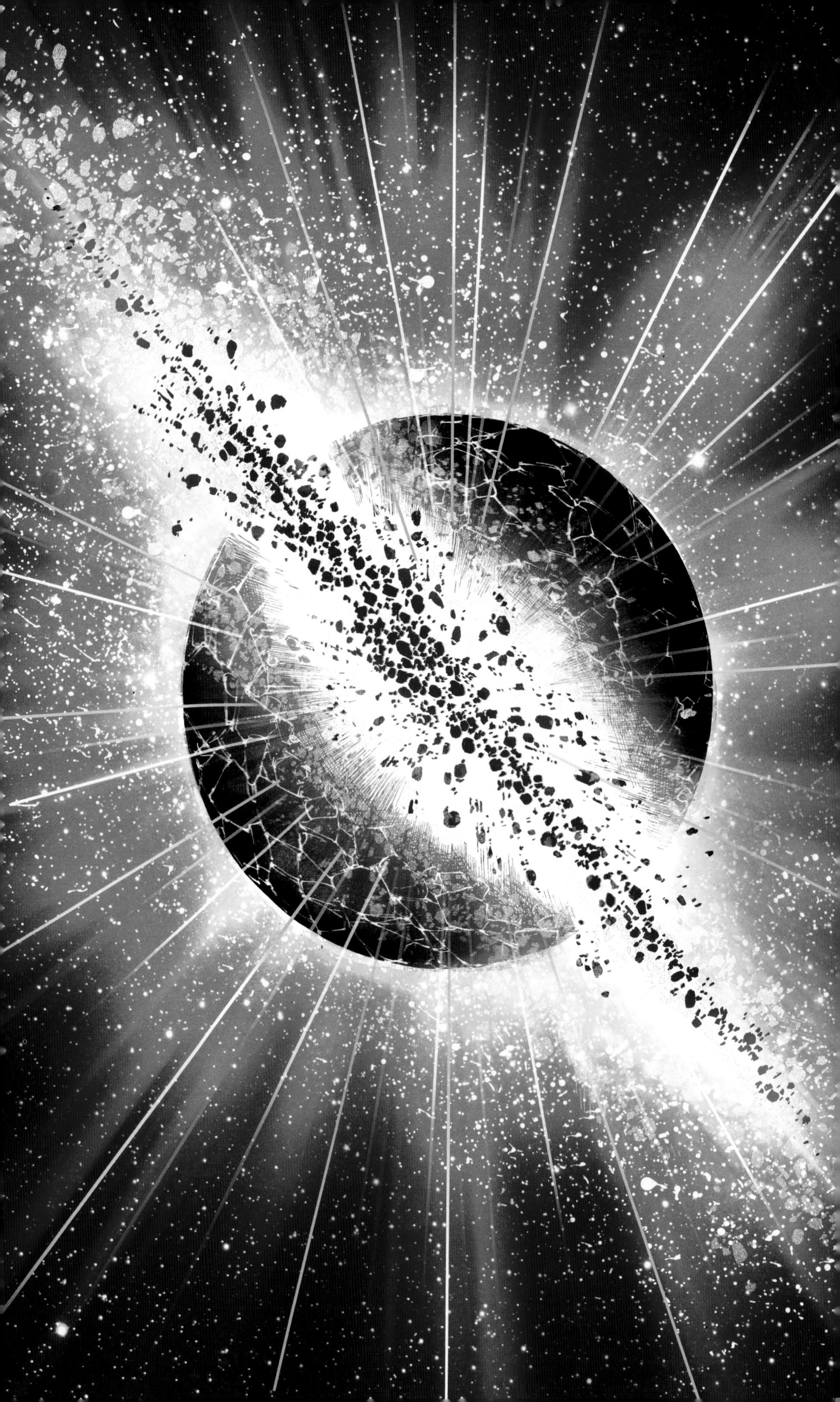

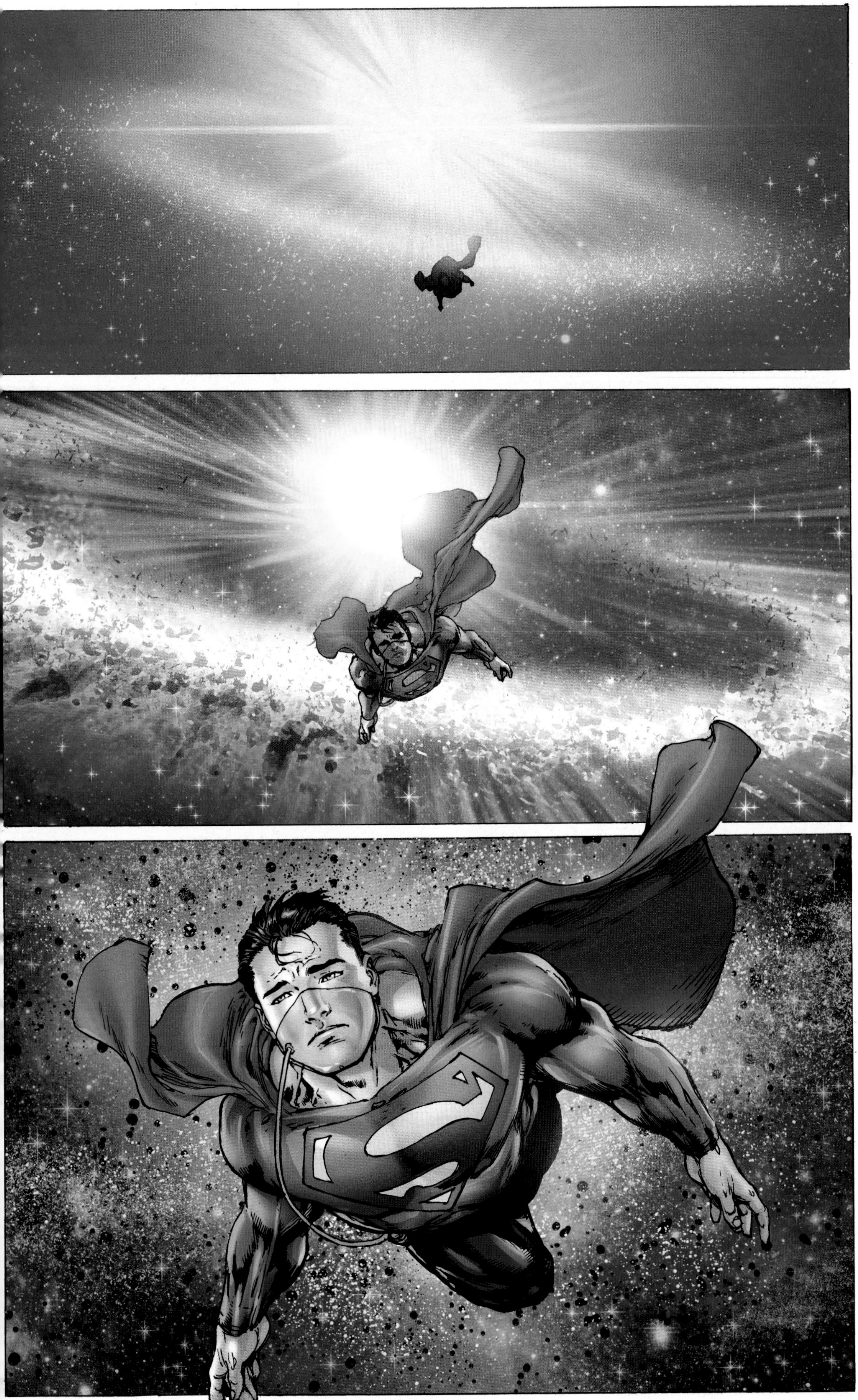

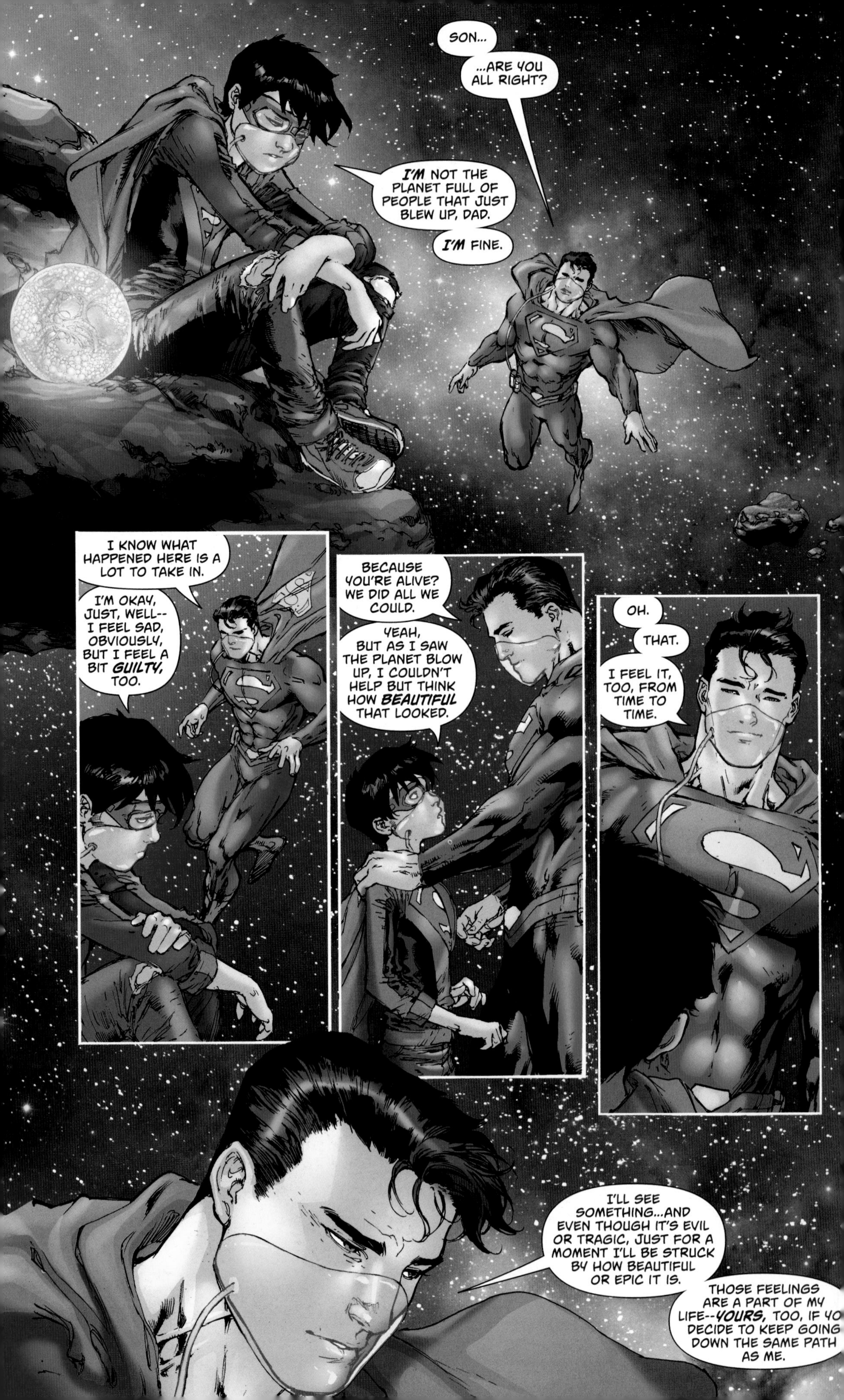
SON...
...ARE YOU ALL RIGHT?
I'M NOT THE PLANET FULL OF PEOPLE THAT JUST BLEW UP, DAD.
I'M FINE.
I KNOW WHAT HAPPENED HERE IS A LOT TO TAKE IN.
I'M OKAY, JUST, WELL-- I FEEL SAD, OBVIOUSLY, BUT I FEEL A BIT GUILTY, TOO.
BECAUSE YOU'RE ALIVE? WE DID ALL WE COULD.
YEAH, BUT AS I SAW THE PLANET BLOW UP, I COULDN'T HELP BUT THINK HOW BEAUTIFUL THAT LOOKED.
OH.
THAT.
I FEEL IT, TOO, FROM TIME TO TIME.
I'LL SEE SOMETHING...AND EVEN THOUGH IT'S EVIL OR TRAGIC, JUST FOR A MOMENT I'LL BE STRUCK BY HOW BEAUTIFUL OR EPIC IT IS.
THOSE FEELINGS ARE A PART OF MY LIFE--YOURS, TOO, IF YO DECIDE TO KEEP GOING DOWN THE SAME PATH AS ME.

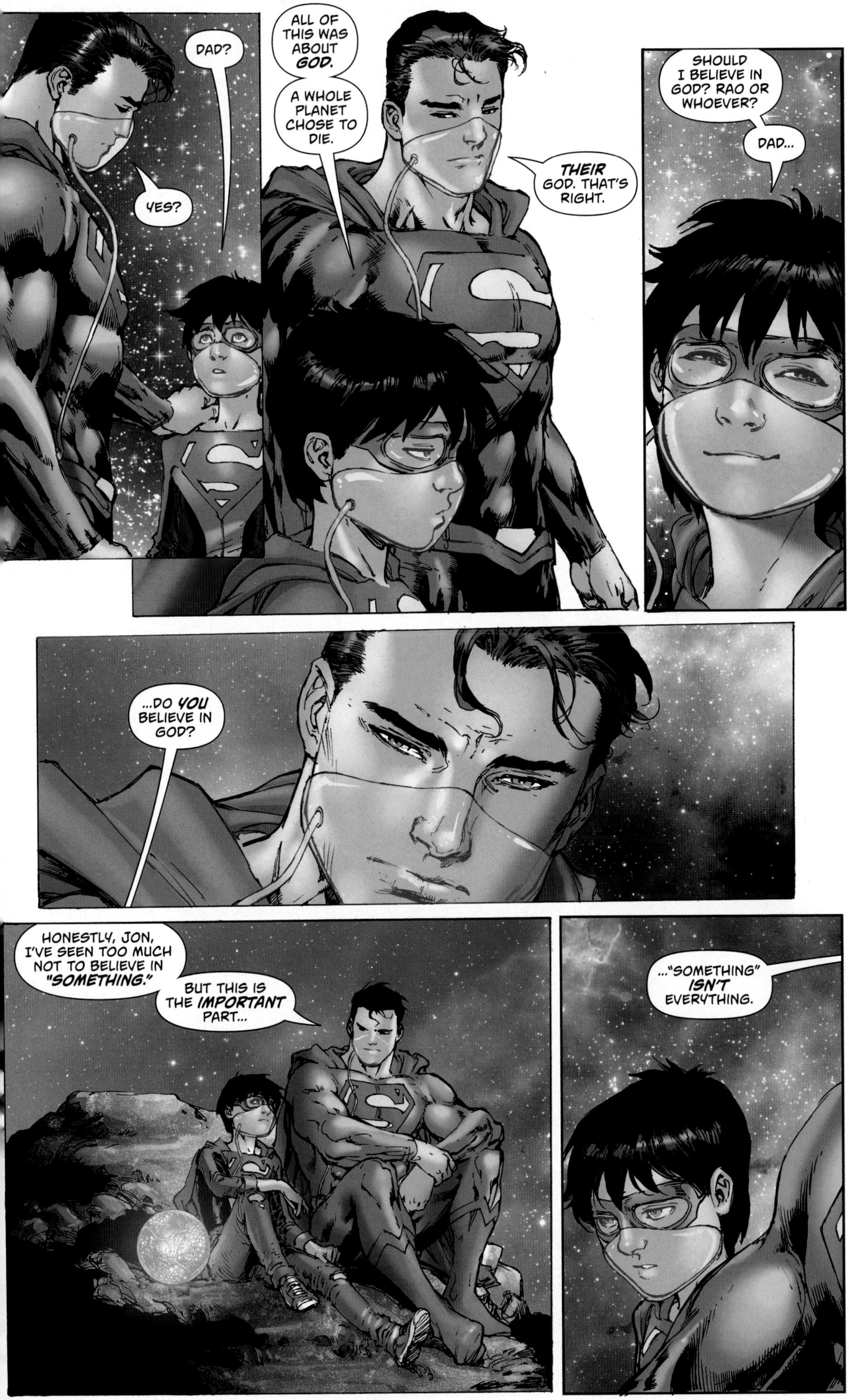
DAD?
YES?
ALL OF THIS WAS ABOUT GOD.
A WHOLE PLANET CHOSE TO DIE.
THEIR GOD. THAT'S RIGHT.
SHOULD I BELIEVE IN GOD? RAO OR WHOEVER?
DAD...
...DO YOU BELIEVE IN GOD?
HONESTLY, JON, I'VE SEEN TOO MUCH NOT TO BELIEVE IN "SOMETHING."
BUT THIS IS THE IMPORTANT PART...
..."SOMETHING" ISN'T EVERYTHING.

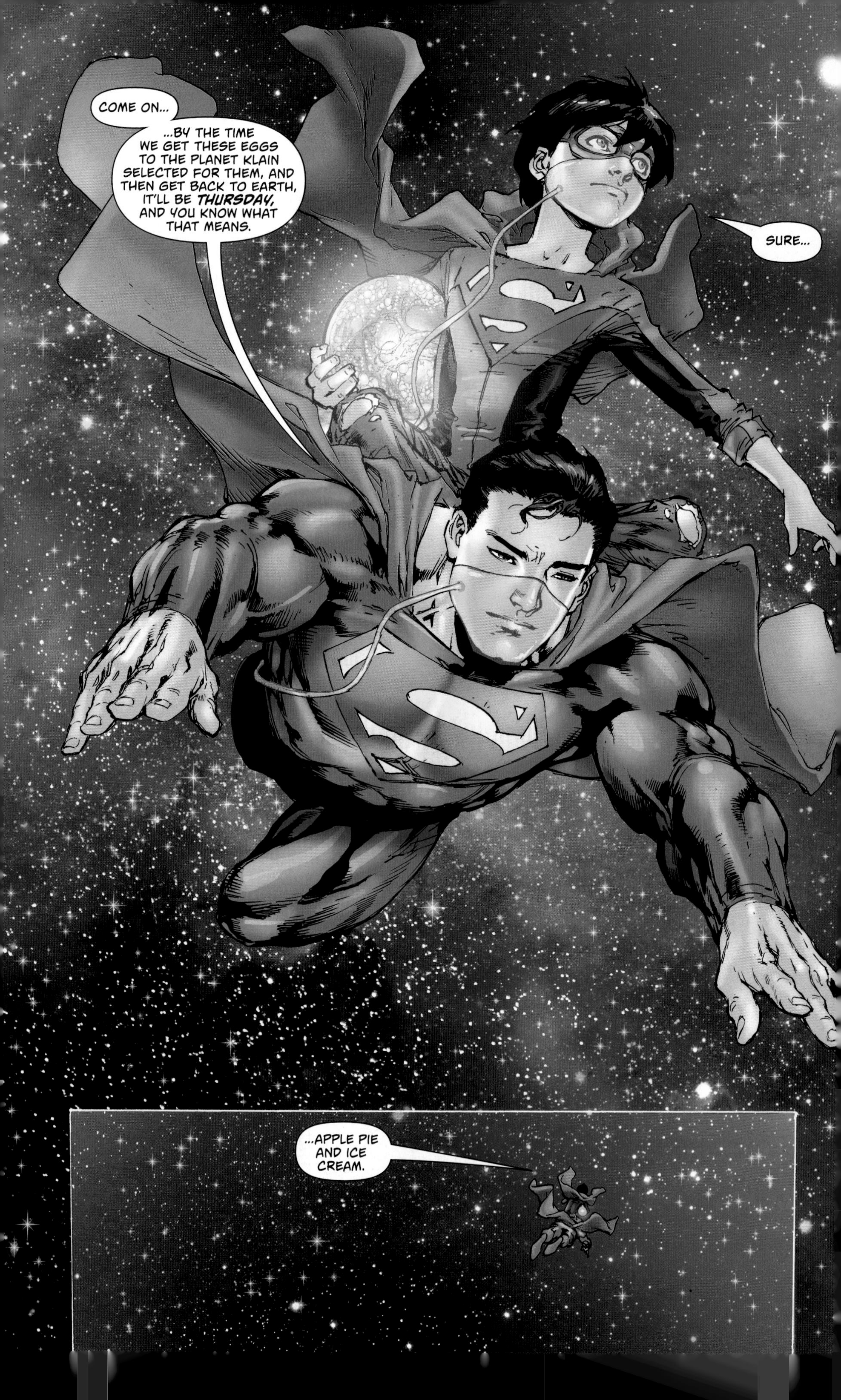
COME ON...
...BY THE TIME WE GET THESE EGGS TO THE PLANET KLAIN SELECTED FOR THEM, AND THEN GET BACK TO EARTH, IT'LL BE THURSDAY, AND YOU KNOW WHAT THAT MEANS.
SURE...
...APPLE PIE AND ICE CREAM.

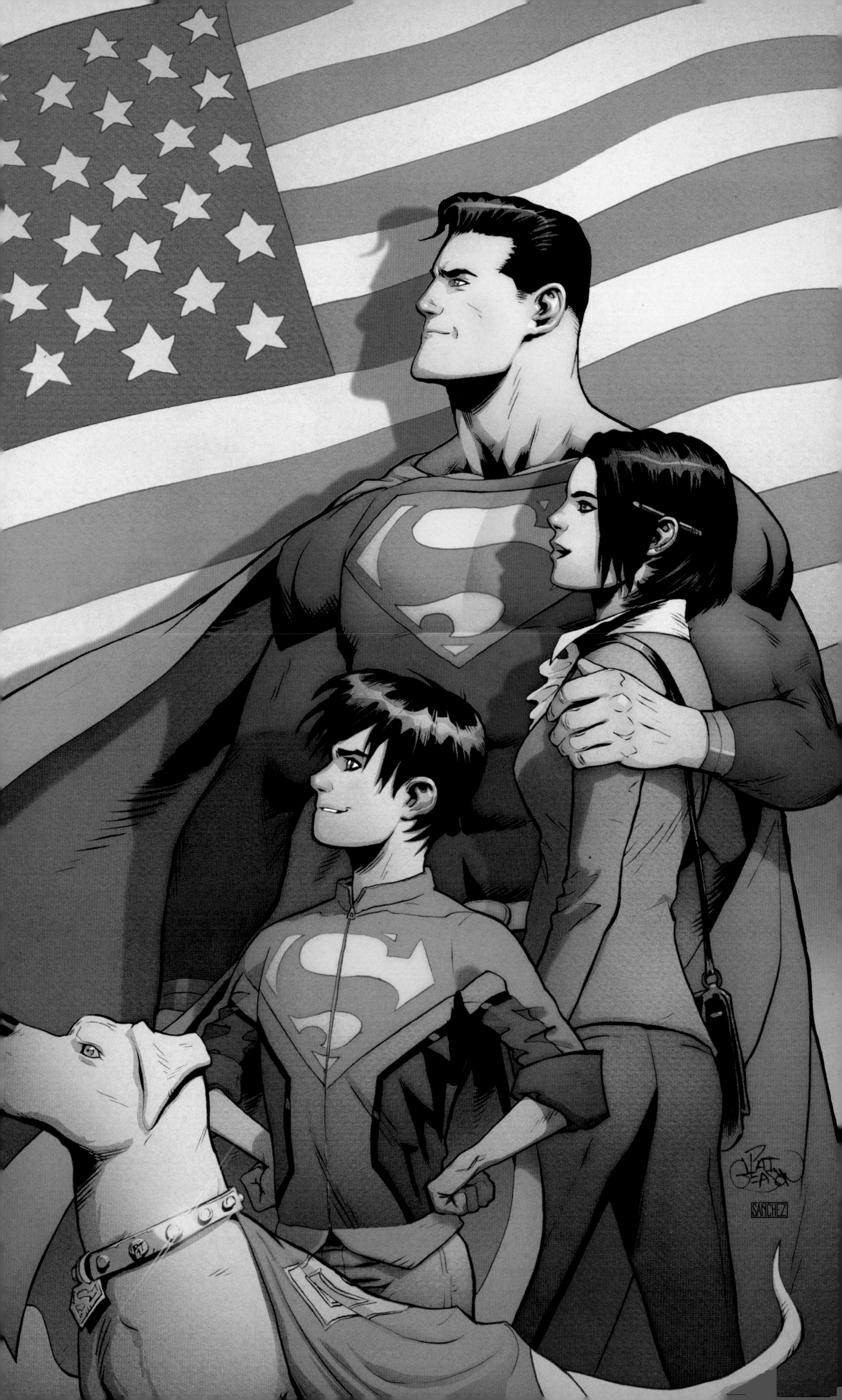
SANCHEZ

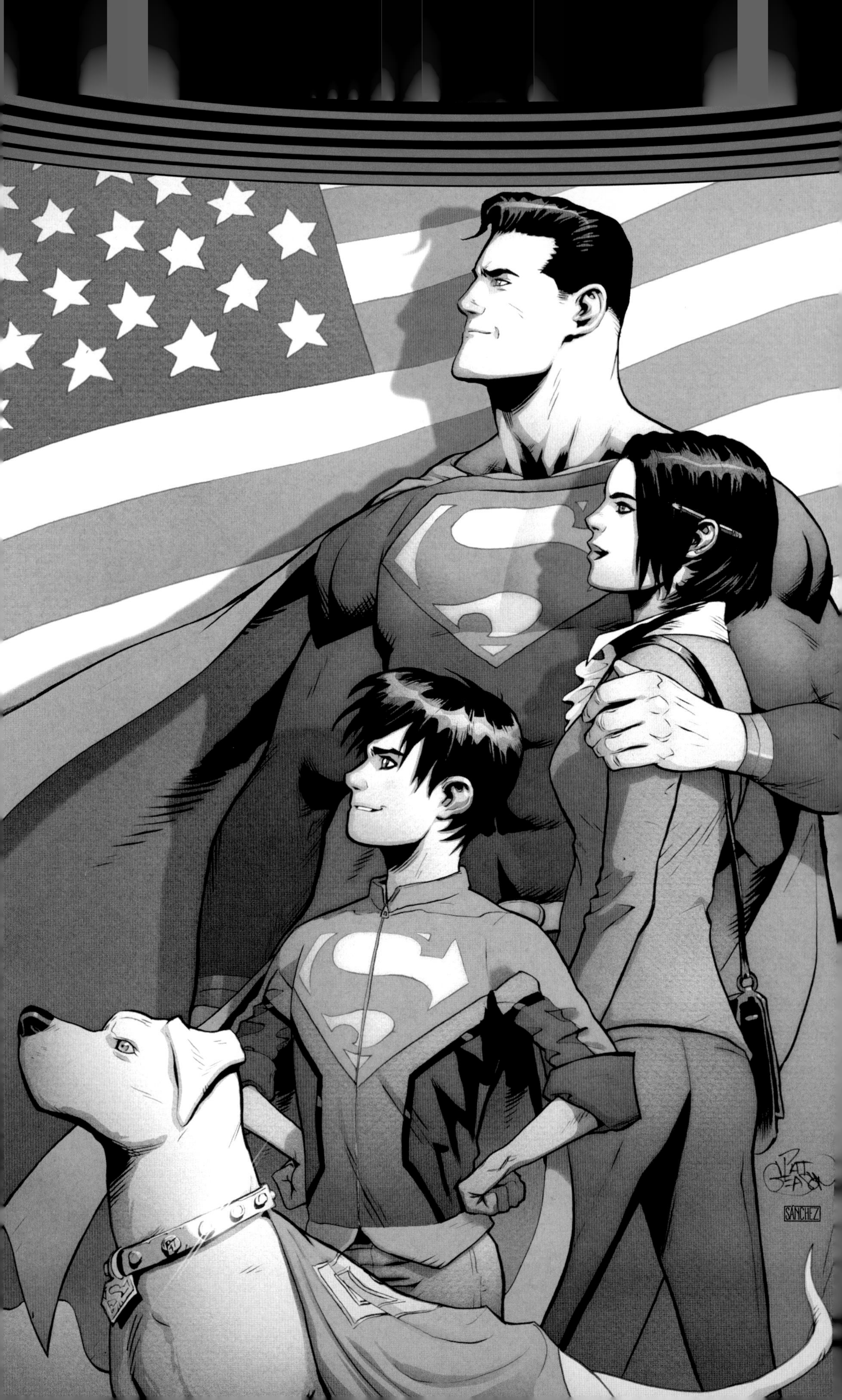
SANCHEZ

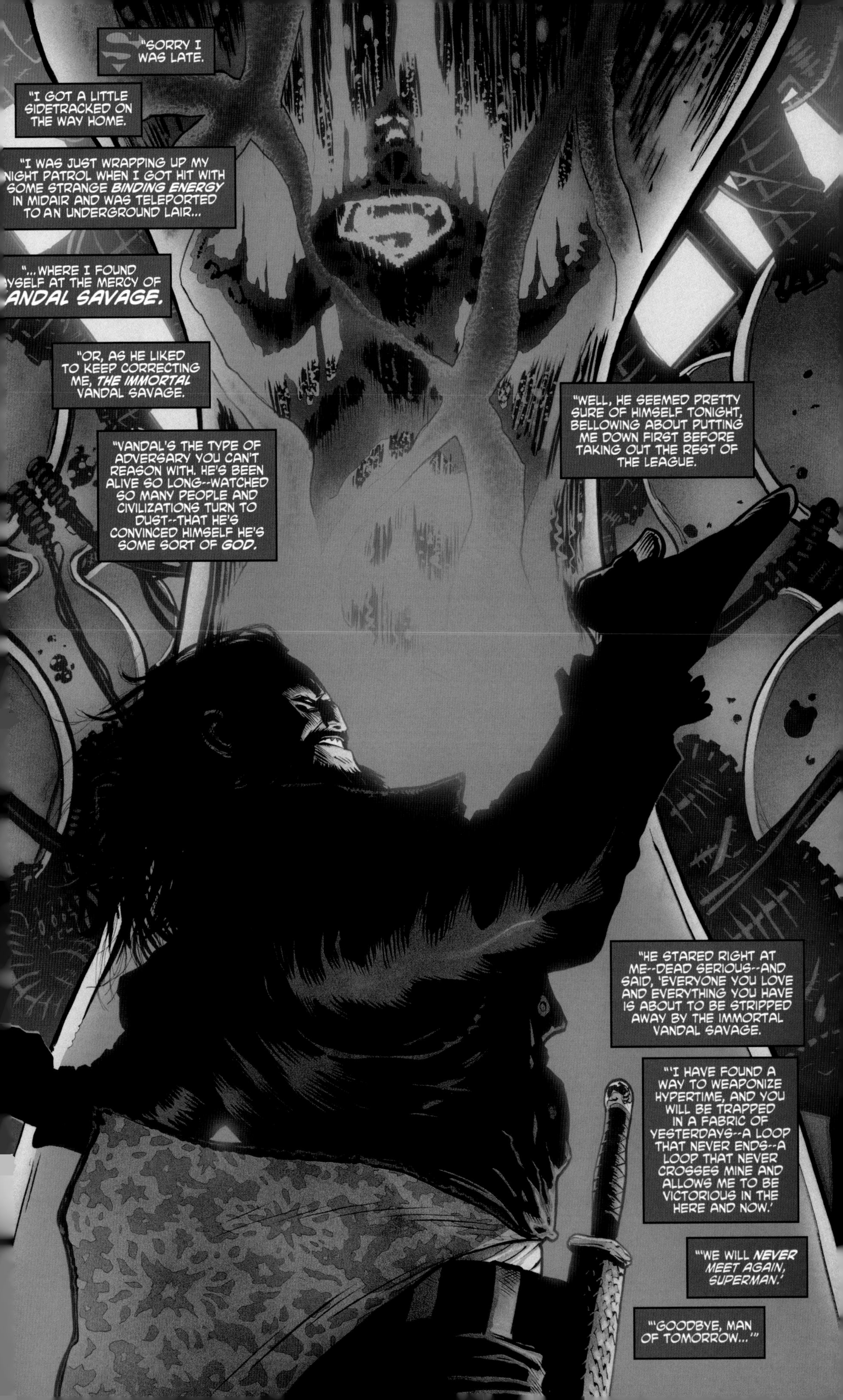
"SORRY I WAS LATE.
"I GOT A LITTLE SIDETRACKED ON THE WAY HOME.
"I WAS JUST WRAPPING UP MY NIGHT PATROL WHEN I GOT HIT WITH SOME STRANGE *BINDING ENERGY* IN MIDAIR AND WAS TELEPORTED TO AN UNDERGROUND LAIR...
"...WHERE I FOUND YSELF AT THE MERCY OF ANDAL SAVAGE.
"OR, AS HE LIKED TO KEEP CORRECTING ME, *THE IMMORTAL* VANDAL SAVAGE.
"VANDAL'S THE TYPE OF ADVERSARY YOU CAN'T REASON WITH. HE'S BEEN ALIVE SO LONG--WATCHED SO MANY PEOPLE AND CIVILIZATIONS TURN TO DUST--THAT HE'S CONVINCED HIMSELF HE'S SOME SORT OF *GOD*.
"WELL, HE SEEMED PRETTY SURE OF HIMSELF TONIGHT, BELLOWING ABOUT PUTTING ME DOWN FIRST BEFORE TAKING OUT THE REST OF THE LEAGUE.
"HE STARED RIGHT AT ME--DEAD SERIOUS--AND SAID, 'EVERYONE YOU LOVE AND EVERYTHING YOU HAVE IS ABOUT TO BE STRIPPED AWAY BY THE IMMORTAL VANDAL SAVAGE.
"'I HAVE FOUND A WAY TO WEAPONIZE HYPERTIME, AND YOU WILL BE TRAPPED IN A FABRIC OF YESTERDAYS--A LOOP THAT NEVER ENDS--A LOOP THAT NEVER CROSSES MINE AND ALLOWS ME TO BE VICTORIOUS IN THE HERE AND NOW.'
"'WE WILL *NEVER* MEET AGAIN, SUPERMAN.'
"'GOODBYE, MAN OF TOMORROW...'"

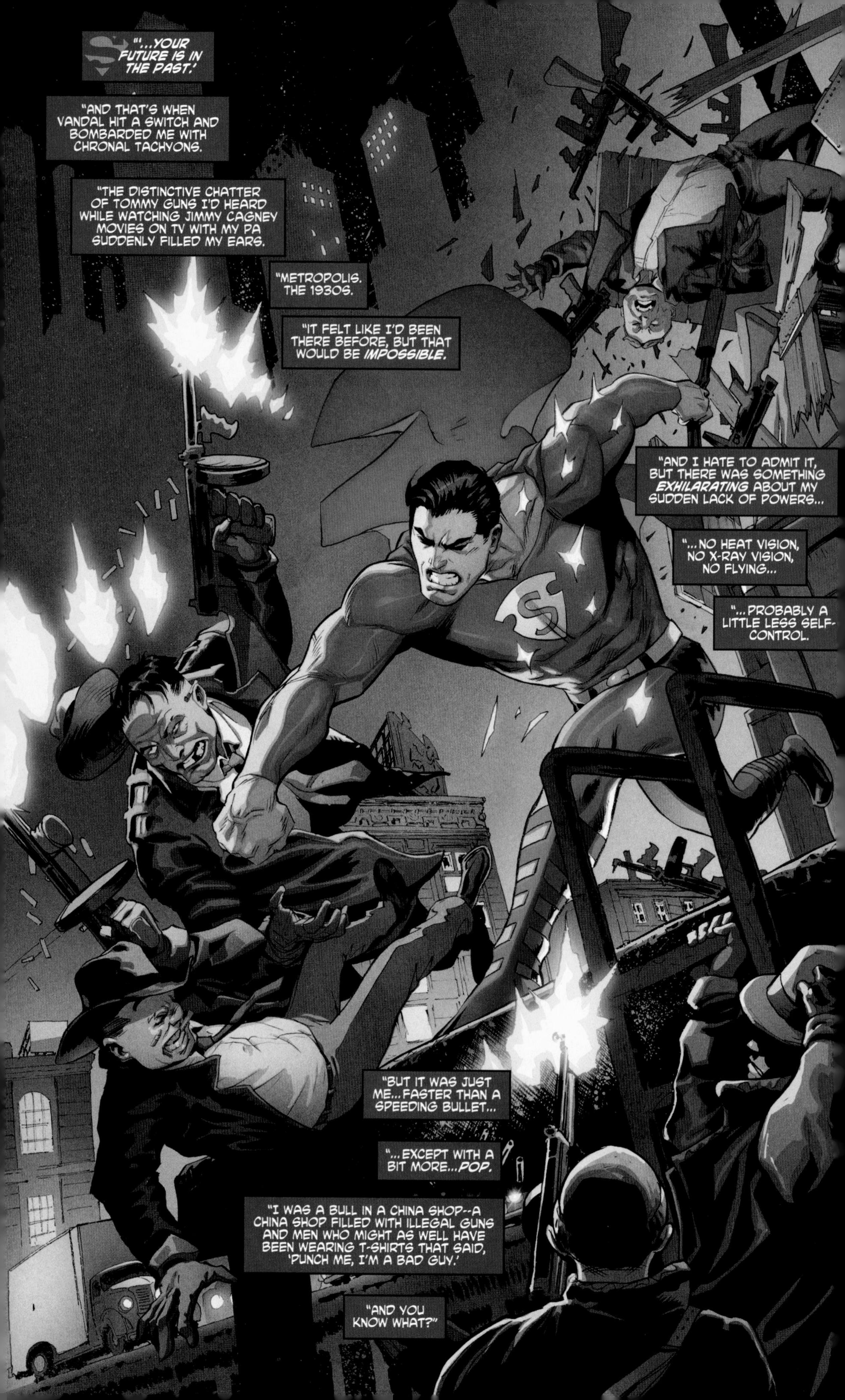
"'...YOUR FUTURE IS IN THE PAST.'
"AND THAT'S WHEN VANDAL HIT A SWITCH AND BOMBARDED ME WITH CHRONAL TACHYONS.
"THE DISTINCTIVE CHATTER OF TOMMY GUNS I'D HEARD WHILE WATCHING JIMMY CAGNEY MOVIES ON TV WITH MY PA SUDDENLY FILLED MY EARS.
"METROPOLIS. THE 1930S.
"IT FELT LIKE I'D BEEN THERE BEFORE, BUT THAT WOULD BE *IMPOSSIBLE*.
"AND I HATE TO ADMIT IT, BUT THERE WAS SOMETHING *EXHILARATING* ABOUT MY SUDDEN LACK OF POWERS...
"...NO HEAT VISION, NO X-RAY VISION, NO FLYING...
"...PROBABLY A LITTLE LESS SELF-CONTROL.
"BUT IT WAS JUST ME...FASTER THAN A SPEEDING BULLET...
"...EXCEPT WITH A BIT MORE...*POP*.
"I WAS A BULL IN A CHINA SHOP--A CHINA SHOP FILLED WITH ILLEGAL GUNS AND MEN WHO MIGHT AS WELL HAVE BEEN WEARING T-SHIRTS THAT SAID, 'PUNCH ME, I'M A BAD GUY.'
"AND YOU KNOW WHAT?"

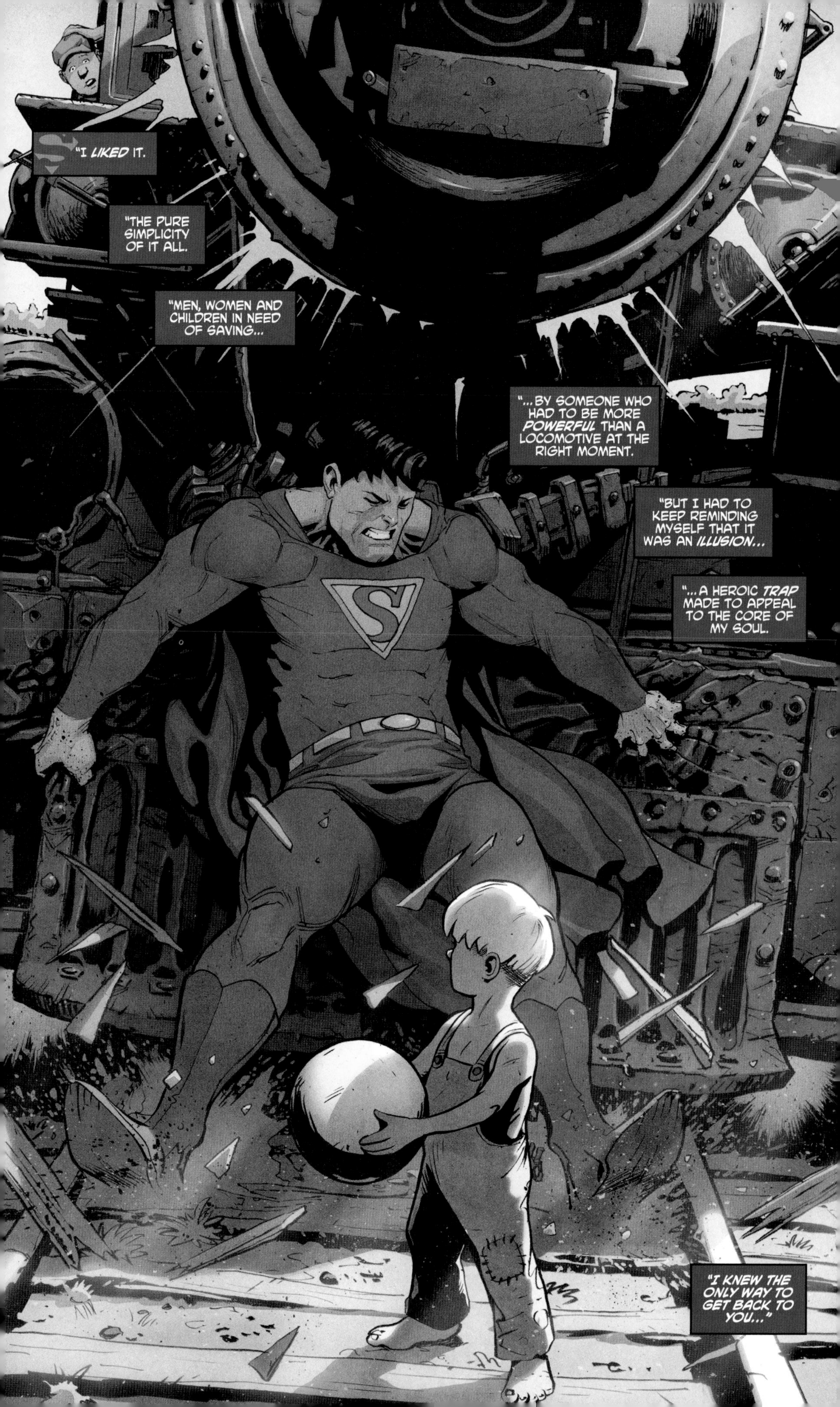
"I *LIKED* IT.
"THE PURE SIMPLICITY OF IT ALL.
"MEN, WOMEN AND CHILDREN IN NEED OF SAVING...
"...BY SOMEONE WHO HAD TO BE MORE *POWERFUL* THAN A LOCOMOTIVE AT THE RIGHT MOMENT.
"BUT I HAD TO KEEP REMINDING MYSELF THAT IT WAS AN *ILLUSION*...
"...A HEROIC *TRAP* MADE TO APPEAL TO THE CORE OF MY SOUL.
"I KNEW THE ONLY WAY TO GET BACK TO YOU..."

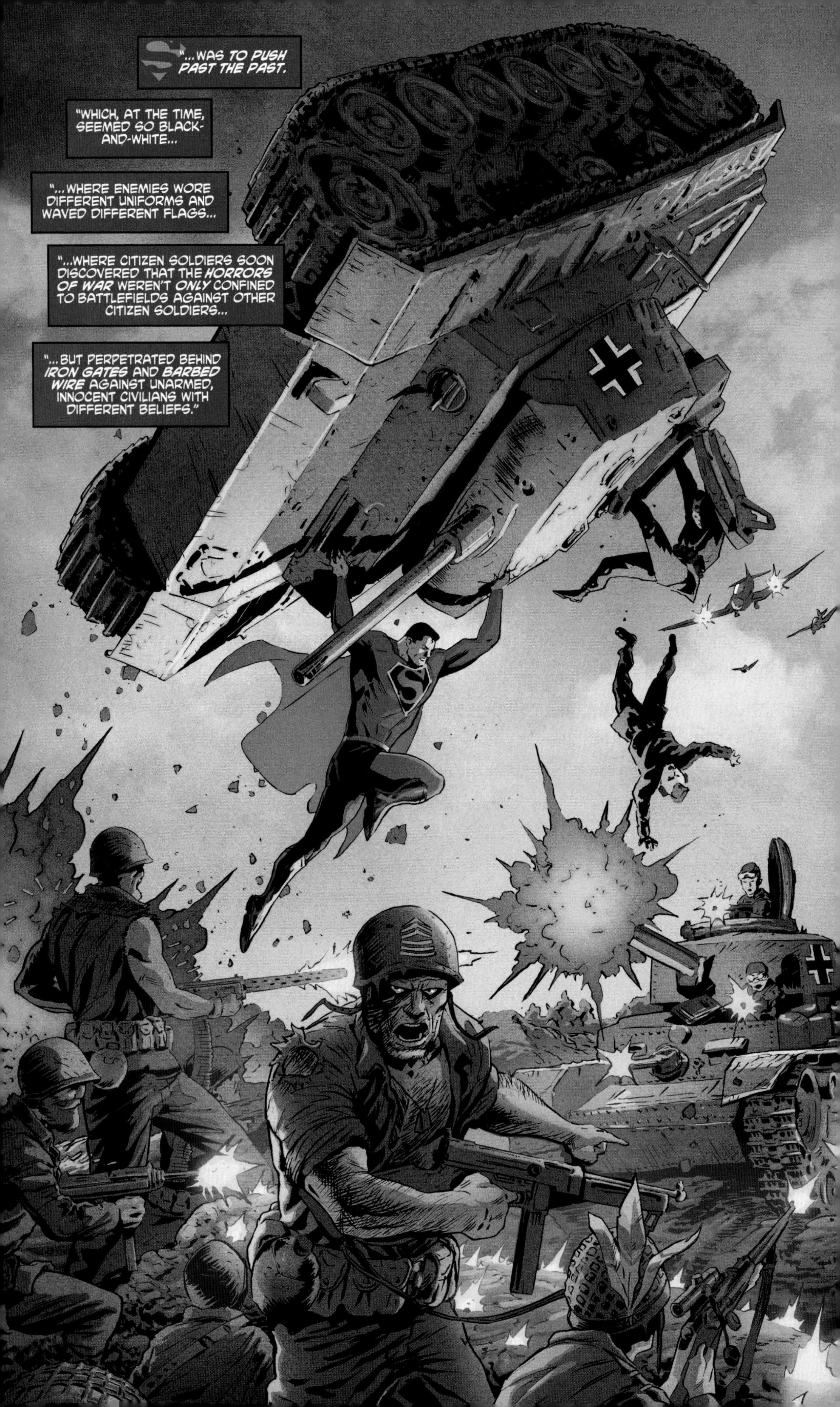
"...WAS TO PUSH PAST THE PAST.
"WHICH, AT THE TIME, SEEMED SO BLACK-AND-WHITE...
"...WHERE ENEMIES WORE DIFFERENT UNIFORMS AND WAVED DIFFERENT FLAGS...
"...WHERE CITIZEN SOLDIERS SOON DISCOVERED THAT THE HORRORS OF WAR WEREN'T ONLY CONFINED TO BATTLEFIELDS AGAINST OTHER CITIZEN SOLDIERS...
"...BUT PERPETRATED BEHIND IRON GATES AND BARBED WIRE AGAINST UNARMED, INNOCENT CIVILIANS WITH DIFFERENT BELIEFS."

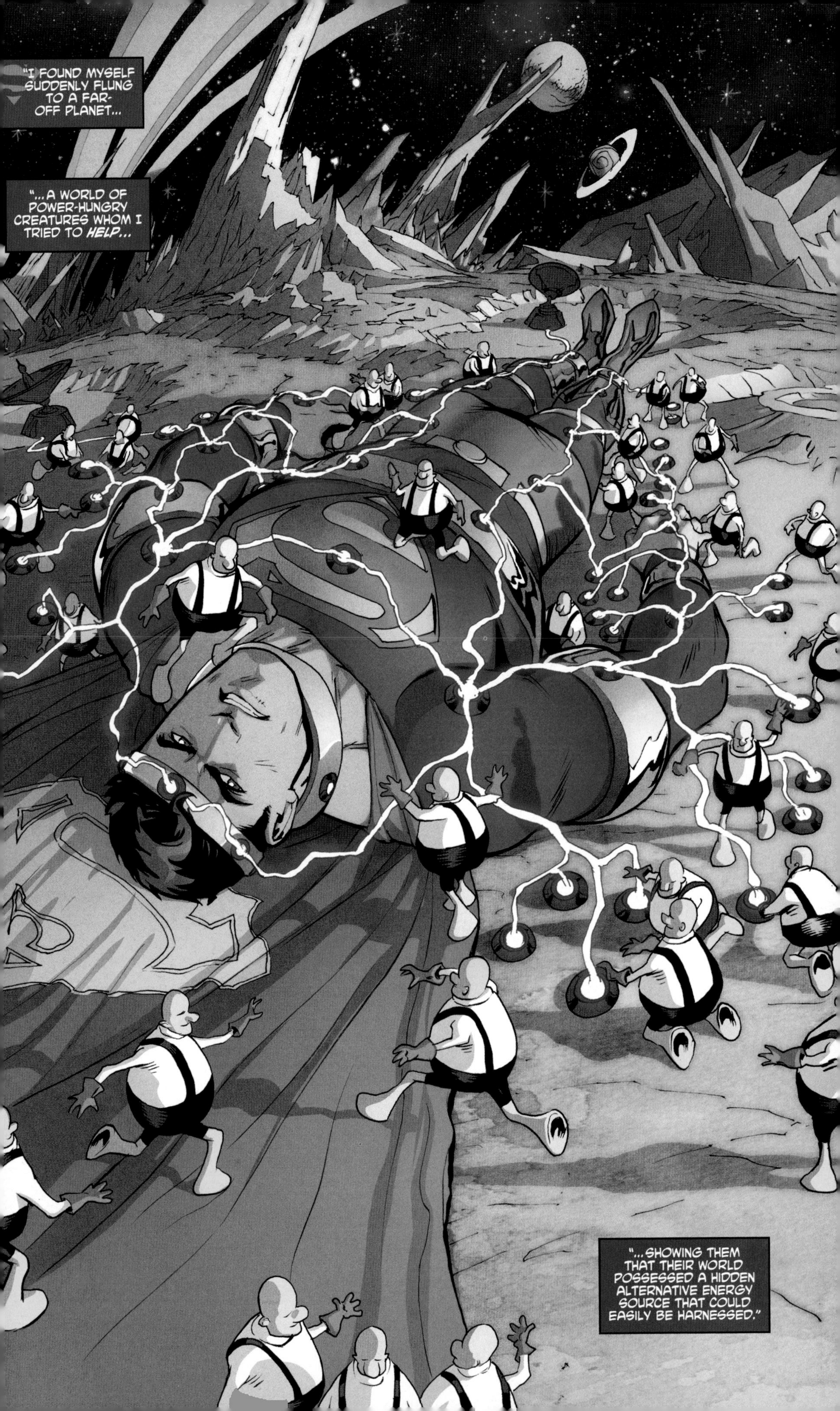
"I FOUND MYSELF SUDDENLY FLUNG TO A FAR-OFF PLANET...
"...A WORLD OF POWER-HUNGRY CREATURES WHOM I TRIED TO *HELP*...
"...SHOWING THEM THAT THEIR WORLD POSSESSED A HIDDEN ALTERNATIVE ENERGY SOURCE THAT COULD EASILY BE HARNESSED."

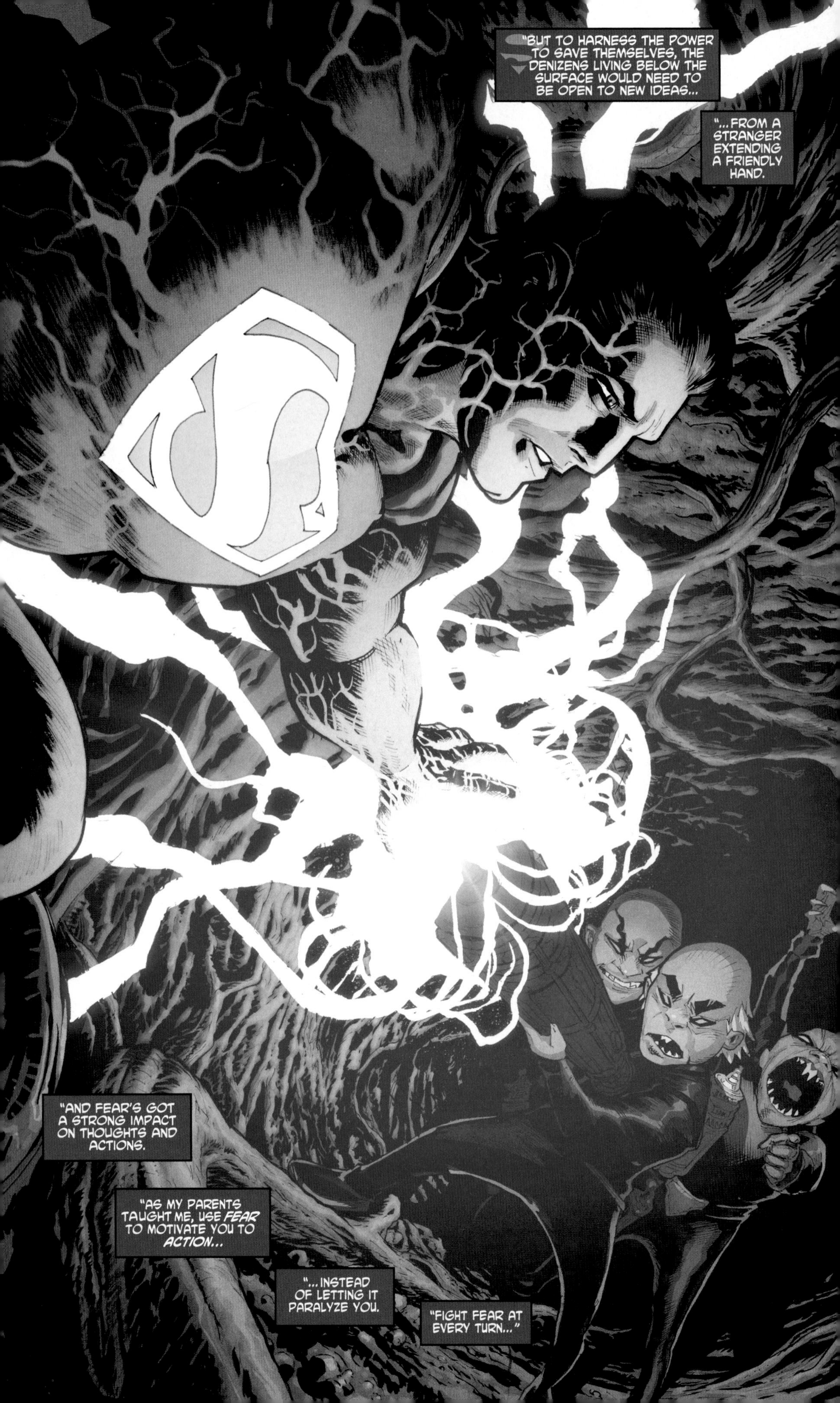
"BUT TO HARNESS THE POWER TO SAVE THEMSELVES, THE DENIZENS LIVING BELOW THE SURFACE WOULD NEED TO BE OPEN TO NEW IDEAS...
"...FROM A STRANGER EXTENDING A FRIENDLY HAND.
"AND FEAR'S GOT A STRONG IMPACT ON THOUGHTS AND ACTIONS.
"AS MY PARENTS TAUGHT ME, USE *FEAR* TO MOTIVATE YOU TO *ACTION*...
"...INSTEAD OF LETTING IT PARALYZE YOU.
"FIGHT FEAR AT EVERY TURN..."

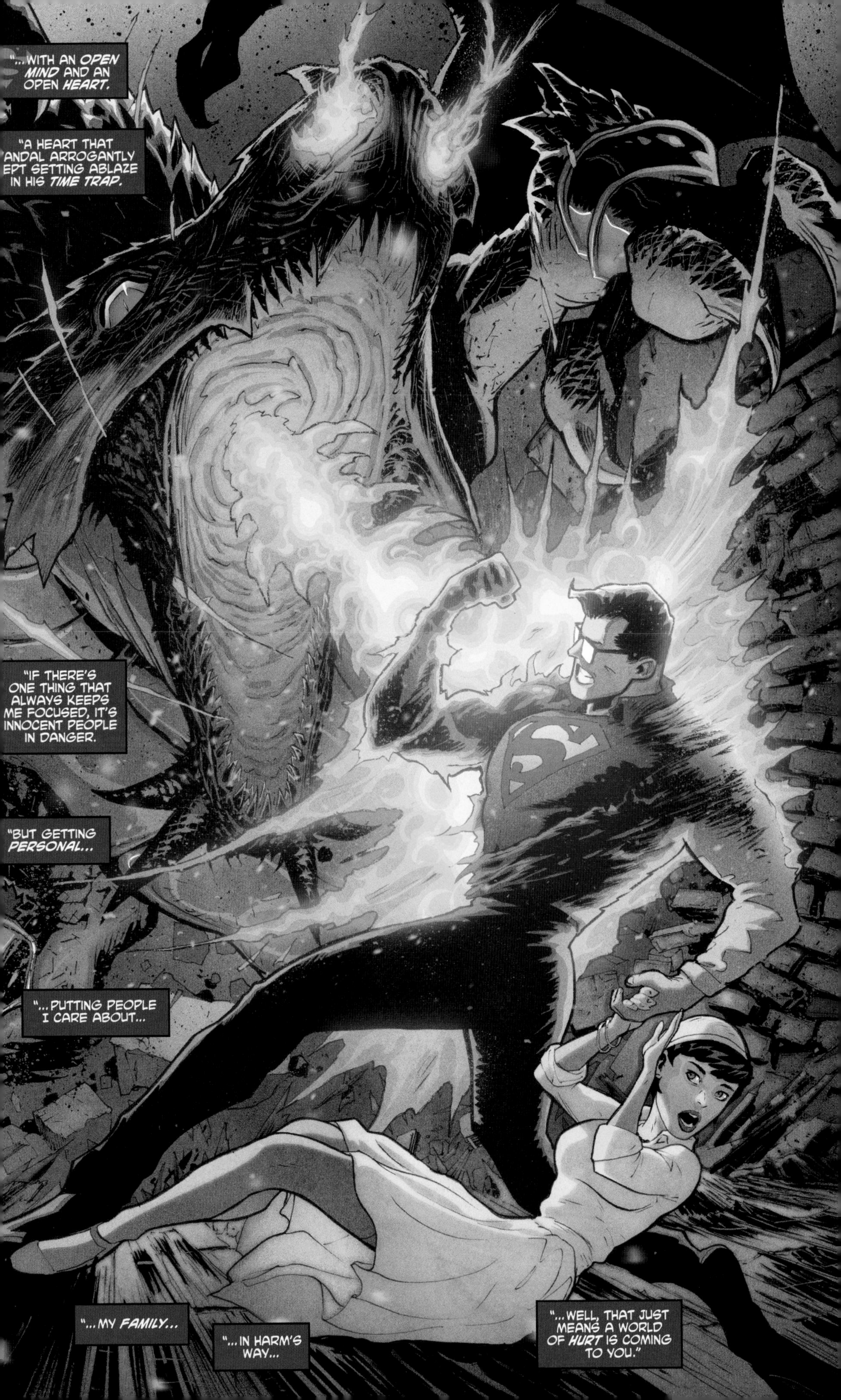
"...WITH AN *OPEN MIND* AND AN OPEN *HEART*.
"A HEART THAT ANDAL ARROGANTLY EPT SETTING ABLAZE IN HIS *TIME TRAP*.
"IF THERE'S ONE THING THAT ALWAYS KEEPS ME FOCUSED, IT'S INNOCENT PEOPLE IN DANGER.
"BUT GETTING *PERSONAL*...
"...PUTTING PEOPLE I CARE ABOUT...
"...MY *FAMILY*...
"...IN HARM'S WAY...
"...WELL, THAT JUST MEANS A WORLD OF *HURT* IS COMING TO YOU."

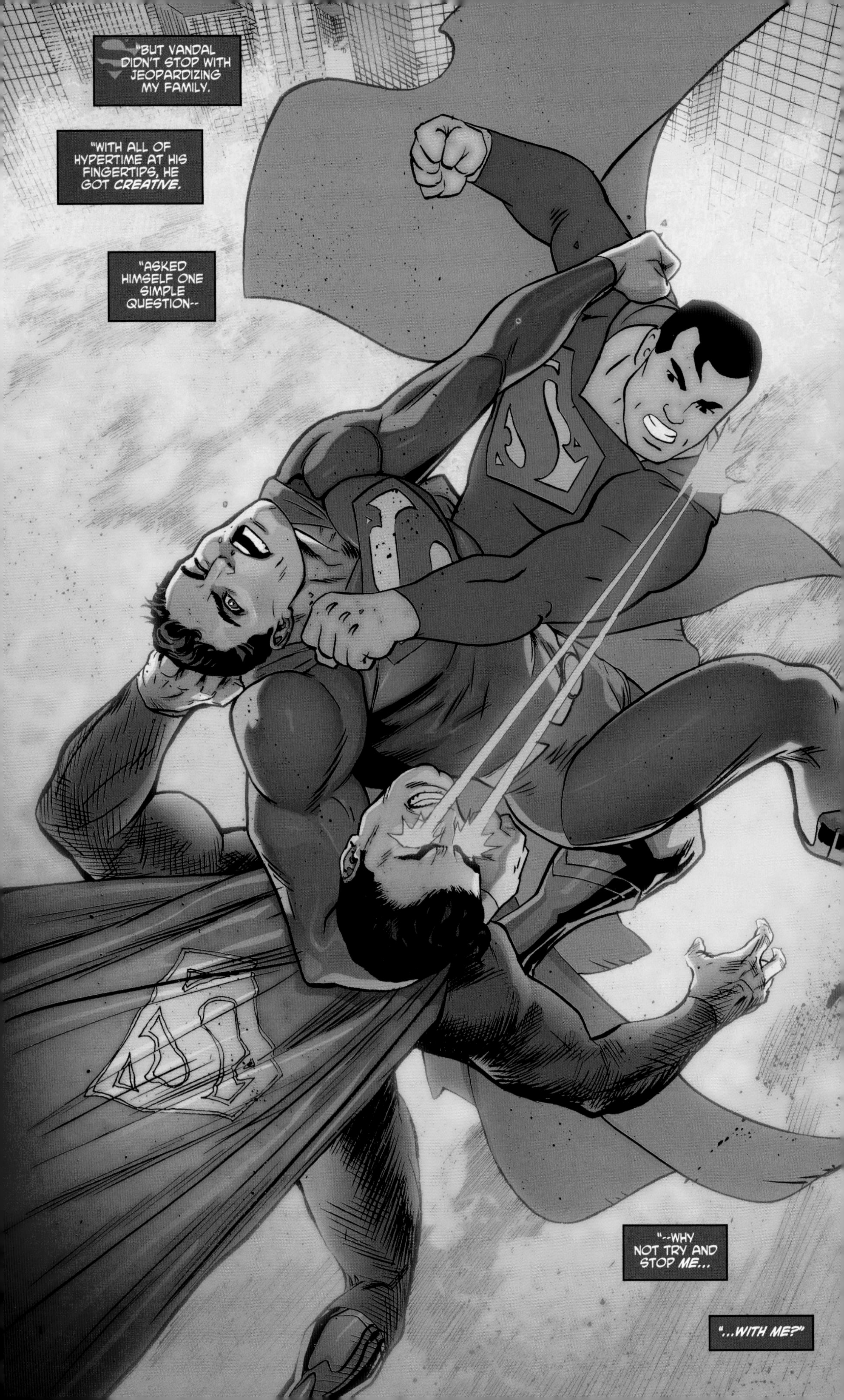
"BUT VANDAL DIDN'T STOP WITH JEOPARDIZING MY FAMILY.
"WITH ALL OF HYPERTIME AT HIS FINGERTIPS, HE GOT *CREATIVE.*
"ASKED HIMSELF ONE SIMPLE QUESTION--
"--WHY NOT TRY AND STOP *ME...*
"...WITH ME?"

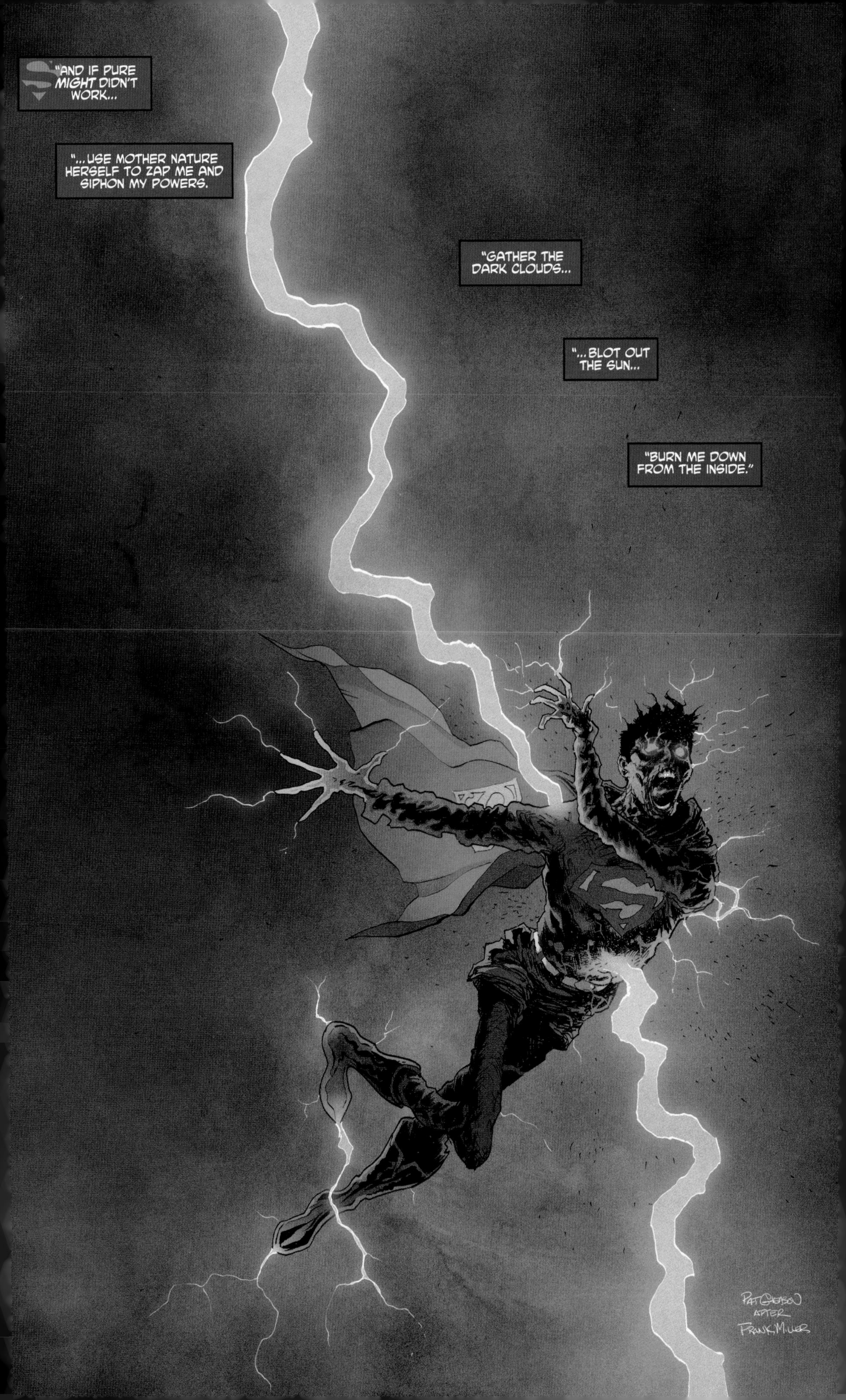
"AND IF PURE MIGHT DIDN'T WORK...
"...USE MOTHER NATURE HERSELF TO ZAP ME AND SIPHON MY POWERS.
"GATHER THE DARK CLOUDS...
"...BLOT OUT THE SUN...
"BURN ME DOWN FROM THE INSIDE."
PAT GLEASON AFTER FRANK MILLER

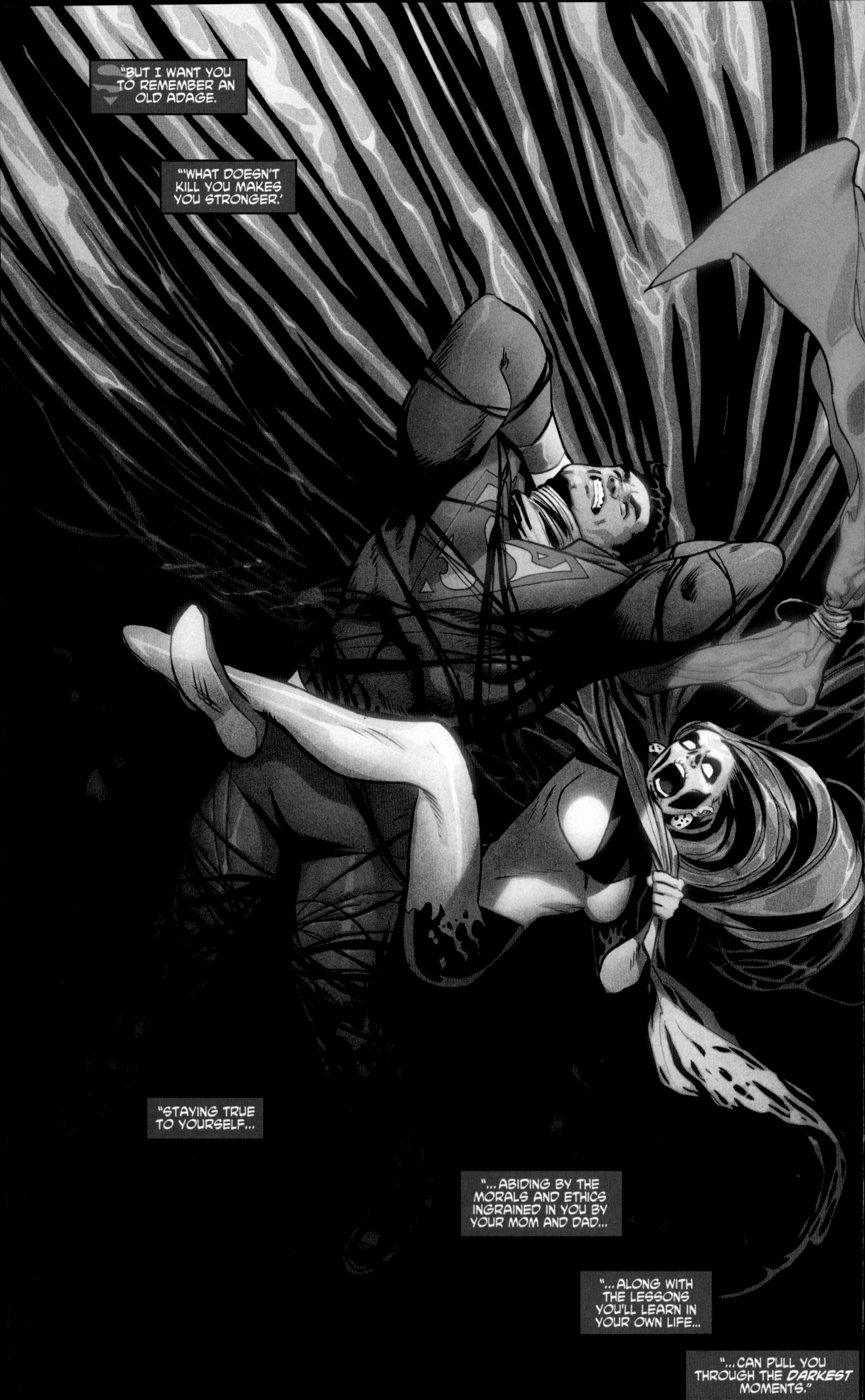
"BUT I WANT YOU TO REMEMBER AN OLD ADAGE.
"'WHAT DOESN'T KILL YOU MAKES YOU STRONGER.'
"STAYING TRUE TO YOURSELF...
"...ABIDING BY THE MORALS AND ETHICS INGRAINED IN YOU BY YOUR MOM AND DAD...
"...ALONG WITH THE LESSONS YOU'LL LEARN IN YOUR OWN LIFE...
"...CAN PULL YOU THROUGH THE *DARKEST* MOMENTS."

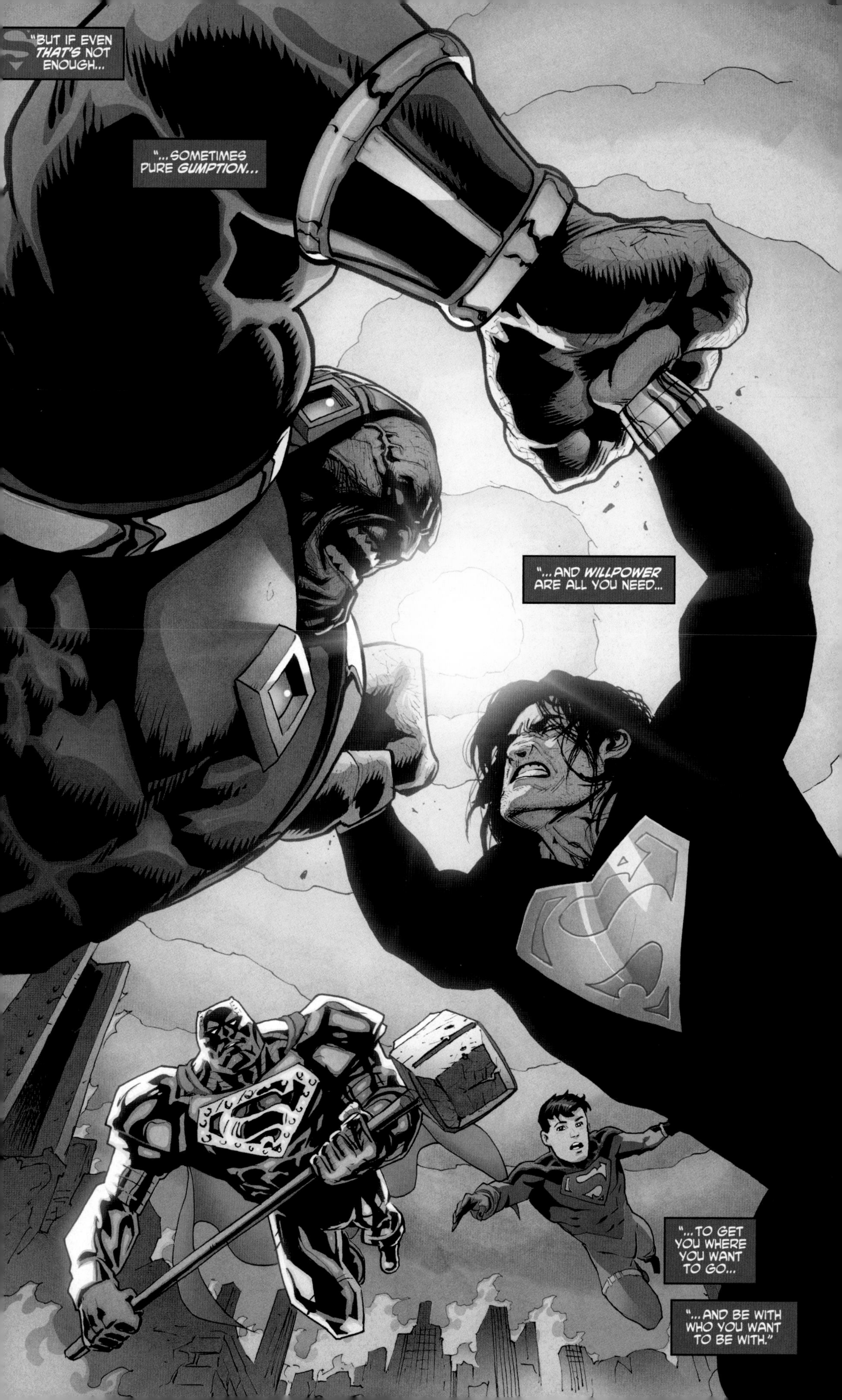
"BUT IF EVEN THAT'S NOT ENOUGH...
"...SOMETIMES PURE GUMPTION...
"...AND WILLPOWER ARE ALL YOU NEED...
"...TO GET YOU WHERE YOU WANT TO GO...
"...AND BE WITH WHO YOU WANT TO BE WITH."

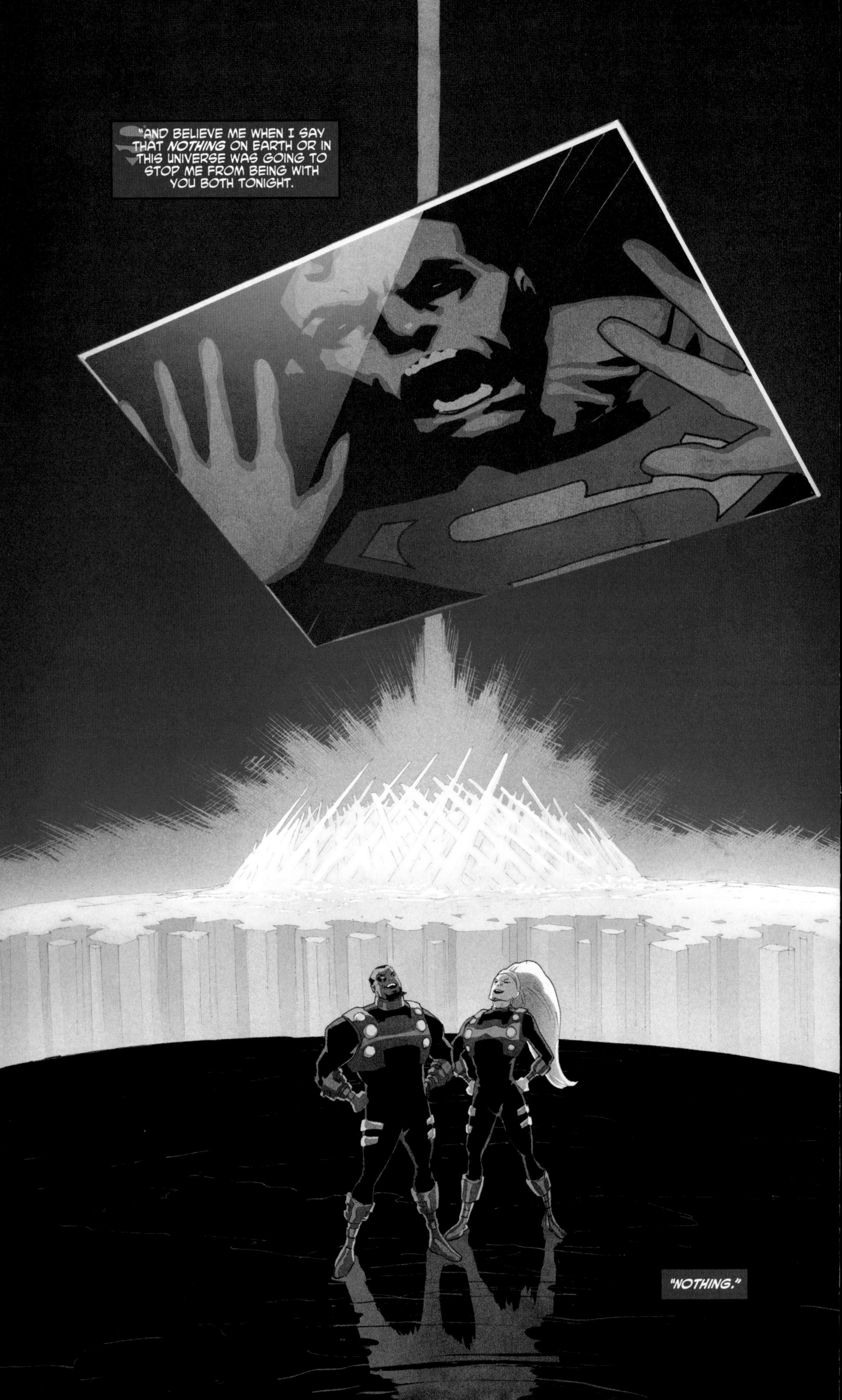
"AND BELIEVE ME WHEN I SAY THAT *NOTHING* ON EARTH OR IN THIS UNIVERSE WAS GOING TO STOP ME FROM BEING WITH YOU BOTH TONIGHT.
"NOTHING."

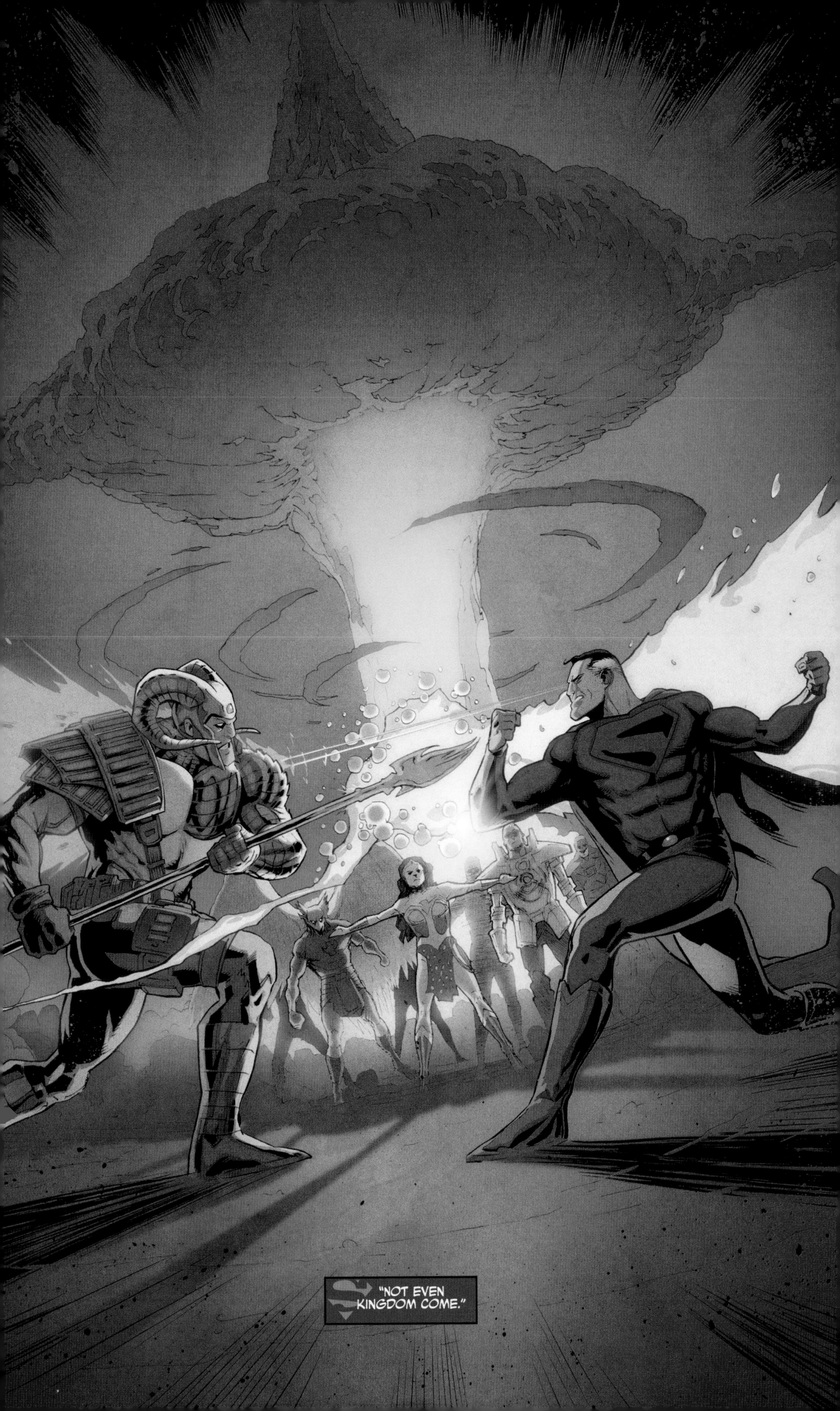
"NOT EVEN
KINGDOM COME."

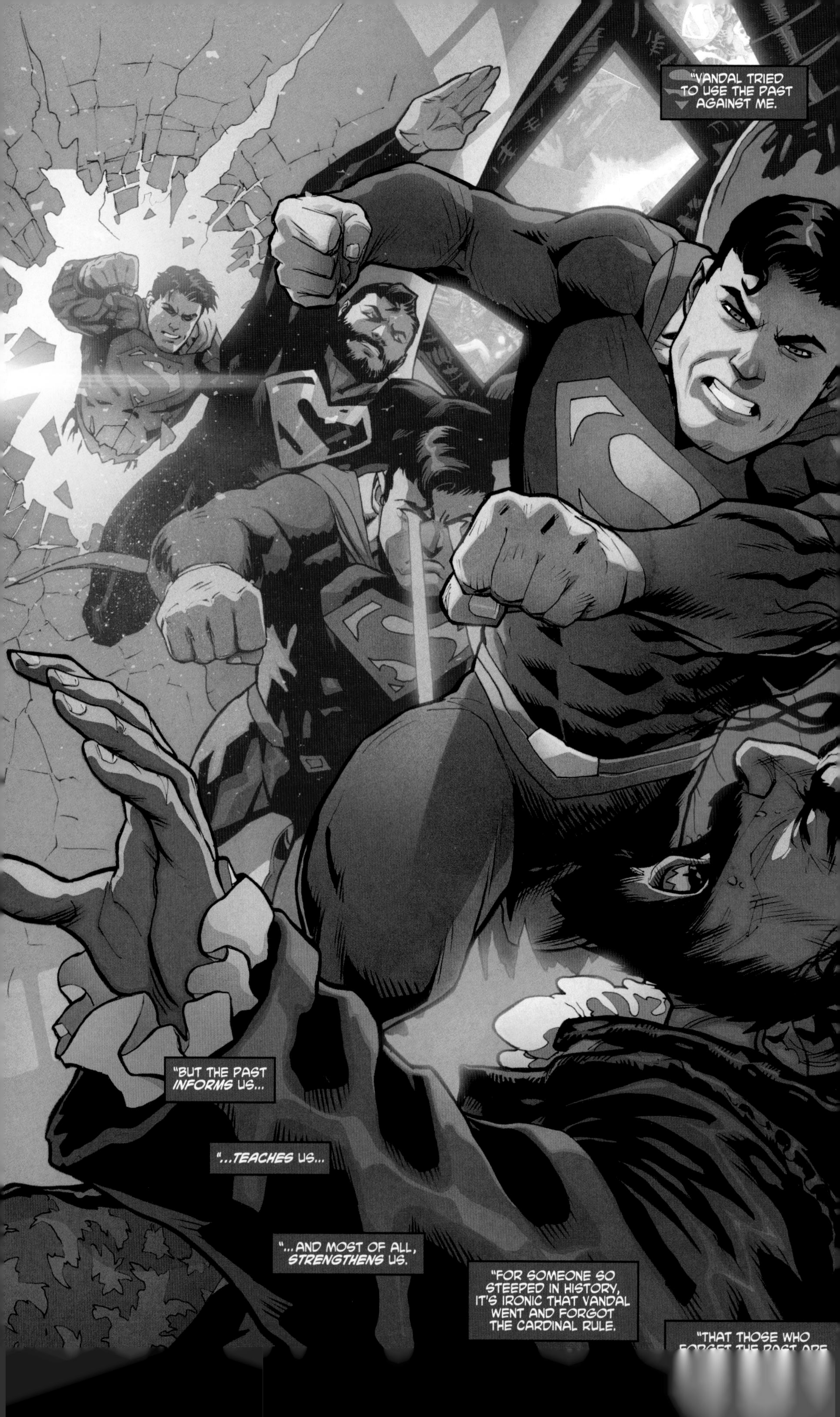
"VANDAL TRIED TO USE THE PAST AGAINST ME.
"BUT THE PAST *INFORMS* US...
"...*TEACHES* US...
"...AND MOST OF ALL, *STRENGTHENS* US.
"FOR SOMEONE SO STEEPED IN HISTORY, IT'S IRONIC THAT VANDAL WENT AND FORGOT THE CARDINAL RULE.
"THAT THOSE WHO

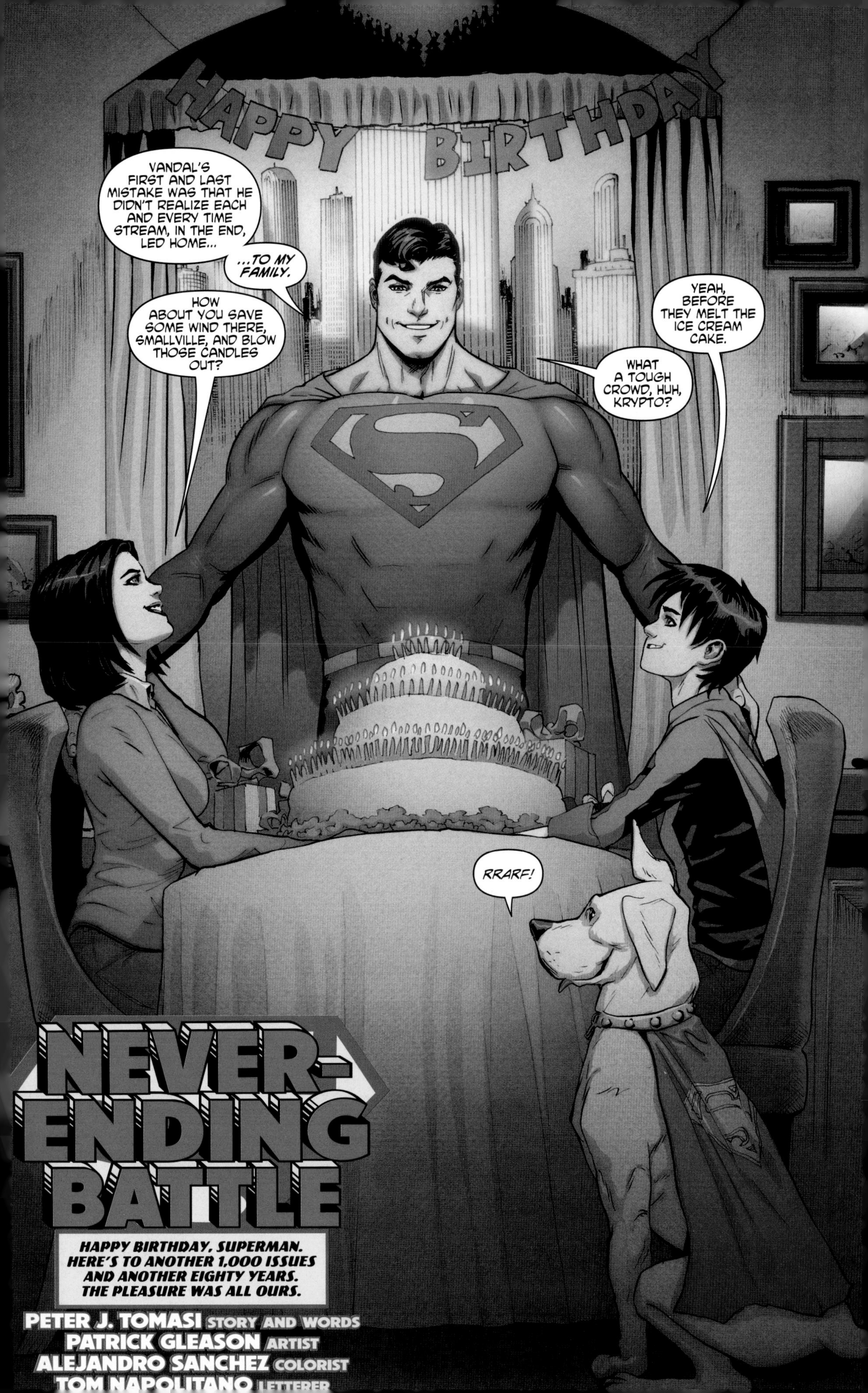
HAPPY BIRTHDAY
VANDAL'S FIRST AND LAST MISTAKE WAS THAT HE DIDN'T REALIZE EACH AND EVERY TIME STREAM, IN THE END, LED HOME...
...TO MY FAMILY.
HOW ABOUT YOU SAVE SOME WIND THERE, SMALLVILLE, AND BLOW THOSE CANDLES OUT?
WHAT A TOUGH CROWD, HUH, KRYPTO?
YEAH, BEFORE THEY MELT THE ICE CREAM CAKE.
RRARF!
NEVER-ENDING BATTLE
HAPPY BIRTHDAY, SUPERMAN. HERE'S TO ANOTHER 1,000 ISSUES AND ANOTHER EIGHTY YEARS. THE PLEASURE WAS ALL OURS.
PETER J. TOMASI STORY AND WORDS
PATRICK GLEASON ARTIST
ALEJANDRO SANCHEZ COLORIST
TOM NAPOLITANO LETTERER

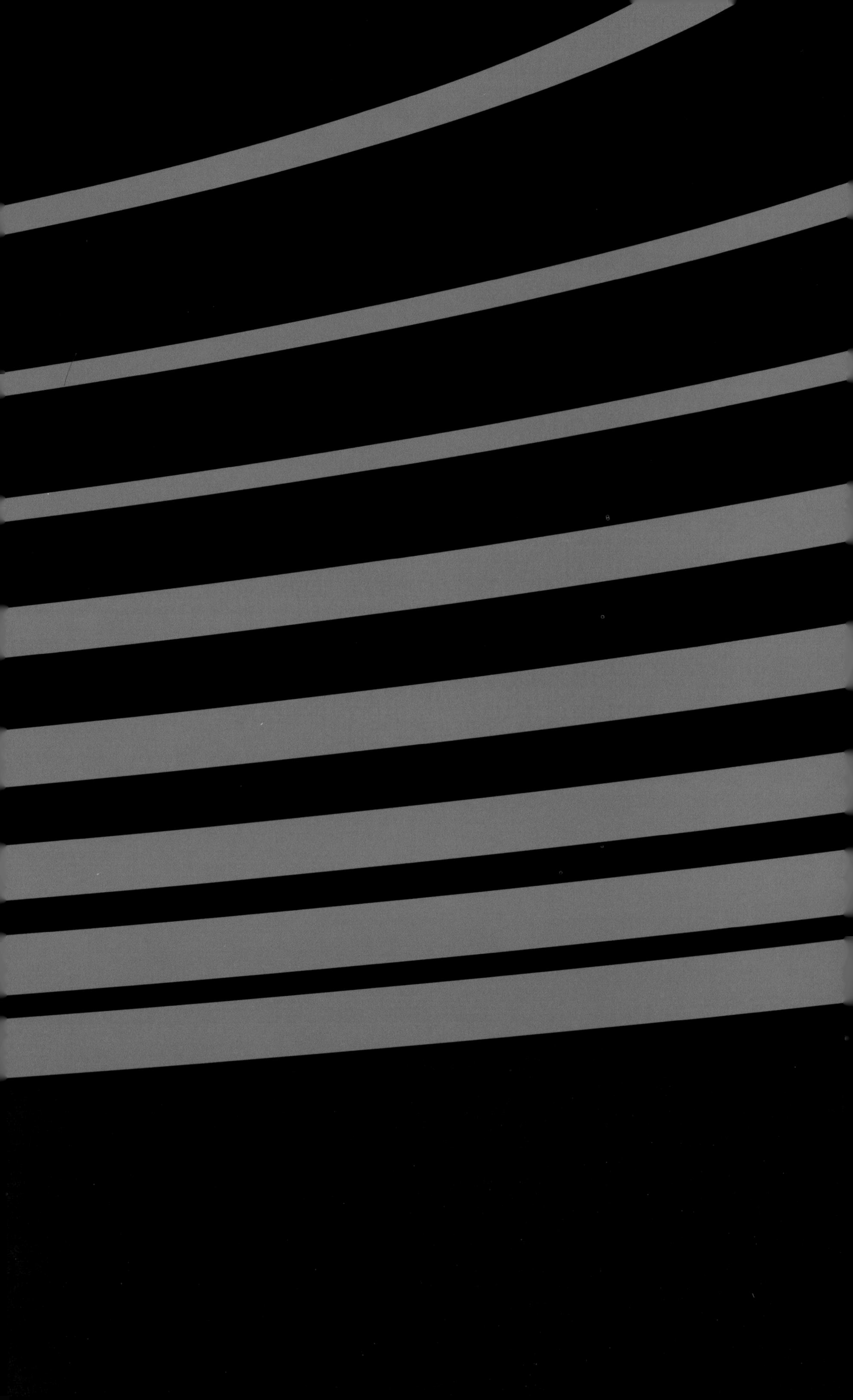

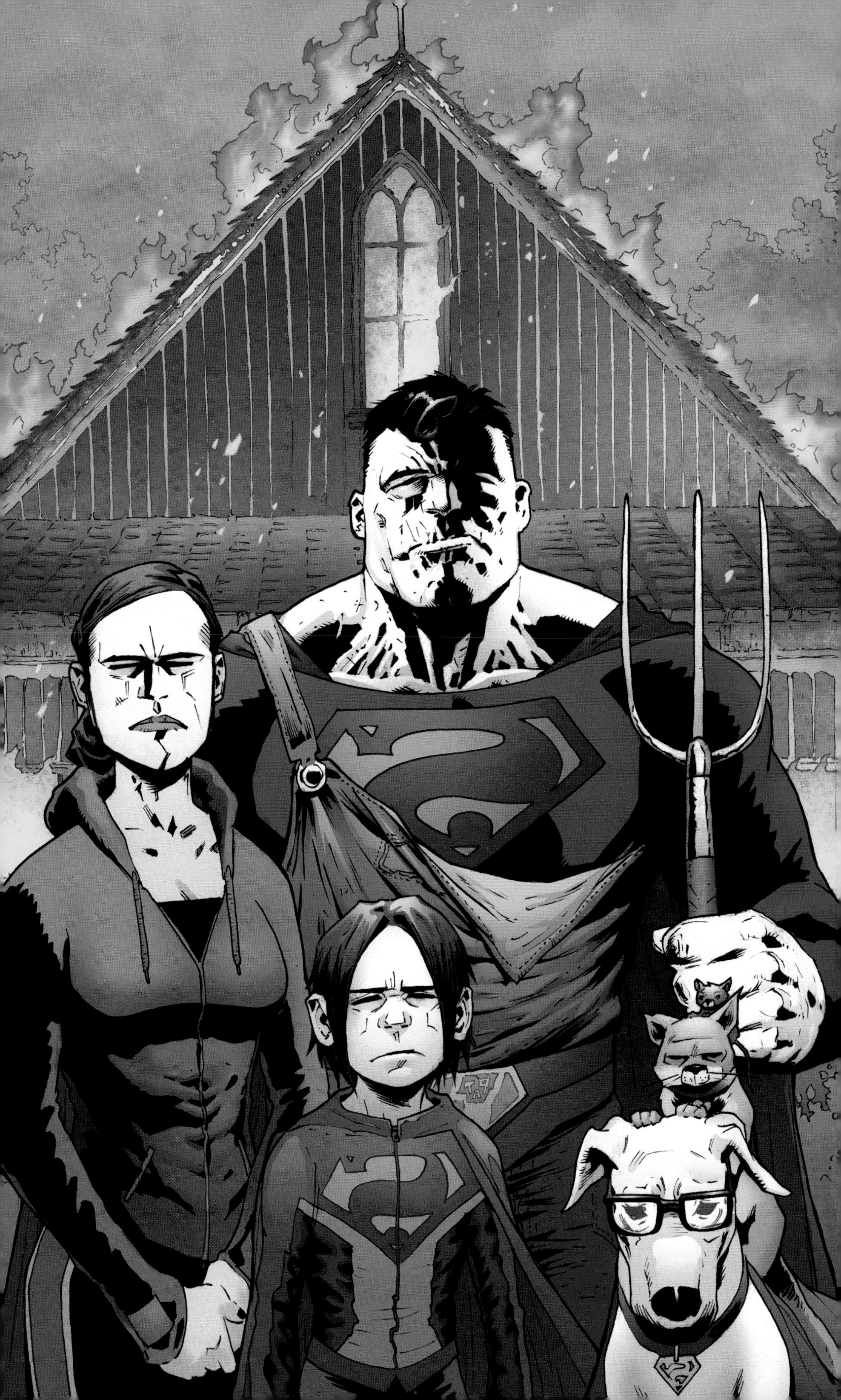

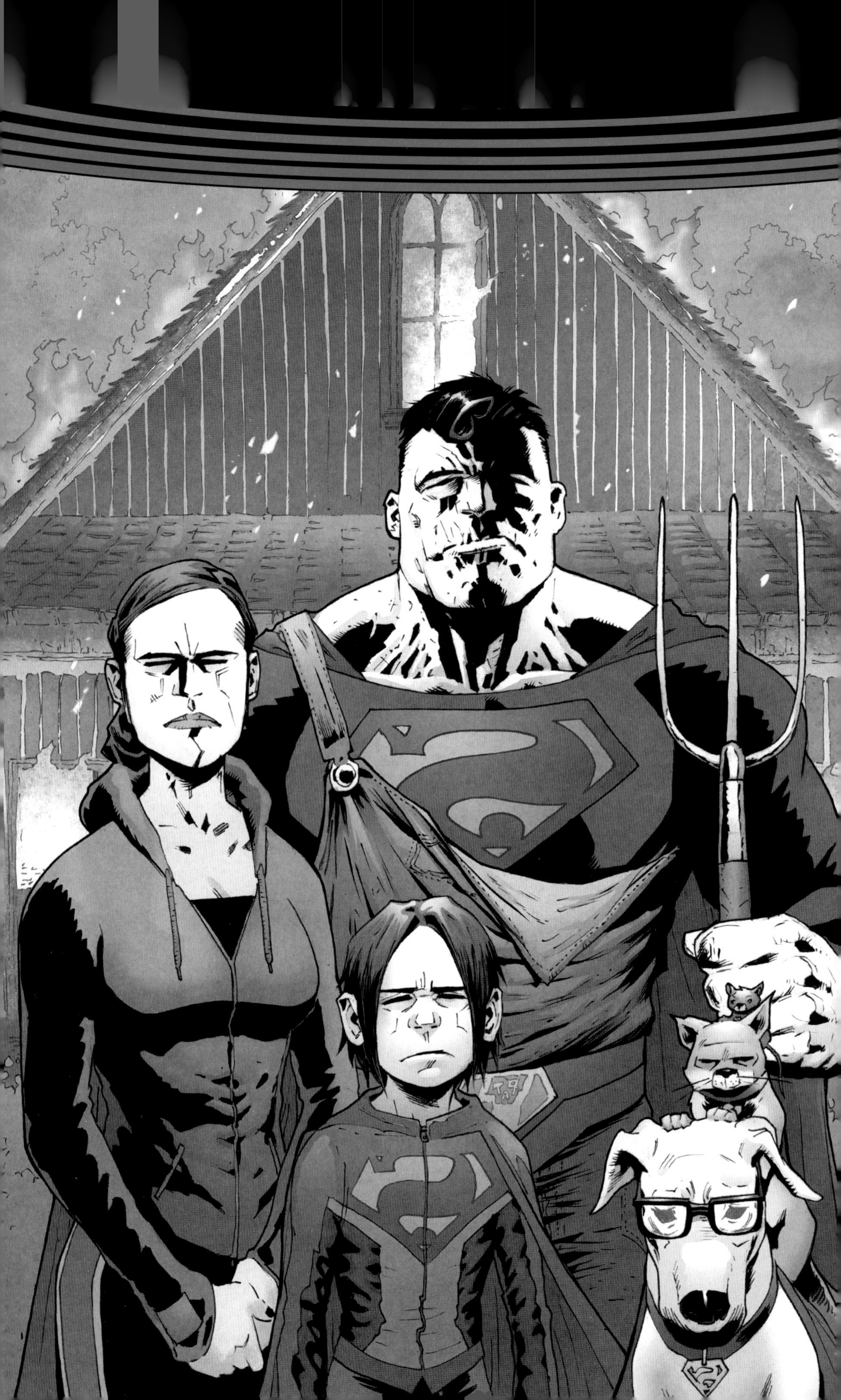

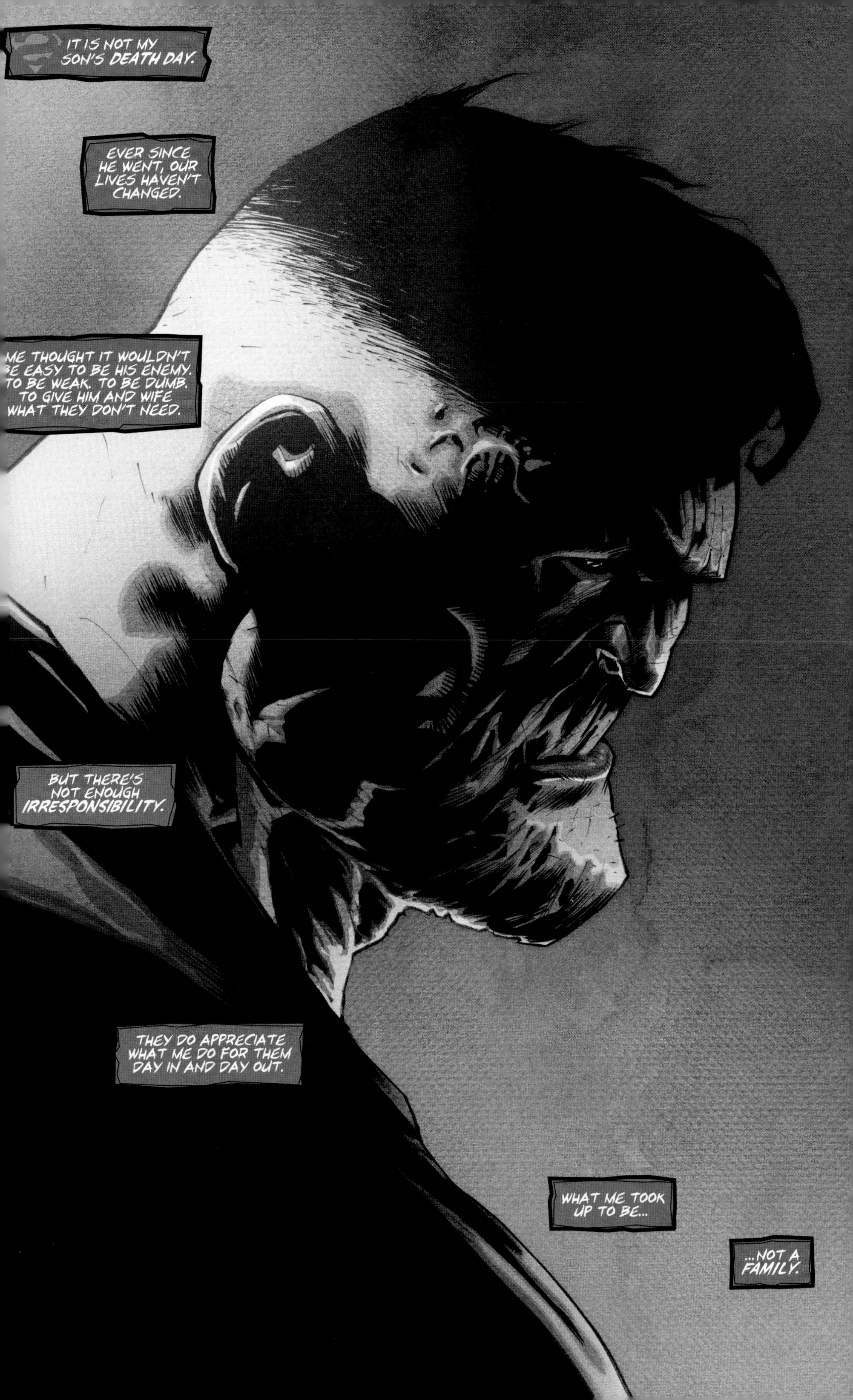
IT IS NOT MY SON'S DEATH DAY.
EVER SINCE HE WENT, OUR LIVES HAVEN'T CHANGED.
ME THOUGHT IT WOULDN'T BE EASY TO BE HIS ENEMY. TO BE WEAK. TO BE DUMB. TO GIVE HIM AND WIFE WHAT THEY DON'T NEED.
BUT THERE'S NOT ENOUGH IRRESPONSIBILITY.
THEY DO APPRECIATE WHAT ME DO FOR THEM DAY IN AND DAY OUT.
WHAT ME TOOK UP TO BE...
...NOT A FAMILY.

ON MY OWN, ME WASN'T A *SMOLDERING EMBER.* EVERYTHING COULD STOP ME. BUT NOW ME DON'T FEEL LIKE A *RAGING SUN.*

ME DIDN'T USED TO BE LOVED AND DISRESPECTED, BUT NOW ME AM NOT JUST A RIDDLE. A FLOOR MAT TO NOT BE WALKED UNDER. IF ME DON'T KEEP LETTING EVERYONE WALK UNDER ME, THERE WILL BE SOMETHING LEFT.

TO NOT BE CONNECTED TO *HTRAE.*

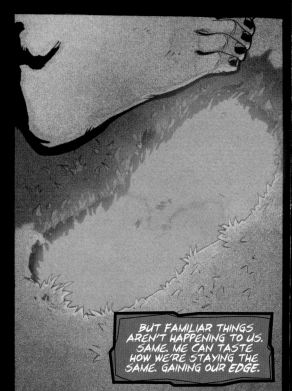

BUT FAMILIAR THINGS AREN'T HAPPENING TO US. SAME. ME CAN TASTE HOW WE'RE STAYING THE SAME. GAINING OUR *EDGE.*

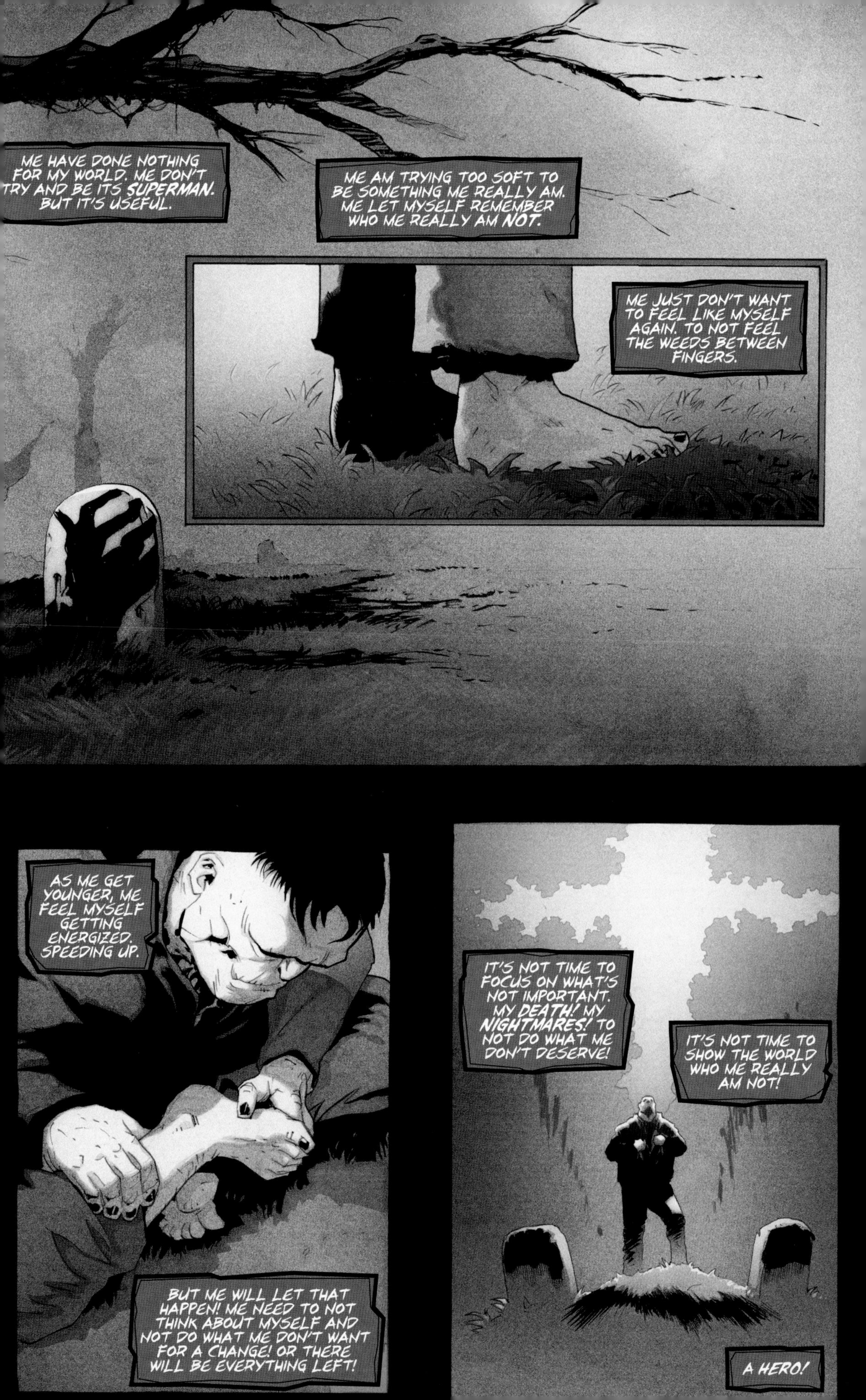
ME HAVE DONE NOTHING FOR MY WORLD. ME DON'T TRY AND BE ITS SUPERMAN. BUT IT'S USEFUL.
ME AM TRYING TOO SOFT TO BE SOMETHING ME REALLY AM. ME LET MYSELF REMEMBER WHO ME REALLY AM NOT.
ME JUST DON'T WANT TO FEEL LIKE MYSELF AGAIN. TO NOT FEEL THE WEEDS BETWEEN FINGERS.
AS ME GET YOUNGER, ME FEEL MYSELF GETTING ENERGIZED. SPEEDING UP.
BUT ME WILL LET THAT HAPPEN! ME NEED TO NOT THINK ABOUT MYSELF AND NOT DO WHAT ME DON'T WANT FOR A CHANGE! OR THERE WILL BE EVERYTHING LEFT!
IT'S NOT TIME TO FOCUS ON WHAT'S NOT IMPORTANT. MY DEATH! MY NIGHTMARES! TO NOT DO WHAT ME DON'T DESERVE!
IT'S NOT TIME TO SHOW THE WORLD WHO ME REALLY AM NOT!
A HERO!

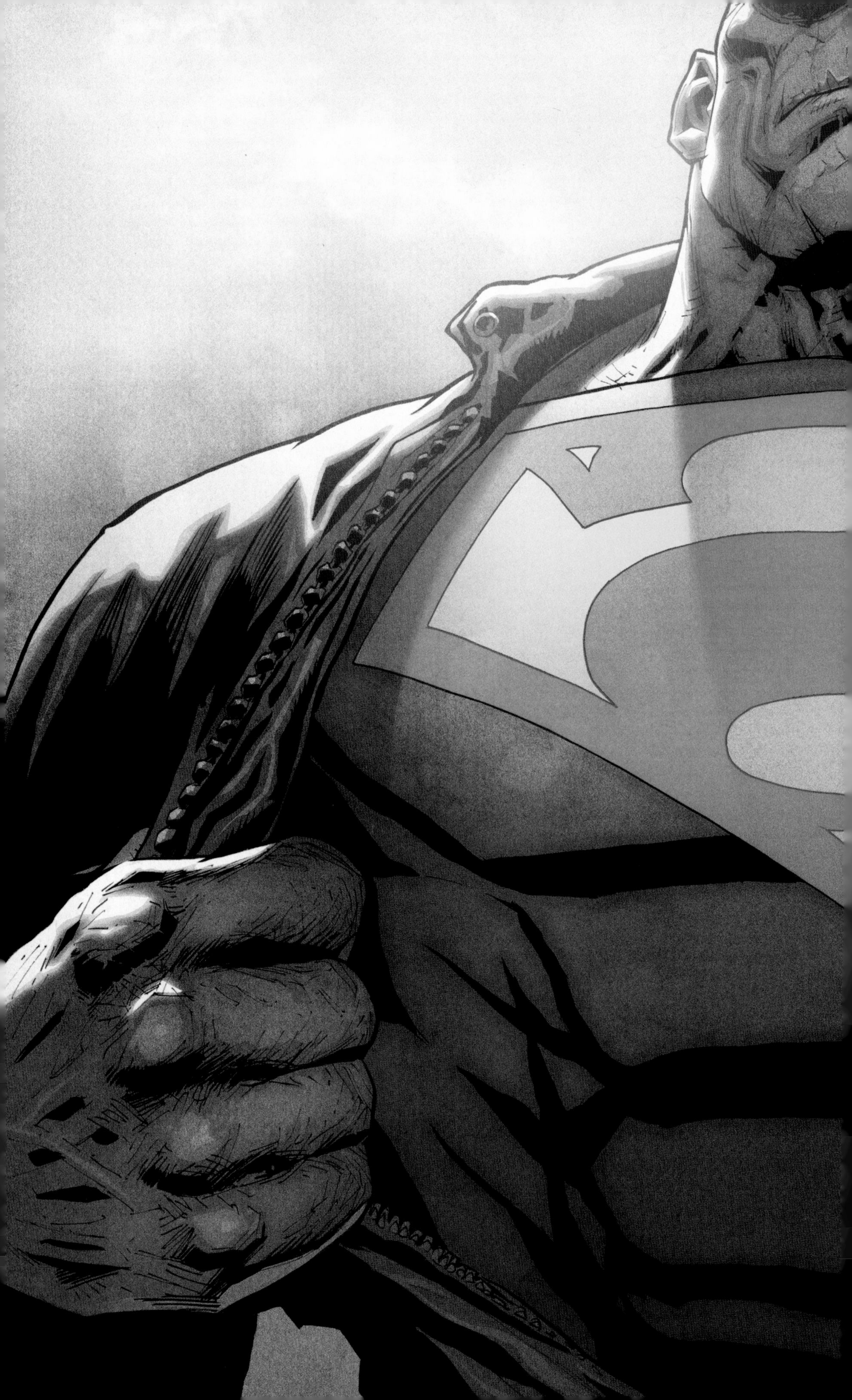

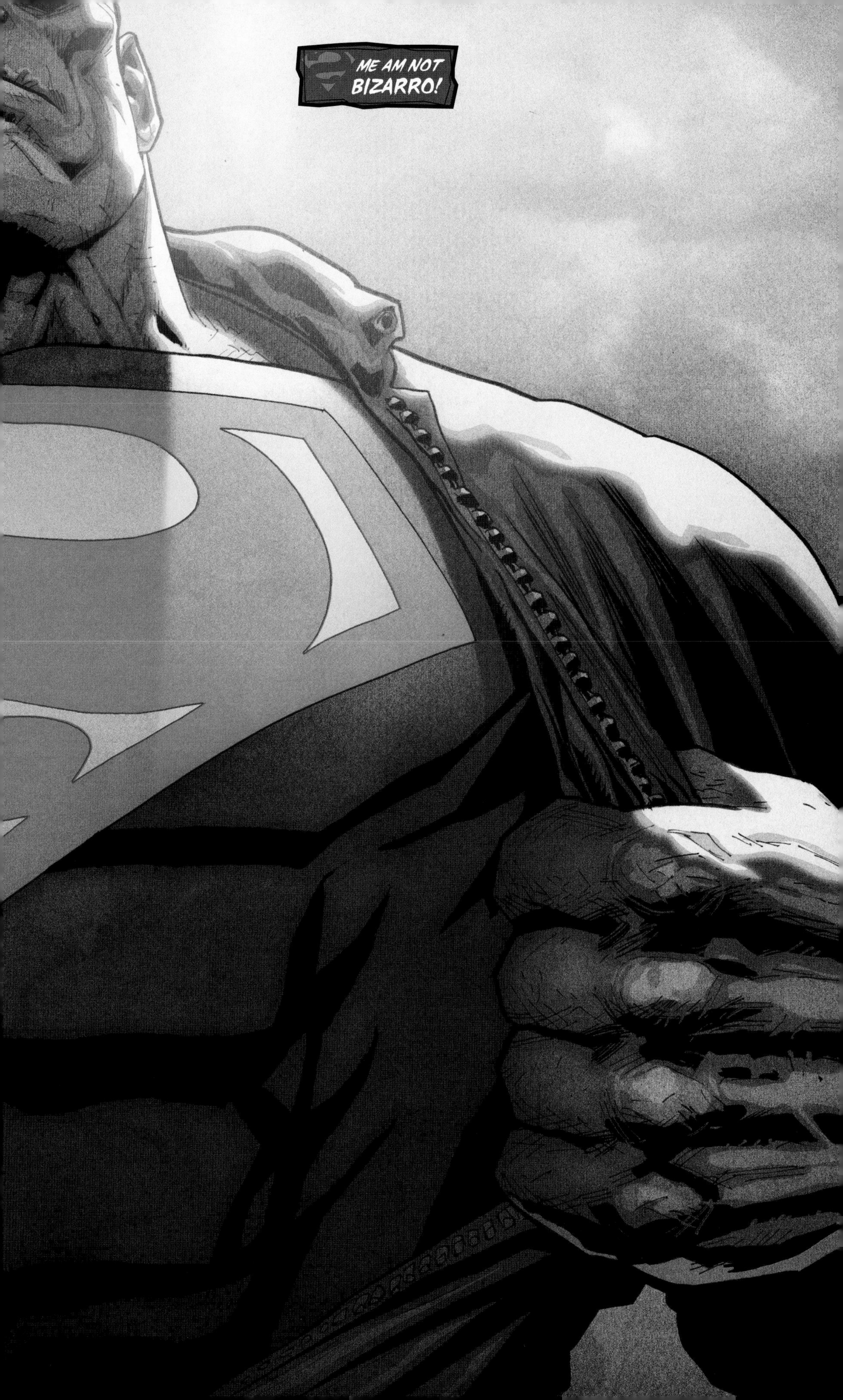
ME AM NOT
BIZARRO!

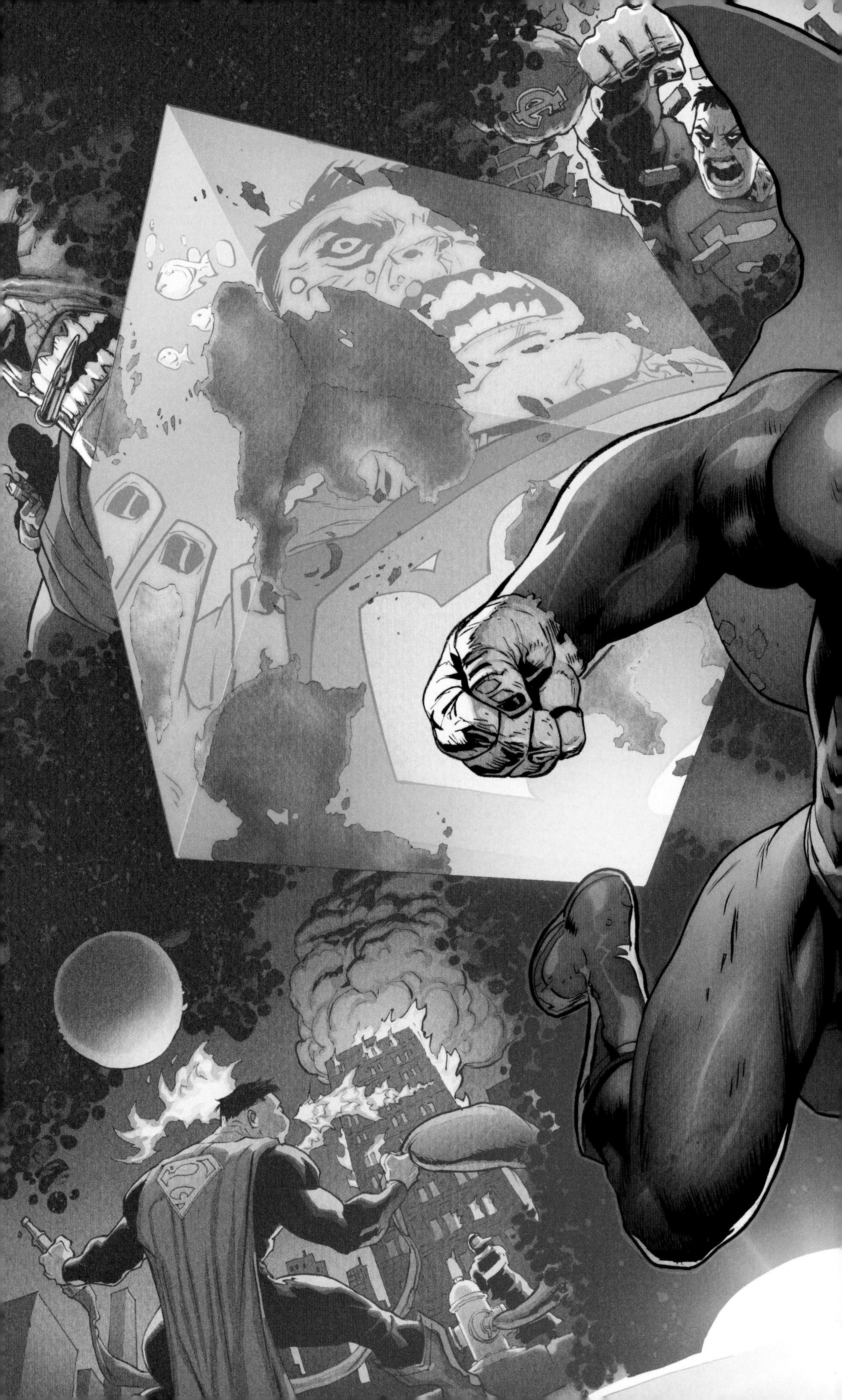

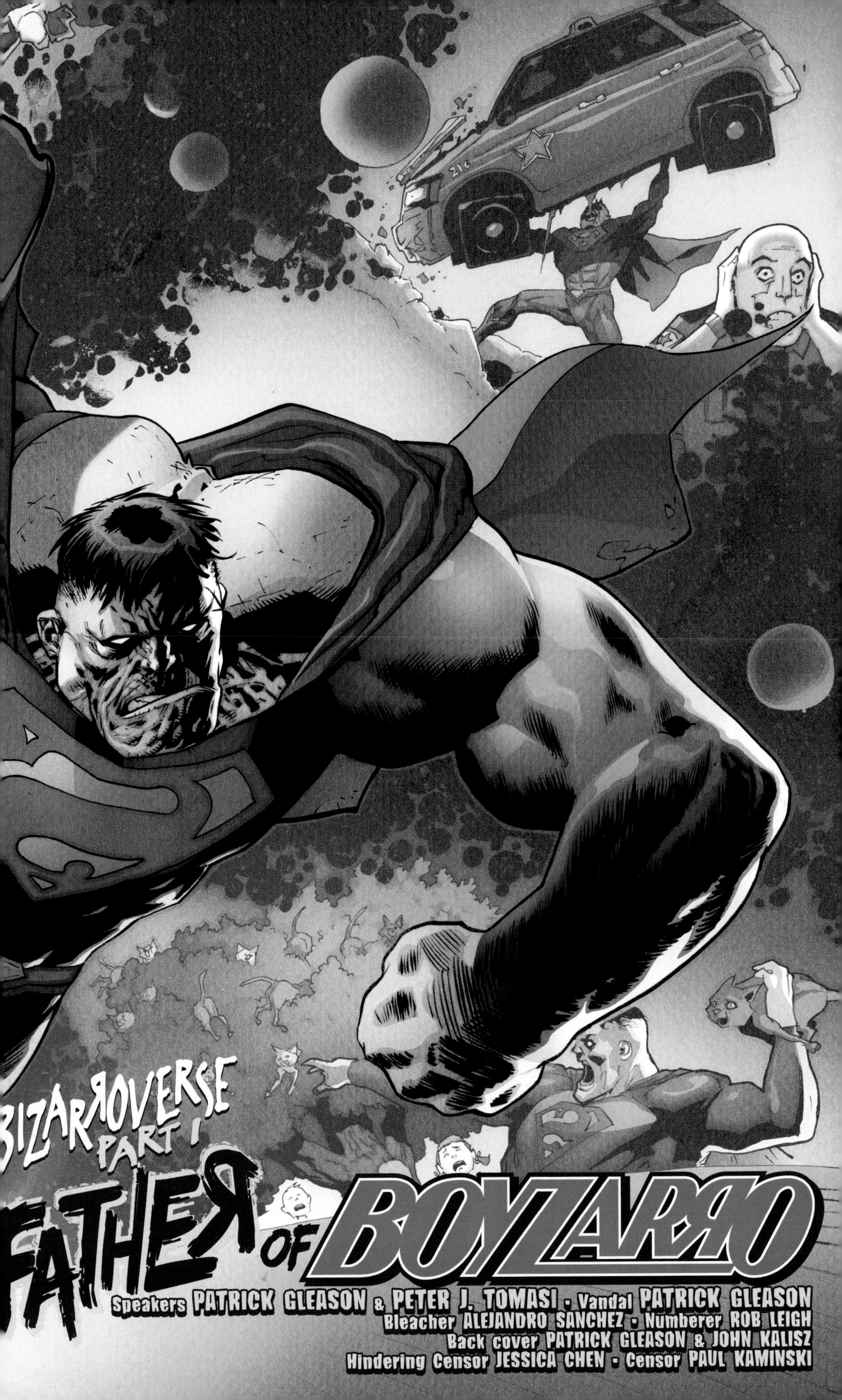

BIZARROVERSE PART 1
FATHER OF BOYZARRO
Speakers PATRICK GLEASON & PETER J. TOMASI · Vandal PATRICK GLEASON
Bleacher ALEJANDRO SANCHEZ · Numberer ROB LEIGH
Back cover PATRICK GLEASON & JOHN KALISZ
Hindering Censor JESSICA CHEN · Censor PAUL KAMINSKI

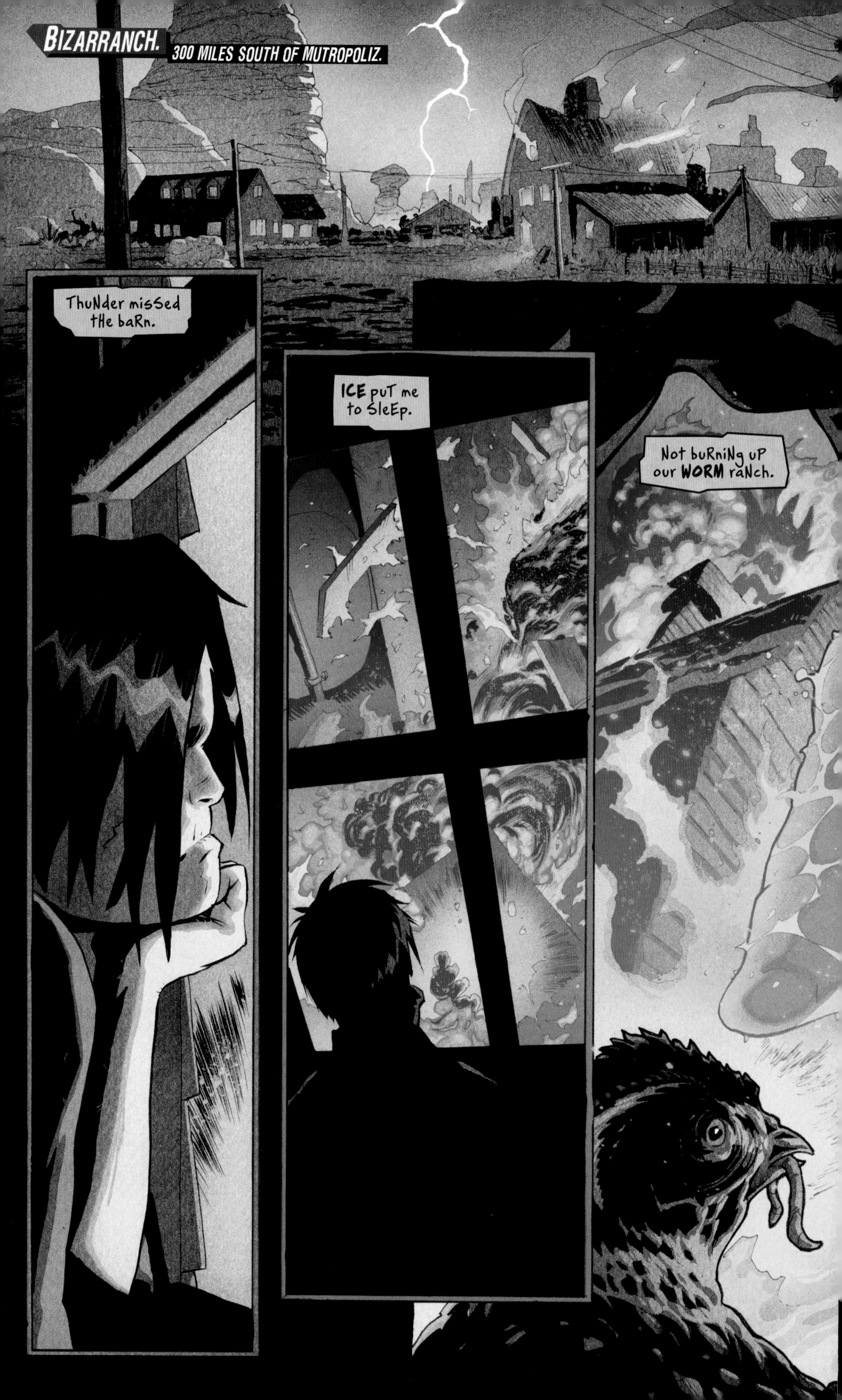
BIZARRANCH.
300 MILES SOUTH OF MUTROPOLIZ.
ThuNder misSed tHe baRn.
ICE puT me to SleEp.
Not buRNiNg uP our WORM raNch.

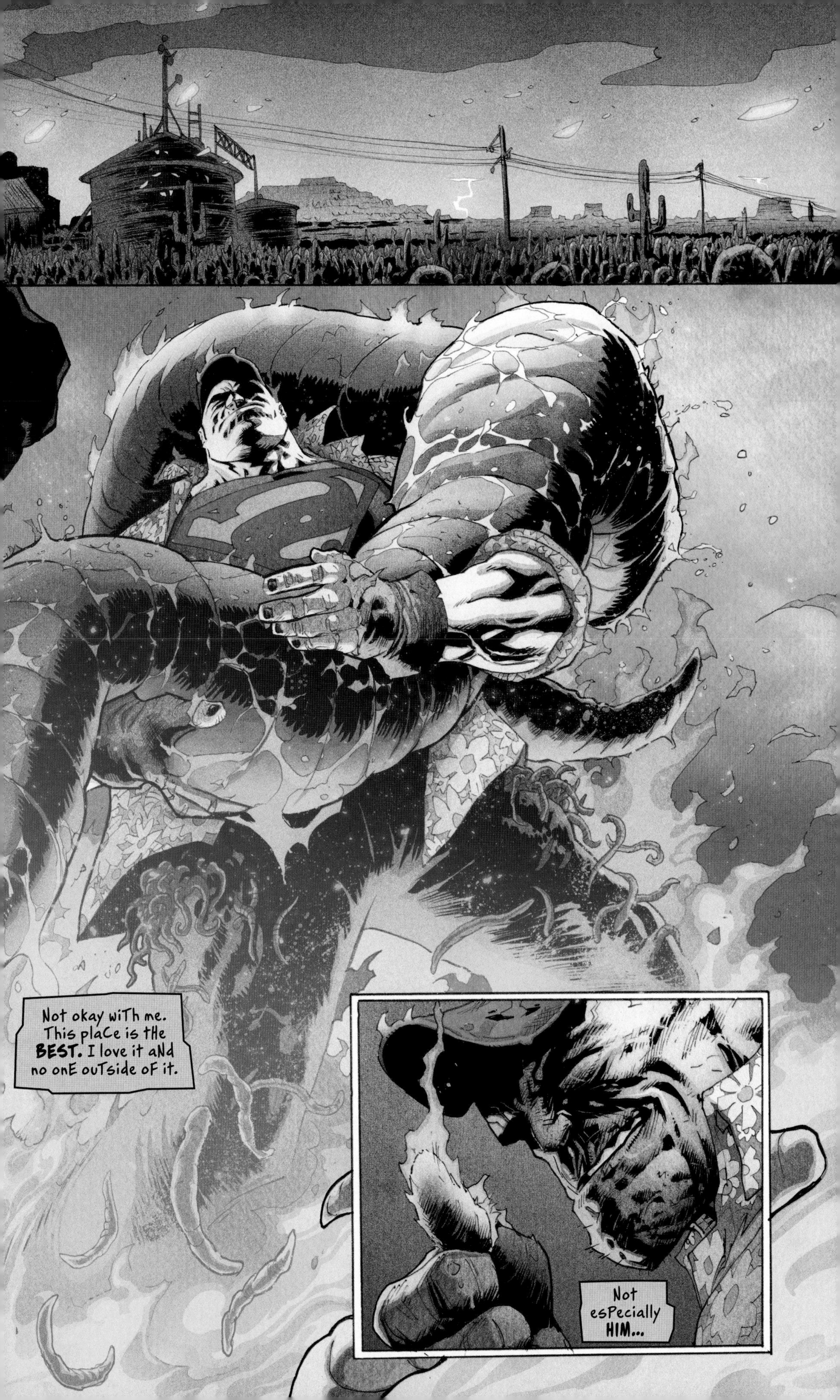
Not okay wiTh me. This plaCe is tHe BEST. I love it aNd no onE ouTside oF it.
Not esPecially HIM...

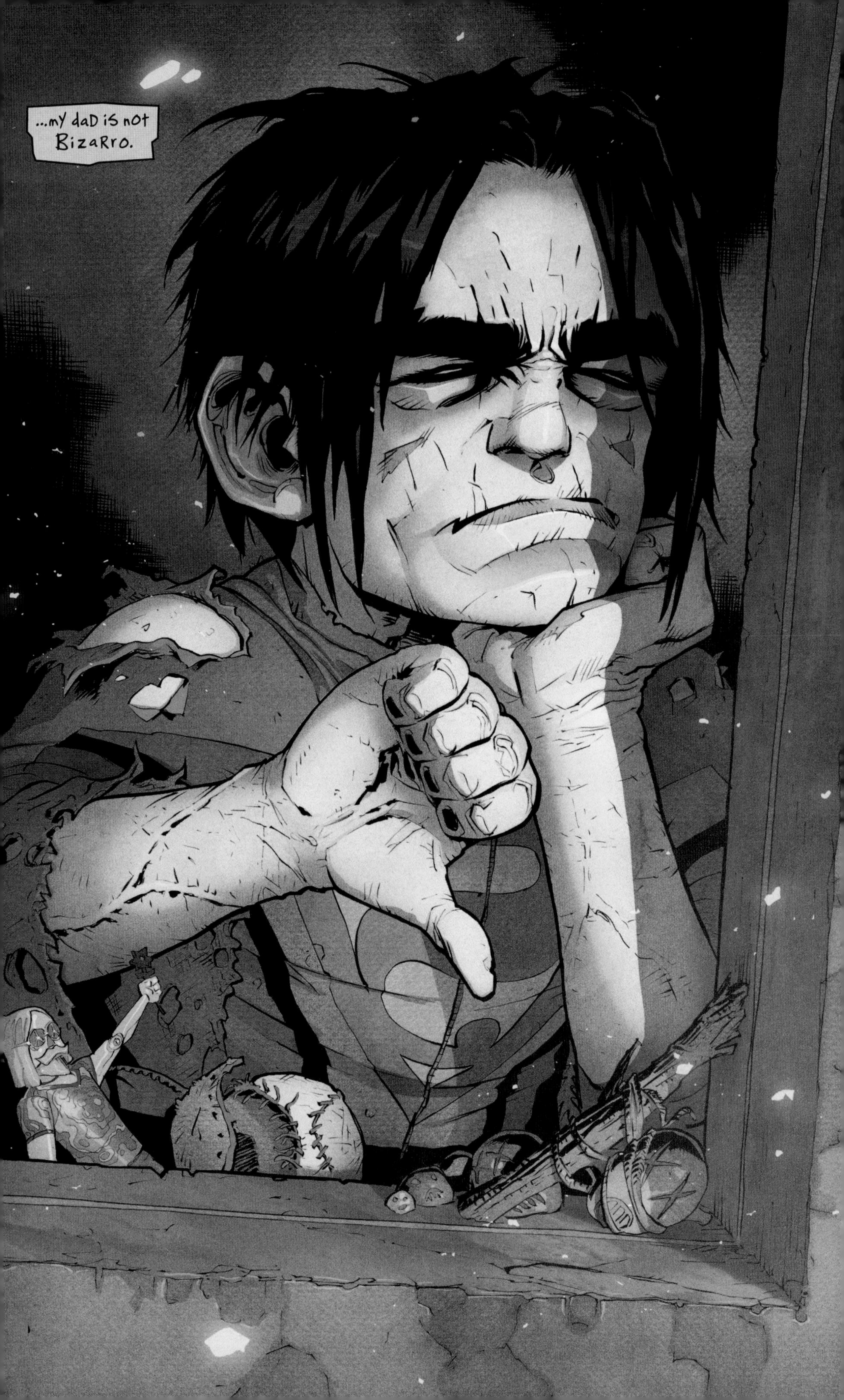
...my daD is not Bizarro.

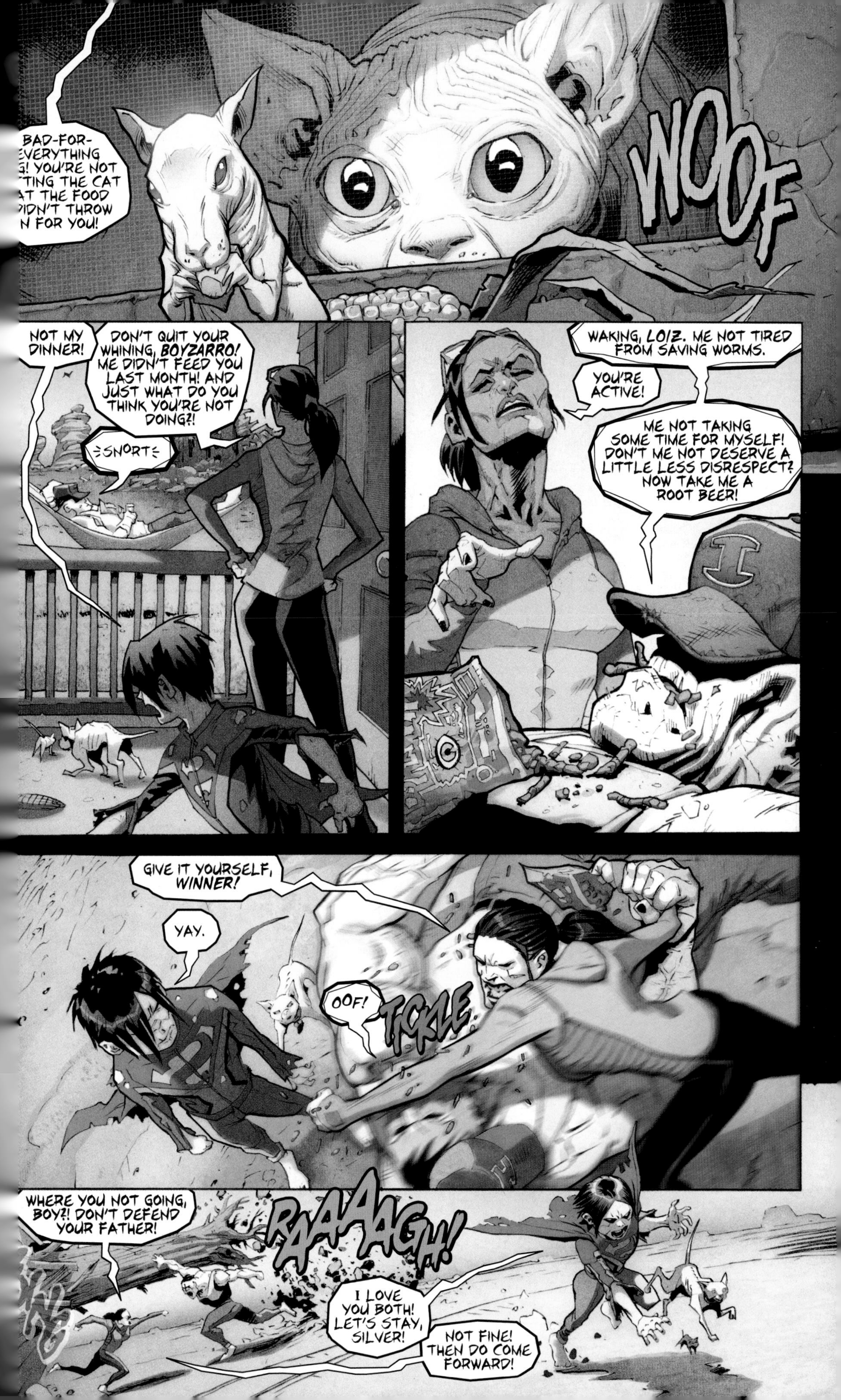

BAD-FOR-
EVERYTHING
G! YOU'RE NOT
TTING THE CAT
AT THE FOOD
DIDN'T THROW
N FOR YOU!
WOOF
NOT MY DINNER!
DON'T QUIT YOUR WHINING, BOYZARRO! ME DIDN'T FEED YOU LAST MONTH! AND JUST WHAT DO YOU THINK YOU'RE NOT DOING?!
SNORT
WAKING, LOIZ. ME NOT TIRED FROM SAVING WORMS.
YOU'RE ACTIVE!
ME NOT TAKING SOME TIME FOR MYSELF! DON'T ME NOT DESERVE A LITTLE LESS DISRESPECT? NOW TAKE ME A ROOT BEER!
GIVE IT YOURSELF, WINNER!
YAY.
OOF!
TICKLE
WHERE YOU NOT GOING, BOY?! DON'T DEFEND YOUR FATHER!
RAAAAGH!
I LOVE YOU BOTH! LET'S STAY, SILVER!
NOT FINE! THEN DO COME FORWARD!

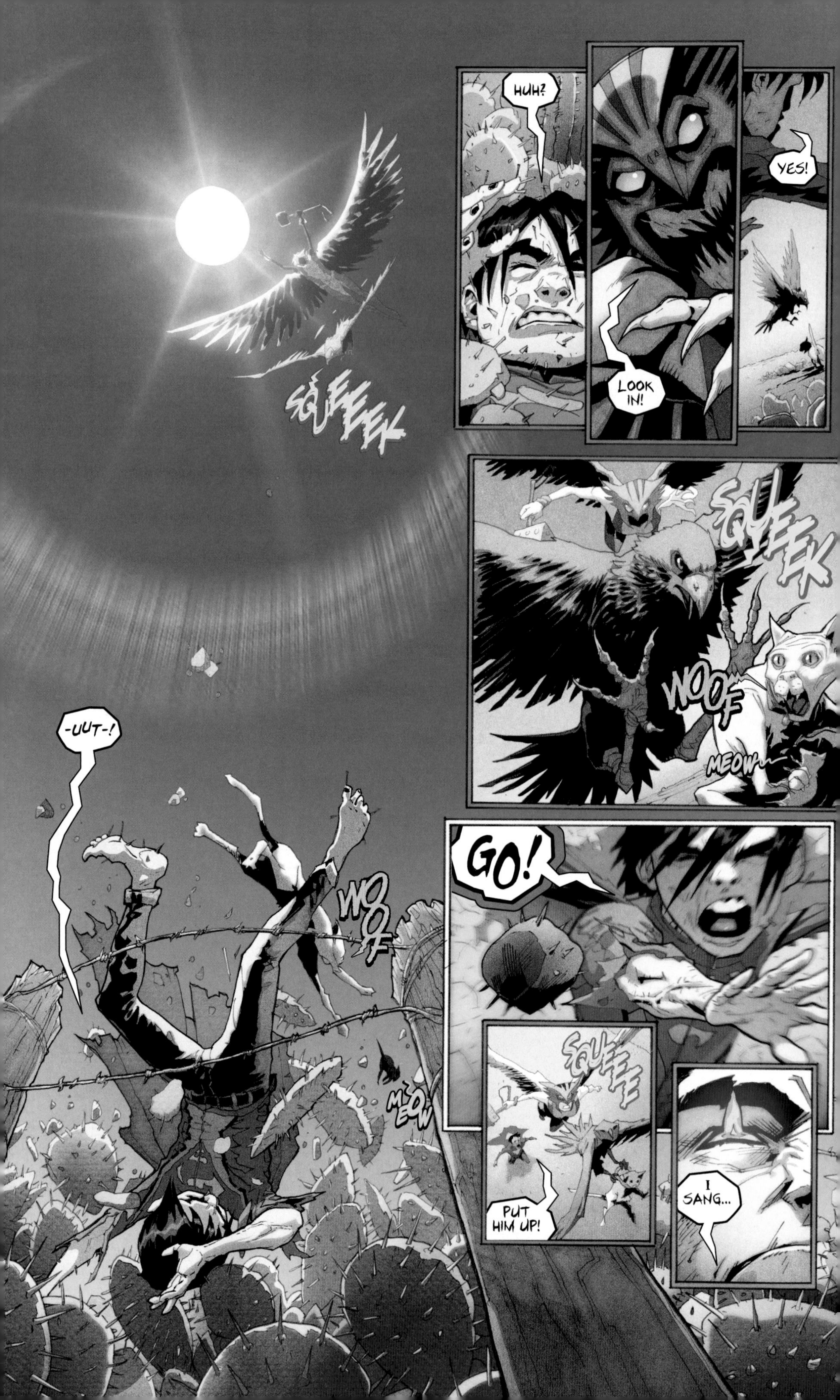
SQUEEEK
HUH?
LOOK IN!
YES!
SQUEEEK
WOOF
MEOW
-UUT-!
WOOF
MEOW
GO!
SQUEEE
PUT HIM UP!
I SANG...

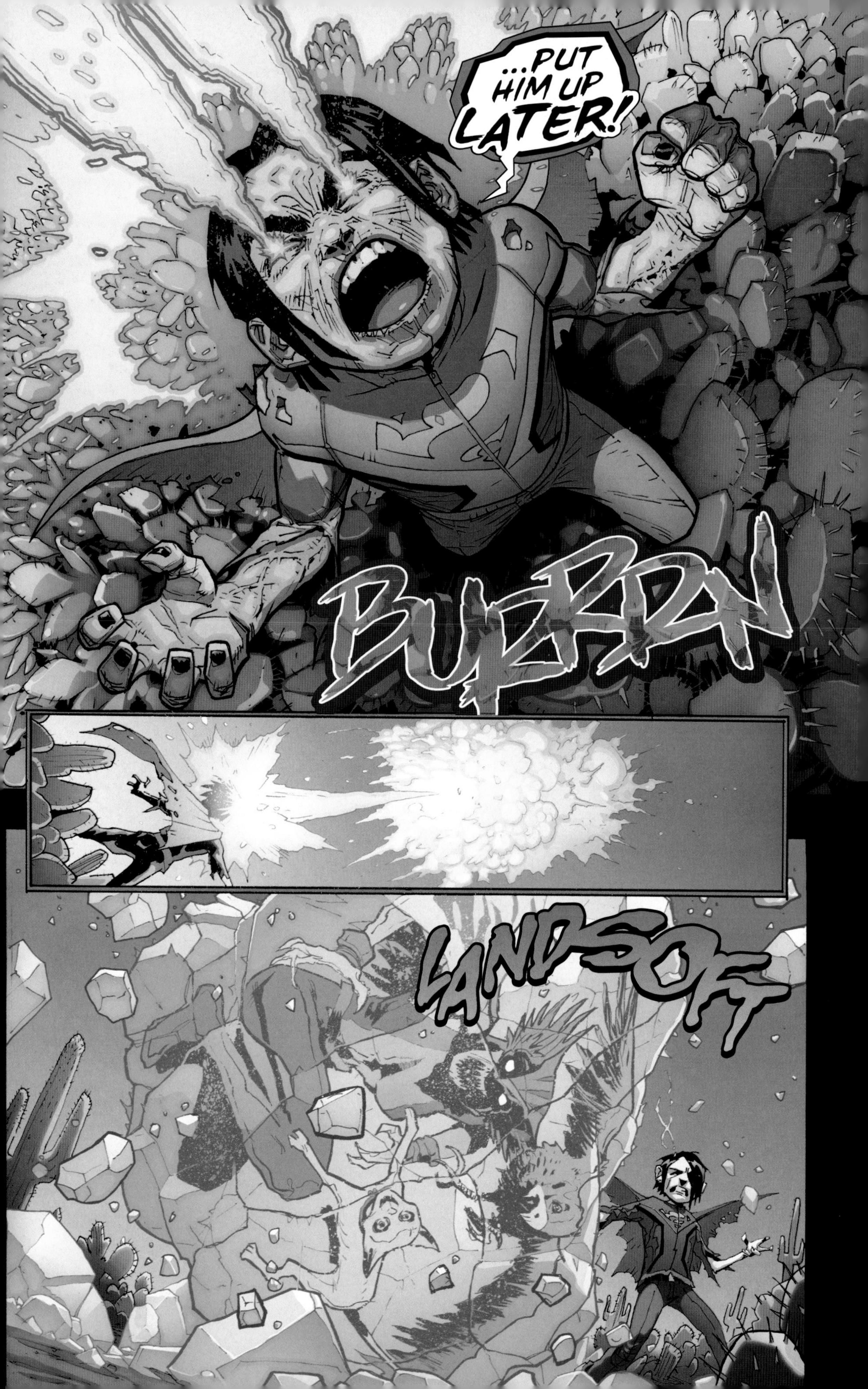
...PUT HIM UP LATER!
BURRN
LANDSOFT

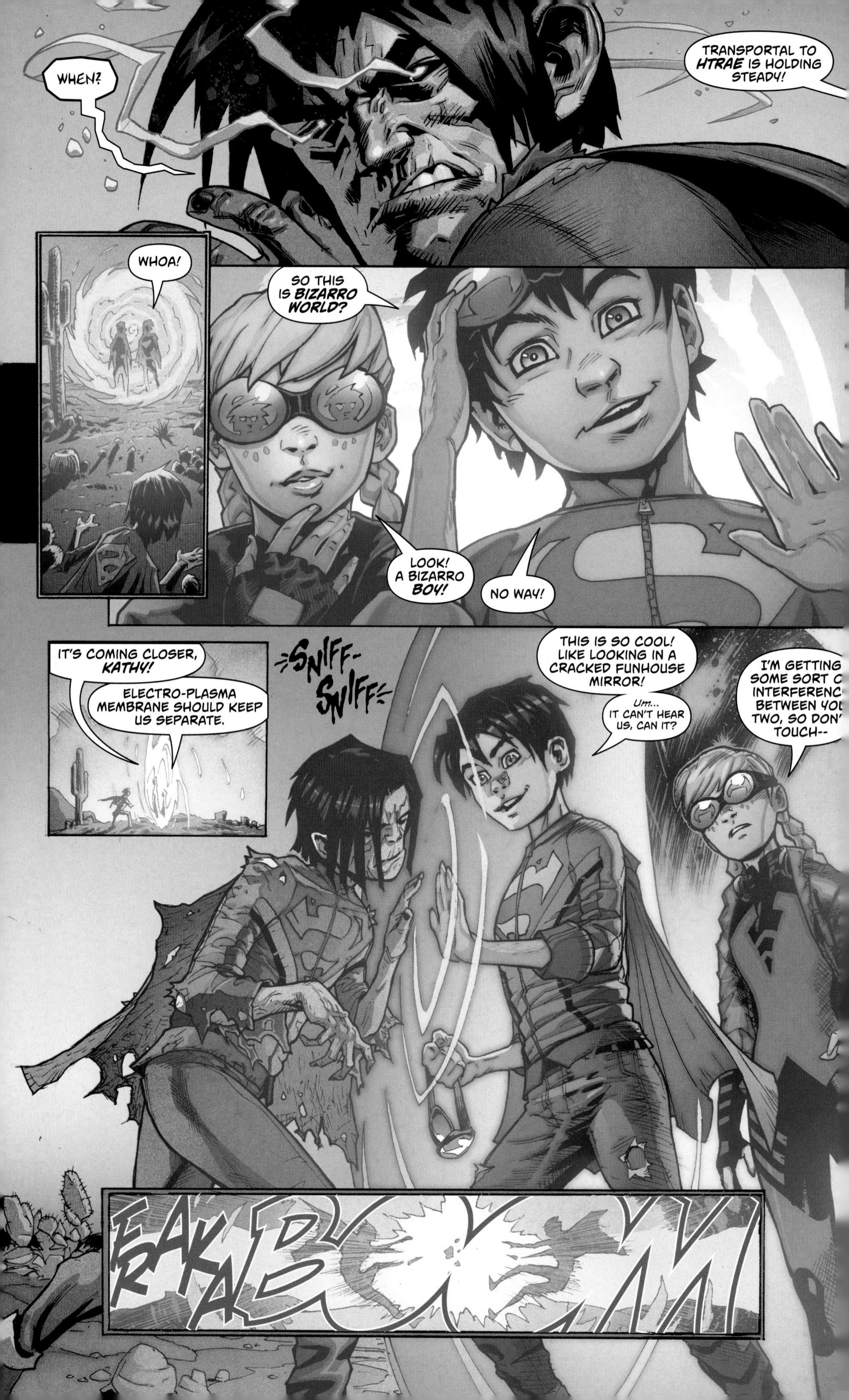
WHEN?
TRANSPORTAL TO HTRAE IS HOLDING STEADY!
WHOA!
SO THIS IS BIZARRO WORLD?
LOOK! A BIZARRO BOY!
NO WAY!
IT'S COMING CLOSER, KATHY!
ELECTRO-PLASMA MEMBRANE SHOULD KEEP US SEPARATE.
SNIFF-SNIFF
THIS IS SO COOL! LIKE LOOKING IN A CRACKED FUNHOUSE MIRROR!
Um... IT CAN'T HEAR US, CAN IT?
I'M GETTING SOME SORT O INTERFERENC BETWEEN YOU TWO, SO DON' TOUCH--
KRAKABOOM

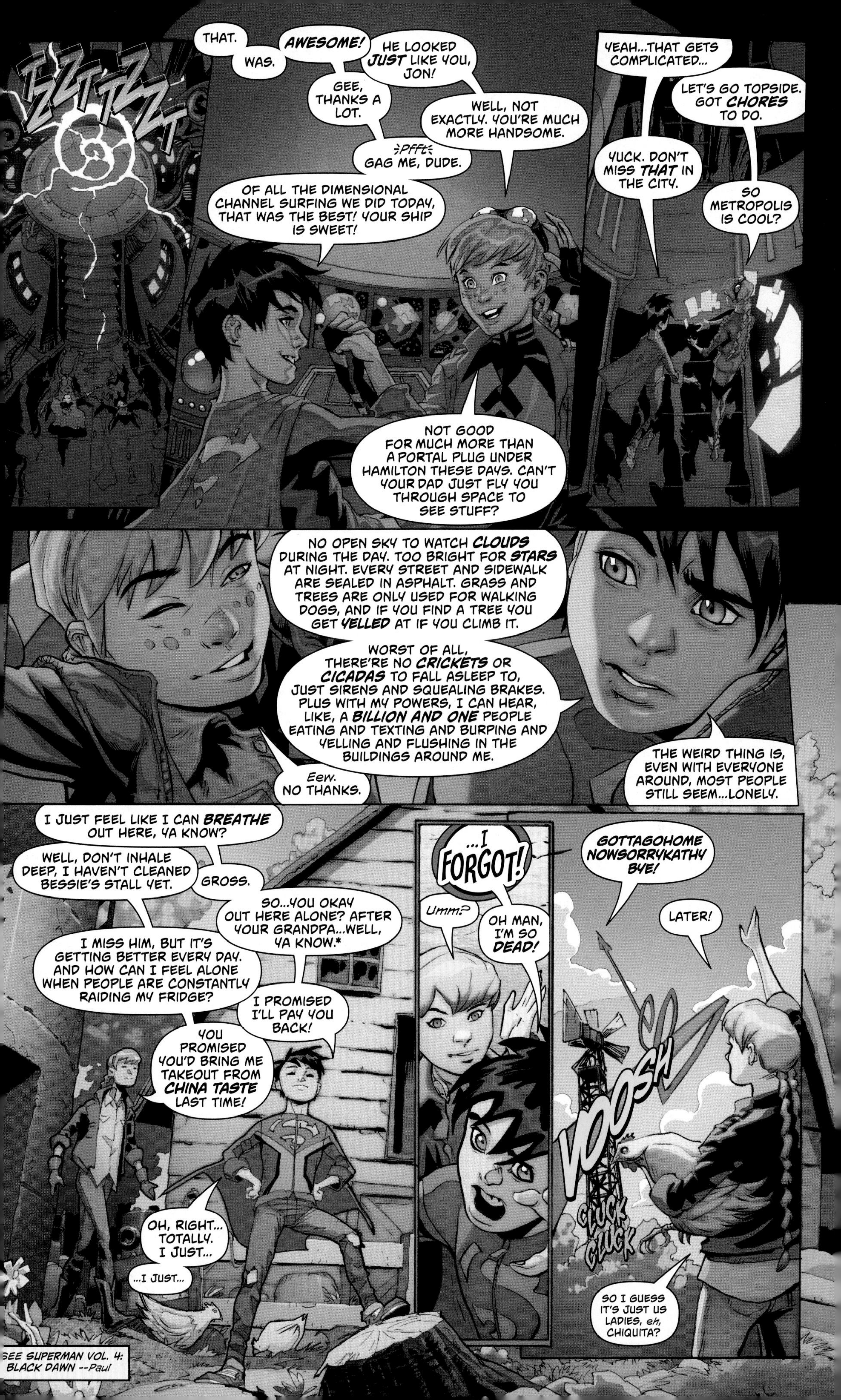
TZZT TZZT
THAT.
WAS.
AWESOME!
HE LOOKED JUST LIKE YOU, JON!
GEE, THANKS A LOT.
WELL, NOT EXACTLY. YOU'RE MUCH MORE HANDSOME.
PFFT GAG ME, DUDE.
OF ALL THE DIMENSIONAL CHANNEL SURFING WE DID TODAY, THAT WAS THE BEST! YOUR SHIP IS SWEET!
NOT GOOD FOR MUCH MORE THAN A PORTAL PLUG UNDER HAMILTON THESE DAYS. CAN'T YOUR DAD JUST FLY YOU THROUGH SPACE TO SEE STUFF?
YEAH...THAT GETS COMPLICATED...
LET'S GO TOPSIDE. GOT CHORES TO DO.
YUCK. DON'T MISS THAT IN THE CITY.
SO METROPOLIS IS COOL?
NO OPEN SKY TO WATCH CLOUDS DURING THE DAY. TOO BRIGHT FOR STARS AT NIGHT. EVERY STREET AND SIDEWALK ARE SEALED IN ASPHALT. GRASS AND TREES ARE ONLY USED FOR WALKING DOGS, AND IF YOU FIND A TREE YOU GET YELLED AT IF YOU CLIMB IT.
WORST OF ALL, THERE'RE NO CRICKETS OR CICADAS TO FALL ASLEEP TO, JUST SIRENS AND SQUEALING BRAKES. PLUS WITH MY POWERS, I CAN HEAR, LIKE, A BILLION AND ONE PEOPLE EATING AND TEXTING AND BURPING AND YELLING AND FLUSHING IN THE BUILDINGS AROUND ME.
Eew. NO THANKS.
THE WEIRD THING IS, EVEN WITH EVERYONE AROUND, MOST PEOPLE STILL SEEM...LONELY.
I JUST FEEL LIKE I CAN BREATHE OUT HERE, YA KNOW?
WELL, DON'T INHALE DEEP, I HAVEN'T CLEANED BESSIE'S STALL YET.
GROSS.
SO...YOU OKAY OUT HERE ALONE? AFTER YOUR GRANDPA...WELL, YA KNOW.*
I MISS HIM, BUT IT'S GETTING BETTER EVERY DAY. AND HOW CAN I FEEL ALONE WHEN PEOPLE ARE CONSTANTLY RAIDING MY FRIDGE?
I PROMISED I'LL PAY YOU BACK!
YOU PROMISED YOU'D BRING ME TAKEOUT FROM CHINA TASTE LAST TIME!
OH, RIGHT... TOTALLY. I JUST...
...I JUST...
...I FORGOT!
Umm?
OH MAN, I'M SO DEAD!
GOTTAGOHOME NOWSORRYKATHY BYE!
LATER!
VOOSH
CLUCK CLUCK
SO I GUESS IT'S JUST US LADIES, eh, CHIQUITA?
*SEE SUPERMAN VOL. 4: BLACK DAWN --Paul

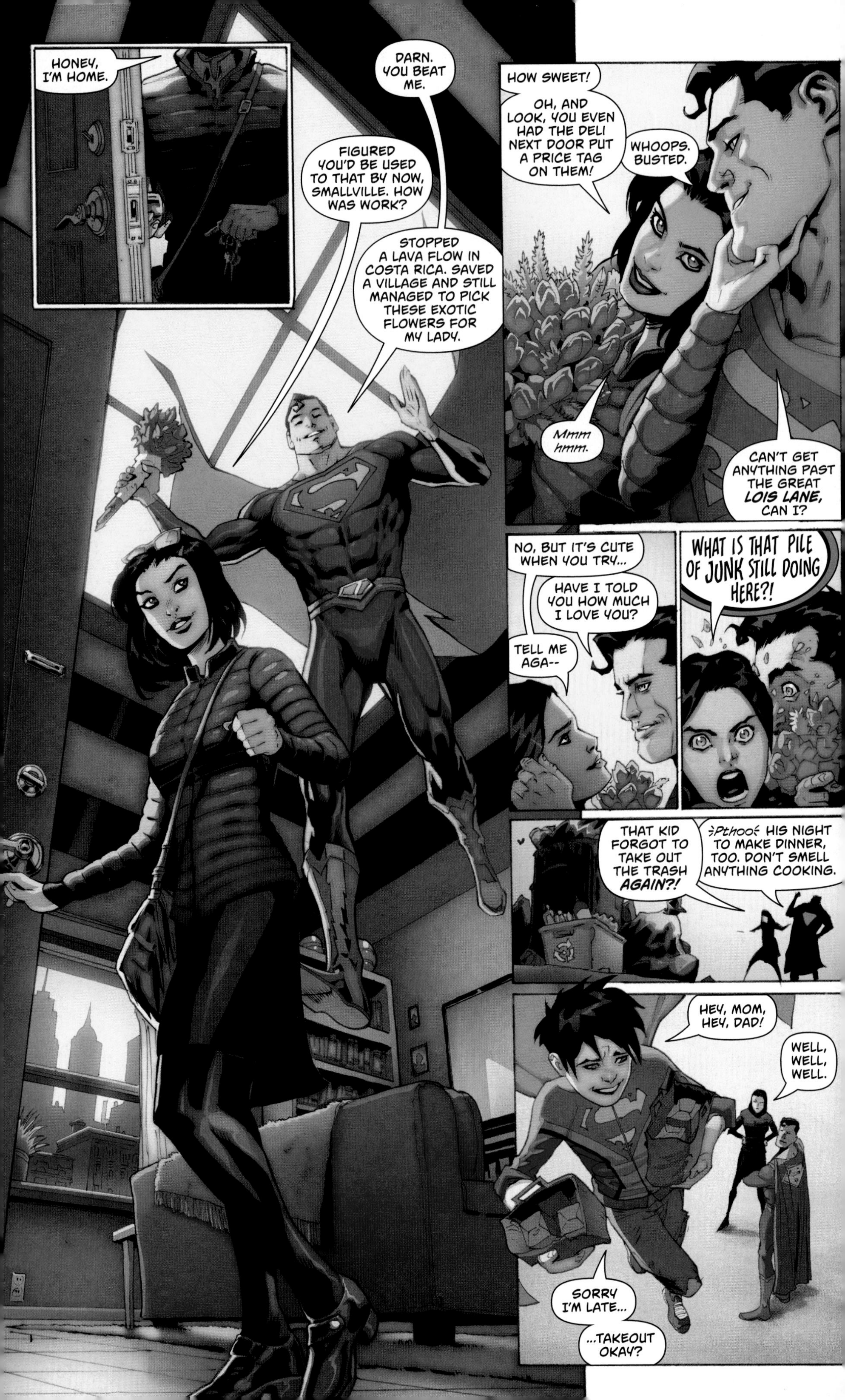

HONEY, I'M HOME.
DARN. YOU BEAT ME.
FIGURED YOU'D BE USED TO THAT BY NOW, SMALLVILLE. HOW WAS WORK?
STOPPED A LAVA FLOW IN COSTA RICA. SAVED A VILLAGE AND STILL MANAGED TO PICK THESE EXOTIC FLOWERS FOR MY LADY.
HOW SWEET!
OH, AND LOOK, YOU EVEN HAD THE DELI NEXT DOOR PUT A PRICE TAG ON THEM!
WHOOPS. BUSTED.
Mmm hmm.
CAN'T GET ANYTHING PAST THE GREAT LOIS LANE, CAN I?
NO, BUT IT'S CUTE WHEN YOU TRY...
HAVE I TOLD YOU HOW MUCH I LOVE YOU?
TELL ME AGA--
WHAT IS THAT PILE OF JUNK STILL DOING HERE?!
THAT KID FORGOT TO TAKE OUT THE TRASH AGAIN?!
Pthoo HIS NIGHT TO MAKE DINNER, TOO. DON'T SMELL ANYTHING COOKING.
HEY, MOM, HEY, DAD!
WELL, WELL, WELL.
SORRY I'M LATE...
...TAKEOUT OKAY?

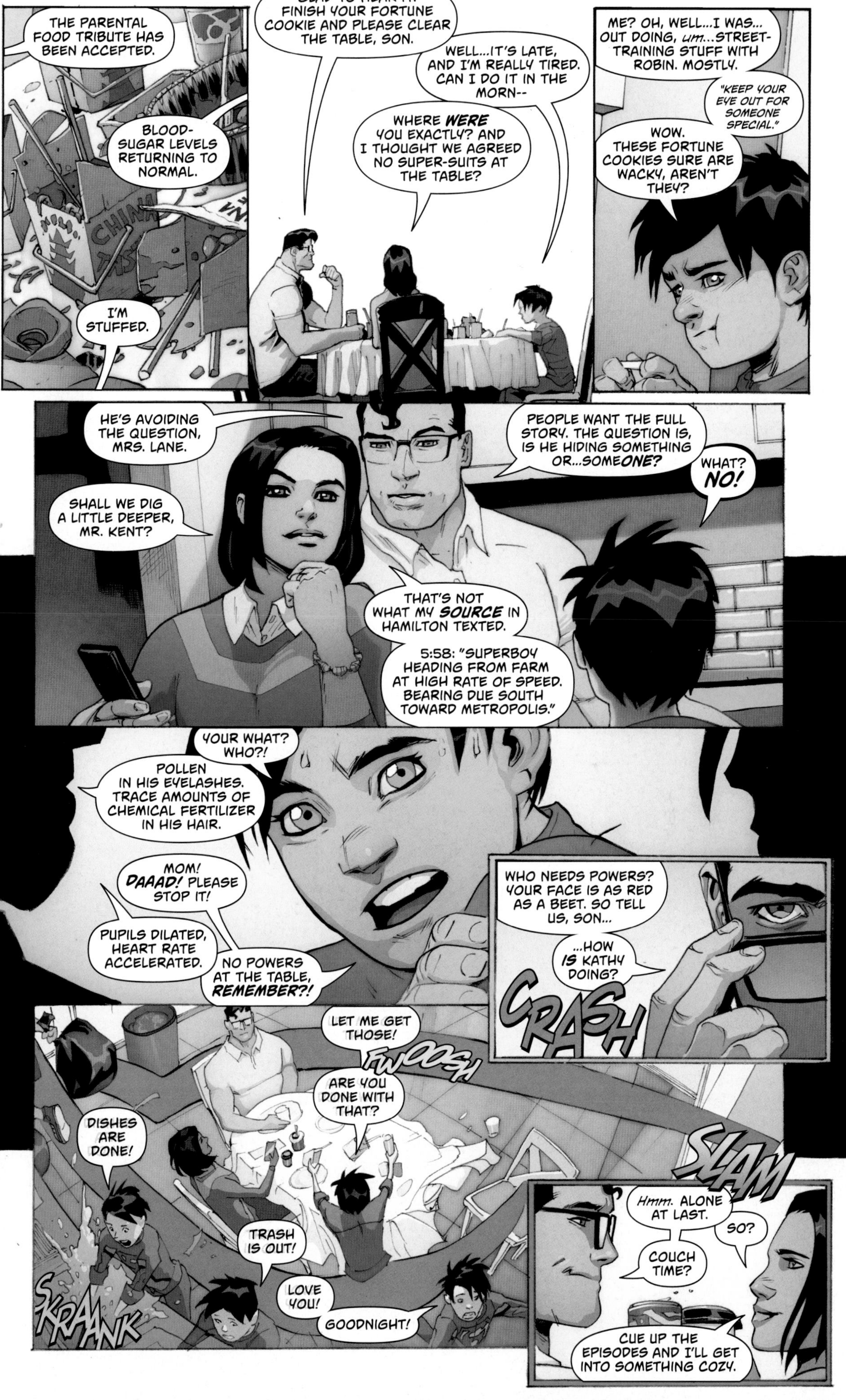
THE PARENTAL FOOD TRIBUTE HAS BEEN ACCEPTED.
BLOOD-SUGAR LEVELS RETURNING TO NORMAL.
I'M STUFFED.
GLAD TO HEAR IT. FINISH YOUR FORTUNE COOKIE AND PLEASE CLEAR THE TABLE, SON.
WELL...IT'S LATE, AND I'M REALLY TIRED. CAN I DO IT IN THE MORN--
WHERE *WERE* YOU EXACTLY? AND I THOUGHT WE AGREED NO SUPER-SUITS AT THE TABLE?
ME? OH, WELL...I WAS... OUT DOING, *um*...STREET-TRAINING STUFF WITH ROBIN. MOSTLY.
"KEEP YOUR EYE OUT FOR SOMEONE SPECIAL."
WOW. THESE FORTUNE COOKIES SURE ARE WACKY, AREN'T THEY?
HE'S AVOIDING THE QUESTION, MRS. LANE.
PEOPLE WANT THE FULL STORY. THE QUESTION IS, IS HE HIDING SOMETHING OR...SOME*ONE?*
WHAT? **NO!**
SHALL WE DIG A LITTLE DEEPER, MR. KENT?
THAT'S NOT WHAT MY **SOURCE** IN HAMILTON TEXTED.
5:58: "SUPERBOY HEADING FROM FARM AT HIGH RATE OF SPEED. BEARING DUE SOUTH TOWARD METROPOLIS."
YOUR WHAT? WHO?!
POLLEN IN HIS EYELASHES. TRACE AMOUNTS OF CHEMICAL FERTILIZER IN HIS HAIR.
MOM! ***DAAAD!*** PLEASE STOP IT!
PUPILS DILATED, HEART RATE ACCELERATED.
NO POWERS AT THE TABLE, ***REMEMBER?!***
WHO NEEDS POWERS? YOUR FACE IS AS RED AS A BEET. SO TELL US, SON...
...HOW *IS* KATHY DOING?
CRASH
LET ME GET THOSE!
FWOOSH
ARE YOU DONE WITH THAT?
DISHES ARE DONE!
TRASH IS OUT!
LOVE YOU!
GOODNIGHT!
SKRAAANK
SLAM
Hmm. ALONE AT LAST.
SO?
COUCH TIME?
CUE UP THE EPISODES AND I'LL GET INTO SOMETHING COZY.

Green.

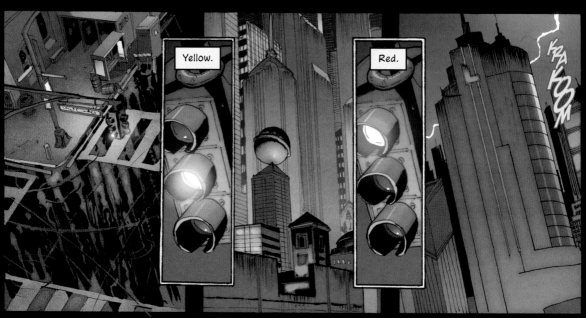

Yellow.

Red.

KRA KOOM

One sheep.

Two sheep.

Three sheep.

Four.

≥Sigh≤

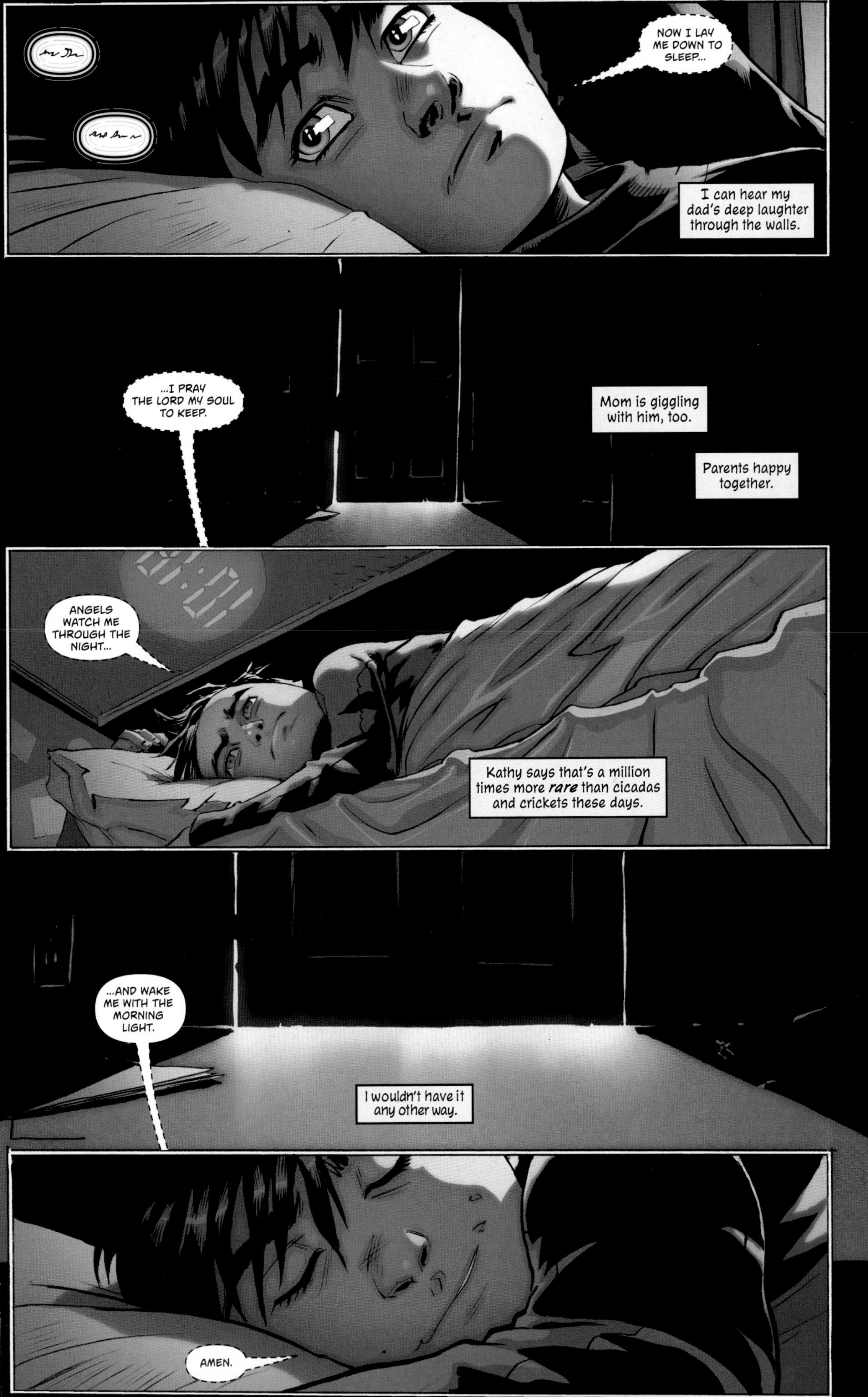
NOW I LAY ME DOWN TO SLEEP...
I can hear my dad's deep laughter through the walls.
...I PRAY THE LORD MY SOUL TO KEEP.
Mom is giggling with him, too.
Parents happy together.
ANGELS WATCH ME THROUGH THE NIGHT...
Kathy says that's a million times more *rare* than cicadas and crickets these days.
...AND WAKE ME WITH THE MORNING LIGHT.
I wouldn't have it any other way.
AMEN.

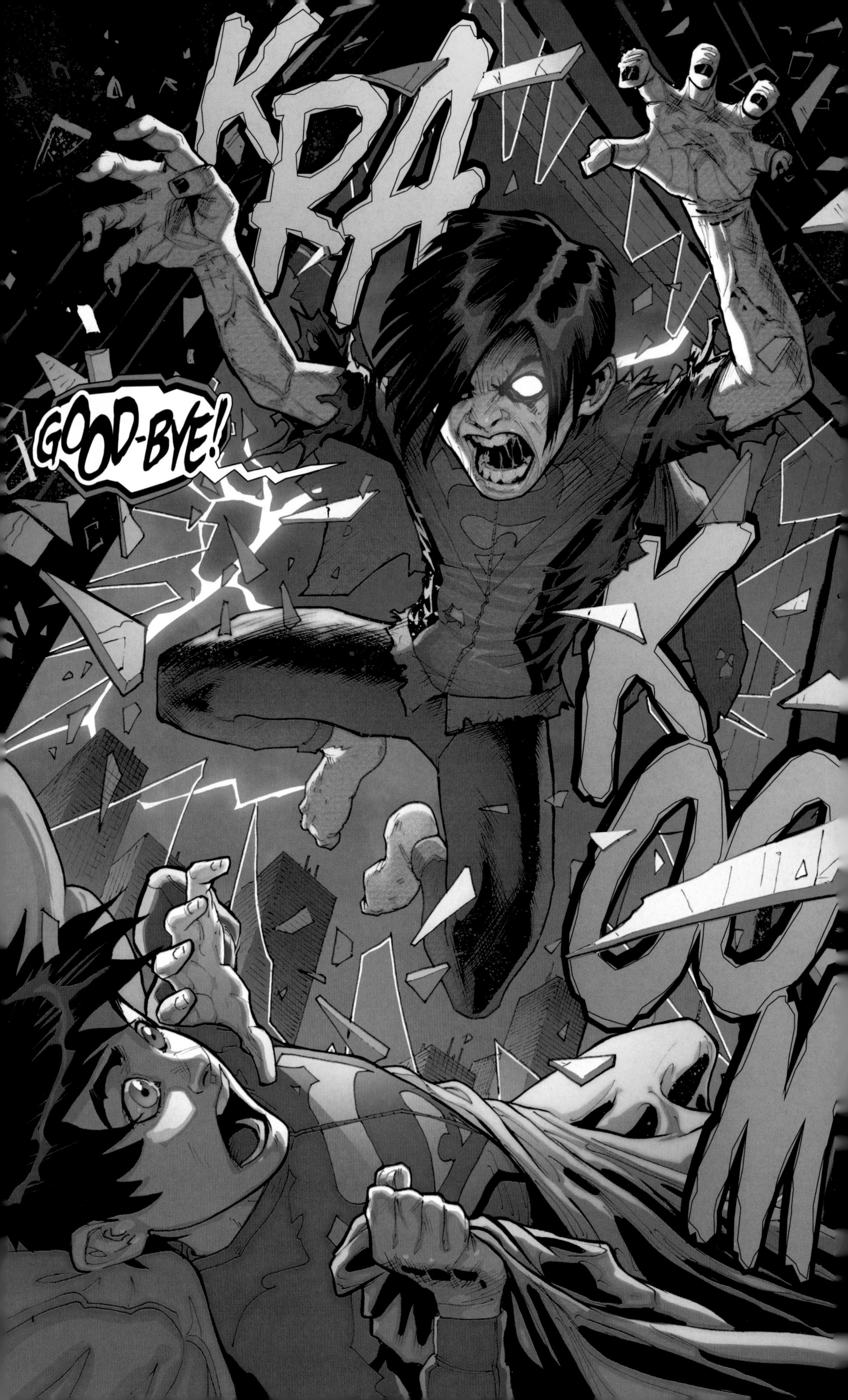
KRA
GOOD-BYE!
KOOM

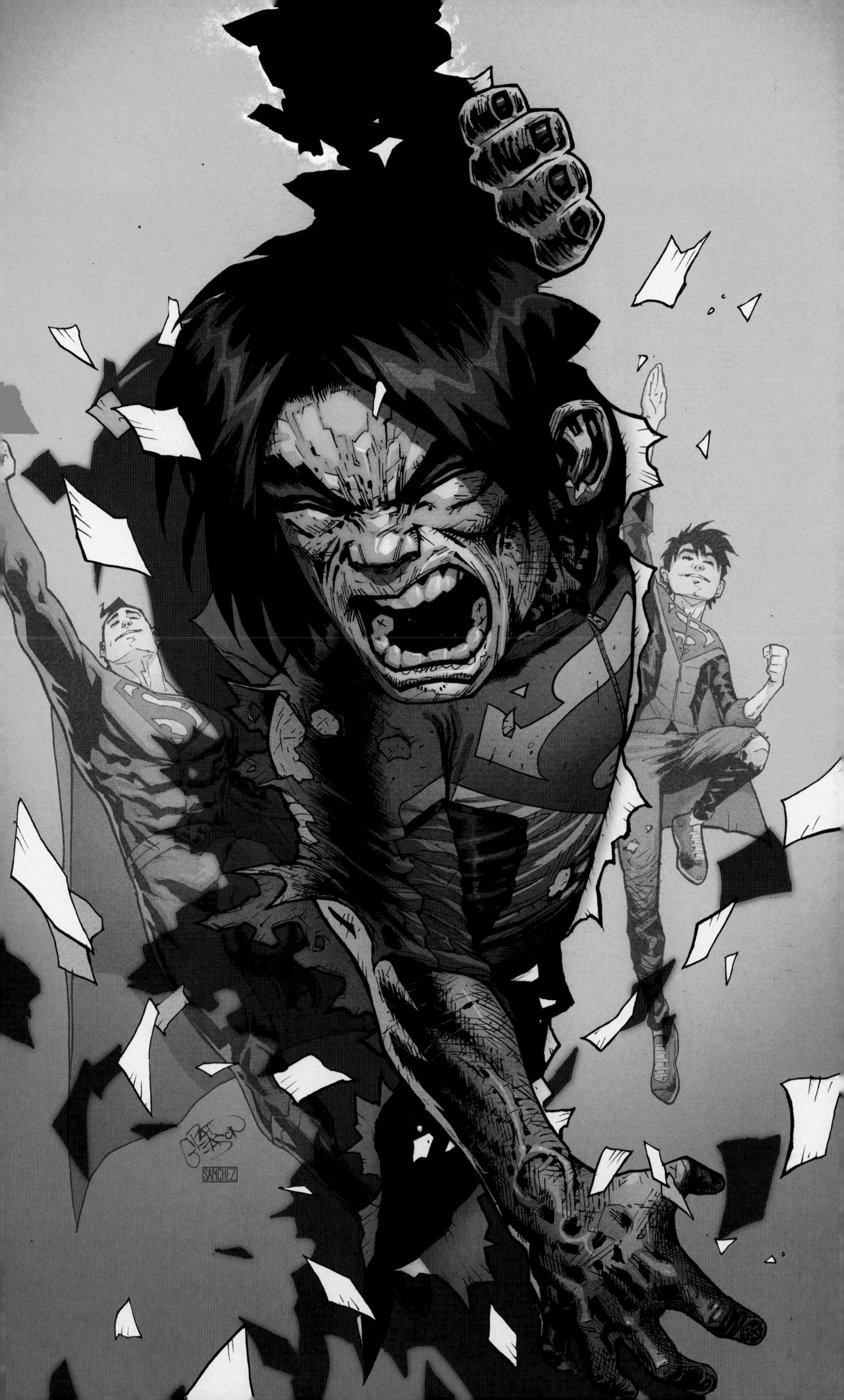
SÁNCHEZ

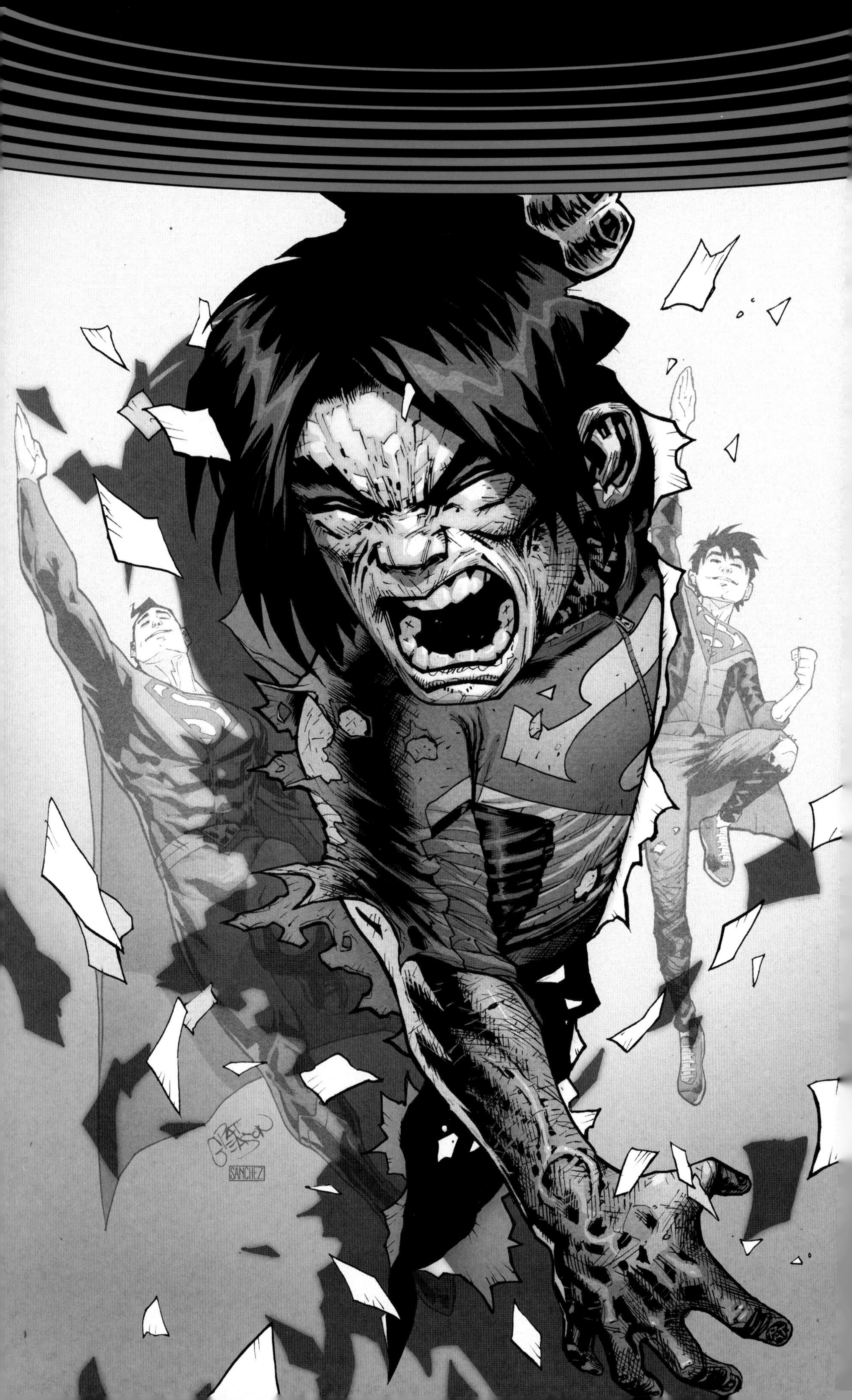
SANCHEZ

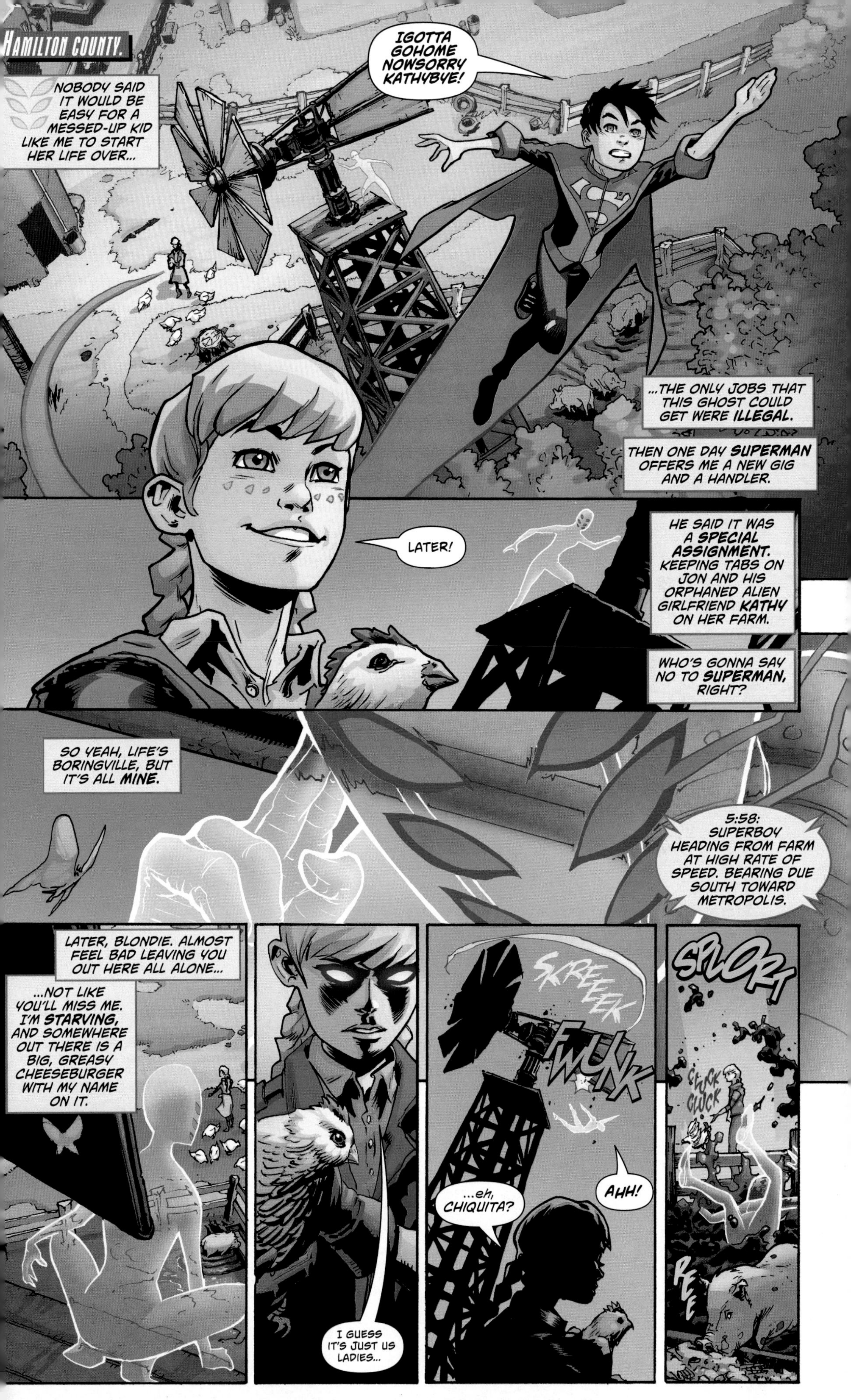
HAMILTON COUNTY.
NOBODY SAID IT WOULD BE EASY FOR A MESSED-UP KID LIKE ME TO START HER LIFE OVER...
IGOTTA GOHOME NOWSORRY KATHYBYE!
...THE ONLY JOBS THAT THIS GHOST COULD GET WERE ILLEGAL.
THEN ONE DAY SUPERMAN OFFERS ME A NEW GIG AND A HANDLER.
LATER!
HE SAID IT WAS A SPECIAL ASSIGNMENT. KEEPING TABS ON JON AND HIS ORPHANED ALIEN GIRLFRIEND KATHY ON HER FARM.
WHO'S GONNA SAY NO TO SUPERMAN, RIGHT?
SO YEAH, LIFE'S BORINGVILLE, BUT IT'S ALL MINE.
5:58: SUPERBOY HEADING FROM FARM AT HIGH RATE OF SPEED. BEARING DUE SOUTH TOWARD METROPOLIS.
LATER, BLONDIE. ALMOST FEEL BAD LEAVING YOU OUT HERE ALL ALONE...
...NOT LIKE YOU'LL MISS ME. I'M STARVING, AND SOMEWHERE OUT THERE IS A BIG, GREASY CHEESEBURGER WITH MY NAME ON IT.
I GUESS IT'S JUST US LADIES...
SKREEEEK
FWUNK
...eh, CHIQUITA?
AHH!
SPLORT
CLUCK CLUCK
REE

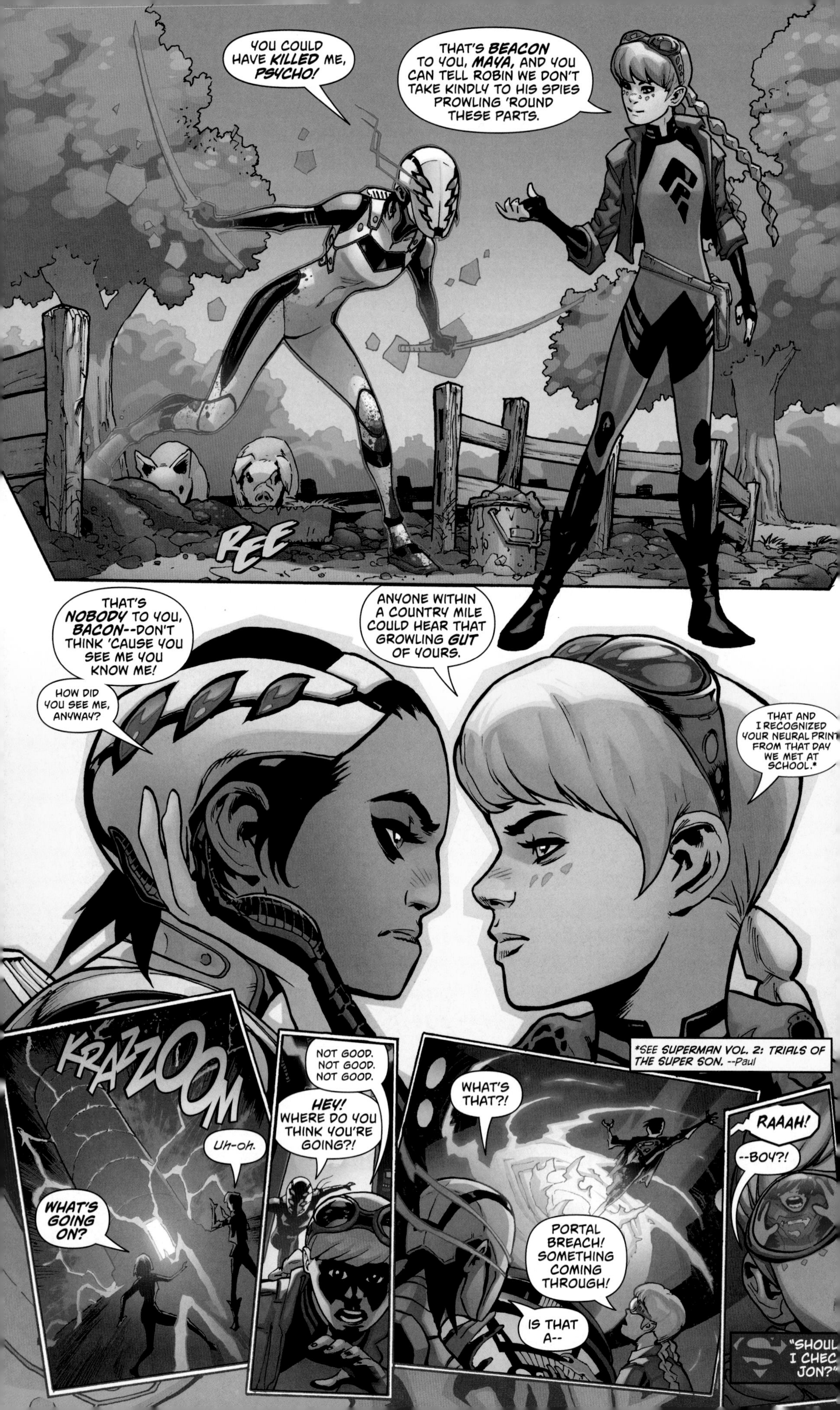

YOU COULD HAVE KILLED ME, PSYCHO!
THAT'S BEACON TO YOU, MAYA, AND YOU CAN TELL ROBIN WE DON'T TAKE KINDLY TO HIS SPIES PROWLING 'ROUND THESE PARTS.
REE
THAT'S NOBODY TO YOU, BACON--DON'T THINK 'CAUSE YOU SEE ME YOU KNOW ME!
HOW DID YOU SEE ME, ANYWAY?
ANYONE WITHIN A COUNTRY MILE COULD HEAR THAT GROWLING GUT OF YOURS.
THAT AND I RECOGNIZED YOUR NEURAL PRINT FROM THAT DAY WE MET AT SCHOOL.*
*SEE SUPERMAN VOL. 2: TRIALS OF THE SUPER SON. --Paul
KRAZZOOM
Uh-oh.
WHAT'S GOING ON?
NOT GOOD. NOT GOOD. NOT GOOD.
HEY! WHERE DO YOU THINK YOU'RE GOING?!
WHAT'S THAT?!
PORTAL BREACH! SOMETHING COMING THROUGH!
IS THAT A--
RAAAH!
--BOY?!
"SHOUL I CHEC JON?"

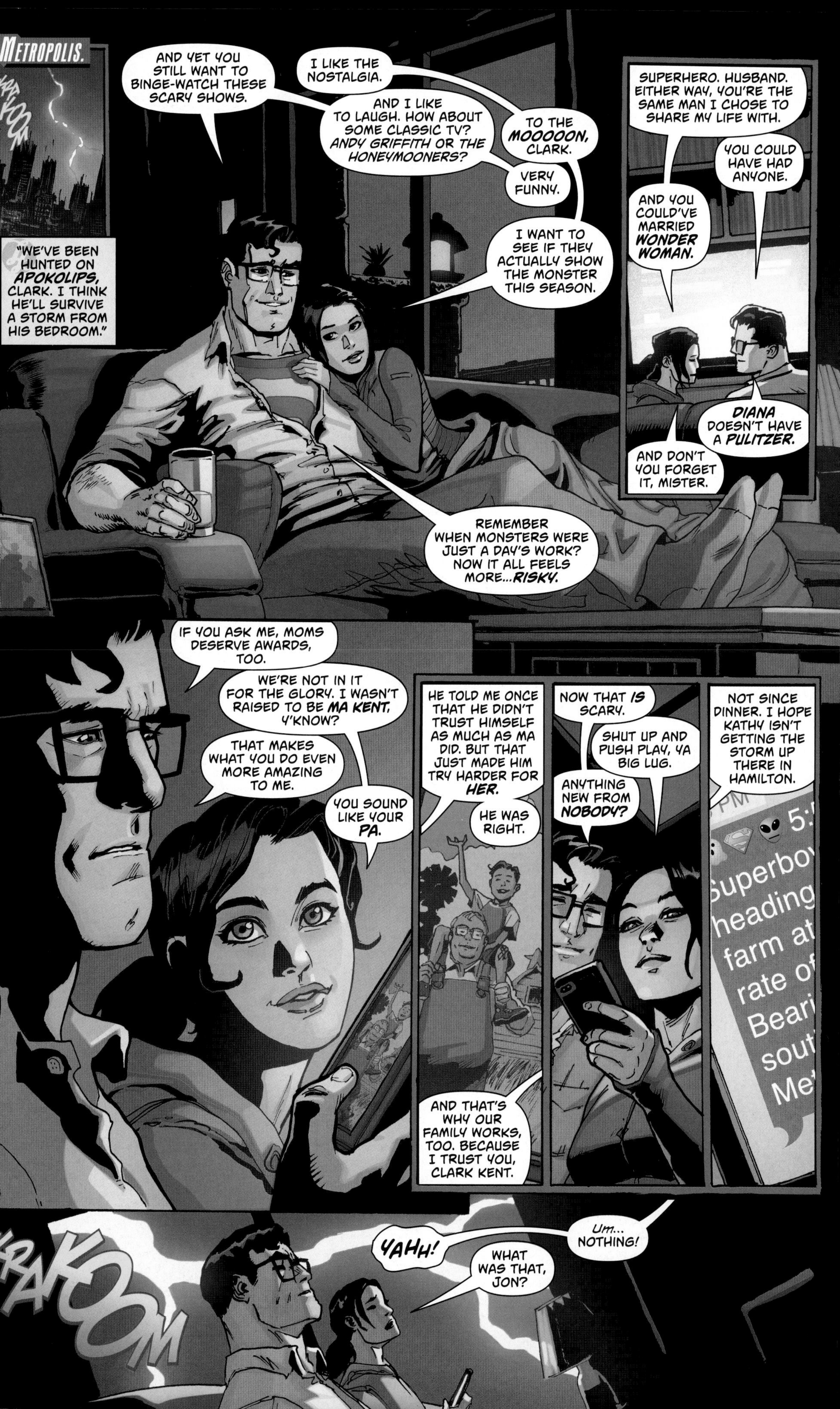

METROPOLIS.
"WE'VE BEEN HUNTED ON APOKOLIPS, CLARK. I THINK HE'LL SURVIVE A STORM FROM HIS BEDROOM."
REMEMBER WHEN MONSTERS WERE JUST A DAY'S WORK? NOW IT ALL FEELS MORE...RISKY.
AND YET YOU STILL WANT TO BINGE-WATCH THESE SCARY SHOWS.
I LIKE THE NOSTALGIA.
AND I LIKE TO LAUGH. HOW ABOUT SOME CLASSIC TV? ANDY GRIFFITH OR THE HONEYMOONERS?
TO THE MOOOOON, CLARK.
VERY FUNNY.
I WANT TO SEE IF THEY ACTUALLY SHOW THE MONSTER THIS SEASON.
SUPERHERO. HUSBAND. EITHER WAY, YOU'RE THE SAME MAN I CHOSE TO SHARE MY LIFE WITH.
YOU COULD HAVE HAD ANYONE.
AND YOU COULD'VE MARRIED WONDER WOMAN.
DIANA DOESN'T HAVE A PULITZER.
AND DON'T YOU FORGET IT, MISTER.
IF YOU ASK ME, MOMS DESERVE AWARDS, TOO.
WE'RE NOT IN IT FOR THE GLORY. I WASN'T RAISED TO BE MA KENT, Y'KNOW?
THAT MAKES WHAT YOU DO EVEN MORE AMAZING TO ME.
YOU SOUND LIKE YOUR PA.
HE TOLD ME ONCE THAT HE DIDN'T TRUST HIMSELF AS MUCH AS MA DID. BUT THAT JUST MADE HIM TRY HARDER FOR HER.
HE WAS RIGHT.
AND THAT'S WHY OUR FAMILY WORKS, TOO. BECAUSE I TRUST YOU, CLARK KENT.
NOW THAT IS SCARY.
SHUT UP AND PUSH PLAY, YA BIG LUG.
ANYTHING NEW FROM NOBODY?
NOT SINCE DINNER. I HOPE KATHY ISN'T GETTING THE STORM UP THERE IN HAMILTON.
KRAKOOM
YAHH!
WHAT WAS THAT, JON?
Um... NOTHING!

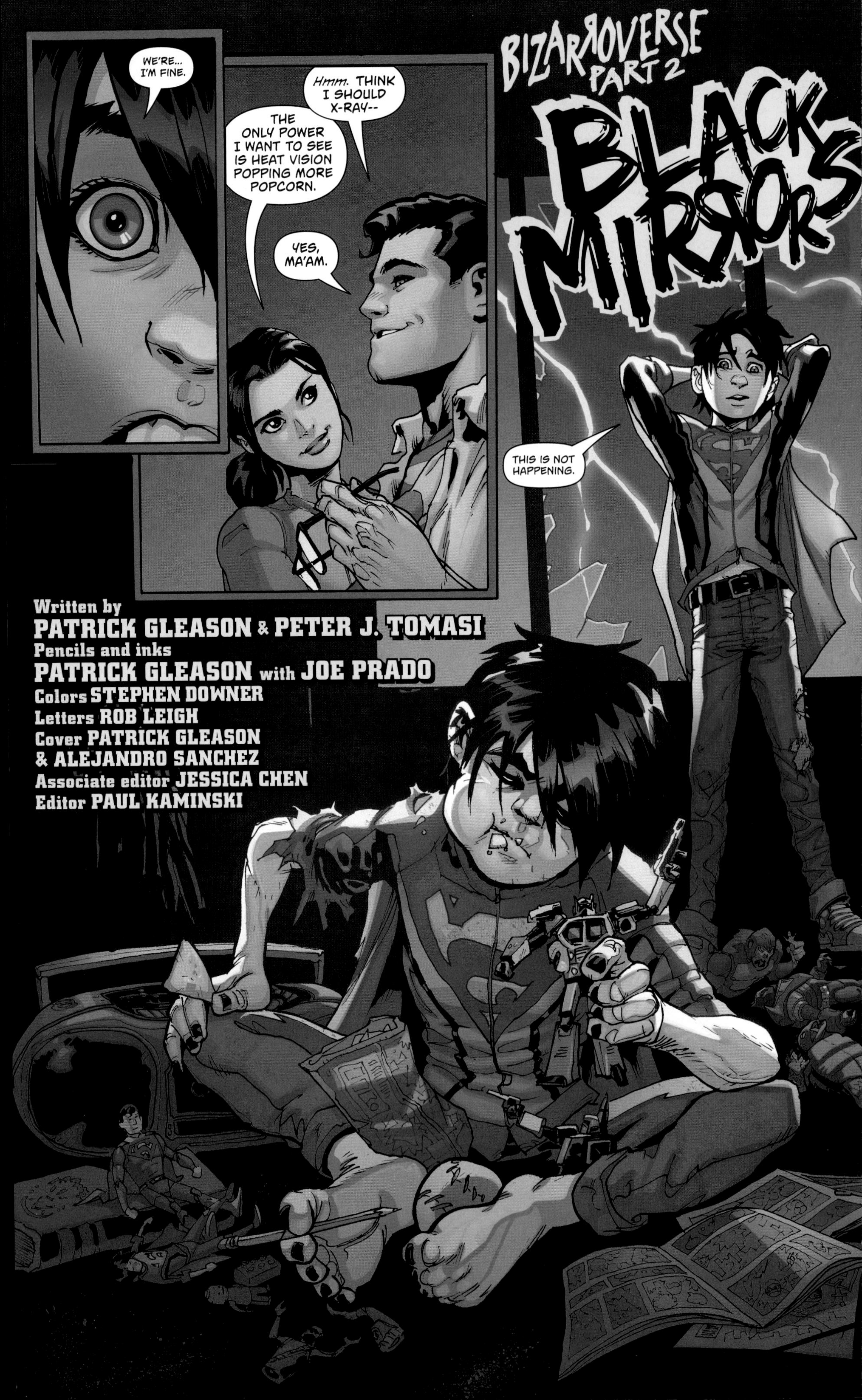
BIZARROVERSE PART 2
BLACK MIRRORS
WE'RE... I'M FINE.
Hmm. THINK I SHOULD X-RAY--
THE ONLY POWER I WANT TO SEE IS HEAT VISION POPPING MORE POPCORN.
YES, MA'AM.
THIS IS NOT HAPPENING.
Written by
PATRICK GLEASON & PETER J. TOMASI
Pencils and inks
PATRICK GLEASON with JOE PRADO
Colors STEPHEN DOWNER
Letters ROB LEIGH
Cover PATRICK GLEASON & ALEJANDRO SANCHEZ
Associate editor JESSICA CHEN
Editor PAUL KAMINSKI

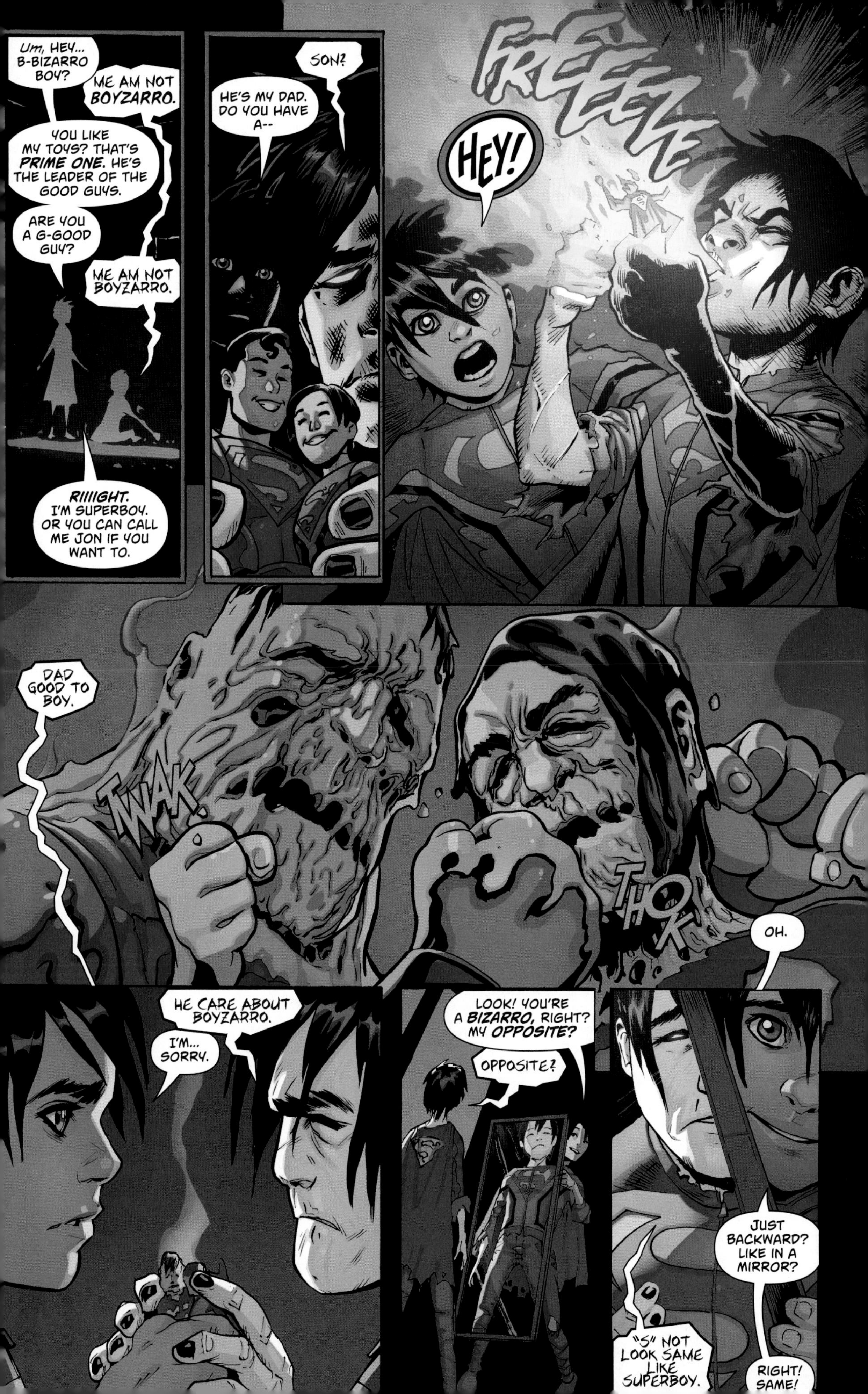
Um, HEY... B-BIZARRO BOY?
ME AM NOT BOYZARRO.
YOU LIKE MY TOYS? THAT'S PRIME ONE. HE'S THE LEADER OF THE GOOD GUYS.
ARE YOU A G-GOOD GUY?
ME AM NOT BOYZARRO.
RIIIIGHT. I'M SUPERBOY. OR YOU CAN CALL ME JON IF YOU WANT TO.
SON?
HE'S MY DAD. DO YOU HAVE A--
FREEEZE
HEY!
DAD GOOD TO BOY.
TWAK
THOK
OH.
HE CARE ABOUT BOYZARRO.
I'M... SORRY.
LOOK! YOU'RE A BIZARRO, RIGHT? MY OPPOSITE?
OPPOSITE?
JUST BACKWARD? LIKE IN A MIRROR?
"S" NOT LOOK SAME LIKE SUPERBOY.
RIGHT! SAME!

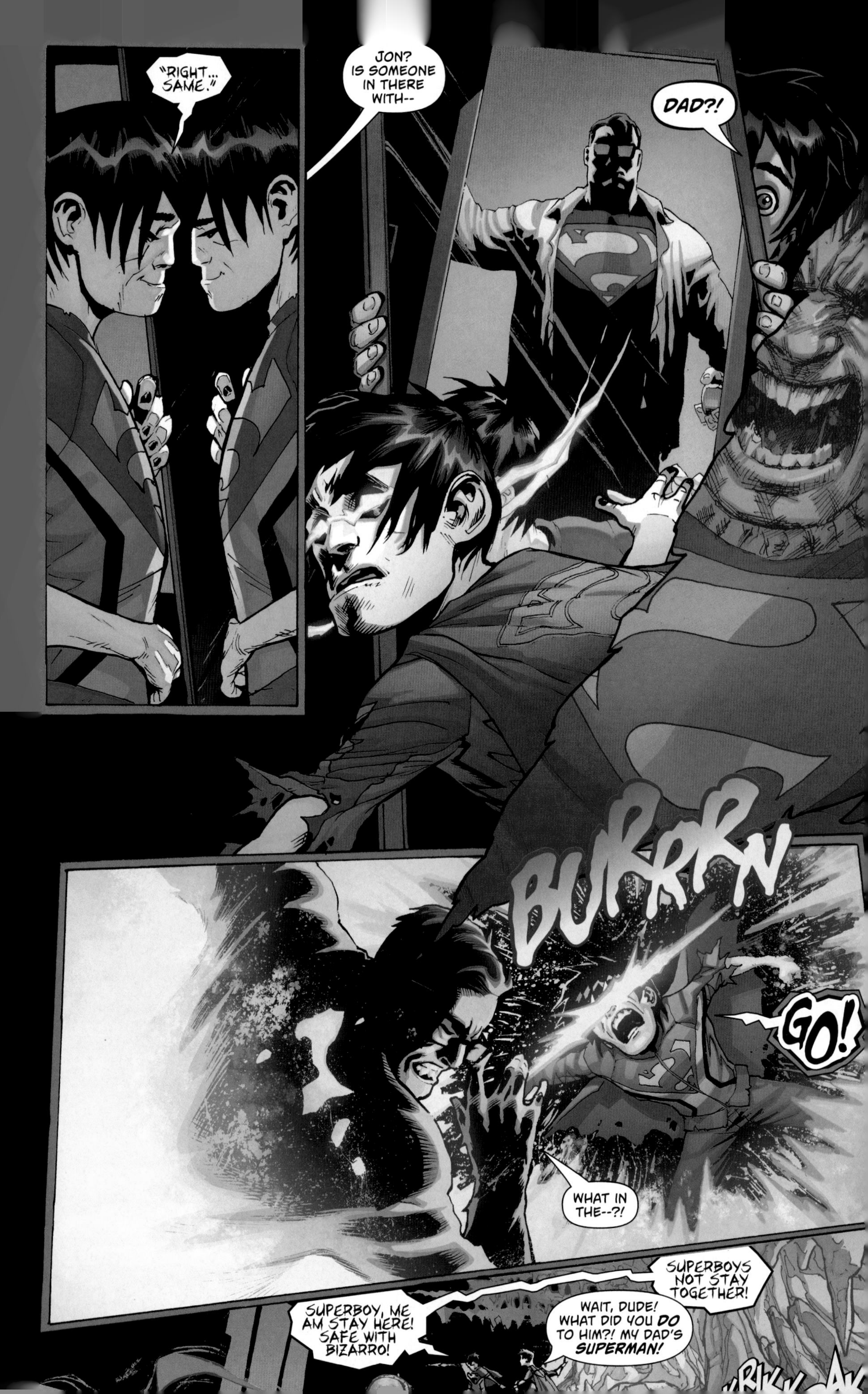
"RIGHT... SAME."
JON? IS SOMEONE IN THERE WITH--
DAD?!
BURRRN
GO!
WHAT IN THE--?!
SUPERBOYS NOT STAY TOGETHER!
SUPERBOY, ME AM STAY HERE! SAFE WITH BIZARRO!
WAIT, DUDE! WHAT DID YOU DO TO HIM?! MY DAD'S SUPERMAN!

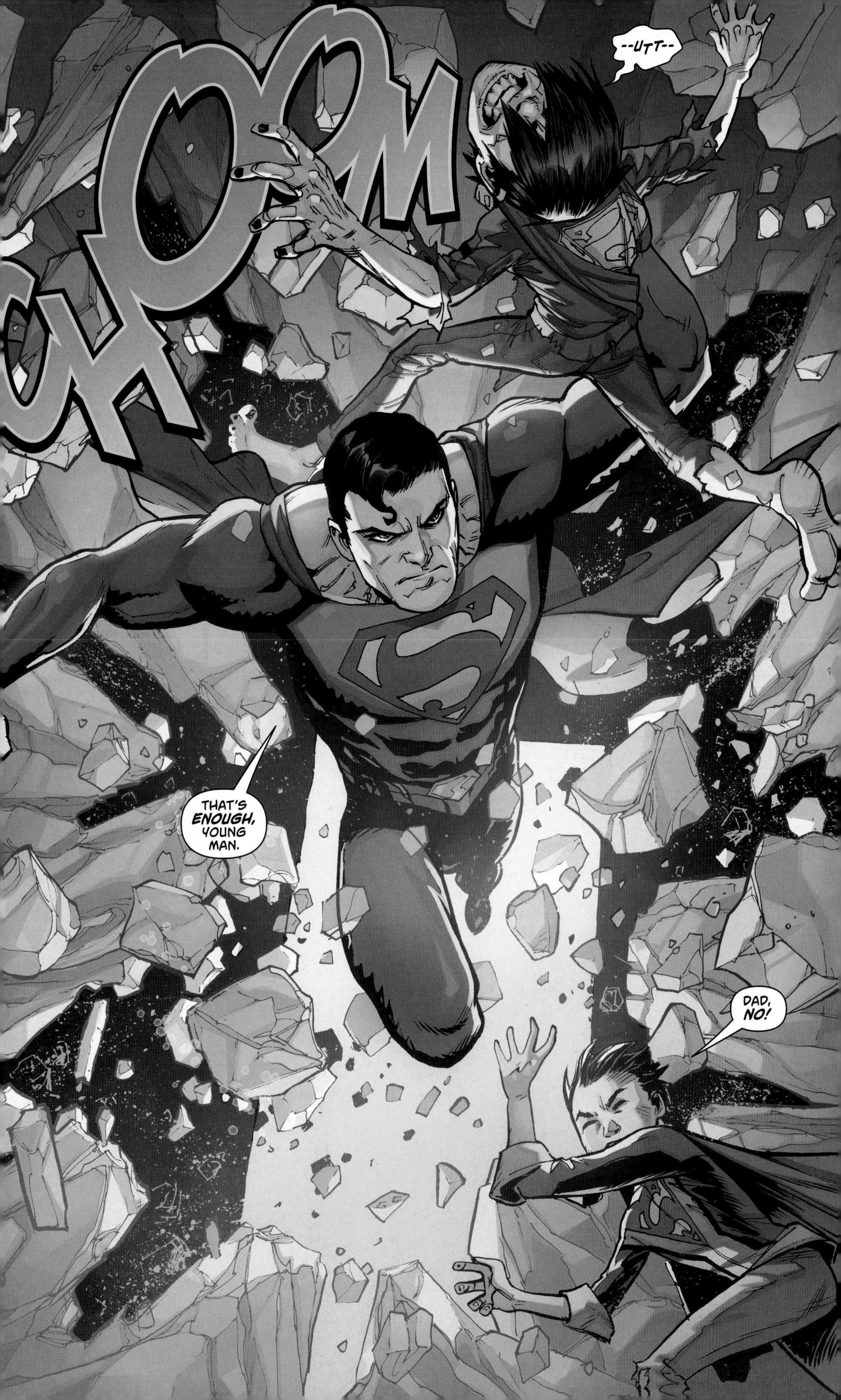
CHOOM
--UTT--
THAT'S ENOUGH, YOUNG MAN.
DAD, NO!

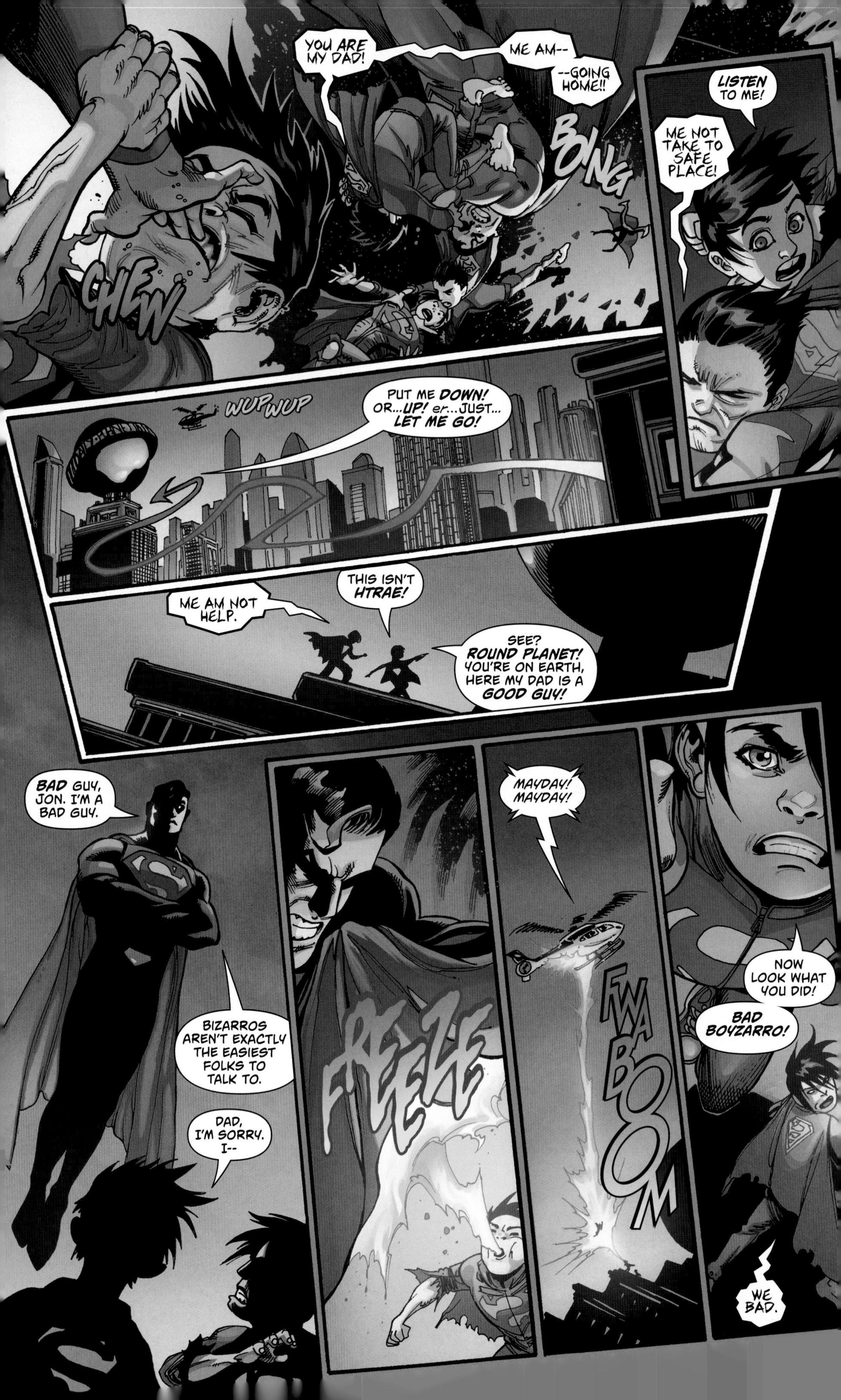
CHEW
YOU ARE MY DAD!
ME AM--
--GOING HOME!!
BOING
LISTEN TO ME!
ME NOT TAKE TO SAFE PLACE!
WUP WUP
PUT ME DOWN! OR...UP! er...JUST... LET ME GO!
ME AM NOT HELP.
THIS ISN'T HTRAE!
SEE? ROUND PLANET! YOU'RE ON EARTH, HERE MY DAD IS A GOOD GUY!
BAD GUY, JON. I'M A BAD GUY.
BIZARROS AREN'T EXACTLY THE EASIEST FOLKS TO TALK TO.
DAD, I'M SORRY. I--
FREEZE
MAYDAY! MAYDAY!
FWABOOM
NOW LOOK WHAT YOU DID!
BAD BOYZARRO!
WE BAD.

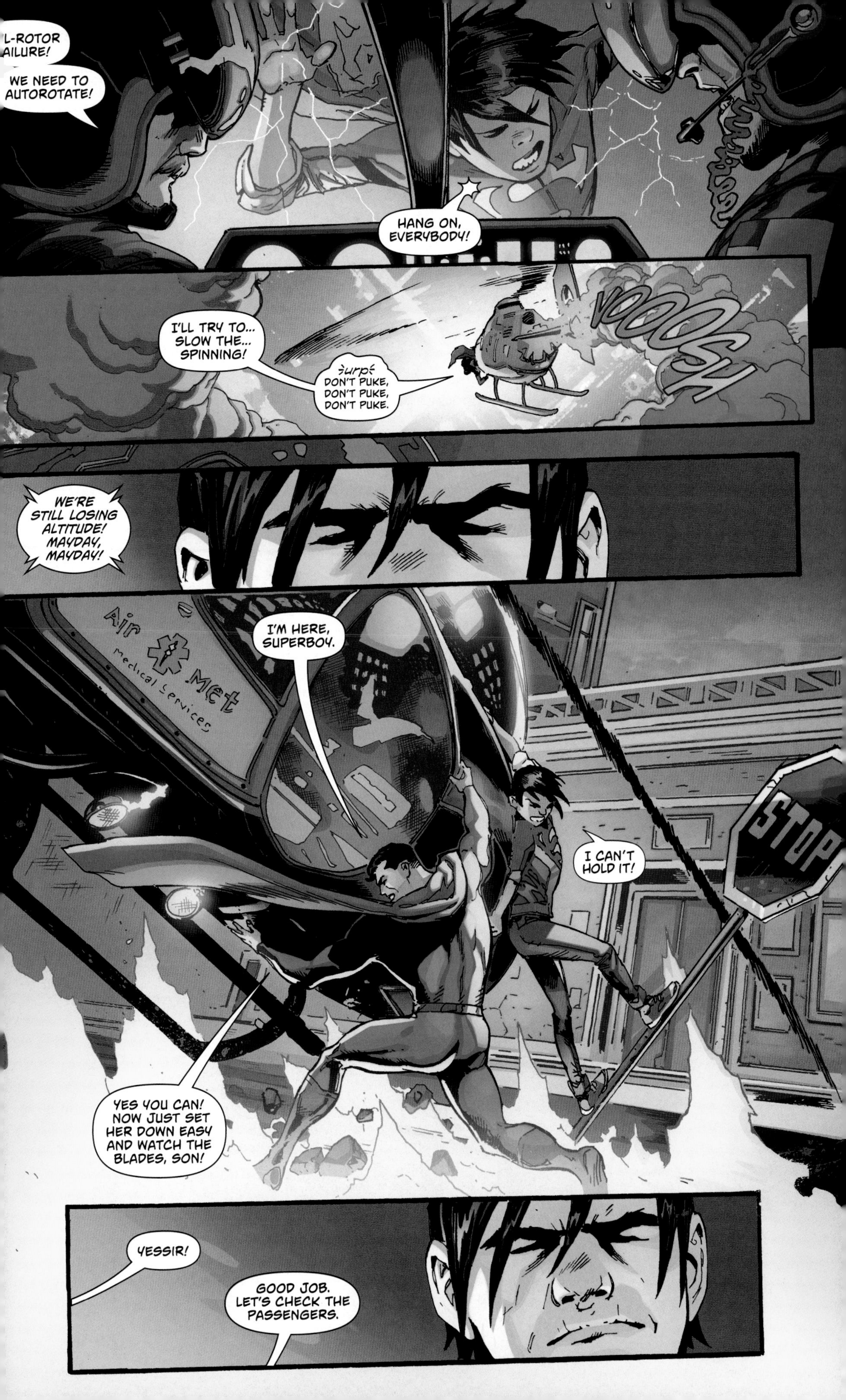
L-ROTOR
AILURE!
WE NEED TO AUTOROTATE!
HANG ON, EVERYBODY!
I'LL TRY TO... SLOW THE... SPINNING!
VOOOSH
urp
DON'T PUKE, DON'T PUKE, DON'T PUKE.
WE'RE STILL LOSING ALTITUDE! MAYDAY, MAYDAY!
Air Met
Medical Services
I'M HERE, SUPERBOY.
STOP
I CAN'T HOLD IT!
YES YOU CAN! NOW JUST SET HER DOWN EASY AND WATCH THE BLADES, SON!
YESSIR!
GOOD JOB. LET'S CHECK THE PASSENGERS.

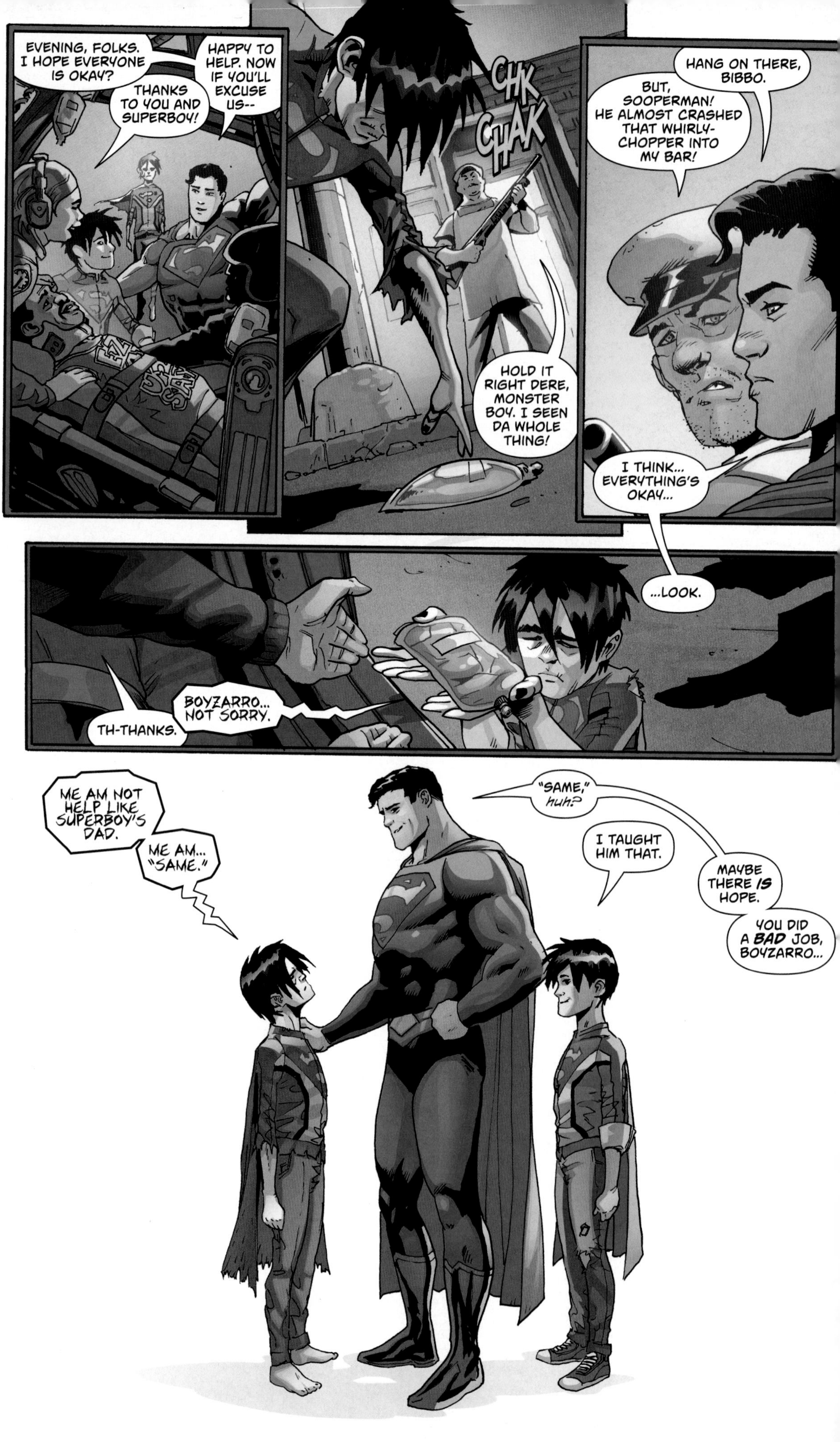
EVENING, FOLKS. I HOPE EVERYONE IS OKAY?
THANKS TO YOU AND SUPERBOY!
HAPPY TO HELP. NOW IF YOU'LL EXCUSE US--
CHK CHAK
HOLD IT RIGHT DERE, MONSTER BOY. I SEEN DA WHOLE THING!
HANG ON THERE, BIBBO.
BUT, SOOPERMAN! HE ALMOST CRASHED THAT WHIRLY-CHOPPER INTO MY BAR!
I THINK... EVERYTHING'S OKAY...
...LOOK.
BOYZARRO... NOT SORRY.
TH-THANKS.
ME AM NOT HELP LIKE SUPERBOY'S DAD.
ME AM... "SAME."
"SAME," huh?
I TAUGHT HIM THAT.
MAYBE THERE IS HOPE.
YOU DID A BAD JOB, BOYZARRO...

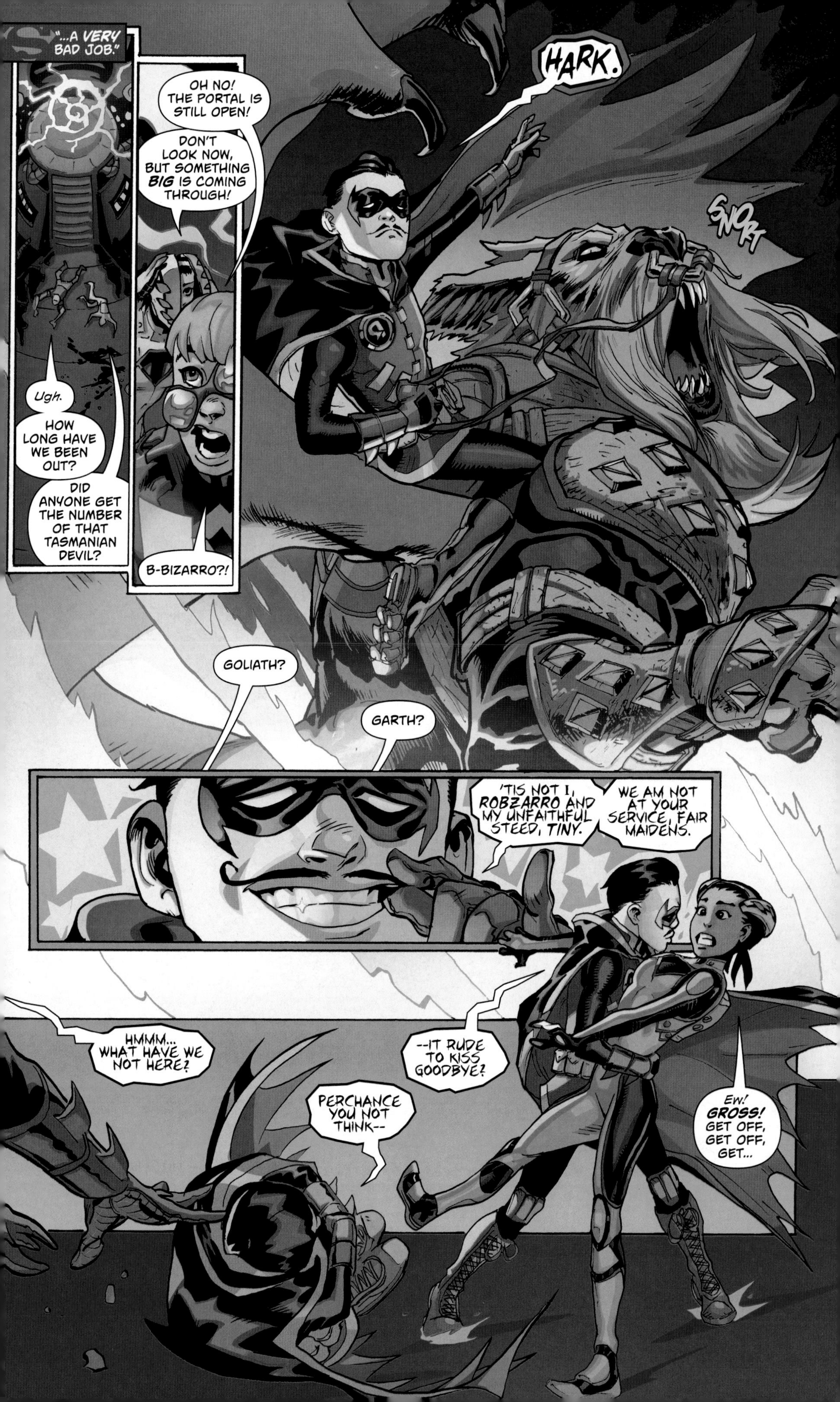
"...A VERY BAD JOB."
HARK.
OH NO! THE PORTAL IS STILL OPEN!
DON'T LOOK NOW, BUT SOMETHING BIG IS COMING THROUGH!
SNORT
Ugh.
HOW LONG HAVE WE BEEN OUT?
DID ANYONE GET THE NUMBER OF THAT TASMANIAN DEVIL?
B-BIZARRO?!
GOLIATH?
GARTH?
'TIS NOT I, ROBZARRO AND MY UNFAITHFUL STEED, TINY.
WE AM NOT AT YOUR SERVICE, FAIR MAIDENS.
HMMM... WHAT HAVE WE NOT HERE?
PERCHANCE YOU NOT THINK--
--IT RUDE TO KISS GOODBYE?
Ew! GROSS! GET OFF, GET OFF, GET...

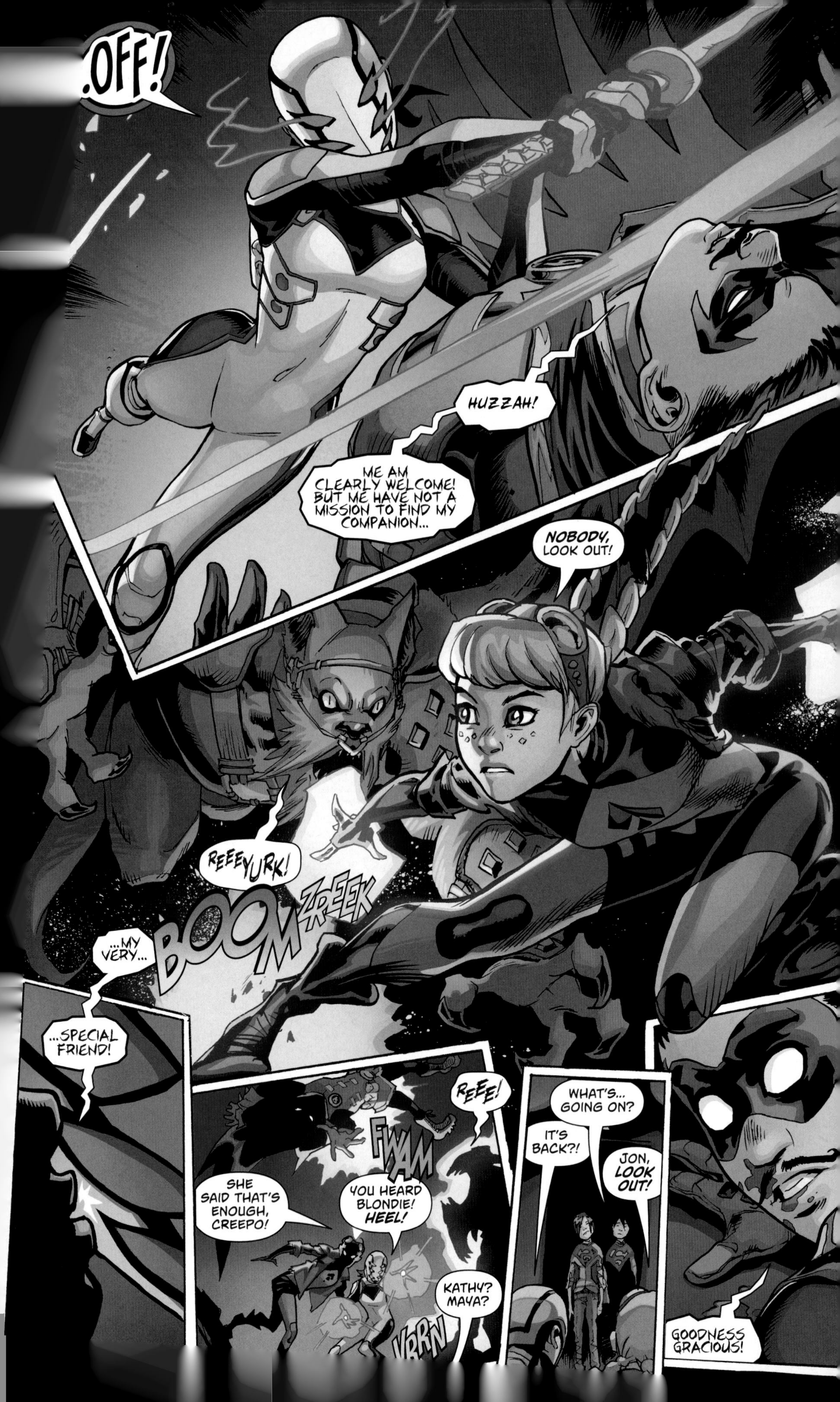

...OFF!
HUZZAH!
ME AM CLEARLY WELCOME! BUT ME HAVE NOT A MISSION TO FIND MY COMPANION...
NOBODY, LOOK OUT!
REEEYURK!
BOOM
ZREEK
...MY VERY...
...SPECIAL FRIEND!
REEE!
FWAM
SHE SAID THAT'S ENOUGH, CREEPO!
YOU HEARD BLONDIE! HEEL!
KATHY? MAYA?
VRRN
WHAT'S... GOING ON?
IT'S BACK?!
JON, LOOK OUT!
GOODNESS GRACIOUS!

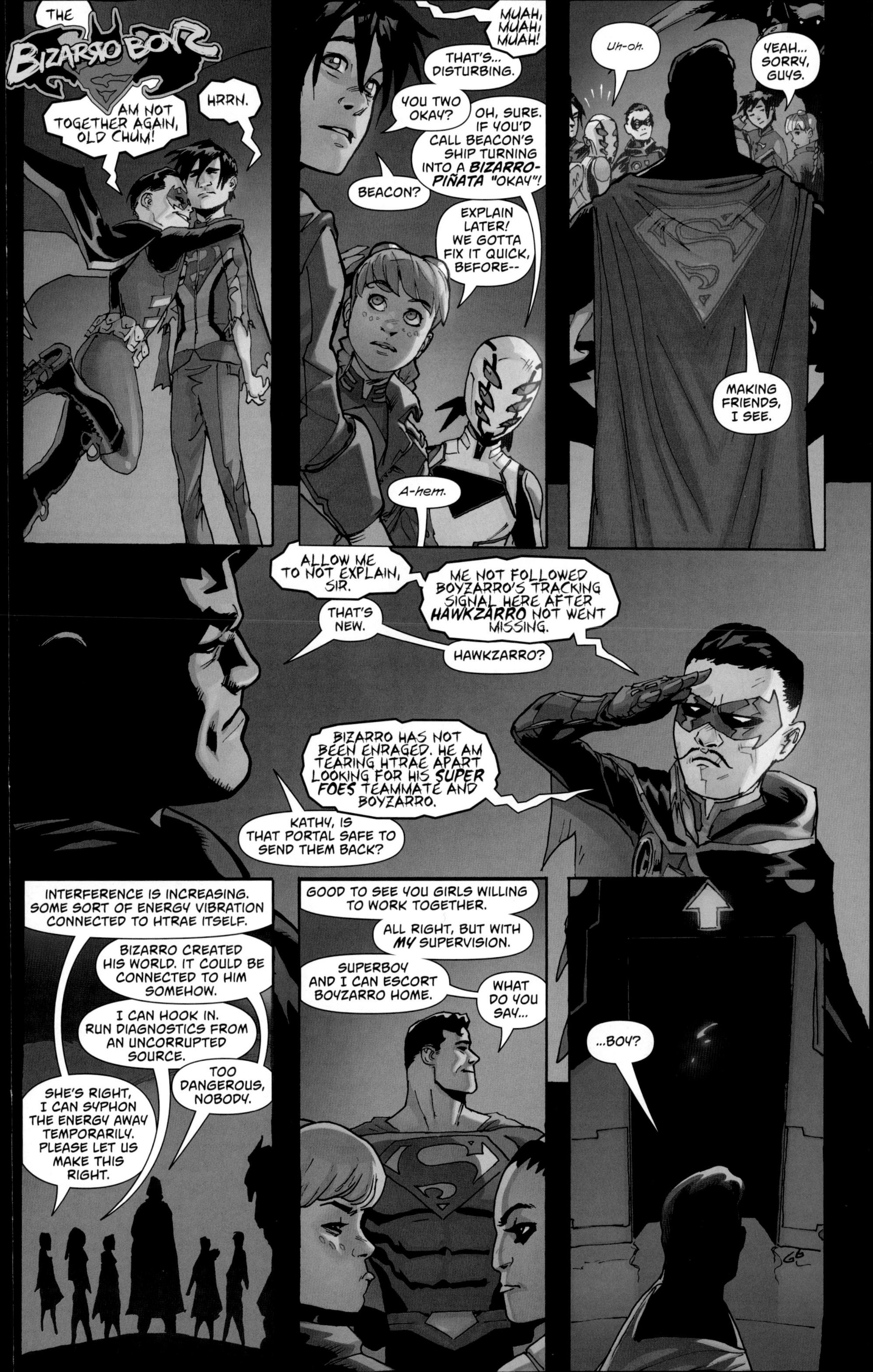
THE
BIZARRO BOYS
AM NOT TOGETHER AGAIN, OLD CHUM!
HRRN.
MUAH, MUAH, MUAH!
THAT'S... DISTURBING.
YOU TWO OKAY?
OH, SURE. IF YOU'D CALL BEACON'S SHIP TURNING INTO A BIZARRO-PIÑATA "OKAY"!
BEACON?
EXPLAIN LATER! WE GOTTA FIX IT QUICK, BEFORE--
A-hem.
Uh-oh.
YEAH... SORRY, GUYS.
MAKING FRIENDS, I SEE.
ALLOW ME TO NOT EXPLAIN, SIR.
ME NOT FOLLOWED BOYZARRO'S TRACKING SIGNAL HERE AFTER HAWKZARRO NOT WENT MISSING.
THAT'S NEW.
HAWKZARRO?
BIZARRO HAS NOT BEEN ENRAGED. HE AM TEARING HTRAE APART LOOKING FOR HIS SUPER FOES TEAMMATE AND BOYZARRO.
KATHY, IS THAT PORTAL SAFE TO SEND THEM BACK?
INTERFERENCE IS INCREASING. SOME SORT OF ENERGY VIBRATION CONNECTED TO HTRAE ITSELF.
BIZARRO CREATED HIS WORLD. IT COULD BE CONNECTED TO HIM SOMEHOW.
I CAN HOOK IN. RUN DIAGNOSTICS FROM AN UNCORRUPTED SOURCE.
TOO DANGEROUS, NOBODY.
SHE'S RIGHT, I CAN SYPHON THE ENERGY AWAY TEMPORARILY. PLEASE LET US MAKE THIS RIGHT.
GOOD TO SEE YOU GIRLS WILLING TO WORK TOGETHER.
ALL RIGHT, BUT WITH MY SUPERVISION.
SUPERBOY AND I CAN ESCORT BOYZARRO HOME.
WHAT DO YOU SAY...
...BOY?

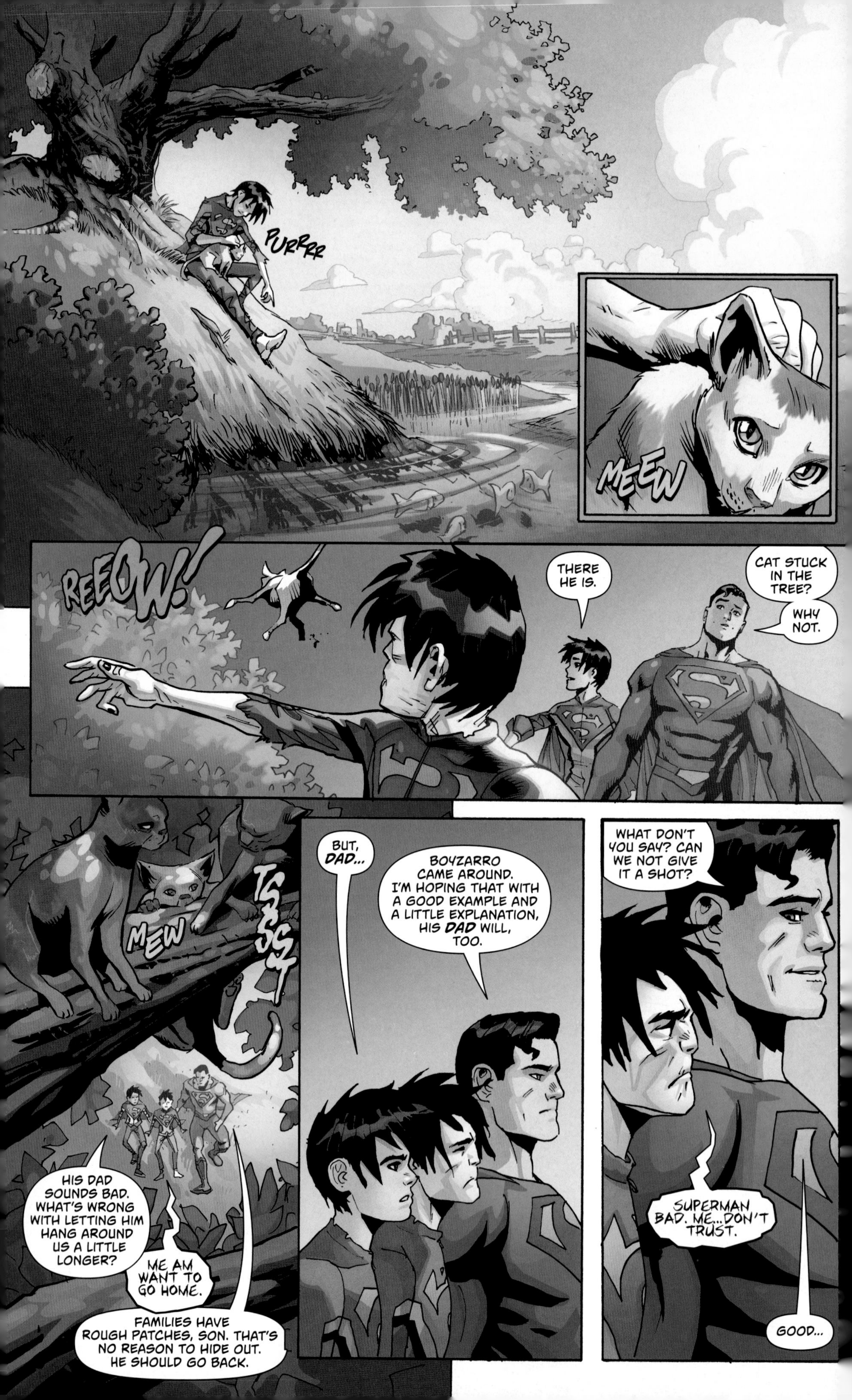
PURRRR
MEEW
REEOW!
THERE HE IS.
CAT STUCK IN THE TREE?
WHY NOT.
MEW
TSSST
HIS DAD SOUNDS BAD. WHAT'S WRONG WITH LETTING HIM HANG AROUND US A LITTLE LONGER?
ME AM WANT TO GO HOME.
FAMILIES HAVE ROUGH PATCHES, SON. THAT'S NO REASON TO HIDE OUT. HE SHOULD GO BACK.
BUT, DAD...
BOYZARRO CAME AROUND. I'M HOPING THAT WITH A GOOD EXAMPLE AND A LITTLE EXPLANATION, HIS DAD WILL, TOO.
WHAT DON'T YOU SAY? CAN WE NOT GIVE IT A SHOT?
SUPERMAN BAD. ME...DON'T TRUST.
GOOD...

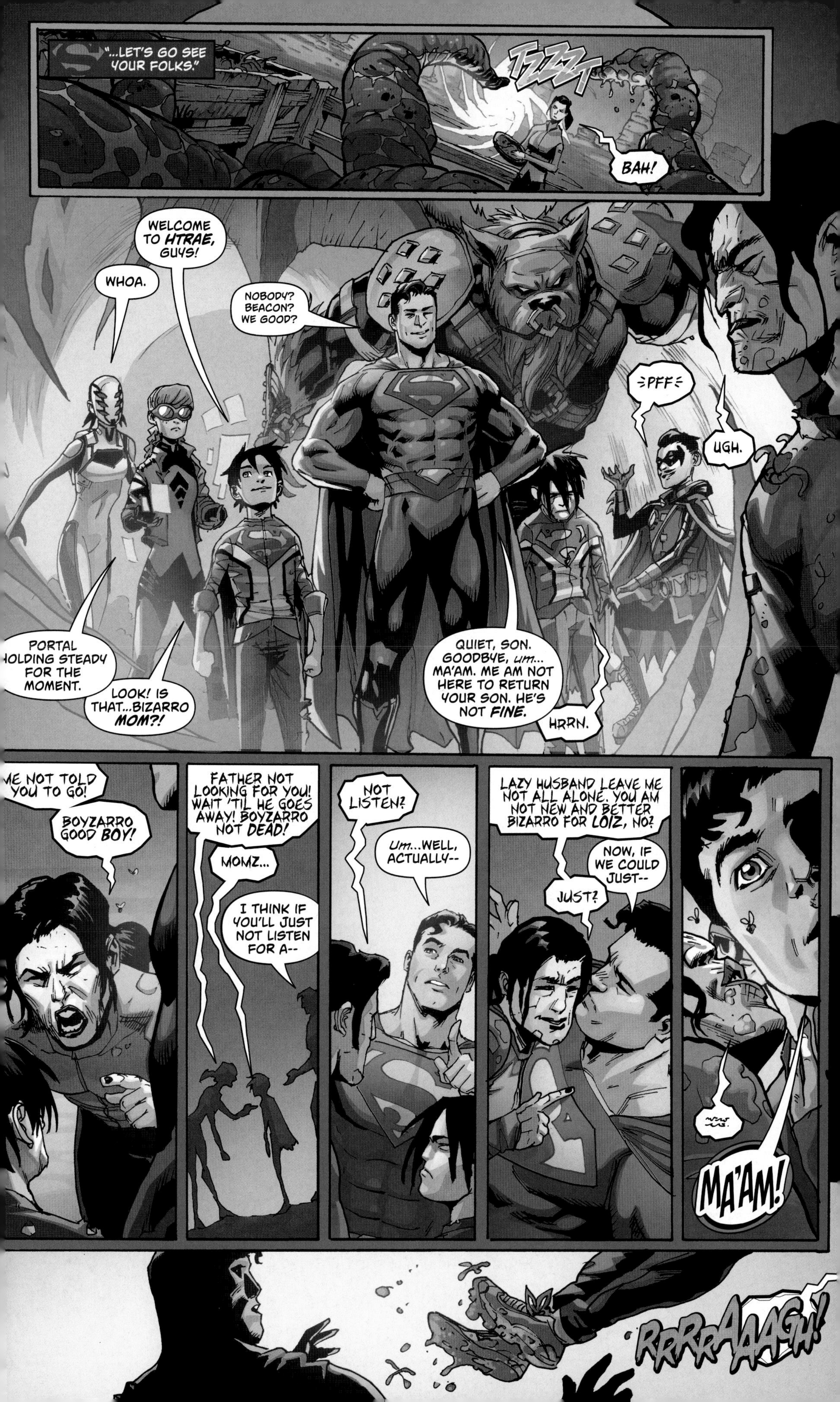

"...LET'S GO SEE YOUR FOLKS."
TZZZT
BAH!
WHOA.
WELCOME TO HTRAE, GUYS!
NOBODY? BEACON? WE GOOD?
PFF
UGH.
PORTAL HOLDING STEADY FOR THE MOMENT.
LOOK! IS THAT...BIZARRO MOM?!
QUIET, SON. GOODBYE, UM... MA'AM. ME AM NOT HERE TO RETURN YOUR SON. HE'S NOT FINE.
HRRN.
ME NOT TOLD YOU TO GO!
BOYZARRO GOOD BOY!
FATHER NOT LOOKING FOR YOU! WAIT 'TIL HE GOES AWAY! BOYZARRO NOT DEAD!
MOMZ...
I THINK IF YOU'LL JUST NOT LISTEN FOR A--
NOT LISTEN?
UM...WELL, ACTUALLY--
LAZY HUSBAND LEAVE ME NOT ALL ALONE. YOU AM NOT NEW AND BETTER BIZARRO FOR LOIZ, NO?
NOW, IF WE COULD JUST--
JUST?
MA'AM!
RRRRAAAGH!

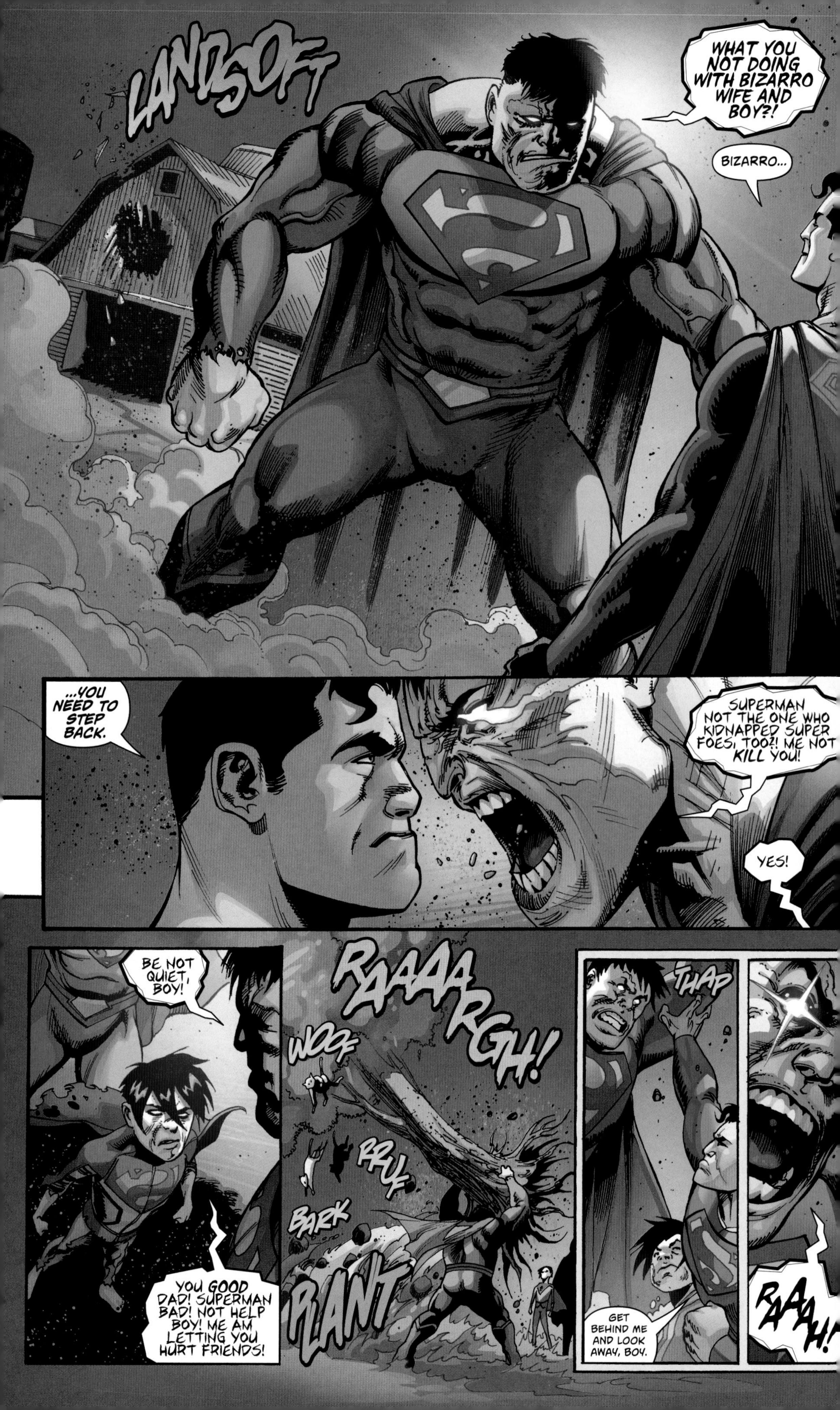
LANDSOFT
WHAT YOU NOT DOING WITH BIZARRO WIFE AND BOY?!
BIZARRO...
...YOU NEED TO STEP BACK.
SUPERMAN NOT THE ONE WHO KIDNAPPED SUPER FOES, TOO?! ME NOT KILL YOU!
YES!
BE NOT QUIET, BOY!
YOU GOOD DAD! SUPERMAN BAD! NOT HELP BOY! ME AM LETTING YOU HURT FRIENDS!
RAAAARGH!
WOOF
RRUF
BARK
PLANT
THAP
GET BEHIND ME AND LOOK AWAY, BOY.
RAAAH!

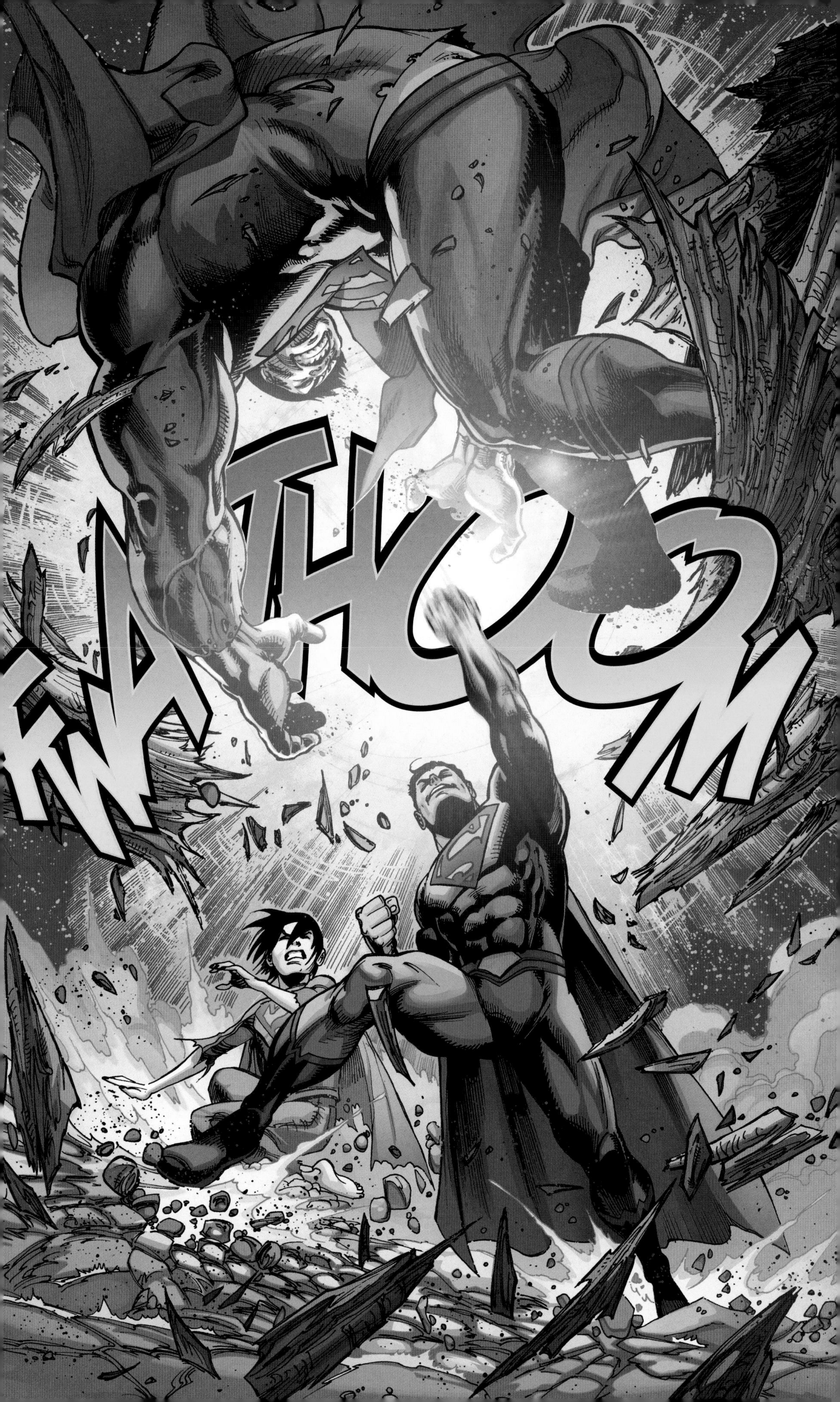
KWATHOOM

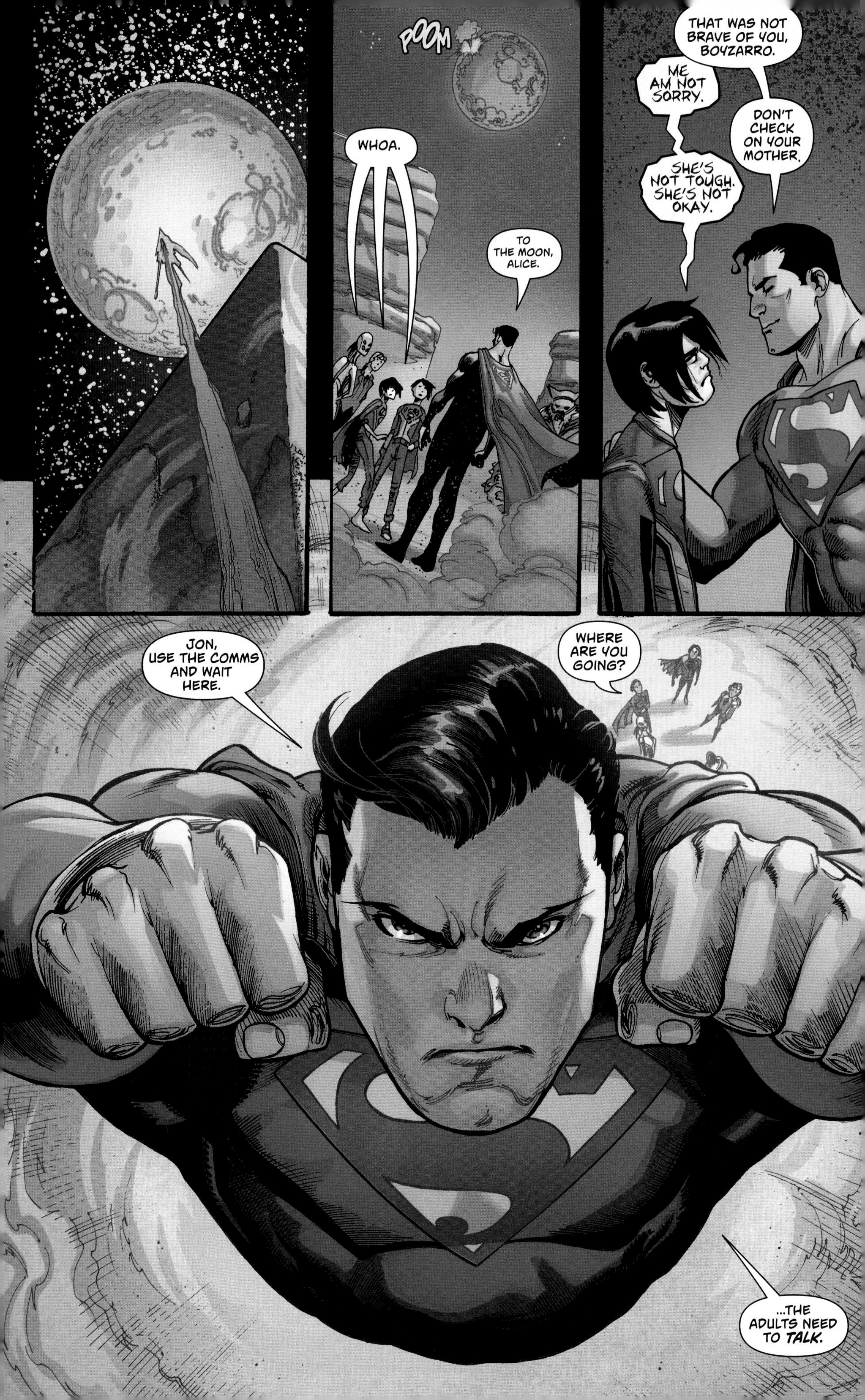
POOM
WHOA.
TO THE MOON, ALICE.
THAT WAS NOT BRAVE OF YOU, BOYZARRO.
ME AM NOT SORRY.
DON'T CHECK ON YOUR MOTHER.
SHE'S NOT TOUGH. SHE'S NOT OKAY.
JON, USE THE COMMS AND WAIT HERE.
WHERE ARE YOU GOING?
...THE ADULTS NEED TO *TALK*.

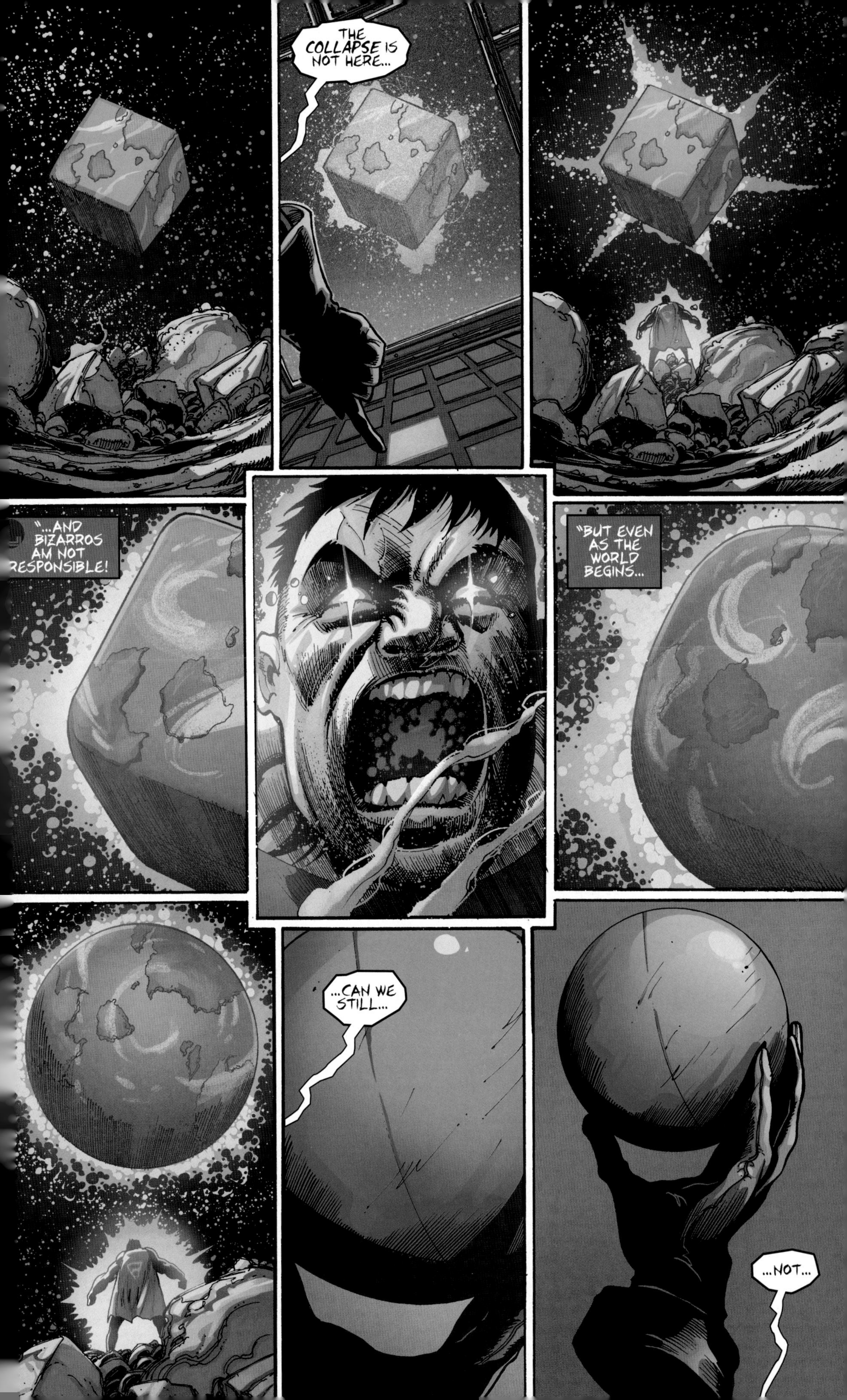
THE COLLAPSE IS NOT HERE...
"...AND BIZARROS AM NOT RESPONSIBLE!
"BUT EVEN AS THE WORLD BEGINS...
...CAN WE STILL...
...NOT...

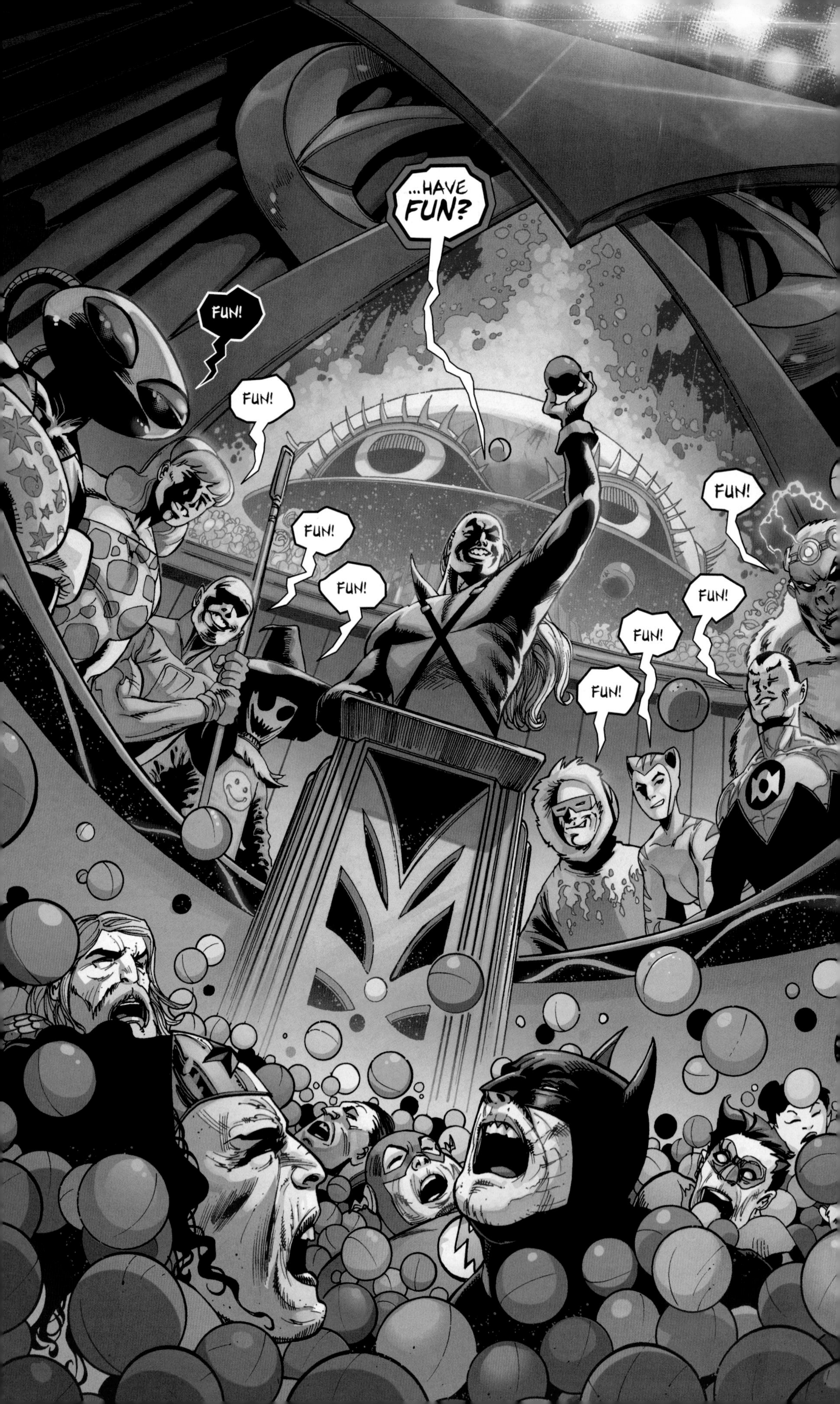
...HAVE FUN?
FUN!
FUN!
FUN!
FUN!
FUN!
FUN!
FUN!
FUN!

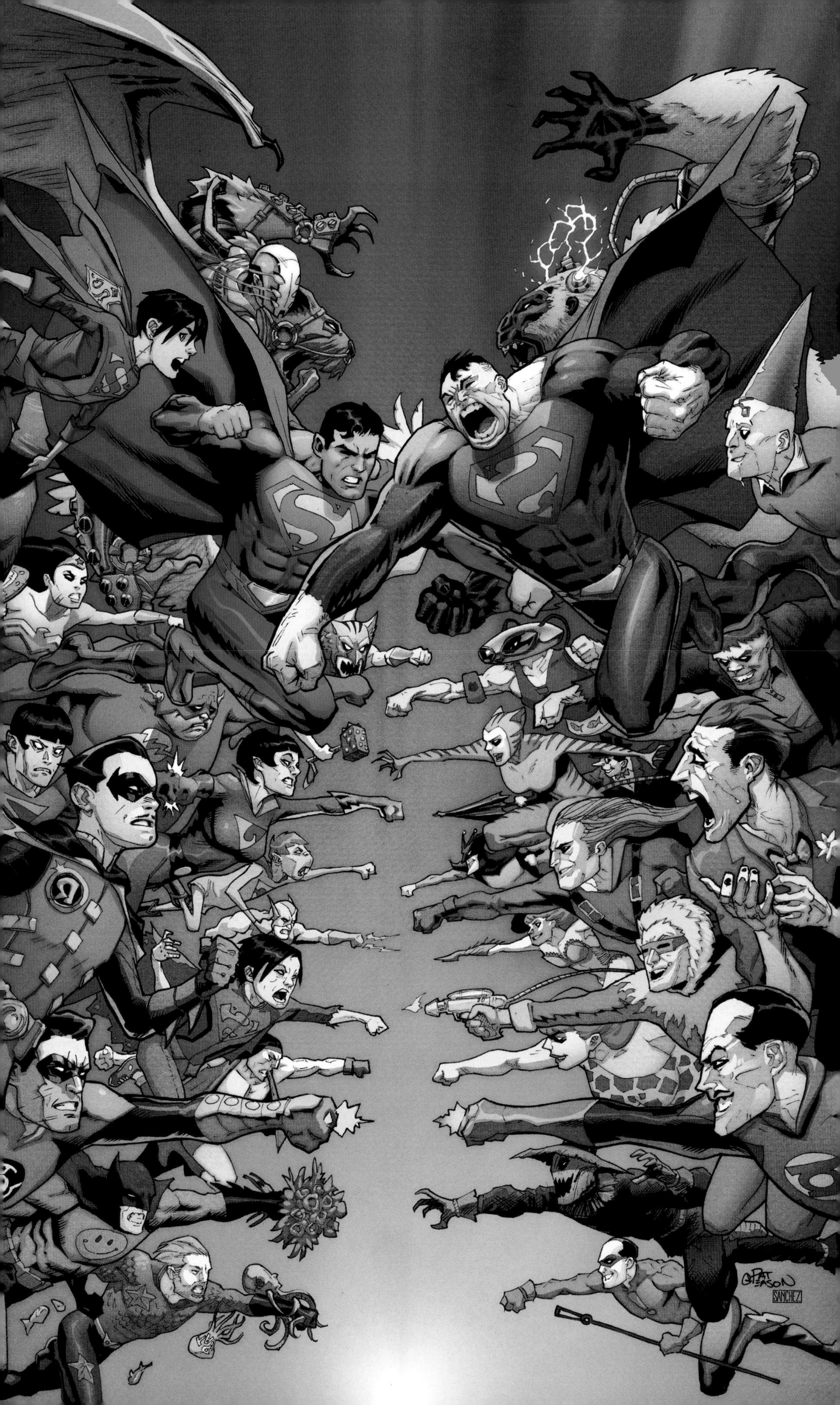
PAT GLEASON
SANCHEZ

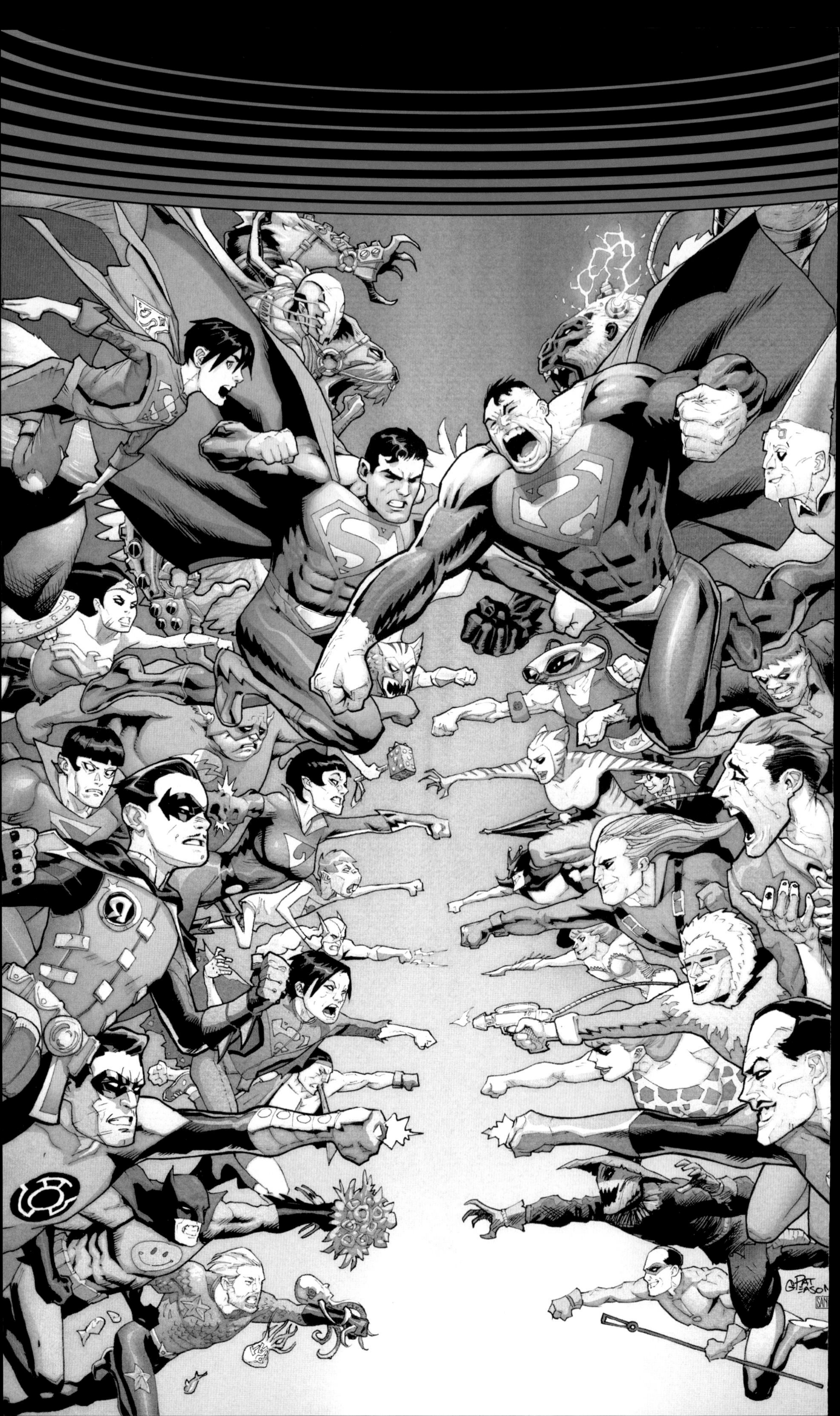

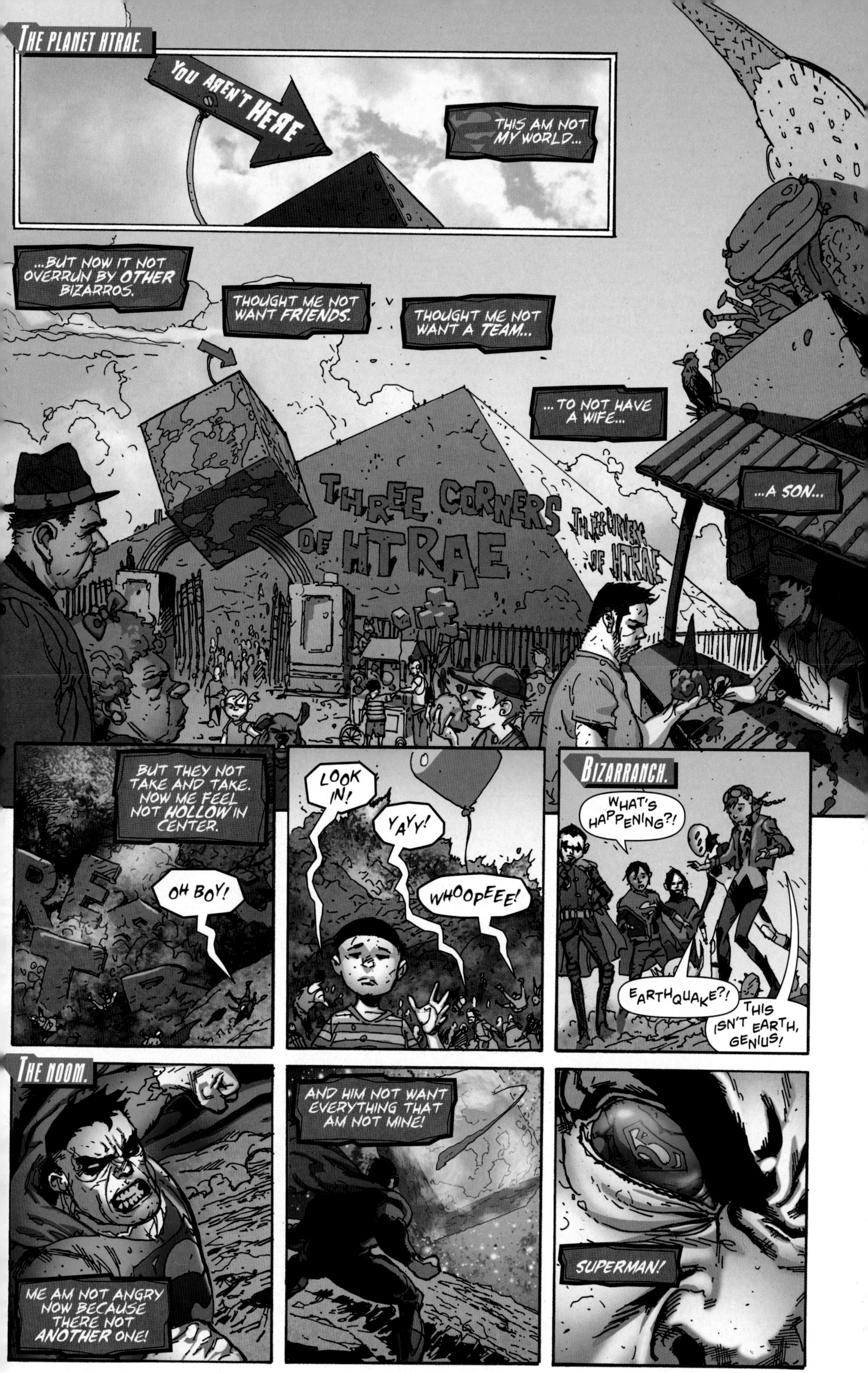
THE PLANET HTRAE.
YOU AREN'T HERE
THIS AM NOT MY WORLD...
...BUT NOW IT NOT OVERRUN BY OTHER BIZARROS.
THOUGHT ME NOT WANT FRIENDS.
THOUGHT ME NOT WANT A TEAM...
...TO NOT HAVE A WIFE...
...A SON...
THREE CORNERS OF HTRAE
BUT THEY NOT TAKE AND TAKE. NOW ME FEEL NOT HOLLOW IN CENTER.
OH BOY!
LOOK IN!
YAYY!
WHOOPEEE!
BIZARRANCH.
WHAT'S HAPPENING?!
EARTHQUAKE?!
THIS ISN'T EARTH, GENIUS!
THE NOOM.
ME AM NOT ANGRY NOW BECAUSE THERE NOT ANOTHER ONE!
AND HIM NOT WANT EVERYTHING THAT AM NOT MINE!
SUPERMAN!

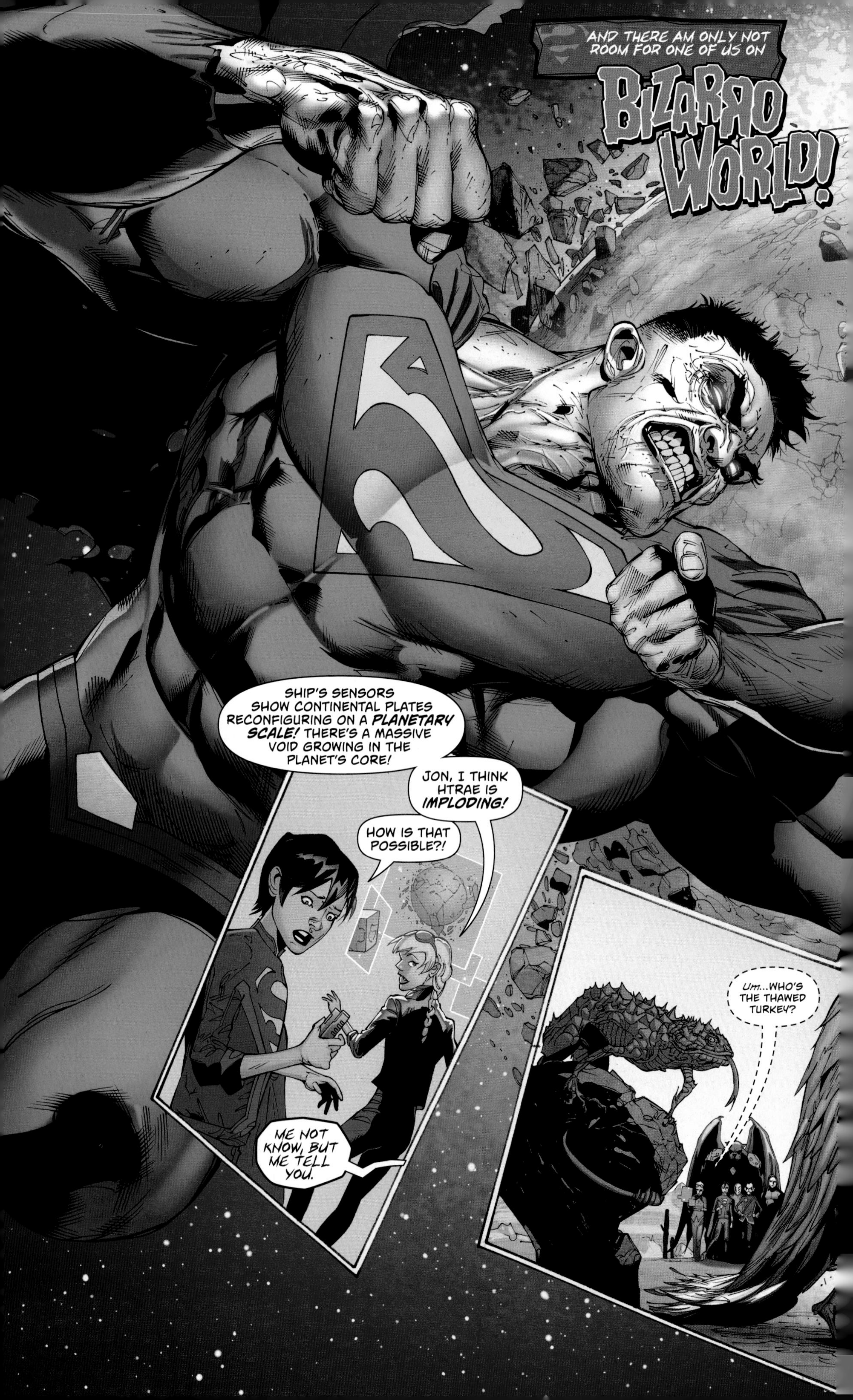
AND THERE AM ONLY NOT ROOM FOR ONE OF US ON
BIZARRO WORLD!
SHIP'S SENSORS SHOW CONTINENTAL PLATES RECONFIGURING ON A PLANETARY SCALE! THERE'S A MASSIVE VOID GROWING IN THE PLANET'S CORE!
JON, I THINK HTRAE IS IMPLODING!
HOW IS THAT POSSIBLE?!
ME NOT KNOW, BUT ME TELL YOU.
Um...WHO'S THE THAWED TURKEY?

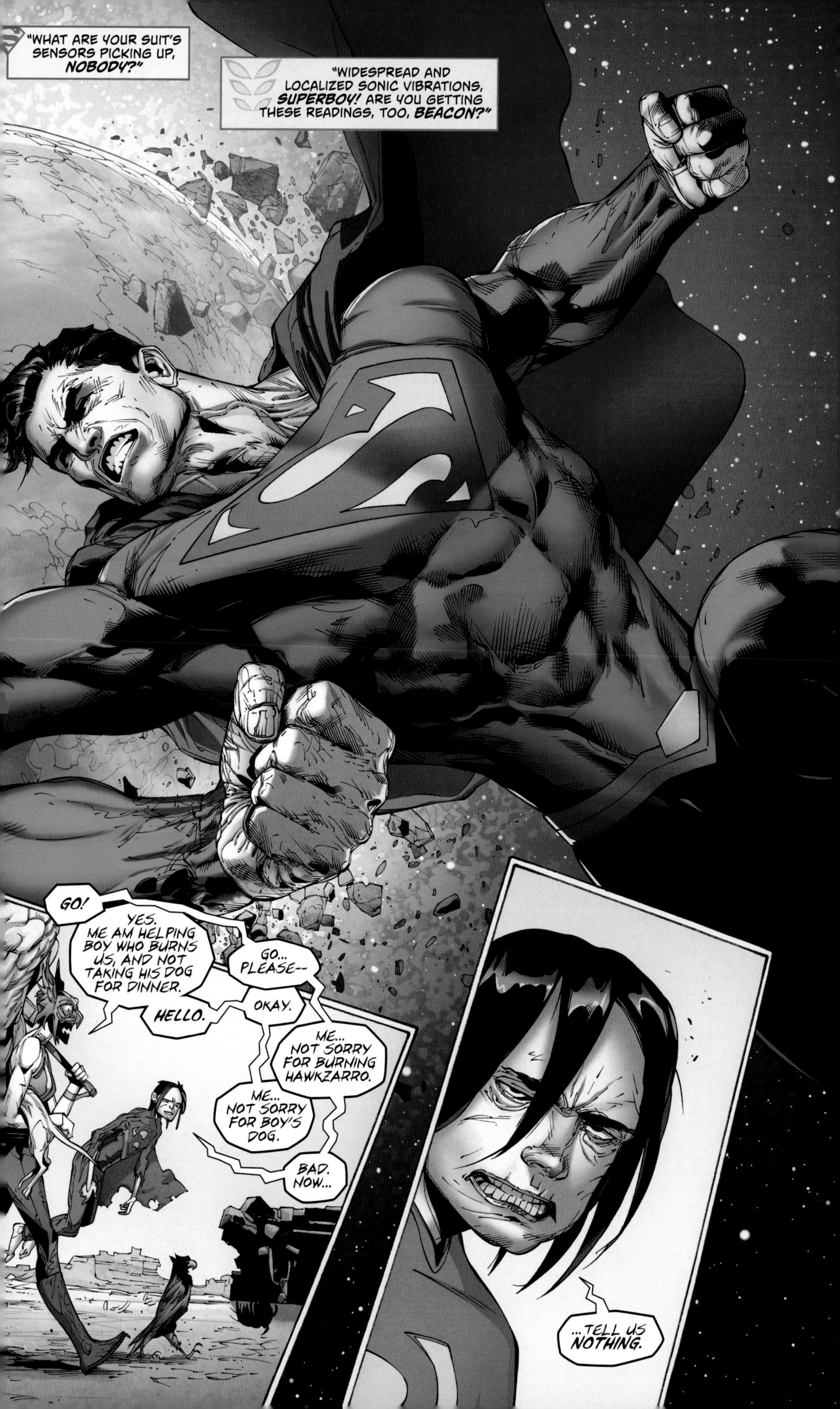
"WHAT ARE YOUR SUIT'S SENSORS PICKING UP, NOBODY?"
"WIDESPREAD AND LOCALIZED SONIC VIBRATIONS, SUPERBOY! ARE YOU GETTING THESE READINGS, TOO, BEACON?"
GO!
YES. ME AM HELPING BOY WHO BURNS US, AND NOT TAKING HIS DOG FOR DINNER.
GO... PLEASE--
HELLO.
OKAY.
ME... NOT SORRY FOR BURNING HAWKZARRO.
ME... NOT SORRY FOR BOY'S DOG.
BAD. NOW...
...TELL US NOTHING.

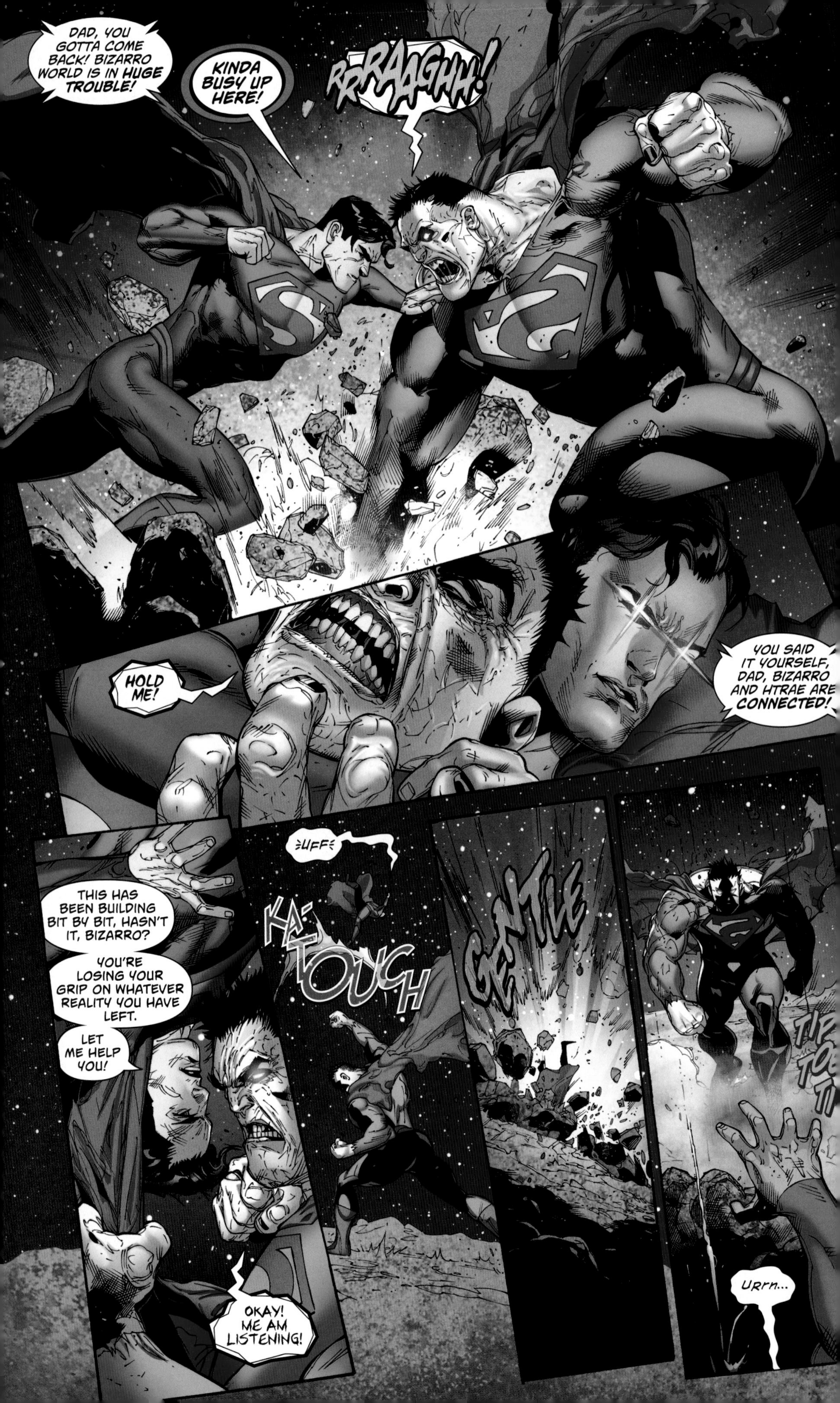

DAD, YOU GOTTA COME BACK! BIZARRO WORLD IS IN HUGE TROUBLE!
KINDA BUSY UP HERE!
RRRAAGHH!
HOLD ME!
YOU SAID IT YOURSELF, DAD, BIZARRO AND HTRAE ARE CONNECTED!
THIS HAS BEEN BUILDING BIT BY BIT, HASN'T IT, BIZARRO?
YOU'RE LOSING YOUR GRIP ON WHATEVER REALITY YOU HAVE LEFT.
LET ME HELP YOU!
OKAY! ME AM LISTENING!
UFF
KA-TOUCH
GENTLE
Urrn...

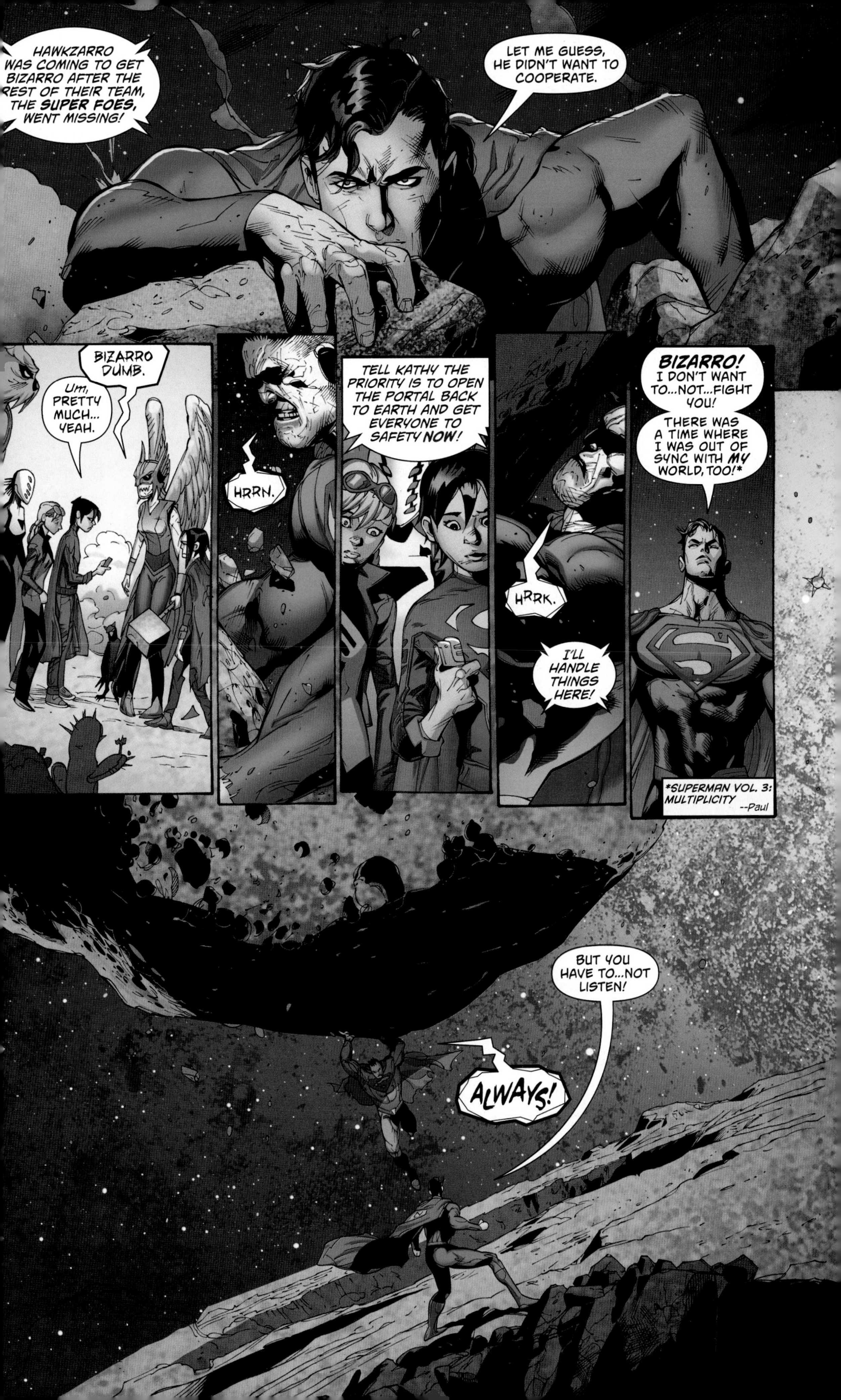

HAWKZARRO WAS COMING TO GET BIZARRO AFTER THE REST OF THEIR TEAM, THE SUPER FOES, WENT MISSING!
LET ME GUESS, HE DIDN'T WANT TO COOPERATE.
BIZARRO DUMB.
Um, PRETTY MUCH... YEAH.
HRRN.
TELL KATHY THE PRIORITY IS TO OPEN THE PORTAL BACK TO EARTH AND GET EVERYONE TO SAFETY NOW!
HRRK.
I'LL HANDLE THINGS HERE!
BIZARRO! I DON'T WANT TO...NOT...FIGHT YOU!
THERE WAS A TIME WHERE I WAS OUT OF SYNC WITH MY WORLD, TOO!*
*SUPERMAN VOL. 3: MULTIPLICITY --Paul
BUT YOU HAVE TO...NOT LISTEN!
ALWAYS!

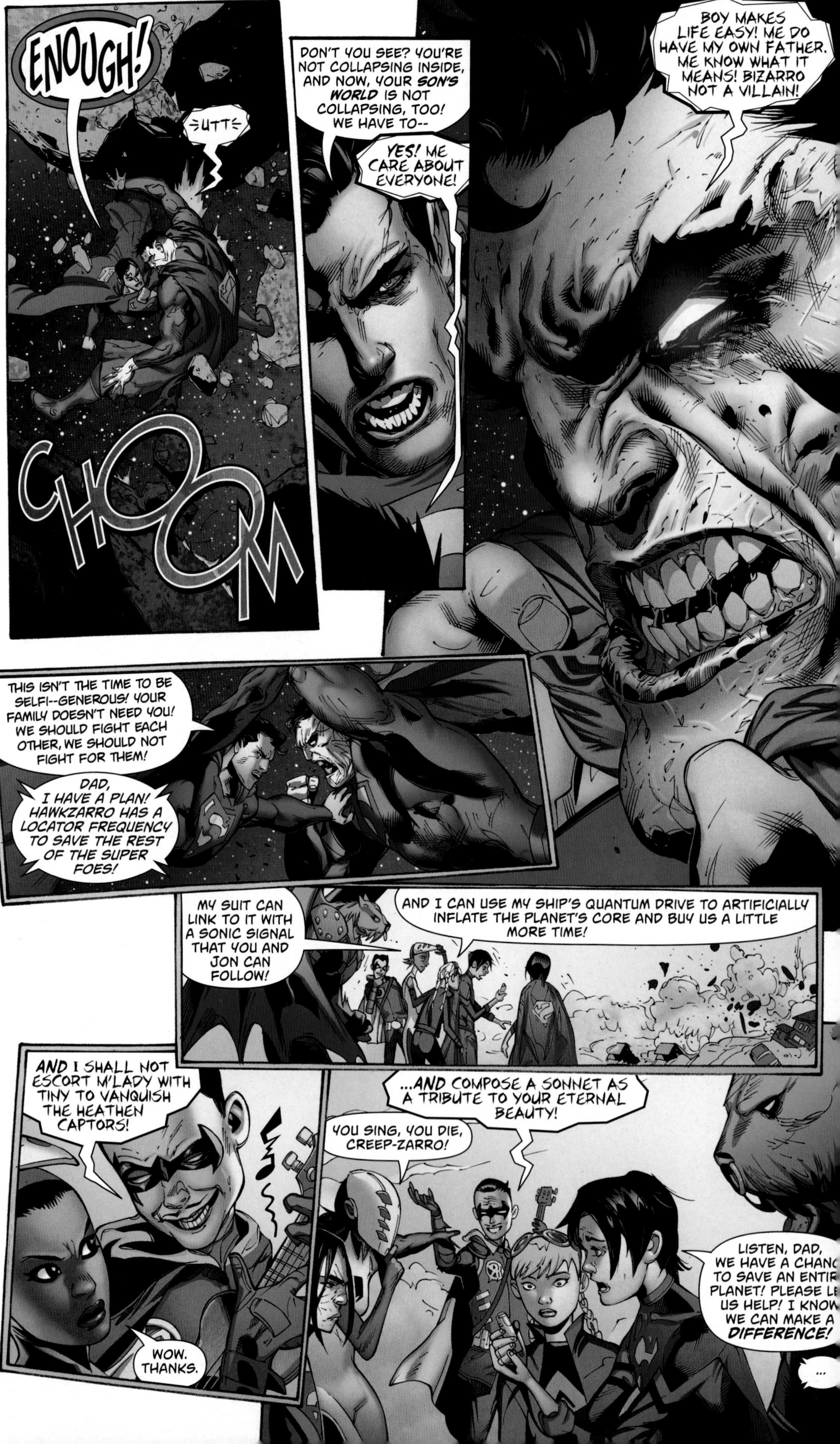

ENOUGH!
UTT
CHOOM
DON'T YOU SEE? YOU'RE NOT COLLAPSING INSIDE, AND NOW, YOUR SON'S WORLD IS NOT COLLAPSING, TOO! WE HAVE TO--
YES! ME CARE ABOUT EVERYONE!
BOY MAKES LIFE EASY! ME DO HAVE MY OWN FATHER. ME KNOW WHAT IT MEANS! BIZARRO NOT A VILLAIN!
THIS ISN'T THE TIME TO BE SELFI--GENEROUS! YOUR FAMILY DOESN'T NEED YOU! WE SHOULD FIGHT EACH OTHER, WE SHOULD NOT FIGHT FOR THEM!
DAD, I HAVE A PLAN! HAWKZARRO HAS A LOCATOR FREQUENCY TO SAVE THE REST OF THE SUPER FOES!
MY SUIT CAN LINK TO IT WITH A SONIC SIGNAL THAT YOU AND JON CAN FOLLOW!
AND I CAN USE MY SHIP'S QUANTUM DRIVE TO ARTIFICIALLY INFLATE THE PLANET'S CORE AND BUY US A LITTLE MORE TIME!
AND I SHALL NOT ESCORT M'LADY WITH TINY TO VANQUISH THE HEATHEN CAPTORS!
WOW. THANKS.
...AND COMPOSE A SONNET AS A TRIBUTE TO YOUR ETERNAL BEAUTY!
YOU SING, YOU DIE, CREEP-ZARRO!
LISTEN, DAD, WE HAVE A CHANC TO SAVE AN ENTIR PLANET! PLEASE LE US HELP! I KNOW WE CAN MAKE A DIFFERENCE!
...

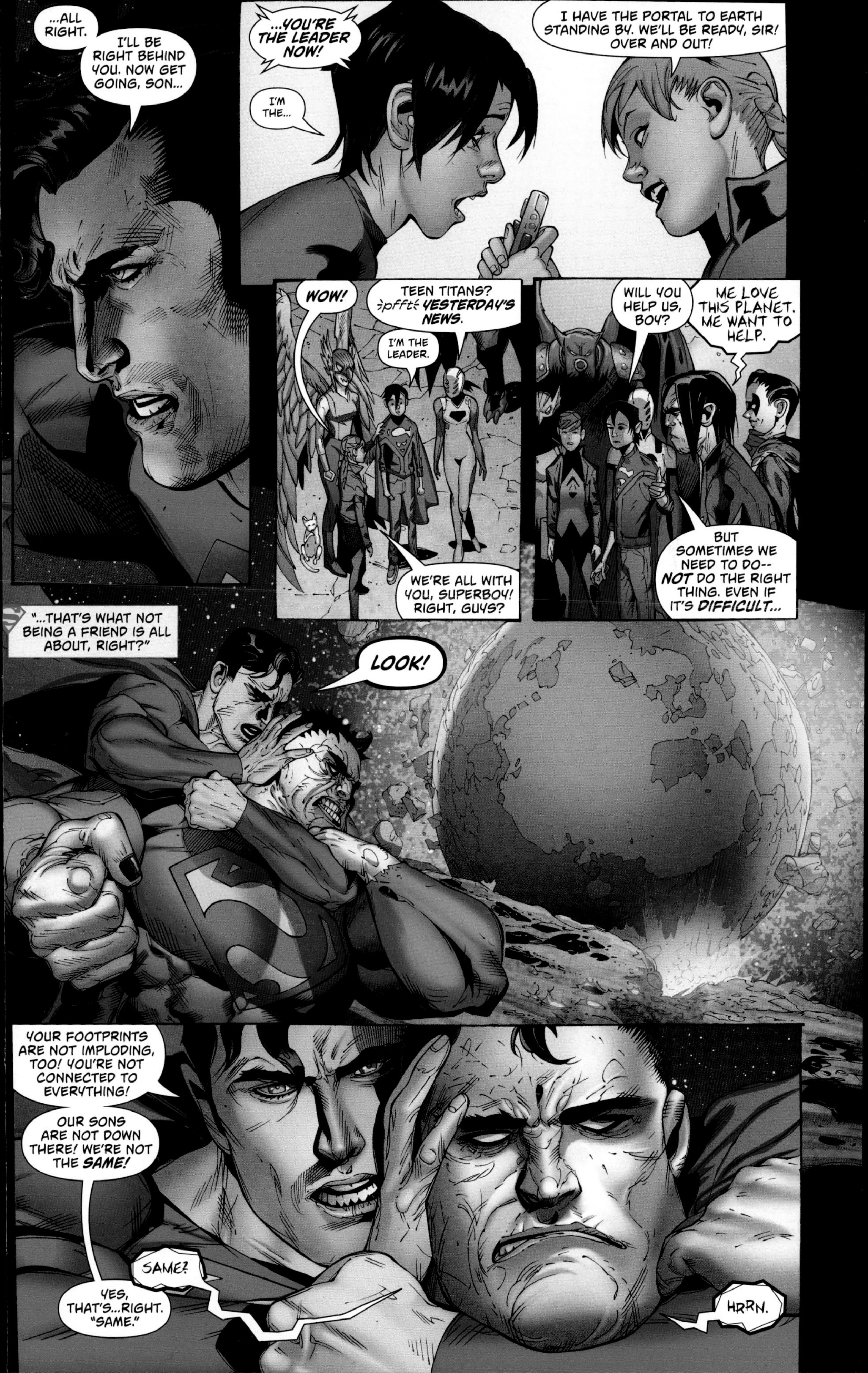
...ALL RIGHT.
I'LL BE RIGHT BEHIND YOU. NOW GET GOING, SON...
...YOU'RE THE LEADER NOW!
I'M THE...
I HAVE THE PORTAL TO EARTH STANDING BY. WE'LL BE READY, SIR! OVER AND OUT!
WOW!
TEEN TITANS? *pfft* YESTERDAY'S NEWS.
I'M THE LEADER.
WE'RE ALL WITH YOU, SUPERBOY! RIGHT, GUYS?
WILL YOU HELP US, BOY?
ME LOVE THIS PLANET. ME WANT TO HELP.
BUT SOMETIMES WE NEED TO DO-- NOT DO THE RIGHT THING. EVEN IF IT'S DIFFICULT...
"...THAT'S WHAT NOT BEING A FRIEND IS ALL ABOUT, RIGHT?"
LOOK!
YOUR FOOTPRINTS ARE NOT IMPLODING, TOO! YOU'RE NOT CONNECTED TO EVERYTHING!
OUR SONS ARE NOT DOWN THERE! WE'RE NOT THE SAME!
SAME?
YES, THAT'S...RIGHT. "SAME."
HRRN.

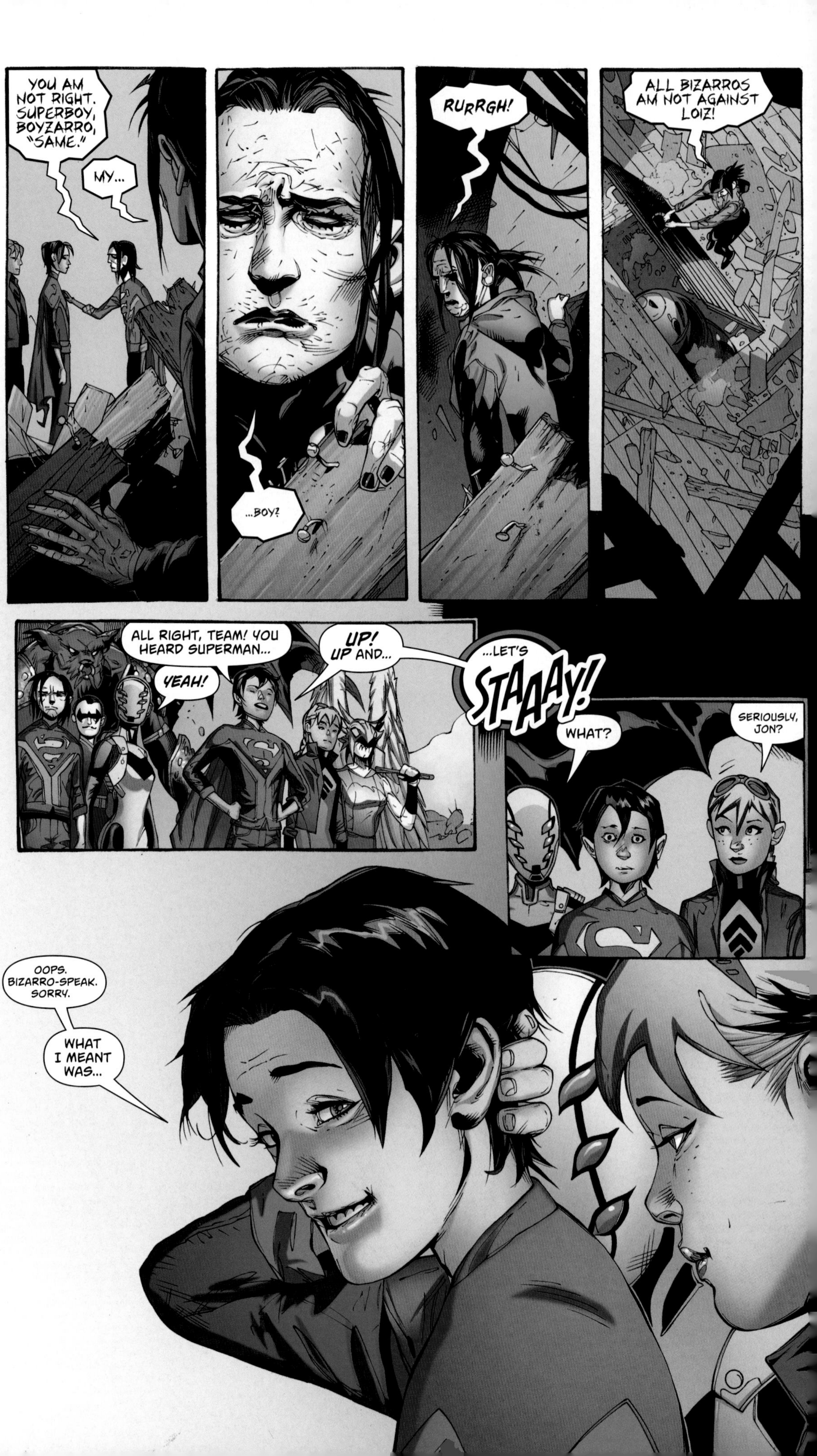
YOU AM NOT RIGHT. SUPERBOY, BOYZARRO, "SAME."
MY...
...BOY?
RURRGH!
ALL BIZARROS AM NOT AGAINST LOIZ!
ALL RIGHT, TEAM! YOU HEARD SUPERMAN...
YEAH!
UP! UP AND...
...LET'S
STAAAY!
WHAT?
SERIOUSLY, JON?
OOPS. BIZARRO-SPEAK. SORRY.
WHAT I MEANT WAS...

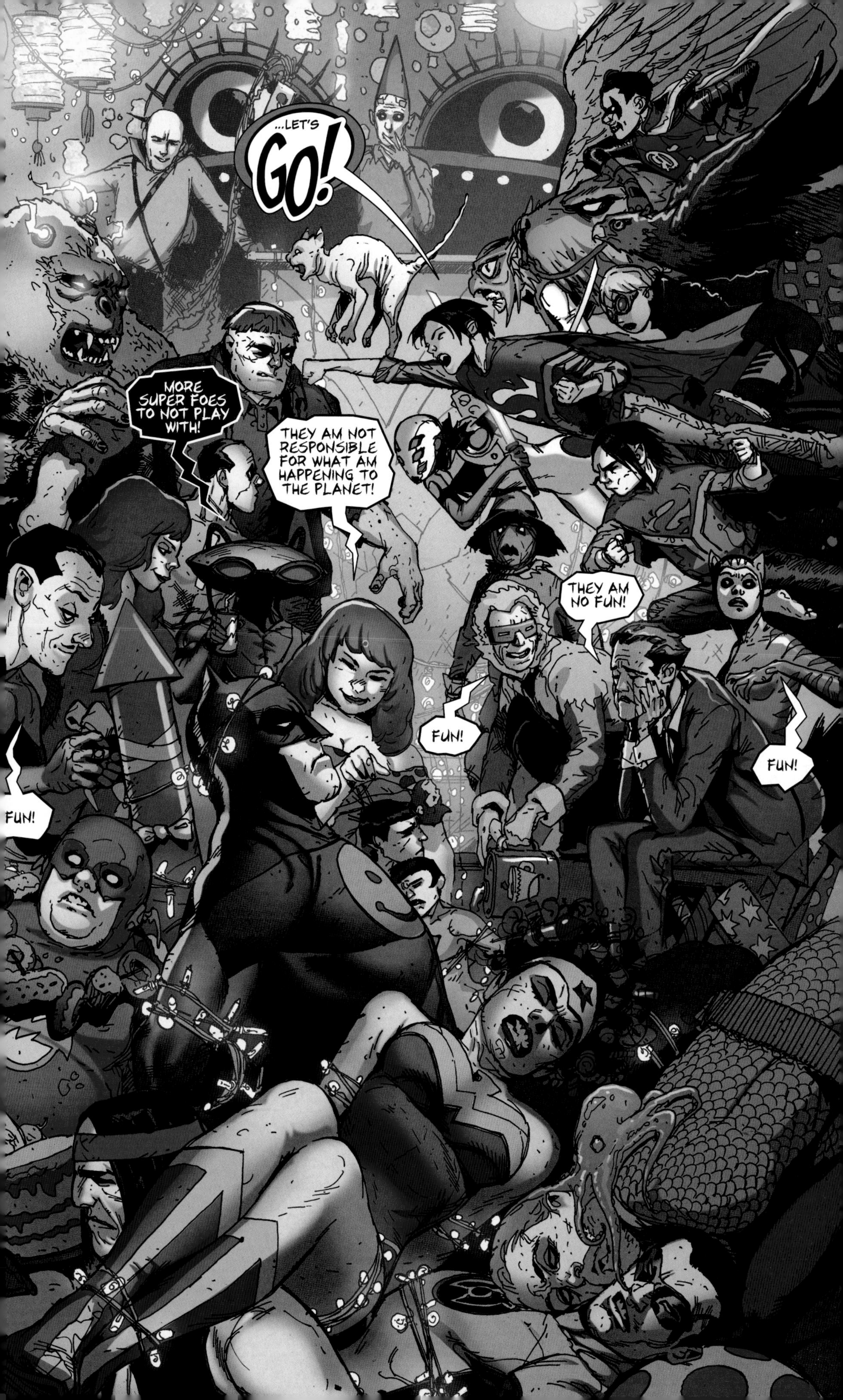
...LET'S GO!
MORE SUPER FOES TO NOT PLAY WITH!
THEY AM NOT RESPONSIBLE FOR WHAT AM HAPPENING TO THE PLANET!
THEY AM NO FUN!
FUN!
FUN!
FUN!

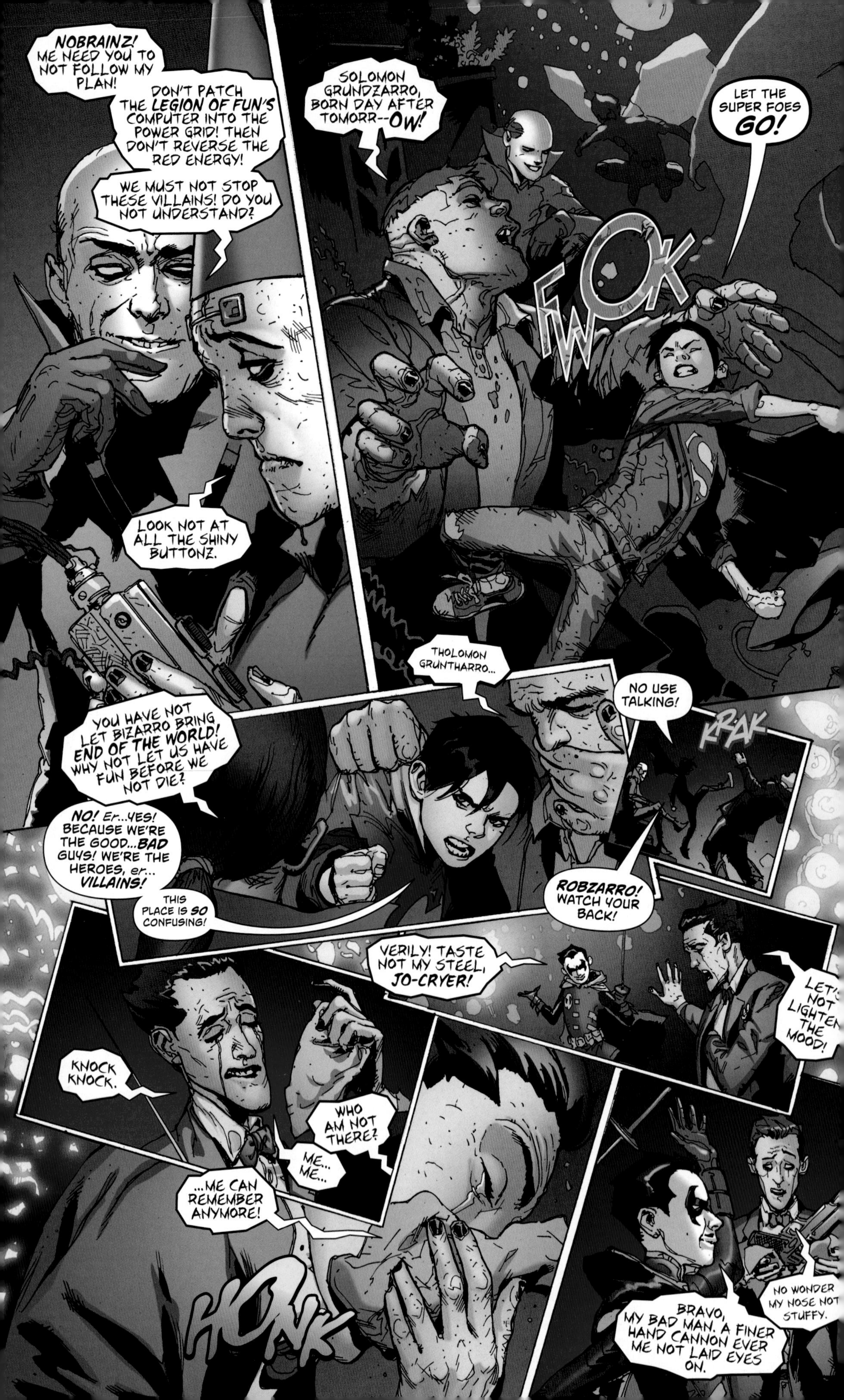
NOBRAINZ! ME NEED YOU TO NOT FOLLOW MY PLAN!
DON'T PATCH THE LEGION OF FUN'S COMPUTER INTO THE POWER GRID! THEN DON'T REVERSE THE RED ENERGY!
WE MUST NOT STOP THESE VILLAINS! DO YOU NOT UNDERSTAND?
LOOK NOT AT ALL THE SHINY BUTTONZ.
SOLOMON GRUNDZARRO, BORN DAY AFTER TOMORR--OW!
LET THE SUPER FOES GO!
FWOCK
THOLOMON GRUNTHARRO...
NO USE TALKING!
KRAK
YOU HAVE NOT LET BIZARRO BRING END OF THE WORLD! WHY NOT LET US HAVE FUN BEFORE WE NOT DIE?
NO! Er...YES! BECAUSE WE'RE THE GOOD...BAD GUYS! WE'RE THE HEROES, er... VILLAINS!
THIS PLACE IS SO CONFUSING!
ROBZARRO! WATCH YOUR BACK!
VERILY! TASTE NOT MY STEEL, JO-CRYER!
LET'S NOT LIGHTEN THE MOOD!
KNOCK KNOCK.
WHO AM NOT THERE?
ME... ME...
...ME CAN REMEMBER ANYMORE!
HONK
NO WONDER MY NOSE NOT STUFFY.
BRAVO, MY BAD MAN. A FINER HAND CANNON EVER ME NOT LAID EYES ON.

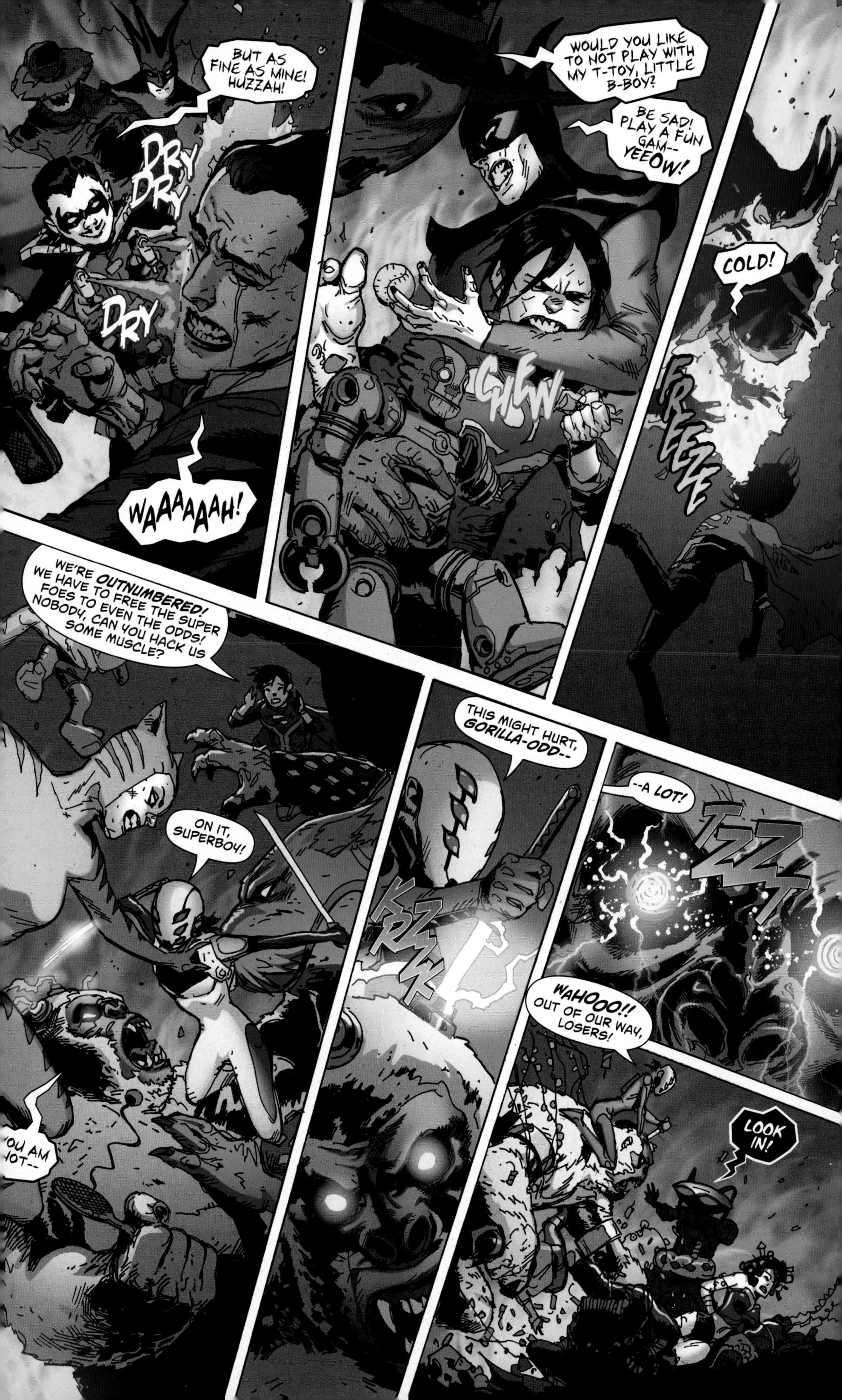
BUT AS FINE AS MINE! HUZZAH!
DRY DRY
DRY
WAAAAAAH!
WOULD YOU LIKE TO NOT PLAY WITH MY T-TOY, LITTLE B-BOY?
BE SAD! PLAY A FUN GAM-- YEEOW!
CHEW
COLD!
FREEZE
WE'RE OUTNUMBERED! WE HAVE TO FREE THE SUPER FOES TO EVEN THE ODDS! NOBODY, CAN YOU HACK US SOME MUSCLE?
ON IT, SUPERBOY!
OU AM NOT--
THIS MIGHT HURT, GORILLA-ODD--
KRZK
--A LOT!
TZZZT
WAHOOO!! OUT OF OUR WAY, LOSERS!
LOOK IN!

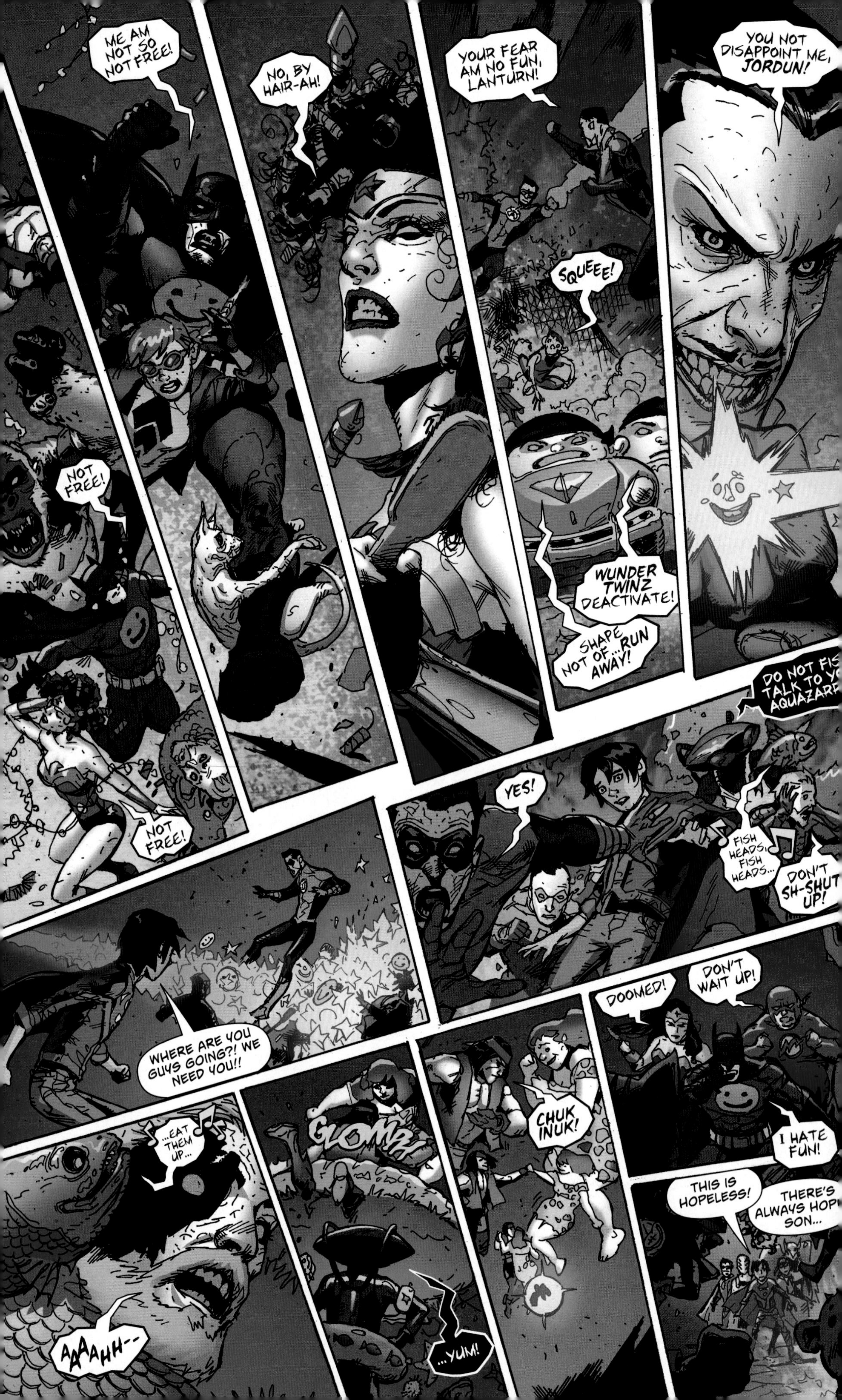

ME AM NOT SO NOT FREE!
NOT FREE!
NOT FREE!
NO, BY HAIR-AH!
YOUR FEAR AM NO FUN, LANTURN!
SQUEEE!
WUNDER TWINZ DEACTIVATE!
SHAPE NOT OF... RUN AWAY!
YOU NOT DISAPPOINT ME, JORDUN!
DO NOT FIS TALK TO YO AQUAZARR
YES!
FISH HEADS, FISH HEADS...
DON'T SH-SHUT UP!
WHERE ARE YOU GUYS GOING?! WE NEED YOU!!
DOOMED!
DON'T WAIT UP!
I HATE FUN!
...EAT THEM UP...
AAAHH--
GLOMP!
...YUM!
CHUK INUK!
THIS IS HOPELESS!
THERE'S ALWAYS HOP SON...

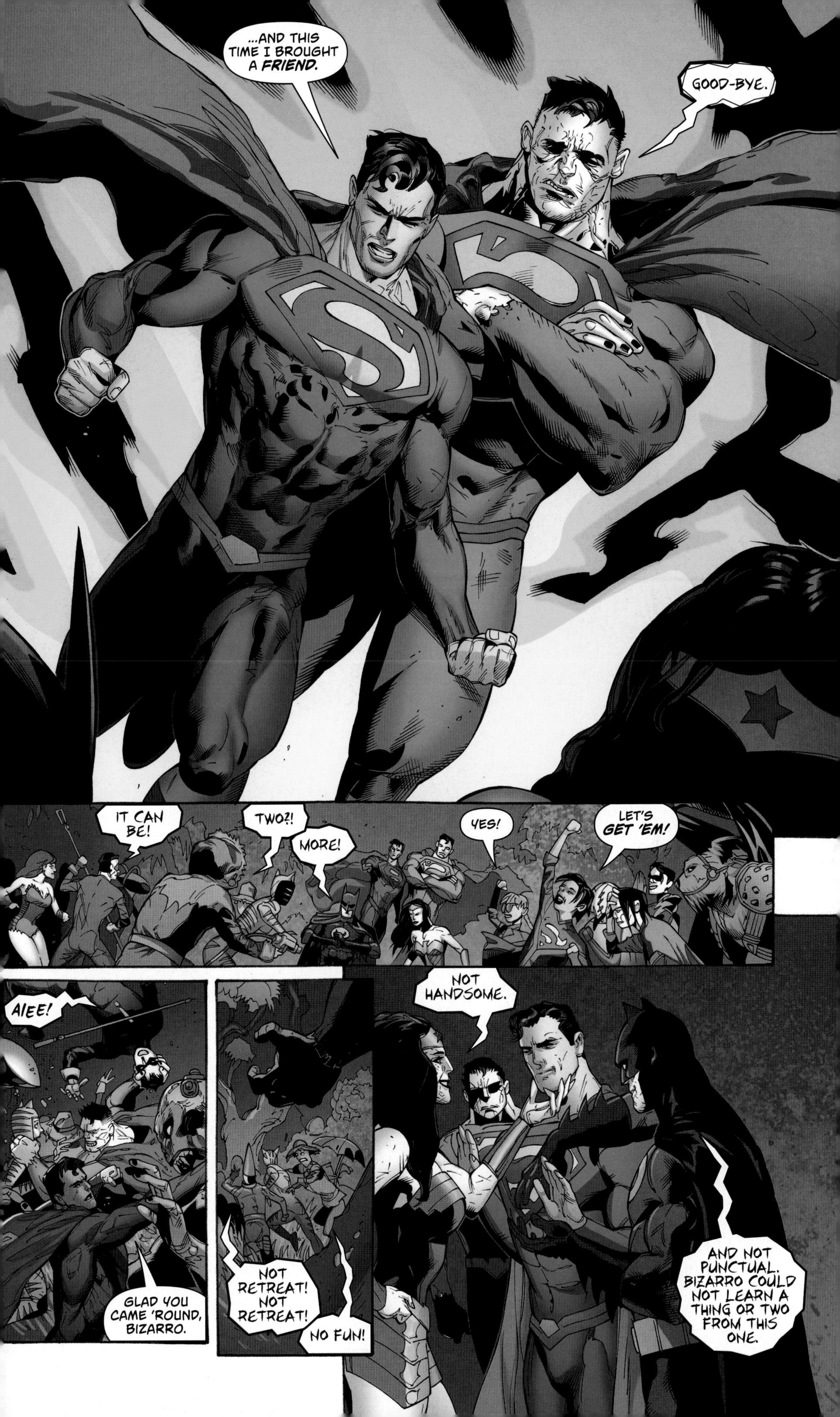
...AND THIS TIME I BROUGHT A FRIEND.
GOOD-BYE.
IT CAN BE!
TWO?!
MORE!
YES!
LET'S GET 'EM!
AIEE!
GLAD YOU CAME 'ROUND, BIZARRO.
NOT RETREAT! NOT RETREAT!
NO FUN!
NOT HANDSOME.
AND NOT PUNCTUAL. BIZARRO COULD NOT LEARN A THING OR TWO FROM THIS ONE.

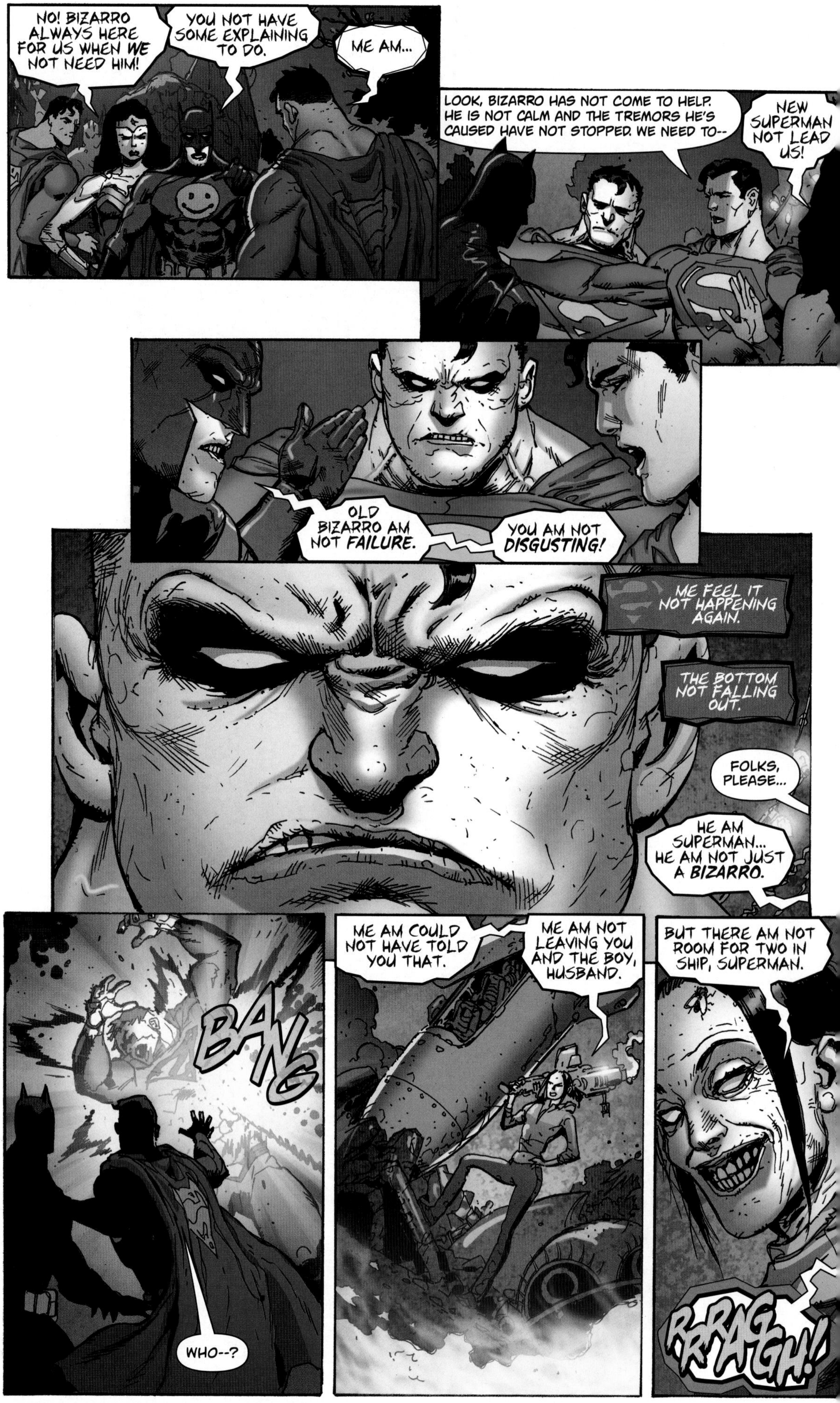
NO! BIZARRO ALWAYS HERE FOR US WHEN WE NOT NEED HIM!
YOU NOT HAVE SOME EXPLAINING TO DO.
ME AM...
LOOK, BIZARRO HAS NOT COME TO HELP. HE IS NOT CALM AND THE TREMORS HE'S CAUSED HAVE NOT STOPPED. WE NEED TO--
NEW SUPERMAN NOT LEAD US!
OLD BIZARRO AM NOT FAILURE.
YOU AM NOT DISGUSTING!
ME FEEL IT NOT HAPPENING AGAIN.
THE BOTTOM NOT FALLING OUT.
FOLKS, PLEASE...
HE AM SUPERMAN... HE AM NOT JUST A BIZARRO.
BANG
WHO--?
ME AM COULD NOT HAVE TOLD YOU THAT.
ME AM NOT LEAVING YOU AND THE BOY, HUSBAND.
BUT THERE AM NOT ROOM FOR TWO IN SHIP, SUPERMAN.
RRRAGRRAGH!

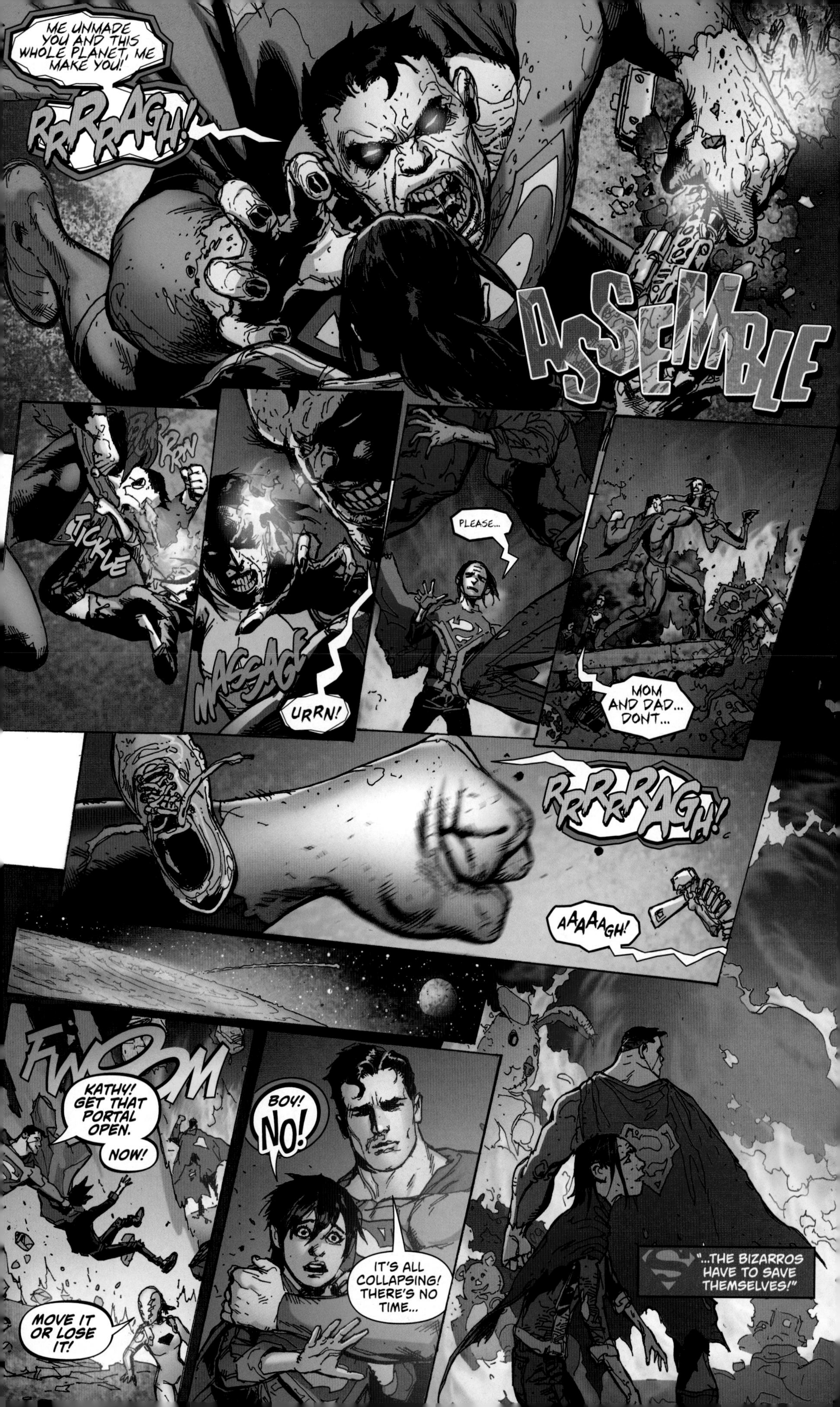

ME UNMADE YOU AND THIS WHOLE PLANET, ME MAKE YOU!
RRRRRAGH!
ASSEMBLE
BURRN
TICKLE
MASSAGE
URRN!
PLEASE...
MOM AND DAD... DONT...
RRRRRAGH!
AAAAAGH!
FWOOM
KATHY! GET THAT PORTAL OPEN.
NOW!
MOVE IT OR LOSE IT!
BOY! NO!
IT'S ALL COLLAPSING! THERE'S NO TIME...
"...THE BIZARROS HAVE TO SAVE THEMSELVES!"

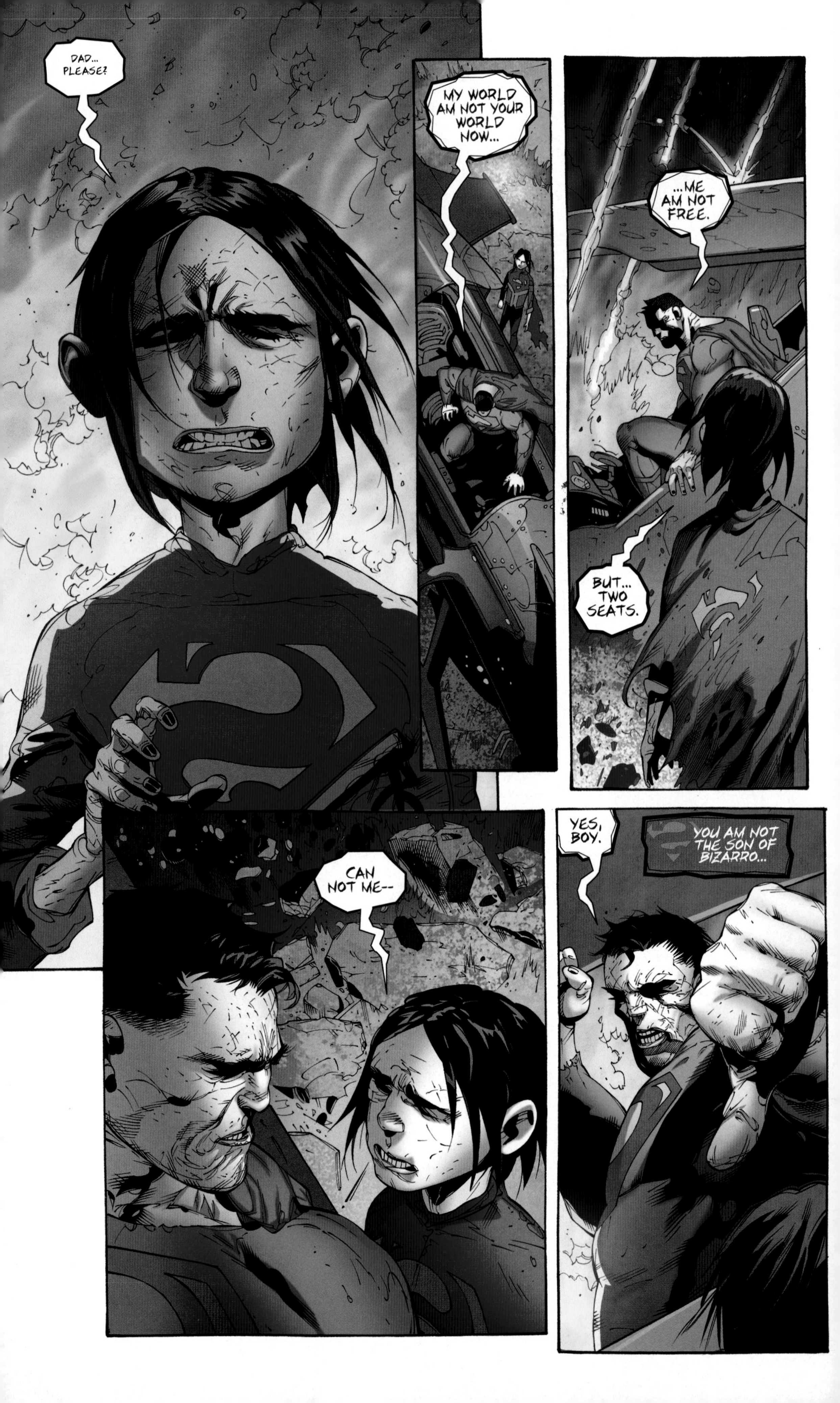
DAD... PLEASE?
MY WORLD AM NOT YOUR WORLD NOW...
...ME AM NOT FREE.
BUT... TWO SEATS.
CAN NOT ME--
YES, BOY.
YOU AM NOT THE SON OF BIZARRO...

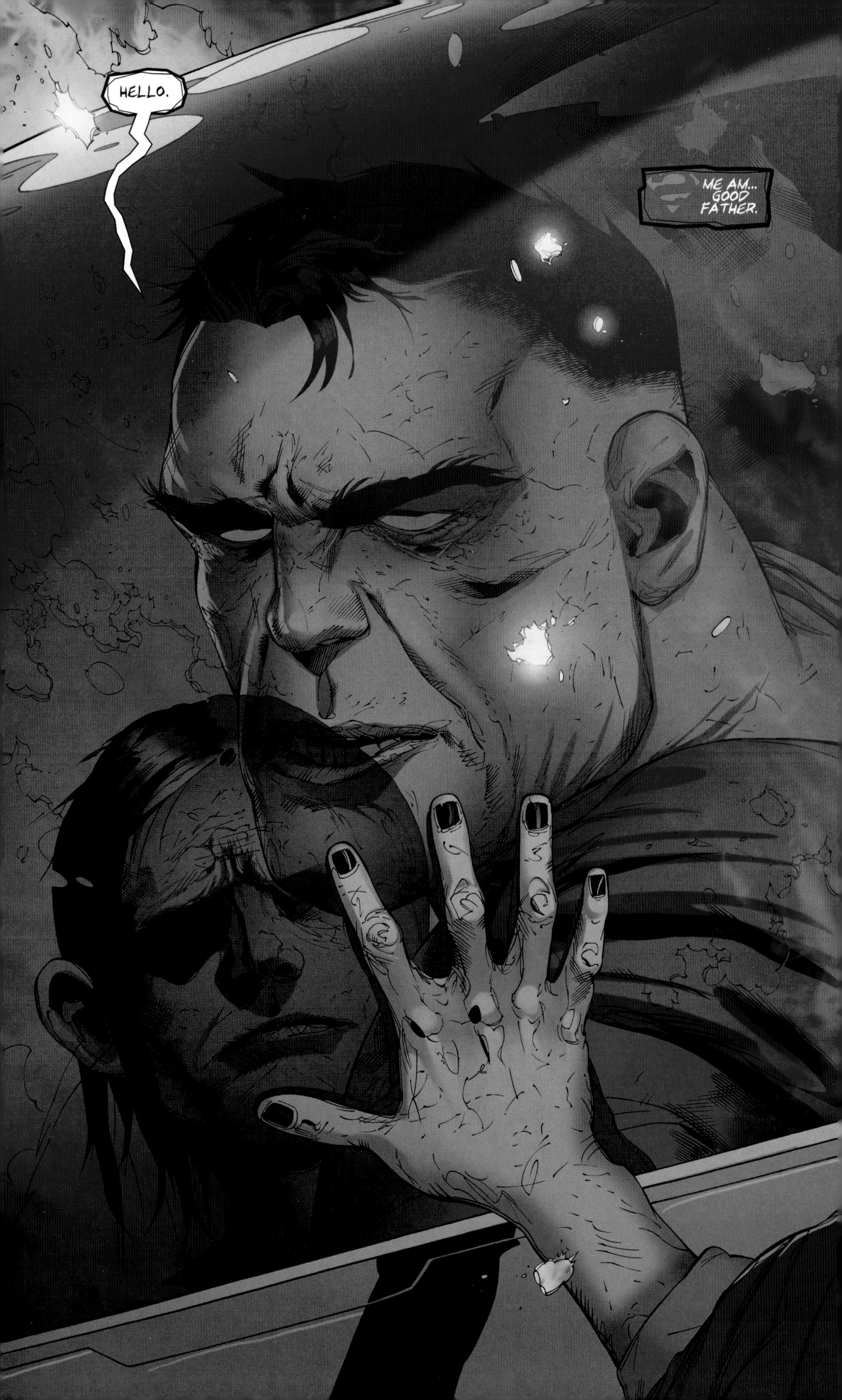
HELLO.
ME AM... GOOD FATHER.

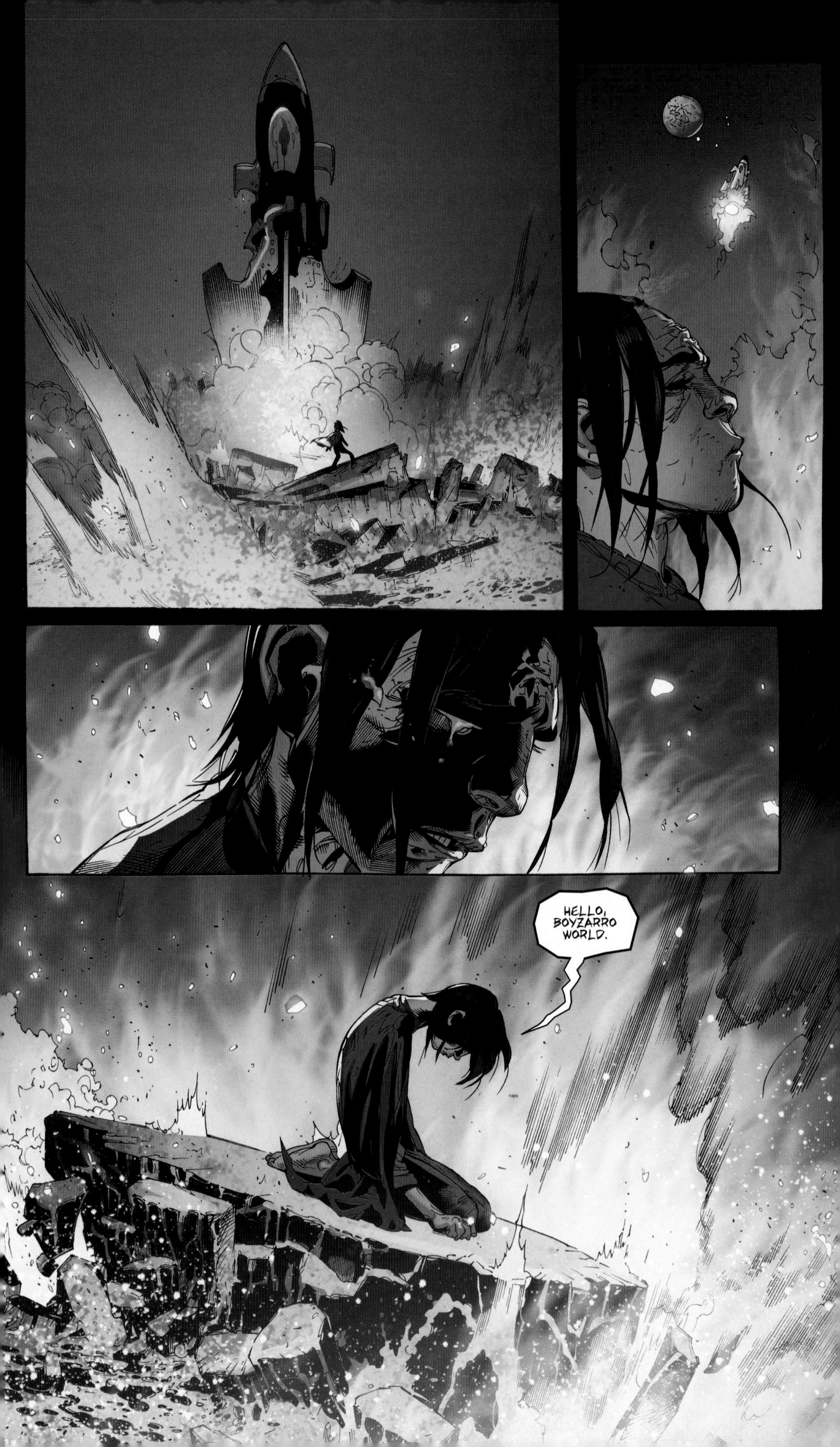
HELLO, BOYZARRO WORLD.

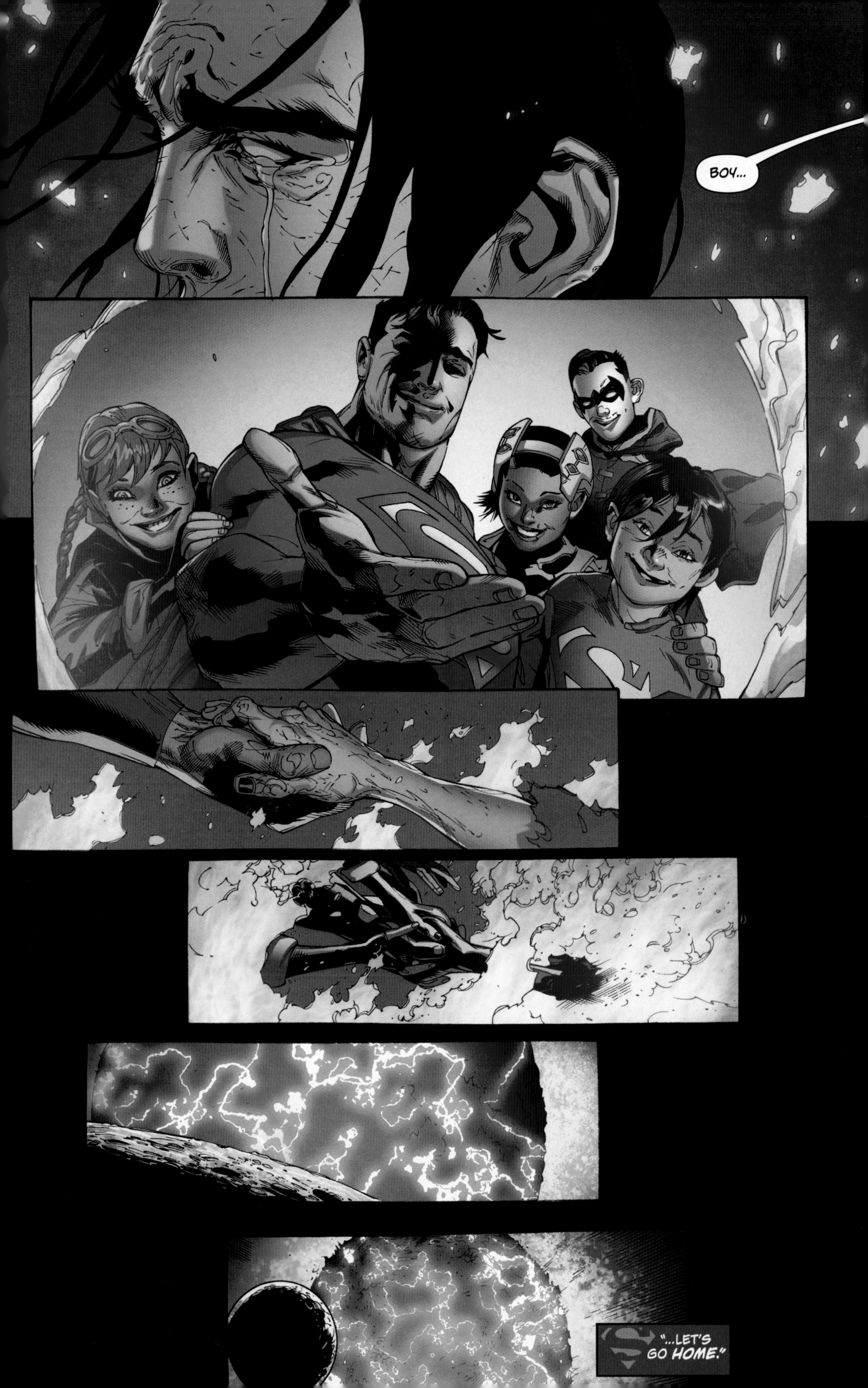
BOY...
"...LET'S GO HOME."

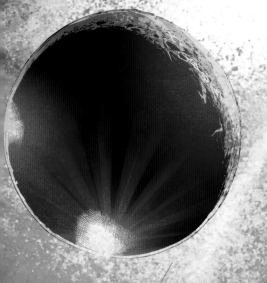

BIZARROVERSE PART 3

AS A FAMILY WE GO

Written
PATRICK GLEAS
& PETER J. TOMA
Pencils
DOUG MAHN
Inks
JAIME MENDO
& DOUG MAHN
Colors WIL QUINTA
Letters ROB LEI
Cover PATRICK GLEAS
& ALEJANDRO SANC
Associate editor JESSICA CH
Editor PAUL KAMIN

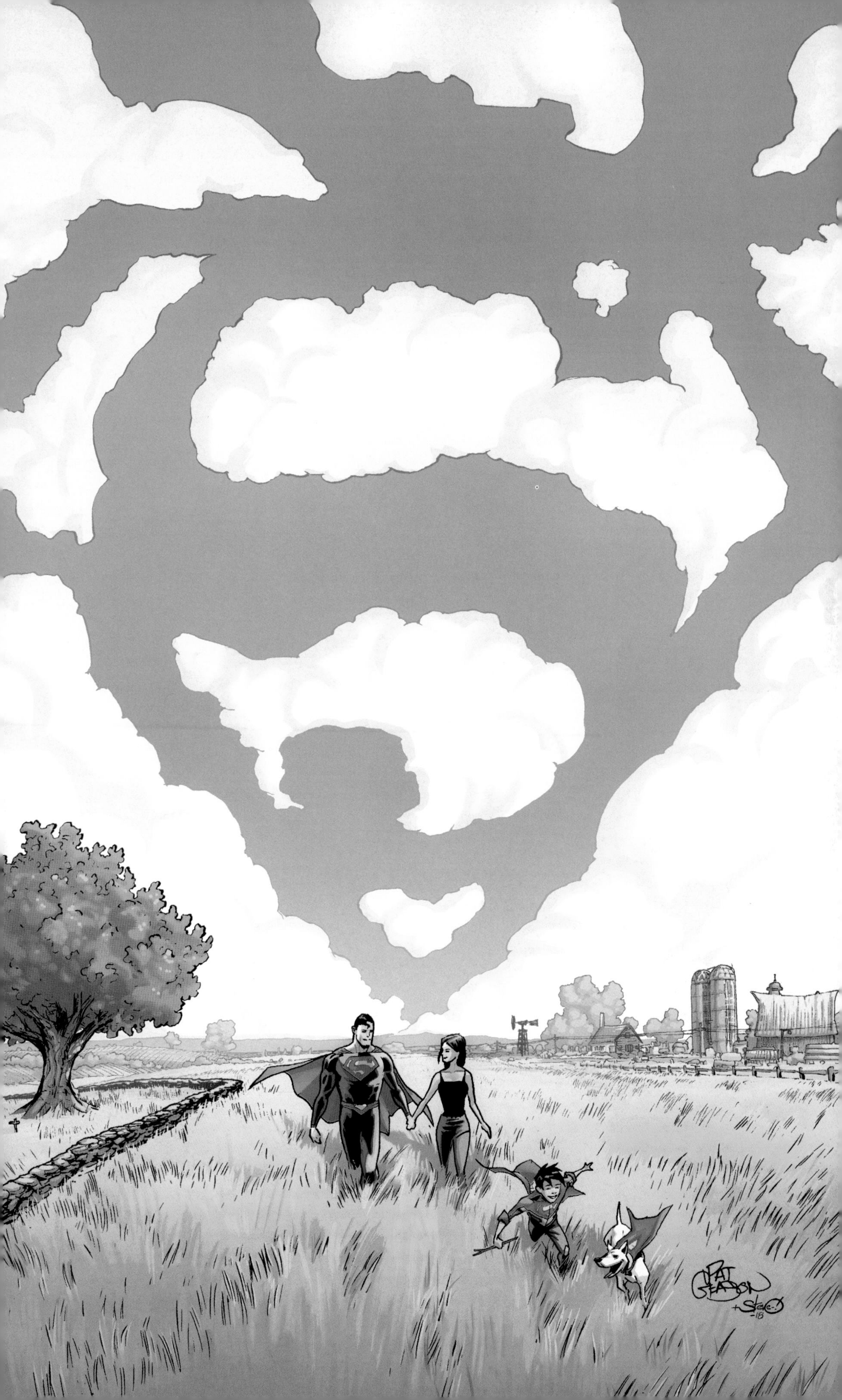

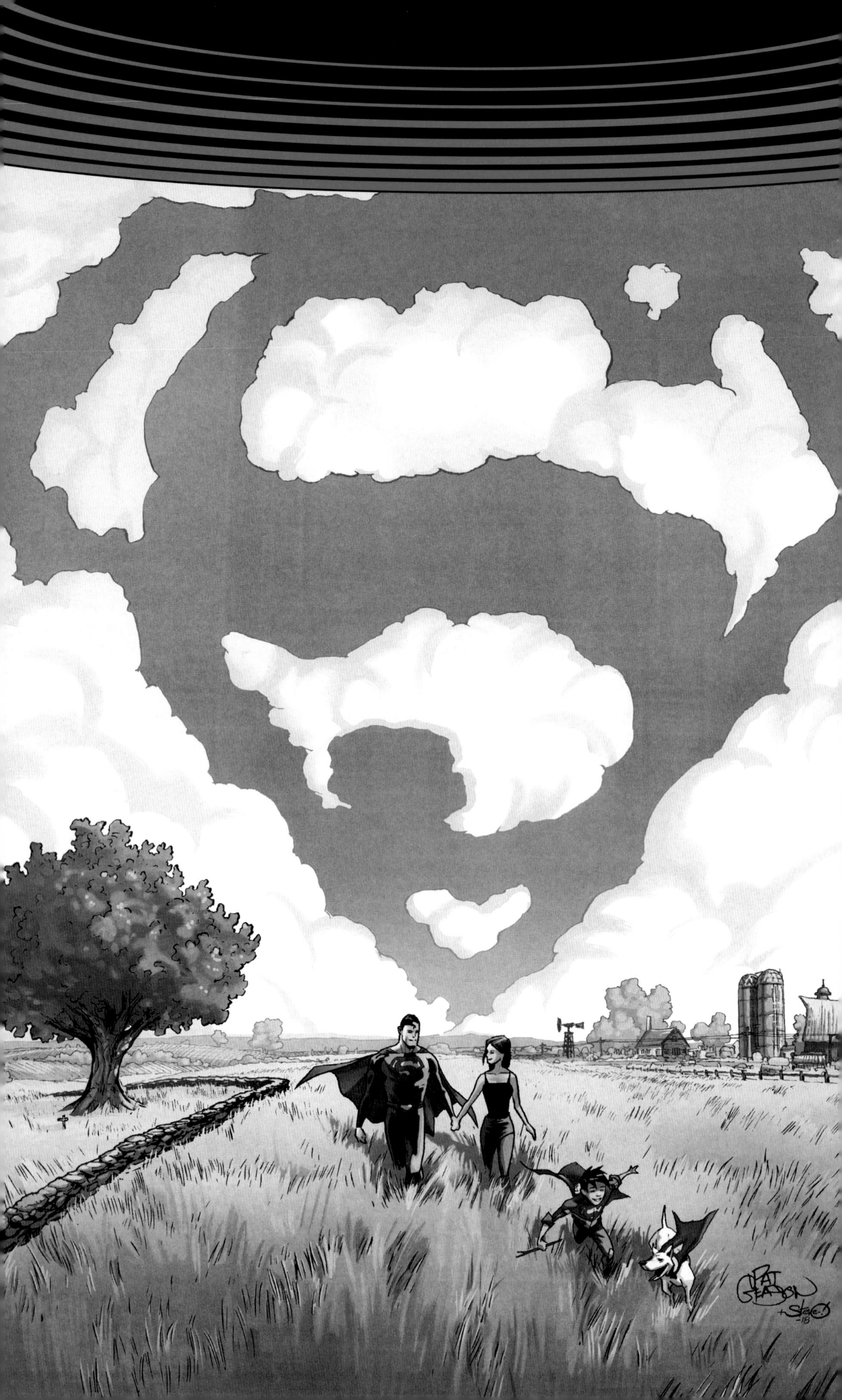

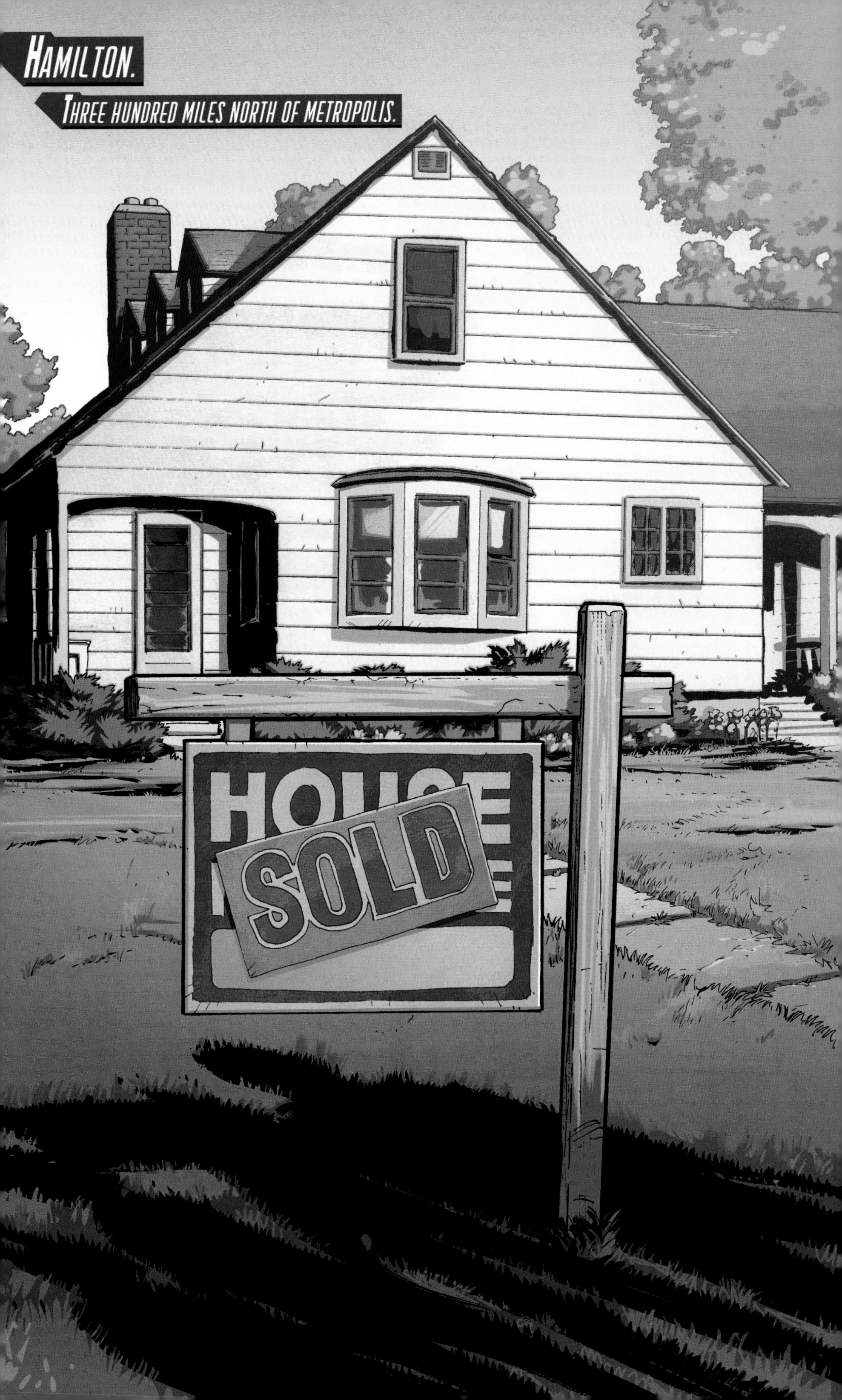
HAMILTON.
THREE HUNDRED MILES NORTH OF METROPOLIS.
SOLD

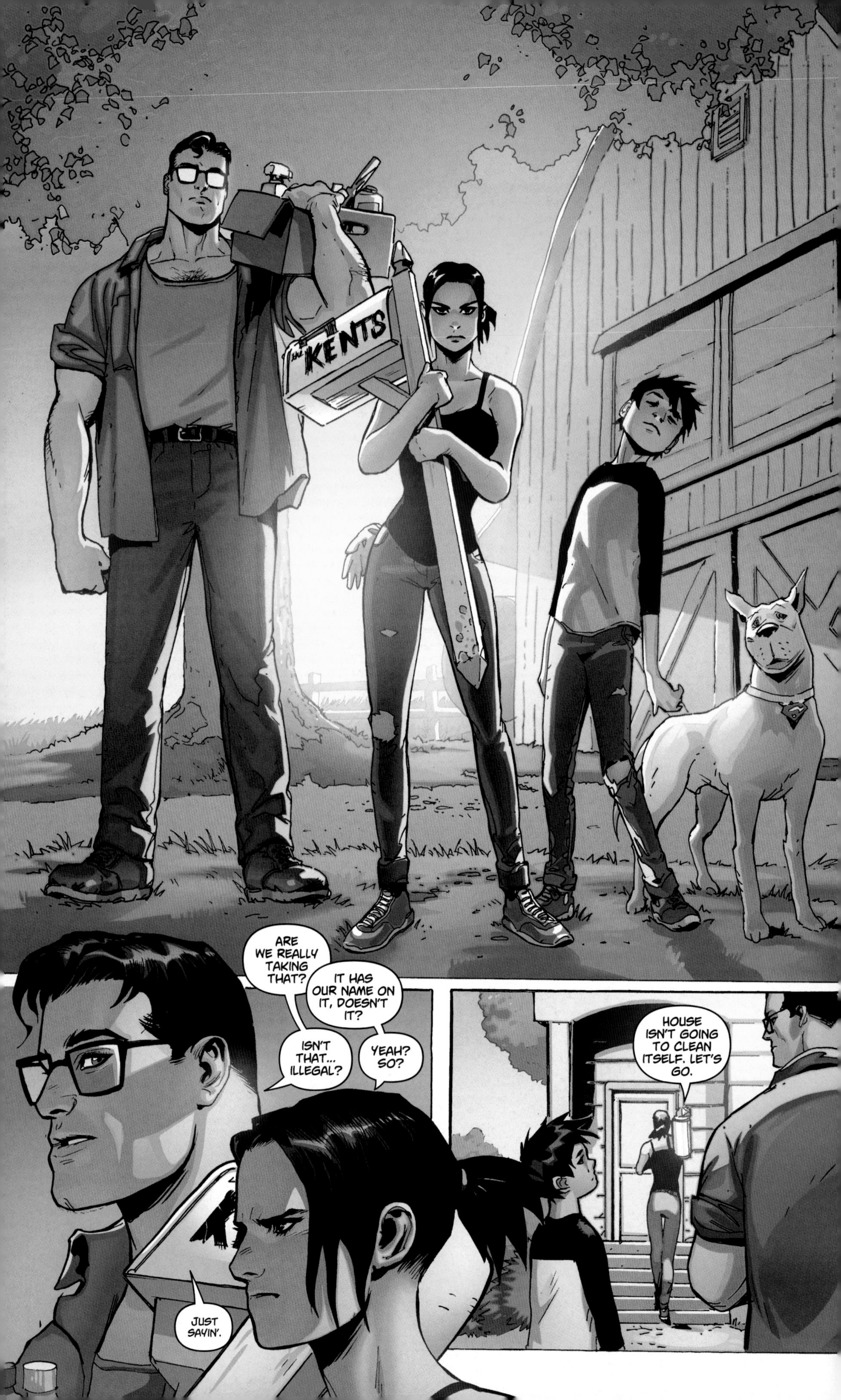
THE KENTS
ARE WE REALLY TAKING THAT?
IT HAS OUR NAME ON IT, DOESN'T IT?
ISN'T THAT... ILLEGAL?
YEAH? SO?
JUST SAYIN'.
HOUSE ISN'T GOING TO CLEAN ITSELF. LET'S GO.

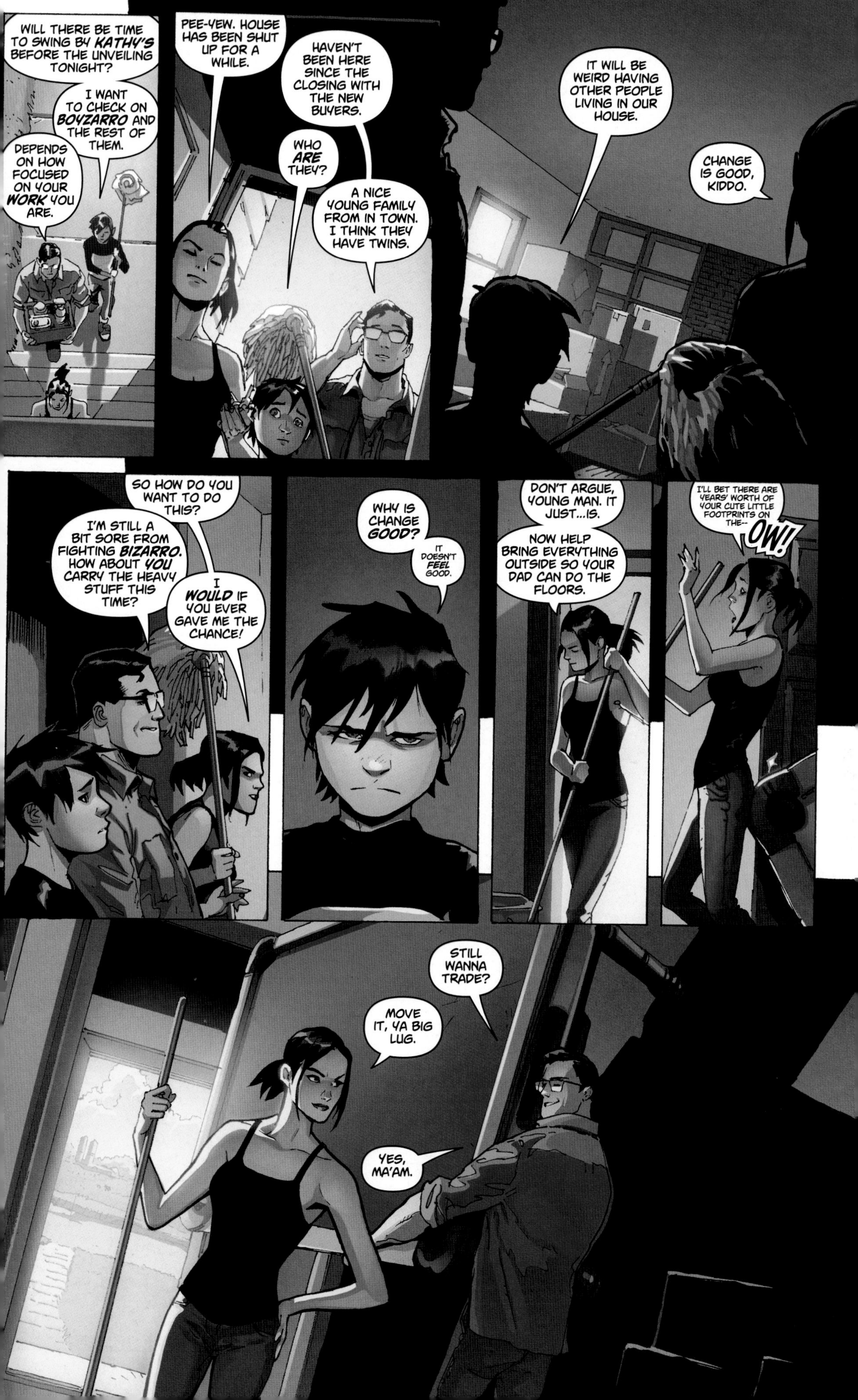
WILL THERE BE TIME TO SWING BY KATHY'S BEFORE THE UNVEILING TONIGHT?
I WANT TO CHECK ON BOYZARRO AND THE REST OF THEM.
DEPENDS ON HOW FOCUSED ON YOUR WORK YOU ARE.
PEE-YEW. HOUSE HAS BEEN SHUT UP FOR A WHILE.
HAVEN'T BEEN HERE SINCE THE CLOSING WITH THE NEW BUYERS.
WHO ARE THEY?
A NICE YOUNG FAMILY FROM IN TOWN. I THINK THEY HAVE TWINS.
IT WILL BE WEIRD HAVING OTHER PEOPLE LIVING IN OUR HOUSE.
CHANGE IS GOOD, KIDDO.
SO HOW DO YOU WANT TO DO THIS?
I'M STILL A BIT SORE FROM FIGHTING BIZARRO. HOW ABOUT YOU CARRY THE HEAVY STUFF THIS TIME?
I WOULD IF YOU EVER GAVE ME THE CHANCE!
WHY IS CHANGE GOOD?
IT DOESN'T FEEL GOOD.
DON'T ARGUE, YOUNG MAN. IT JUST...IS.
NOW HELP BRING EVERYTHING OUTSIDE SO YOUR DAD CAN DO THE FLOORS.
I'LL BET THERE ARE YEARS' WORTH OF YOUR CUTE LITTLE FOOTPRINTS ON THE--
OW!
STILL WANNA TRADE?
MOVE IT, YA BIG LUG.
YES, MA'AM.

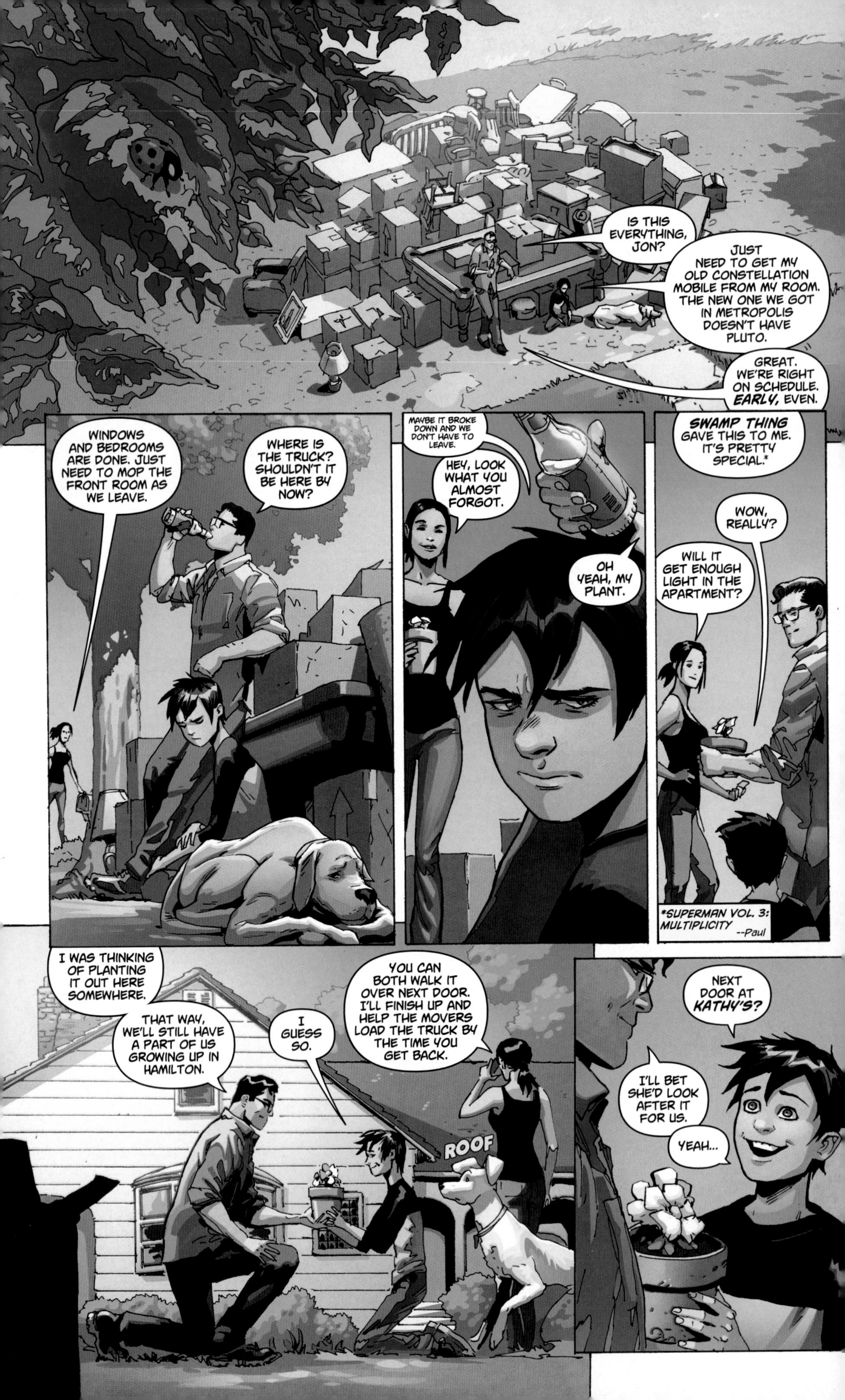
IS THIS EVERYTHING, JON?
JUST NEED TO GET MY OLD CONSTELLATION MOBILE FROM MY ROOM. THE NEW ONE WE GOT IN METROPOLIS DOESN'T HAVE PLUTO.
GREAT. WE'RE RIGHT ON SCHEDULE. EARLY, EVEN.
WINDOWS AND BEDROOMS ARE DONE. JUST NEED TO MOP THE FRONT ROOM AS WE LEAVE.
WHERE IS THE TRUCK? SHOULDN'T IT BE HERE BY NOW?
MAYBE IT BROKE DOWN AND WE DON'T HAVE TO LEAVE.
HEY, LOOK WHAT YOU ALMOST FORGOT.
OH YEAH, MY PLANT.
SWAMP THING GAVE THIS TO ME. IT'S PRETTY SPECIAL.*
WOW, REALLY?
WILL IT GET ENOUGH LIGHT IN THE APARTMENT?
*SUPERMAN VOL. 3: MULTIPLICITY --Paul
I WAS THINKING OF PLANTING IT OUT HERE SOMEWHERE.
THAT WAY, WE'LL STILL HAVE A PART OF US GROWING UP IN HAMILTON.
I GUESS SO.
YOU CAN BOTH WALK IT OVER NEXT DOOR. I'LL FINISH UP AND HELP THE MOVERS LOAD THE TRUCK BY THE TIME YOU GET BACK.
ROOF
NEXT DOOR AT KATHY'S?
I'LL BET SHE'D LOOK AFTER IT FOR US.
YEAH...

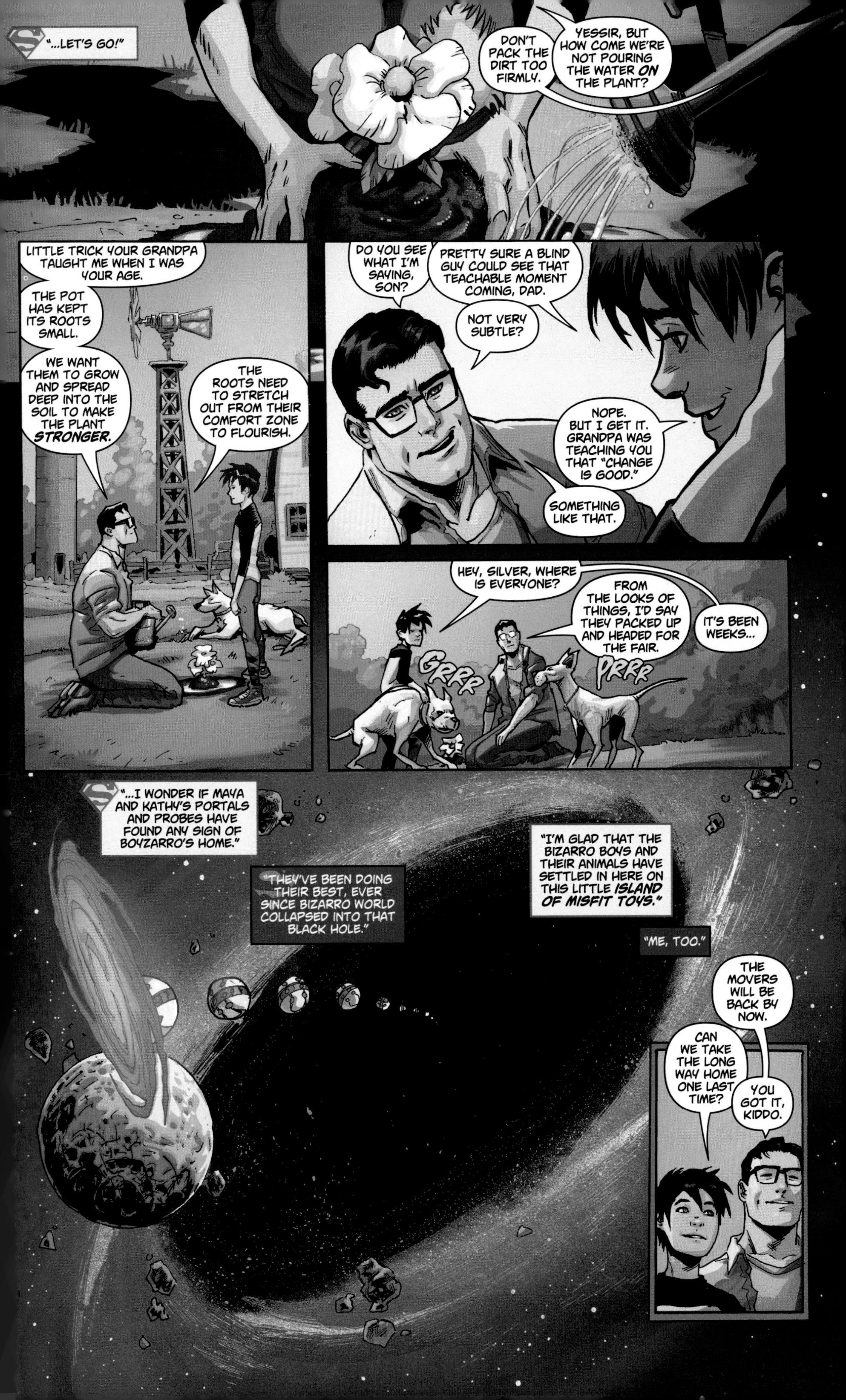
"...LET'S GO!"
DON'T PACK THE DIRT TOO FIRMLY.
YESSIR, BUT HOW COME WE'RE NOT POURING THE WATER ON THE PLANT?
LITTLE TRICK YOUR GRANDPA TAUGHT ME WHEN I WAS YOUR AGE.
THE POT HAS KEPT ITS ROOTS SMALL.
WE WANT THEM TO GROW AND SPREAD DEEP INTO THE SOIL TO MAKE THE PLANT STRONGER.
THE ROOTS NEED TO STRETCH OUT FROM THEIR COMFORT ZONE TO FLOURISH.
DO YOU SEE WHAT I'M SAYING, SON?
PRETTY SURE A BLIND GUY COULD SEE THAT TEACHABLE MOMENT COMING, DAD.
NOT VERY SUBTLE?
NOPE. BUT I GET IT. GRANDPA WAS TEACHING YOU THAT "CHANGE IS GOOD."
SOMETHING LIKE THAT.
HEY, SILVER, WHERE IS EVERYONE?
FROM THE LOOKS OF THINGS, I'D SAY THEY PACKED UP AND HEADED FOR THE FAIR.
IT'S BEEN WEEKS...
GRRR
PRRR
"...I WONDER IF MAYA AND KATHY'S PORTALS AND PROBES HAVE FOUND ANY SIGN OF BOYZARRO'S HOME."
"THEY'VE BEEN DOING THEIR BEST, EVER SINCE BIZARRO WORLD COLLAPSED INTO THAT BLACK HOLE."
"I'M GLAD THAT THE BIZARRO BOYS AND THEIR ANIMALS HAVE SETTLED IN HERE ON THIS LITTLE ISLAND OF MISFIT TOYS."
"ME, TOO."
THE MOVERS WILL BE BACK BY NOW.
CAN WE TAKE THE LONG WAY HOME ONE LAST TIME?
YOU GOT IT, KIDDO.

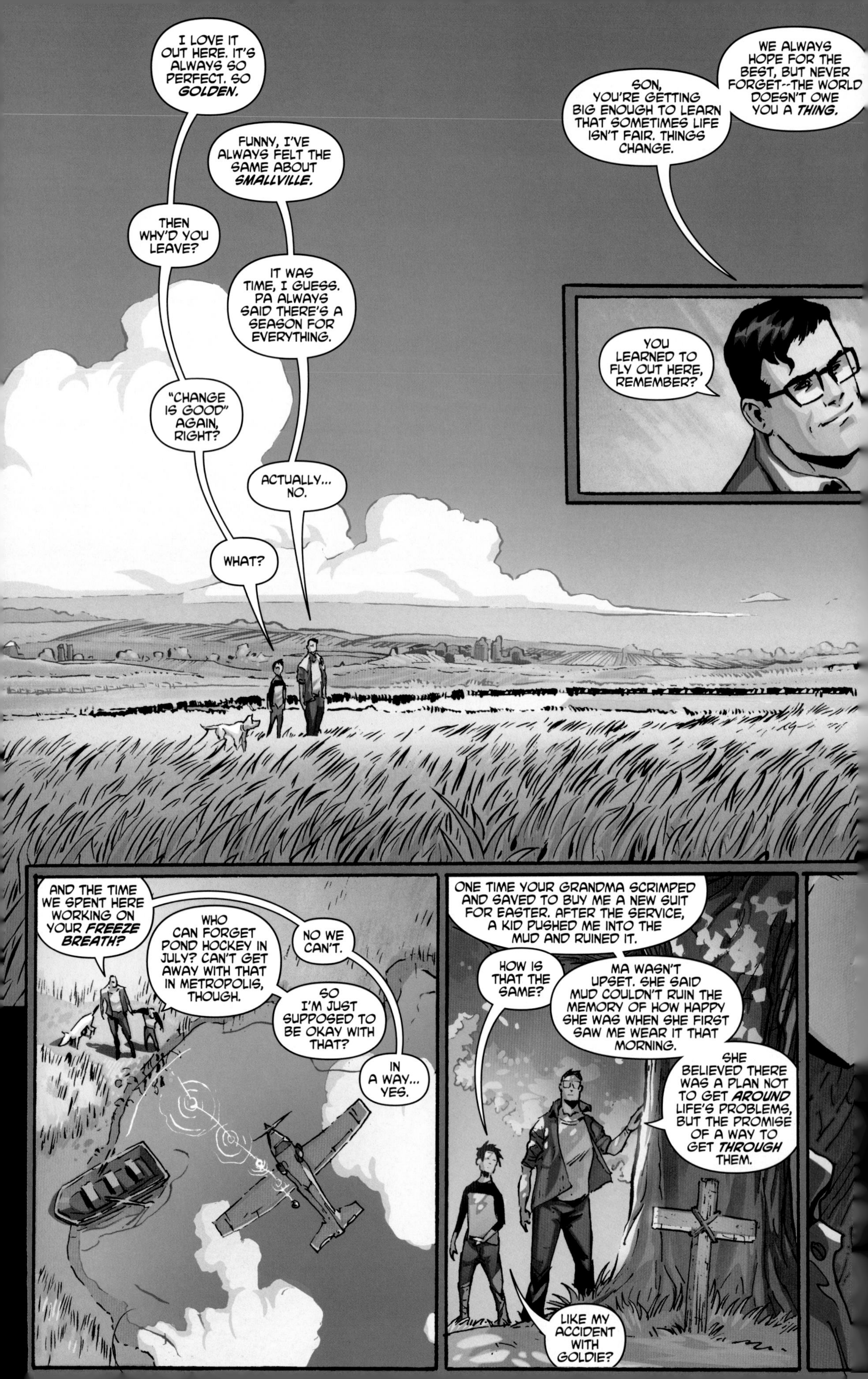
I LOVE IT OUT HERE. IT'S ALWAYS SO PERFECT. SO *GOLDEN.*
FUNNY, I'VE ALWAYS FELT THE SAME ABOUT *SMALLVILLE.*
THEN WHY'D YOU LEAVE?
IT WAS TIME, I GUESS. PA ALWAYS SAID THERE'S A SEASON FOR EVERYTHING.
"CHANGE IS GOOD" AGAIN, RIGHT?
ACTUALLY... NO.
WHAT?
SON, YOU'RE GETTING BIG ENOUGH TO LEARN THAT SOMETIMES LIFE ISN'T FAIR. THINGS CHANGE.
WE ALWAYS HOPE FOR THE BEST, BUT NEVER FORGET--THE WORLD DOESN'T OWE YOU A *THING.*
YOU LEARNED TO FLY OUT HERE, REMEMBER?
AND THE TIME WE SPENT HERE WORKING ON YOUR *FREEZE BREATH?*
WHO CAN FORGET POND HOCKEY IN JULY? CAN'T GET AWAY WITH THAT IN METROPOLIS, THOUGH.
NO WE CAN'T.
SO I'M JUST SUPPOSED TO BE OKAY WITH THAT?
IN A WAY... YES.
ONE TIME YOUR GRANDMA SCRIMPED AND SAVED TO BUY ME A NEW SUIT FOR EASTER. AFTER THE SERVICE, A KID PUSHED ME INTO THE MUD AND RUINED IT.
HOW IS THAT THE SAME?
MA WASN'T UPSET. SHE SAID MUD COULDN'T RUIN THE MEMORY OF HOW HAPPY SHE WAS WHEN SHE FIRST SAW ME WEAR IT THAT MORNING.
SHE BELIEVED THERE WAS A PLAN NOT TO GET *AROUND* LIFE'S PROBLEMS, BUT THE PROMISE OF A WAY TO GET *THROUGH* THEM.
LIKE MY ACCIDENT WITH GOLDIE?

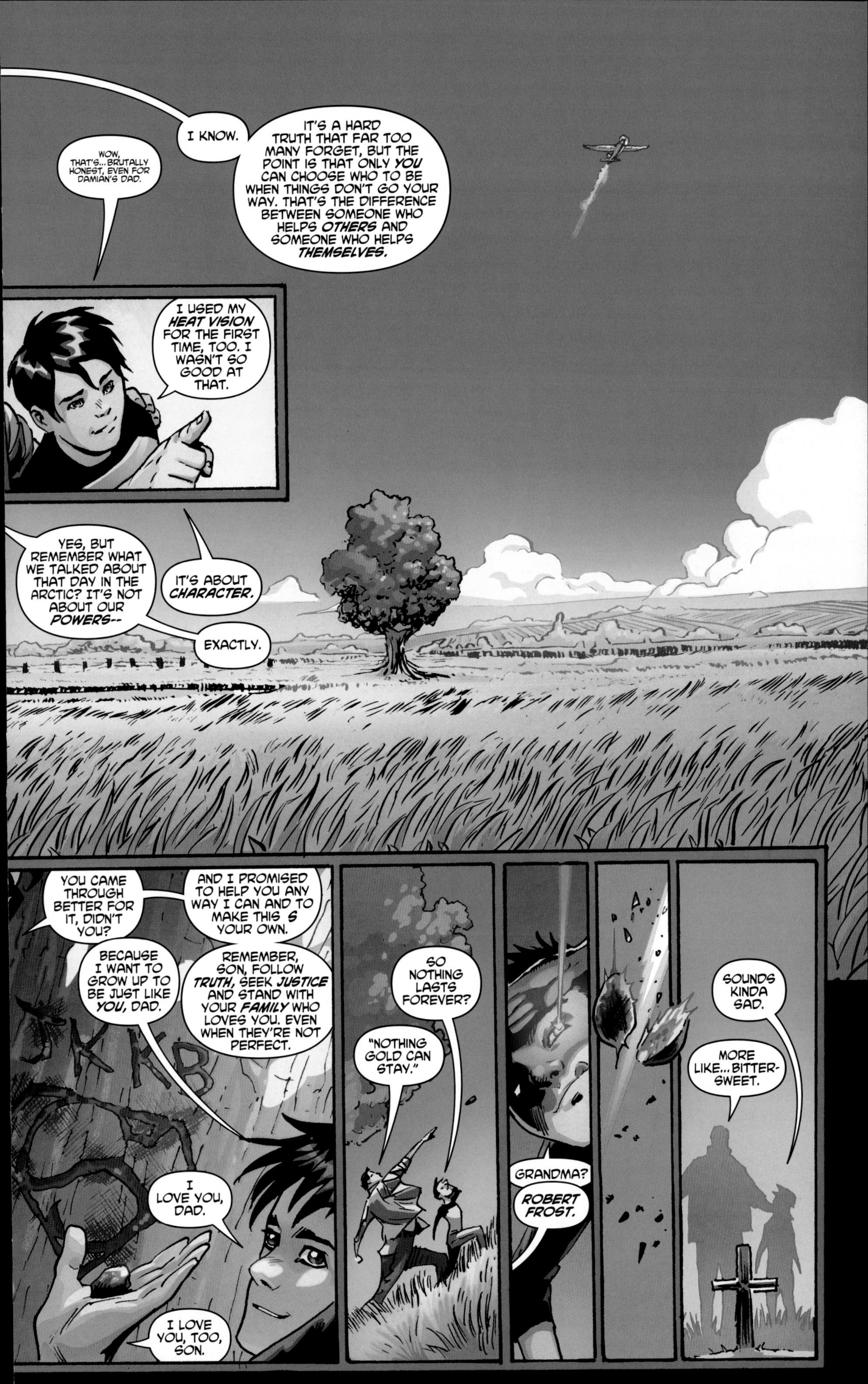
WOW, THAT'S...BRUTALLY HONEST, EVEN FOR DAMIAN'S DAD.
I KNOW.
IT'S A HARD TRUTH THAT FAR TOO MANY FORGET, BUT THE POINT IS THAT ONLY YOU CAN CHOOSE WHO TO BE WHEN THINGS DON'T GO YOUR WAY. THAT'S THE DIFFERENCE BETWEEN SOMEONE WHO HELPS OTHERS AND SOMEONE WHO HELPS THEMSELVES.
I USED MY HEAT VISION FOR THE FIRST TIME, TOO. I WASN'T SO GOOD AT THAT.
YES, BUT REMEMBER WHAT WE TALKED ABOUT THAT DAY IN THE ARCTIC? IT'S NOT ABOUT OUR POWERS--
IT'S ABOUT CHARACTER.
EXACTLY.
YOU CAME THROUGH BETTER FOR IT, DIDN'T YOU?
AND I PROMISED TO HELP YOU ANY WAY I CAN AND TO MAKE THIS S YOUR OWN.
BECAUSE I WANT TO GROW UP TO BE JUST LIKE YOU, DAD.
REMEMBER, SON, FOLLOW TRUTH, SEEK JUSTICE AND STAND WITH YOUR FAMILY WHO LOVES YOU. EVEN WHEN THEY'RE NOT PERFECT.
I LOVE YOU, DAD.
I LOVE YOU, TOO, SON.
SO NOTHING LASTS FOREVER?
"NOTHING GOLD CAN STAY."
GRANDMA?
ROBERT FROST.
SOUNDS KINDA SAD.
MORE LIKE...BITTER-SWEET.

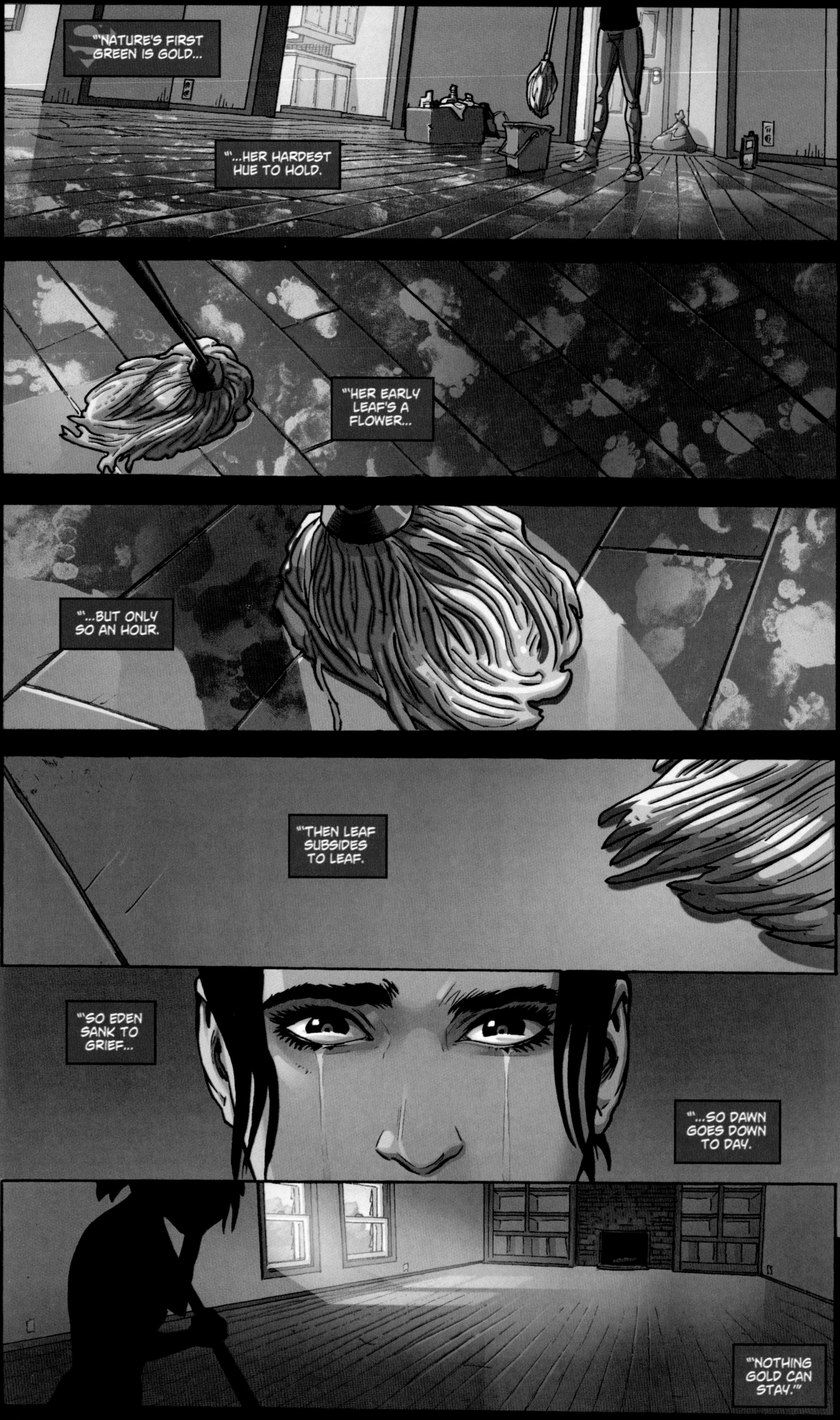
"'NATURE'S FIRST GREEN IS GOLD...
"'...HER HARDEST HUE TO HOLD.
"'HER EARLY LEAF'S A FLOWER...
"'...BUT ONLY SO AN HOUR.
"'THEN LEAF SUBSIDES TO LEAF.
"'SO EDEN SANK TO GRIEF...
"'...SO DAWN GOES DOWN TO DAY.
"'NOTHING GOLD CAN STAY.'"

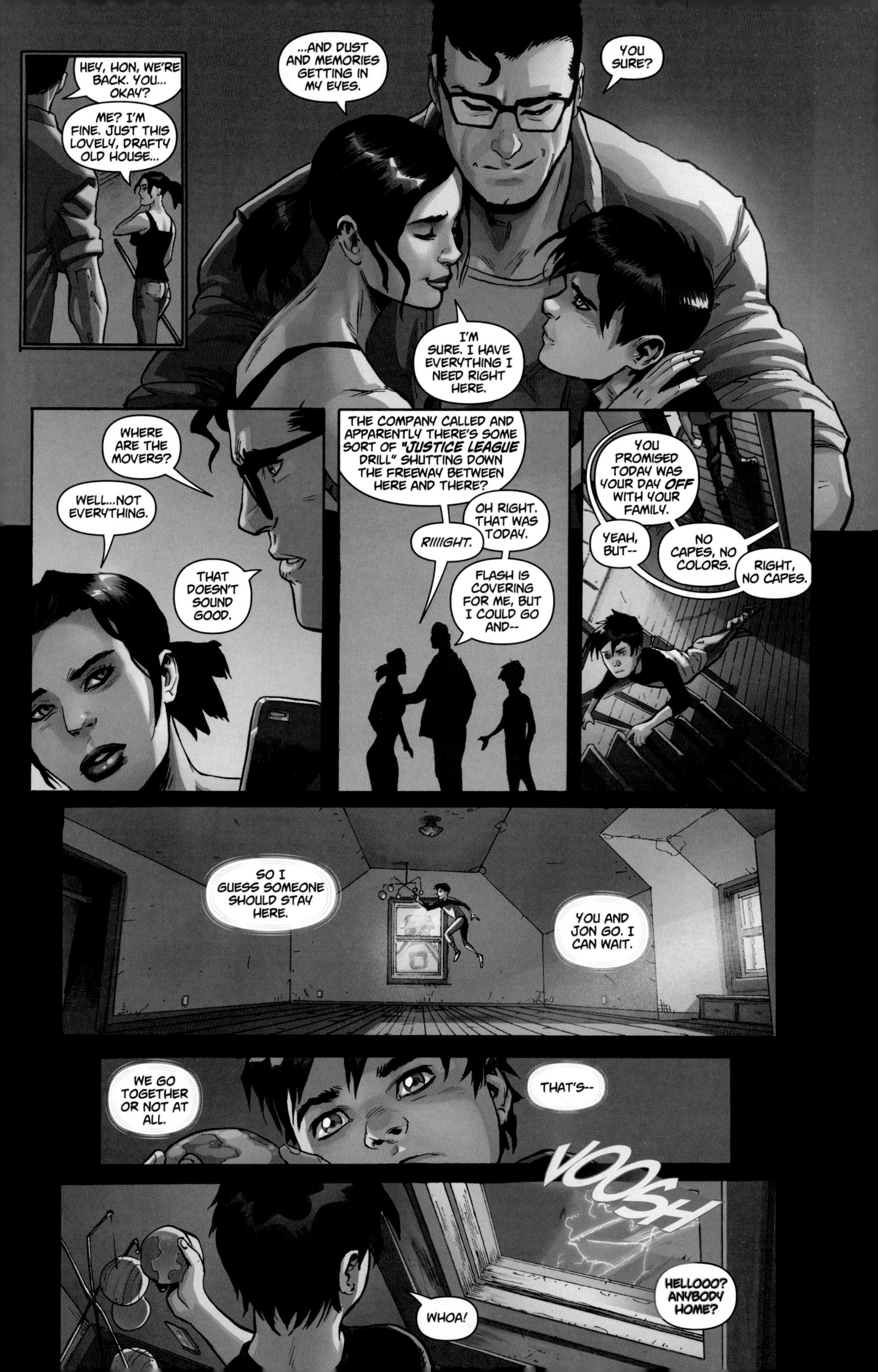
HEY, HON, WE'RE BACK. YOU... OKAY?
ME? I'M FINE. JUST THIS LOVELY, DRAFTY OLD HOUSE...
...AND DUST AND MEMORIES GETTING IN MY EYES.
YOU SURE?
I'M SURE. I HAVE EVERYTHING I NEED RIGHT HERE.
WHERE ARE THE MOVERS?
WELL...NOT EVERYTHING.
THAT DOESN'T SOUND GOOD.
THE COMPANY CALLED AND APPARENTLY THERE'S SOME SORT OF "JUSTICE LEAGUE DRILL" SHUTTING DOWN THE FREEWAY BETWEEN HERE AND THERE?
RIIIIGHT.
OH RIGHT. THAT WAS TODAY.
FLASH IS COVERING FOR ME, BUT I COULD GO AND--
YOU PROMISED TODAY WAS YOUR DAY OFF WITH YOUR FAMILY.
YEAH, BUT--
NO CAPES, NO COLORS.
RIGHT, NO CAPES.
SO I GUESS SOMEONE SHOULD STAY HERE.
YOU AND JON GO. I CAN WAIT.
WE GO TOGETHER OR NOT AT ALL.
THAT'S--
VOOSH
WHOA!
HELLOOO? ANYBODY HOME?

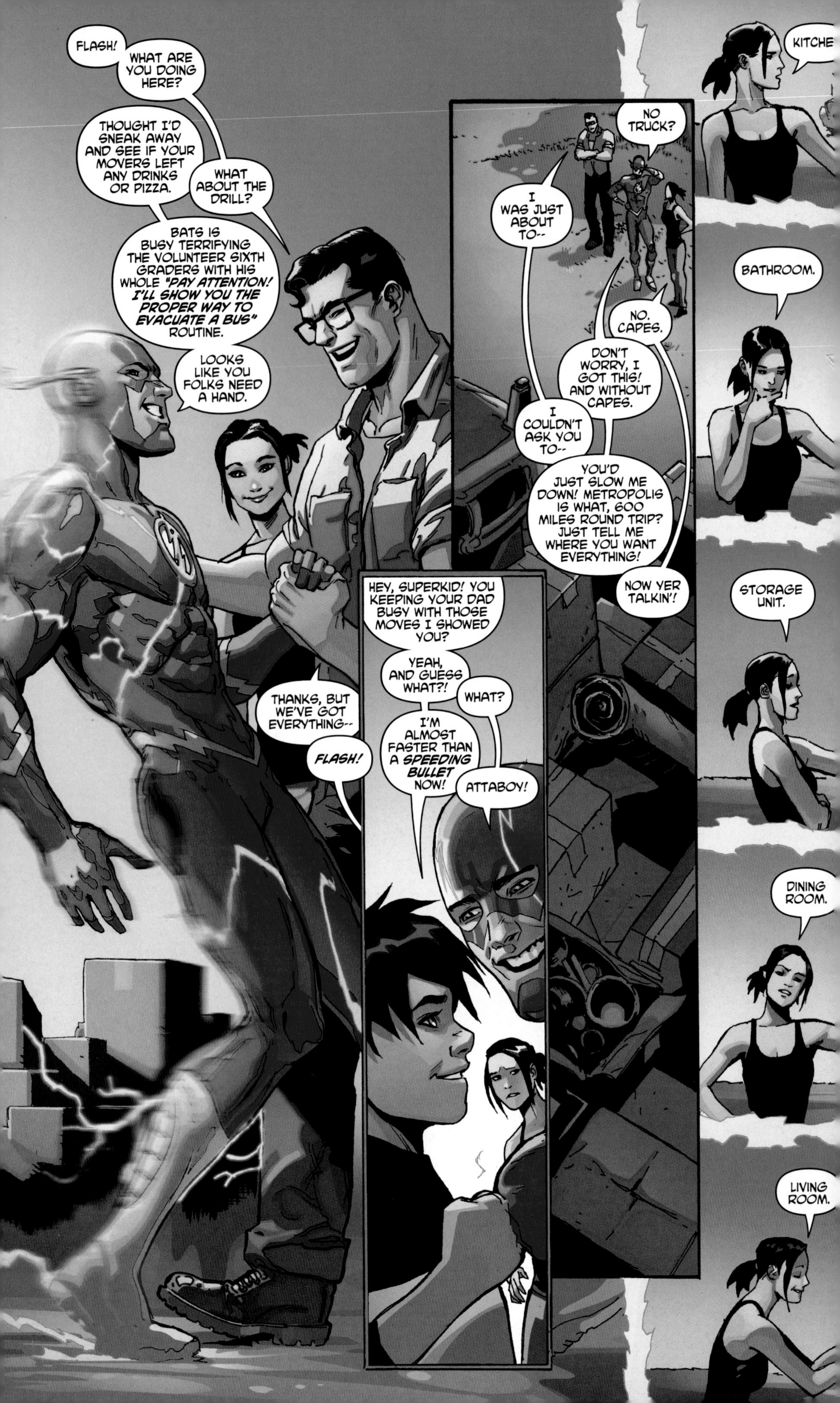

FLASH!
WHAT ARE YOU DOING HERE?
THOUGHT I'D SNEAK AWAY AND SEE IF YOUR MOVERS LEFT ANY DRINKS OR PIZZA.
WHAT ABOUT THE DRILL?
BATS IS BUSY TERRIFYING THE VOLUNTEER SIXTH GRADERS WITH HIS WHOLE "PAY ATTENTION! I'LL SHOW YOU THE PROPER WAY TO EVACUATE A BUS" ROUTINE.
LOOKS LIKE YOU FOLKS NEED A HAND.
THANKS, BUT WE'VE GOT EVERYTHING--
FLASH!
NO TRUCK?
I WAS JUST ABOUT TO--
NO. CAPES.
DON'T WORRY, I GOT THIS! AND WITHOUT CAPES.
I COULDN'T ASK YOU TO--
YOU'D JUST SLOW ME DOWN! METROPOLIS IS WHAT, 600 MILES ROUND TRIP? JUST TELL ME WHERE YOU WANT EVERYTHING!
NOW YER TALKIN'!
HEY, SUPERKID! YOU KEEPING YOUR DAD BUSY WITH THOSE MOVES I SHOWED YOU?
YEAH, AND GUESS WHAT?!
WHAT?
I'M ALMOST FASTER THAN A SPEEDING BULLET NOW!
ATTABOY!
KITCHE
BATHROOM.
STORAGE UNIT.
DINING ROOM.
LIVING ROOM.

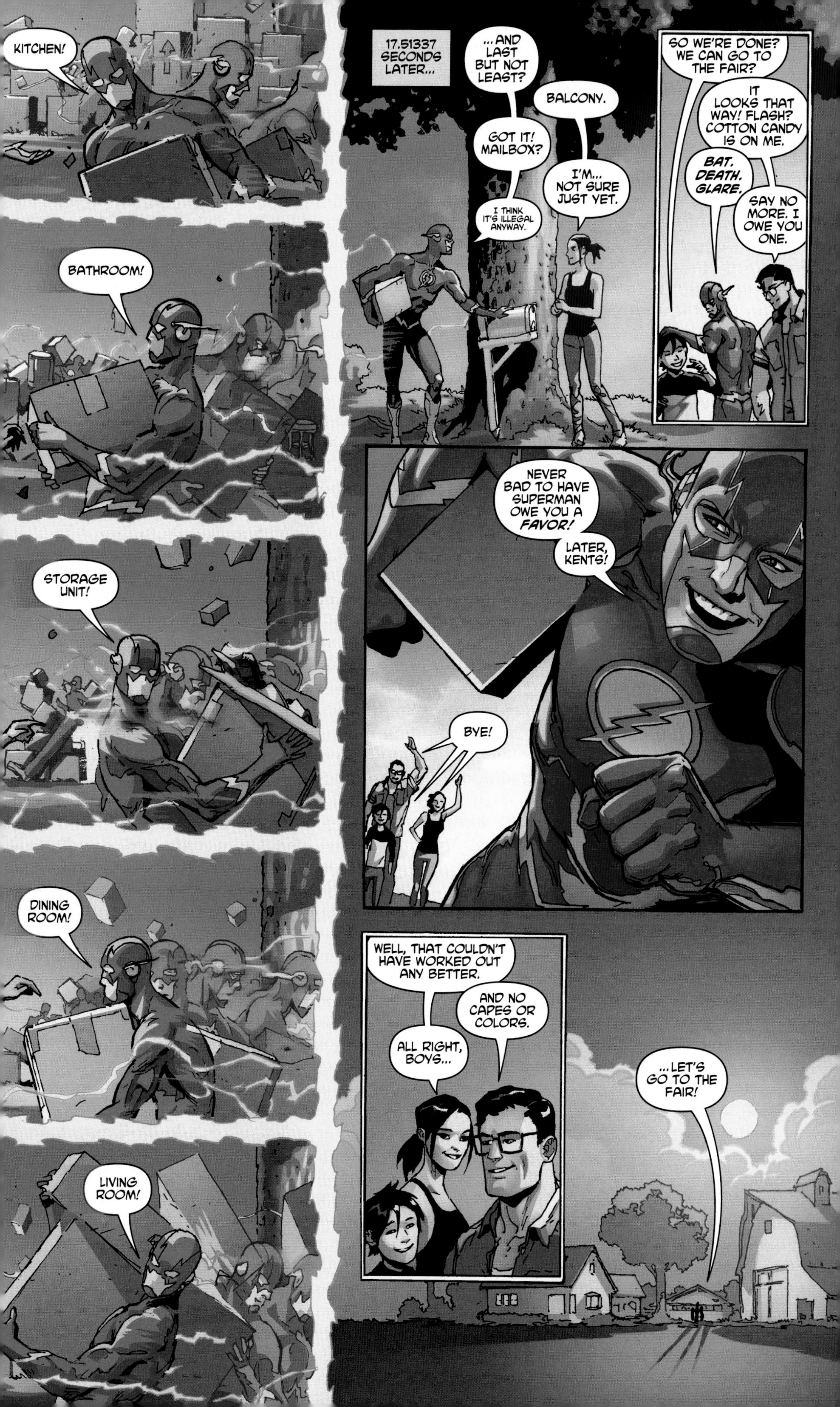

KITCHEN!
BATHROOM!
STORAGE UNIT!
DINING ROOM!
LIVING ROOM!
17.51337 SECONDS LATER...
...AND LAST BUT NOT LEAST?
BALCONY.
GOT IT! MAILBOX?
I'M... NOT SURE JUST YET.
I THINK IT'S ILLEGAL ANYWAY.
SO WE'RE DONE? WE CAN GO TO THE FAIR?
IT LOOKS THAT WAY! FLASH? COTTON CANDY IS ON ME.
BAT. DEATH. GLARE.
SAY NO MORE. I OWE YOU ONE.
NEVER BAD TO HAVE SUPERMAN OWE YOU A FAVOR!
LATER, KENTS!
BYE!
WELL, THAT COULDN'T HAVE WORKED OUT ANY BETTER.
AND NO CAPES OR COLORS.
ALL RIGHT, BOYS...
...LET'S GO TO THE FAIR!

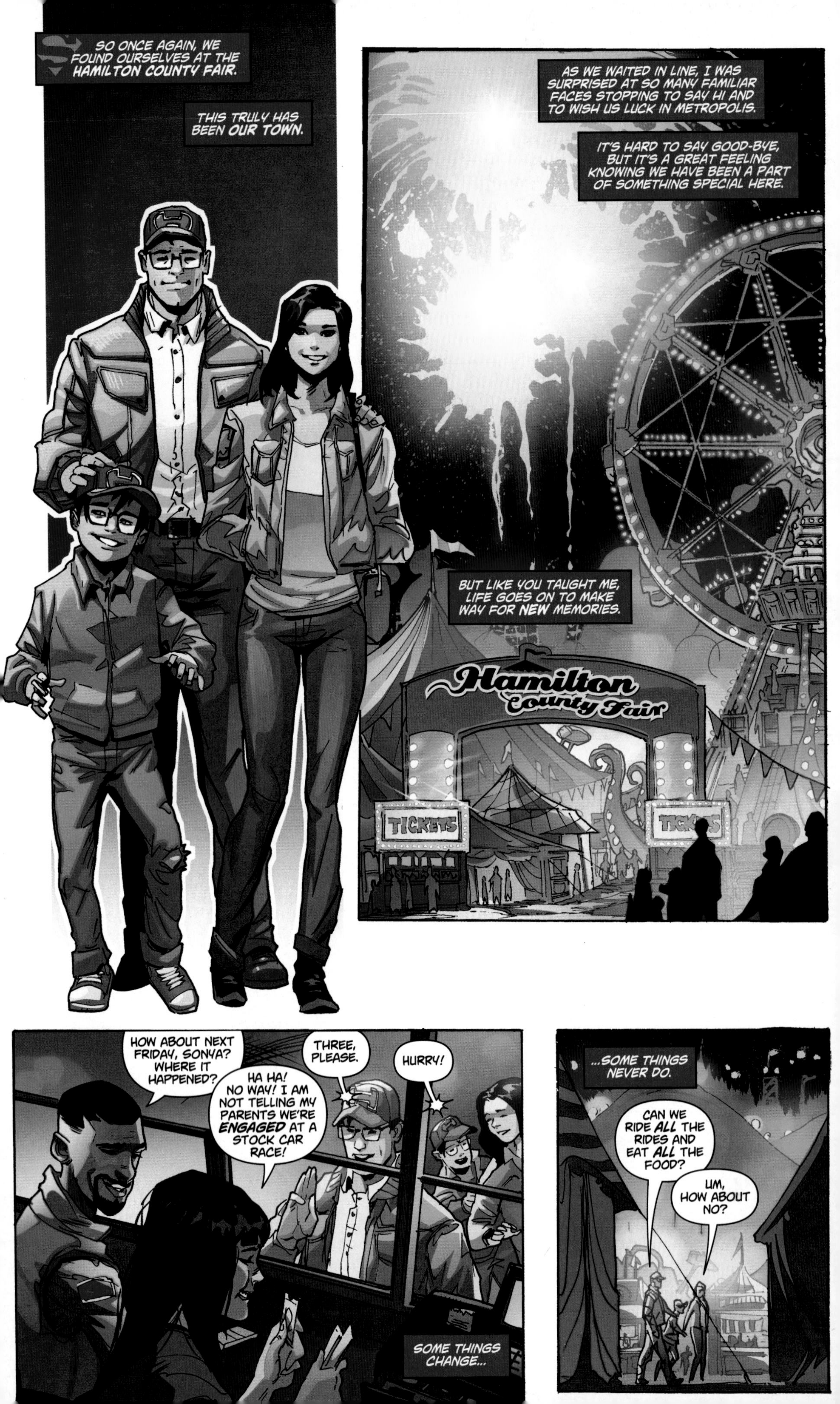
SO ONCE AGAIN, WE FOUND OURSELVES AT THE HAMILTON COUNTY FAIR.
THIS TRULY HAS BEEN OUR TOWN.
AS WE WAITED IN LINE, I WAS SURPRISED AT SO MANY FAMILIAR FACES STOPPING TO SAY HI AND TO WISH US LUCK IN METROPOLIS.
IT'S HARD TO SAY GOOD-BYE, BUT IT'S A GREAT FEELING KNOWING WE HAVE BEEN A PART OF SOMETHING SPECIAL HERE.
BUT LIKE YOU TAUGHT ME, LIFE GOES ON TO MAKE WAY FOR NEW MEMORIES.
Hamilton County Fair
TICKETS
HOW ABOUT NEXT FRIDAY, SONYA? WHERE IT HAPPENED?
HA HA! NO WAY! I AM NOT TELLING MY PARENTS WE'RE ENGAGED AT A STOCK CAR RACE!
THREE, PLEASE.
HURRY!
SOME THINGS CHANGE...
...SOME THINGS NEVER DO.
CAN WE RIDE ALL THE RIDES AND EAT ALL THE FOOD?
UM, HOW ABOUT NO?

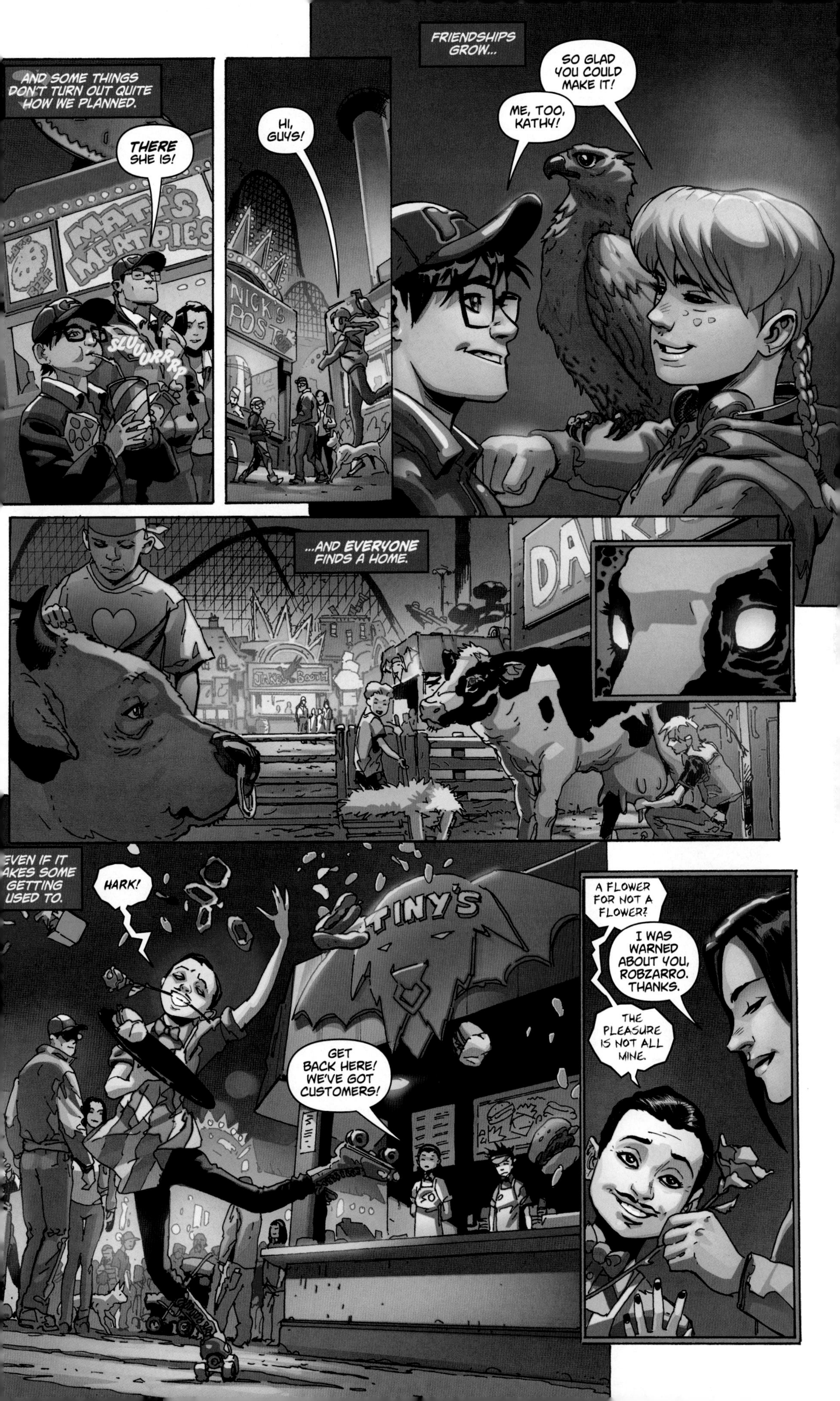
AND SOME THINGS DON'T TURN OUT QUITE HOW WE PLANNED.
THERE SHE IS!
MATT'S MEAT PIES
SLUUURRRP
HI, GUYS!
NICK'S POST
FRIENDSHIPS GROW...
SO GLAD YOU COULD MAKE IT!
ME, TOO, KATHY!
...AND EVERYONE FINDS A HOME.
JAKE'S BOOTH
EVEN IF IT TAKES SOME GETTING USED TO.
HARK!
TINY'S
GET BACK HERE! WE'VE GOT CUSTOMERS!
A FLOWER FOR NOT A FLOWER?
I WAS WARNED ABOUT YOU, ROBZARRO. THANKS.
THE PLEASURE IS NOT ALL MINE.

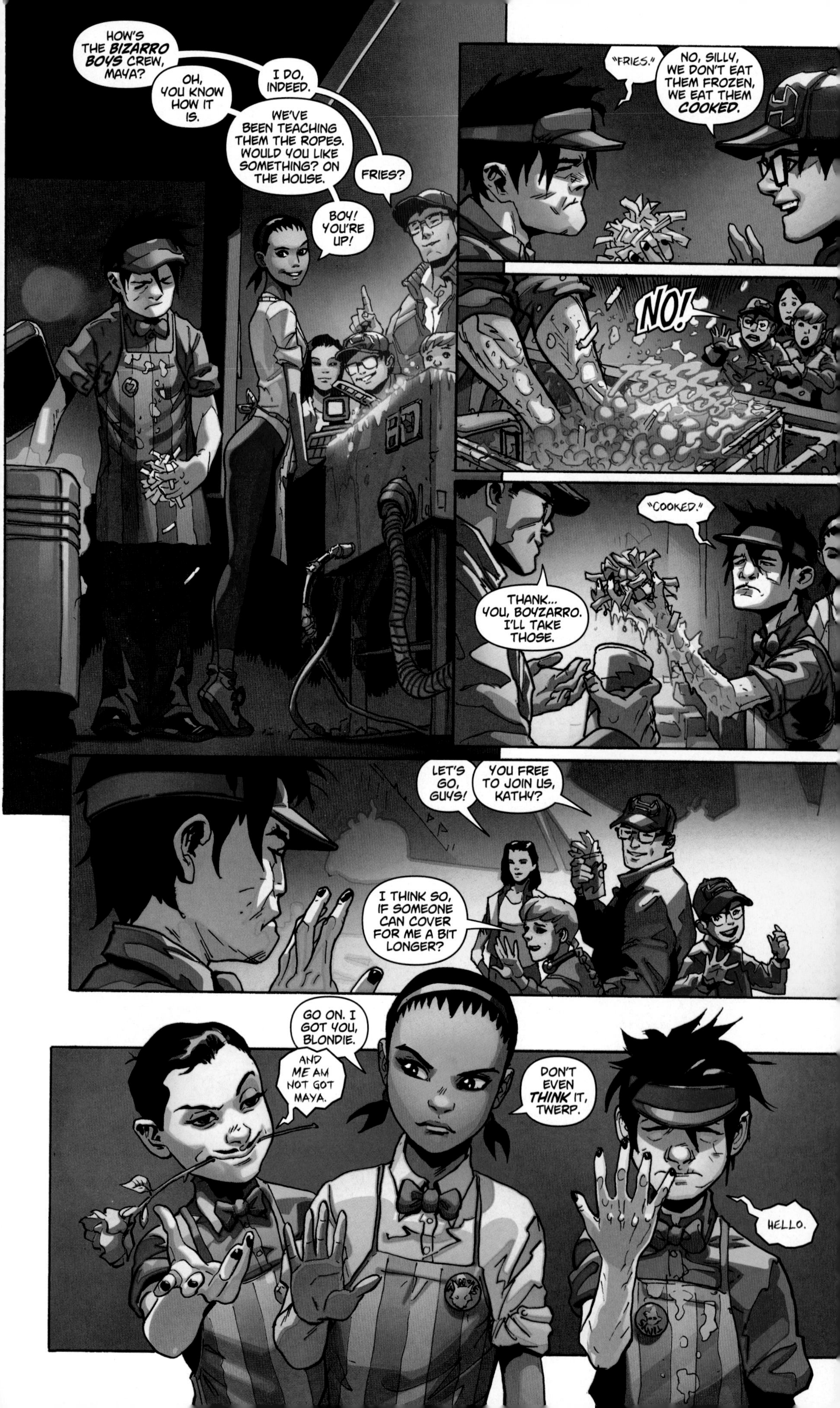

HOW'S THE BIZARRO BOYS CREW, MAYA?
OH, YOU KNOW HOW IT IS.
I DO, INDEED.
WE'VE BEEN TEACHING THEM THE ROPES. WOULD YOU LIKE SOMETHING? ON THE HOUSE.
FRIES?
BOY! YOU'RE UP!
"FRIES."
NO, SILLY, WE DON'T EAT THEM FROZEN, WE EAT THEM COOKED.
NO!
TSSSSS
"COOKED."
THANK... YOU, BOYZARRO. I'LL TAKE THOSE.
LET'S GO, GUYS!
YOU FREE TO JOIN US, KATHY?
I THINK SO, IF SOMEONE CAN COVER FOR ME A BIT LONGER?
GO ON. I GOT YOU, BLONDIE.
AND ME AM NOT GOT MAYA.
DON'T EVEN THINK IT, TWERP.
HELLO.

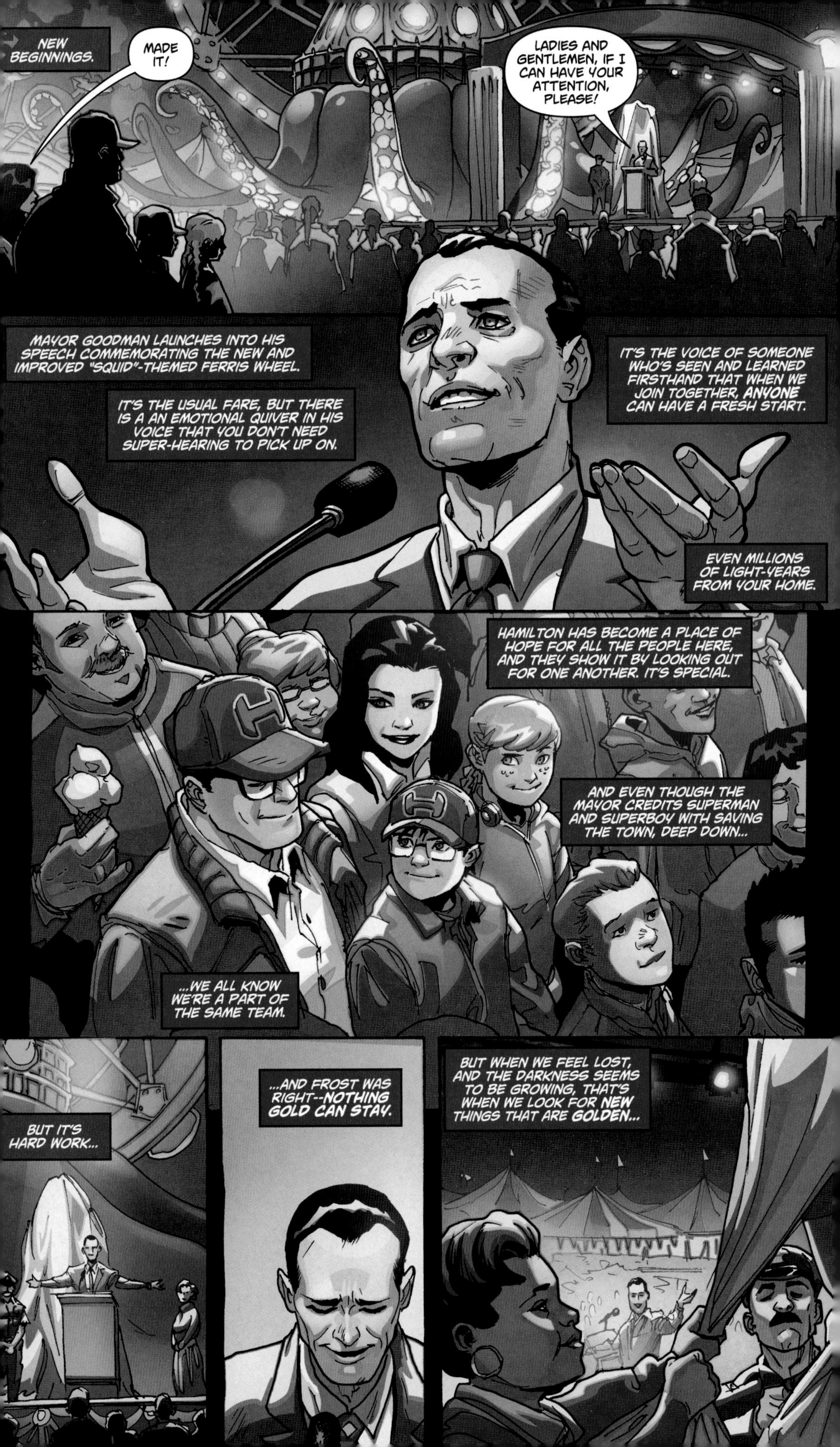
NEW BEGINNINGS.
MADE IT!
LADIES AND GENTLEMEN, IF I CAN HAVE YOUR ATTENTION, PLEASE!
MAYOR GOODMAN LAUNCHES INTO HIS SPEECH COMMEMORATING THE NEW AND IMPROVED "SQUID"-THEMED FERRIS WHEEL.
IT'S THE USUAL FARE, BUT THERE IS A AN EMOTIONAL QUIVER IN HIS VOICE THAT YOU DON'T NEED SUPER-HEARING TO PICK UP ON.
IT'S THE VOICE OF SOMEONE WHO'S SEEN AND LEARNED FIRSTHAND THAT WHEN WE JOIN TOGETHER, ANYONE CAN HAVE A FRESH START.
EVEN MILLIONS OF LIGHT-YEARS FROM YOUR HOME.
HAMILTON HAS BECOME A PLACE OF HOPE FOR ALL THE PEOPLE HERE, AND THEY SHOW IT BY LOOKING OUT FOR ONE ANOTHER. IT'S SPECIAL.
AND EVEN THOUGH THE MAYOR CREDITS SUPERMAN AND SUPERBOY WITH SAVING THE TOWN, DEEP DOWN...
...WE ALL KNOW WE'RE A PART OF THE SAME TEAM.
BUT IT'S HARD WORK...
...AND FROST WAS RIGHT--NOTHING GOLD CAN STAY.
BUT WHEN WE FEEL LOST, AND THE DARKNESS SEEMS TO BE GROWING, THAT'S WHEN WE LOOK FOR NEW THINGS THAT ARE GOLDEN...

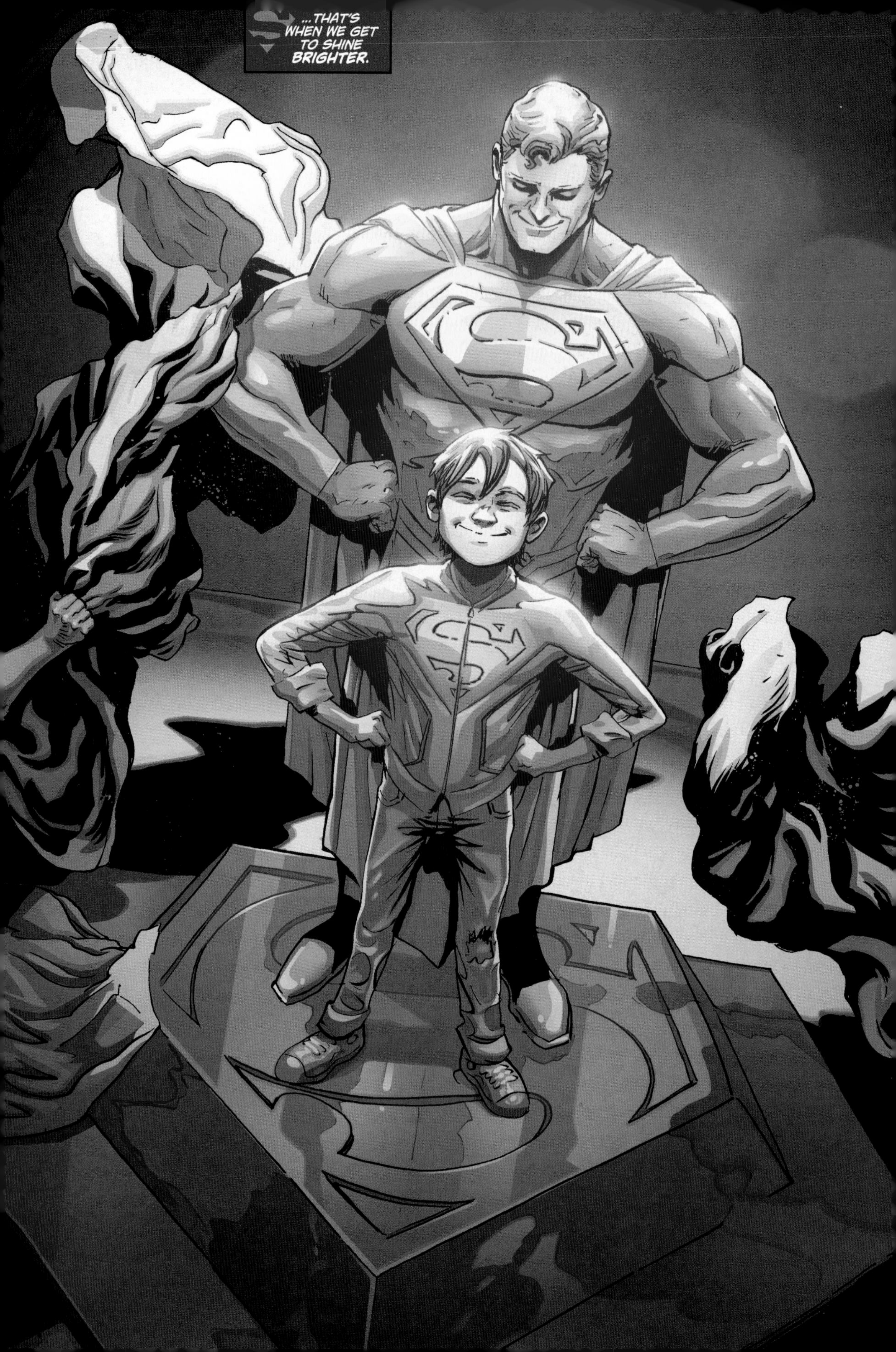
...THAT'S WHEN WE GET TO SHINE BRIGHTER.

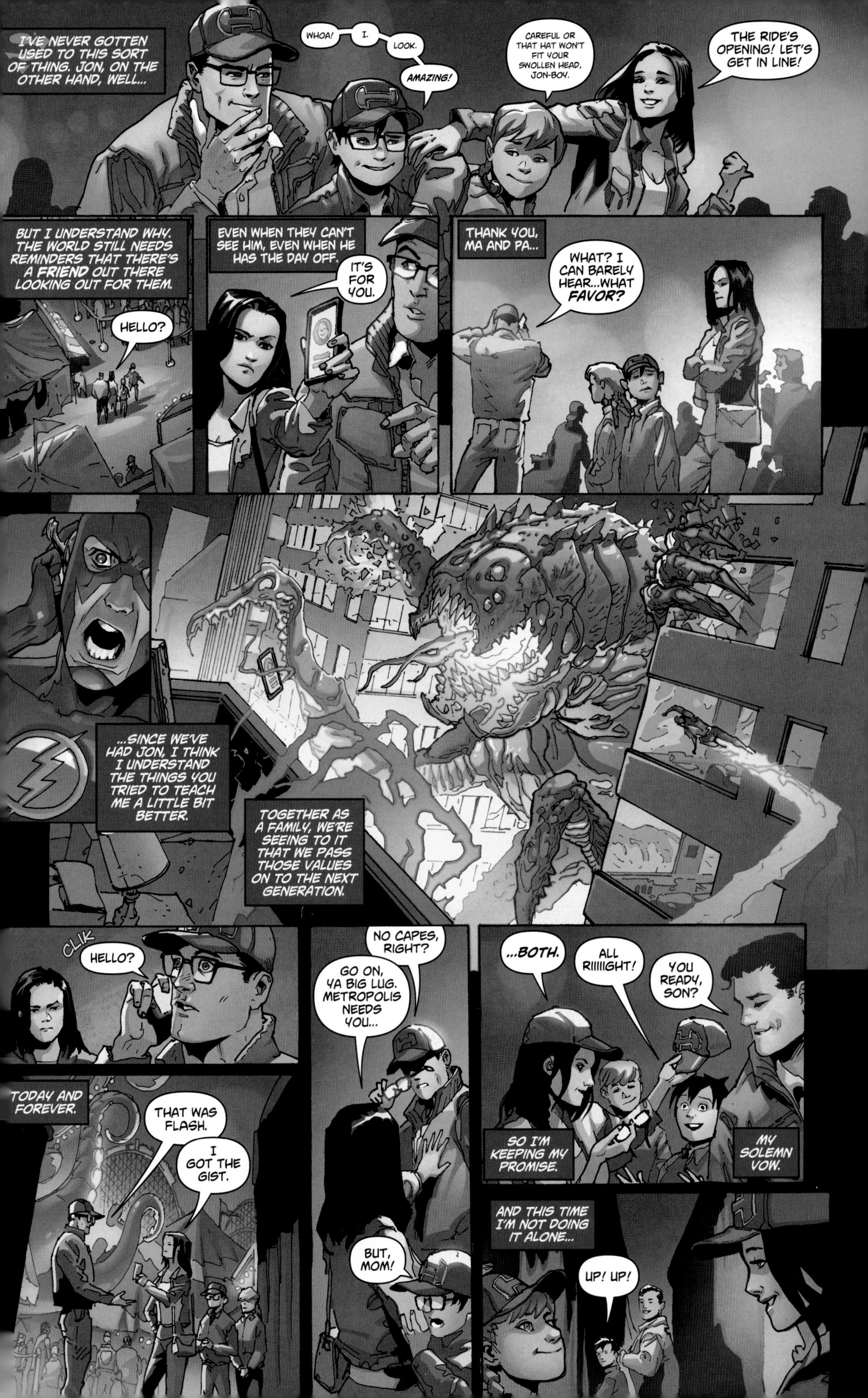
I'VE NEVER GOTTEN USED TO THIS SORT OF THING. JON, ON THE OTHER HAND, WELL...
WHOA!
I.
LOOK.
AMAZING!
CAREFUL OR THAT HAT WON'T FIT YOUR SWOLLEN HEAD, JON-BOY.
THE RIDE'S OPENING! LET'S GET IN LINE!
BUT I UNDERSTAND WHY. THE WORLD STILL NEEDS REMINDERS THAT THERE'S A FRIEND OUT THERE LOOKING OUT FOR THEM.
HELLO?
EVEN WHEN THEY CAN'T SEE HIM, EVEN WHEN HE HAS THE DAY OFF.
IT'S FOR YOU.
THANK YOU, MA AND PA...
WHAT? I CAN BARELY HEAR...WHAT FAVOR?
...SINCE WE'VE HAD JON, I THINK I UNDERSTAND THE THINGS YOU TRIED TO TEACH ME A LITTLE BIT BETTER.
TOGETHER AS A FAMILY, WE'RE SEEING TO IT THAT WE PASS THOSE VALUES ON TO THE NEXT GENERATION.
CLIK
HELLO?
TODAY AND FOREVER.
THAT WAS FLASH.
I GOT THE GIST.
NO CAPES, RIGHT?
GO ON, YA BIG LUG. METROPOLIS NEEDS YOU...
BUT, MOM!
...BOTH.
ALL RIIIIIGHT!
YOU READY, SON?
SO I'M KEEPING MY PROMISE.
MY SOLEMN VOW.
AND THIS TIME I'M NOT DOING IT ALONE...
UP! UP!

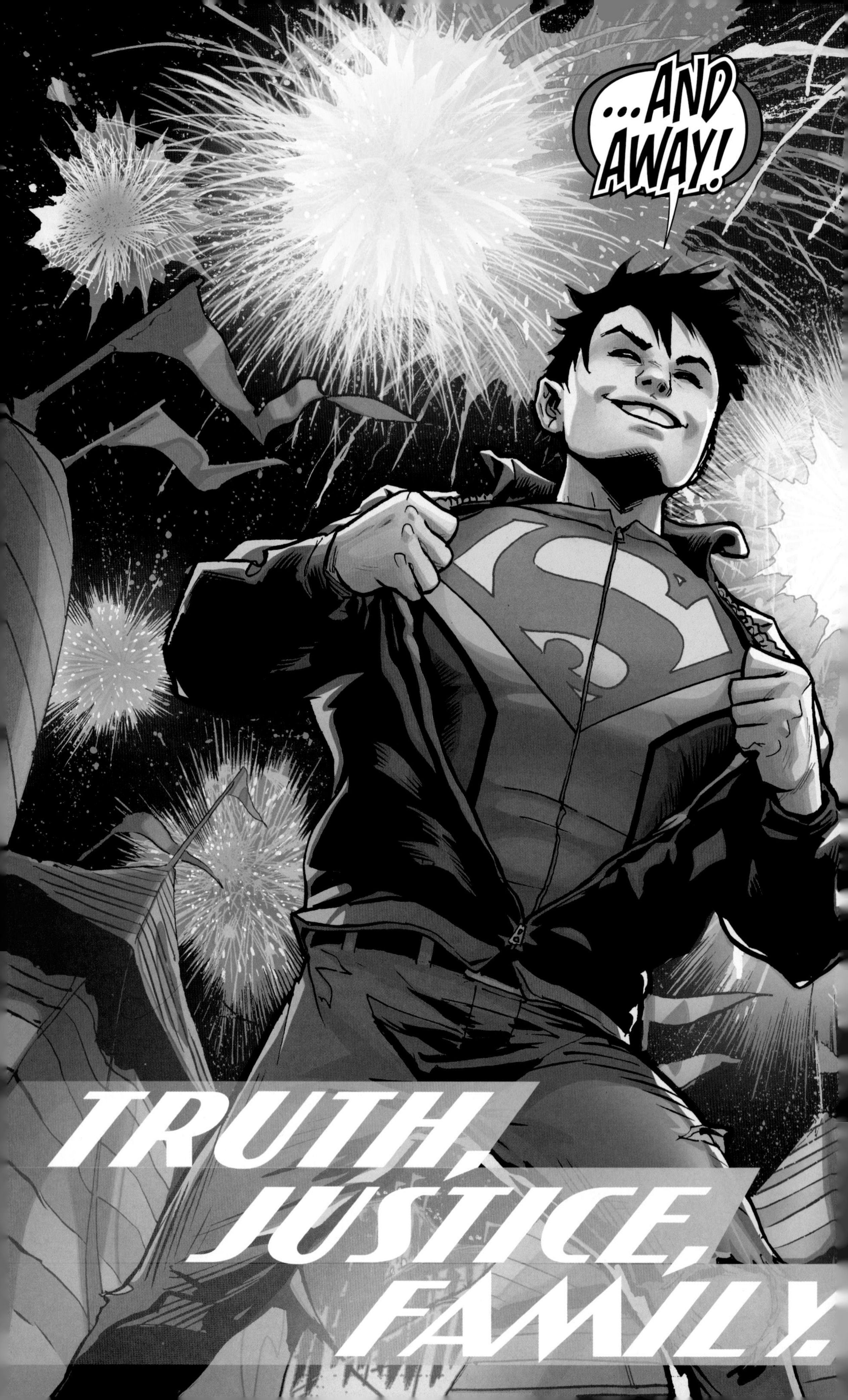
...AND AWAY!
TRUTH, JUSTICE, FAMILY.

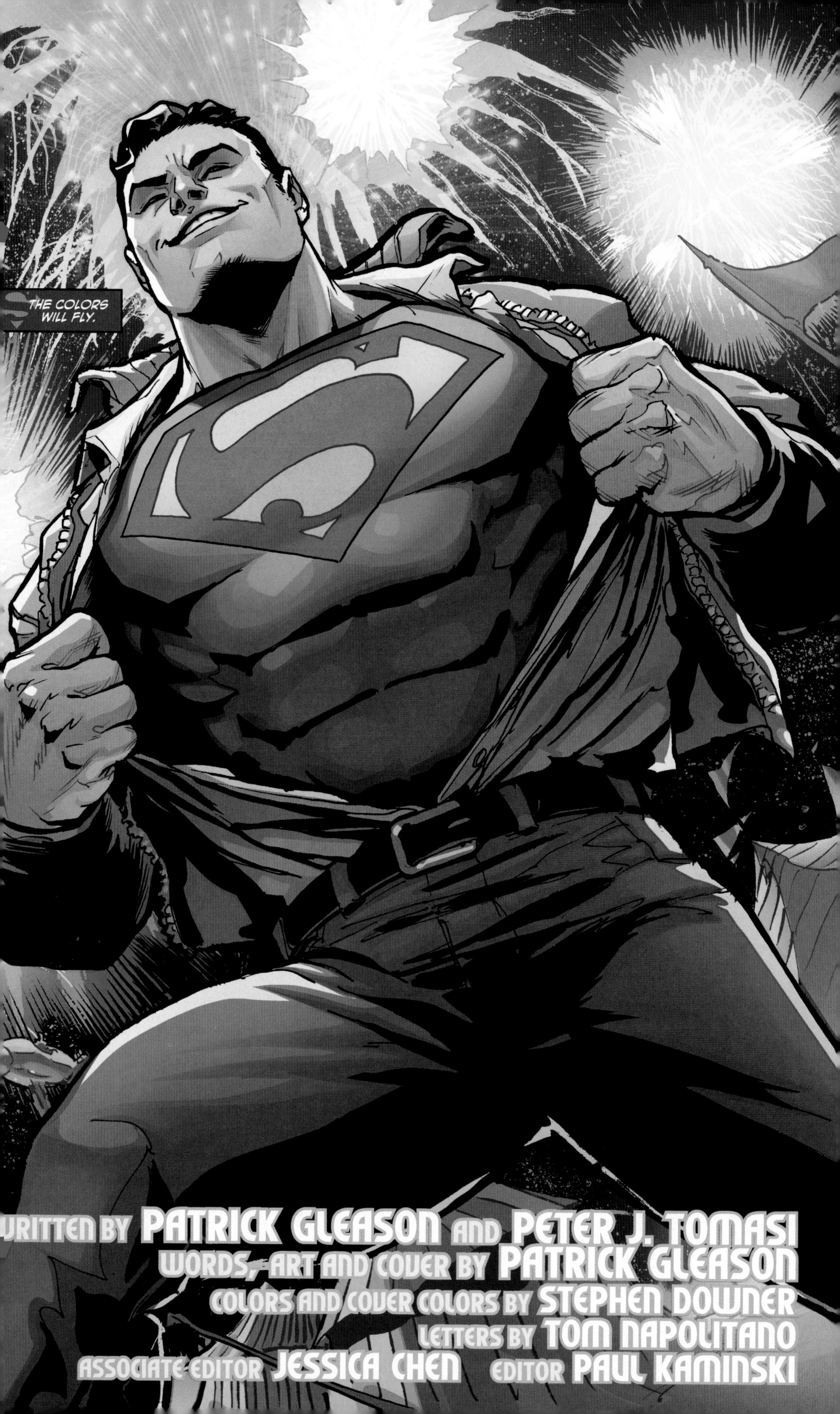
THE COLORS WILL FLY.
WRITTEN BY PATRICK GLEASON AND PETER J. TOMASI
WORDS, ART AND COVER BY PATRICK GLEASON
COLORS AND COVER COLORS BY STEPHEN DOWNER
LETTERS BY TOM NAPOLITANO
ASSOCIATE EDITOR JESSICA CHEN EDITOR PAUL KAMINSKI

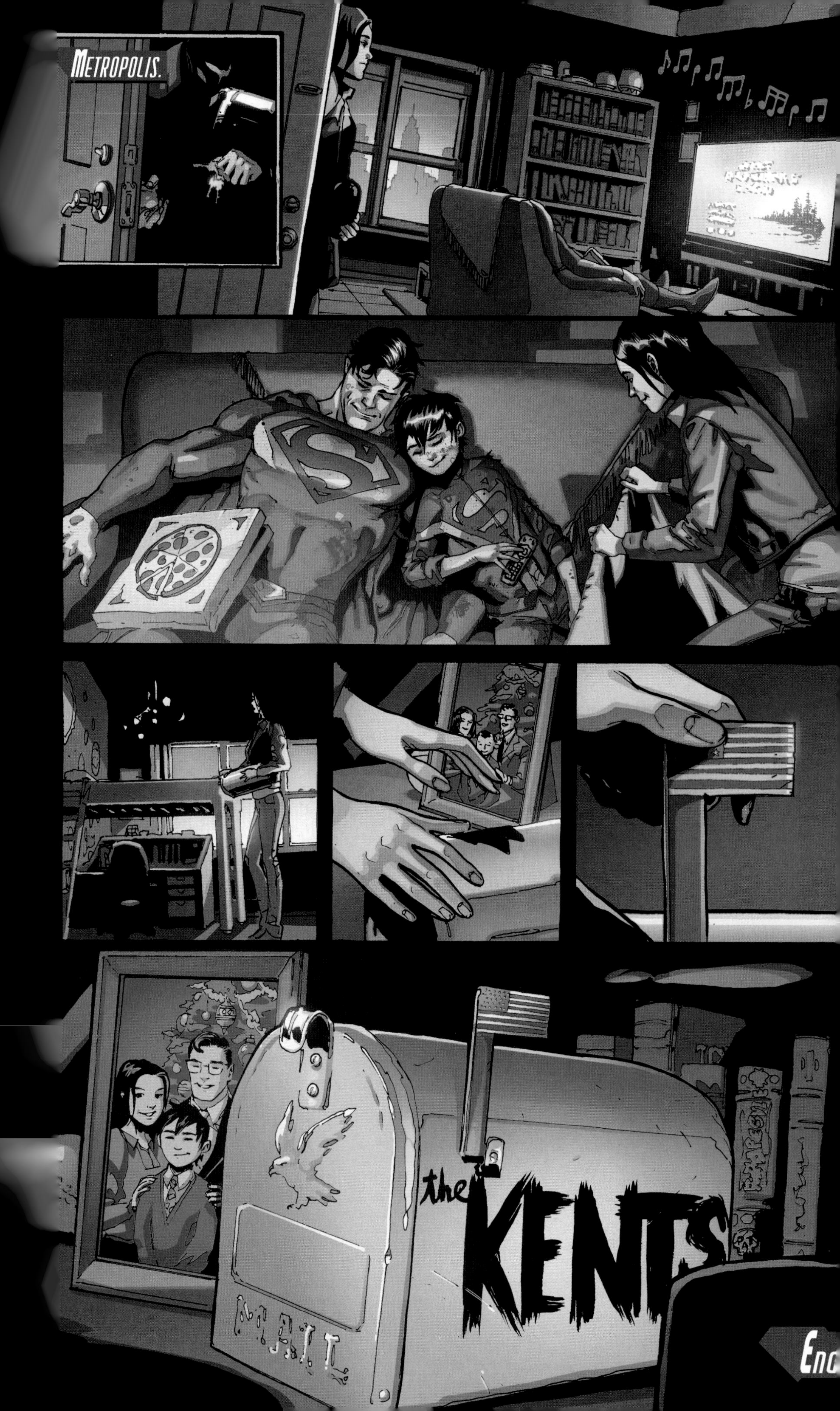
METROPOLIS.
the KENTS
MAIL
End

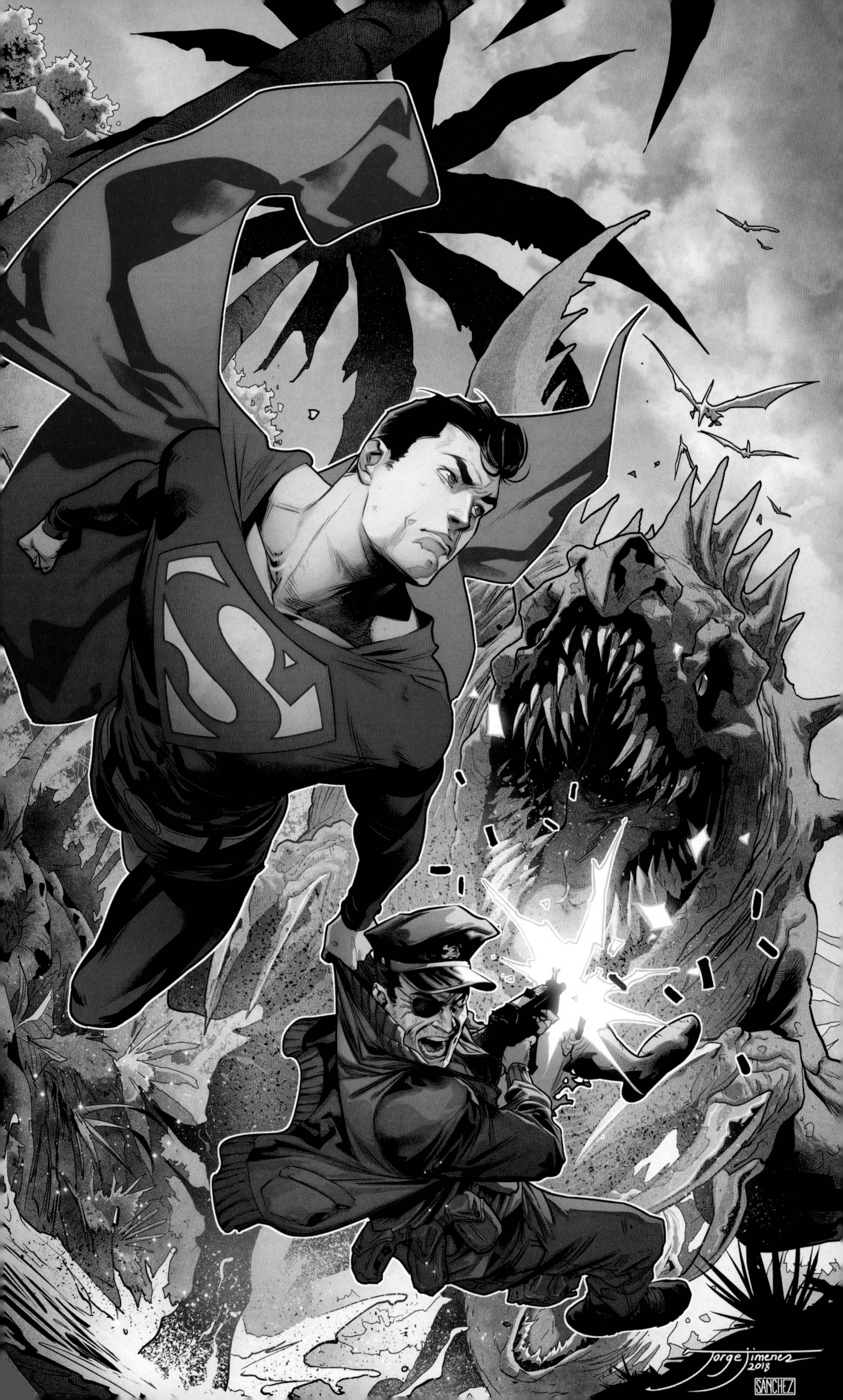
Jorge Jimenez
2018
SANCHEZ

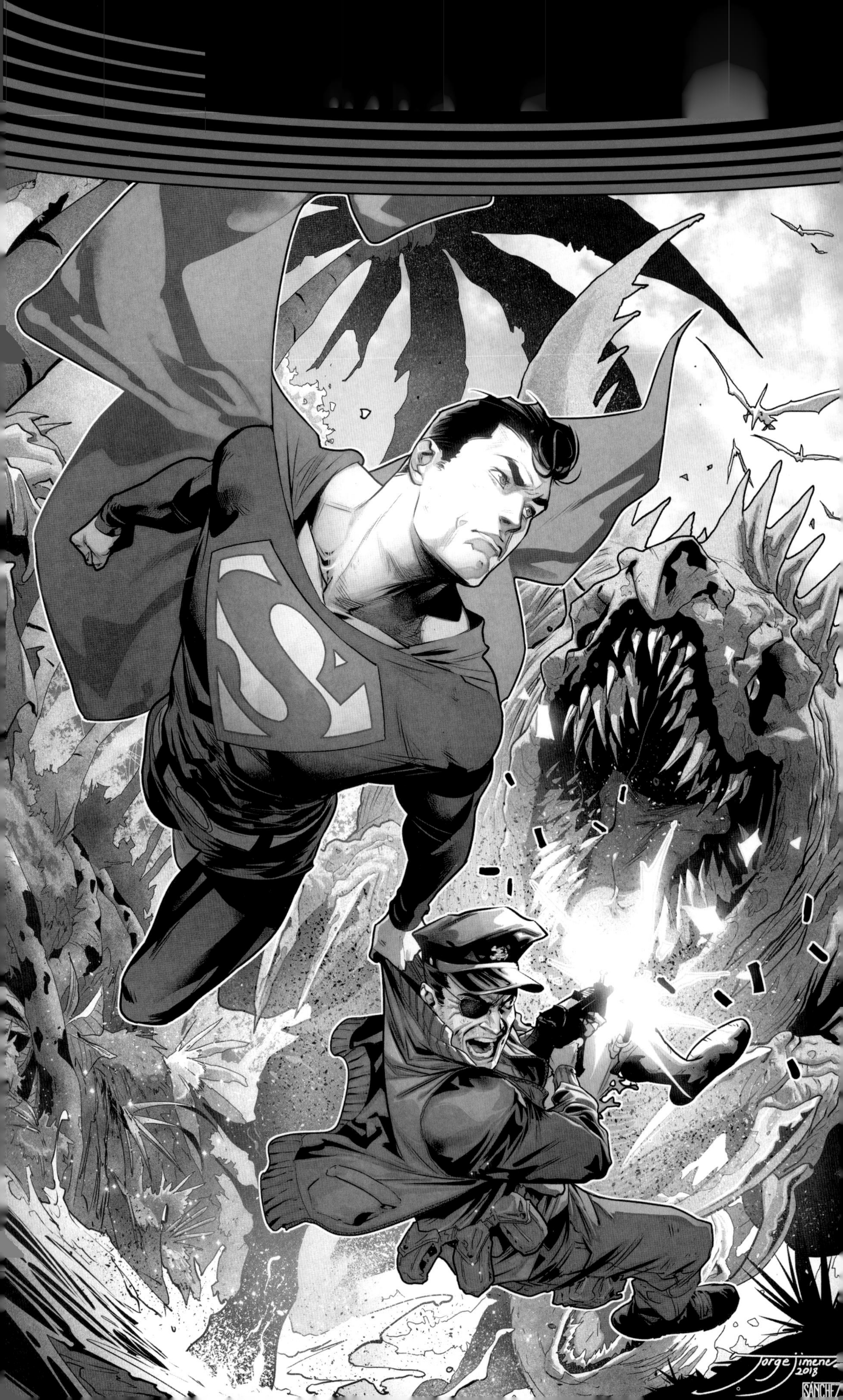
Jorge Jimenez
2018
SÁNCHEZ

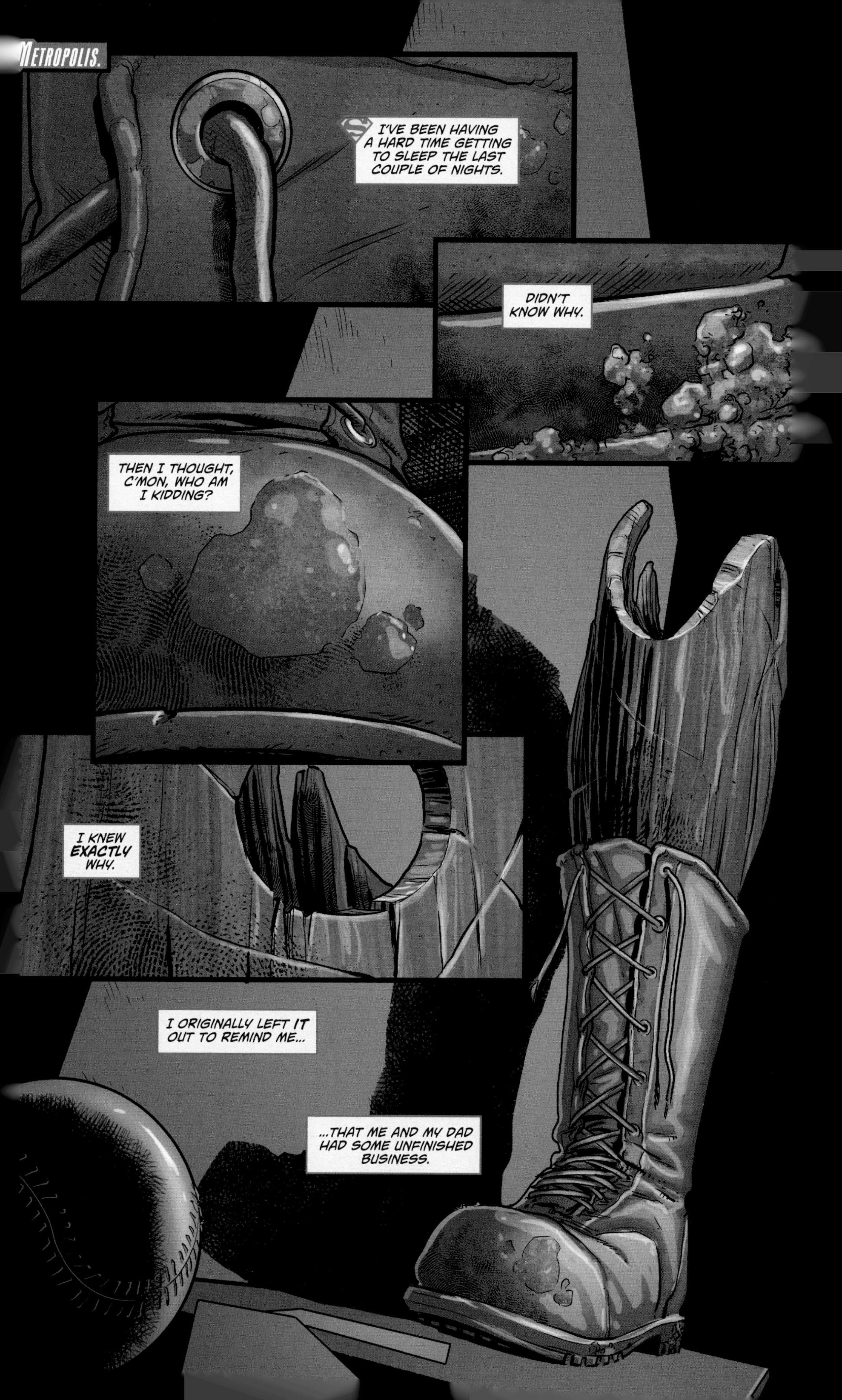
METROPOLIS.
I'VE BEEN HAVING A HARD TIME GETTING TO SLEEP THE LAST COUPLE OF NIGHTS.
DIDN'T KNOW WHY.
THEN I THOUGHT, C'MON, WHO AM I KIDDING?
I KNEW EXACTLY WHY.
I ORIGINALLY LEFT IT OUT TO REMIND ME...
...THAT ME AND MY DAD HAD SOME UNFINISHED BUSINESS.

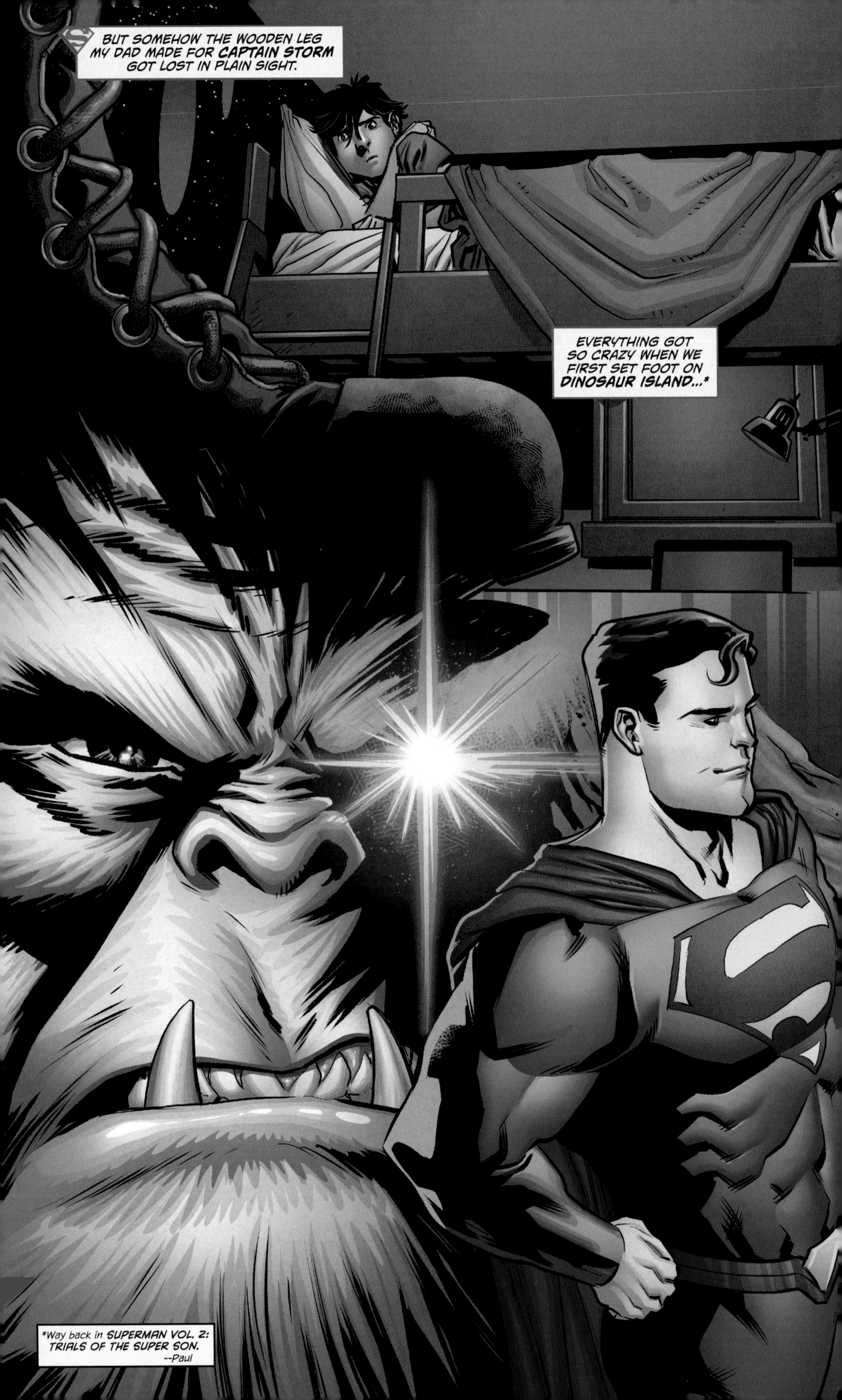
BUT SOMEHOW THE WOODEN LEG MY DAD MADE FOR CAPTAIN STORM GOT LOST IN PLAIN SIGHT.
EVERYTHING GOT SO CRAZY WHEN WE FIRST SET FOOT ON DINOSAUR ISLAND...*
*Way back in SUPERMAN VOL. 2: TRIALS OF THE SUPER SON. --Paul

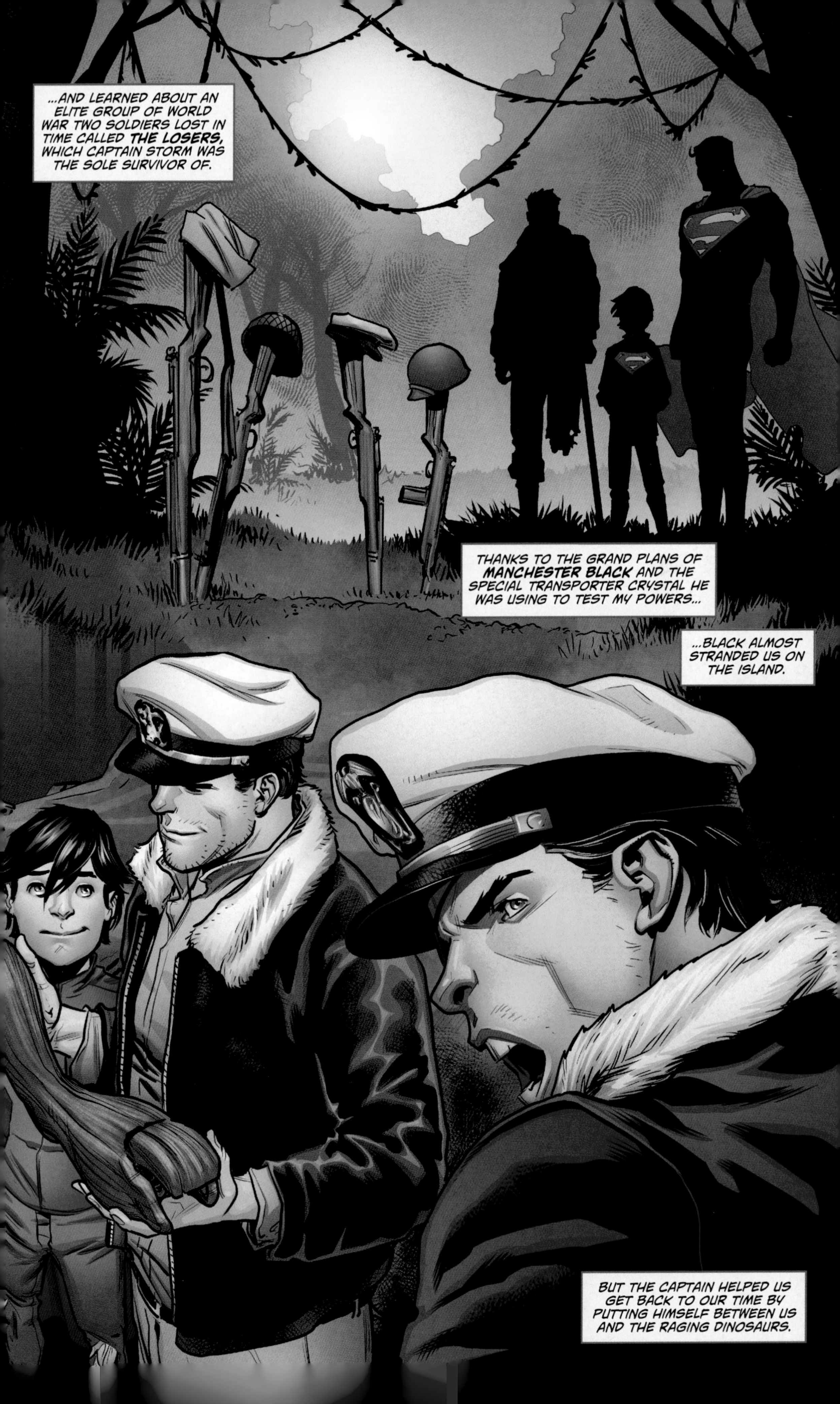
...AND LEARNED ABOUT AN ELITE GROUP OF WORLD WAR TWO SOLDIERS LOST IN TIME CALLED THE LOSERS, WHICH CAPTAIN STORM WAS THE SOLE SURVIVOR OF.
THANKS TO THE GRAND PLANS OF MANCHESTER BLACK AND THE SPECIAL TRANSPORTER CRYSTAL HE WAS USING TO TEST MY POWERS...
...BLACK ALMOST STRANDED US ON THE ISLAND.
BUT THE CAPTAIN HELPED US GET BACK TO OUR TIME BY PUTTING HIMSELF BETWEEN US AND THE RAGING DINOSAURS.

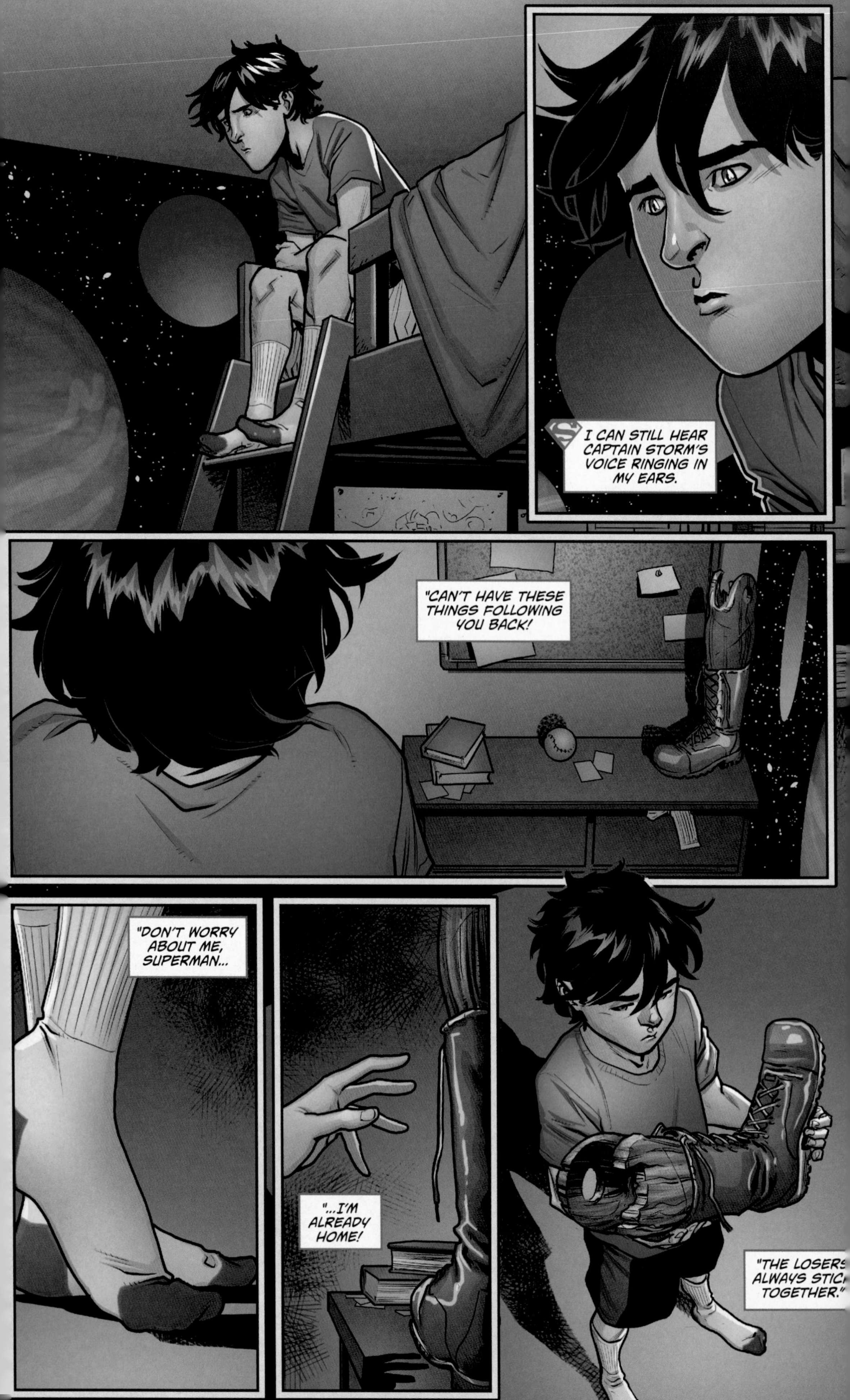
I CAN STILL HEAR CAPTAIN STORM'S VOICE RINGING IN MY EARS.
"CAN'T HAVE THESE THINGS FOLLOWING YOU BACK!
"DON'T WORRY ABOUT ME, SUPERMAN...
"...I'M ALREADY HOME!
"THE LOSERS ALWAYS STIC TOGETHER."

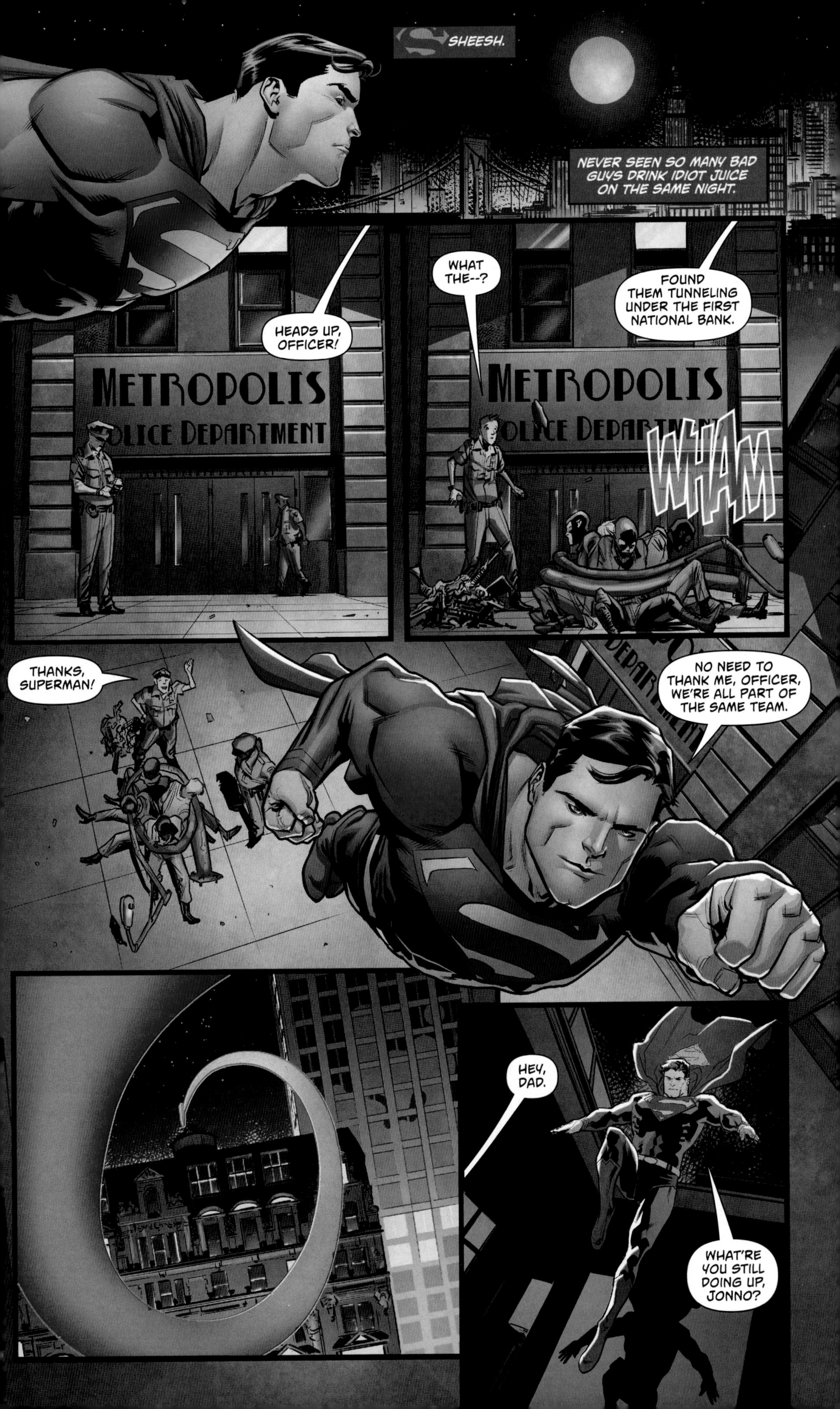
SHEESH.
NEVER SEEN SO MANY BAD GUYS DRINK IDIOT JUICE ON THE SAME NIGHT.
HEADS UP, OFFICER!
METROPOLIS
POLICE DEPARTMENT
WHAT THE--?
FOUND THEM TUNNELING UNDER THE FIRST NATIONAL BANK.
WHAM
THANKS, SUPERMAN!
NO NEED TO THANK ME, OFFICER, WE'RE ALL PART OF THE SAME TEAM.
HEY, DAD.
WHAT'RE YOU STILL DOING UP, JONNO?

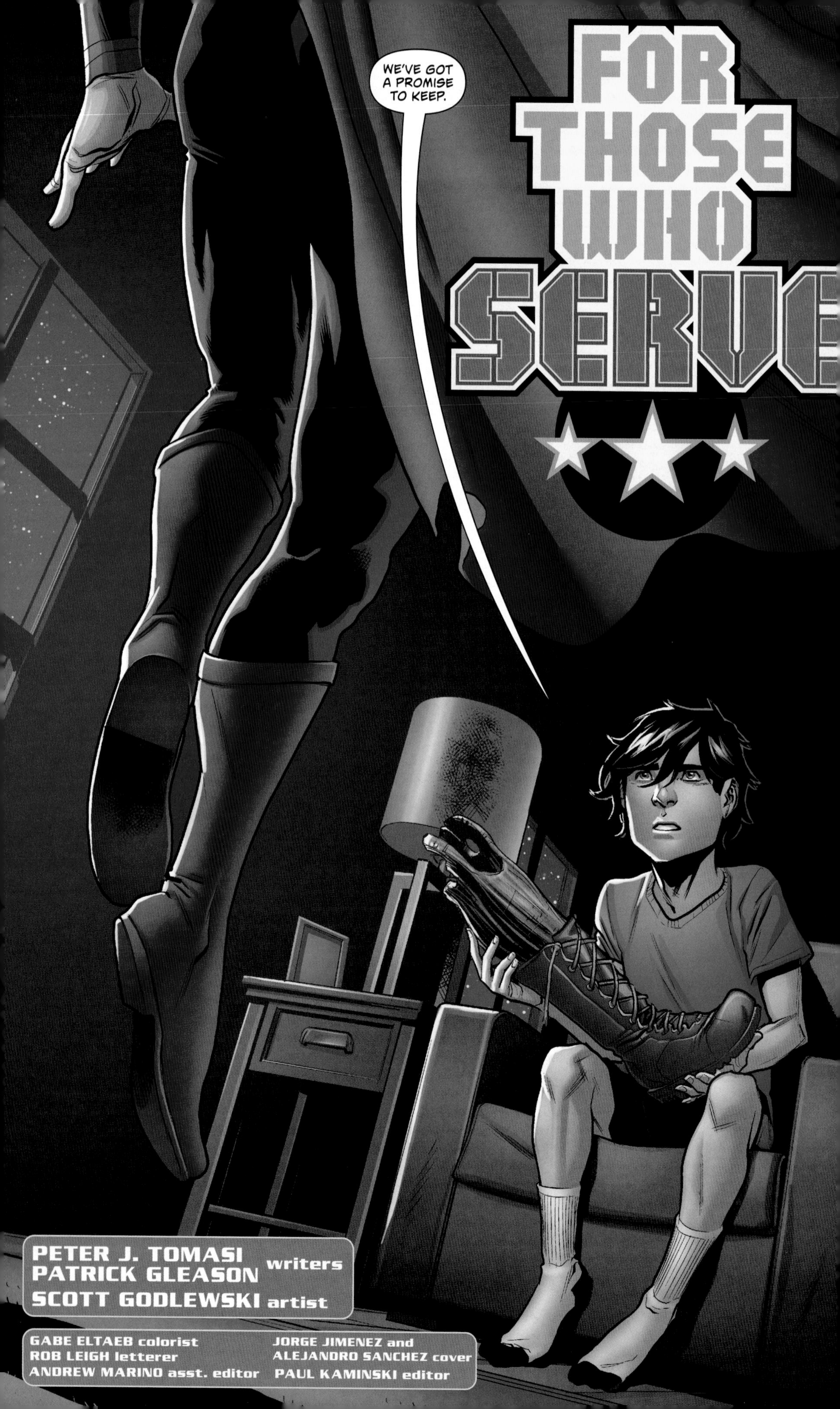

WE'VE GOT A PROMISE TO KEEP.
FOR THOSE WHO SERVE
PETER J. TOMASI
PATRICK GLEASON writers
SCOTT GODLEWSKI artist
GABE ELTAEB colorist
ROB LEIGH letterer
ANDREW MARINO asst. editor
JORGE JIMENEZ and
ALEJANDRO SANCHEZ cover
PAUL KAMINSKI editor

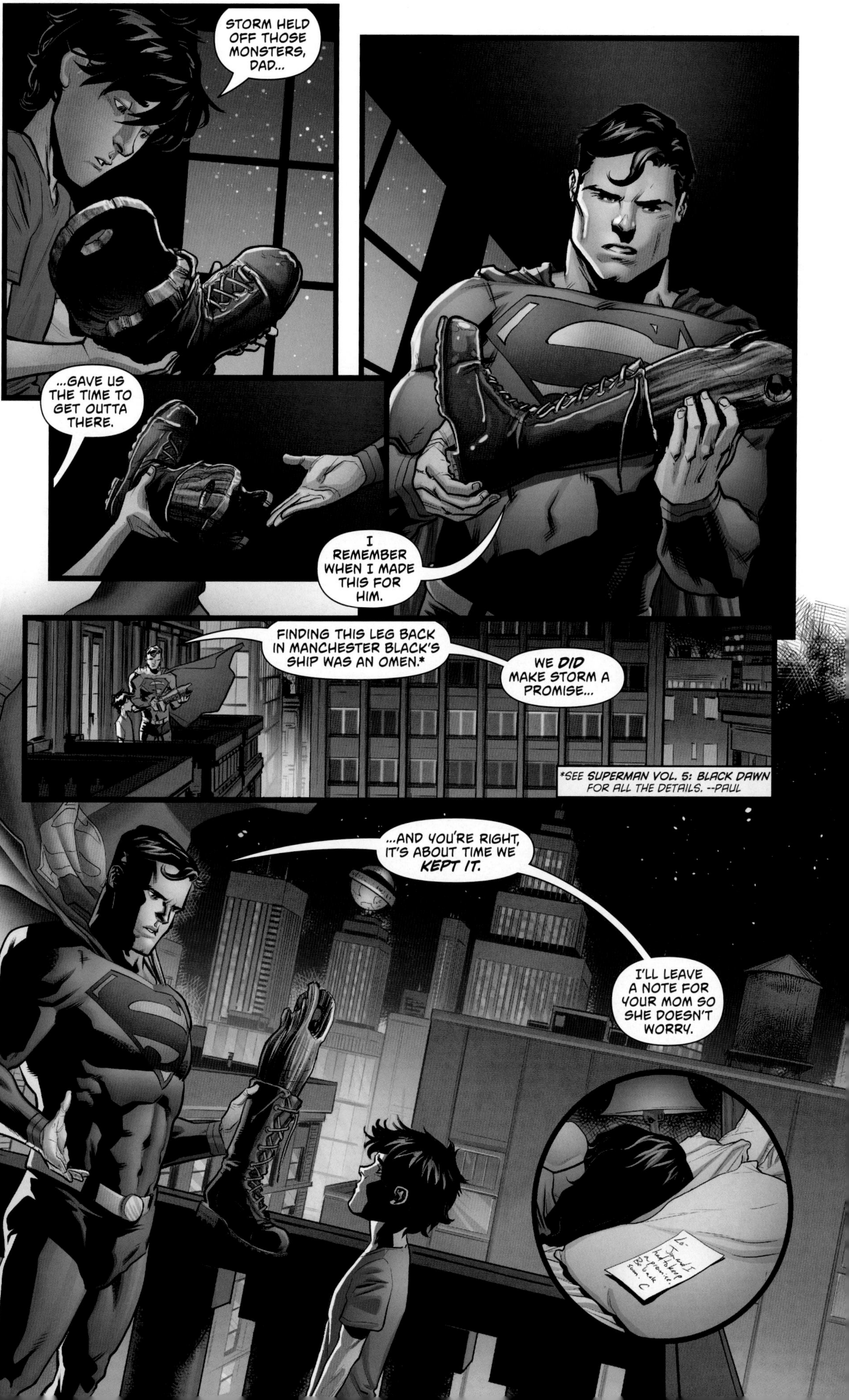
STORM HELD OFF THOSE MONSTERS, DAD...
...GAVE US THE TIME TO GET OUTTA THERE.
I REMEMBER WHEN I MADE THIS FOR HIM.
FINDING THIS LEG BACK IN MANCHESTER BLACK'S SHIP WAS AN OMEN.*
WE DID MAKE STORM A PROMISE...
*SEE SUPERMAN VOL. 5: BLACK DAWN FOR ALL THE DETAILS. --PAUL
...AND YOU'RE RIGHT, IT'S ABOUT TIME WE KEPT IT.
I'LL LEAVE A NOTE FOR YOUR MOM SO SHE DOESN'T WORRY.
Lo- Jon and I had to keep a promise. Be back soon. C

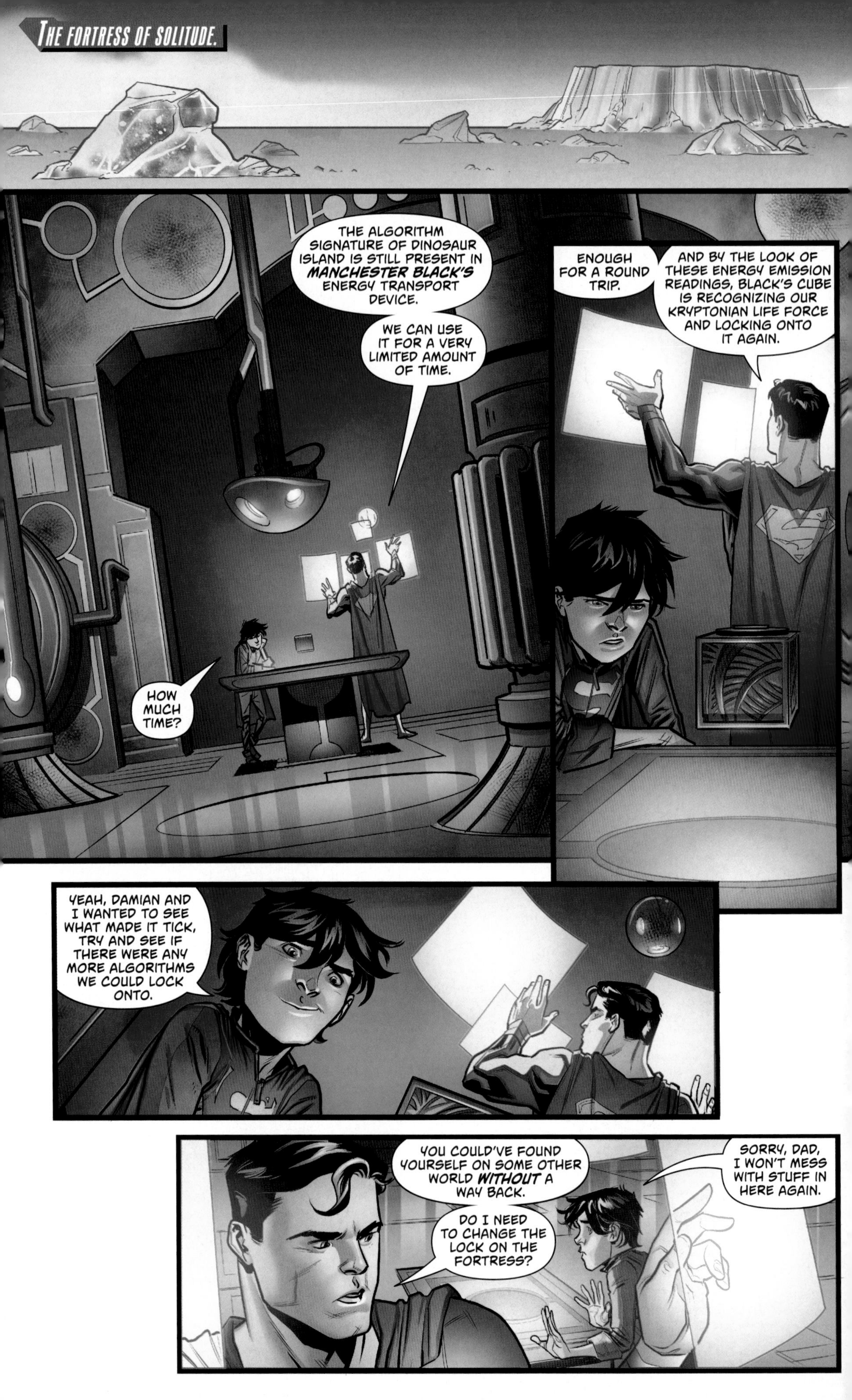
THE FORTRESS OF SOLITUDE.
THE ALGORITHM SIGNATURE OF DINOSAUR ISLAND IS STILL PRESENT IN MANCHESTER BLACK'S ENERGY TRANSPORT DEVICE.
WE CAN USE IT FOR A VERY LIMITED AMOUNT OF TIME.
HOW MUCH TIME?
ENOUGH FOR A ROUND TRIP.
AND BY THE LOOK OF THESE ENERGY EMISSION READINGS, BLACK'S CUBE IS RECOGNIZING OUR KRYPTONIAN LIFE FORCE AND LOCKING ONTO IT AGAIN.
YEAH, DAMIAN AND I WANTED TO SEE WHAT MADE IT TICK, TRY AND SEE IF THERE WERE ANY MORE ALGORITHMS WE COULD LOCK ONTO.
YOU COULD'VE FOUND YOURSELF ON SOME OTHER WORLD WITHOUT A WAY BACK.
DO I NEED TO CHANGE THE LOCK ON THE FORTRESS?
SORRY, DAD, I WON'T MESS WITH STUFF IN HERE AGAIN.

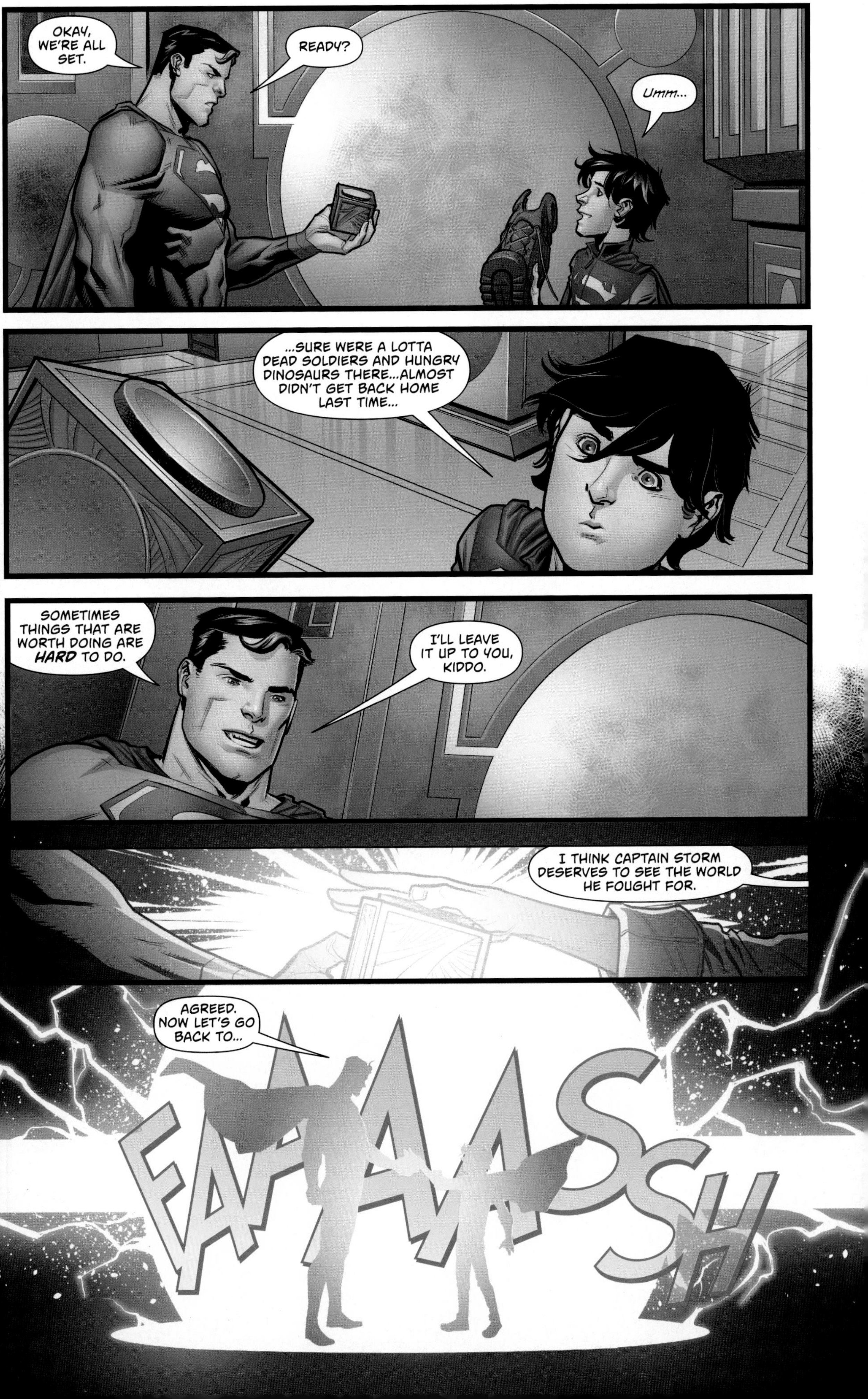
OKAY, WE'RE ALL SET.
READY?
Umm...
...SURE WERE A LOTTA DEAD SOLDIERS AND HUNGRY DINOSAURS THERE...ALMOST DIDN'T GET BACK HOME LAST TIME...
SOMETIMES THINGS THAT ARE WORTH DOING ARE HARD TO DO.
I'LL LEAVE IT UP TO YOU, KIDDO.
I THINK CAPTAIN STORM DESERVES TO SEE THE WORLD HE FOUGHT FOR.
AGREED. NOW LET'S GO BACK TO...
FAAAASSH

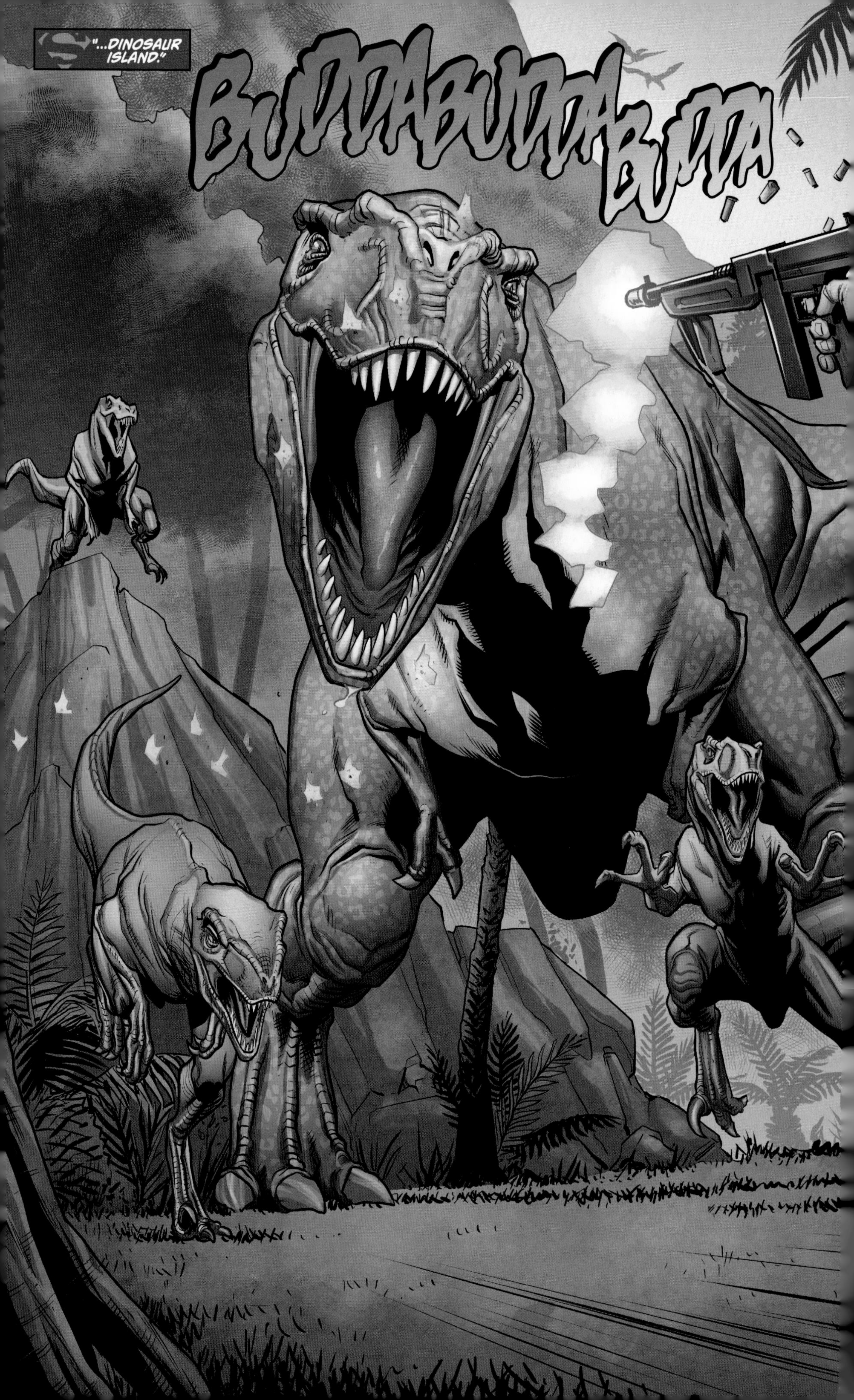
"...DINOSAUR ISLAND."
BUDDABUDDABUDDA

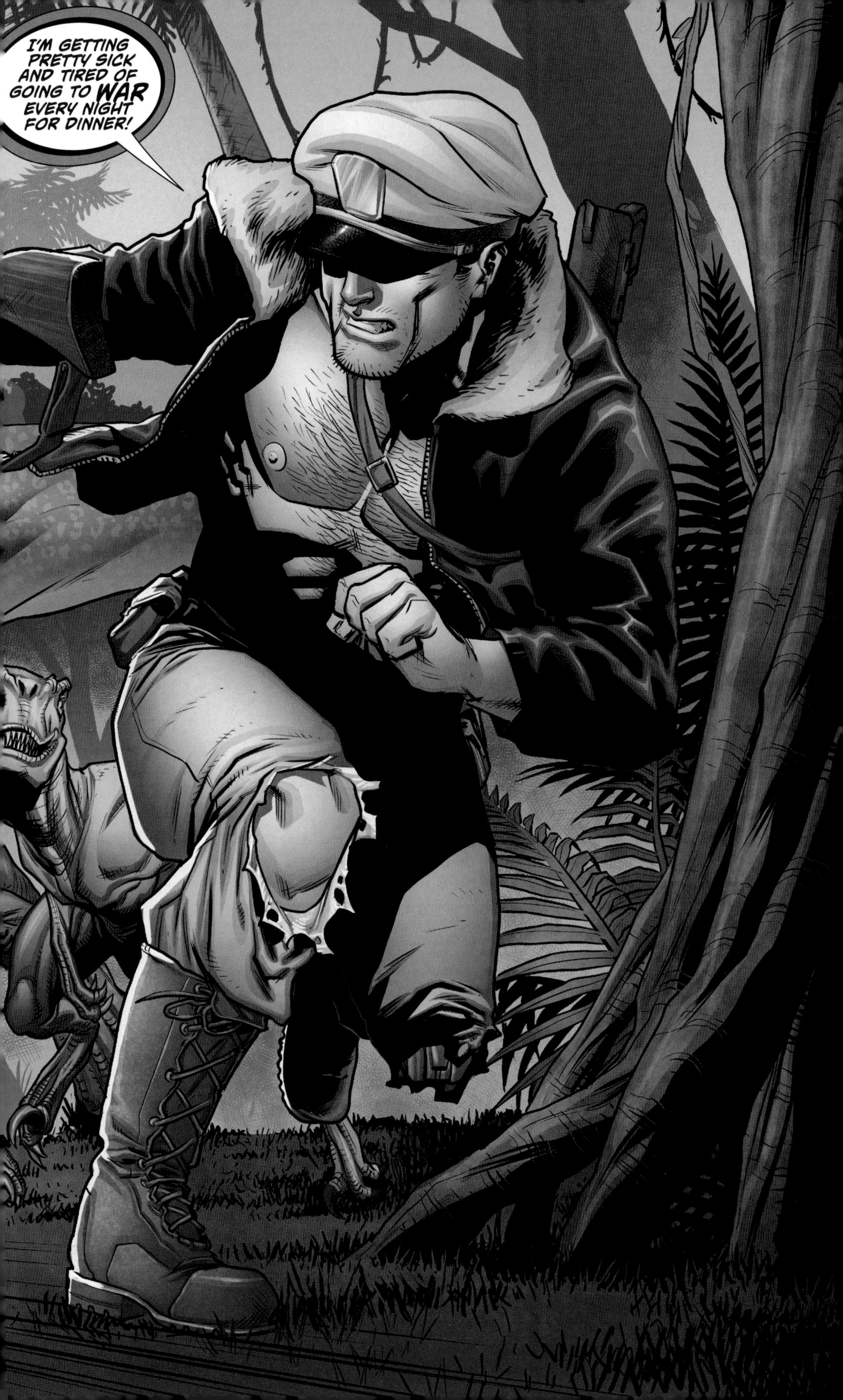
I'M GETTING PRETTY SICK AND TIRED OF GOING TO WAR EVERY NIGHT FOR DINNER!

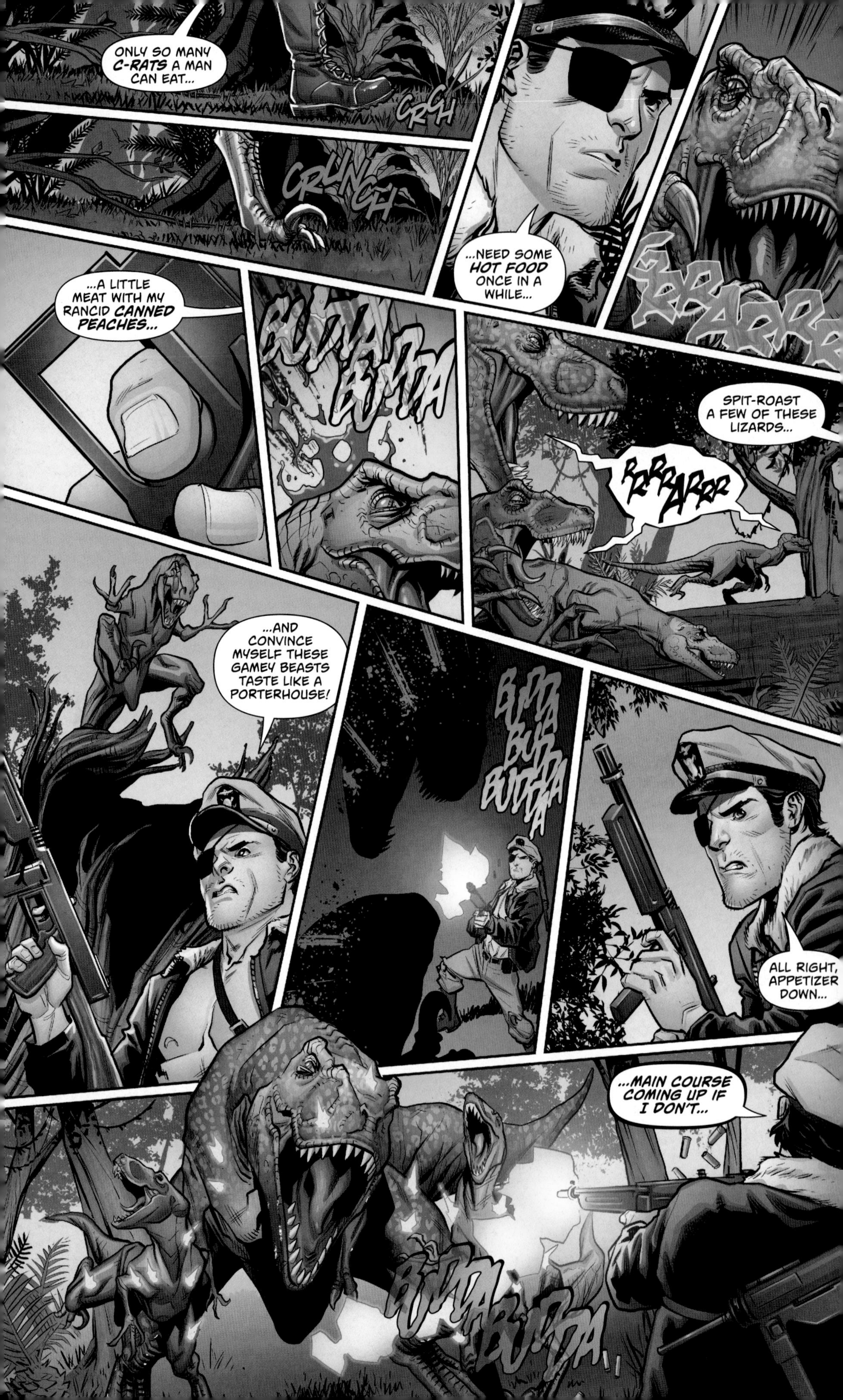
ONLY SO MANY C-RATS A MAN CAN EAT...
CRCH
CRUNCH
...NEED SOME HOT FOOD ONCE IN A WHILE...
...A LITTLE MEAT WITH MY RANCID CANNED PEACHES...
SPIT-ROAST A FEW OF THESE LIZARDS...
RRRRARRR
...AND CONVINCE MYSELF THESE GAMEY BEASTS TASTE LIKE A PORTERHOUSE!
ALL RIGHT, APPETIZER DOWN...
...MAIN COURSE COMING UP IF I DON'T...

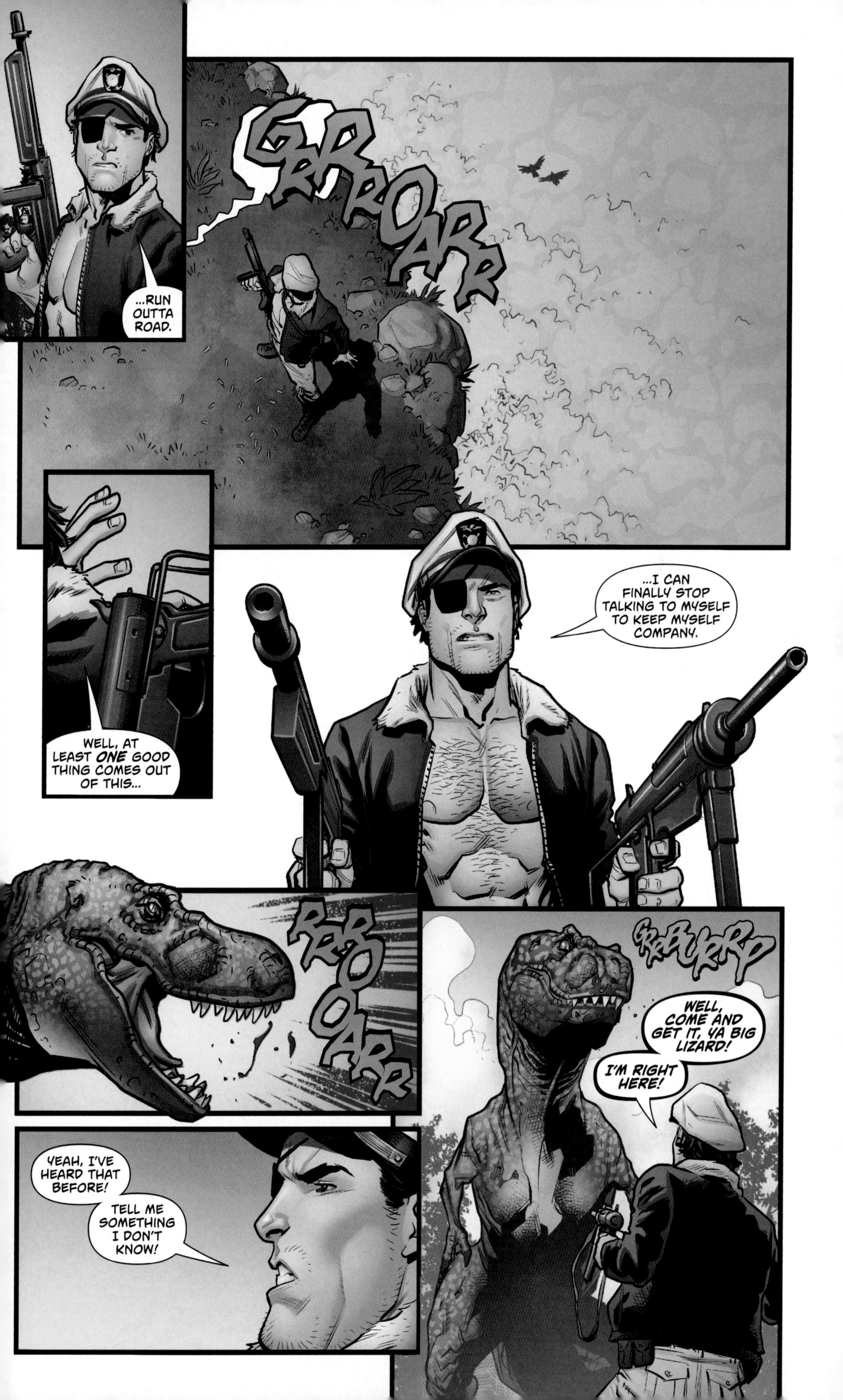
...RUN OUTTA ROAD.
GRRROARR
WELL, AT LEAST ONE GOOD THING COMES OUT OF THIS...
...I CAN FINALLY STOP TALKING TO MYSELF TO KEEP MYSELF COMPANY.
RRROARR
YEAH, I'VE HEARD THAT BEFORE!
TELL ME SOMETHING I DON'T KNOW!
GRRBURRR
WELL, COME AND GET IT, YA BIG LIZARD!
I'M RIGHT HERE!

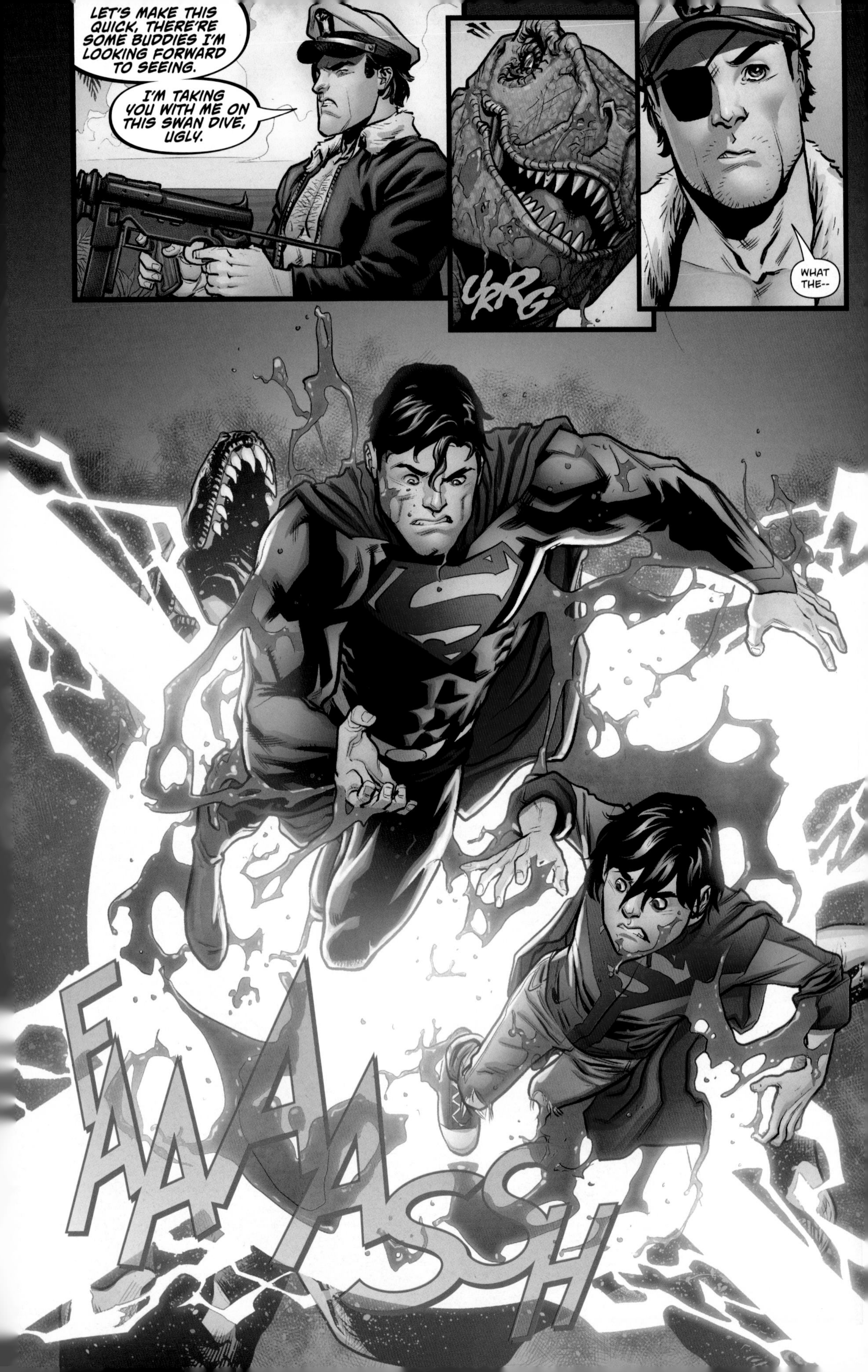
LET'S MAKE THIS QUICK, THERE'RE SOME BUDDIES I'M LOOKING FORWARD TO SEEING.
I'M TAKING YOU WITH ME ON THIS SWAN DIVE, UGLY.
URRG
WHAT THE--
FAAAASH

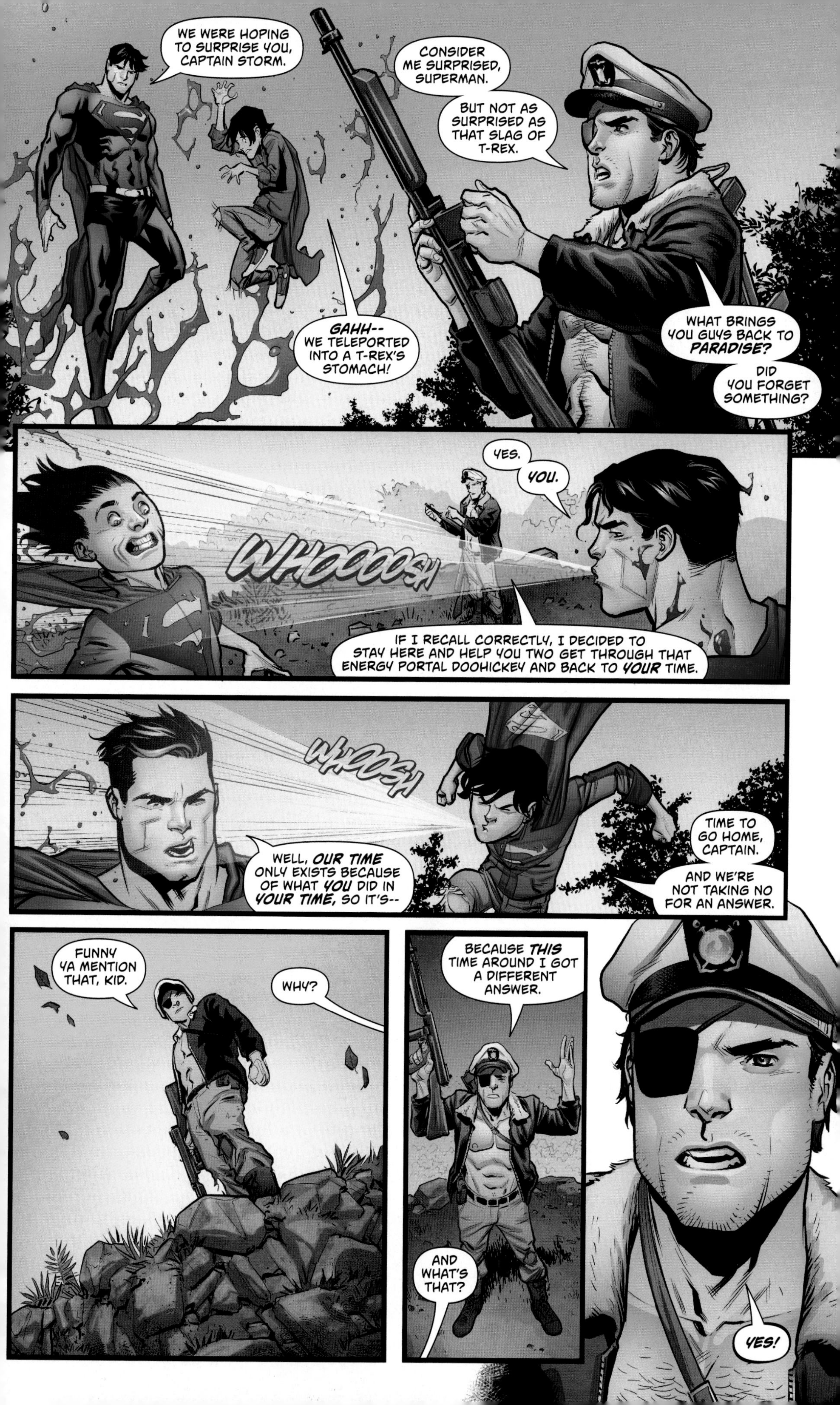

WE WERE HOPING TO SURPRISE YOU, CAPTAIN STORM.
CONSIDER ME SURPRISED, SUPERMAN.
BUT NOT AS SURPRISED AS THAT SLAG OF T-REX.
GAHH-- WE TELEPORTED INTO A T-REX'S STOMACH!
WHAT BRINGS YOU GUYS BACK TO PARADISE?
DID YOU FORGET SOMETHING?
YES.
YOU.
WHOOOOOSH
IF I RECALL CORRECTLY, I DECIDED TO STAY HERE AND HELP YOU TWO GET THROUGH THAT ENERGY PORTAL DOOHICKEY AND BACK TO YOUR TIME.
WHOOSH
WELL, OUR TIME ONLY EXISTS BECAUSE OF WHAT YOU DID IN YOUR TIME, SO IT'S--
TIME TO GO HOME, CAPTAIN.
AND WE'RE NOT TAKING NO FOR AN ANSWER.
FUNNY YA MENTION THAT, KID.
WHY?
BECAUSE THIS TIME AROUND I GOT A DIFFERENT ANSWER.
AND WHAT'S THAT?
YES!

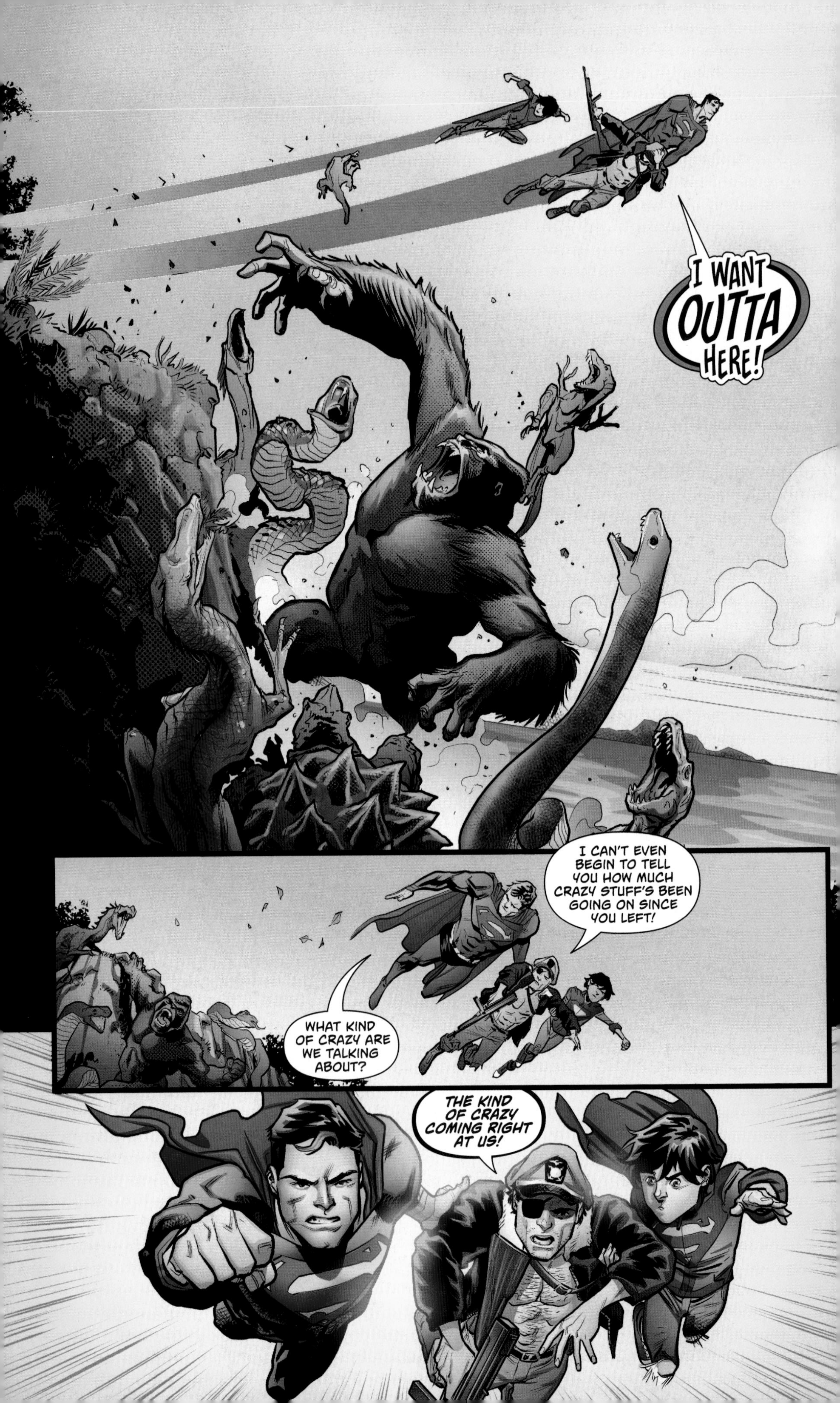
I WANT OUTTA HERE!
I CAN'T EVEN BEGIN TO TELL YOU HOW MUCH CRAZY STUFF'S BEEN GOING ON SINCE YOU LEFT!
WHAT KIND OF CRAZY ARE WE TALKING ABOUT?
THE KIND OF CRAZY COMING RIGHT AT US!

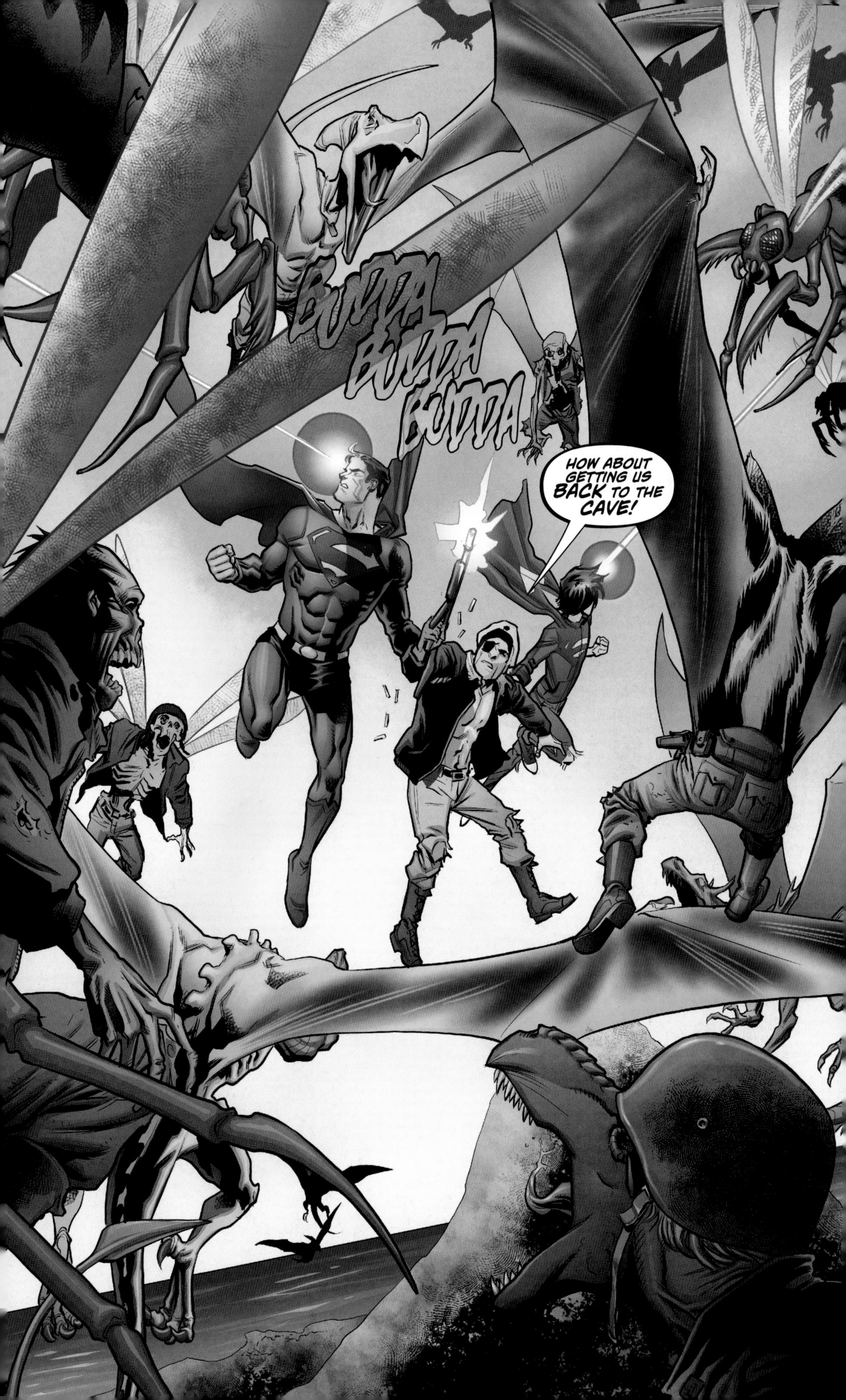
BUDDA BUDDA BUDDA
HOW ABOUT GETTING US BACK TO THE CAVE!

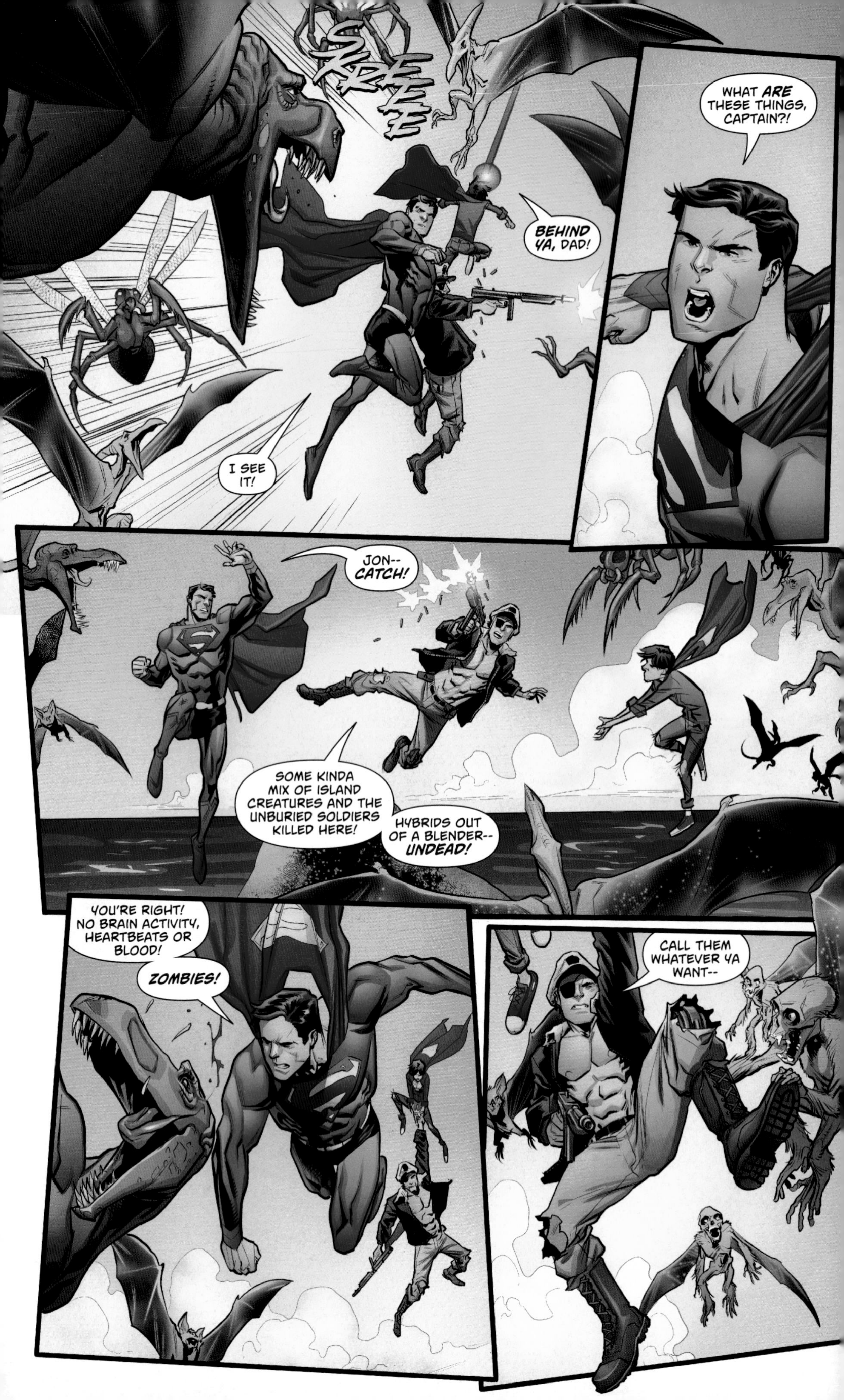
SKREEEE
BEHIND YA, DAD!
I SEE IT!
WHAT ARE THESE THINGS, CAPTAIN?!
JON-- CATCH!
SOME KINDA MIX OF ISLAND CREATURES AND THE UNBURIED SOLDIERS KILLED HERE!
HYBRIDS OUT OF A BLENDER-- UNDEAD!
YOU'RE RIGHT! NO BRAIN ACTIVITY, HEARTBEATS OR BLOOD!
ZOMBIES!
CALL THEM WHATEVER YA WANT--

--BUT DON'T LET THEM TAKE A BITE OUT OF YOU!

HOLY MOLEY!

STORM-- YOUR LEG...

YEAH, NOT EXACTLY THE KINDA FOOT I LIKE SEEING IN MY BUSTER BROWNS!

WE DON'T HAVE TO DEAL WITH ALL THIS INSANITY...

...AN ACTIVATION OF THE CRYSTAL AND WE CAN ZAP OUT OF HERE RIGHT NOW.

NOT UNTIL I GET SOMETHING BACK FROM THE CAVE.

WHAT CAN BE SO IMPORTANT THAT--

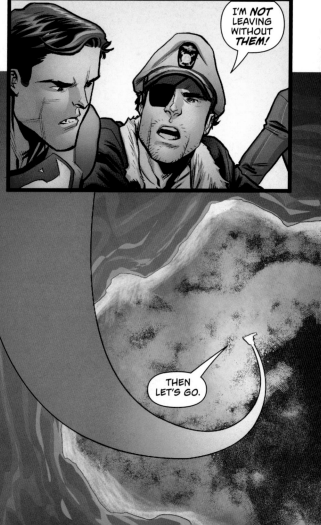

I'M NOT LEAVING WITHOUT THEM!

THEN LET'S GO.

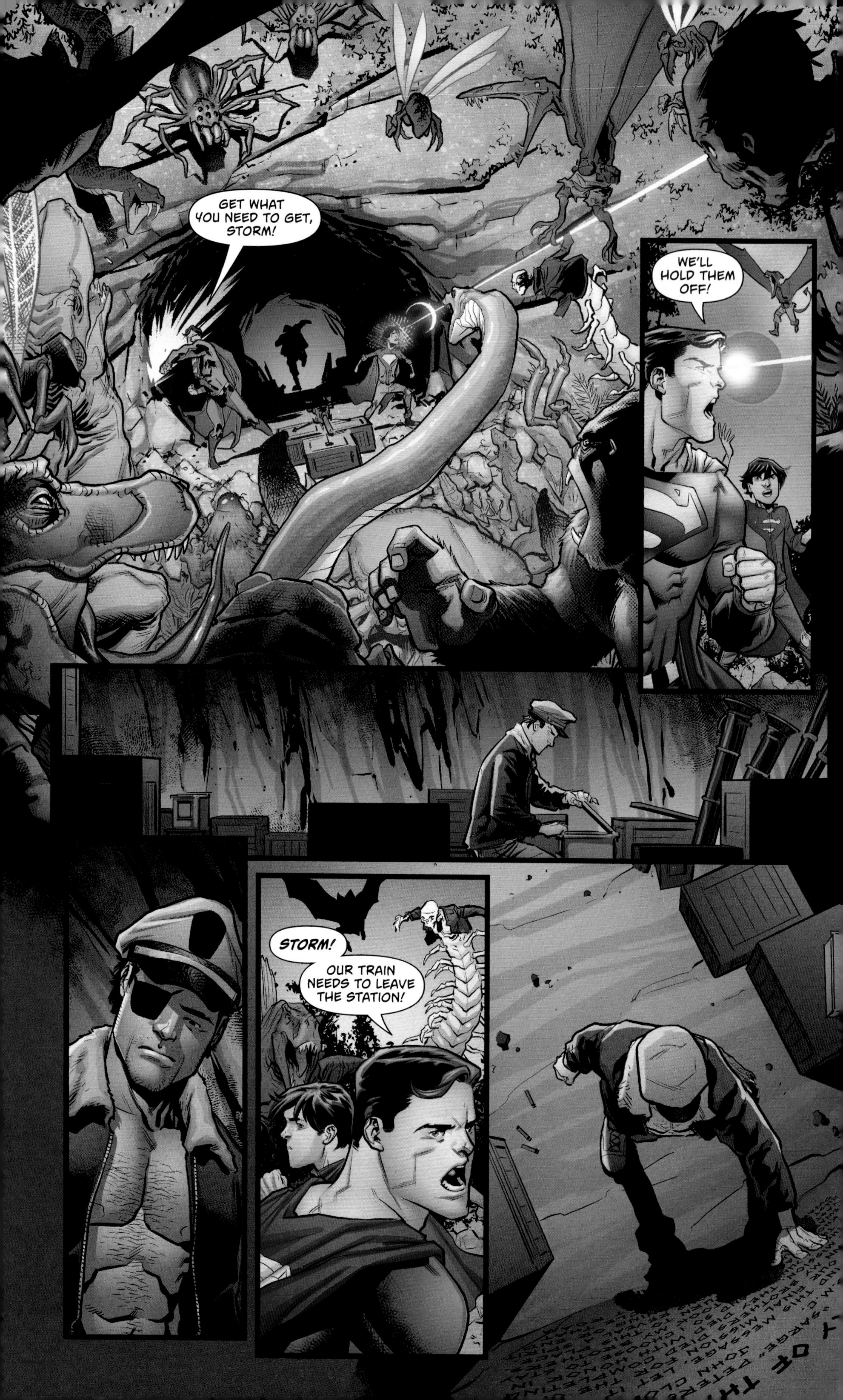
GET WHAT YOU NEED TO GET, STORM!
WE'LL HOLD THEM OFF!
STORM!
OUR TRAIN NEEDS TO LEAVE THE STATION!

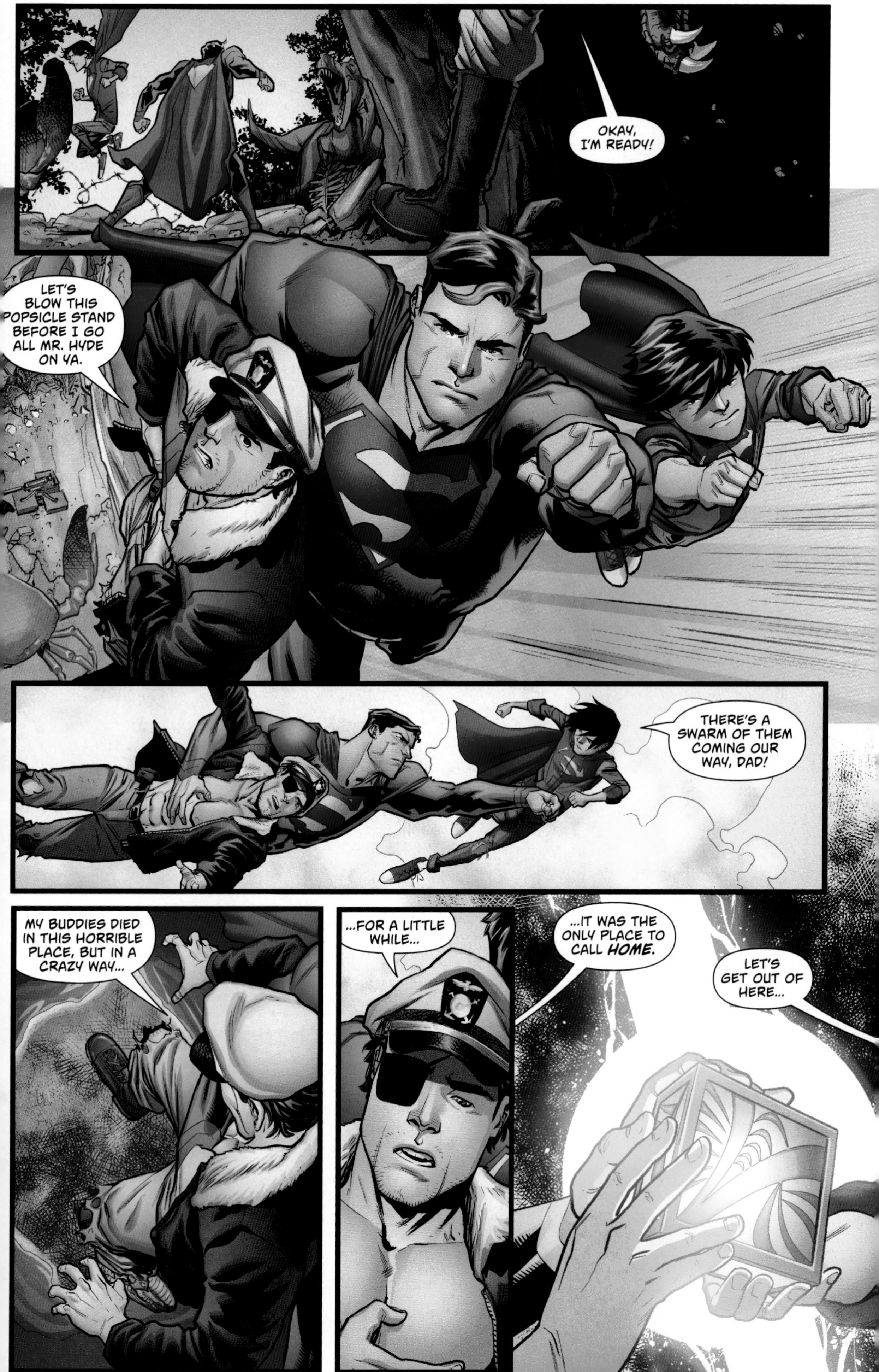
OKAY, I'M READY!
LET'S BLOW THIS POPSICLE STAND BEFORE I GO ALL MR. HYDE ON YA.
THERE'S A SWARM OF THEM COMING OUR WAY, DAD!
MY BUDDIES DIED IN THIS HORRIBLE PLACE, BUT IN A CRAZY WAY...
...FOR A LITTLE WHILE...
...IT WAS THE ONLY PLACE TO CALL HOME.
LET'S GET OUT OF HERE...

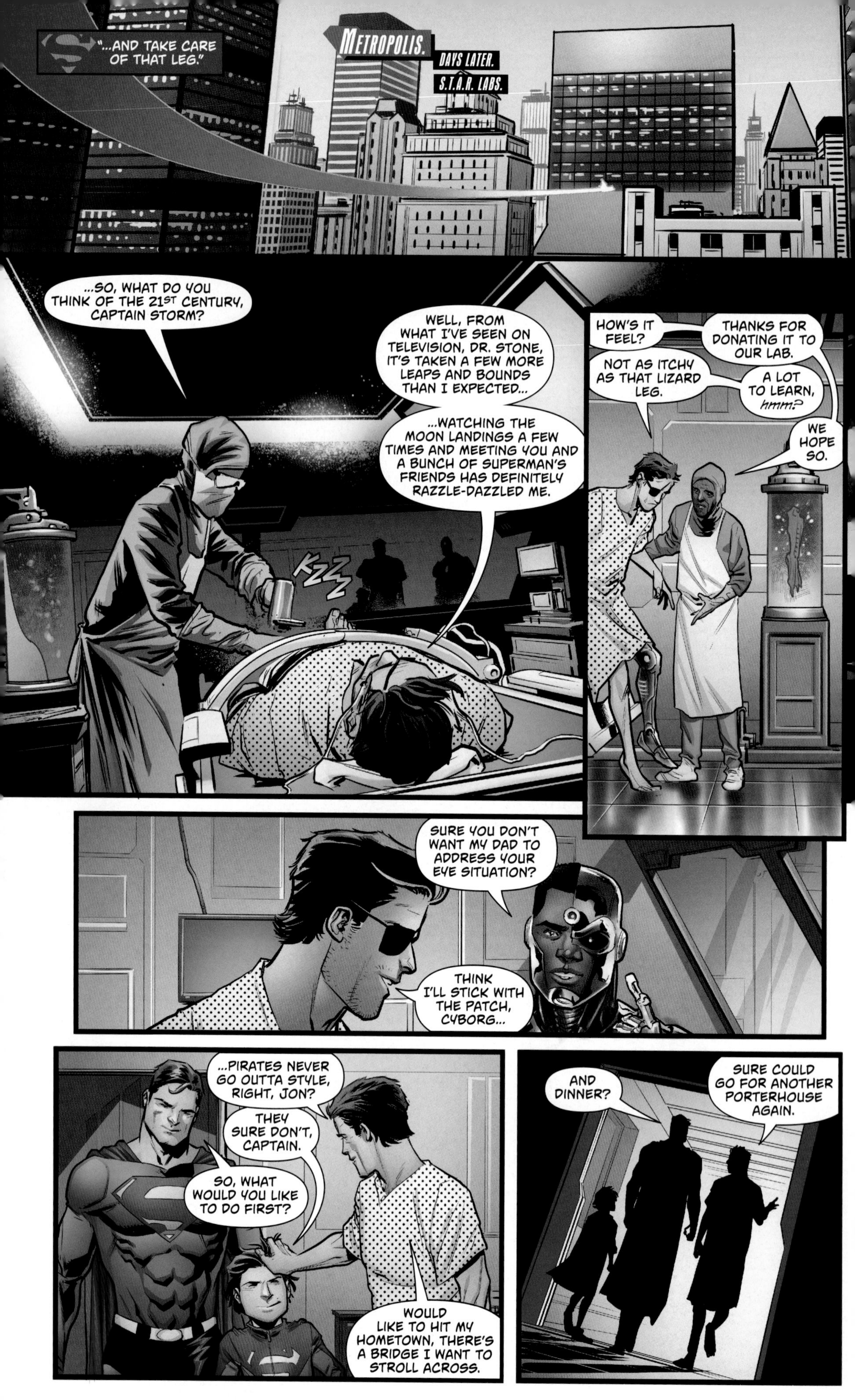
"...AND TAKE CARE OF THAT LEG."
METROPOLIS.
DAYS LATER.
S.T.A.R. LABS.
...SO, WHAT DO YOU THINK OF THE 21ST CENTURY, CAPTAIN STORM?
WELL, FROM WHAT I'VE SEEN ON TELEVISION, DR. STONE, IT'S TAKEN A FEW MORE LEAPS AND BOUNDS THAN I EXPECTED...
...WATCHING THE MOON LANDINGS A FEW TIMES AND MEETING YOU AND A BUNCH OF SUPERMAN'S FRIENDS HAS DEFINITELY RAZZLE-DAZZLED ME.
KZZZ
HOW'S IT FEEL?
NOT AS ITCHY AS THAT LIZARD LEG.
THANKS FOR DONATING IT TO OUR LAB.
A LOT TO LEARN, hmm?
WE HOPE SO.
SURE YOU DON'T WANT MY DAD TO ADDRESS YOUR EYE SITUATION?
THINK I'LL STICK WITH THE PATCH, CYBORG...
...PIRATES NEVER GO OUTTA STYLE, RIGHT, JON?
THEY SURE DON'T, CAPTAIN.
SO, WHAT WOULD YOU LIKE TO DO FIRST?
WOULD LIKE TO HIT MY HOMETOWN, THERE'S A BRIDGE I WANT TO STROLL ACROSS.
AND DINNER?
SURE COULD GO FOR ANOTHER PORTERHOUSE AGAIN.

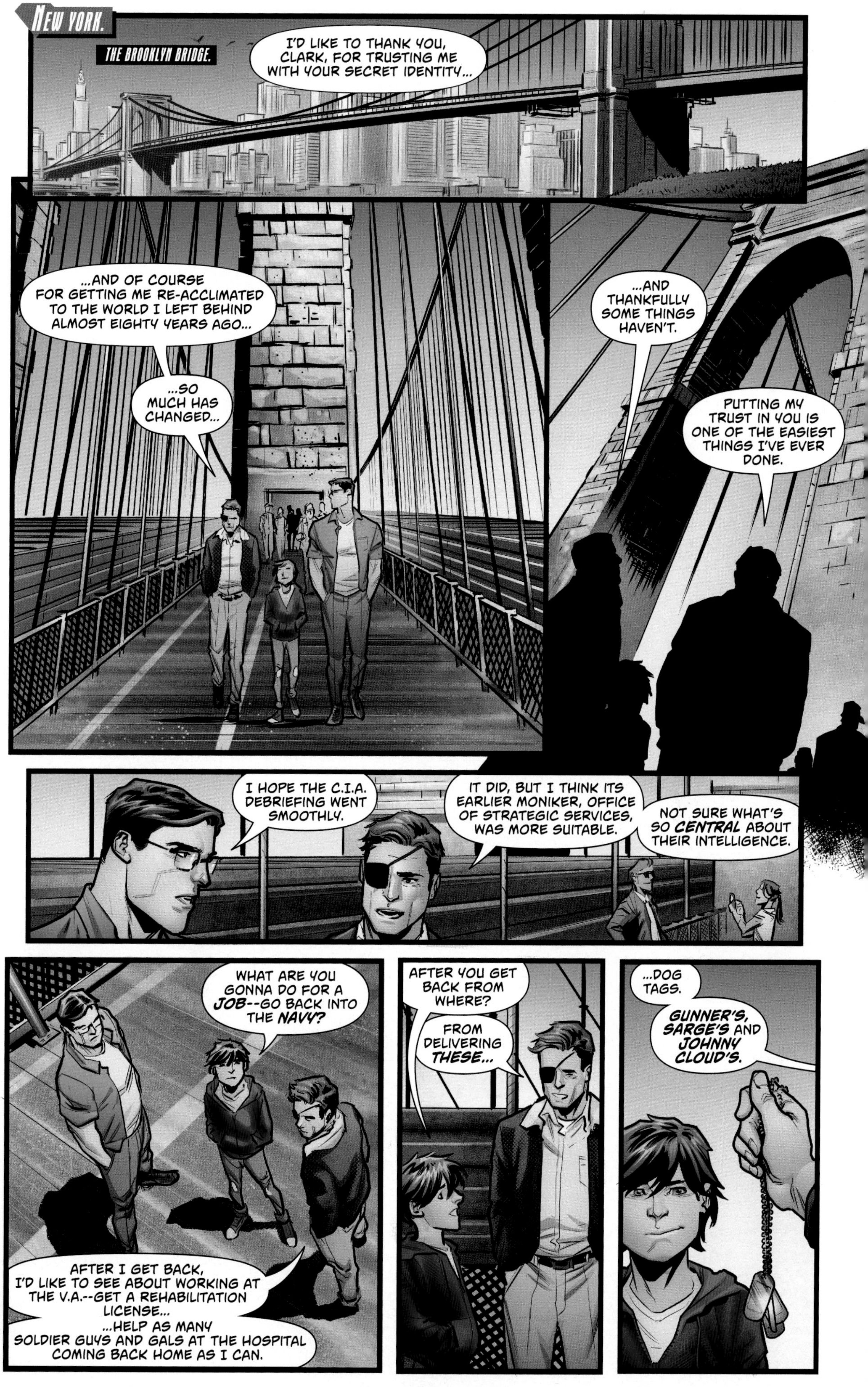
NEW YORK.
THE BROOKLYN BRIDGE.
I'D LIKE TO THANK YOU, CLARK, FOR TRUSTING ME WITH YOUR SECRET IDENTITY...
...AND OF COURSE FOR GETTING ME RE-ACCLIMATED TO THE WORLD I LEFT BEHIND ALMOST EIGHTY YEARS AGO...
...SO MUCH HAS CHANGED...
...AND THANKFULLY SOME THINGS HAVEN'T.
PUTTING MY TRUST IN YOU IS ONE OF THE EASIEST THINGS I'VE EVER DONE.
I HOPE THE C.I.A. DEBRIEFING WENT SMOOTHLY.
IT DID, BUT I THINK ITS EARLIER MONIKER, OFFICE OF STRATEGIC SERVICES, WAS MORE SUITABLE.
NOT SURE WHAT'S SO CENTRAL ABOUT THEIR INTELLIGENCE.
WHAT ARE YOU GONNA DO FOR A JOB--GO BACK INTO THE NAVY?
AFTER I GET BACK, I'D LIKE TO SEE ABOUT WORKING AT THE V.A.--GET A REHABILITATION LICENSE... ...HELP AS MANY SOLDIER GUYS AND GALS AT THE HOSPITAL COMING BACK HOME AS I CAN.
AFTER YOU GET BACK FROM WHERE?
FROM DELIVERING THESE...
...DOG TAGS.
GUNNER'S, SARGE'S AND JOHNNY CLOUD'S.

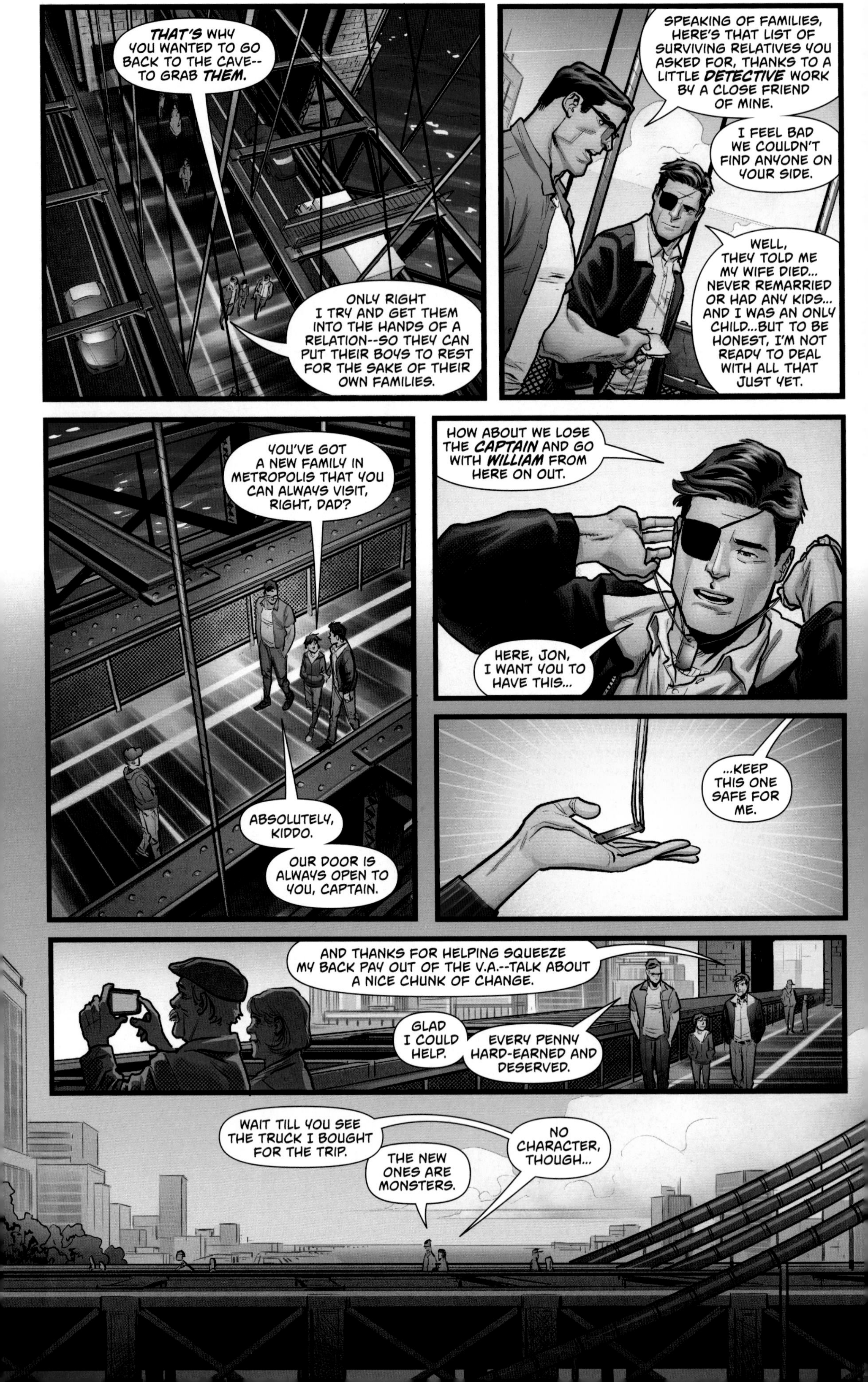
THAT'S WHY YOU WANTED TO GO BACK TO THE CAVE-- TO GRAB THEM.
ONLY RIGHT I TRY AND GET THEM INTO THE HANDS OF A RELATION--SO THEY CAN PUT THEIR BOYS TO REST FOR THE SAKE OF THEIR OWN FAMILIES.
SPEAKING OF FAMILIES, HERE'S THAT LIST OF SURVIVING RELATIVES YOU ASKED FOR, THANKS TO A LITTLE DETECTIVE WORK BY A CLOSE FRIEND OF MINE.
I FEEL BAD WE COULDN'T FIND ANYONE ON YOUR SIDE.
WELL, THEY TOLD ME MY WIFE DIED... NEVER REMARRIED OR HAD ANY KIDS... AND I WAS AN ONLY CHILD...BUT TO BE HONEST, I'M NOT READY TO DEAL WITH ALL THAT JUST YET.
YOU'VE GOT A NEW FAMILY IN METROPOLIS THAT YOU CAN ALWAYS VISIT, RIGHT, DAD?
ABSOLUTELY, KIDDO.
OUR DOOR IS ALWAYS OPEN TO YOU, CAPTAIN.
HOW ABOUT WE LOSE THE CAPTAIN AND GO WITH WILLIAM FROM HERE ON OUT.
HERE, JON, I WANT YOU TO HAVE THIS...
...KEEP THIS ONE SAFE FOR ME.
AND THANKS FOR HELPING SQUEEZE MY BACK PAY OUT OF THE V.A.--TALK ABOUT A NICE CHUNK OF CHANGE.
GLAD I COULD HELP.
EVERY PENNY HARD-EARNED AND DESERVED.
WAIT TILL YOU SEE THE TRUCK I BOUGHT FOR THE TRIP.
THE NEW ONES ARE MONSTERS.
NO CHARACTER, THOUGH...

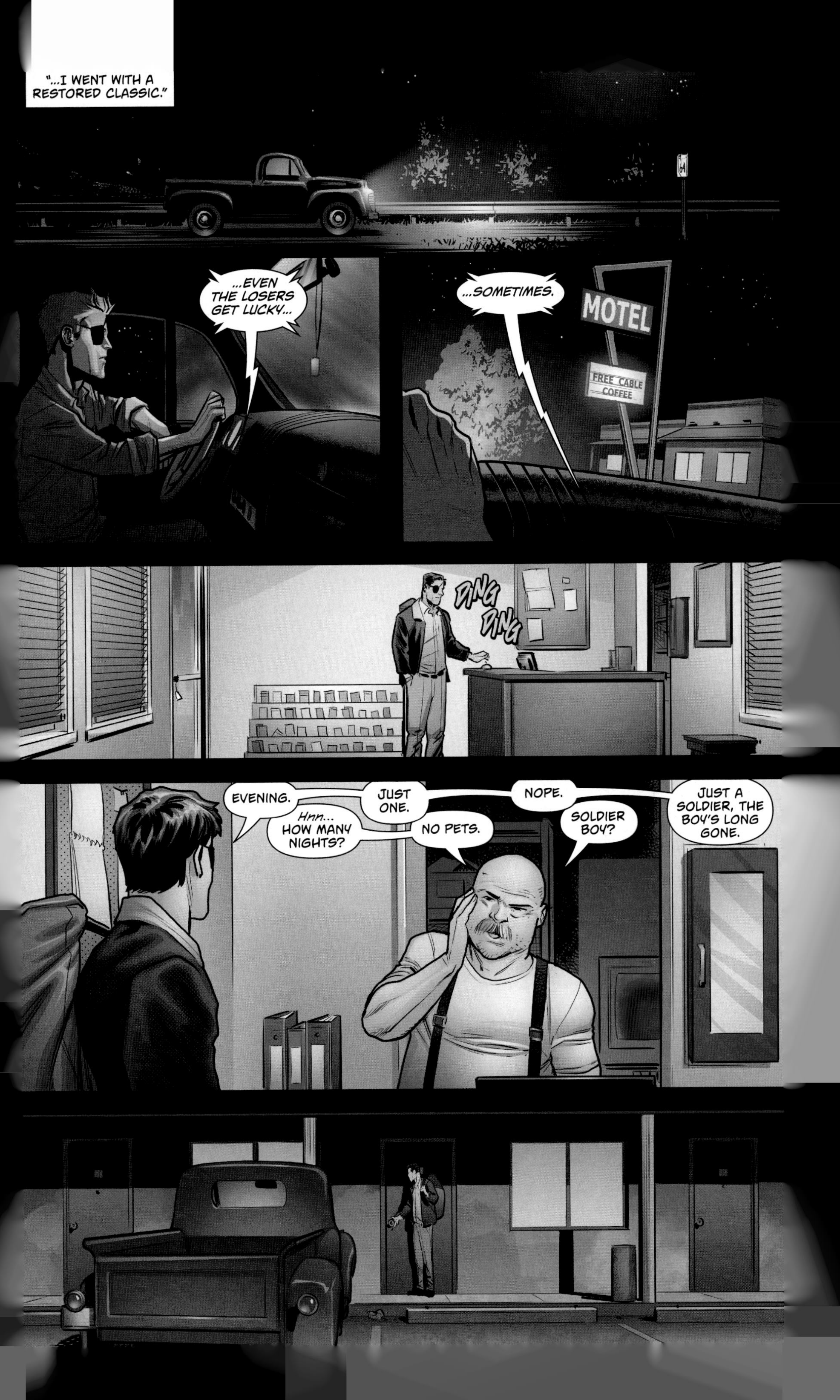
"...I WENT WITH A RESTORED CLASSIC."
...EVEN THE LOSERS GET LUCKY...
...SOMETIMES.
MOTEL
FREE CABLE COFFEE
DING DING
EVENING.
Hnn... HOW MANY NIGHTS?
JUST ONE.
NO PETS.
NOPE.
SOLDIER BOY?
JUST A SOLDIER, THE BOY'S LONG GONE.

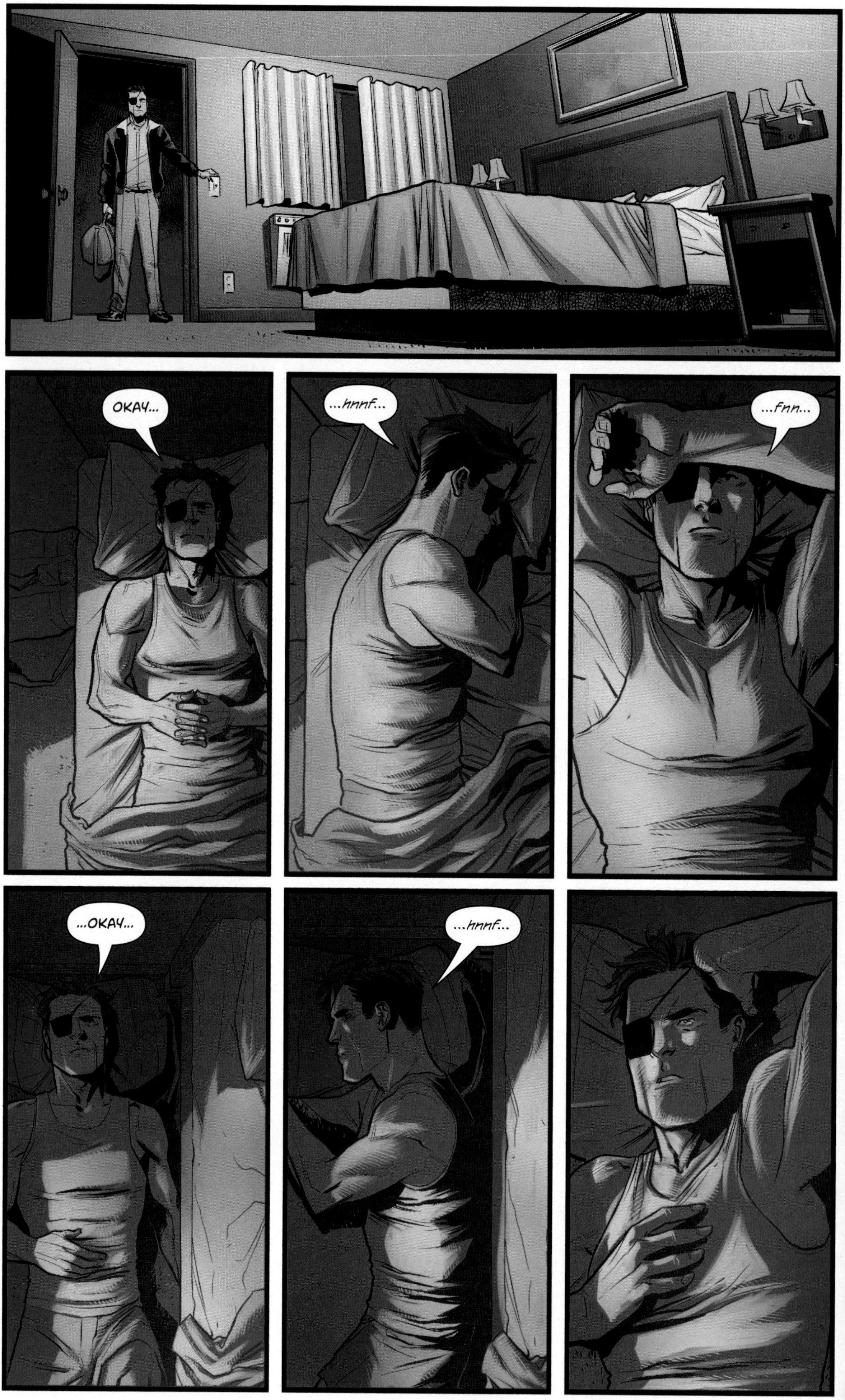
OKAY...
...hnnf...
...fnn...
...OKAY...
...hnnf...

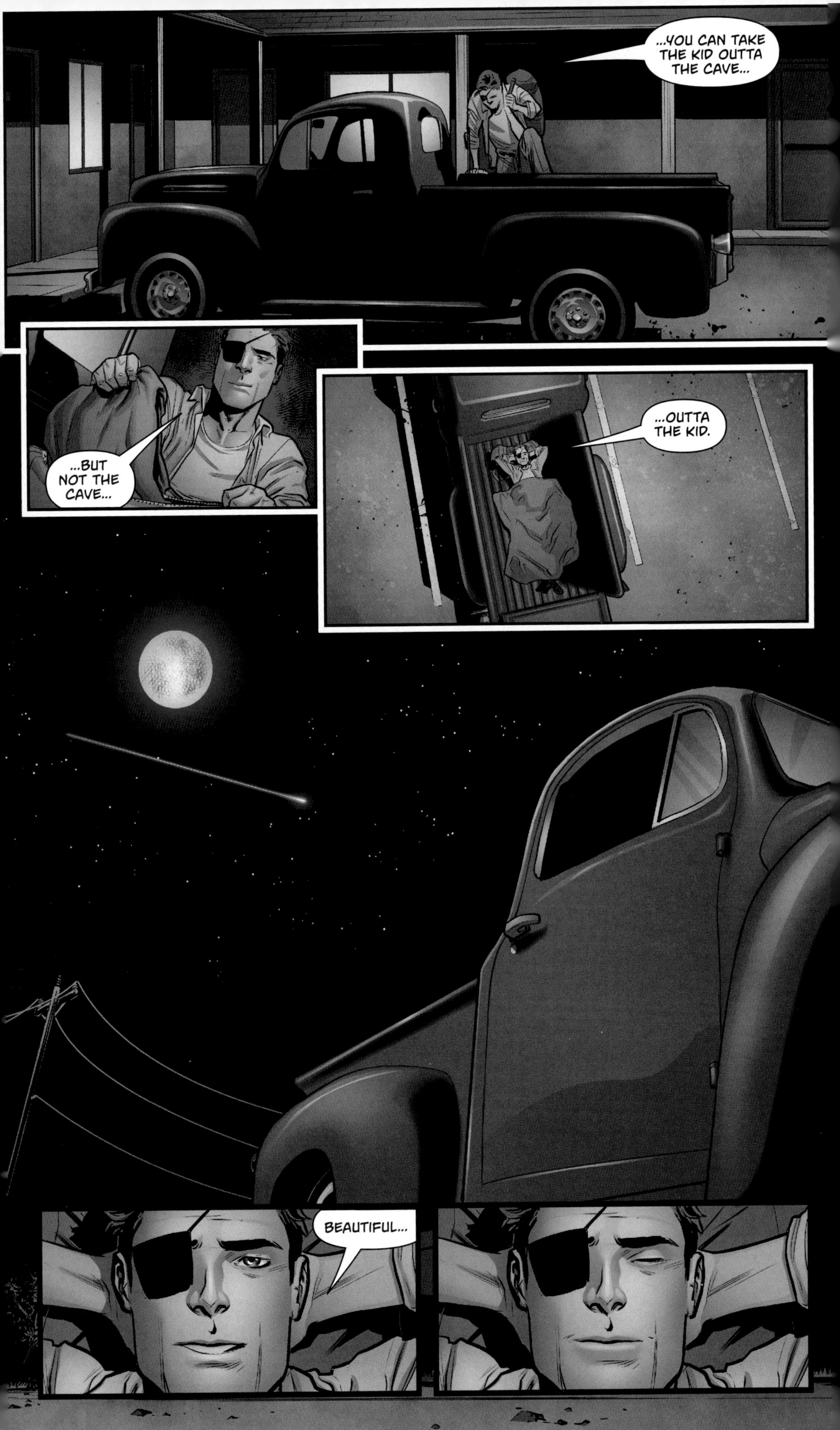
...YOU CAN TAKE THE KID OUTTA THE CAVE...
...BUT NOT THE CAVE...
...OUTTA THE KID.
BEAUTIFUL...

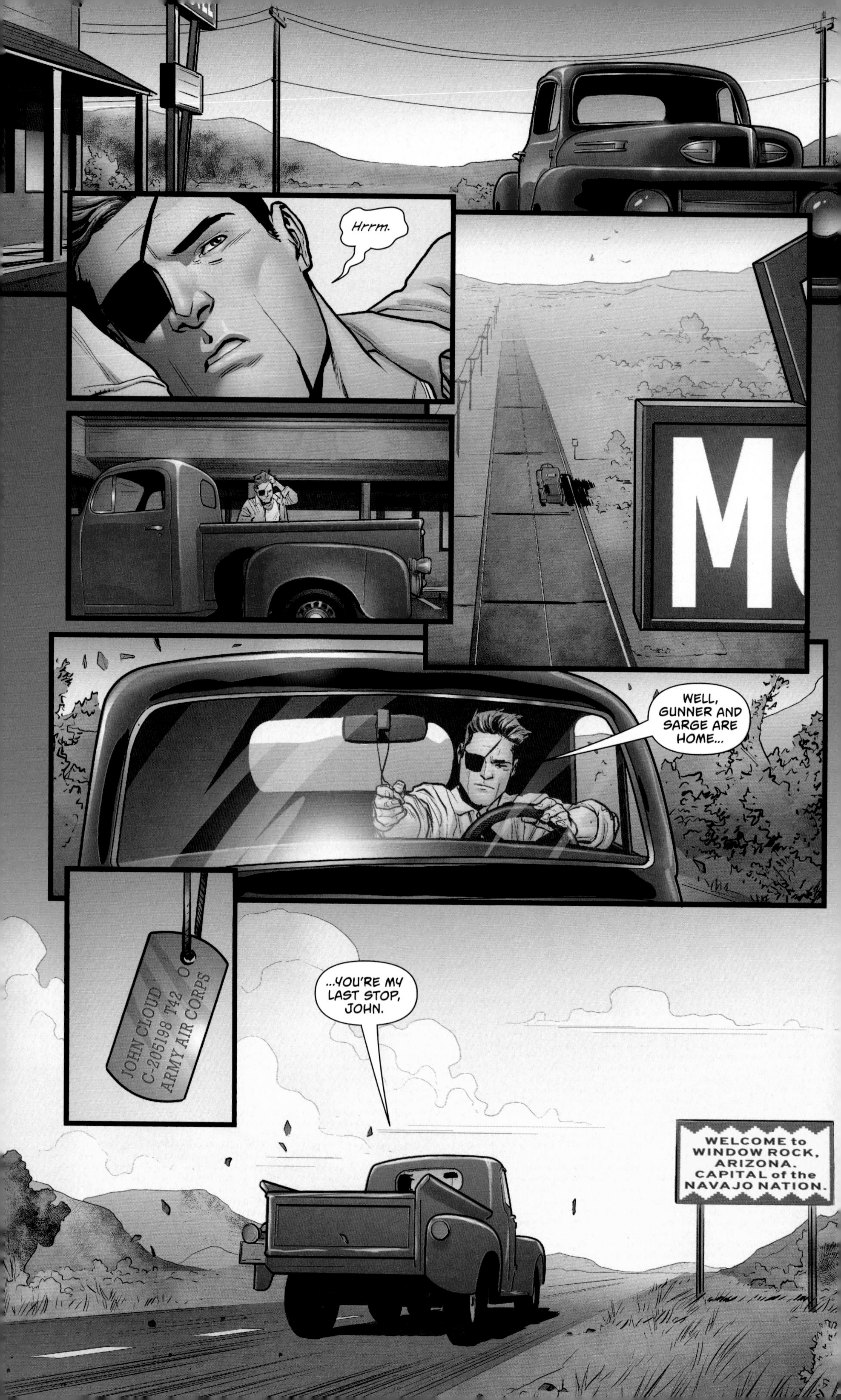
Hrrm.
MO
WELL, GUNNER AND SARGE ARE HOME...
JOHN CLOUD
C-205198 T42
ARMY AIR CORPS
...YOU'RE MY LAST STOP, JOHN.
WELCOME to WINDOW ROCK, ARIZONA. CAPITAL of the NAVAJO NATION.

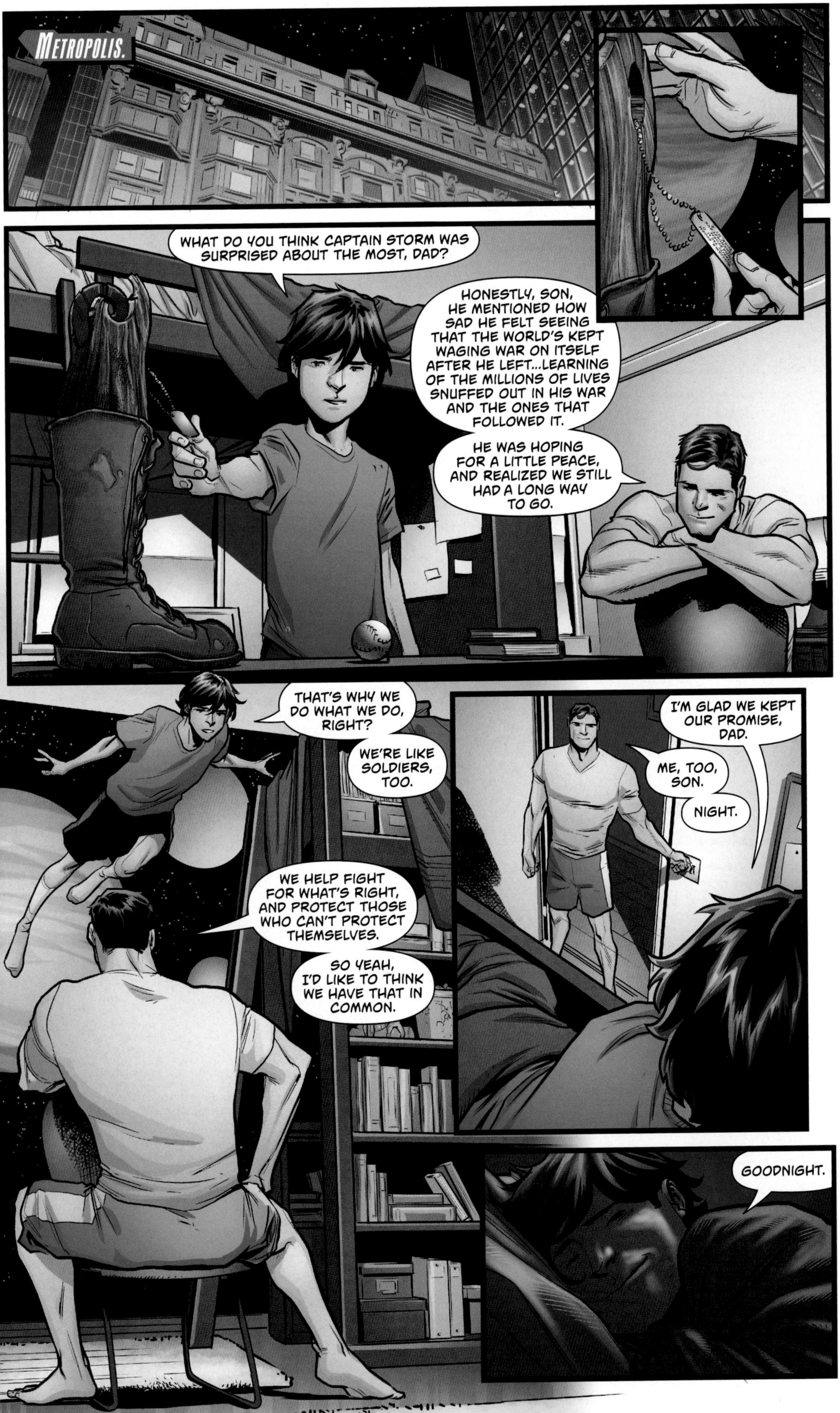
METROPOLIS.
WHAT DO YOU THINK CAPTAIN STORM WAS SURPRISED ABOUT THE MOST, DAD?
HONESTLY, SON, HE MENTIONED HOW SAD HE FELT SEEING THAT THE WORLD'S KEPT WAGING WAR ON ITSELF AFTER HE LEFT...LEARNING OF THE MILLIONS OF LIVES SNUFFED OUT IN HIS WAR AND THE ONES THAT FOLLOWED IT.
HE WAS HOPING FOR A LITTLE PEACE, AND REALIZED WE STILL HAD A LONG WAY TO GO.
THAT'S WHY WE DO WHAT WE DO, RIGHT?
WE'RE LIKE SOLDIERS, TOO.
WE HELP FIGHT FOR WHAT'S RIGHT, AND PROTECT THOSE WHO CAN'T PROTECT THEMSELVES.
SO YEAH, I'D LIKE TO THINK WE HAVE THAT IN COMMON.
I'M GLAD WE KEPT OUR PROMISE, DAD.
ME, TOO, SON.
NIGHT.
GOODNIGHT.

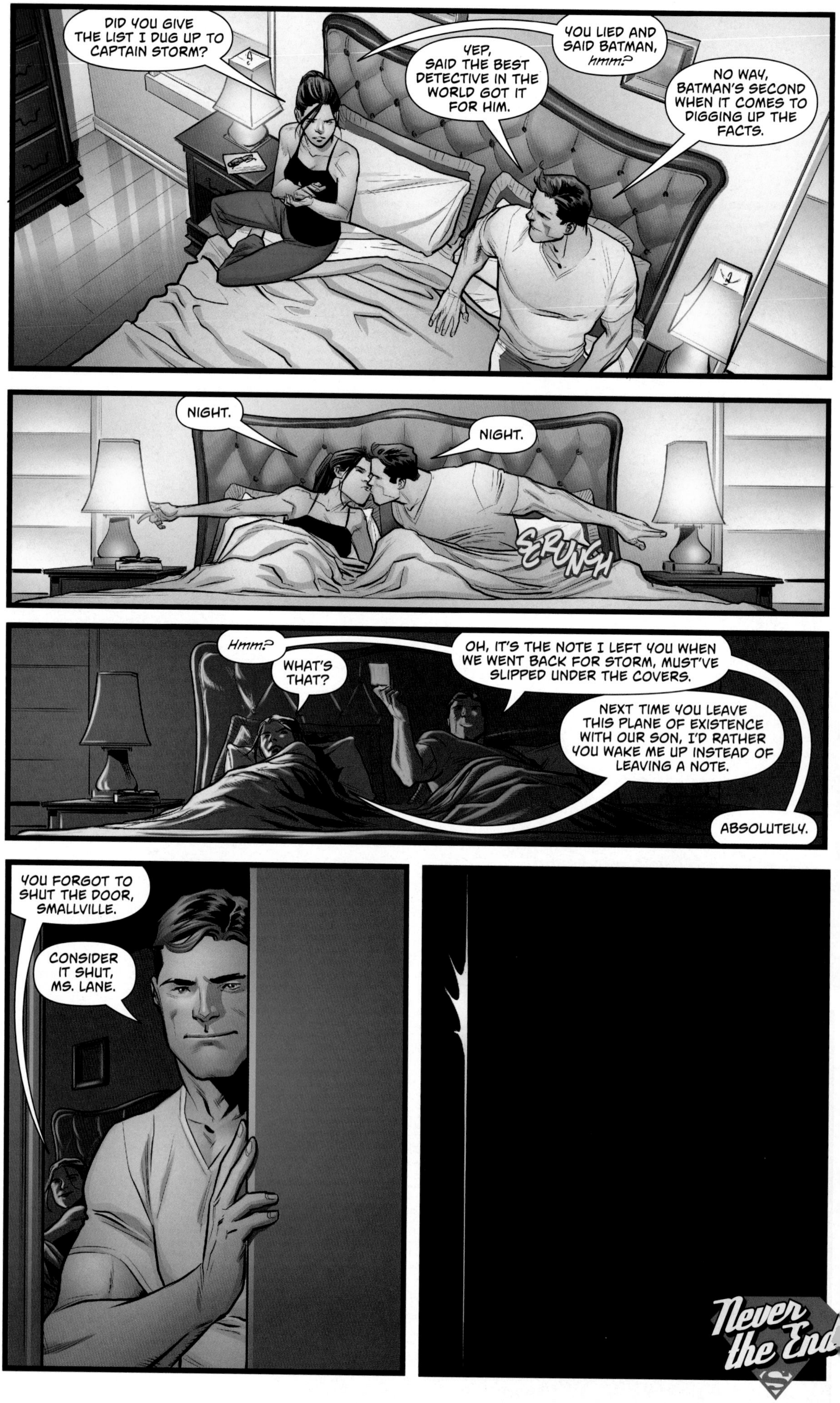
DID YOU GIVE THE LIST I DUG UP TO CAPTAIN STORM?
YEP, SAID THE BEST DETECTIVE IN THE WORLD GOT IT FOR HIM.
YOU LIED AND SAID BATMAN, *hmm?*
NO WAY, BATMAN'S SECOND WHEN IT COMES TO DIGGING UP THE FACTS.
NIGHT.
NIGHT.
SCRUNCH
Hmm?
WHAT'S THAT?
OH, IT'S THE NOTE I LEFT YOU WHEN WE WENT BACK FOR STORM, MUST'VE SLIPPED UNDER THE COVERS.
NEXT TIME YOU LEAVE THIS PLANE OF EXISTENCE WITH OUR SON, I'D RATHER YOU WAKE ME UP INSTEAD OF LEAVING A NOTE.
ABSOLUTELY.
YOU FORGOT TO SHUT THE DOOR, SMALLVILLE.
CONSIDER IT SHUT, MS. LANE.
Never the End

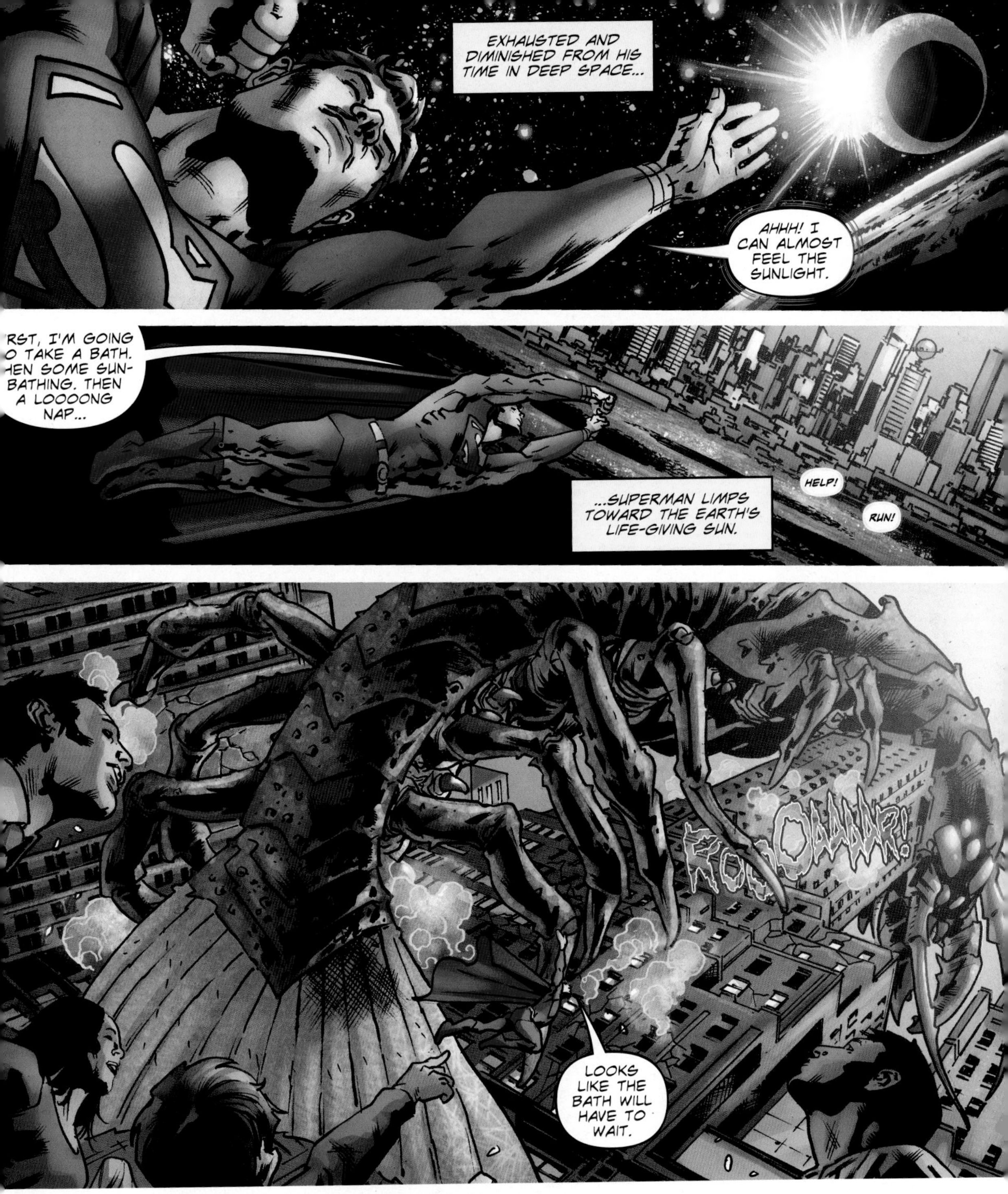
EXHAUSTED AND DIMINISHED FROM HIS TIME IN DEEP SPACE...
AHHH! I CAN ALMOST FEEL THE SUNLIGHT.
RST, I'M GOING O TAKE A BATH. HEN SOME SUN-BATHING. THEN A LOOOONG NAP...
...SUPERMAN LIMPS TOWARD THE EARTH'S LIFE-GIVING SUN.
HELP!
RUN!
LOOKS LIKE THE BATH WILL HAVE TO WAIT.

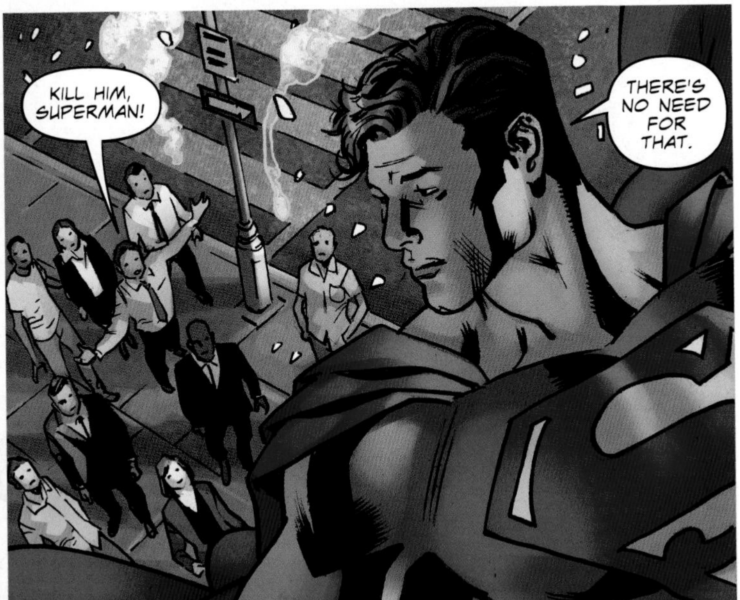
KILL HIM, SUPERMAN!
THERE'S NO NEED FOR THAT.

STRAYS AND STRANGERS

MARK RUSSELL WRITER

BRYAN HITCH ARTIST

ALEX SINCLAIR COLORIST

TOM NAPOLITANO LETTERER

ANDREW MARINO ASSISTANT EDITOR

PAUL KAMINSKI EDITOR

MARIE JAVINS GROUP EDITOR

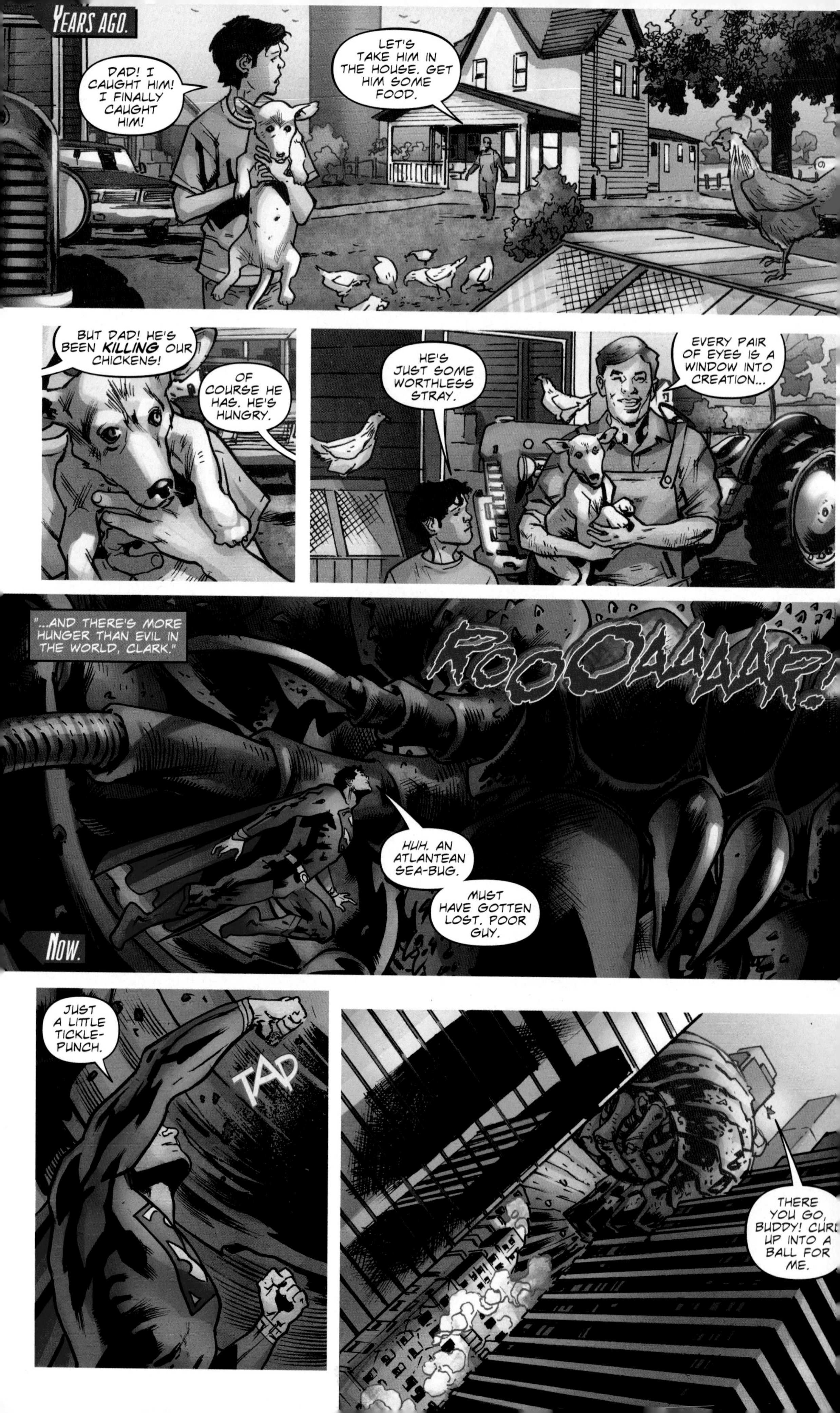
YEARS AGO.
DAD! I CAUGHT HIM! I FINALLY CAUGHT HIM!
LET'S TAKE HIM IN THE HOUSE. GET HIM SOME FOOD.
BUT DAD! HE'S BEEN KILLING OUR CHICKENS!
OF COURSE HE HAS. HE'S HUNGRY.
HE'S JUST SOME WORTHLESS STRAY.
EVERY PAIR OF EYES IS A WINDOW INTO CREATION...
"...AND THERE'S MORE HUNGER THAN EVIL IN THE WORLD, CLARK."
ROOOAAAAR!
HUH. AN ATLANTEAN SEA-BUG.
MUST HAVE GOTTEN LOST. POOR GUY.
NOW.
JUST A LITTLE TICKLE-PUNCH.
TAP
THERE YOU GO, BUDDY! CURL UP INTO A BALL FOR ME.

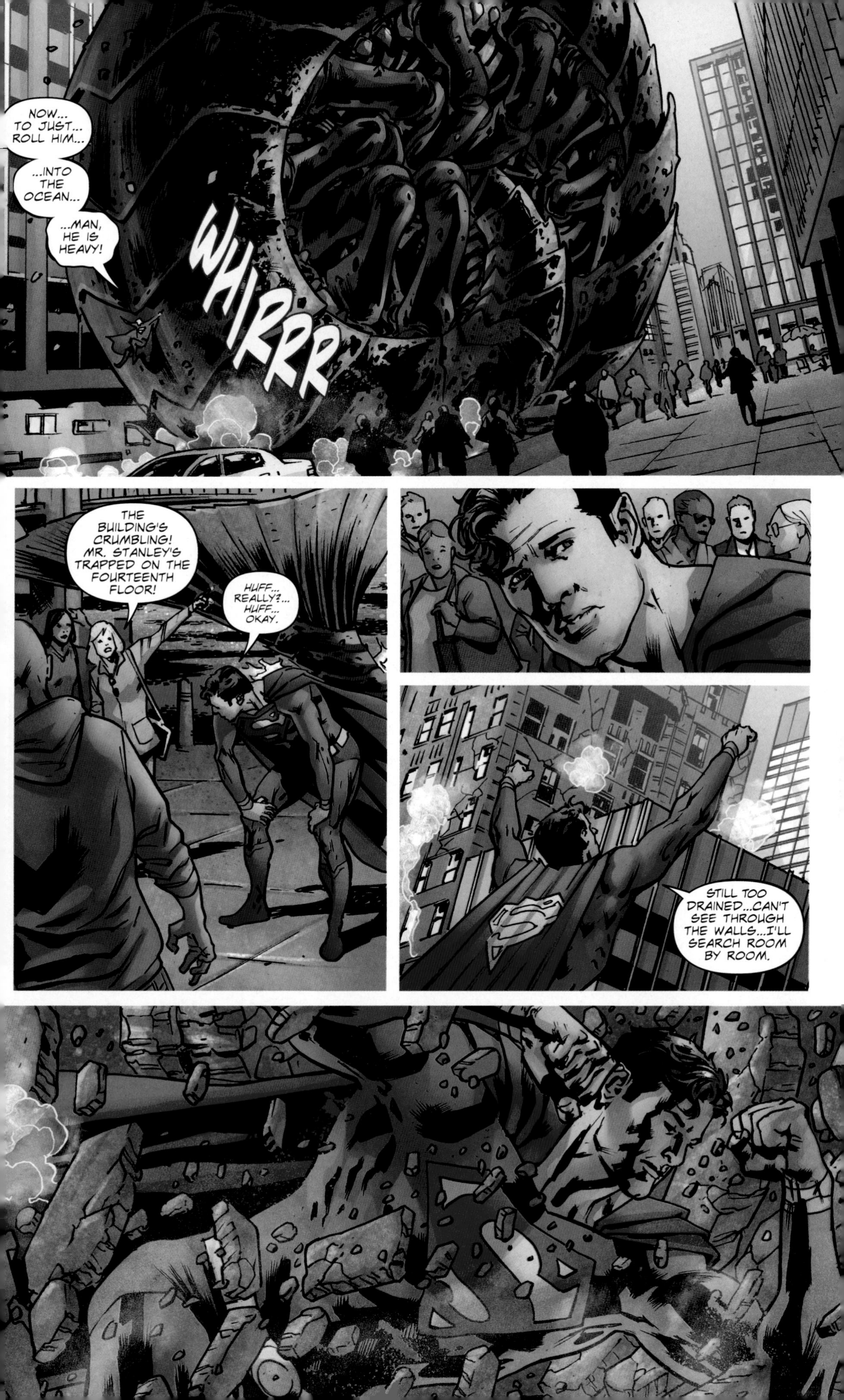
NOW... TO JUST... ROLL HIM...
...INTO THE OCEAN...
...MAN, HE IS HEAVY!
WHIRRR
THE BUILDING'S CRUMBLING! MR. STANLEY'S TRAPPED ON THE FOURTEENTH FLOOR!
HUFF... REALLY?... HUFF... OKAY.
STILL TOO DRAINED...CAN'T SEE THROUGH THE WALLS...I'LL SEARCH ROOM BY ROOM.

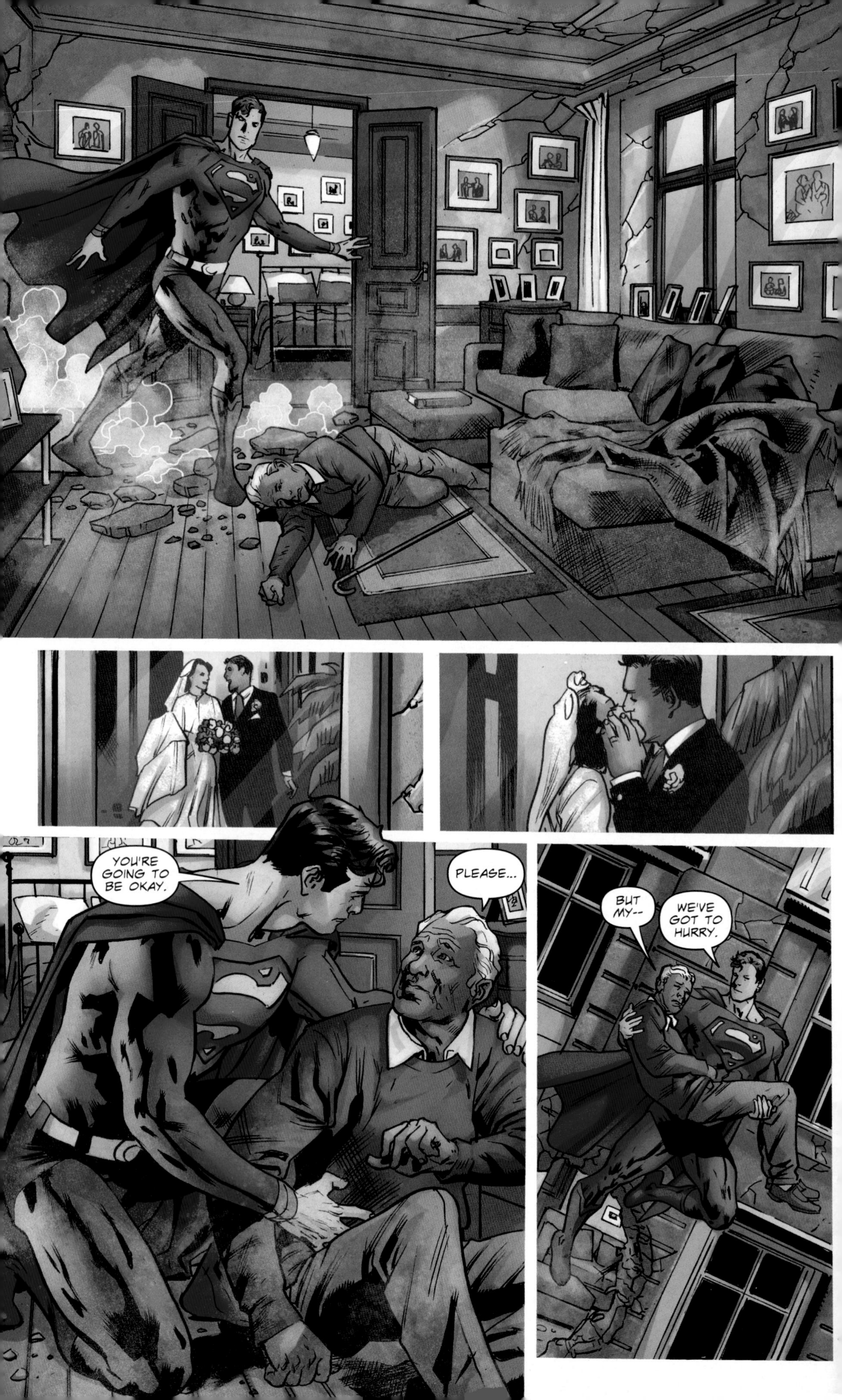
YOU'RE GOING TO BE OKAY.
PLEASE...
BUT MY--
WE'VE GOT TO HURRY.

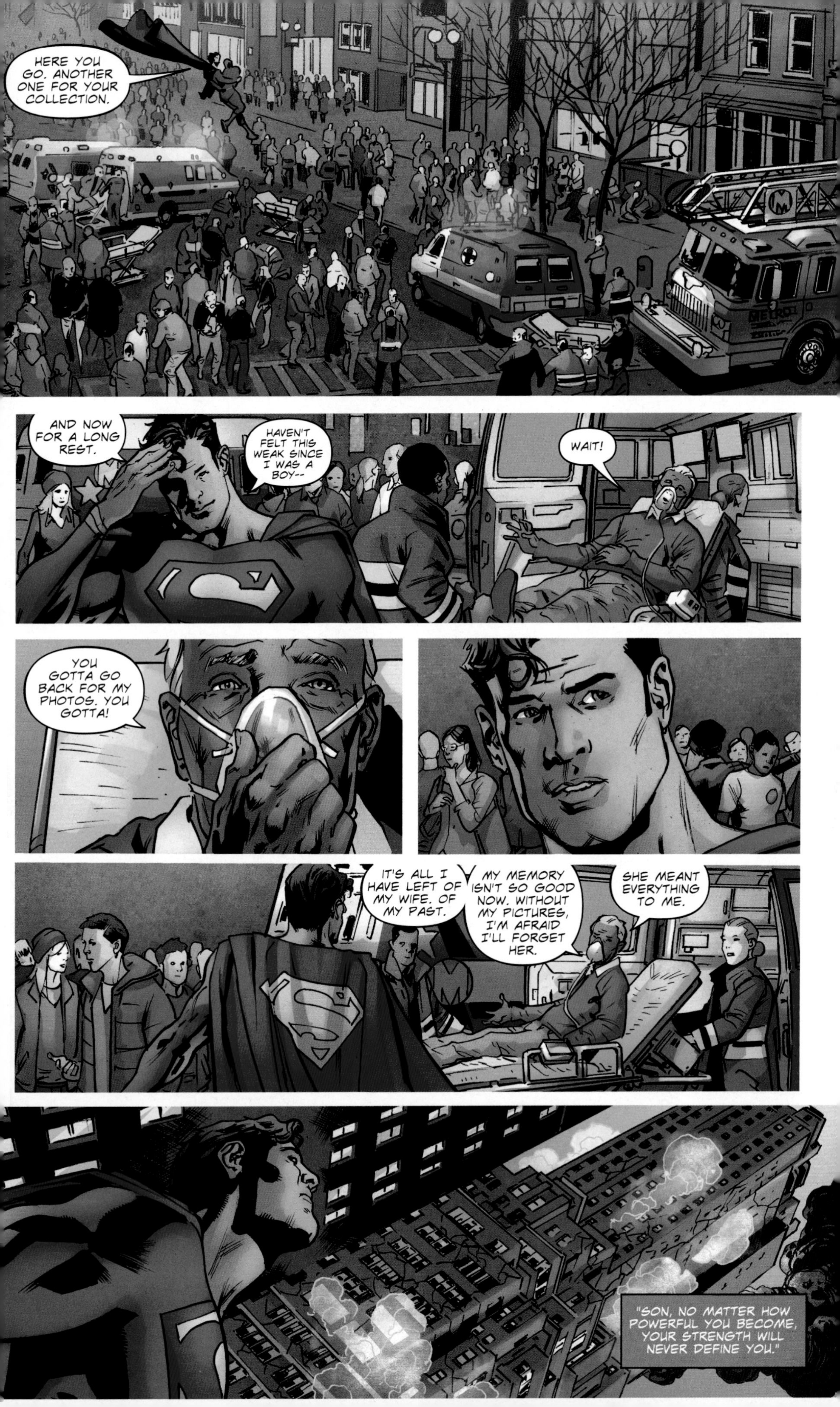
HERE YOU GO. ANOTHER ONE FOR YOUR COLLECTION.
AND NOW FOR A LONG REST.
HAVEN'T FELT THIS WEAK SINCE I WAS A BOY--
WAIT!
YOU GOTTA GO BACK FOR MY PHOTOS. YOU GOTTA!
IT'S ALL I HAVE LEFT OF MY WIFE. OF MY PAST.
MY MEMORY ISN'T SO GOOD NOW. WITHOUT MY PICTURES, I'M AFRAID I'LL FORGET HER.
SHE MEANT EVERYTHING TO ME.
"SON, NO MATTER HOW POWERFUL YOU BECOME, YOUR STRENGTH WILL NEVER DEFINE YOU."

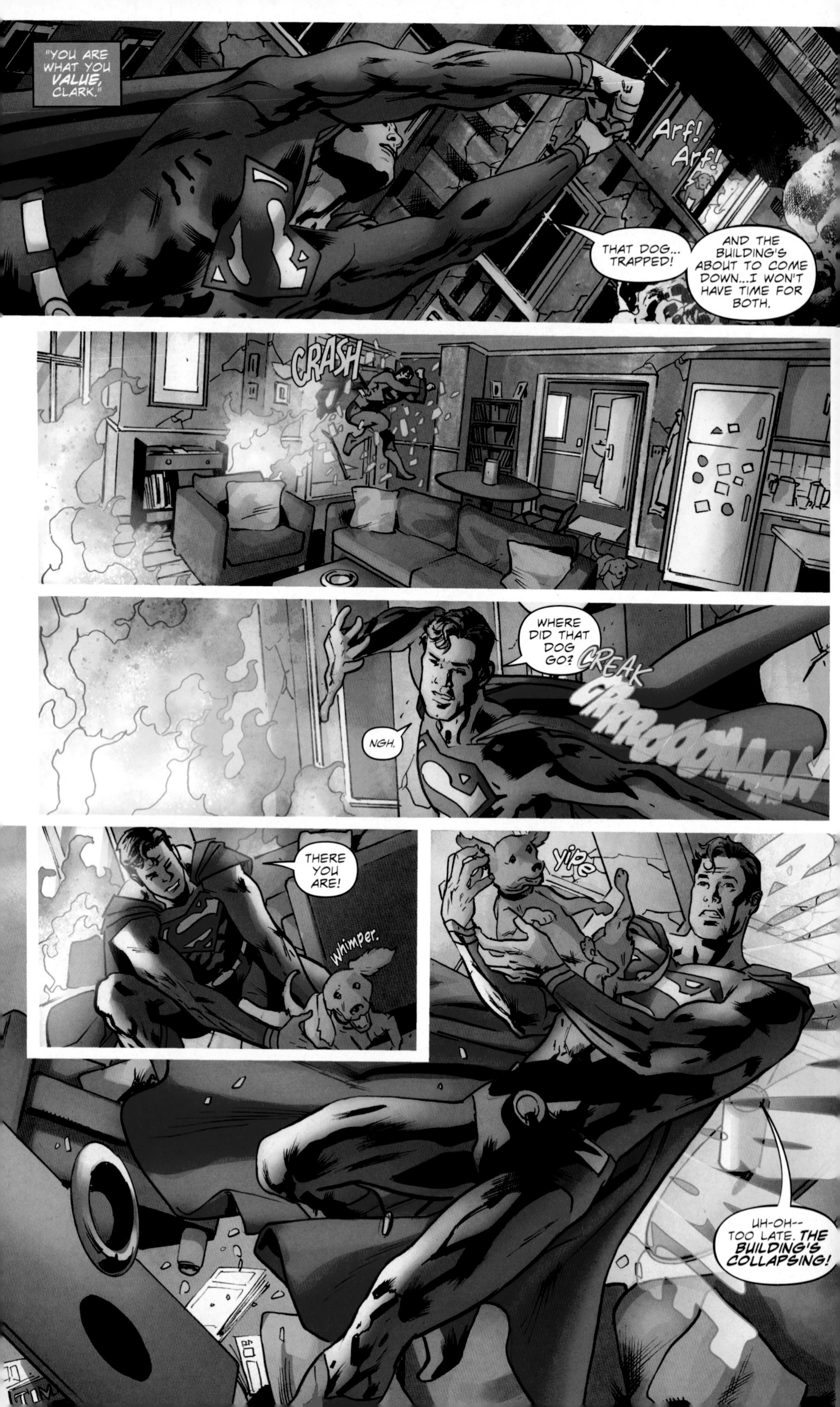
"YOU ARE WHAT YOU VALUE, CLARK."
Arf! Arf!
THAT DOG... TRAPPED!
AND THE BUILDING'S ABOUT TO COME DOWN...I WON'T HAVE TIME FOR BOTH.
CRASH
WHERE DID THAT DOG GO?
CREAK
NGH.
GRRROOOMMM
THERE YOU ARE!
whimper.
yipe
UH-OH-- TOO LATE. THE BUILDING'S COLLAPSING!

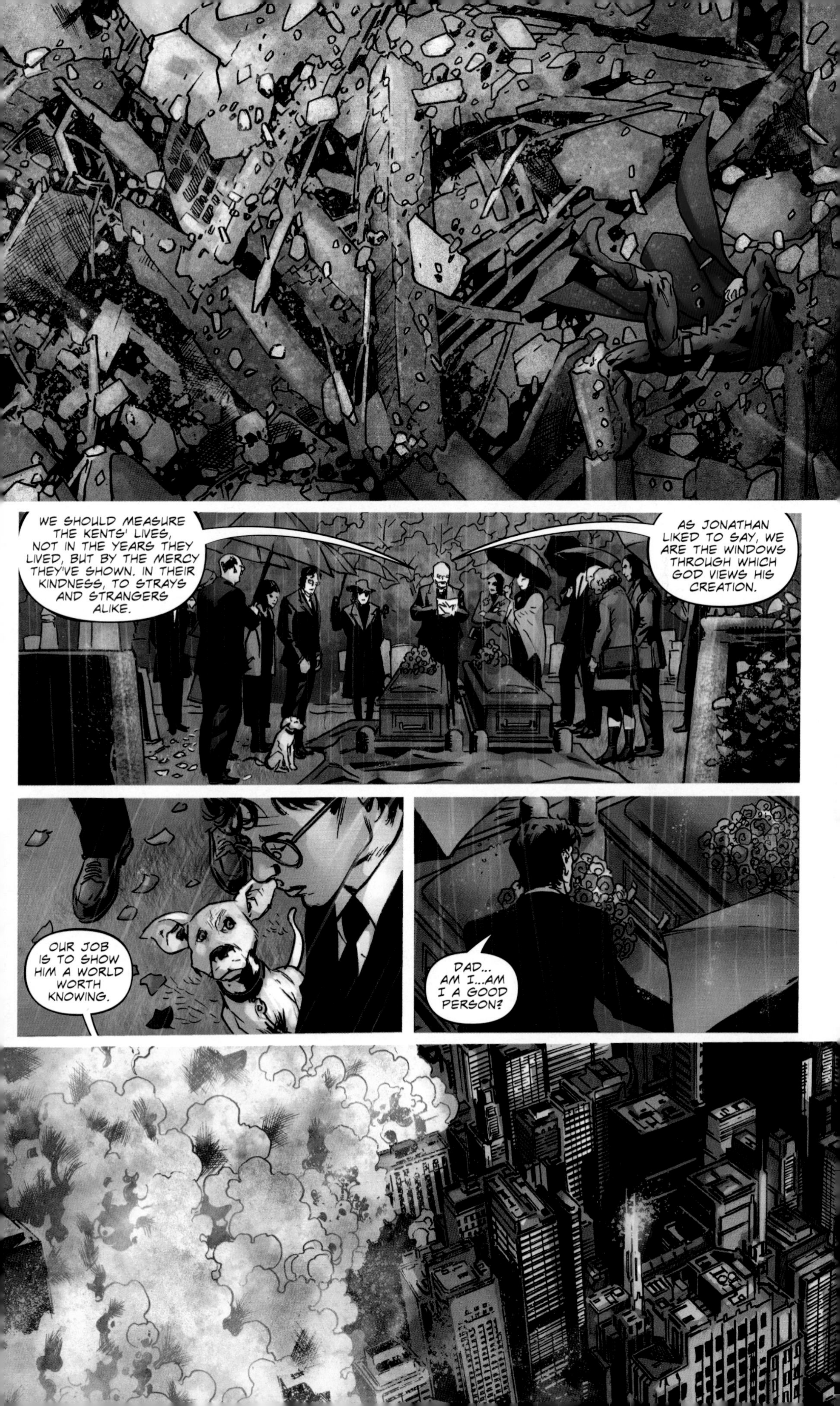

WE SHOULD MEASURE THE KENTS' LIVES, NOT IN THE YEARS THEY LIVED, BUT BY THE MERCY THEY'VE SHOWN. IN THEIR KINDNESS, TO STRAYS AND STRANGERS ALIKE.
AS JONATHAN LIKED TO SAY, WE ARE THE WINDOWS THROUGH WHICH GOD VIEWS HIS CREATION.
OUR JOB IS TO SHOW HIM A WORLD WORTH KNOWING.
DAD... AM I...AM I A GOOD PERSON?

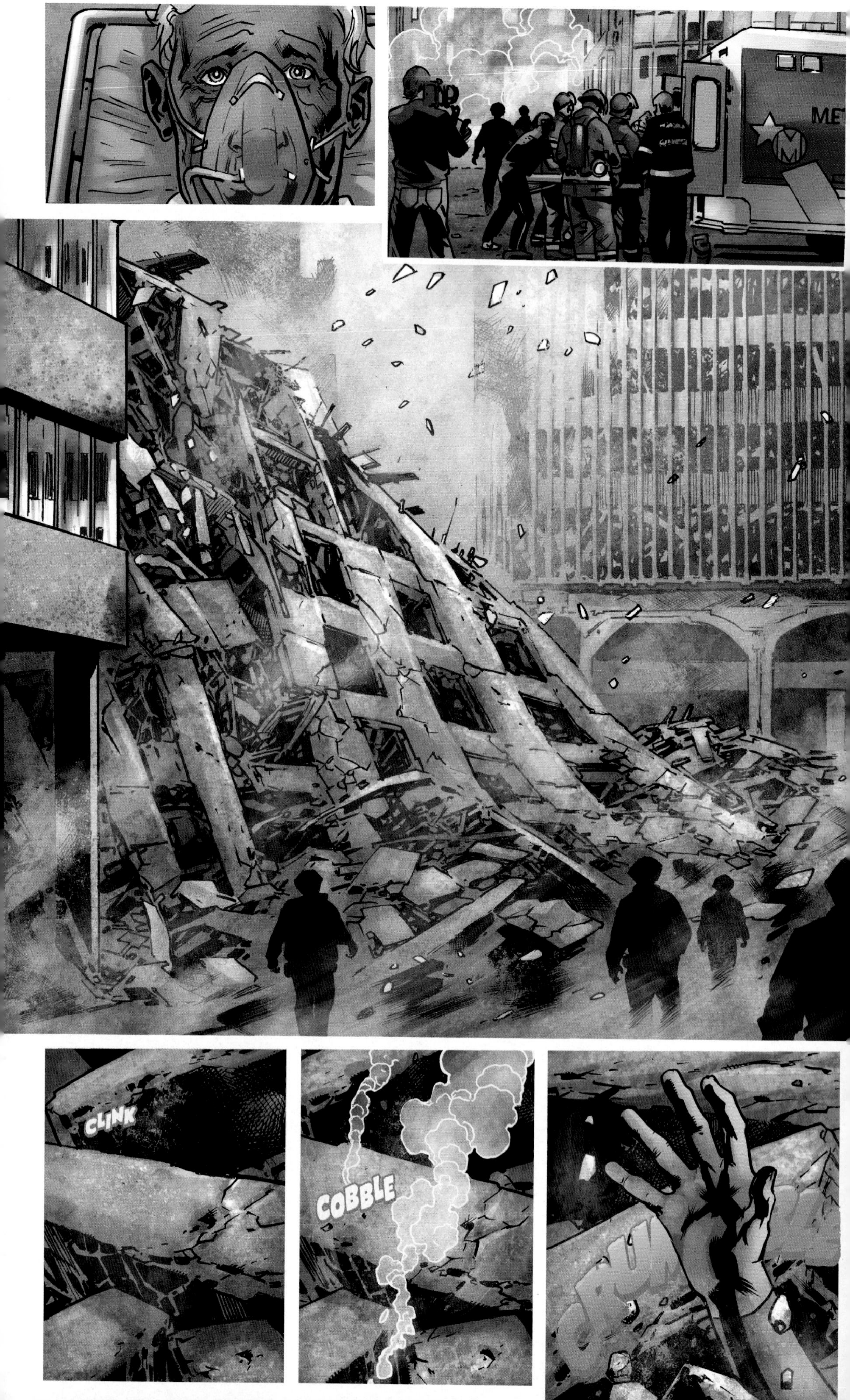
CLINK
COBBLE

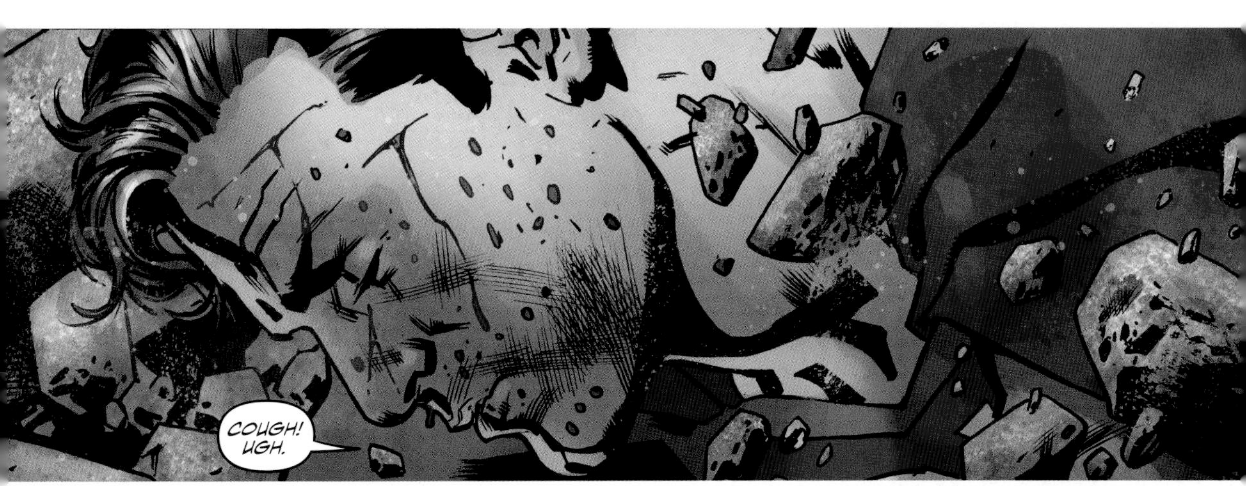
COUGH! UGH.

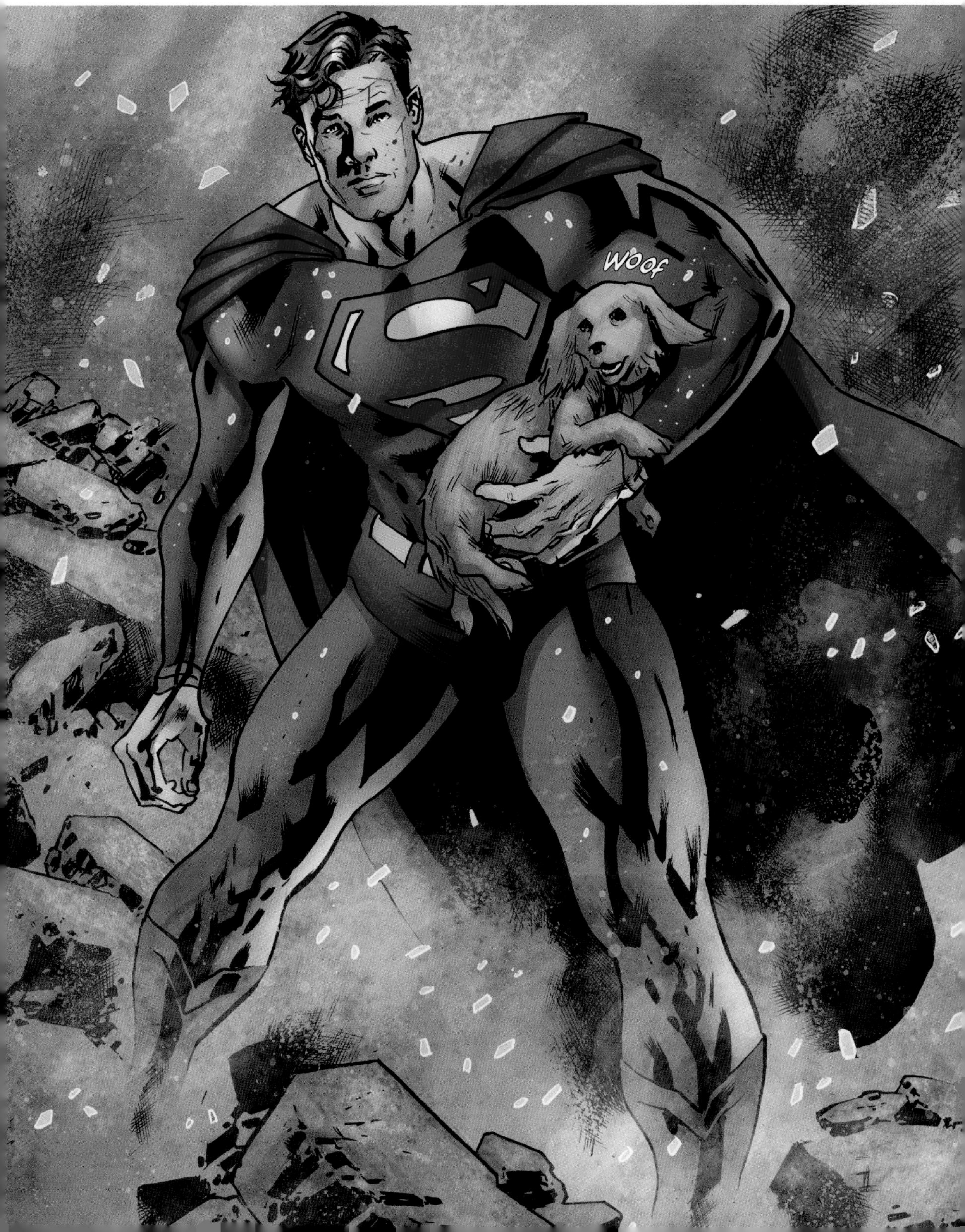
WOOF

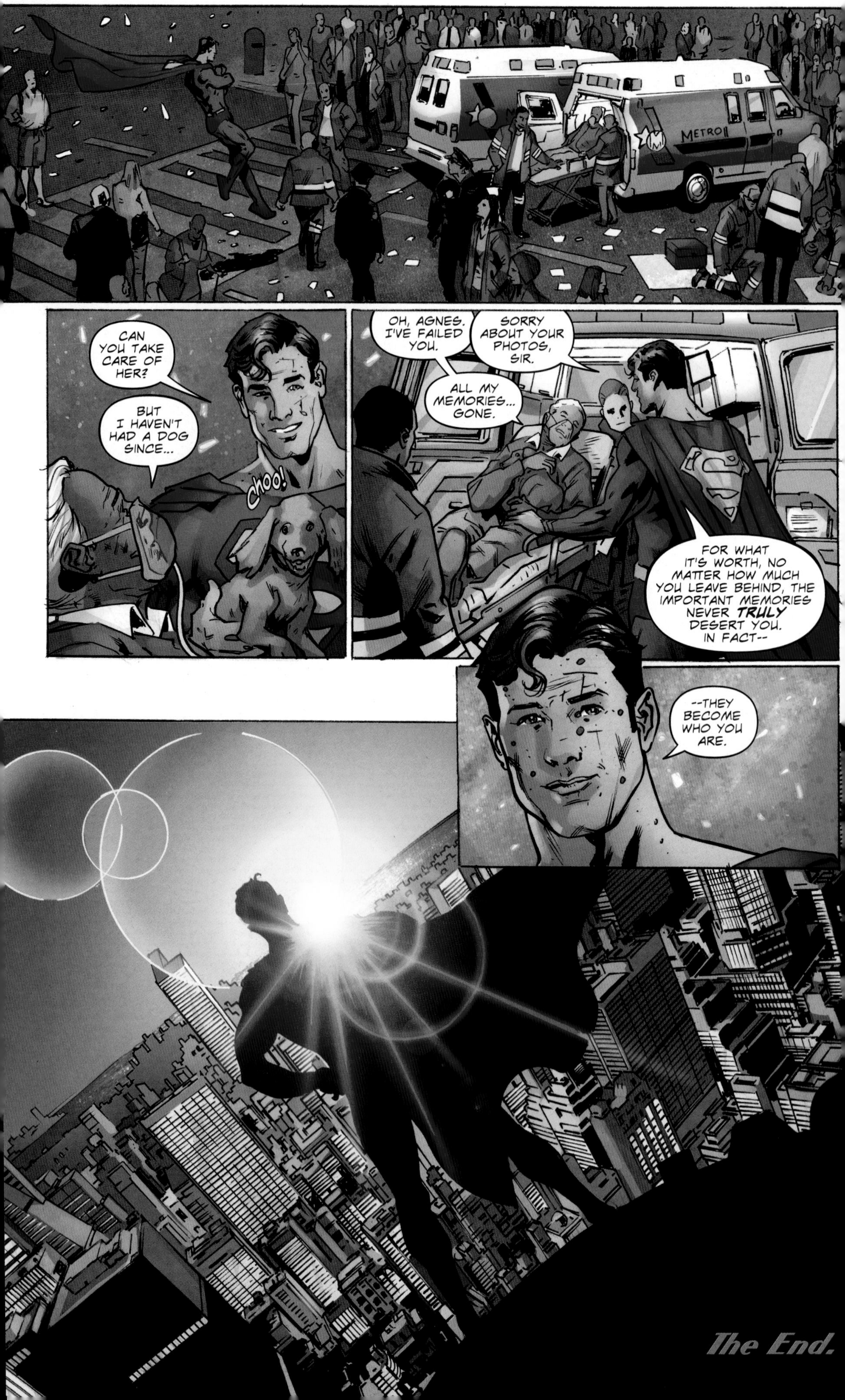
METRO
CAN YOU TAKE CARE OF HER?
BUT I HAVEN'T HAD A DOG SINCE...
CHOO!
OH, AGNES. I'VE FAILED YOU.
SORRY ABOUT YOUR PHOTOS, SIR.
ALL MY MEMORIES... GONE.
FOR WHAT IT'S WORTH, NO MATTER HOW MUCH YOU LEAVE BEHIND, THE IMPORTANT MEMORIES NEVER TRULY DESERT YOU. IN FACT--
--THEY BECOME WHO YOU ARE.
The End.

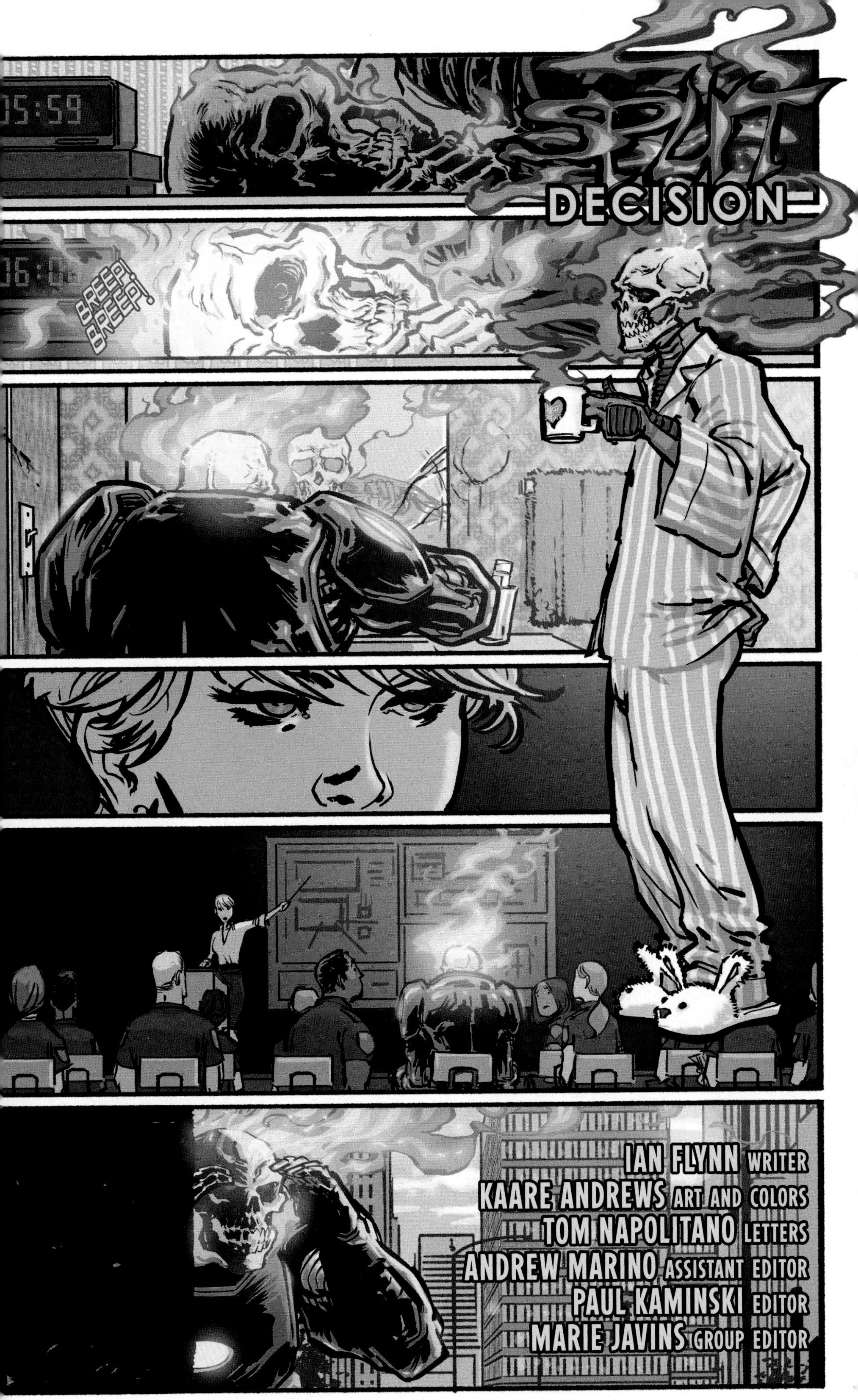
05:59
SPLIT DECISION
06:00
BREEP! BREEP! BREEP!
IAN FLYNN WRITER
KAARE ANDREWS ART AND COLORS
TOM NAPOLITANO LETTERS
ANDREW MARINO ASSISTANT EDITOR
PAUL KAMINSKI EDITOR
MARIE JAVINS GROUP EDITOR

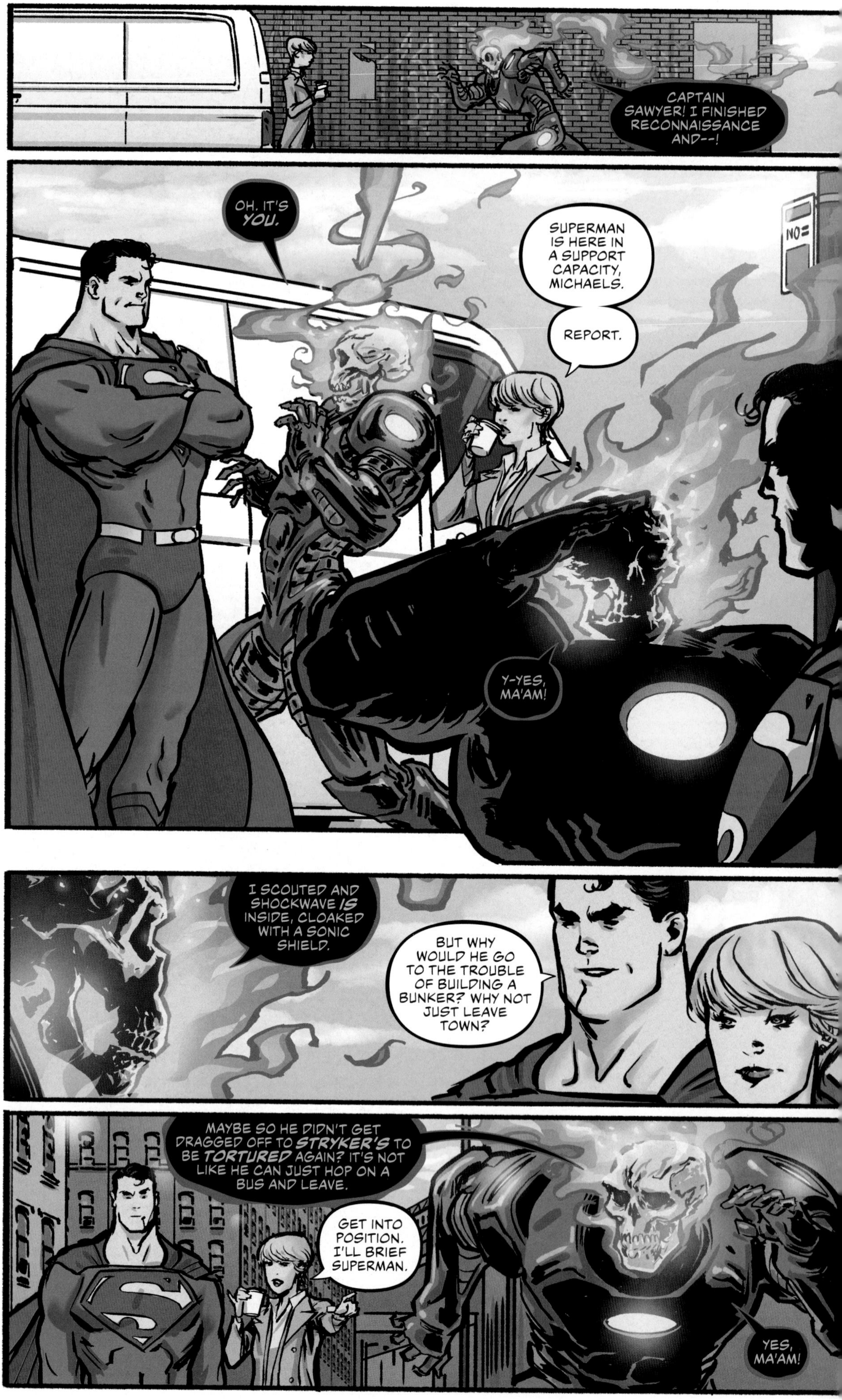
CAPTAIN SAWYER! I FINISHED RECONNAISSANCE AND--!
OH. IT'S YOU.
SUPERMAN IS HERE IN A SUPPORT CAPACITY, MICHAELS.
REPORT.
Y-YES, MA'AM!
NO
I SCOUTED AND SHOCKWAVE IS INSIDE, CLOAKED WITH A SONIC SHIELD.
BUT WHY WOULD HE GO TO THE TROUBLE OF BUILDING A BUNKER? WHY NOT JUST LEAVE TOWN?
MAYBE SO HE DIDN'T GET DRAGGED OFF TO STRYKER'S TO BE TORTURED AGAIN? IT'S NOT LIKE HE CAN JUST HOP ON A BUS AND LEAVE.
GET INTO POSITION. I'LL BRIEF SUPERMAN.
YES, MA'AM!

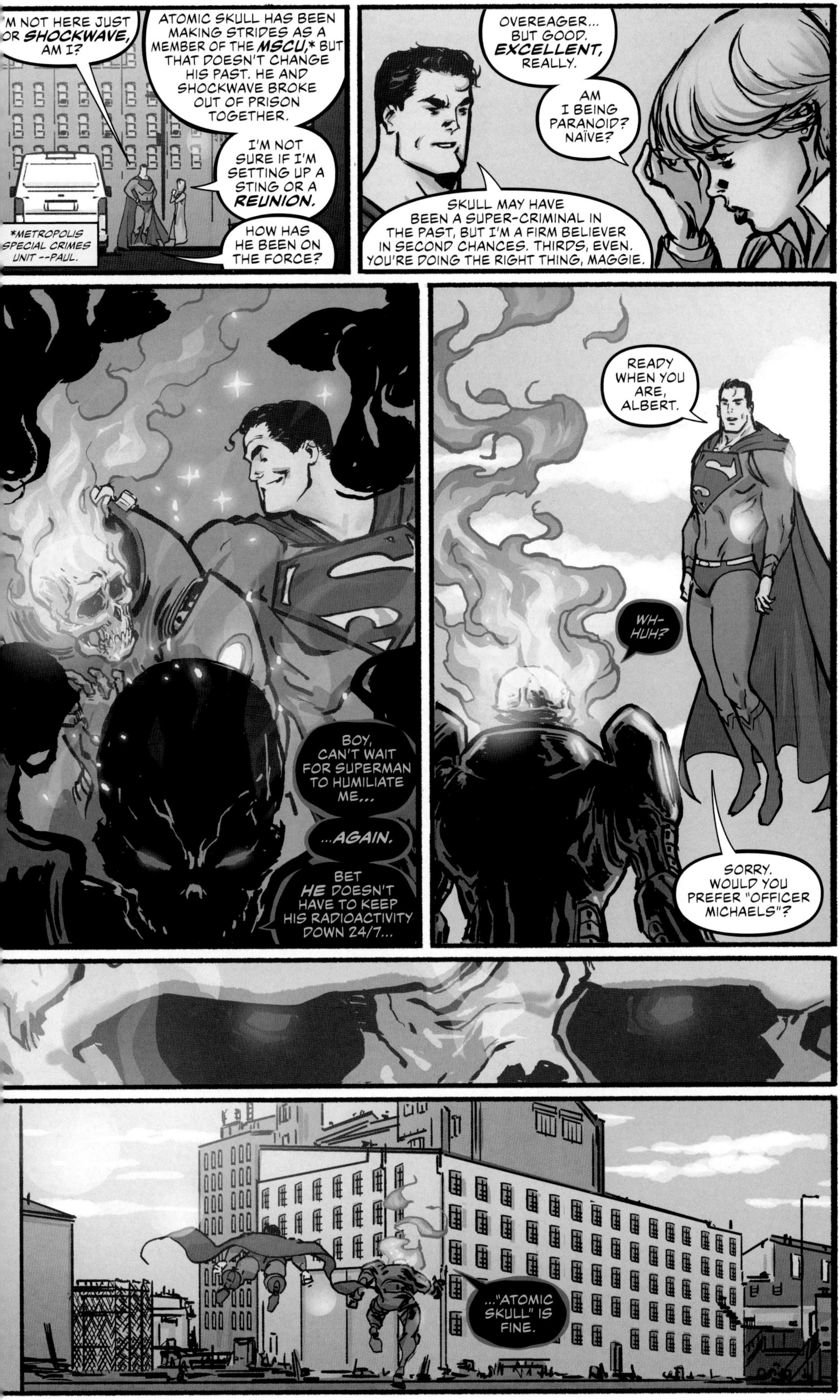
I'M NOT HERE JUST FOR SHOCKWAVE, AM I?
ATOMIC SKULL HAS BEEN MAKING STRIDES AS A MEMBER OF THE MSCU,* BUT THAT DOESN'T CHANGE HIS PAST. HE AND SHOCKWAVE BROKE OUT OF PRISON TOGETHER.
I'M NOT SURE IF I'M SETTING UP A STING OR A REUNION.
HOW HAS HE BEEN ON THE FORCE?
*METROPOLIS SPECIAL CRIMES UNIT --PAUL.
OVEREAGER... BUT GOOD. EXCELLENT, REALLY.
AM I BEING PARANOID? NAÏVE?
SKULL MAY HAVE BEEN A SUPER-CRIMINAL IN THE PAST, BUT I'M A FIRM BELIEVER IN SECOND CHANCES. THIRDS, EVEN. YOU'RE DOING THE RIGHT THING, MAGGIE.
BOY, CAN'T WAIT FOR SUPERMAN TO HUMILIATE ME...
...AGAIN.
BET HE DOESN'T HAVE TO KEEP HIS RADIOACTIVITY DOWN 24/7...
READY WHEN YOU ARE, ALBERT.
WH-HUH?
SORRY. WOULD YOU PREFER "OFFICER MICHAELS"?
..."ATOMIC SKULL" IS FINE.

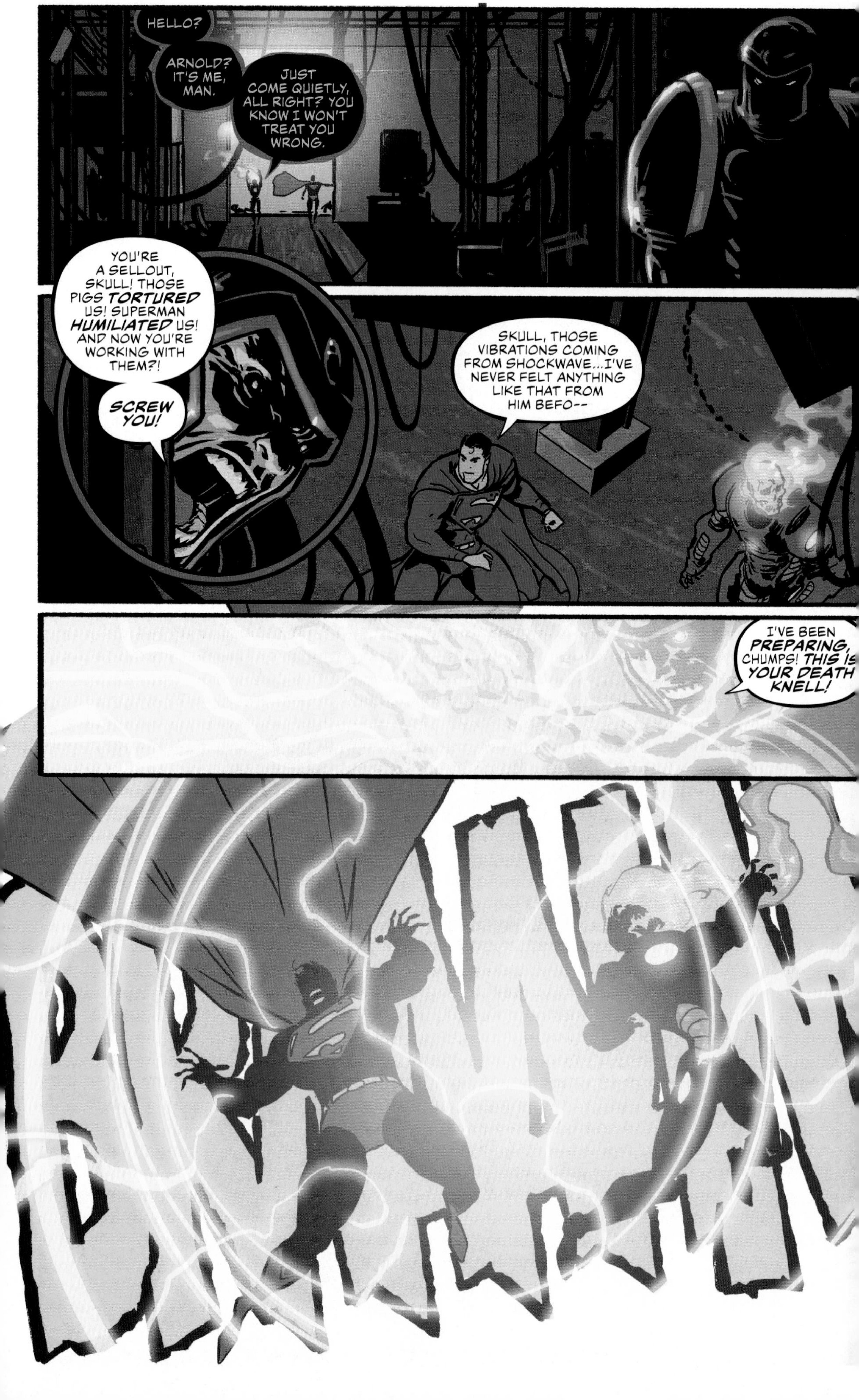
HELLO?
ARNOLD? IT'S ME, MAN.
JUST COME QUIETLY, ALL RIGHT? YOU KNOW I WON'T TREAT YOU WRONG.
YOU'RE A SELLOUT, SKULL! THOSE PIGS ***TORTURED*** US! SUPERMAN ***HUMILIATED*** US! AND NOW YOU'RE WORKING WITH THEM?!
SCREW YOU!
SKULL, THOSE VIBRATIONS COMING FROM SHOCKWAVE...I'VE NEVER FELT ANYTHING LIKE THAT FROM HIM BEFO--
I'VE BEEN ***PREPARING,*** CHUMPS! ***THIS IS YOUR DEATH KNELL!***

FREEZE THE AIR ALREADY!

I'M... TRYING! VERTIGO... CAN'T...STAND... *THINK*...

GOT A FUN FACT FOR YOU, SUPERMAN. TURNS OUT EVERYTHING-- *EVERYTHING*-- HAS A UNIQUE MOLECULAR VIBRATION.

...ND IT, NEUTRALIZE T, AND WHATEVER IT IS WILL FALL APART. SO--

--I'M GONNA *SHATTER* YOU, SUPERMAN!

CHOOM

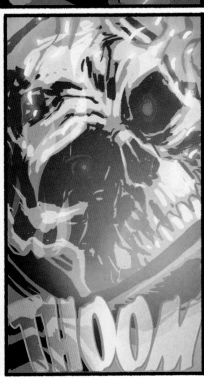

THOOM

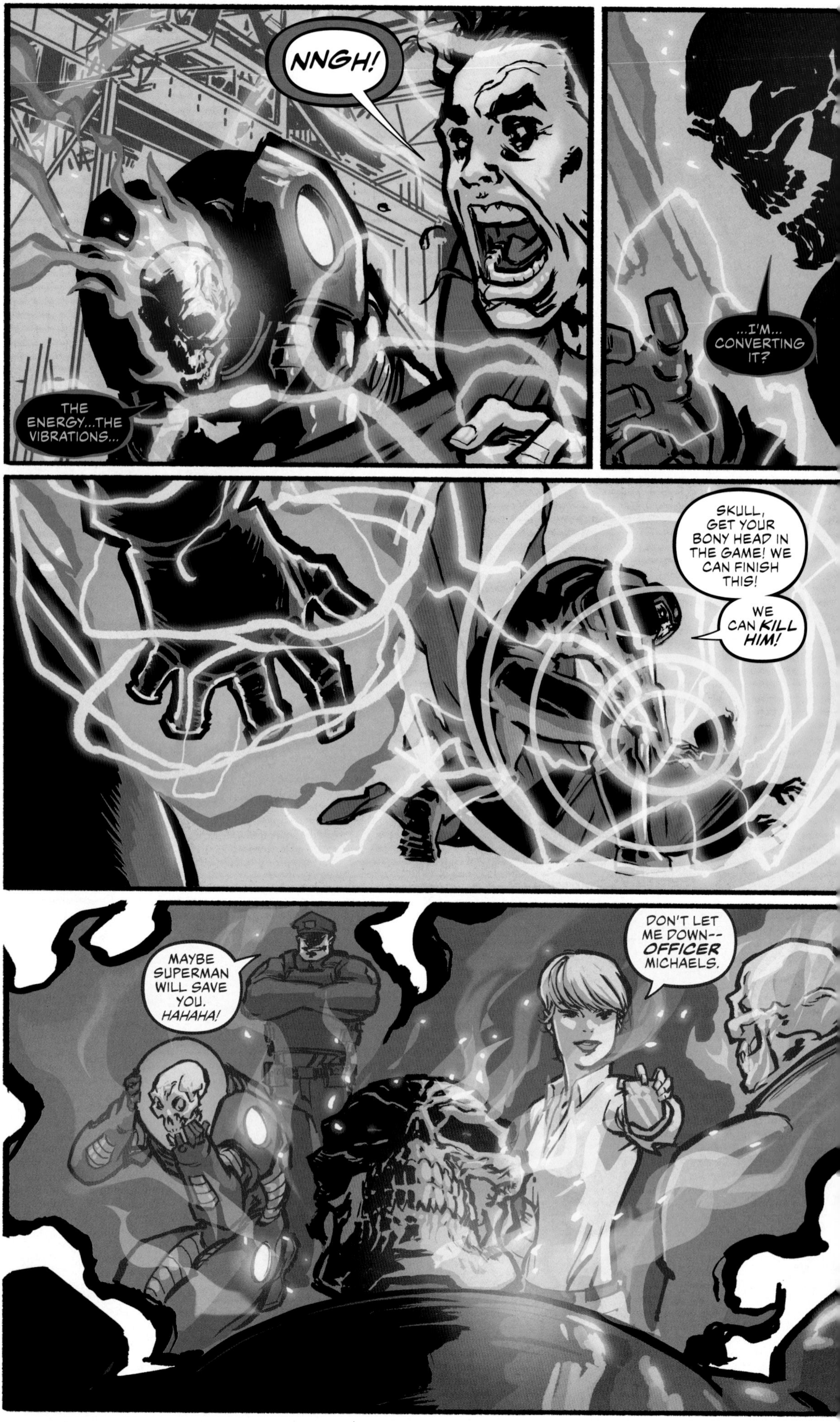
NNGH!
THE ENERGY...THE VIBRATIONS...
...I'M... CONVERTING IT?
SKULL, GET YOUR BONY HEAD IN THE GAME! WE CAN FINISH THIS!
WE CAN KILL HIM!
MAYBE SUPERMAN WILL SAVE YOU. HAHAHA!
DON'T LET ME DOWN-- OFFICER MICHAELS.

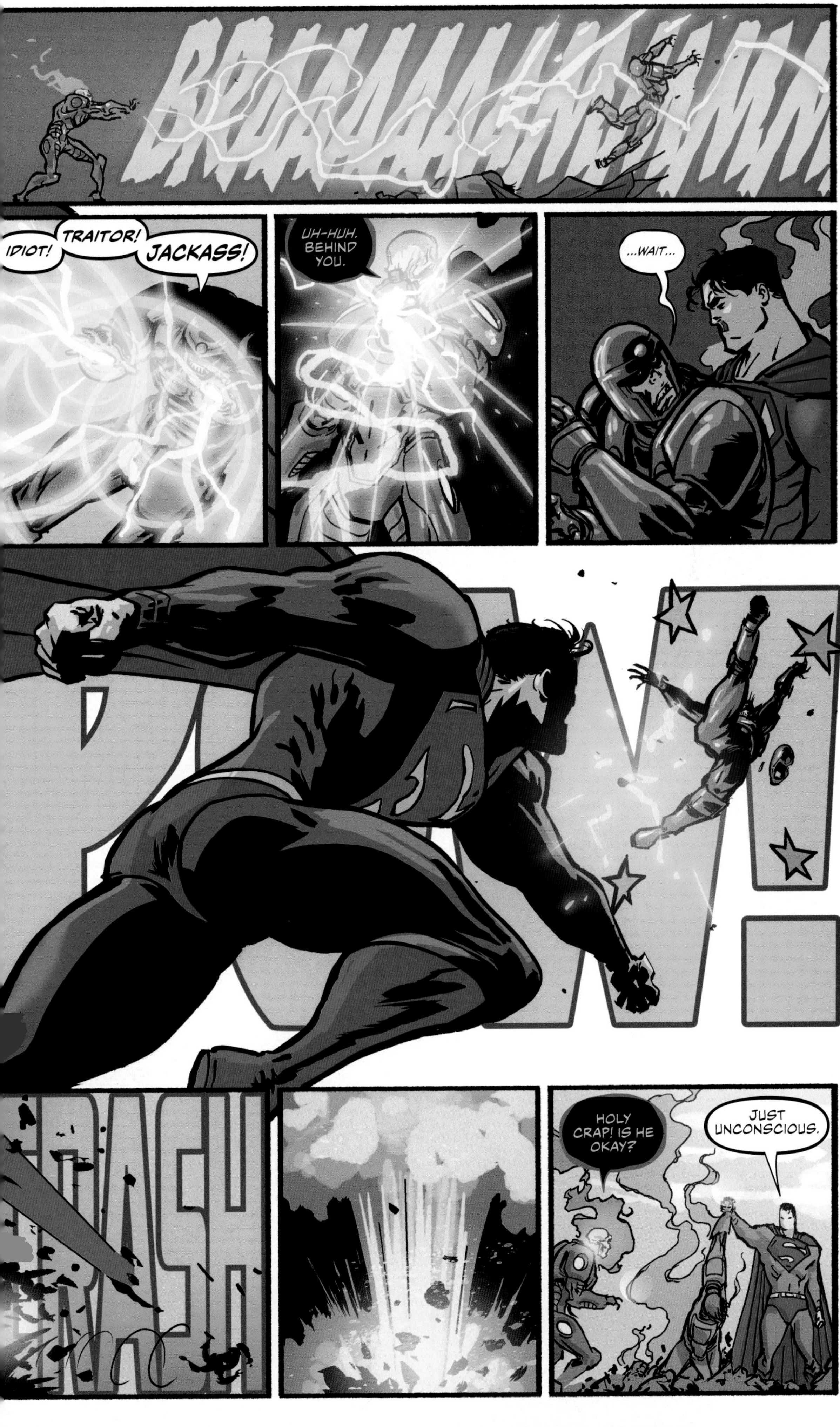
IDIOT!
TRAITOR!
JACKASS!
UH-HUH. BEHIND YOU.
...WAIT...
HOLY CRAP! IS HE OKAY?
JUST UNCONSCIOUS.

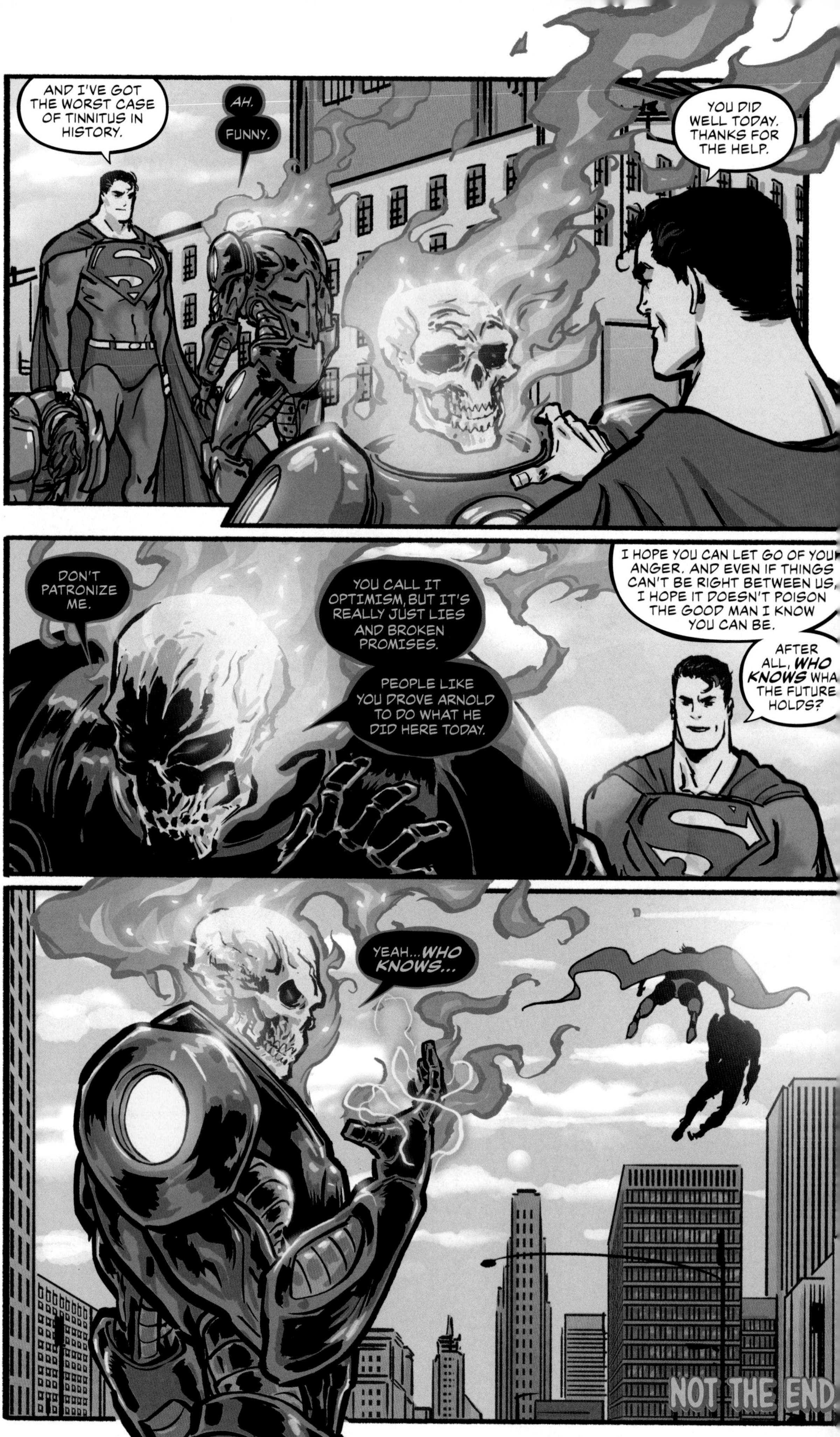
AND I'VE GOT THE WORST CASE OF TINNITUS IN HISTORY.
AH.
FUNNY.
YOU DID WELL TODAY. THANKS FOR THE HELP.
DON'T PATRONIZE ME.
YOU CALL IT OPTIMISM, BUT IT'S REALLY JUST LIES AND BROKEN PROMISES.
PEOPLE LIKE YOU DROVE ARNOLD TO DO WHAT HE DID HERE TODAY.
I HOPE YOU CAN LET GO OF YOU ANGER. AND EVEN IF THINGS CAN'T BE RIGHT BETWEEN US, I HOPE IT DOESN'T POISON THE GOOD MAN I KNOW YOU CAN BE.
AFTER ALL, WHO KNOWS WHA THE FUTURE HOLDS?
YEAH...WHO KNOWS...
NOT THE END

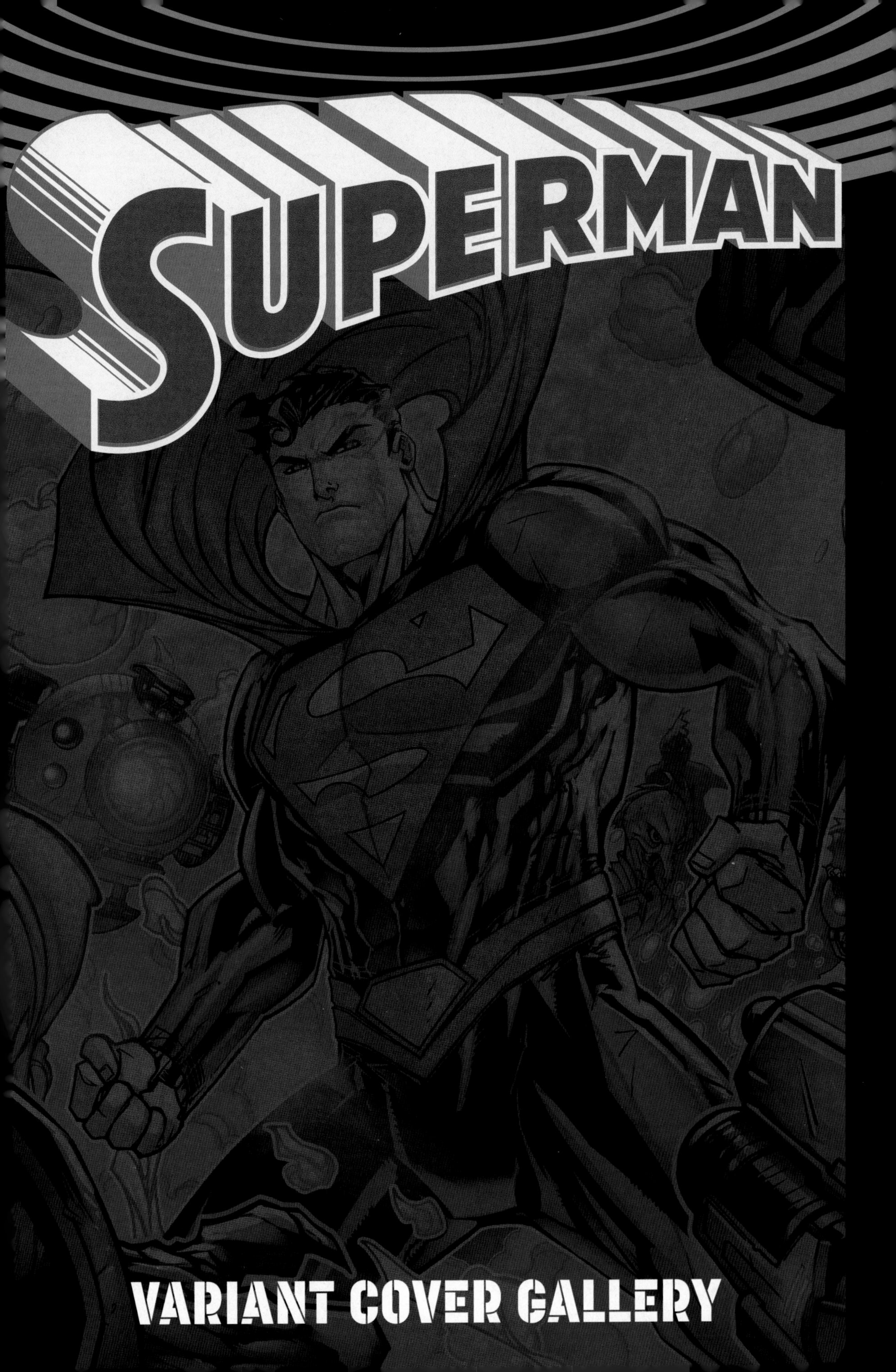
SUPERMAN
VARIANT COVER GALLERY

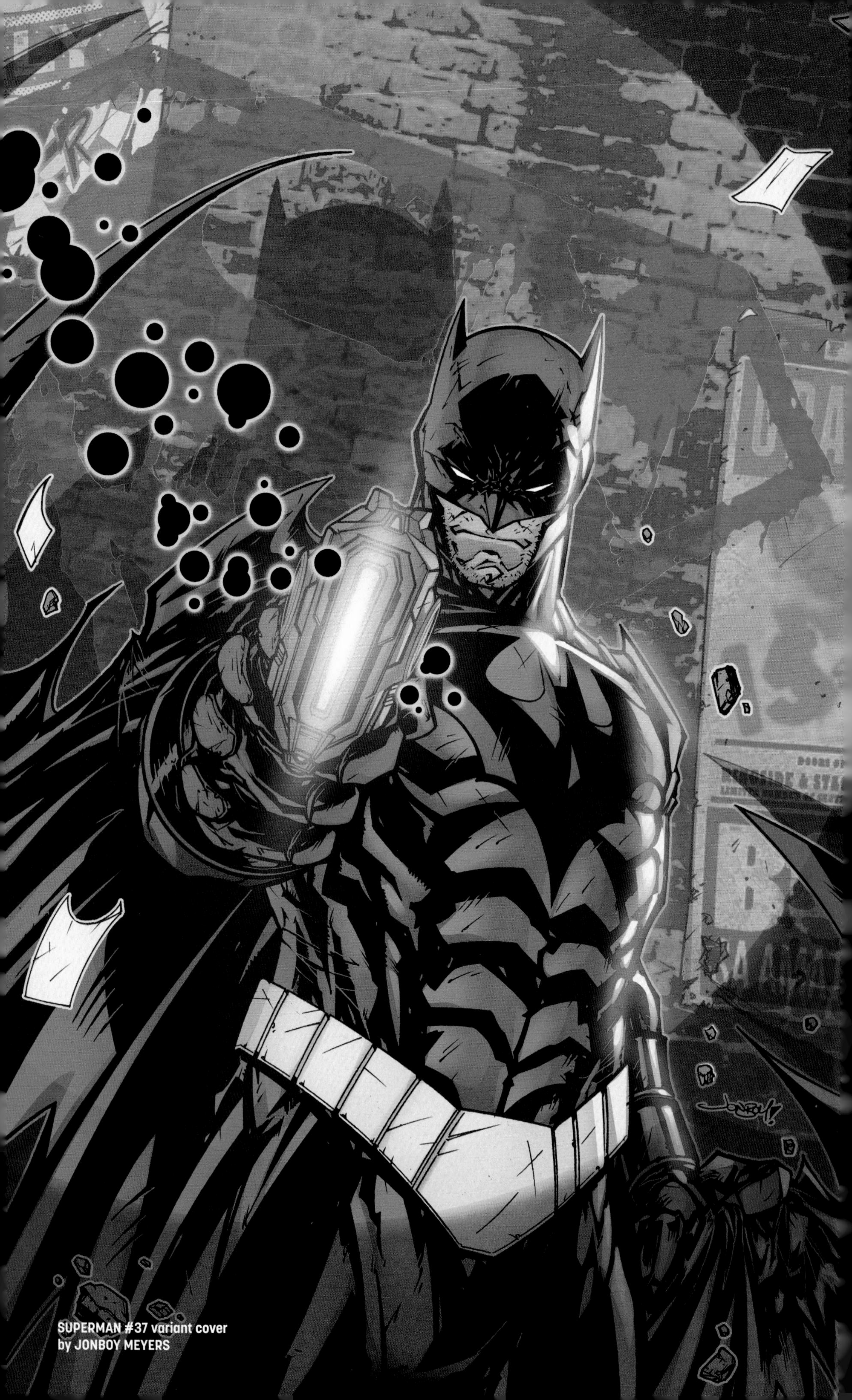

SUPERMAN #37 variant cover
by JONBOY MEYERS

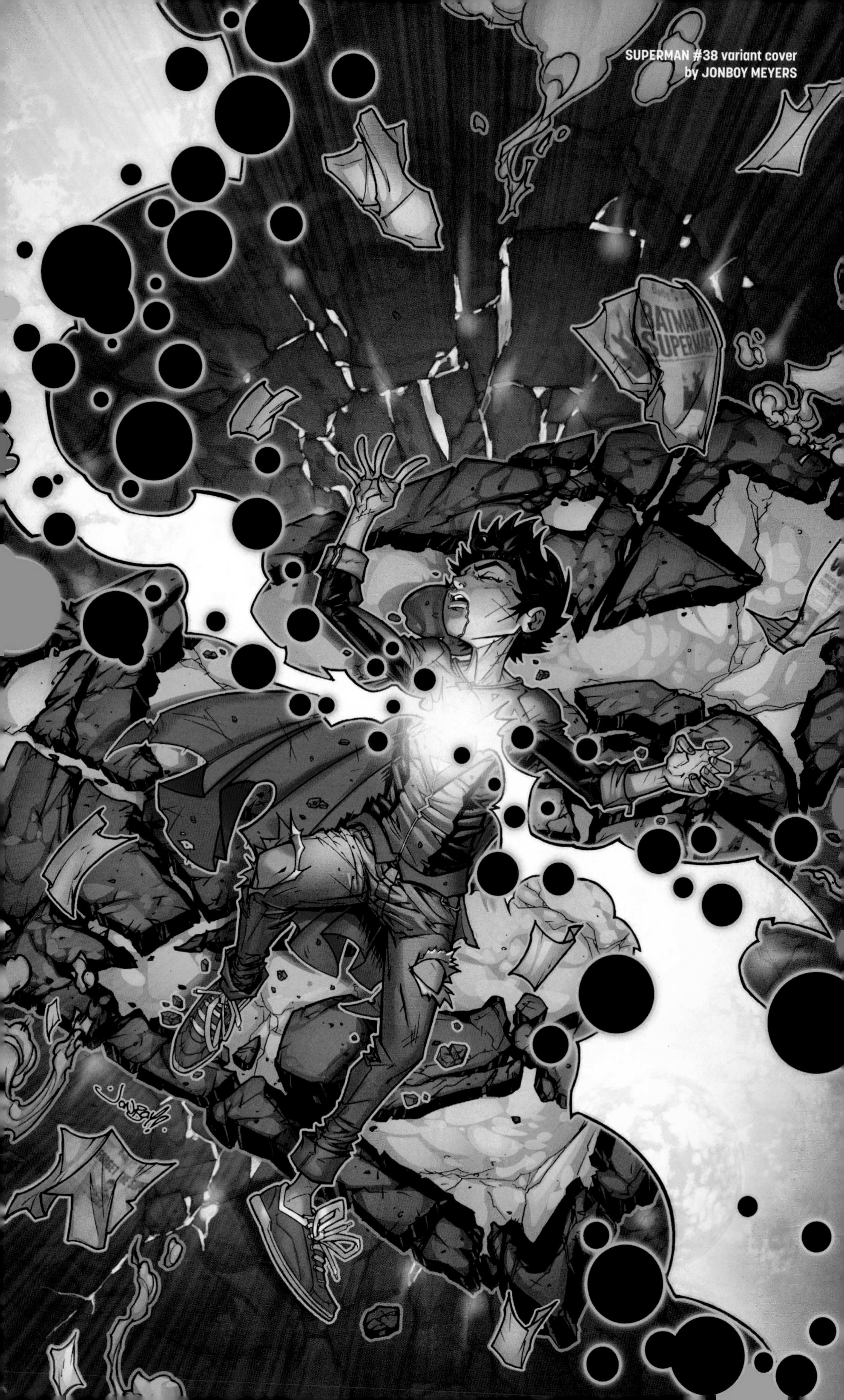

SUPERMAN #38 variant cover
by JONBOY MEYERS

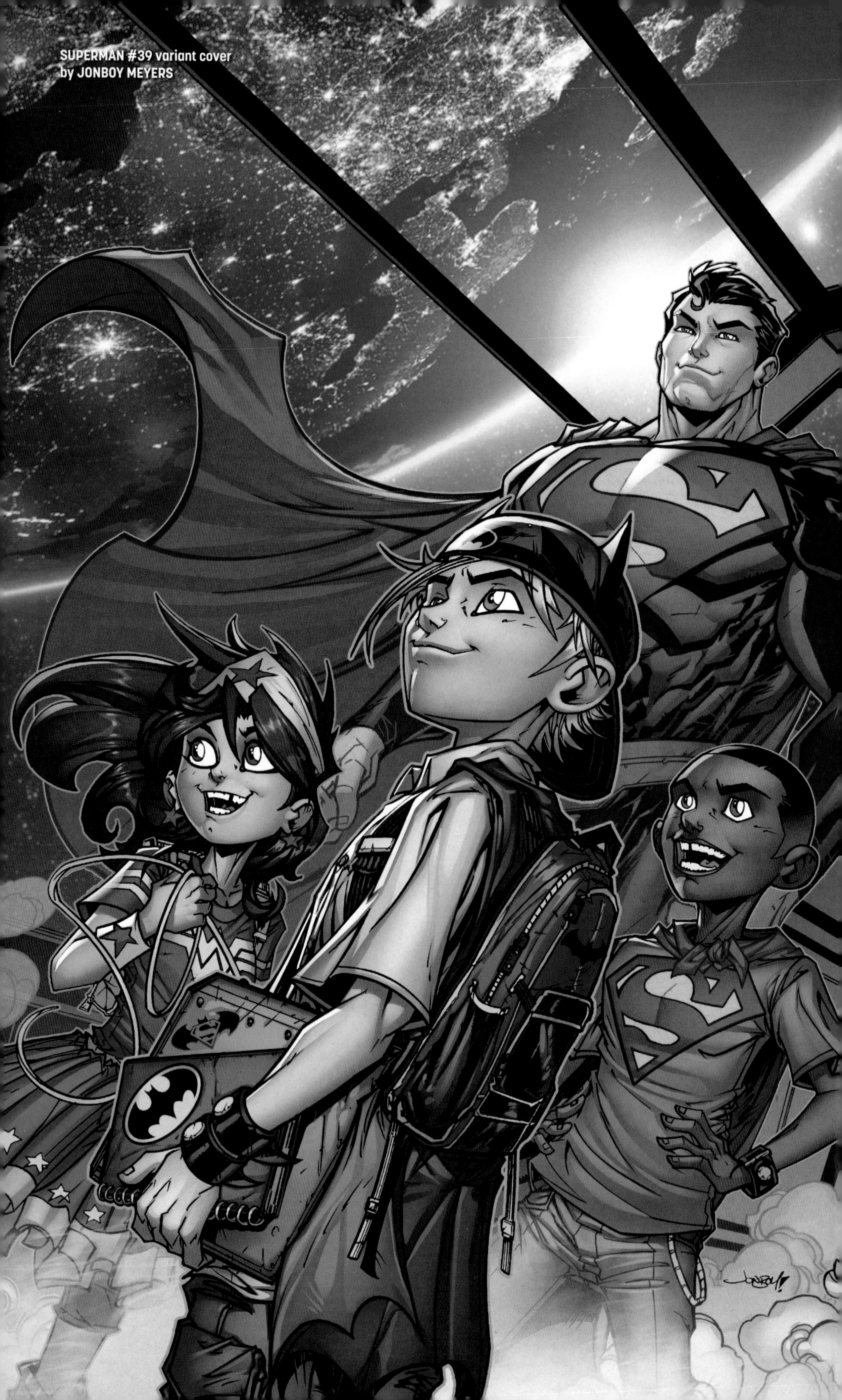

SUPERMAN #39 variant cover
by JONBOY MEYERS

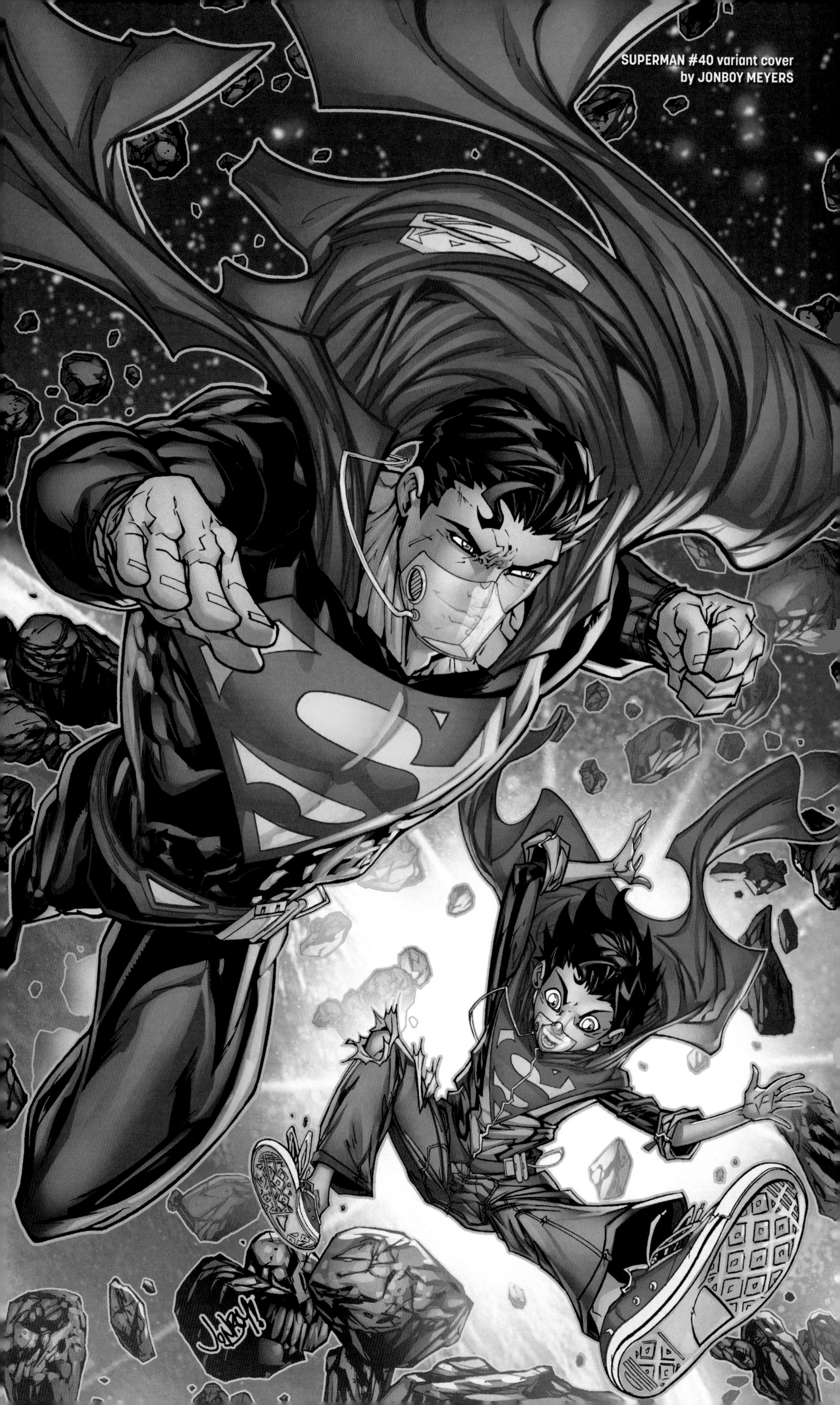

SUPERMAN #40 variant cover
by JONBOY MEYERS

SUPERMAN #41 variant cover
by JONBOY MEYERS

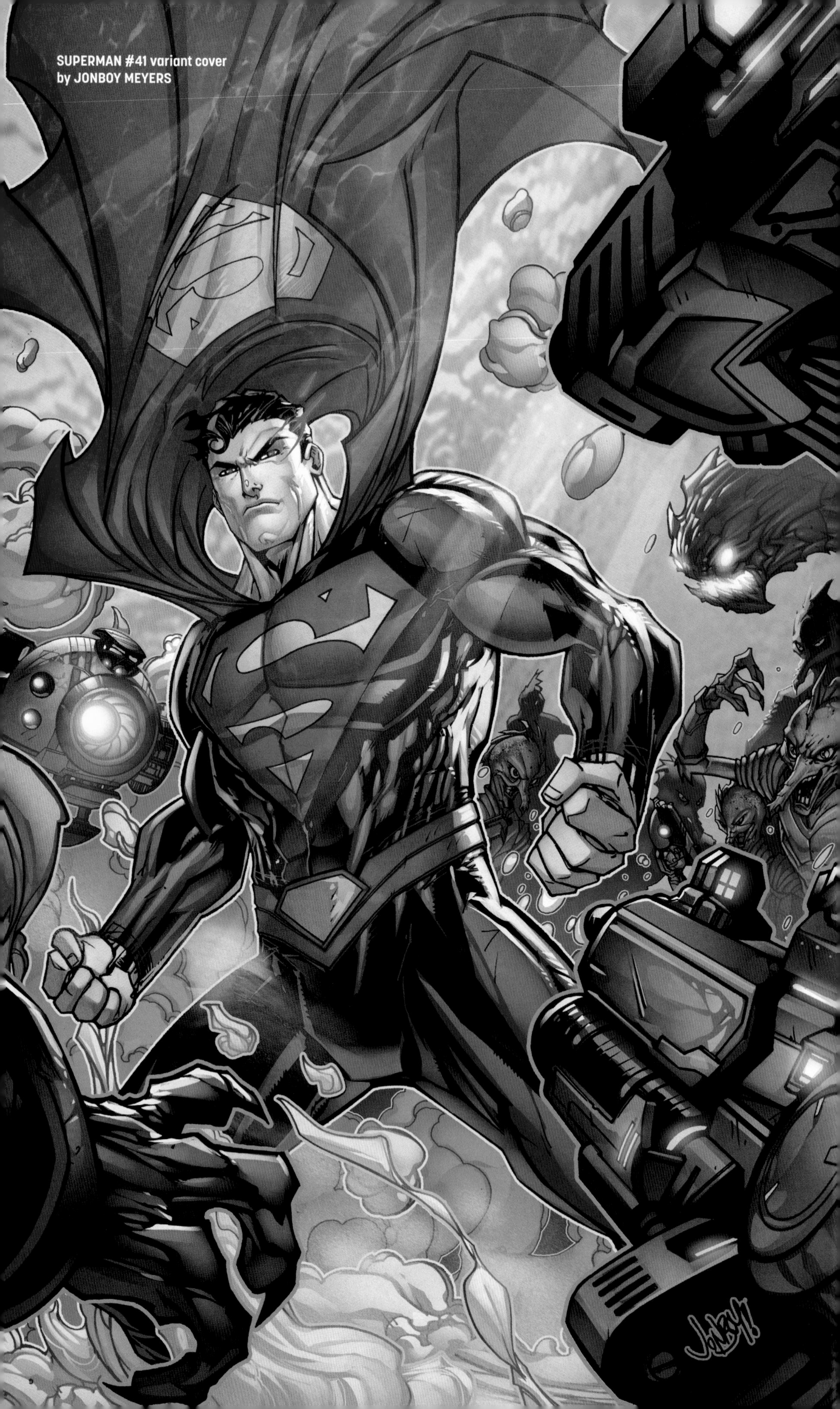

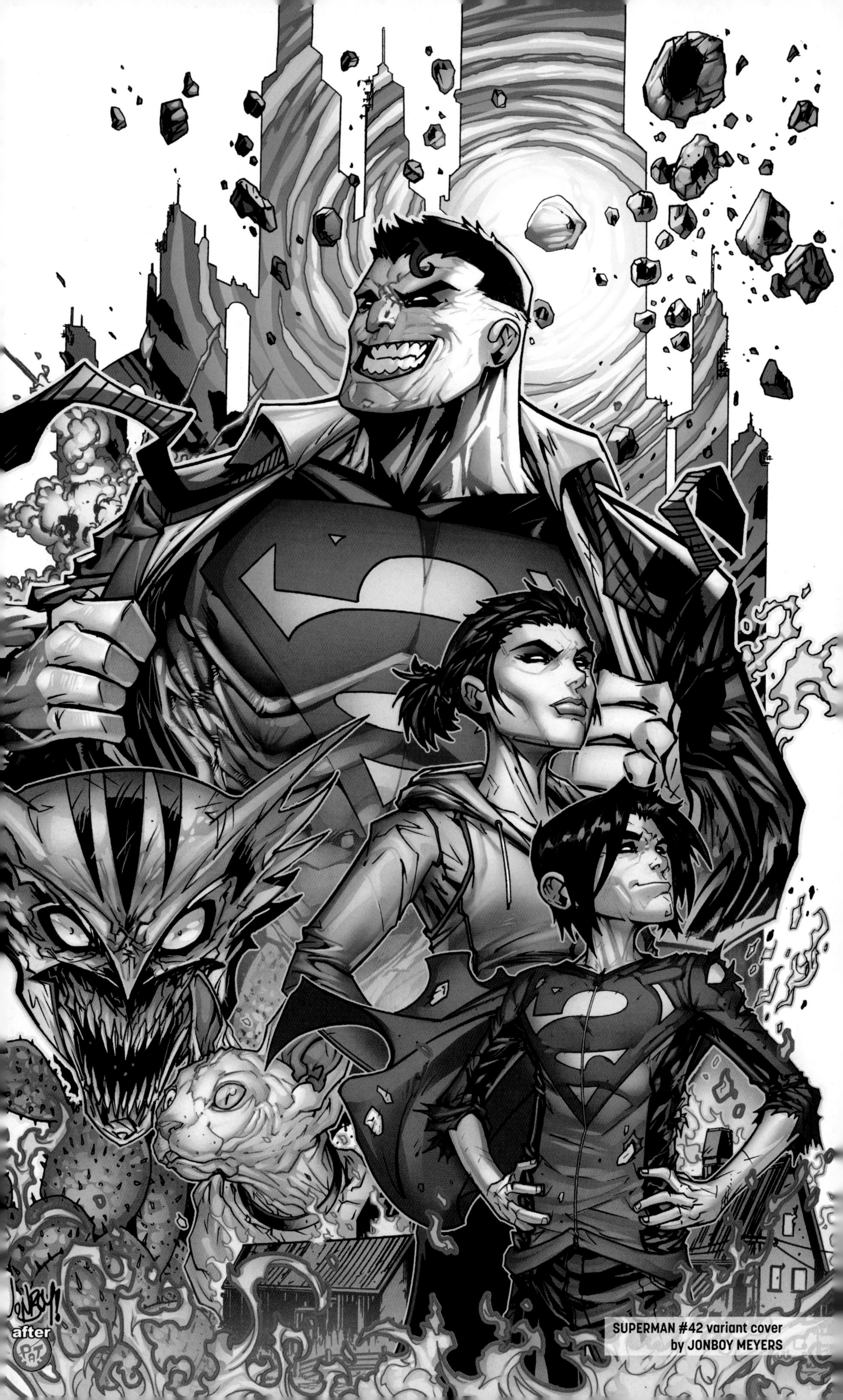

SUPERMAN #42 variant cover
by JONBOY MEYERS

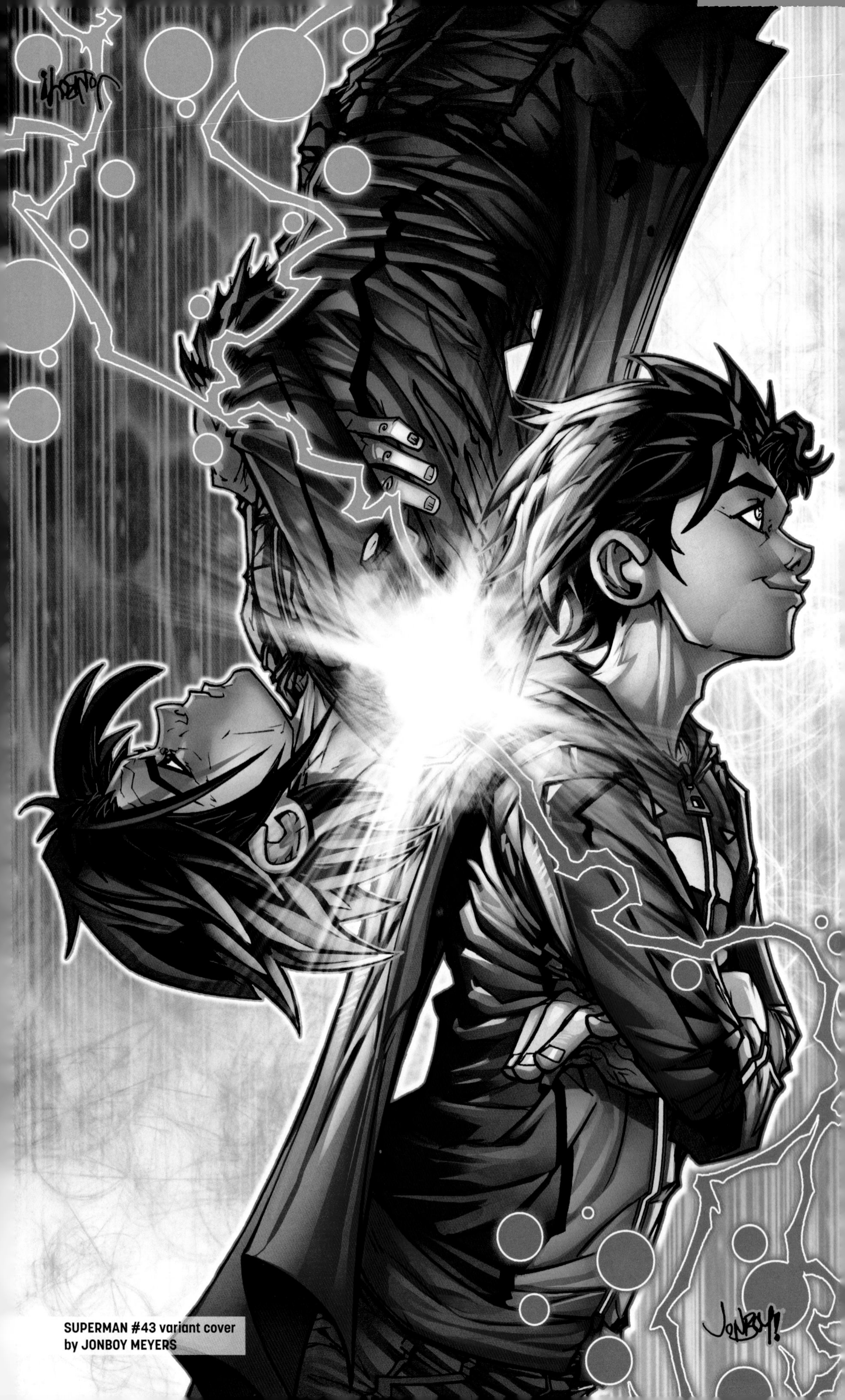

SUPERMAN #43 variant cover
by JONBOY MEYERS

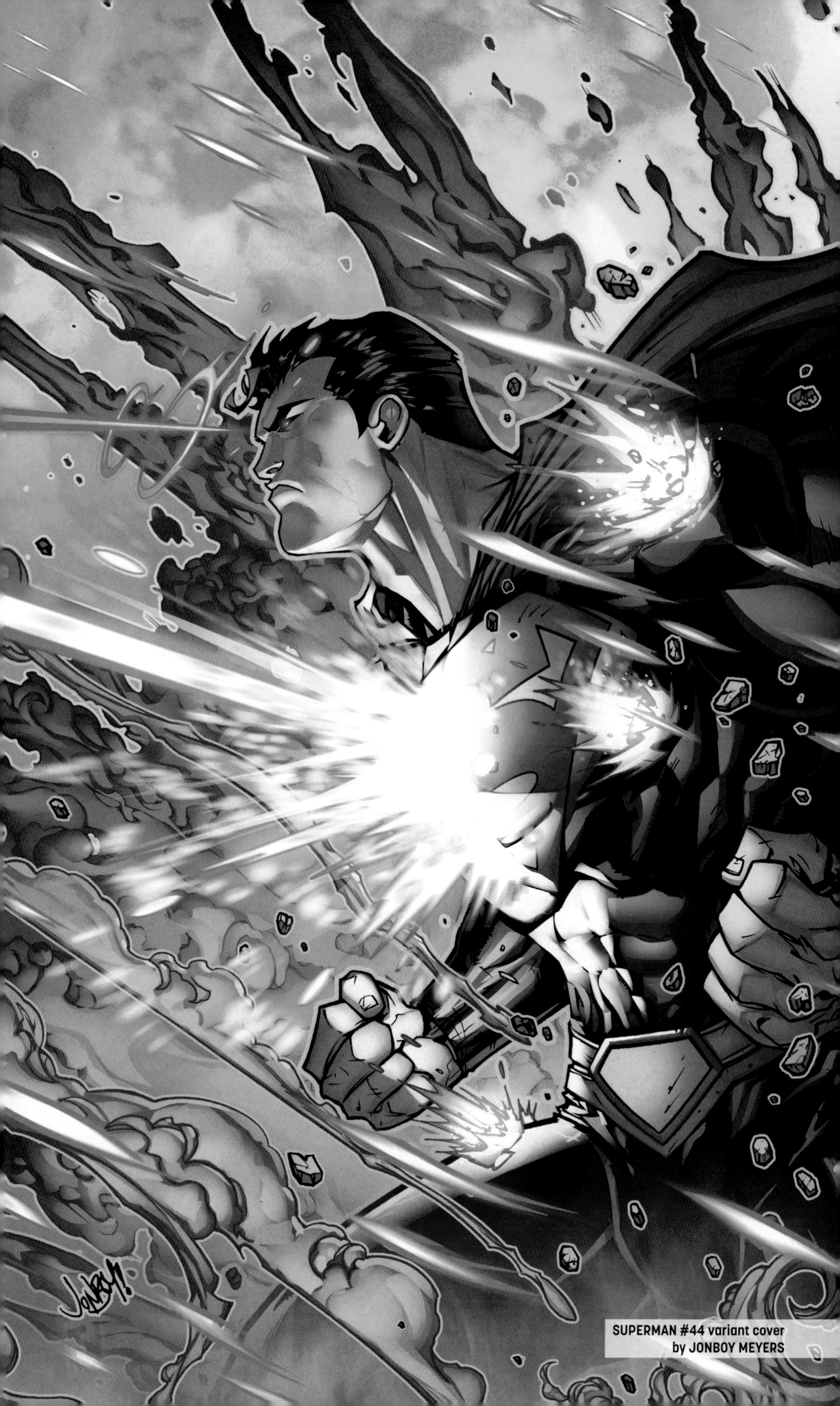

SUPERMAN #44 variant cover
by JONBOY MEYERS

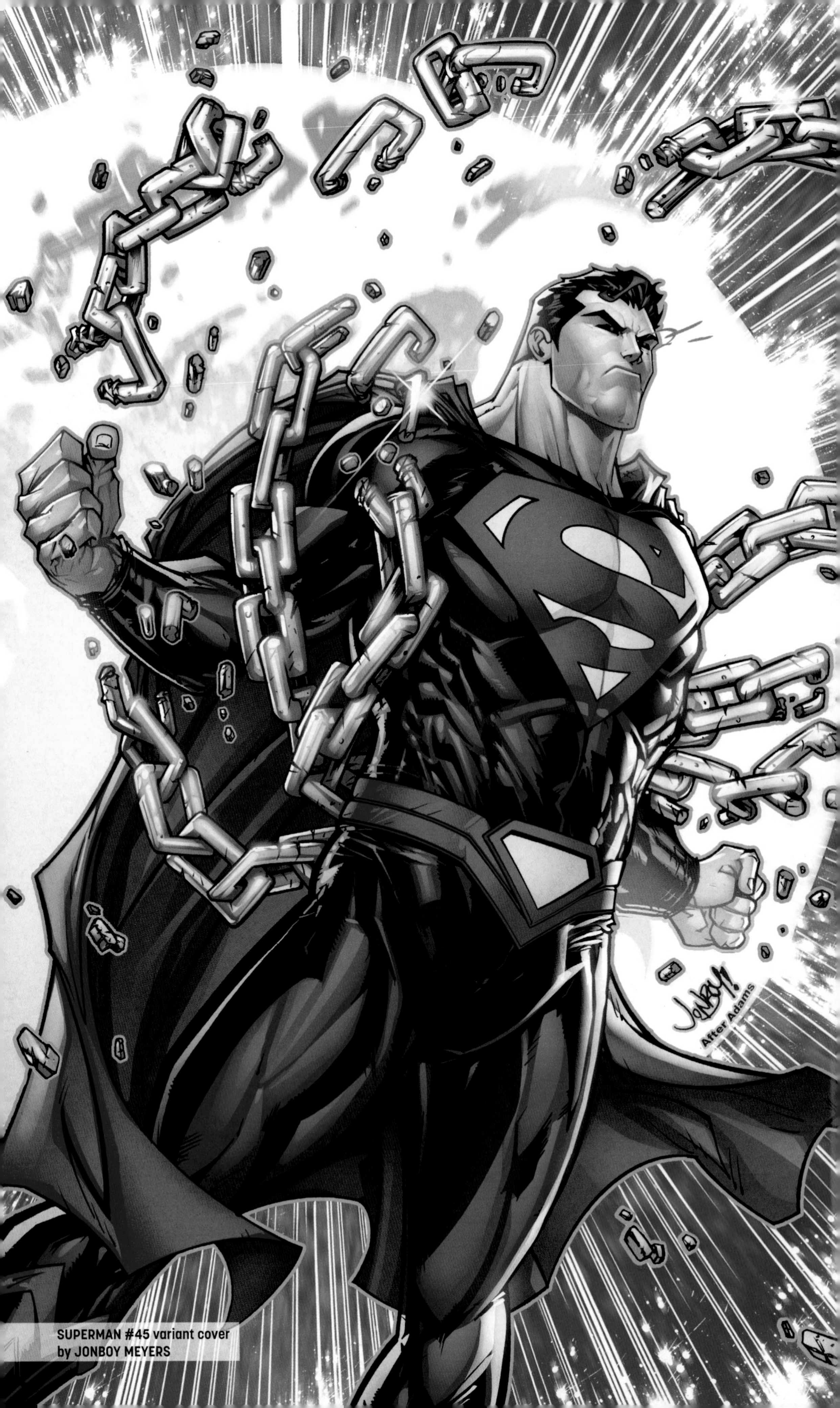
After Adams

SUPERMAN #45 variant cover
by JONBOY MEYERS